DATE DUE

Counseling and Psychotherapy

Counseling
and
Psychotherapy

Les Parrott III, Ph.D.
Seattle Pacific University

The McGraw-Hill Companies, Inc.

New York   St. Louis   San Francisco   Auckland   Bogotá   Caracas
Lisbon   London   Madrid   Mexico City   Milan   Montreal   New Delhi
Paris   San Juan   Singapore   Sydney   Tokyo   Toronto

McGraw-Hill

A Division of The **McGraw-Hill** Companies

COUNSELING AND PSYCHOTHERAPY

Acknowledgments appear on pages 401–403 and on this page by reference.

This book is printed on acid-free paper.

2 3 4 5 6 7 8 9 0 FGR FGR 9 0 9 8 7

ISBN 0-07-048581-x

This book was set in Palatino by Graphic World.
The editor was Brian McKean; the editing manager was Peggy Rehberger;
the production supervisor was Denise L. Puryear;
the design manager was Joseph A. Piliero;
the cover was designed by BC Graphics.
The photo editor was Debra Hershkowitz.
The permissions editor was Elsa Peterson.
Project supervision was done by Graphic World Publishing Services.

Library of Congress Cataloging-in-Publication Data

Parrott, Les.
    Counseling and psychotherapy / Les Parrott III.
        p.   cm.
    Includes bibliographical references and index.
    ISBN 0-07-048581-X
    1. Counseling.   2. Psychotherapy.   I. Title.
BF637.C6P275   1997
158'.3--dc20   96-27915

http//www.mhcollege.com

About the Author

LES PARROTT III, PH.D., is Associate Professor of Psychology at Seattle Pacific University. With his wife, Dr. Leslie Parrott, he also codirects the Center for Relationship Development on the campus of Seattle Pacific University, a groundbreaking program dedicated to teaching the basics of good relationships. Les received his Ph.D. in clinical psychology from the Graduate School of Psychology at Fuller Theological Seminary. His clinical training included work at the University of Southern California Medical Center and a two-year post-doctoral fellowship at the University of Washington School of Medicine. The author of more than fifty articles, Les has also written several books, including *How to Write Psychology Papers, The Career Counselor* (with Leslie), *Helping the Struggling Adolescent, Love's Unseen Enemy, High-Maintenance Relationships, Saving Your Marriage Before It Starts* (with Leslie), and *Becoming Soul Mates* (with Leslie).

To Leslie
My Soul Mate

Contents

PREFACE   xi

Part 1
THE PRACTICE OF COUNSELING

Chapter 1   The Realm of Counseling   3
Chapter 2   Becoming an Effective Counselor   24
Chapter 3   Legal and Ethical Issues for the Beginning Counselor   44
Chapter 4   Contemporary Issues in Counseling   56

Part II
MAJOR THERAPEUTIC THEORIES

Chapter 5   Introduction: Your Personal Theory of Therapy   79
Chapter 6   Psychoanalytic Therapy   87
Chapter 7   Adlerian Therapy   119
Chapter 8   Existential Therapy   154
Chapter 9   Person-Centered Therapy   182
Chapter 10 Gestalt Therapy   211
Chapter 11 Transactional Analysis   242
Chapter 12 Behavioral Therapy   278
Chapter 13 Rational Emotive and Other Cognitive Therapies   317
Chapter 14 Reality Therapy   355
Chapter 15 Conclusion: Comparing the Major Therapeutic
              Theories   380

ACKNOWLEDGMENTS   401
NAME INDEX   405
SUBJECT INDEX   419

Preface

"All beginnings are hard." So reads the first sentence of Chaim Potok's novel *In the Beginning.* He elaborates through his main character, David, who as a 9-year-old boy, burst into tears because a passage of a Bible commentary had proved too difficult for him to understand. But David's mentor spoke to him in a gentle voice: "Be patient, David, you cannot swallow all the world at one time."

As a teacher, I resonate with that sentiment. And I hope that as a beginning counseling student you do too. Perhaps you have already decided on a career in counseling. Maybe you are still considering such a decision. Or maybe you are interested in the study of professional counseling because an introductory knowledge of this field will augment other endeavors. Whatever your aspirations and position, I trust that you are beginning this journey one step at a time. For truly, the art and science of counseling cannot be swallowed whole.

Along with your professor, this book will help you break the field of counseling into manageable pieces that can more easily be studied, critiqued, and eventually assimilated into your own understanding and application of an approach to counseling and psychotherapy. I hope that along the way you will seriously consider the limitations and contributions of the various therapeutic systems this book presents and that you will slowly start to acquire the foundation of a counseling style that fits your values and personality. This will require keeping an open mind as you read, not jumping to conclusions or making assumptions before fully grasping each therapeutic approach.

The truth is, it takes most professional counselors many years of study and experience to develop a sound rationale for systematically adhering to certain therapeutic concepts and techniques. So avoid the temptation to advocate one approach to the exclusion of all others at this beginning stage. An introductory course in counseling is not enough to make that kind of decision and there is no reason to unduly limit yourself to a single theory when there are many other fruitful approaches that can be drawn upon. You will soon discover that each and every theory offers a unique approach to understanding human predicaments and provides the counselor with healing tools for resolving them. So although it may be difficult, I encourage you to not judge each theory as right or wrong. Instead, make it your goal to learn from them all and in time your own personal theory of psychotherapy will develop and emerge, one step at a time.

HOW THIS BOOK IS ORGANIZED

This text is divided into two parts. "Part One: The Practice of Counseling," provides a foundation for understanding the field of counseling. This includes exploring the realm of counseling (where counseling comes from and what counselors do), the qualities of effective counseling, the legal and ethical issues in counseling, and contemporary issues in counseling (such as cross-cultural counseling).

"Part Two: Major Therapeutic Theories," presents the basic concepts of the most influential theories of modern counseling. This overview of the divergent forms of counseling and therapy will allow you to evaluate the unique contributions and limitations of each therapeutic system, applying it to psychological struggles.

In writing this book, I have included a number of features to help you understand and better remember the material.

- Each chapter begins with an outline of the main points. I suggest that you read the outline first, to gain a concept of where the chapter is headed.
- Special boxes are used at various points in the text to amplify and enrich the main narrative. To avoid having them perceived merely as extras, I refer to each box at the point in the text where it is most relevant to the topic under discussion.
- Many chapters include photographic essays showing highlights of counseling theorist's professional and personal life.
- Each theory chapter contains a glossary of key terms to explain any technical language with which you may not be familiar. The key terms are readily accessible in the chapter you are studying rather than at the end of the book.
- Notable quotes by many famous counselors, psychotherapists, and others are highlighted in the margins throughout the text.
- References are cited in the text by authors' last names and dates of publication (e.g., Freud, 1940). This method of citation not only documents the various sources of information cited in the text but is also useful for consultation when pursuing particular topics in more detail.
- The Subject Index and Name Index, appearing at the end of the text, provide you with an alphabetized listing of all terms, subject matter, and people's names along with their page citations.

- A Study Guide accompanies the textbook. It contains many helpful exercises and suggestions for studying to promote learning.
- A workbook/study guide, *Exercises for Effective Counseling and Psychotherapy* by Les Parrott III and Siang-Yang Tan (Graduate School of Psychology, Fuller Theological Seminary) accompanies the textbook. It includes exercises and cases with emphasis on micro-skills approach, and suggestions for better and more effective studying.

Throughout the writing of this text, many people have played a critical role in making my job easier. For help with research, my gratitude goes to Tad Beckwith, Susan Hamilton, Kari Newbill, and Laurie Nouguier. Luke Reinsma brought clarity and cadence to my sentences in several drafts. Many friends and colleagues served as sounding boards, consultants, and encouragers at various stages of this project: Roy Barsness, Nathan Brown, Timothy Clinton, Gary Collins, Dennis Guernsey, Allen Ivey, Mary Bradford Ivey, Don MacDonald, Ginger MacDonald, Del McHenry, David Myers, Leslie Parrott, Sr., Charles Ridley, and Míchaél Roe, among others. I owe a great debt to Virginia Powers-Lagac for her work on the instructor's manual and Siang-Yang Tan for his contribution to the student manual. The assistance of Marcia Craig and Debra Hershkowitz is also appreciated. From conception to finished book, Johnna Reitz, Susan Elia, Brian McKean, Jane Vaicunas and the rest of the McGraw-Hill team have been a pleasure to work with. Their efforts and dedication have increased the quality of this book in countless ways. I am also indebted to the following manuscript reviewers: Daniel Cowley, Webster University; A. Michael Dougherty, Western Carolina University; Ed Jacobs, West Virginia University; Hannah Lerman, University of Southern California; Eileen Nelson, James Madison University; Virginia Powers-Lagac, Our Lady of the Elms College; Eldon Ruff, Indiana University, South Bend; Jill Shoen, South Dakota State University; Kenneth Wegner, Boston College.

It is now time to conclude introductory remarks and embark on your journey. As you study modern counseling and psychotherapy, the persons, places, and perspectives will be filled in with greater understanding by the student who stays the course. My best.

Les Parrott

Counseling and Psychotherapy

PART ONE

The Practice of Counseling

CHAPTER 1

The Realm of Counseling

Chapter Outline

Vienna and Beyond
The Deep Roots of Counseling
What Is Counseling?
Counseling or Psychotherapy?
Functions of Counselors
Therapeutic Training and Settings
Professional Growth and Development
A Summary Word

Following the mayhem of the American and French Revolutions in the late 18th century, a revolution began in 19th-century Europe without the firing of guns, the leading of troops, or the seizing of political power. It began with a single man who irreversibly changed the way Western civilization thinks. He provided new paradigms on which a great number of other ideas and behavior patterns are based. He defined issues that are points of reference for modern men and women. He set in place the paradigms on which decisions for educating children are made, people evaluated, events interpreted, values determined, actions motivated, documents negotiated. For better or for worse, almost nothing in life has escaped his influence. The intellectual giant who revolutionized the thinking of the Western world was a neurologist-turned-psychiatrist whose life is forever identified with Vienna, Austria. His name is Sigmund Freud (1856–1939).

Freud is a household name on both sides of the Atlantic today. Who has not heard of a "Freudian slip" or an "unconscious motive"? He established the unconscious as a motivator and believed that human personality was built like a block wall, one brick at a time. A flawed personality was the result of imperfect bricks buried in a hidden tier far below the capstone, the fault of the brick layer rather than of the troubled adult.

Freud ranks among the most influential thinkers in history. His theories changed the way Western civilization thinks about human nature. His work on the origin and treatment of mental illness has formed the point of departure, if not the basis, for 20th-century psychiatry. His theories on sexual development have led to the open discussion of the subject in modern media. His theories on sex and violence as basic factors in personality have had a major impact on the writing of novels, the making of movies, and much of daytime and evening television fare, to say nothing of billboard advertising and magazine subject matter. It is difficult to find a part of our lives Freud has not touched.

Knowledge is the eye of desire and can become the pilot of the soul.

—Will Durant

And it is equally difficult to understand modern counseling and psychotherapy without exploring—if only briefly—its origins. So the first few pages of this text are devoted to an excavation, if you will, of some of the most influential developments. Even the deep roots of healing that predate Freud will be exposed for your examination. But we begin with an excavation site rich in artifacts that will soon take us to several intriguing locales beyond the borders of Western culture.

VIENNA AND BEYOND

As Athens was the cultural center of the Greek World, Rome the capital of the Empire, and Jerusalem the Holy City for Jews and Christians, Vienna, on the south bank of the Danube at the foot of the Austrian Alps, is considered by many to be the birthplace of psychiatry, psychoanalysis, and psychotherapy, as well as the source from which other counseling methods have taken root, developed, and spread.

Sigmund Freud and Alfred Adler (1870–1937) lived in Vienna. They attended medical school there. And it was in Vienna that they honed their therapeutic skills and developed their theories based on research that came from their patient relationships. Even Victor Frankl, the 26-year-old Jewish psychiatrist who was sent to a Nazi death camp during World War II and who survived to develop and practice his logotherapy, was president of the same Vienna medical association that Freud once headed.

Freud's influence, however, moved out from over Vienna to hover above other great centers of learning dedicated to the greater understanding of the mind and its healing. Carl Jung (1875–1961) received his medical degree from The University of Zurich and began his practice and research in Basel, the town of his birth. As an early disciple of Freud, Jung later broke with him over his mentor's excessive focus on sexual instincts. Their friendship ended, but Jung stayed in his home town to become a professor of medical psychology at the University of Basel.

In 1938 Freud moved to London to escape the wrath of the Germans who had overrun Austria, and it was in London that his daughter, Anna Freud (1895–1982), continued her work after her father's death. Inevitably the influence of Freud's work in psychotherapy crossed the Atlantic and came to rest in New York City, where existentialists such as Rollo May and humanists such as Carl Rogers did some of their work. Eventually, the working places of leaders in the field of mind healing spread widely to include such locales as San Francisco (Eric Berne), Mexico City (Eric Fromm), and Johannesburg in the Republic of South Africa (Frederick Perls, who later moved to California).

All of these diverse places had some things in common, however. They were cities instead of rural settings. This means there were many people who needed their services, and costs could be covered by people who could afford it, or by enlightened governmental agencies who made funds available. Each of these cities had strong medical schools with a bias toward research. The concentration of these ground-breaking practitioners in geographical centers made interaction among themselves possible and afforded access for the aggregate of followers who needed to be near the leader. And from these centers of leadership in psychotherapy and research, the practice of those who followed the various schools of thought spread out to cover the Western world and beyond.

As a result, today we take the "talking cure" for granted. Counseling and psychotherapy have reached nearly every part of the modern globe. From great metropolises to small towns on nearly every continent, the healing craft begun by Freud in Vienna is being conducted, in one form or another, by thousands of practitioners. If the truth be known, however, Freud and the other theorists you will study in this text were not the first to offer therapeutic help. Counseling has a long, long past.

THE DEEP ROOTS OF COUNSELING

In reality, the desire to help others—to counsel—is as old as time and not limited to Western cultures. To a considerable extent, the contemporary history of psychotherapy has been developmentally blind to its heritage and culturally bound by its borders. Because its roots are deeply embedded in the rich soil of European-American thought and theory, modern counseling has developed without significant contribution from healers and thinkers who represent the non-Western world. In fact, it has been estimated that over 90% of all psychologists who have ever lived are from the Western world (Lonner & Malpass, 1994). Even today, for a variety of reasons some members of ethnic minority groups will choose informal sources of help for emotional problems (Mays & Albee, 1993). Help is sought, not from a professional counselor, but from acupuncturists, herbalists, family physicians, clergy, friends, and family members who share a world view with the person—and who are thus culturally sensitive.

Even before Freud, then, there were ancient counterparts to today's counselors, many of them beyond the borders of Europe. The chieftains of old tribal societies, for example, offered counsel to those in need (Gibson & Mitchell, 1986). The Native American and other tribal groups relied on the shaman,

Navajo medicine man administering chant
to mother and baby for better health.
(Corbis-Bettmann)

believing much more in spiritual and holistic healing than a conventional "counselor." Historically, Asians, Africans, and South Americans all looked to various kinds of mind healers. Although psychological theory and elaborate counseling techniques were not necessarily developed and systematized, these individuals were sought out for their intuitive wisdom and insight.

From the classical Greek and Roman eras to early modern times, counselors were philosophers, physicians, or priests. Plato (427–347 B.C.), one of the first to organize psychological insights into a systematic theory, dealt with questions about children, parenting, education, decision making, attitudes, and so on. Plato's most famous student, Aristotle (384–323 B.C.), also contributed to what was to become therapeutic understanding. Hippocrates and other Greek physicians contributed insight into the helping professions as well.

The ancient Hebrew people accepted the importance of personal identity and responsibility. The first-century Christian societies emphasized humanistic ideals that were later basic to the counseling movement. In the Middle Ages therapeutic interventions—wise or unwise—were increasingly implemented by the Church.

Although many modern historians point to Freud as the founder and catalyst of psychotherapy, a number of people who preceded Freud, in addition to the ancients, made significant contributions to counseling as we know it. One European antecedent to Freud was Paul Dubois (1848–1918), a Swiss physician and psychotherapist who treated psychotic patients by talking with them in a reasonable manner. At about the time Freud was beginning his work, Pierre Janet (1848–1947), a well-known and respected psychotherapist, founded a new system of "dynamic psychiatry" (Corsini & Wedding, 1995). And it was Josef Breuer (1842–1925), a well-known Viennese physician 14 years older than Freud, who taught him about *catharsis*, a method of removing hysterical symptoms through talking them out. The emergence of counseling as a psychologically based profession also owes a debt to William Wundt, who distinguished psychology as a separate science in 1879 by opening his Psychological Institute at the University of Leipzig, thereby launching a systematic inquiry into human behavior. The beginning of psychiatry as a specialty of medicine was another important development in this period (Gibson & Mitchell, 1986).

Inherent in every form of psychotherapy is an attempt by the therapist to help clients translate their problems into more helpful and less demoralizing terms.

—Jerome Frank

It should also be pointed out that early in the evolution of psychoanalysis, women such as Ruth Mack Brunswick, Marie Bonaparte, Helene Deutsch, Edith Jacobson, and Theresa Benedek developed new understandings of the psychology of women that went beyond the early psychoanalytic focus on sexuality. And other women, including Karen Horney and Clara Thompson, would later challenge the givens of the Freudian psychoanalytic scheme that had contributed to the myths about women. All of these factors, from ancient societies' reliance on counselors to European antecedents, contributed to the birth and growth of Freud's psychoanalysis and the general emergence of the practice of counseling and psychotherapy, eventually leading to its explosive growth in the United States.

As America entered the 20th century, life became more complex; the demands for psychological adjustment, more intense. The changing values, increased pace, and contradictions in rural versus metropolitan norms of the early 20th century created the backdrop for the development of professional counseling. Pastors who had considered the pulpit as the center of their work now needed training for the proper use of their new counseling rooms. Doctors who thought their work was medicine suddenly learned that people were their business. Teachers were called on, not simply to teach, but to understand children. The revolution was on, and professional counselors were helping to see it through.

The common thread uniting these historical eras even beyond the borders of Western civilization is the concept of the psychotherapist as the "doctor of the interior" (Cushman, 1993, p. 22). This is true not only for psychodynamic theories but also for the diverse post–World War II era modalities included in this book: humanistic, behavioral, cognitive, and so on. Counselors shape, maintain, and facilitate healing in the private quarters contained in every individual.

Helene Deutsch (1884–1982).
(Copyright © Karsh, Ottawa/Woodfin Camp & Associates)

Today therapeutic interventions are being welcomed everywhere from prisons to churches. The variety of approaches, theories, and fads has grown at a bewildering rate; by now there are more than 200 different psychotherapeutic systems (Gabbard, 1995). New strategies and techniques are developing in unexpected forms and at a rapid pace (see Sidebar 1-1). The future of counseling and psychotherapy reaches to the horizon and beyond.

WHAT IS COUNSELING?

With this brief overview of counseling's historical roots, it is appropriate that we define, as much as possible, exactly what counseling is and how most practitioners understand their various functions.

Counseling is a word everyone understands, but no two people understand it in quite the same way. It is easier to practice the art and science of counseling than it is to describe it (London, 1964; Meehl, 1994). Conventional dictionaries offer little help. If you look up counseling, you'll find something like "the art of

Sidebar 1-1

THERAPY ON WHEELS

Hurtling down life's fast lane, executives and professionals often don't have time to bare their souls to a psychotherapist. Enter Dr. Ursula Strauss and Dr. Shelley Lennox, two psychologists who have come up with a scheme as original to psychology as takeout food and the Big Mac were to the culinary arts. They chauffeur their patients to work and analyze them all at the same time.

For $175 a session, a uniformed driver and either Dr. Strauss or Dr. Lennox pick up the executive at a suburban home in a van with an interior customized as a therapist's office—a burgundy couch faced by two bucket seats, a small coffee table graced by fresh flowers, and a clock on the wall. As Dr. Strauss or Dr. Lennox listen to the patient's problems, the driver, who is sealed off from the therapeutic conversations, heads to the executive's Manhattan office.

Neither the honks of a log jammed Long Island Expressway nor the jolts of Manhattan's cratered streets seems to distract their patients, the psychologists say. For executives who cannot spare the rush hour, the psychologists are willing to do lunch scheduling, parking near the patient's building and saving the trip to a therapist's office. They will even schedule a session on the way to an airport.

Their business, Mobile Psychological Services, has grown to 50 patients, 6

Psychologists Dr. Ursula Strauss *(right)* and Dr. Shelley Lennox
provide therapy in a van for people on the run.
(Jim Estrin/NYT Pictures)

Continued.

Sidebar 1-1—cont'd

therapists, 3 drivers and 4 vans and they are already thinking franchises.

The American Psychological Association knows of no other enterprise quite like this, and a spokesman, Doug Fizel, said he has heard no particular criticisms or endorsements of the idea.

"There's greater concern about therapy over the phone, therapy over radio, therapy on television," he said. "At least in a van the therapist is there. With the other forms of therapy, there's no direct contact and the therapist can't pick up non-verbal cues from the patient."

Dr. Strauss and Dr. Lennox feel they are filling an unmet need. "There were these patients who always had the same problem: they had to cancel, they had to be out of town," said Dr. Strauss, who still spends most of her week seeing patients

in her Bronx and Westchester offices, which have no wheels.

For patients who are in emotional crisis, Dr. Strauss and Dr. Lennox prefer to use their offices, but the van, they say, is fine for routine psychotherapy and for helping people with problems like substance abuse or phobias.

Stockbrokers, bankers and lawyers, she said, are often Type A personalities who work hard and work others hard and come to her to learn "how to handle it all." Of course, she said, she is aware that her service is feeding their neuroses, gratifying their need to squeeze everything into their pressured life style. "It's an irony that's not lost on us," she said. "But as one of the patients said, 'It's either this or nothing.'"

As a result of van treatment, Dr. Lennox added, the patients should learn to "appreciate the importance of providing the time for a therapy session" and forgo the van.

By Joseph Berger, *The New York Times,* Friday, January 13, 1995. Reprinted with permission.

advising." The definition is not particularly wrong; it is simply too broad to be useful. Many people advise. Psychologists, social workers, salespeople, psychics, school guidance personnel, pastors, attorneys, camp leaders, dentists, bartenders, and even friends advise. Professional counseling is more than merely an art of giving advice.

Consider the variety of definitions provided by scholars. The similarities and differences in these references indicate how difficult it is to locate a succinct definition of counseling. Here is a small sampling of the hundreds we have to choose from:

- Counseling is the artful application of scientifically derived psychological knowledge and techniques for the purpose of changing human behavior (Burke, 1989).
- Counseling is a helping relationship that includes someone seeking help and someone willing to give help who is trained to help in a setting that permits help to be given and received (Cormier & Hackney, 1987).
- Counseling consists of whatever ethical activities a counselor undertakes in an effort to help the client engage in those types of behavior that will lead to a resolution of the client's problems (Krumboltz, 1965).

- Psychotherapy is a situation in which two people interact and try to come to an understanding of one another, with the specific goal of accomplishing something beneficial for the complaining person (Bruch, 1981).

A commonly accepted and easily remembered definition of counseling does not exist because counseling is a dynamic, ever-evolving profession. The term itself is value laden and therefore "responsive to a nexus of interlocking pressures and concerns" (Belkin, 1988, p. 120). The numerous attempts to define counseling, however, have revealed many of its consistent and fundamental elements. In his insightful work *Persuasion and Healing,* Jerome Frank (1973) describes common factors that cut across the spectrum of counseling and psychotherapy. Common features include the counselor having a personal commitment to help clients; being given a certain degree of authority and thus inspiring faith and hope in clients; acting as a mediator between suffering clients and the larger society; helping clients release emotions, rethink problems, and restore morale simply by listening in an empathic manner; offering a framework for change by providing an explanatory scheme that helps clients understand suffering; and being actively involved in the process of change, usually over a number of sessions.

A word means what you want it to mean.

—Lewis Carroll

Other scholars have also highlighted common features in the diverse pool of counseling definitions (see Gottman & Markman, 1978). Most assume, for example, that counselors are *trained as professionals.* They have a base of knowledge and a bank of proven techniques and procedures as resources for their work. Counselors do not rely upon folk wisdom or intuition, the way one does over an informal cup of coffee with a friend. Competent counselors are in touch with current developments in their profession, and they have a repertoire of professional skills that have been gained through education and application (Beutler & Kendall, 1995).

Another common notion is that counseling is *an art as well as a science.* Professional counselors may rely upon research to direct their practice and inform their effectiveness, but they balance their scientific knowledge with the art of warm relationships. They see people, not as subjects or cases, but as people. In the same vein, professional counselors maintain *high ethical standards in their practices.* They recognize the need for clear-cut codes of ethical conduct and a means of accountability. They hold high moral standards and values. They understand the importance of clients' rights and act in full recognition of their professional limits. Of course, all of this is *directed toward positive change.* The desired results of therapy are behavioral, emotional, or attitudinal change. Counselors help clients learn and practice new ways of thinking and living. They help clients make choices and act on them. Effective counseling results in improved relationships, better coping skills, and personal growth (Cavaliere, 1995).

Sidebar 1-2

ARE YOU RELUCTANT TO SEEK HELP?

Society encourages people to be independent and autonomous when they experience emotional struggles. Consequently, the decision to see a counselor or psychotherapist compounds some people's stress. How willing are you to seek professional help during periods of inner conflict?

    The following scale was developed to assess a person's willingness to see a counselor. Read each statement carefully and indicate your degree of agreement using the scale below. In responding, please be completely candid.

> 0 = Disagreement
> 1 = Probable Disagreement
> 2 = Probable Agreement
> 3 = Agreement

_____ 1. Although there are clinics for people with psychological troubles, I would not have much faith in them.

_____ 2. If a good friend asked my advice about a mental health problem I might recommend that he or she see a counselor.

_____ 3. I would feel uneasy going to a psychologist because of what some people would think.

_____ 4. A person with a strong character can get over psychological conflicts by him- or herself, and would have little need of a professional counselor.

_____ 5. There are times when I have felt completely lost and would have welcomed professional advice for a personal or emotional problem.

_____ 6. Considering the time and expense involved in psychotherapy, it would have doubtful value for a person like me.

_____ 7. I would willingly confide intimate matters to an appropriate person if I thought it might help me or a member of my family.

_____ 8. I would rather live with certain psychological struggles than go through the ordeal of getting professional treatment.

_____ 9. Emotional difficulties, like many things, tend to work out by themselves.

_____ 10. There are certain problems that should not be discussed outside of one's immediate family.

_____ 11. A person with a serious emotional disturbance would probably feel most secure in a good mental hospital.

_____ 12. If I believed I was having a mental breakdown, my first inclination would be to get professional attention.

_____ 13. Keeping one's mind on a job is a good solution for avoiding personal worries and concerns.

_____ 14. Having been a psychiatric patient is a blot on a person's life.

_____ 15. I would rather be advised by a close friend than by a psychologist, even for an emotional problem.

_____ 16. A person with an emotional problem is not likely to solve it alone; he or she *is* likely to solve it with professional help.

_____ 17. I resent a person—professionally trained or not—

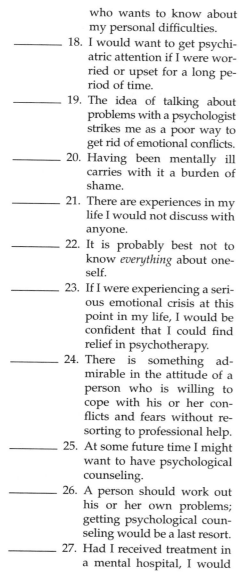

who wants to know about my personal difficulties.

———— 18. I would want to get psychiatric attention if I were worried or upset for a long period of time.

———— 19. The idea of talking about problems with a psychologist strikes me as a poor way to get rid of emotional conflicts.

———— 20. Having been mentally ill carries with it a burden of shame.

———— 21. There are experiences in my life I would not discuss with anyone.

———— 22. It is probably best not to know *everything* about oneself.

———— 23. If I were experiencing a serious emotional crisis at this point in my life, I would be confident that I could find relief in psychotherapy.

———— 24. There is something admirable in the attitude of a person who is willing to cope with his or her conflicts and fears without resorting to professional help.

———— 25. At some future time I might want to have psychological counseling.

———— 26. A person should work out his or her own problems; getting psychological counseling would be a last resort.

———— 27. Had I received treatment in a mental hospital, I would

not feel that it had to be "covered up."

———— 28. If I thought I needed psychiatric help, I would get it no matter who knows about it.

———— 29. It is difficult to talk about personal affairs with highly educated people such as doctors, teachers, and clergymen.

Scoring procedure: Begin by reversing the numerical value for items 1, 3, 4, 6, 8, 9, 10, 13, 14, 15, 17, 19, 20, 21, 22, 24, 26, and 29; that is, 0 earns 3 points, 1 earns 2 points, 2 earns 1 point and 3 earns 0 points. After reversing the scores of these items, add the numbers for all 29 items.

Interpreting your score: Low scores of 29 to 49 express a negative attitude toward seeking professional help. This does not mean that you presently have problems that require professional help; it simply means if you did, you would be reluctant to see a therapist. You may feel that a social stigma is attached to seeking help or that it is a sign of personal weakness. Medium scores of 50 to 63 indicate that you believe professional help can be useful, but you are somewhat unsure about whether you would actually use it. A high score of 64 to 87 suggests that you have a positive attitude toward seeking a counselor or psychotherapist for help.

If you expect to counsel others, the experience of being a client can give you firsthand knowledge of what your clients are likely to undergo. In addition, personal therapy can help you come to grips with unresolved situations, blind spots, unfinished business, and interpersonal conflicts. As a future counselor, you can learn few things more important than how you carry old feelings into present situations.

E. Fischer & J. Turner (1970). Attitudes toward seeking professional help: Development and research utility of an attitude scale. *Journal of Consulting and Clinical Psychology, 35,* 82–83. Copyright © 1970 American Psychological Association. Reprinted by permission of the author.

COUNSELING OR PSYCHOTHERAPY?

There is a line in *The Music Man* that says "People from Iowa can stand toe to toe, for days and days, and never see eye to eye." The same could be said of scholars who debate the distinctive features of counseling and psychotherapy. Some believe the distinction between counseling and psychotherapy is vital. Others see it as useless. Although I will use the terms more or less interchangeably in this text, it is helpful to understand the common perceptions of the two terms.

Counseling has traditionally been viewed as less intensive than psychotherapy; it has focused more on preventive mental health, whereas psychotherapy has concerned itself with reparative intervention. The goals of counseling have been oriented toward education and developmental concerns, whereas the goals of psychotherapy have generally been remedial. Work settings have also been used as a means of distinction between counseling and psychotherapy. Psychotherapists, according to traditional expectations, are more apt to work in hospital settings or in private practice, whereas counselors are more likely to work in educational settings (George & Cristiani, 1990). Some consider the number of interventions to be a deciding factor (Gelso & Fretz, 1992). About 12 to 15 sessions constitute counseling, whereas interventions beyond that point are psychotherapy.

Some view the difference as a matter of degree on a continuum, with counseling and psychotherapy at opposite ends (Brammer, Abrego, & Shostrom, 1993). Counseling is characterized by such terms as "educational," "vocational," "supportive," "situational," "problem solving," "conscious," "oriented in the present," emphasis on "normal," and "short term." Psychotherapy, on the other end of the continuum, can be characterized by such terms as "reconstructive," "in depth," "oriented in the past," "analytical," "emphasis on dysfunction," and "long term." But in the middle range of this continuum, where the interventions are less defined, the terms *counseling* and *psychotherapy* are often options for describing the same thing.

A word is not a crystal, transparent and unchanged, it is the skin of a living thought and may vary greatly in color and content according to the circumstances and the time in which it is used.

—Oliver Wendell Holmes

Despite efforts and the desire to make distinctions, however, current trends are blurring the fine lines between counseling and psychotherapy (Lipsey & Wilson, 1993). Counselors, for example, are now working with more severe populations in such places as hospitals, mental health agencies, and correctional institutions. In some states, counselors are moving more and more into private practice. There is so much overlap that broad generalizations about differences between the two are of little value. Despite attention to particular differences, most professionals in the field agree that counselors practice what psychotherapists consider psychotherapy, and psychotherapists practice what counselors consider counseling. Thus clear-cut distinctions between counseling and psychotherapy are virtually impossible to defend (Moldawsky, 1990). Patterson (1973) flatly states *"there are no essential differences between counseling and psychotherapy"* (italics in original; p. xiv).

FUNCTIONS OF COUNSELORS

After this cursory examination of counseling's roots and an attempt to define more clearly what counseling is, we now turn to what counselors do. You see, contemporary counselors do more than counsel. They function as consultants, trainers, supervisors, and so on. Blocher (1987) outlines several district counselor delivery modes. Along with traditional one-to-one counseling, for example, counselors provide assistance to their clients through *group therapy*, which has become increasingly popular. At one time, groups were considered a time-saving way of providing service to more people. Today, group therapy is often used as a treatment of choice for clients whose struggles revolve around dysfunctional interpersonal relationships or problems in communication. A group setting can have advantages over one-to-one counseling. Groups more closely simulate a person's natural social situation, and they can provide the type of social support individual counseling may not offer.

Consultation is another rapidly growing delivery mode used by counselors. For example, counselors frequently consult with parents, teachers, school administrators, youth workers, ministers, police officers, and others who work or live with troubled people. They may also consult with volunteer workers in such organizations as Big Brothers or Big Sisters. In each of these cases the counselor works with a person who is attempting to help another person who is not seen by the counselor. Some call it "indirect helping" (Blocher & Biggs, 1983) or "triadic consultation" (Tharp & Wetzel, 1969). Blocher (1987) notes several advantages of such consultation. First, it is an effective means of creating a relationship with hard-to-reach clients—people who simply will not see a counselor directly but can receive help through others. Consultation allows counselors to meet those needs indirectly. Second, consultation multiplies the scope of a counselor's services. Consulting with teachers in a school, for example, increases the number of people who are served. People working collaboratively with a counselor can affect many lives. Finally, consultation has a ripple effect, often reaching beyond the identified client, benefiting others who encounter the person with whom the counselor has consulted. Consultation with a parent about one child, for example, may ultimately benefit the entire family.

Another important service provided by many effective counselors is *training*. Not every psychological problem is the result of deep-seated, intrapsychic conflict or dysfunction. Clients' emotional struggles are often the result of not practicing basic coping strategies and skills. Some people never learn how to contend with stressful situations. Their problems are the result not of pathology, but of a lack of understanding of essential life skills (Gazda, 1984). Counselors can "give psychology away" by converting psychological principles into teachable skills and disseminating these skills through training efforts (Larson, 1984, p. 2). Teaching and training people in coping skills is sometimes the preferred method of treatment (Carkhuff, 1971; Phillips, 1978).

Organizational development is another increasingly used mode of intervention. Counselors are concerned with the healthy development of organizations because organizations shape the lives of clients in significant ways. Children, for example spend thousands of hours in schools. Adults spend many of their waking hours in business and industrial environments. It is not surprising, then, that the problems people bring to counselors often arise out of stresses originating in organizations. The competent counselor recognizes the importance of developing organizational environments that further human goals and fulfill human needs effectively (Jewell, 1985). Counselors in a school setting, for example, can work with teachers and administrators in implementing everything from curricular changes to the physical structure of the classroom. The goal of organizational development is "to improve the quality of the environment of a given organization in order both to improve the performance of the organization and to enhance the psychological development and well-being of its members" (Blocher, 1987, p. 10).

Supervision allows established counselors to advance their profession by training new and less experienced counselors (Bernard & Goodyear, 1994; Osipow, Walsh, & Tosi, 1984). In supervision, master counselors evaluate the skills of other counselors and provide them with constructive comments. Every competent training program places counseling students in observational settings such as practicums and internships, where they work with a supervisor who evaluates their performance. For this reason, many established counselors are likely eventually to provide supervision for novice counselors. For some counselors it is a part of their job description. Directors of counseling agencies, for example, often supervise junior-level counselors who work under them.

It should be clear, then, that the contemporary counselor does more than counsel. Whereas one-on-one, face-to-face counseling is still a predominant mode of service delivery, today's counselors are not limited to a single treatment strategy. Group therapy, consultation, training, organizational development, and supervision are becoming standard specialties in the counseling profession.

THERAPEUTIC TRAINING AND SETTINGS

We now come to a critically important issue: how persons become a specific type of counselor and the settings in which they do their work.

A study at the Unviersity of Montana recently revealed that people are confused about the role and training of professional people-helpers (Warner & Bradley, 1991). When asked about the difference between a psychologist and a psychiatrist, for example, many people are at a loss. There are a great variety of professional therapists, trained at numerous levels and working in diverse settings. It is no wonder that students of counseling need a clearer understanding of the types of mental health service providers.

To be ignorant of what occurred before you were born is to remain always a child.

—Marcus Tullius Cicero

Most professional counselors or psychotherapists earn either a Master's degree or a Doctoral degree in Counseling or Clinical Psychology. Interdisciplinary in substance and scope, counseling is typically taught in graduate programs by a diverse group of specialized professionals (Belkin, 1988;

Christensen & Jacobson, 1994). The faculty of a typical counseling department may include clinical psychologists, counseling psychologists, school and family counselors, psychiatric social workers, psychometricians, philosophers of education, community psychologists, vocational counselors, and social workers.

Cormier and Cormier (1985) suggest that counselors in training typically demonstrate growth and proficiency in *self-development,* that is, in a heightened awareness of attitudes and behaviors that may facilitate or interfere with a helping relationship; in *skill development,* such as in counseling techniques, strategies, and style; and in *process development,* such as in becoming aware of the effect of particular counseling interentions on clients. Each of these areas is crucial to effective counseling and is therefore the focus of most counselor training programs.

Of course, the type of degree and the specialization within the program will determine what kind of professional one becomes. Since there is considerable overlap among the various concentrations in all mental health professions, it is important to understand the legal and functional distinctions that makes each unique. In brief, mental health practitioners are classified by the following descriptions (see also Sidebar 1-3).

Psychiatrists are medical doctors who have advanced training in mental health and psychopathology. Some psychiatrists who specialize in prescribing psychotropic medication have had little training in psychotherapy or counseling, whereas others do psychotherapy in addition to or instead of using medication. Still others are trained in psychoanalysis and have gone through the process themselves. Certification in psychiatry by the American Board of Psychiatry and Neurology is preferred but not required in all situations.

Psychoanalysts are trained specifically in Freudian psychoanalysis. Reputable institutes of psychoanalytic training require at least 3 years of training. Many insist that the trainee be licensed as a psychologist or psychiatrist.

Psychologists hold a Ph.D., Ed.D., or a Psy.D. from an approved institution of higher education. Not all psychologists are trained as counselors or psychotherapists, however. Many psychologists specialize in a range of related studies, including animal behavior, social psychology, lifespan development, geriatrics, and organizational psychology.

Clinical psychologists are trained in helping people solve major psychological problems. Their doctoral work includes internship training in psychological assessment and psychotherapy. Although requirements vary from state to state, generally clinical psychologists are required to pass comprehensive written and oral examinations. Licensed by the states in which they practice, clinical psychologists work in a number of settings including hospitals, prisons, clinics, and private practice.

Counseling psychologists are usually trained at the doctoral level to help people solve psychological problems related to such areas as personal adjustment, marriage, family, career, and school. They are licensed in the same way as clinical psychologists but usually do not work with more severe forms of psychological disturbance. Counseling psychologists often work in school settings and in private practice.

School psychologists are often trained at the doctoral level and work with educators and others to promote the intellectual, social, and emotional growth of school-age children. They may evaluate and treat children, generate programs, and consult with teachers and school officials. Their work settings include schools, nurseries, and daycare centers.

Industrial/organizational psychologists are trained at the doctoral level and are concerned with developing general theories or models that increase the effectiveness of organizations and make sense of the often confusing and complex patterns of interaction in the workplace. They use theories and experience in solving specific work behavior problems such as absenteeism or low productivity.

Marriage and family therapists earn a Master's or Doctorate in Marital and Family Therapy and in most states become licensed as Marriage, Family and Child Counselors (MFCC). Their training and practice is based on a theory of systems (i.e., interactions between a person and their social environment) rather than a model of individual therapy.

Social workers usually earn a Bachelor of Social Work from an accredited undergraduate school and then a Master's degree in Social Work. In many states they must become licensed to practice as a clinical social worker, a specialty focusing primarily on individual and family treatment. Social workers practice in a number of environments including medical settings, rehabilitative centers, correctional centers, private practice, and facilities for both the mentally and physically challenged.

> *There are some things which cannot be learned quickly, and time, which is all we have, must be paid heavily for their acquiring.*
>
> —Ernest Hemingway

Psychiatric nurses earn an Associates or Baccalaureate degree, pass a comprehensive examination, and specialize in psychiatric services. They provide front-line care in psychiatric hospitals, community mental health clinics, day treatment settings, and so on. In many states a nurse with an M.S.N. (Master of Science in Nursing) and psychiatric/mental health certification is also a third-party reimbursable and can do private practice (they cannot do this with a B.S.N. [Bachelor of Science in Nursing]).

Pastoral counselors are ministers who have been trained primarily in theology but have also acquired education and experience in counseling. They maintain a vision of spiritual wholeness rooted in their belief in the healing power of God. Many have been trained in one of over 350 clinical pastoral education centers in the United States.

Vocational counselors usually earn a master's degree. Concerned with much more than matching a person with a specific job, they work with people in helping them choose, enter, and progress in their vocations.

Occupational counselors may earn a Bachelor of Arts (B.A.) or a master's degree and gain clinical experience through an internship. They primarily help children and adults suffering from physical challenges to make the most of their resources.

School counselors earn an advanced degree in counseling psychology and work primarily with people needing to clarify educational and career issues. They work primarily, but not exclusively, in school settings.

Sidebar 1-3

SOURCES OF THERAPEUTIC SERVICES

Therapists work in a variety of organizational settings. Foremost among them are the following:

- *Private practitioners*—Self-employed therapists are listed in the Yellow Pages under their professional category, such as psychologists or psychiatrists. Private practitioners tend to be relatively expensive, but they also tend to be highly experienced therapists.
- *Community mental health centers*—These centers have salaried psychologists, psychiatrists, and social workers on staff. The centers provide a variety of services and often have staff available on weekends and at night to deal with emergencies. These centers may be the only resource for clients with limited

Reprinted from Weiten, Lloyd, & Lashley, *Psychology applied to modern life: Adjustment in the 90s* (3rd ed.). Pacific Grove, GA: Brooks/Cole.

funds because many provide treatment for clients on a sliding fee schedule.

- *Hospitals*—Several kinds of hospitals provide therapeutic services. There are both public and private mental hospitals that specialize in the care of people with psychological disorders. Many general hospitals have psychiatric units and those that do not will usually have psychiatrists and psychologists on staff and on call. Although hospitals tend to concentrate on inpatient treatment, many provide outpatient therapy as well.
- *Human service agencies*—Various social service agencies employ therapists to provide short-term counseling. Depending on your community, you may find agencies that deal with family problems, juvenile problems, drug problems, and so forth.
- *Schools and workplaces*—Most high schools and colleges have counseling centers where students can get help with personal problems. Similarly, some large businesses offer in-house counseling to their employees.

Substance abuse counselors earn a B.A. or a master's degree and help individuals suffering from addictions to drugs and alcohol. They usually work in treatment centers for substance abuse.

Paraprofessional counselors have intensive but limited training in helping approaches. They have gained some supervised field experience and almost always work under the direct supervision of a professional.

PROFESSIONAL GROWTH AND DEVELOPMENT

Before I conclude this introductory chapter, it is important for me to make one more point clear: Competent counselors are dedicated to life-long professional development. They recognize that the completion of a degree, even a doctorate, does not signal the end of personal and professional growth; only continuing education will enable them to maintain a vital and satisfying career in counseling. Whereas these academic milestones are important and worthy of celebration, proficient counselors maintain involvement in organizations that keep

American Psychological
Association, Washington, D. C.
*(Anice Hoachlander/
Hoachlander Photography Associates)*

American Counseling Association,
Alexandria, Virginia.
(Mattox Commercial Photography)

them accountable and current in their profession. Even counselors who have endured years of graduate courses, internships, postdoctoral fellowships, and a rigorous licensure exam come to understand the old adage, "The more I learn, the more I need to know."

There are many opportunities for counselors to sharpen their skills and further their understanding of counseling (Davison & Lazarus, 1994). Each year books are published for practicing counselors. But one of the best resources for professional development is membership in a counseling organization that provides resources through news publications, scholarly journals, workshops, and conventions.

Established more than 100 years ago, the American Psychological Association (APA) is the oldest organization of this kind and is made up of more than 70,000 members. The APA is composed of more than 50 divisions covering a range of interests. The Division for Counseling Psychology (Division 17) publishes the *Journal of Counseling Psychology,* the *Journal of Vocational Behavior,* the *Journal of Professional Psychology,* and the *Counseling Psychologist.* Membership dues and fees include subscriptions to *The APA Monitor,* psychology's newspaper, and the *American Psychologist,* the official journal of the APA.

> *An education isn't how much you have committed to memory, or even how much you know. It's being able to differentiate between what you do know and what you don't.*
>
> —Anatole France

In 1951 several professional associations for counselors and student personnel workers joined to form the American Personnel and Guidance Association. In 1984 it became the American Association for Counseling and Development, and in 1992 it again changed its name to the American Counseling Association (ACA). Boasting a membership of more than 55,000 from all fields of counseling, the ACA is made up of 16 divisions that include such specialties as multicultural counseling and development, career development, and mental health. The ACA disseminates counseling news and research through the *Journal of Counseling and Development* and the newsletter *Guidepost*. In addition, most of the ACA divisions publish journals dedicated specifically to concerns of that division.

The ACA and the APA hold annual regional and national conventions. The national meetings are large, with workshops, paper sessions, and symposia scheduled almost every hour. Joining these organizations and attending their conventions is an important part of a counselor's professional development and accountability. To keep counselors in check, both the APA and the ACA also have specific ethical guidelines, which will be addressed specifically in another chapter.

Students planning on an advanced degree in counseling or clinical psychology can begin their life-long process of professional accountability and development by joining these professional organizations as student affiliates. For a fraction of the cost of professional membership, students can receive special newsletters and reduced rates on journals. The address for APA is: 750 First St., N.E., Washington, DC 20002-4242. Students interested in the ACA can write to: ACA Student Membership, 5999 Stevenson Ave., Alexandria, VA 22304-3303.

A SUMMARY WORD

The study of counseling is like following the flow of a great river where territorial conflicts are fought, bridges are constructed for commercial advantage, and alliances are made with various tributaries that serve the purposes of the main stream. But in the meanwhile, most of life is lived on the banks of the river by people who have learned how to adjust to circumstances beyond their control as they make a living, raise families, and strive to keep order in their lives. It is on these banks, among these people, that qualified professional counselors find their fullest opportunities for service. It is also here that most become fulfilled by the rewards of a profession that truly can make a difference.

Before moving on to the next chapter, review what counseling is. Set your mind free from misunderstandings, conflicts, and overlapping of the various kinds of counseling within the total realm, and satisfy yourself on what counselors do. This process will take time, but it is worth the effort before turning to the important issues in the next chapter.

REFERENCES

Belkin, G. S. (1988). *An introduction to counseling* (3rd ed.). Dubuque, IA: Wm. C. Brown.

Bernard, J. M., & Goodyear, R. K. (1994). *Fundamentals of clinical supervision.* New York: Allyn & Bacon.

Beutler, L. E., & Kendall, P. C. (1995). Introduction to the special section: The case for training in the provision of psychological therapy. *Journal of Consulting and Clinical Psychology, 63,* 179–181.

Blocher, D. H. (1987). *The Professional Counselor.* New York: Macmillan.

Blocher, D. H., & Biggs, D. (1983). *Counseling psychology in community settings.* New York: Springer.

Brammer, L. M., Abrego, P. J., & Shostrom, E. L. (1993). *Therapeutic counseling and psychotherapy* (6th ed.). Englewood Cliffs, NJ: Prentice-Hall.

Bruch, H. (1981). Teaching and learning of psychotherapy. *Canadian Journal of Psychiatry, 26,* 86–92.

Burke, J. F. (1989). *Contemporary approaches to psychotherapy and counseling: The self-regulation and maturity model.* Pacific Grove, CA: Brooks/Cole.

Carkhuff, R. R. (1971). Training as a preferred mode of treatment. *Journal of Counseling Psychology, 13,* 123–131.

Cavaliere, F. (June, 1995). APA brochure offers tips on choosing a psychologist. *The APA Monitor, 9,* 11.

Christensen, A., & Jacobson, N. S. (1994). Who (or what) can do psychotherapy: The status and challenge of nonprofessional therapies. *Psychological Science, 5,* 8–14.

Cormier, W. H., & Cormier, L. S. (1985). *Interviewing strategies for helpers.* Monterey, CA: Brooks/Cole.

Cormier, L. S., & Hackney, H. (1987). *The professional counselor: A process guide to helping.* Englewood Cliffs, NJ: Prentice-Hall.

Corsini, R. J., & Wedding, D. (1995). *Current psychotherapies* (5th ed.). Itasca, IL: F. E. Peacock.

Cushman, P. (1992). Psychotherapy to 1992: A historically situated interpretation. In D. K. Freedheim, H. J. Freudenberger, J. W. Kessler, S. B. Messner, D. R. Peterson, H. H. Strupp, & P. L. Wachtel (Eds.), *A history of psychotherapy: A century of change.* Washington, DC: American Psychological Association.

Davison, G. C., & Lazarus, A. A. (1994). Clinical innovation and evaluation: Integrating practice with inquiry. *Clinical Psychology: Science and Practice, 1,* 157–168.

Frank, J. (1973). *Persuasion and healing.* New York: Schocken Books.

Gabbard, G. (1995). Are all psychotherapies equally effective? *The Menninger Letter, 3,* 1–2.

Gazda, G. M. (1984). Multiple impact training: A life skills approach. In D. Larson (Ed.), *Teaching psychological skills.* Monterey, CA: Brooks/Cole.

Gelso, C. J., & Fretz, B. R. (1992). *Counseling psychology.* Fort Worth, TX: Harcourt Brace Jovanovich.

George, R. L., & Cristiani, T. S. (1990). *Counseling theory and practice* (3rd ed.). Englewood Cliffs, NJ: Prentice-Hall.

Gibson, R. L., & Mitchell, M. H. (1986). *Introduction to counseling and guidance* (2nd ed.). New York: Macmillan.

Gottman, J., & Markman, H. (1978). Experimental designs in psychotherapy research. In S. Garfield & A. Bergin (Eds.), *Handbook of psychotherapy and behavior change: An empirical analysis.* New York: Wiley.

Jewell, L. N. (1985). *Contemporary Industrial/Organizational Psychology.* New York: West Publishing.

Krumboltz, J. D. (1965). Behavioral counseling: Rationale and research. *Personnel and Guidance Journal, 44,* 383–387.

Larson, D. (1984). *Teaching psychological skills.* Monterey, CA: Brooks/Cole.

Lipsey, M., & Wilson, D. (1993). The efficacy of psychological, education, and behavioral treatment: Confirmation from meta-analysis. *American Psychologist, 48,* 1181–1209.

London, P. (1964). *The modes and morals of psychotherapy.* Washington, DC: Hemisphere.

Lonner, W. J., & Malpass, R. (1994). *Psychology and culture.* New York: Allyn & Bacon.

Mays, V. M., & Albee, G. W. (1993). Psychotherapy and ethnic minorities. In D. K. Freedheim (Ed.), *History of psychotherapy.* Washington, DC: American Psychological Association.

Meehl, P. E. (1993). If Freud could define psychoanalysis, why can't ABPP do it? *Psychoanalysis and Contemporary Thought, 16,* 299–326.

Moldawsky, S. (1990). Is solo practice really dead? *American Psychologist, 45,* 544–546.

Osipow, S. H., Walsh, W. B., & Tosi, D. J. (1984). *A survey of counseling methods* (Rev ed.). Homewood, IL: Dorsey Press.

Patterson, C. H. (1973). *Theories of counseling and psychotherapy* (2nd ed.). New York: Harper & Row.

Phillips, L. (1978). *The social skills basis of psychopathology.* New York: Grune & Stratton.

Tharp, R. G., & Wetzel, R. J. (1969). *Behavior modification in the natural environment.* New York: Academic Press.

Warner, D. L., & Bradley, J. R. (1991). Undergraduate psychology students' views of counselors, psychiatrists, and psychologists: A challenge to academic psychologists. *Professional Psychology: Research and Practice, 22,* 138–140.

CHAPTER 2

Becoming an
Effective Counselor

Chapter Outline

Personal Qualities of Effective Counselors
Common Pitfalls Faced by Beginning Counselors
A Summary Word

Karl Wallenda, a great tightrope aerialist, fell to his death in 1978, while walking a 75-foot-high wire in downtown San Juan, Puerto Rico. Shortly after this
tragedy, his wife, also an aerialist, discussed that fatal walk. She recalled that all
Karl thought about for three straight months before his attempt was falling. It
was the first time he'd ever thought about failure in his work and, from her
point of view, he put all his energies into *not falling* rather than walking the
tightrope. Karl was virtually destined to make a mistake.

The counselor who focuses more on his or her potential for failure than on
success is, like Karl Wallenda, also likely to fall. The counselor in training is especially tempted to invest a disproportionate amount of time and energy in trying to avoid mistakes instead of focusing on what it takes to be effective. Do
you have a secret fear of making therapeutic blunders? If so, you are not alone.
In this chapter we attempt to alleviate this kind of anxiety by exploring the personal qualities of effective counselors—by paying attention, not so much to
what they do, as to *who* they are. We then turn our attention to some of the most
common mistakes the beginning therapist makes. The goal is to help you become aware of these pitfalls, avoid them, and put your energy into becoming
the most effective counselor you can be.

PERSONAL QUALITIES OF EFFECTIVE COUNSELORS

What makes counselors effective? Is it their theoretical orientation? Their
therapeutic techniques and skills? Not as much as you might guess. After

reviewing nearly 100 studies on the effectiveness of counselors, Truax and Mitchell (1971) concluded that therapeutic techniques can be useful only when the counselor's personality is inherently helpful. In other words, a counselor's *personal qualities* are at least as essential to therapeutic outcomes as the counselor's knowledge, theory, and skill (Jevne, 1981). Theoretical orientation, interviewing skills, and even professional experience are not the critical determinants for effective therapy. The counselor's personality is the single most important criterion for effectiveness (Perez, 1979; Seligman, 1995).

Before developing this point further, however, a word of caution is in order: a person's traits cannot compensate for inadequate knowledge or poor therapeutic skills. "A helpful personality that lacks knowledge and helping skills is like a good driver who operates an unsafe car" (Cavanaugh, 1990, p. 72). Although personal qualities cannot substitute for adequate training, the point is that the most effective practitioners possess certain personal qualities that transcend their therapeutic techniques and cut across theoretical lines (Bergin & Lambert, 1978; Small, 1990).

What are these qualities that make a difference? In a classic 4-year study conducted with counselors who worked with hospital patients, it was discovered that patients improved when their therapists showed high levels of warmth, genuineness, and empathy, regardless of their theoretical orientation. When these qualities were lacking, the hospital patients grew worse (Rogers, Gendlin, Kiesler, & Truax, 1967). These early findings have been bolstered by subsequent research, both with patients and with counselees who were not hospitalized (see Corrigan, Dell, Lewis, & Schmidt, 1980; Gelso & Carter, 1994; Loesch, Crane, & Rucker, 1978; Row, Murphy, & DeCsipkes, 1975).

Through the years numerous studies have contributed to the list of basic qualities shared by effective counselors. In fact, discovering these qualities is one of the most popular of dissertation topics among students seeking advanced degrees in therapy (Patterson & Eisenberg, 1983). Perhaps because of this extensive research on the subject, the list of personal qualities that improve the possibilities of healing keeps growing. Many authors, including Corey and Corey (1982), Carkhuff and Berenson (1977), Trotzer (1977), Kottler (1983), Patterson and Eisenberg (1983), and Sexton and Whiston (1994) have compiled several lists that include such qualities as a sense of humor, a high energy level, self-confidence, neutrality, flexibility, analytical thinking, creativity, enthusiasm, compassion, and honesty. The following, however, is an annotated list of what seem to be, according to the studies, the eight most important qualities in an effective counselor. Of course, perfection in these personal qualities is not required, only an awareness of one's own personality and a willingness to confront what is detrimental and to cultivate what is needed. These eight qualities are psychological health, genuine interest in others, empathic ability, personal warmth, personal power, self-awareness, tolerance of ambiguity, and an awareness of values.

> Good counselors lack no clients.
> —Shakespeare

Psychological Health

No one expects professional counselors to be paragons of psychological health; the crucial factor is the counselor's sense of well-being and his or her willingness to be in process. Counselors are models of behavior. If they do not demonstrate psychological health they become part of the problem, rather than part of the solution (Cavanaugh, 1990). Of all the personality variables studied in positive mental health research, *meaning and purpose* are most predictive of well-being. Counselors need a positive philosophy for living, a sense of meaning and purpose that give them inner strength to adjust to circumstances beyond their control. Abraham Maslow, who turned psychology on its heels by being the first to study personal health, said, "Human beings need values and a philosophy of life to live by in the same sense that they need sunlight, calcium, or love." A positive philosophy of life helps generate the strength to overcome the unavoidable struggles along the way—not that people with optimum mental health are immune to difficulties, failures, and tragedies, but they possess the capacity to incorporate meaning into their struggles and to rise above them.

Another mark of mental health is a sense of *personal responsibility*. Some experts view an avoidance of personal responsibility as the essence of *all* emotional disturbance. When people avoid responsibility for themselves, they either blame selected people or they generalize the blame on the nebulous "they,"

Abraham Maslow (1908–1970).
(Corbis-Bettmann)

whether the government, General Motors, or a special interest group such as the environmentalists or the loggers. Either way, they become unnecessarily dependent by making someone else responsible for their needs, their pain, or their failure. Healthy counselors are not passive victims looking to lay the blame on someone else; rather, they are on a quest for more mastery in their lives. They model responsibility and avoid the attitude of "You think *you've* got problems!" Albert Bandura (1977) calls this ability to be in control of one's life *perceived self-efficacy*. Studies have shown that the greater one's perceived self-efficacy, the better one's general psychological adjustment (Heppner & Anderson, 1985; Seligman, 1990).

Sidebar 2-1

THE SELF-ACTUALIZING THERAPIST

The ideal outcome of counseling is to help clients become more self-actualizing or more fully functioning. If this is a goal for clients, some writers (e.g., Carkhuff & Berenson, 1977) believe it should be an objective for counselors also. You can only lead someone as far as you have traveled yourself. Maslow's quest to discover the characteristics of highly functioning people revealed the following traits (Patterson, 1985):

- *Being reality based.* The self-actualizing person detects phoniness and has an accurate, nondistorted perception of reality.
- *Being accepting of self, others, and nature.* Self-actualizing persons respect and esteem themselves and others.
- *Being spontaneous.* Self-actualizing persons are not conformists, but neither are they anticonformist for the sake of being so.
- *Being problem centered.* Self-actualizing persons have a sense of mission in their lives.
- *Having a need for privacy.* Self-actualizing persons enjoy solitude.
- *Being autonomous.* Self-actualizing persons do not depend on others or their culture for satisfaction.
- *Having a continued freshness of appreciation.* Self-actualizing persons experience pleasure and wonder in their everyday world.
- *Being mystical.* Self-actualizing persons have meaningful experiences of ecstasy and awe.
- *Being compassionate.* Self-actualizing persons have strong feelings of sympathy and regard for other human beings in general.
- *Being relational.* Self-actualizing persons have a circle of deep friendships with other healthy persons.
- *Being nondiscriminatory.* Self-actualizing persons are humble and ready to learn from anyone.
- *Being highly ethical.* Self-actualizing persons clearly distinguish means from ends.
- *Having a sense of humor.* Self-actualizing persons have a spontaneous and thoughtful sense of humor that is neither hostile nor sarcastic.
- *Being creative.* Self-actualizing persons have a fresh, creative way of looking at things.

Effective counselors are on a quest toward self-actualization to better help others in their self-actualizing journey. It is not expected that counselors rate high on each of these qualities, but rather that they be aware of where they are in the process and what they must do to move on.

Psychological health is also marked by being at peace in the present. Maslow said: "Some people spend their entire lives indefinitely preparing to live." (see Sidebar 2-1.) This is not true, however, with people who enjoy positive mental health. These individuals find joy in the journey toward their destination; they are not simply waiting to arrive. Healthy people have launched themselves fully into the stream of life and find it stimulating, meaningful, and enjoyable (Rogers, 1961). They read, write, travel, and play. They enjoy the company of diverse friends as well as the privacy of being alone (Cavanaugh, 1990). In summary, whereas ineffective counselors are relatively uneasy with the character of their inner life, effective counselors are on relatively good terms with their own emotional experience (Allen, 1967; Cormier & Hackney, 1987; Gurman, 1972).

Genuine Interest in Others

One's desire to be a professional counselor can be equated with an authentic interest in helping people, the emphasis being as much on the word *authentic* as on the phrase *helping people*. Unfortunately, some persons pursue the profession of counseling for the wrong reasons. As T. S. Eliot wrote in his play, *Murder in the Cathedral*, "The last temptation is the greatest treason; to do the right deed for the wrong reason." There are many self-serving reasons for would-be counselors to enter the helping profession: for personal advancement, for example, for recognition, or even because of a need for self-therapy (Pietrofesa, Hoffman, & Splete, 1984).

Effective counselors, on the other hand, are authentic; they are genuinely interested in helping people gain better mental health. Carl Rogers (1951) called this quality of authenticity *congruence* and defined it as consistency between a counselor's real self and what a counselor says and does. A counselor cannot fake authenticity: it is not something you do, but something you are.

Genuine concern for others is part of a lifestyle (Egan, 1990). It is integral to the persona, to the role one chooses to play in life, as Carl Jung put it. It cannot be mustered up for the moment like a manufactured smile. Being genuine means stripping away masks and being real. It means not playing a role (MacDevitt, 1987). The point is that energy spent on role playing or keeping a facade on straight absorbs energy that might have been used in alleviating problems. Counselors cannot help clients achieve authenticity without *being* authentic themselves (see Sidebar 2-2). Burdened with the lack of honesty in the "outside" world, clients do not want to relate to another unreal person who is playing the role of counselor (Dreyfus, 1967). They cannot be open, trusting, and honest with a counselor who does not mirror these same qualities. Genuiness underlies the entire counseling relationship, and it is at the core of an effective counselor's being. Only when those who hope to practice counseling appreciate the centrality of genuiness, can they apply therapeutic theories and techniques effectively (Pietrofesa et al., 1984).

> The counselor's personality is the fulcrum on which are balanced knowledge of behavior dynamics and therapeutic skill.
>
> —Michael E. Cavanaugh

Sidebar 2-2

BEING "ROLE-FREE"

Effective therapists do not take refuge in the role of playing counselor. They do not use the facade of being a counselor to substitute for competence or to fool the client. Gibb (1968, 1978) suggests several ways counselors can become "role-free." Here are a few of his suggestions:

- Communicate without distorting your messages.
- Listen to others without distorting their messages.
- Reveal your true motivations.
- Be spontaneous and free in your communications.
- Strive for interdependence rather than dependence with clients.
- Be concrete in your communications.
- Be willing to commit yourself to others.

Empathic Abilities

Empathy is the ability to put oneself in the shoes of other people and see the world as they see it. Unlike sympathy, which merely projects feelings onto other people, empathy allows one sensitively to enter another's feelings and accurately understand them. Sympathy is standing on the shore, seeing a person struggling in the water and throwing out a life-ring. Empathy, on the other hand, is jumping into the water and risking one's own safety to help the struggling person. Empathy is risky because it will change you. Once you empathize with an alcoholic, for example, you won't look at alcoholism in the same way again (Parrott, 1994).

Contemporary writers view empathy in a number of ways. Empathy has been described as thinking "*with,* rather than *for* or *about* the client" (Brammer & Shostrom, 1982, p. 160), or as the process of grasping with great clarity the meaning clients want to convey (Tyler, 1969). Some have said that empathy is "the ability to understand and to accurately communicate the meanings of the client's cognitive and affective responses about his or her self and the environment" (Osipow, Walsh, & Tosi, 1984, p. 18). One of the best explanations of empathy comes from Carl Rogers (1957), who said empathy is "to sense the client's private world as if it were your own, but without ever losing the 'as if' quality—that is empathy" (p. 99).

Studied extensively, empathy has proved to be crucial to positive outcomes in counseling (Aspey, 1975; Barrett-Lennard, 1962; Ridley, Mendoza, & Kanitz, 1994). It helps build rapport, elicit information from clients, and foster their goals (Egan, 1990). Carkhuff (1969) and Pierce developed a Discrimination Inventory that presents a scale for assessing a counselor's level of empathy. On the scale, a counselor's responses are rated on the following five levels:

Level 1: The counselor communicates no awareness of even the most obvious, expressed surface feelings of clients.

Level 2: The counselor may communicate some awareness of obvious, surface feelings of clients, but the level of meaning is distorted.

Level 3: The counselor responds with accurate understandings of the surface feelings of clients but may not respond to or may misinterpret the deeper feelings.

Level 4: The counselor communicates an understanding of the expressions of clients at a level deeper than they were expressed, enabling them to experience and express those feelings at a deeper level.

Level 5: The counselor is "tuned in" to clients and responds with accuracy to all their deeper as well as their surface feelings.

Empathy says: "If I were her I would act as she does." According to Carkhuff (1969), empathy is the key ingredient in a helping relationship. "Without an empathic understanding of the helpee's world and his difficulties as he sees them, there is no basis for helping" (p. 173).

Personal Warmth

Personal warmth refers to one's psychological climate and the conditions of the therapeutic interview. But there is a significant distinction to be made between the liberation of personal warmth and the oppressiveness of "humidity" that can suffocate potential: "The warm counselor is caring and freeing; the humid counselor is needy and possessive" (Cavanaugh, 1990, p. 85). A counselor with personal warmth shows interest, concern, and attention but allows for personal space as well. His or her caring is nonpossessive and does not judge or evaluate (Bergin & Garfield, 1971; Rausch & Bordin, 1957; Truax & Carkhuff, 1967). Rogers (1951) called this quality *unconditional positive regard*—the complete acceptance of clients' characteristics and behaviors.

The purpose of nonpossessive warmth is to preserve clients' self-respect and to provide a trusting and safe atmosphere. Warmth stimulates clients' trust and helps them recognize that they can be liked in spite of unattractive characteristics (Bergin & Garfield, 1971; Osipow et al., 1984). Clients count on the therapist being consistently nonjudgmental. This stability allows them to express themselves freely without fearing a reaction of disapproval, shock, or criticism. In addition, warmth begets warmth, melting human defenses. "It is a rare human being who does not respond to warmth with warmth and to hostility with hostility. It is probably the most important principle for the beginning therapist to understand" (Truax & Carkhuff, 1967, p. 36).

> Anyone with a modicum of human warmth, common sense, some sensitivity to human problems, and a desire to help can benefit many candidates for psychotherapy.
>
> —Jerome D. Frank

An attitude of warmth accepts what is, rather than demands what should be. It is the capacity to suspend critical judgment (Egan, 1990). The opposite of contempt, an accepting attitude involves neither approval nor disapproval of clients' personality characteristics or behavior. In acceptance there are no reservations, conditions, evaluations, and judgments of clients' feelings (Boy & Pine, 1982). This kind of acceptance is often revealed

Warmth and acceptance is often revealed nonverbally.
(Courtesy of Seattle Pacific University)

through nonverbal behaviors (Cavanaugh, 1990; Gazda, 1973; LaCrosse, 1975). Smiles, head nods, hand gestures, eye contact, and a slight forward tilt of the body can all contribute to counselors being judged as warm by their clients. In other words, clients are very much aware of their counselors' nonverbal behaviors and use these signals to interpret their warmth (see Sidebar 2-3).

Whatever specific approach a counselor uses, the likelihood of his or her success in the counseling dialog is strengthened by a capacity for personal warmth (Kanfer & Goldstein, 1991). According to Goldstein and Higginbotham (1991), without the expression of warmth, particular strategies and helping interventions may be "technically correct but therapeutically impotent" (p. 48).

NONVERBAL CUES OF PERSONAL WARMTH AND COLDNESS

Warmth is communicated primarily through nonverbal behaviors such as voice tone, eye contact, facial expressions, gestures, and touch. It is important to remember that clients from non-Western cultures may perceive these North American nonverbal signals of warmth and cold differently.

Nonverbal cue	Warmth	Coldness
Tone of voice	Soft, soothing	Callous, reserved, hard
Facial expression	Smiling, interested	Poker-faced, frowning, disinterested
Posture	Relaxed, leaning toward the other person	Tense, leaning away from the other person
Eye contact	Looking directly into the other person's eyes	Avoiding eye contact
Touching	Touching the other softly and discreetly	Avoiding all touch
Gestures	Open, welcoming	Closed, as if guarding oneself
Physical proximity	Close	Distant

From D. W. Johnson (1981). *Reaching out: Interpersonal effectiveness and self-actualization* (2nd ed.) Englewood Cliffs, NJ: Prentice-Hall. Reprinted by permission.

Self-Awareness

The ancient dictum of Socrates to "know thyself" is critical to becoming an effective counselor. Self-knowledge allows counselors to identify personal limits and become more objective. It empowers counselors to know "what they are doing, why they are doing it, which problems are theirs, and which belong to the client" (Cavanaugh, 1990, p. 73). When counselors know themselves and are comfortable with themselves, they are more at ease in working with others (Baldwin & Satir, 1987; Brennan & Piechowski, 1991). Self-awareness keeps counselors from allowing themselves to interfere with the therapeutic process. For this reason, many graduate training programs in counseling rightly encourage their students to undergo personal therapy themselves. Counselors in training can also become more self-aware by keeping a journal, in which they can record thoughts, feelings, experiences, stories, poems, dreams, and drawings. Our written expressions are often different from what we might disclose verbally, and they can teach us much about who we are (Watson & Tharp, 1993). Cormier and Cormier (1985) say "it is just as important to keep track of our own personal growth as it is to keep track of what technique or change program we are using with a client" (p. 13).

Regardless of the means for achievement, there is no debating that counseling is more effective when counselors are aware of their personal issues. Belkin (1988) points to three critical areas deserving of self-study for the counselor: security, trust, and courage. A responsible self-examination can lead to heightened self-awareness by asking questions that target these important areas of the inner self. To begin with, ask, "Do I feel secure?" Counselors who are secure have little need to pass judgment on others, and they are confident enough to allow clients to develop at their own rates and in their own directions. It has also been found that insecure therapists are less accurate in their ability to recall words and feelings expressed in counseling interviews (Milliken & Kirchner, 1971). Next, ask yourself, "Do I trust other people?" The counselor who is suspicious and cynical is not likely to relate to clients in ways that are conducive to healthy change and growth. Mistrustful counselors project feelings and ideas onto clients that do not exist. For example, a therapist who is feeling angry projects this feeling onto the client and asks, "Why are you so negative today?" The third question in this self-study trilogy is, "Do I have the courage to confront challenges?" Counselors must have the courage to confront themselves—to examine their true motives, their feelings, and limitations. Counselors must also have the courage to confront their clients and be willing, at times, to subjugate their own feelings and desires to be liked, respected, and admired in favor of the therapeutic process of the clients.

Tolerance of Ambiguity

Much of the counselor's world is abstract and ambiguous. Clients are often not fully aware of their real problems, and they sometimes complain of vague, indefinable symptoms. Their feelings may vacillate daily without reason. On top of these ambiguities, there are other uncertainties endemic to the practice of counseling itself. For instance, there is no single way of approaching a given therapeutic issue. The counselor cannot prescribe a proven antidote the way a physician can scribble out a prescription on a pad. The path to healing is often unique to a particular client, and there are no precise road maps for the counselor to follow. The uncertainty of the journey requires stamina, poise, and a high tolerance for ambiguity.

The light of the body is the eye.
—Matthew 6:22

According to a German proverb, "Patience is a bitter plant, but it bears sweet fruit." Counselors who have a high tolerance for ambiguity understand this principle of patience, and their therapeutic labors show it. Effective counselors—counselors who are tolerant of ambiguity—consistently practice patience with their clients, gently working to move the process along. At times, they abandon their search for cause and effect and come to terms with the ambiguity of diagnostic changes and the uncertainty of tentative treatment plans (Tramel, 1981). In short, less successful counselors are less tolerant of ambiguous material in the counseling interview than are more effective counselors.

Awareness of Values

Long ago, in a classic study in a nursery school, children were shown a poker chip and then asked to compare the size of the chip to the size of an adjustable circle of light, until the chip and the circle of light were perceived as being the same size. The children were then told they could exchange their poker chips for candy. After the children understood this proposition, they were again asked to compare the size of the chips to the circle of light. This time, the chips seemed much larger to the children (Lambert, Solomon, & Watson, 1949). Quite clearly, our personal values color our perceptions (see Sidebar 2-4).

Values are the convictions or beliefs that determine our goals and how we attempt to meet them. They guide our actions and prescribe our outlook on life. If you value success and accomplishment, for example, you will probably be a hard worker, striving for advancement. If you place a high value on social activities, you are more likely to seek a work setting requiring a more minimal commitment. Becoming aware of one's values is critically important to being an effective counselor. A particular combination of values constitutes a world view, which will influence counseling activities in numerous ways.

Sidebar 2-4

	Rank	Value
WHAT DO YOU VALUE?	_____	Beautiful world
A few years ago three sociologists de-signed a television program called *The Great American Values Test* to conduct an experiment on the possible influence of television on values. To take their test, study the list in the right column and place a number to the left of each value that describes its importance to you (1 = most important; 18 = least important). In completing this test, think carefully and work slowly. If you change your mind, don't hesitate to change your answer.	_____	Comfortable life
	_____	Equality
	_____	Exciting life
	_____	Family security
	_____	Freedom
	_____	Happiness
	_____	Inner harmony
	_____	Mature love
You may find it interesting to com-pare your rankings with a sample of adults in the state of Washington who re-sponded to this test. From top to bottom, they responded: 15, 8, 12, 17, 1, 3, 5, 11, 14, 13, 16, 18, 10, 4, 7, 9, 6, 2.	_____	National security
	_____	Pleasure
	_____	Recognition from others
	_____	Salvation
S. J. Ball-Rokeach, M. Rokeach, & J. W. Grube (1984). The great American values test: Can television alter basic beliefs? *Psychology Today, 18,* 34–41.	_____	Self-respect
	_____	Sense of accomplishment
	_____	True friendship
	_____	Wisdom
	_____	World peace

To begin with, effective counselors have thought through their values and live by them. Carl Rogers (1969, 1977) found that most people who seek out therapy follow external value judgments, which are not necessarily their own. They deny their own personal convictions in favor of convictions others have taught them to hold. This is not true, however, of the effective counselor, who is particularly aware of personal convictions and has the courage to uphold them. A review of research related to a variety of helping professionals, including teachers, clergy, school counselors, and counselors in training, concluded that the helper's awareness of values is a significant factor in predicting the effectiveness of the help (Combs, 1986; Kelly, 1990). Of course, the effective counselor also strives to understand and appreciate the values of others. After all, it was Eric Fromm who said that the test of love is loving the stranger at our gates—the individual with values different from our own.

Of course, not all values have an impact on the helping process. Cormier and Cormier (1985), for example, suggest that "the counselor who values sailing can probably work with a client who values being a landlubber without any problem" (p. 17). It is those values that reflect morality, ethics, and lifestyle that have a greater probability of entering into the helping process.

Can counselors avoid conveying these values to their clients? Should they? Some professionals believe that the counselor should communicate no value orientation while counseling, that he or she should strive to be morally neutral in their counseling and focus only on the clients' values. They believe that the influence of the counselor's values would prevent clients from constructing their own internalized values (George & Cristiani, 1990; Ibrahim, 1991).

At the same time, some professionals have long called for an abandonment of this position (e.g., Patterson, 1958; Rosenthal, 1955; Samler, 1960; Williamson, 1958). They believe counselors cannot escape their values, that they cannot pretend to abandon or lack a value system in a counseling setting (George and Cristiani, 1990)—in short, that it is impossible to be "value-free" with clients (Cormier & Cormier, 1985). The counselor's values will be a part of the therapeutic work, either consciously or unconsciously (Coonerty, 1991; Rokeach & Regan, 1980). Okun (1982) asserts that "in an interpersonal relationship, whether or not it is a helping relationship, values are transmitted either covertly or overtly between the participants" (p. 229). In other words, values may sometimes be communicated in subtle ways, but they *are* communicated. Nonverbal cues of approval and disapproval, for example, convey value messages whether or not the therapist intends to or not (Corey, Corey, & Callanan, 1984). Given this inevitable communication of values, many professionals favor an open and explicit value orientation in counseling. They treat changing values of clients as part of the counseling process and argue that, no matter how passive and valueless the counselor may appear, the value systems of clients are influenced and gradually become congruent with the counselor's system of values.

> The deepest principle in human nature is the craving for appreciation.
>
> —William James

In fact, although many counselors believe their values should be kept out of therapy as much as possible, research indicates that clients who improve most perceptibly tend to conform their values with those of the counselor. According to one study, when clients were grouped by how similar their values were to the values of the counselor, it was found that clients in a medium similarity group improved more than those in either high similarity or low similarity groups (Cook, 1966). These and other findings suggest that seeing themselves as too similar or too different from the other has an adverse effect on their interactions.

Because values are an integral part of personality, they are blended into the counselor's formula for effectiveness. Counselors who hold world views radically different from those of their clients and who are unaware of these differences "are most likely to impute negative traits to their clients" (Sue, 1978, p. 458). The effective counselor, who is aware of personal values and respects clients' welfare when those values clash, may be expected to refer clients to a more compatible therapist.

• • •

These qualities of an effective counselor—psychological health, genuine interest in others, empathic ability, personal warmth, self-awareness, tolerance of ambiguity, and an awareness of values—take time to acquire. Perhaps the word *becoming* in the title of this chapter should be underlined. Becoming effective as a counselor is not a product, but a process. No one is error free. Nevertheless, the remainder of this chapter is devoted to the identification of the most probable hurdles in a counselor's path and how they may be avoided.

COMMON PITFALLS FACED
BY BEGINNING COUNSELORS

When a promising young executive at IBM lost over $10 million in a venture under his authority, both he and his immediate bosses were understandably devastated. However, when IBM's founder and president, Tom Watson, called the shattered executive into his office for a review of what happened, the man blurted out, "I guess you want my resignation?" "You can't be serious," Watson replied. "We've just spent $10 million educating you!" Thankfully, most mistakes are not as costly as the one this IBM executive made. And most schools and counseling centers cannot absorb $10 million mistakes. However, the good news is that there is no such thing as learning without making mistakes. As a counselor in training, you will be expected to make mistakes, and you will be expected to learn from your mistakes (Gambrill, 1990). Learning to counsel is like learning to ski: if you're not falling down, you're not learning.

The following is not an exhaustive list of blunders made by beginning counselors, nor is it a catalog of the worst possible therapeutic errors. Rather, this list is representative of some of the most common mistakes made by beginning therapists. The list is designed to stimulate your thinking and heighten your awareness of difficulties that may lie around the corner.

Premature Problem Solving

Like a complex puzzle with interlocking pieces, a client's struggle cannot normally be diagnosed and cured in a brief time. A problem that has been escalating for years cannot be understood and healed in minutes. Trying to solve the problem before it is fully understood, however, is one of the most common therapeutic mistakes.

Consider Traci, a college student with a 3.8 grade point average who says, "I'm really depressed and I think it's because I bombed my English mid-term." As her counselor reviewed her symptoms, the self-assessment seemed accurate. Traci expected to receive high marks, and falling short had indeed been traumatic for her. The counselor mused silently over the signs of an over-achiever whose academic performance was unrealistic. The therapist searched gently, asking questions and listening for answers that might or might not enforce the hypothesis. The student admitted she was impatient with herself. She wanted to be valedictorian. The counselor seemed to have nailed the problem squarely, and it was time in the counseling process to dispute her unrealistic goal of valedictorian. She had obviously inflicted herself with disquieting pressure that caused mild depression, and the counselor spent the next five sessions trying to whittle away at her unrealistic standards. It seemed progress was underway. Later in the week, however, the counselor received a message on the office answering machine that changed everything. It was from Traci's roommate who said, "I know I probably shouldn't be calling you, but I was afraid that Traci hadn't told you she's bulimic." All of a sudden, the counselor's theory about Traci's overachieving disintegrated.

> We understand only that which we love.
>
> —Goethe

A seasoned counselor knows it is normally not easy, in one or two sessions, to identify clearly and to diagnose the underlying problems in a dysfunctional person. It may take that long for clients to trust the counselor enough to reveal the most revealing factors in their situation. The effective counselor is therefore continually saying, "Is there something else I may be missing?"

Not Setting Limits

In an effort to be understanding and tolerant, most beginning counselors have difficulty setting their own personal limits—dealing appropriately with such issues as repeated calls on the phone by clients, for example, with missed appointments, and clients not paying fees on time. Another potential problem area is the amount of time the counselor spends with clients in each session. Some clients may attempt to test the limits by continuing to talk past the appointed end of the session. But giving clients 60 or 70 minutes when 50 were promised may raise questions in their minds. These clients will wonder whether you are strong enough to be their therapist if you can't handle their end-of-session ramblings. Do not be afraid to set limits and courteously hold to them (Cloud & Townsend, 1992).

Fear of Silence

The inexperienced counselor is often afraid of silence. The compulsion to say something during an awkward silence is natural and part of the human need to fill the gaps of everyday conversation. In counseling, however, silence is not a sign that the counselor needs to say something. Silence does not mean that something has gone wrong. When the counselor senses that the wheels of thought and feeling are turning, he or she should give clients time to reflect and contemplate. The effective counselor allows this process to happen without interruption. A nervous counselor who gets anxious during silence, on the other hand, will derail a train of thought by interrupting the productive silence.

Many clients have difficulty expressing themselves on sensitive subjects, and interrupting them before they have finished what they are trying to say is degrading. The effective counselor rehearses what he or she is going to say next, but holds it in check until clients have fully completed the momentary struggle of thinking and talking about something that probably makes them feel very vulnerable.

There are times, of course, when silence is not productive. Some clients, for example, may be socially anxious and, for this reason, they may be unable to express themselves easily. Naive about how therapy works, other clients may expect the therapist to do all of the talking. But more often, silence works to a positive purpose. Some of counseling's most therapeutic moments occur during periods of quiet contemplation. The inexperienced counselor needs to remember that it takes clients much longer to incorporate what you have said than the time it has taken to say it. When clients are quiet they are often in the therapeutic process. So become comfortable with silence and learn to maintain eye contact with your clients, nodding your head as a nonverbal expression of listening and understanding (Brammer & MacDonald, 1996).

> We can only know ourselves through knowing others and we can only know others through knowing ourselves.
>
> —Sydney Harris

Interrogating

By relying too heavily on asking questions, the inexperienced counselor may cause clients to feel interrogated rather than understood. But interrogation and counseling are not synonymous: little therapeutic help takes place during an inquisition. The counselor in training, therefore, needs to learn to refrain from subjecting clients to a barrage of questions. Excessive probing can make them feel beleaguered, and eventually they may clam up.

It is important to understand that good information can be obtained without interrogation. In response to a client who says, "My father was angry at me for most of the afternoon," numerous questions could follow: How often does your father become angry? What does he do when he is angry? How does that make you feel? A therapist can obtain much of this information and more by saying something like, "I get the impression you have experienced your father's anger more than once." An open-ended statement like this lets clients know they are understood, and it invites further disclosure without the risk of putting them on the spot.

The point is that it is possible for the skilled counselor to elicit information without a series of threatening questions. When he or she actively tries to understand clients' experiences, this helps them genuinely open up. Relevant information then becomes more readily accessible, and a stronger therapeutic alliance is built.

Impatience

Every therapist watches with hope for signs of progress. Every counselor wants clients to improve as soon as possible. Impatience in the inexperienced counselor shows up in an eagerness to push unprepared clients into a treatment strategy before their time has come. Although there are certain "Aha" moments in counseling, most therapeutic improvement is gradual, often slow. Gradual change is not an indicator of poor therapy (Cunningham, Davis, Bremner, Dunn, & Rzasa, 1993). Transformation in the mind takes time. A person who is grieving the loss of a loved one, for example, cannot be forced to snap out of it. Nor can a person struggling with an eating disorder be expected to reverse habits quickly that have been a long time building. The problem may be radical, but it is inevitable that the cure will be gradual.

In fact, clients who are rushed into making rapid changes will be set up for further failure. Being pushed to show signs of improvement too soon may result in extreme defensiveness, regression, or a premature termination of therapy altogether. Thus the beginning counselor must be sensitive to issues of personal impatience, for most clients cannot and will not make dramatic changes quickly. Nor should they.

Moralizing

Therapists are not required to compromise their convictions, to relinquish the beliefs, values, and morals that are their own. Nevertheless, regardless of clients' behaviors, a professional counselor may refrain from passing judgments on the personhood of the clients. A primary goal of therapy is not to condemn, but to understand. Understanding, of course, does not in and of itself condone behavior; it does not mean the therapist becomes amoral. Understanding means simply accepting people by keeping an open, nonjudgmental mind. Research has shown that the counselor who is not open-minded continues to believe incorrect things about clients, even in light of new and different information (Anderson, Lepper, & Ross, 1980).

Clients are rarely helped by a moralizing counselor. In fact, in the majority of cases passing moral judgment decreases the probability of healthy change. "When you criticize me," Carl Rogers once said, "I intuitively dig in to defend myself. However, when you accept me like I am, I suddenly find I am willing to change" (1961, p. 90). Although holding firm to personal convictions, the effective counselor does not mistake preaching for counseling. When a counselor cannot seem to refrain from personal judgment of a client, referral once again becomes an option.

Reluctance to Refer

No counselor is expected to work with all the potential clients who come for help. The beginning counselor must learn, early on, that referral to another competent counselor is a part of doing good therapeutic work. If for any reason—shortage of time, skill, or capacity to be emotionally present—a counselor is unable to meet clients' needs, referral is not only a necessity but an ethical obligation.

The unexamined life is not worth living.

—Socrates

Careful referral involves more than giving clients the name of another counselor, however. Clients should be given a choice among therapists who are qualified to deal with their problems. And to protect against abandonment, the counselor should follow up on the referral to determine whether or not the appropriate connection has been made.

A SUMMARY WORD

Fear of failure is one of the greatest obstacles that confronts the inexperienced counselor. Every therapist, regardless of experience and training, will make mistakes. Even Freud, Rogers, Ellis, and all the great theorists with whom we will become acquainted in this text were not immune to error. The counselor in training needs space to make mistakes that can turn into lessons. No supervisor expects to see a perfect set of attitudes and techniques from an intern, even one with a diploma in hand. Thus the inexperienced counselor needs to learn to be patient, as he or she initially struggles to gain professional momentum.

Consider the genius and inventor Thomas Edison, who was one day faced with two special dejected assistants telling him, "We've just completed our seven hundredth experiment and we still don't have a light bulb. We have failed." But Edison did not agree. "We haven't failed," he said. "We now know seven hundred things not to do. We are becoming experts."

Edison's wisdom applies to beginning counselors. Each "mistake" you make brings you one step closer to reaching your goal. It is hoped that you will avoid the mistakes outlined in the latter half of this chapter and journey closer to the qualities of effectiveness noted in the first half, but you are certain to stumble from time to time. After all, counseling is a serious business. What you do as a future counselor can make a significant difference in the lives of your clients. For this reason you can accept your anxieties as normal. As you log more and more counseling experience and as you progress in counselor education, your errors will decrease and your confidence will increase.

REFERENCES

Anderson, C. A., Lepper, M. R., & Ross, L. (1980). Perseverance of social theories: The role of explanation in the persistence of discredited information. *Journal of Personality and Social Psychology, 39,* 1037–1049.

Allen, T. (1967). Effectiveness of counselor trainees as a function of psychological openness. *Journal of Counseling Psychology, 14,* 35–40.

Aspey, D. N. (1975). Empathy. *The Counseling Psychologist, 5,* 10–14.

Baldwin, M., & Satir, V. (1987). *The use of self.* New York: Hawthorn Press.

Bandura, A. (1977). Self-efficacy: Toward a unifying theory of behavioral change. *Psychological Review, 84,* 191–215.

Barrett-Lennard, G. T. (1962). Dimensions of therapist response as causal factors in therapeutic change. *Psychological Monographs, 76* (43, Whole No. 562).

Belkin, G. S. (1988). *Introduction to Counseling.* (3rd ed.). Dubuque, IA: Wm. C. Brown.

Bergin, A. E., & Garfield, S. L. (Eds.). (1971). *Handbook of psychotherapy and behavior change: An empirical analysis.* New York: Wiley.

Bergin, A. E., & Lambert, M. J. (1978). The evaluation of therapeutic outcomes. In S. L. Garfield & A. E. Bergin (Eds.), *Handbook of psychotherapy and behavior change: An empirical analysis* (p. 139–189). New York: Wiley.

Boy, A., & Pine, G. (1982). *Client-centered counseling: A renewal.* Boston: Allyn & Bacon.

Brammer, L. M., & MacDonald, G. (1996). *The helping relationship: Process and skills* (6th ed.). Englewood Cliffs, NJ: Prentice-Hall.

Brammer, L. M., & Shostrom, E. L. (1982). *Therapeutic psychology: Fundamentals of counseling and psychotherapy* (4th ed.). Englewood Cliffs, NJ: Prentice-Hall.

Brennan, T. P., & Piechowski, M. M. (1991). A developmental framework for self-actualization: Evidence from case studies. *Journal of Humanistic Psychology, 31,* 43–64.

Carkhuff, R. R. (1969). *Helping and human relations.* New York: Holt, Rinehart & Winston.

Carkhuff, R. R., & Berenson, B. G. (1977). *Beyond counseling and therapy* (2nd ed.). New York: Hold, Rinehart & Winston.

Cavanaugh, M. E. (1990). *The counseling experience.* Prospect Heights, IL: Waveland Press.

Cloud, H., & Townsend, J. (1992). *Boundaries: When to say yes and when to say no.* Grand Rapids: Zondervan.

Combs, A. (1986). What makes a good helper. *Person-Centered Review, 1,* 51–61.

Cook, R. E. (1966). A comparative study of motivational intentions associated with the committing of problem behaviors. *Dissertation Abstracts International, 27* (3-A), 666–667.

Coonerty, S. M. (1991). Change in the change agents growth in the capacity to heal. In R. C. Curtis & G. Stricker (Eds.), *How people change: Inside and outside therapy* (pp. 81–97). New York: Plenum.

Corey, G., & Corey, M. S. (1982). *Groups: Process and practice* (2nd ed.). Monterey, CA: Brooks/Cole.

Corey, G., Corey, M. S., & Callanan, P. (1984). *Professional and ethical issues in counseling and psychotherapy* (2nd ed.). Monterey, CA: Brooks/Cole.

Cormier, W. H., & Cormier, L. S. (1985). *Interviewing strategies for helpers* (2nd ed.). Monterey, CA: Brooks/Cole.

Cormier, L. S., & Hackney, H. (1987). *The professional counselor: A process guide to helping.* Englewood Cliffs, NJ: Prentice-Hall.

Corrigan, J. D., Dell, D. M., Lewis, K. N., & Schmidt, L. D. (1980). Counseling as a social influence process: A review. *Journal of Counseling Psychology, 27,* 395–441.

Cunningham, C., Davis, J. R., Bremner, R., Dunn, K. W., & Rzasa, T. (1993). Coping modeling problem solving versus mastery modeling: Effects on adherence, in-session process, and skill acquisition in a residential parent-training program. *Journal of Consulting and Clinical Psychology, 23*.

Dreyfus, E. A. (1967). Humanness: A therapeutic variable. *Personnel and Guidance Journal, 45*, 573–528.

Egan, G. (1990). *The skilled helper: A systematic approach to effective helping.* Monterey, CA: Brooks/Cole.

Gambrill, E. (1990). *Critical thinking in clinical practice.* San Francisco: Jossey-Bass.

Gazda, G. (1973). *Human relations development: A manual for educators.* Boston: Allyn & Bacon.

Gelso, C. J., & Carter, J. A. (1994). Components of the psychotherapy relationship: Their interaction and unfolding. *Journal of Counseling Psychology, 41*, 296–309.

George, R. L., & Cristiani, T. S. (1990). *Counseling theory and practice* (3rd ed.). Englewood Cliffs, NJ: Prentice-Hall.

Gibb, J. R. (1968). The counselor as a role-free person. In C. A. Parker (Ed.), *Counseling theories and counselor education.* Boston: Houghton Mifflin.

Gibb, J. R. (1978). *Trust: A new view of personal and organizational development.* Los Angeles: The Guild of Tutors Press.

Goldstein, A. P., & Higginbotham, H. N. (1991). Relationship-Enhancement Methods. In F. H. Kanfer & A. P. Goldstein (Eds.), *Helping people change* (p. 20–29). New York: Pergamon Ress.

Gurman, A. S. (1972). Therapists' mood patterns and therapeutic facilitativeness. *Journal of Counseling Psychology, 19*, 169–170.

Heppner, P. P., & Anderson, W. P. (1985). The relationship between problem-solving self appraisal and psychological adjustment. *Cognitive Therapy and Research, 9*, 415–427.

Ibrahim, F. A. (1991). Contributions of cultural worldview to generic counseling and development. *Journal of Counseling and Development 70*, 13–19.

Jevne, R. (1981). Counselor competencies and selected issues in a Canadian counselor education program. *Canadian Counselor, 15*, 57–63.

Kanfer, F. H., & Goldstein, A. P. (1991). *Helping people change: A textbook of methods* (4th ed.). New York: Pergamon Press.

Kelly, T. A. (1990). The role of values in psychotherapy: A critical review of process and outcome effects. *Clinical Psychology Review, 10*, 171–186.

Kottler, J. A. (1983). *Pragmatic group leadership.* Monterey, CA: Brooks/Cole.

LaCrosse, M. B. (1975). Nonverbal behavior and perceived counselor attractiveness and persuasiveness. *Journal of Counseling Psychology, 22*, 563–566.

Lambert, W. W., Solomon, R. L., & Watson, P. D. (1949). Reinforcement and extinction as factors in size estimation. *Journal of Experimental Psychology, 39*, 637–641.

Loesch, L. C., Crane, B. B., & Rucker, B. B. (1978). Counselor trainee effectiveness: More puzzle pieces. *Counselor Education and Supervision, 17*, 19–204.

MacDevitt, J. W. (1987). Therapist's personal therapy and professional self-awareness. *Psychotherapy, 24*, 693–703.

Milliken, R. L., & Kirchner, R. (1971). Counselor's understanding of student's communication as a function of the counselor's perceptual defense. *Journal of Counseling Psychology, 18*, 14–18.

Okun, B. F. (1982). *Effective helping: Interviewing and counseling techniques* (2nd ed.). Monterey, CA: Brooks/Cole.

Osipow, S. H., Walsh, W. B., & Tosi, D. J. (1984). *A survey of counseling methods.* Homewood, IL: Dorsey Press.

Parrott, L. (1994). *Love's unseen enemy.* Grand Rapids, MI: Zondervan.

Patterson, C. (1958). The place of values in counseling and psychotherapy. *Journal of Counseling Psychology, 5,* 216–223.

Patterson, C. H. (1985). *The therapeutic relationship: Foundations for an eclectic psychotherapy.* Monterey, CA: Brooks/Cole.

Patterson, L. E., & Eisenberg, S. (1983). *The counseling process* (3rd ed.). Boston: Houghton Mifflin.

Perez, J. F. (1979). *Family counseling: Theory and practice.* New York: Van Nostrand.

Pietrofesa, J. J., Hoffman, A., & Splete, H. H. (1984). *Counseling: An introduction* (2nd ed.). Boston: Houghton Mifflin.

Rausch, H. L., & Bordin, E. S. (1957). Warmth in personality development and in psychotherapy. *Psychiatry, 20,* 351–363.

Ridley, C. R., Mendoza, D., & Kanitz, B. (1994). Multicultural training: Reexamination, operationalization, and integration. *The Counseling Psychologist, 22,* 227–289.

Rogers, C. R. (1951). *Client-centered therapy.* Boston: Houghton Mifflin.

Rogers, C. R. (1957). The necessary and sufficient conditions of therapeutic personality change. *Journal of Consulting Psychology, 21,* 95–103.

Rogers, C. R. (1961). *On becoming a person: A therapist's view of psychotherapy.* Boston: Houghton Mifflin.

Rogers, C. R. (1969). *Freedom to learn.* Columbus, OH: Charles E. Merrill.

Rogers, C. R. (1977). *Carl Rogers on personal power.* New York: Delacorte Press.

Rogers, C. R., Gendlin, E. T., Kiesler, D. V., & Truax, C. B. (1967). *The therapeutic relationship and its impact.* Madison, WI: University of Wisconsin Press.

Rokeach, M. (1973). *The nature of human values.* New York: Free Press.

Rokeach, M., & Regan, J. F. (1980). The role of values in the counseling situation. *Personnel and Guidance Journal, 58,* 576–582.

Rosenthal, R. (1995). Progress in clinical psychology: Is there any? *Clinical Psychology Science and Practice, 2(2),* 183–192.

Rowe, W., Murphy, H. B., & DeCsipkes, R. A. (1975). The relationship of counseling characteristic and counseling effectiveness. *Review of Educational Research, 45,* 231–246.

Samler, J. (1960). Change in values: A goal in counseling. *Journal of Counseling Psychology, 7,* 32–39.

Seligman, M. E. P. (1990). *Learned optimism.* New York: Knopf.

Seligman, M. E. P. (1995). The effectiveness of psychotherapy: The Consumer Reports Study. *American Psychologist, 50,* 965–974.

Sexton, T. L., & Whiston, S. C. (1994). The status of a counseling relationship: An empirical review. *The Counseling Psychologist, 22,* 6–78.

Small, J. (1990). *Becoming naturally therapeutic.* New York: Bantam.

Sue, D. W. (1978). World views and counseling. *Personnel and Guidance Journal,* 458–462.

Tramel, D. (1981). A lesson from the physicists. *Personnel and Guidance Journal, 59,* 425–429.

Trotzer, J. P. (1977). *The counselor and the group.* Monterey, CA: Brooks/Cole.

Truax, C. B., & Carkhuff, R. R. (1967). *Toward effective counseling and psychotherapy.* Chicago: Aldine.

Truax, C. B., & Mitchell, K. M. (1971). Research on certain therapist interpersonal skills in relation to process and outcome. In A. E. Bergin & S. Garfield (Eds.), *Handbook of psychotherapy and behavior change* (p. 299–344). New York: Wiley.

Tyler, L. E. (1969). *The work of the counselor.* New York: Appleton-Century-Crofts.

Watson, D. L., & Tharp, R. G. (1993). *Self-directed behavior: Self-modification for personal adjustment* (6th ed.). Pacific Grove, CA: Brooks/Cole.

Williamson, E. (1958). Value orientation in counseling. *Personnel and Guidance Journal, 36,* 520–528.

CHAPTER 3

Legal and Ethical Issues for the Beginning Counselor

Chapter Outline

Foundations of Legal and Ethical Practice
The Client–Counselor Relationship
Confidentiality and Privileged Communication
When in Doubt
Ethical Principles and Guidelines

Construction on the Golden Gate Bridge, that great engineering feat which was to connect San Francisco with Marin County, was interrupted by outrage from people over the frequent fatalities and maimings of workmen who fell from the span to the icy waters of the bay several hundred feet below. Newspapers fanned the public flame with gruesome pictures and heart-rendering stories of the men and the impact of their deaths among widows and fatherless children. The bridge was less than half finished, and there had already been 24 such accidents.

The sponsors and underwriters responded to the widespread distress by installing a configuration of strong nets beneath the entire working area. Accidental deaths were reduced to only four during the remainder of the construction. This was good, but there was also an unexpected result. Knowing the safety net was there, the physical confidence of the men increased, their equilibrium was substantially improved, and the total number of accidents of all kinds was greatly reduced.

The same idea applies in the counseling room. Counselors work with more personal confidence and will more nearly protect themselves from relational disasters when they are aware of the configuration of safety nets provided for those who work within the legal and ethical guidelines of their profession. Both the therapist and the client are protected by these nets.

Few professionals are more vulnerable to encountering potential legal troubles and ethical dilemmas than counselors (Cohen, 1992; Wilson & Ranft, 1993).

The voluminous numbers of articles and books on the subject are a silent witness to the perils. In this chapter, the basic legal and ethical issues pertaining to the counselor–client relationship will be introduced.

FOUNDATIONS OF LEGAL AND ETHICAL PRACTICE

A legal and ethical counseling practice is grounded on something counselors *are*, not something counselors *do*. The bedrock of legal and ethical counseling is *virtue*—a term rarely heard in psychology (Gelso & Fretz, 1992). Virtue should not be confused with a principle or rule, "rather it is a habit, disposition, or trait that a person may possess or aspire to possess. A moral virtue is an acquired habit or disposition to do what is morally right or praiseworthy" (Beauchamp & Childress, 1983, p. 261). The virtuous counselor, however, does not acquire ethical behavior through good intentions. The counselor with character begins by being legally and ethically competent. A sound counseling practice is built on knowing the law and understanding client rights (Hatton, Balente, & Rink, 1977). Virtue is nourished by deep roots anchored in the bedrock of the self. Virtue is grounded in an enlightened knowledge of the law; a clearly understood set of ethical, professional standards that are securely anchored from within; and personal values and beliefs which drive the morality of client relationships (Cooper, 1992).

Jordan and Meara (1990) present the idea of *virtue ethics,* which focuses on *being* as much as on *doing.* Virtuous counselors emphasize "not so much what is permitted as what is preferred" (p. 112). Personal values of the counselor are a basis for empowering the practice of ethical behavior (Wrenn, 1958). A counselor's ethical behavior involves more than subscribing to a code of ethics, for good ethics are built on a genuine concern for the client's welfare (Corey, Corey, & Callanan, 1993).

Counselors have an obligation to their clients and to their profession to be accountable for the quality of the professional services they offer. Legally, the therapist must possess the degree of learning, skill, and ability that others similarly situated ordinarily possess; must exercise reasonable care and diligence in the application of knowledge and skill to the patient's needs; and must use his or her best judgment in the treatment and care of patients (*Stone v. Procter* 1963; quoted in Furrow, 1980, p. 23). Effective counselors are transparent and fully honest with themselves about the limits of their own expertise (Pope & Vasquez, 1991). The American Psychological Association (1992) requires professionals to "provide services and only use techniques for which they are qualified by training and experience" (p. 390). Being competent as a therapist does not mean being able to treat every person that needs counseling. A responsible therapist will accept only clients that can benefit from the training and skill the therapist has acquired. Research has shown that inept counseling can indeed be worse than no treatment at all (Bergin,

Perfect virtue is to do
unwitnessed that which we
should be capable of doing
before all the world.
—François de La Rochefoucauld

1963). Competency includes knowing what issues you cannot treat because you are not qualified by training and experience. Simply reading a book or attending a weekend workshop devoted to a particular topic does not qualify a counselor to begin unsupervised therapy in a new treatment area. If a counselor wishes to expand an area of professional competence, supervision from a clearly qualified professional is essential. Failure to practice at a reasonable level of competence may result in accusations of malpractice (Jobes & Berman, 1993). Generally, malpractice is defined as "a failure to meet prevailing, professionally accepted standards of practice" (Blocher, 1987, p. 30).

When a counselor recognizes that a client's needs are beyond his or her expertise, the counselor is responsible for making referrals to other qualified counselors. In making referrals of clients, counselors need to help clients understand the reasons for the referral and the distinctive qualifications of the professional to whom the referral is made. If, for example, a counselor is referring a depressed client to a psychiatrist who specializes in psychotropic medication, the counselor should explain that a psychiatrist is practicing a medical specialty and that the psychiatrist may prescribe much needed medication to help the client better manage the depressive symptoms (Cormier & Cormier, 1991).

THE CLIENT–COUNSELOR RELATIONSHIP

The essential element in a therapeutic relationship is trust. Counseling deals with deeply personal issues and requires a high level of risk-taking on the part of clients. Without a reasonable level of trust, the therapeutic relationship cannot be very effective. Counselor effectiveness is proportionate to the level of trustworthiness between therapist and clients. As trust is diminished so is healing.

Informed consent is the basis of a trusting relationship and a cornerstone of counselor ethics. Through informed consent, clients are told what can be expected during treatment, how long it may take, and how much it will probably cost. They are also informed of their right to agree or decline to participate in any aspect of counseling (Green, 1993). The information is communicated, not in professional jargon, but in language that is easily understood. Informed consent also gives clients opportunities to ask questions. According to Schutz (1982), a therapist should "describe the therapeutic program recommended, indicating also the anticipated benefits of the program, the foreseeable material risks of treatment, and the likely results of no treatment" (p. 24).

> You can fool some of the people all the time, and all of the people some of the time, but you cannot fool all of the people all the time.
> —Abraham Lincoln

According to Cormier and Hackney (1987), counselors are responsible for providing the following information to clients at the outset of counseling:

1. A description of his or her role and qualifications as counselor.
2. An explanation of the process of counseling and any particular procedures or approaches to be used, and their purpose.

3. A description of any discomfort or risks that may evolve.
4. A description of any reasonably expected benefits.
5. A disclosure of other approaches or strategies that also may be useful.
6. An offer to answer inquiries about counseling or procedures at any time.
7. A statement that the client can withdraw consent and discontinue participation in a procedure or in therapy at any time.

Psychotherapy continues to battle the mistaken notion that therapists have "magical" powers—that therapists are latter-day miracle workers. Much of the public must be educated regarding the realities of counseling and professionals need to help dispel erroneous thinking about counseling. "Therapists," says Schutz (1982), "should attempt to create reasonable expectations for the public about what psychotherapy can and cannot do" (p. 95).

What about associating with clients outside of the therapeutic setting? "Deep down in his mind," according to Frieda Fromm-Reichmann (1950), "no patient wants a nonprofessional relationship with his therapist, regardless of the fact that he may express himself to the contrary" (p. 46). A relationship with a client outside of the therapeutic context will almost always complicate treatment (Borys & Pope, 1989). It leads to a tangled web of dual or multiple roles. To protect the welfare of clients, counselors must avoid dual relationships (Newman, 1993; Otero & O'Meara, 1991). Otherwise, he or she will run the risk of clouding objectivity and interfering with the therapeutic process. Dual relationships also increase the probability of sexual intimacies in psychotherapy, so often publicized (Bates & Brodesky, 1989; Cornell, 1994; Pope, 1990; Williams, 1992), as in Sidebar 3-1.

CONFIDENTIALITY & PRIVILEGED COMMUNICATION

A 15-year-old sat in the office of an inexperienced counselor. "Look, I need your help," he said. "Can I tell you a secret without you telling anyone else?" Sensing something serious and wanting the adolescent to open up, the new counselor agreed to keep quiet.

"My dad is a total jerk, and I can't handle it anymore. I got a ticket to California, and I'm gone, man. I want you to give me a week and then give my mom this." He handed over two folded sheets of white notebook paper, stapled shut.

The counselor tried to change the boy's mind or at least get him to talk with his father first. She offered to mediate the conversation, but, standing firm, the boy finally left unconvinced. Even though the counselor had agreed not to break the secret, she wondered if she shouldn't tell someone.

Problems of confidentiality are the most frequent source of ethical dilemmas for counselors (Pope & Vetter, 1992). Confidentiality can be defined as a relationship built on trust in which a client reveals private or secret information to a counselor with confidence it will not be passed on. Confidentiality assumes the counselor, "having grown powerful as a result of such knowledge, discloses

SEX IN THE FORBIDDEN ZONE

It is, in a way, the ideal setting for extraordinary intimacy. Patient and therapist are isolated from the world, focused on each other intently, exploring long-buried emotions. In successful psychotherapy, patients usually undergo something called transference, in which they come to see the therapist as an all-loving parent they can trust completely. The process can stir feelings in the therapist, too; power is a potent aphrodisiac. Freud warned that therapists should struggle against such "countertransference" and not abuse the patient's longing for love. Yet even some of his closest disciples couldn't withstand the temptations of the couch. Carl Jung took two patients as his mistresses. Otto Rank had a long affair with [a] patient.

History is replete with such indiscretions between psychotherapists and pa-

Indiscretion between therapist and client was portrayed in "The Prince of Tides."
(Columbia Pictures Archive Photos/
Fotos International)

tients, and they've become the standard plot line for popular films from "The Prince of Tides" to "Basic Instinct. . . ." [Books like *Sex in the Forbidden Zone* and *Sex in the Therapy Hour* have explored therapeutic sexual ethics in detail. Nobody knows how widespread sex between therapists and clients really is, but one thing is certain:] A spate of widely publicized cases [is] forcing the [therapeutic] profession to take stronger action. "A lot more cases are being reported," says Shirley Siegel, cofounder of the group Stop Abuse By Counselors in Seattle. "Women are much more willing to come forward and report embarrassing situations." Eight states have enacted laws making sex between patients and therapists a crime, and several more are weighing criminal sanctions. Professional associations are also getting tougher about disciplining ethics abuse. The APA now publicizes the fact that in the last 10 years, it has expelled or suspended 113 members, mostly for sexual misconduct. . . .

Almost inevitably, patients who sleep with their therapists end up more emotionally scarred than when they began treatment. Sexually abused patients "look very much like incest survivors," says [psychiatrist Nanette] Gartrell. Many find it difficult to trust subsequent therapists, and most blame themselves for the encounter. In one national survey, it was found that 11 percent of patients who had sex with their therapists were hospitalized as a result; 14 percent attempted suicide and 1 percent succeeded. "When a therapist engages in sex with a patient, he or she is engaging in a potentially homicidal activity," [former chairman of the APA's ethics committee Kenneth] Pope says, "far more than getting into a car drunk and driving."

the information to others only at the behest or with the consent of the [client]" (Dulchin & Segal, 1982, p. 13). This means that counselors do not talk to anyone about a client or even reveal that they are seeing a client without prior written permission from the client (Knapp & VandeCreek, 1987).

There is no justifiable excuse for inadvertent slips that reveal information shared in confidence. Even nondamaging information is to be protected (Abeles, 1992; Kompf, 1993). It is unethical, for example, to show a client's IQ test results to a counseling center receptionist—even if they are the highest IQ scores you have ever seen. Gelso and Fretz (1992) state that "any information obtained in professional relationships is to be treated confidentially" (p. 56). Clients deserve to have their personal information protected by strict confidentiality. It frees clients from worrying over who might hear the private information they discuss with the therapist. Confidentiality protects clients from having confessional gossip or tidbits about themselves passed on. Pure confidentiality is a hallmark of professional counseling (Sheeley & Herlihy, 1986).

Confidentiality, however, does have limits (Denkowski & Denkowski, 1982; MacNair, 1992). Confidentiality is an ethical principle rather than a legal statute. Confidentiality, according to Siegel (1979), involves "professional ethics rather than any legalism and indicates an explicit promise or contract to reveal nothing about an individual except under conditions agreed to by the source or subject" (p. 251). Legally, the concept of confidentiality is known as privileged communication. It spells out the legal conditions for breaking confidence with a client (DeKraai & Sales, 1982; Herlihy & Sheeley, 1987).

> You may be deceived if you trust too much, but you will live in torment if you don't trust enough.
>
> —Frank Crane

Shah (1969) defines privileged communication as "the legal right which exists by statute and which protects the client from having his confidences revealed publicly from the witness stand during legal proceedings without his permission" (p. 57). Lawyers, physicians, ministers, and psychologists are among the few professionals who have a legal right to claim privileged communication.

Ethical dilemmas, such as the one at the beginning of this section, also arise because of a conflict between what is best for the client and what is best for other involved people. Blocher (1987) states that "when a counselor encourages a client to believe that a communication will be held in full and complete confidence, the only ethical ground for breaking that confidence is danger to human life" (p. 27). In other words, privileged communication does not hold up in cases where the counselor has reasonable cause to believe that the person is in such a psychological state as to be dangerous to himself (i.e., suicidal) or to the person or property of another. For example, health and mental health professionals have a duty to warn the sexual partners of clients with AIDS if the clients refuse to do so themselves (Cohen, 1990; Harding, Gray, & Neal, 1993; Lamb, Clark, Drumheller, Frizzell, & Surrey, 1989). The next chapter will have much more to say about AIDS as a counseling issue.

In such cases, counselors have a "duty to warn" (see Sidebar 3-2) by disclosing information that can prevent a threatened danger (Gehring, 1982; Leslie, 1983). Berger (1982) concludes that a confidence should be broken when the client is in danger to himself or others, when the client is engaged in criminal actions, when the counselor is so ordered by the court, and when it is in the best interests of a child or an elder who is a victim of abuse.

Clients should be apprised of the limits of confidentiality at the outset of therapy. Counselors should also obtain client permission before tape recording a session or sharing information with a supervisor (McGuire, Graves, & Blau, 1985). Of course, supervisors, like counselors, are obligated to respect the confidentiality of client communication. "When a clear policy exists and is explained to the client before confidences are accepted, many ethical and professional problems can be avoided" (Blocher, 1987, p. 26).

| Law is reason free from passion.

—Aristotle

Sidebar 3-2

PRIVILEGE AND PUBLIC PERIL: THE DUTY TO WARN

In August 1969, Prosejit Poddar informed his counselor that he was planning to kill his girlfriend. Poddar was a voluntary outpatient at the Cowell Memorial Hospital on the Berkeley campus of the University of California. The therapist later called the campus police and told them of this threat. He asked the campus police to observe Poddar and watch for danger signs that might require psychiatric hospitalization.

The campus officers did take Poddar into custody for questioning, but they later released him because he was "rational." Poddar's counselor followed up his call with a formal letter requesting the assistance of the chief of the campus police. Later, the counselor's supervisor asked that the letter be returned, ordered that the letter and the therapist's case notes be destroyed, and asked that no further action be taken in the case. No warning was given, either to the intended victim or to her parents, of Tatiana's peril.

Two months later, on October 27, 1969, Poddar killed Tatiana Tarasoff. In what is now a landmark court case referred to as the Tarasoff decision, Tatiana Tarasoff's parents filed suit against the Board of Regents and employees of the university for failing to notify the intended victim of the threat. A lower court dismissed the suit; the parents appealed; and the California Supreme Court ruled in favor of the parents in 1976 and held that a failure to warn the intended victim was irresponsible.

This case resulted in the establishment of laws requiring psychotherapists to warn individuals when they become aware of intentions to harm: "We conclude that the public policy favoring protection of the confidential character of patient–psychotherapist communication must yield to the extent that exposure is essential to avert danger to others. The protection privilege ends where the public peril begins." (Beauchamp & Childress, 1983, p. 283).

WHEN IN DOUBT

Few things damage social dignity as much as physically stumbling over some unseen object. Missing a step is humiliating. But, assuming no one is hurt, it is always humorous to onlookers when the elegantly dressed stumble and fall. When a professional and proper musician, for example, steps onto a platform with music in hand, stumbles, and sends sheets of music into the air, it takes a good emcee to recover from the embarrassment and have the audience laughing with him instead of at him. Unfortunately, qualified counselors also stumble professionally but it is never a laughing matter. Misjudgment occurs when counselors do not utilize accessible resources for understanding and practicing the legal and ethical standards of counseling—consultation with other colleagues.

When in doubt, consult an experienced colleague. Legal and ethical considerations can be complex and confusing, so effective counselors regularly consult with other professionals on issues that are unclear (Sileo & Kopala, 1993; Taylor & Gazda, 1991). Consultation can take the form of a brief phone call or be as extensive as bringing in a colleague to observe your sessions. Counselors can also obtain guidance by phone consultations with state and national counseling associations such as the American Counseling Association or the American Psychological Association.

In addition to consulting with professional colleagues, competent counselors also commonly make referrals to other counselors who can meet the needs of a particular client more effectively than themselves. MacDonald (1992) has compiled a list of situations likely to call for referral (based on Cormier & Cormier, 1991; Seligman, 1986). A referral may be necessary when the following situations arise:

- Your client wishes to pursue matters that are contrary to your value system, to professional ethics, or to legal codes.
- You lack essential knowledge and/or skills for the best modes of treatment for each client.
- Personality differences between you and your client prevent working together effectively.
- Interpersonal connections with the client outside of counseling might create a conflict of interest (e.g., being asked to counsel a family member of an associate).
- You and your client are making little progress toward treatment goals and prospects for making greater progress are dim.

In addition, it is a good idea to refer a person for a thorough physical examination as part of the counseling evaluation (Cavanaugh, 1990). It can also be helpful to enlist the aid of a minister, priest, or rabbi, especially when the person communicates a need for spiritual comfort during crisis interventions. Referral to a counselor of the same sex may help a client feel more comfortable. A woman whose husband has just left her may make more progress, for example, with a female therapist. Referral can be appropriate and helpful in a number of situations, for both ancillary work with the primary counselor as well as a final referral when the counselor is doubtful about her or his ability to meet the needs of the client effectively.

ETHICAL PRINCIPLES AND GUIDELINES

Determining what is or is not ethical behavior is often difficult, not only for the novice counselor, but for the experienced practitioner as well. Thankfully, the helping professions offer several guidelines and codes of ethical behavior to lead them through perpelexing ethical dilemmas. These codes include *Code of Ethics,* published in 1989 by the National Board of Certified Counselors (NBCC); the *AAMFT Code of Ethics,* adopted by the American Association for Marriage and Family Therapists (1991); *Code of Ethics for Mental Health Counselors,* adopted in 1987 by the American Mental Health Counselors Association (AMHCA) and supported by the National Academy for Certified Clinical Mental Health Counselors (NACCMHC); *Ethical Guidelines for Group Counselors,* approved in 1989 by the Association for Specialists in Group Work (ASGW); *Ethical Principles of Psychologists and Code of Conduct Standards,* adopted by the American Counseling Association (1988); and *Ethical Standards for School Counselors,* adopted in 1984 by the American School Counselors Association (ASCA). Not only have these national professional groups provided ethical guidelines for their members, but many state counseling and psychological associations have also adopted their own versions of ethical standards.

> | Where law ends, tyranny begins.
> —William Pitt

Perhaps the most widely used guidelines for ethical behavior come from the American Psychological Association (1992) and the American Counseling Association (1995). These documents should be consulted by any practitioner in doubt about specific ethical questions. Both sets of guidelines are reprinted in the study guide that accompanies this book.

REFERENCES

Abeles, N. (1992). An ethical dilemma: Disclosure of test items to parents. *Psychotherapy in Private Practice, 10,* 23–26.

American Association for Counseling and Development. (1981). *Ethical standards.* Alexandria, VA: Author.

American Association for Marriage and Family Therapy. (1991). *AAMFT code of ethics.* Washington, DC: Author.

American Counseling Association. (1988). *Ethical standards.* Alexandria, VA: Author.

American Counseling Association. (1995). *Code of ethics and standards of practice.* Alexandria, VA: Author.

American Mental Health Counselors Association. (1987). *Code of ethics for mental health counselors.* Alexandria, VA: Author.

American Psychological Association. (1992). Ethical principles of psychologist. *American Psychologist, 47,* 1597–1611.

American School Counselors Association. (1984). *Ethical standards for school counselors.* Washington, DC: Author.

Association for Specialists in Group Work. (1989). *Ethical guidelines for group counselors.* Alexandria, VA: Author.

Bates, C. M., & Brodesky, A. M. (1989). *Sex in the therapy hour: A case of professional incest.* New York: Guilford Press.

Beauchamp, T. L., & Childress, J. S. (1983). *Principles of biomedical ethics* (2nd ed.). New York: Oxford University Press.

Berger, M. (1982). Ethics and the therapeutic relationship. In M. Rosenbaum (Ed.), *Ethics and values in psychotherapy* (pp. 67–95). New York: Free Press.

Bergin, A. E. (1963). The effects of psychotherapy: Negative effects revisited. *Journal of Counseling Psychology, 10,* 244–249.

Blocher, D. H. (1987). *The professional counselor.* New York: Macmillan.

Borys, D. S., & Pope, K. S. (1989). Dual relationships between therapist and client: A national study of psychologists, psychiatrists, and social workers. *Professional Psychology: Research and Practice, 20,* 283–293.

Cavanaugh, M. E. (1990). *The counseling experience.* Prospect Heights, IL: Waveland Press, Inc.

Cohen, E. D. (1990). Confidentiality, counseling, and clients who have AIDS: Ethical foundations of a model rule. *Journal of Counseling and Development, 68,* 282–286.

Cohen, K. (1992). Some legal issues in counseling and psychotherapy. *British Journal of Guidance and Counseling, 20,* 10–26.

Cooper, G. F. (1992). Ethical issues in counseling and psychotherapy: The background. *British Journal of Guidance and Counseling, 20,* 1–9.

Corey, G., Corey, M. S., & Callanan, P. (1993). *Issues and ethics in the helping professions* (4th ed.). Pacific Grove, CA: Brooks/Cole.

Cormier, W. H., & Cormier, L. S. (1991). *Interviewing strategies for helpers* (3rd ed.). Monterey, CA: Brooks/Cole.

Cormier, L. S., & Hackney, H. (1987). *The professional counselor: A process guide to helping.* Englewood Cliffs, NJ: Prentice-Hall.

Cornell, W. F. (1994). Dual relationships in transactional analysis: Training, supervision, and therapy. *Transactional Analysis Journal, 24,* 21–30.

DeForest, C., & Stone, G. L. (1980). Effects of sex and intimacy level on self-disclosure. *Journal of Counseling Psychology, 27,* 93–96.

DeKraai, M. B., & Sales, B. D. (1982). Confidential communications of psychotherapists. *Psychotherapy, 21,* 293–318.

Denkowski, K. M., & Denkowski, G. C. (1982). Client-counselor confidentiality: An update of rationale, legal status, and implications. *Personnel and Guidance Journal, 60,* 371–375.

Dulchin, J., & Segal, A. J. (1982). The ambiguity of confidentiality in a psychoanalytic institute. *Psychiatry, 45,* 13–25.

Fromm-Reichmann F. (1950). *Principles of intensive psychotherapy.* Chicago: University of Chicago Press.

Furrow, B. R. (1980). *Malpractice in psychotherapy.* Lexington, MA: Lexington Books.

Gehring, D. D. (1982). The counselor's "duty to warn." *Personnel and Guidance Journal, 61,* 208–210.

Gelso, C. J., & Fretz, B. R. (1992). *Counseling psychology.* Fort Worth, TX: Harcourt Brace Jovanovich.

Green, S. W. (1993). Long-term psychotherapy and informed consent. *Hospital and Community Psychiatry, 44,* 1005–1006.

Harding, A.K., Gray, L. A. & Neal, N. (1993). Confidentiality limits with clients who have HIV: A review of ethical and legal guidelines and professional policies. *Journal of Counseling and Development, 71,* 297–305.

Hatton, C. L., Balente, S. M., & Rink, A. (1977). *Suicide: Assessment and intervention.* Englewood Cliffs, NJ: Prentice-Hall.

Hendrick, S. S. (1981). Self-disclosure and marital satisfaction. *Journal of Personality and Social Psychology, 40,* 1150–1159.

Herlihy, B., & Sheeley, B. L. (1987). Privileged communication in selected helping professions: A comparison among statutes. *Journal of Counseling and Development, 65,* 479–483.

Jobes, D. A., & Berman, A. L. (1993). Suicide and malpractice liability: Assessing and revising policies, procedures, and practice in outpatient settings. *Professional Psychology: Research & Practice, 24,* 91–99.

Jordan, A. E., & Meara, N. M. (1990). Ethics and the professional practice of psychologists: The role of virtues and principles. *Professional Psychology Research and Practice, 21,* 107–114.

Knapp, S., & VandeCreek, L. (1987). *Privileged communications in the mental health professions.* New York: Van Nostrand Reinhold.

Kompf, M. (1993). Ethical considerations in teacher disclosure: Persons and methods. *Teaching & Teacher Education, 9,* 519–528.

Lamb, D. H., Clark, C., Drumheller, P., Frizzell, K., & Surrey, L. (1989). Applying Tarasoff to AIDS-related psychotherapy issues. *Professional Psychology: Research and Practice, 20,* 37–43.

Leslie, R. (1983, Nov./Dec.). Tarasoff decision extended. *California Therapist,* p. 6.

MacDonald, D. (1992). *Making effective referrals.* Unpublished manuscript.

MacNair, R. R. (1992). Ethical dilemmas of child abuse reporting: Implications for mental health counselors. *Journal of Mental Health Counseling, 14,* 127–136.

McGuire, J. M., Graves, S., & Blau, B. (1985). Depth of self-disclosure as a function of assured confidentiality and videotape recording. *Journal of Counseling and Development, 64,* 259–263.

National Board of Certified Counselors. (1989). *Code of ethics.* Alexandria, VA.

Newman, J. L. (1993). Ethical issues in consultation. *Journal of Counseling and Development, 72,* 148–156.

Otero, Z. T. M., & O'Meara, D. P. (1991). Mental injury litigation: The roles of the lawyer and the psychologist. *Medical Psychotherapy: An International Journal, 4,* 17–26.

Pope, K. S. (1988). How clients are harmed by sexual contact with mental health professionals: The syndrome and its prevalence. *Journal of Counseling and Development, 67,* 222–226.

Pope, K. S. (1990). Therapist-patient sexual involvement: A review of the research. *Clinical Psychology Review, 10,* 477–490.

Pope, K. S., & Vasquez, M. J. T. (1991). *Ethics in psychotherapy and counseling: A practical guide for psychologists.* San Francisco: Jossey-Bass.

Pope, K. S., & Vetter, V. A. (1992). Ethical dilemmas encountered by members of the American Psychological Association. *American Psychologist, 47,* 397–411.

Remley, T. (1992). *ACA legal series.* Alexandria, VA: American Counseling Association.

Rutter, P. (1989). *Sex in the forbidden zone: When men in power—therapists, doctors, clergy, teachers and others—betray women's trust.* Los Angeles: Jeremy P. Tarcher.

Schutz, B. (1982). *Legal liability in psychotherapy.* San Francisco: Jossey-Bass.

Seligman, L. (1986). *Diagnosis and treatment planning in counseling.* New York: Human Sciences.

Shah, S. (1969). Privileged communications, confidentiality, and privacy: Privileged communications. *Professional Psychology, 1,* 56–69.

Sheeley, B. L., & Herlihy, B. (1986). The ethics of confidentiality and privileged communication. *Journal of Counseling and Human Service Professions, 1,* 141–148.

Siegel, M. (1979). Privacy, ethics and confidentiality. *Professional Psychology, 10,* 249–258.

Sileo, F. J., & Kopala, M. (1993). An A-B-C-D-E worksheet for promoting beneficence when considering ethical issues. *Counseling & Values, 37,* 89–95.

Taylor, R. E., & Gazda, G. M. (1991). Concurrent individual and group therapy: The ethical issues. *Journal of Group Psychotherapy, Psychodrama & Sociometry, 44,* 51–59.

Williams, M. H. (1992). Exploitation and inference: Mapping the damage from therapist-patient sexual involvement. *American Psychologist, 47,* 412–421.

Wilson, L. S., & Ranft, V. A. (1993). The state of ethical training for counseling psychology doctoral students. *Counseling Psychologist, 21,* 445–456.

Wrenn, C. G. (1962). The culturally encapsulated counselor. *Harvard Educational Review, 32,* 444–449.

CHAPTER 4

Contemporary Issues in Counseling

Chapter Outline

Multicultural Counseling
Gender Differences
The Differently Abled
Religious Clients
AIDS
Older Adults
A Summary Word

Professional counseling is forever changing as the emphases on certain concerns within society shift. For example, increases in pollution, decreases in the Earth's resources, changing roles of women, innovations in media and technology, changing insurance policies (see Sidebar 4-1) poverty, AIDS, homelessness, and aging are among the concerns that will change and are changing the face of psychotherapy (Hackney & Wrenn, 1990). This chapter explores some of the most current issues in the realm of professional counseling: multicultural issues, gender differences, the differently abled, religious clients, AIDS, and counseling older adults. To be clear, this is an introduction, a brief overview, of these issues, not an in-depth analysis.

MULTICULTURAL COUNSELING

Culture consists of everything people have learned to do, believe, value, and enjoy in their collective lives. According to Sue and Sue (1990), it is the totality of ideals, beliefs, skills, tools, customs, and institutions into which each member of society is born. Contemporary counselors have come to understand that a client's culture must be carefully understood and considered if counseling is to be effective (Atkinson, Morten, & Sue, 1989; Devore & Schlesinger, 1991;

REHAB CENTERS RUN DRY

KICKING THE HABIT OF 30-DAY,
INPATIENT TREATMENT, SUBSTANCE-
ABUSE CLINICS RETOOL FOR
MANAGED CARE

By Elizabeth Gleick

Five years ago, Sierra Tucson was the model of a happy farm for substance abusers. Thousands of people from across the country came to the manicured 325-acre "campus" to deal with their addictions to alcohol, drugs, food, sex or gambling among the saguaros and sagebrush in the foothills of Arizona's Santa Catalina mountains. It was a Cadillac of the substance-abuse centers, and a company-provided Cadillac at that: employee health insurance routinely covered most of the costs of the standard 30-day stay there. Today, Sierra Tucson is a different place. Where there used to be 313 beds for people with a host of mental-health problems, now there are only 70. The management has added to its offerings Miraval, a holistic health spa along the lines of the nearby tony Canyon Ranch. Some of those who still visit Sierra Tucson to cope with addictions do much of their therapy in short, intensive workshops. And more than three-quarters of them now pay the $650-a-night tab out of their own pockets.

Welcome to rehab centers in the age of managed care. "It was like a cloudburst," admits Keith Arnold, Sierra Tucson's director of marketing. "It decimated the business. We've changed our marketing strategy and now go after the self-paying"—read rich—"client." These days, it is difficult to get in-patient coverage at all for detoxification. "The number of in-patient treatment programs has declined precipitously," says Monica Oss, editor of *Open Minds,* a behavioral-health-industry newsletter. "Between 1988 and 1993, the

average number of patient bed days dropped from 35 to 17."

As a result, across the country facilities like Sierra Tucson have been forced to reinvent themselves. In 1994 the Hartford Institute of Living, in Connecticut, merged with Hartford Hospital to avoid extinction. The nonprofit giants, the Betty Ford Center in Rancho Mirage, California, and the Hazelden Foundation in Minnesota, have both increased the amount of financial aid they offer to needy patients. McLean Hospital in Belmont, Massachusetts, a 185-year-old Harvard-affiliated facility, long ago famous as a haven for addled and addicted Brahmins, has seen its average patient stay drop from 57 days to 14 since 1989 and now fills 70% of its beds with Medicaid and Medicare patients.

When it comes to substance-abuse treatment, however, unlike other forms of medical care, many doctors and insurers have discovered a rare parcel of common ground: nearly all acknowledge that some of the changes being imposed by managed care are long overdue. "There was a lot of waste," concedes Dr. Michael Sheehy, president of patrician Silver Hill in New Canaan, Connecticut, who says that the arbitrariness of month-long stays "made no clinical sense." Dr. William Goldman, medical director of U.S. Behavioral Health, one of the largest companies in the country, agrees. "Most of the free-standing psychiatric hospitals in the '80s provided only one service-24-hour, acute hospital care," he says. "It became apparent to payers that treatment usually ended, particularly with substance abuse, when the limit was reached on one's insurance coverage. Patients always got better on the thirtieth day."

Though addiction specialists concede that some scamming went on in the for-profit recovery business, they nevertheless caution that for some patients, one month in a placid, nurturing environment, away from all the temptations of their old

Continued.

routine, is the best medicine. Dr. Frederic Schiffer, who recalls treating cocaine addicts at McLean, says he saw his patients four times a week for four weeks. "They needed the time to be held in a kind environment," he claims. "The grounds were very therapeutic. We would walk the grounds and talk."

As always, with managed care, it comes down to whose judgment prevails—the doctor or the insurer. Dr. Lloyd Sederer, senior vice president of Clinical Services at McLean, who believes that for the most part the benefit rollbacks have not caused undue harm, nevertheless is growing weary of the hours he spends dickering with insurance companies. "We have clinical responsibility but not the fiscal control," he says. "The next step is to give us a fixed budget and goals and then let us deliver our services to meet those goals."

Rehab facilities are now obliged to offer an array of treatment options. Some have patients live on the grounds, but with only round-the-clock supervision rather than round-the-clock nursing and medical care. Other patients attend therapy programs during the day but sleep elsewhere. "After 10 or 14 days of hospitalization," explains Sederer, "the staff know they must find other services, like partial hospitalization and ambulatory programs. The concept is continuous care."

But the wrong treatment choice can carry real risks. Silver Hill's Sheehy tells a story about an alcoholic patient who attended four to six hours of therapy a day, then retired to a nearby inn each night. One evening the patient bought a bottle of Jack Daniel's on his way home from the clinic, got drunk, then fell down the stairs,

From *Time*, February 5, 1996, pp. 44–45.

nearly crashing through a window. And for many addicts, detoxification is only the beginning of treatment. Often, substance abuse overlays a more serious psychiatric problem that needs lengthy treatment. In a short stay, says Jerry Spicer, president of Hazelden, "you can deal with detox, but you can't bring about a recovery. It comes down to trying to treat a chronic illness as an acute one." "What you lose," agrees McLean's Sederer, "is the ability to see patients to the next stage of recovery."

"He loses the ability to do that," counters Dr. John Ludden, of Harvard Pilgrim Health Care, an HMO, "but we don't." Ludden maintains that when done right, the new treatment protocols can still provide a safe haven for patients. But "the hospital psychiatrist is no longer the center of the universe," says Ludden, though even he acknowledges that "there are managed-care companies that perhaps have been overzealous in their intrusion." In some plans that make aggressive use of the "medical necessity" clause in their contracts, reports Sheehy, "we're clearly losing people we can't get in or keep in long enough."

Betty Ford Center president John Schwarzlose says it is routine to receive a call from the patient's managed-care company after five to eight days. Is the patient ambulatory? they want to know. Is he or she doing better? Then the struggle begins. Some companies refuse to divulge their benefit criteria, which also vary from plan to plan and state to state. "Our physicians talk to their physicians," says Schwarzlose. "Then we call the patient in to see our financial counselors," because, increasingly, the insurer's response to continuing inpatient addiction treatment, he explains, is to "just say no." But for now, at least, managed care has mostly succeeded in cutting the fat out of substance-abuse care, while saving the vital organs.

Goldrick, Pearce, & Giordano, 1982; Lee & Richardson, 1991; Sue and Sue, 1990; Vontress, 1971). Racial and ethnic factors, for example, can prevent counselors from establishing a therapeutic relationship with clients from different cultures (Carter, 1991; Ridley, 1995; Sue, 1977). "Ethnicity," according to Aponte (1990, p. 3) "can be part of the solution or the problem for the client."

Research indicates that ethnic-minority clients often do not take advantage of counseling services and, when they do, they frequently terminate the thera-peutic relationship prematurely. For example, the termination rate for Asian Americans, African Americans, Chicanos, and Native Americans has been found to be 50% after only the first counseling session. The termination rate for Anglo clients in the same situation is 30% (Sue, 1977; Sue, Fujino, Hu, Takeuchi, & Zane 1991; Sue & McKinney, 1975; Sue, McKinney, Allen, & Hall, 1974). Clients of coun-selors who have received training in cross-cultural counseling, however, are less likely to terminate from therapy prematurely (Lopez, Lopez, & Fong, 1991; Wade and Bernstein, 1991).

> In times of change, the learners inherit the earth while the learned find themselves beautifully equipped to live in a world that no longer exists.
>
> —Eric Hoffer

Cross-cultural counseling has been defined as a relationship in which the client and the counselor do not share the same cultural background, values, norms, roles, lifestyles, and methods of communicating (Ponterotto, Casas,

Cross-cultural counseling.
(Irene Bayer/Monkmeyer)

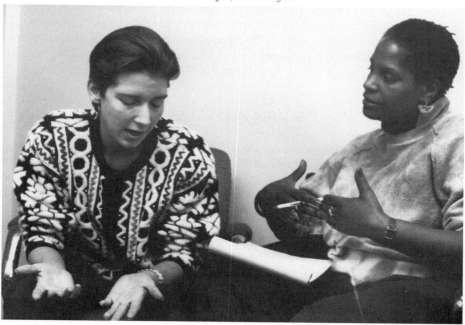

Suzuki, & Alexander, 1995). Sue and Sue (1990, p. 167–168) have identified the following characteristics they see as vital to being a culturally skilled counselor:

1. Culturally skilled counselors have moved from being culturally unaware to being aware and sensitive to their own cultural heritage and to valuing and respecting differences. Rather than being "ethnocentric" and believing in the superiority of their own cultural heritage, they show acceptance and respect for cultural differences.
2. Culturally skilled counselors are aware of their own values and biases, and how they may affect minority clients. These counselors try not to hold preconceived notions about minority clients. They actively avoid unwarranted labeling and stereotyping.
3. Culturally skilled counselors are comfortable with differences that exist between themselves and their clients in terms of race and beliefs. They do not see differences as being deviant. Every person, regardless of his or her culture or differences, is equally human.
4. Culturally skilled counselors are sensitive to circumstances that may dictate referral of the minority client to a member of his or her own culture or to another counselor in general. They are not threatened by the prospect of referring a client to someone else because of their own limitations in cross-cultural counseling.
5. Culturally skilled counselors acknowledge their own prejudicial attitudes, beliefs, and feelings. They do not deny that they have been socialized in a racist society and they accept responsibility for their own racism.

Certain factors present themselves in cross-cultural counseling that are not operative in other counseling relationships. Counselors, regardless of ethnic background, who plan to work with those whose cultural heritage is different from their own must take seriously these factors and learn to deal with them effectively (Pedersen, 1994; Sue, Arredondo, & McDavis, 1992).

GENDER DIFFERENCES

Just as race or national origin can be a hurdle for counselors in helping relationships, so can gender differences. A feminist counseling approach has arisen precisely because male therapists often do not take into account women's issues, and it has made us painfully aware of sexist notions applied to therapy. Important differences in the therapeutic treatment received by men and women are often overlooked. For instance, women are more likely than men to seek professional counseling (Gove & Tudor, 1973; Williams, 1987; Worell & Remer, 1992). In part, this may reflect a higher rate of mental illness among women for some disorders (e.g., abuse survival, depression, severe anxieties, phobias, and eating disorders), but it is also likely that women are more willing than men to admit that they have psychological problems and that they need help in solving them (Hubbard, 1992). In fact, some studies indicate that women engage in more open and personal self-disclosure than do men; and, of course, this is to their advantage (Antill & Cotton, 1986; DeForest & Stone, 1980; Good, Gilbert, & Scher, 1990; Greenblatt, Hasenauer, & Freimuth, 1980; Hendrick, 1981; O'Brien, 1988).

The counseling profession has only recently begun to consider the importance of gender differences. Most counseling theories have been developed by males and most therapists are male. As a result women in therapy may be encouraged, directly or indirectly, to adopt traditional, male-oriented views. For example, there may be a tendency for male therapists to encourage women to adapt, adjust, or conform to their surroundings passively (Broverman, Broverman, Clarkson, Rosenkrantz, & Vogel, 1970; Williams, 1992; Hare-Mustin, 1983; Schlossberg & Pietrofesa, 1973). This inhibition of activity and the resulting suppression of anger, in fact, may predispose women to depression more than men. Inadvertantly or not, counseling has fostered a societal context that puts women at increased risk for emotional distress.

> A little philosophy inclineth
> men's minds to atheism, but
> depth in philosophy bringeth
> men's minds about to religion.
>
> —Francis Bacon

Male therapists are often not sufficiently sensitive to how much some of the stress experienced by women derives from the world in which they live (American Psychological Association, 1975; Asher, 1975; Scher & Good, 1990). Specific life experiences of women, such as domestic abuse, sexual harassment, menstrual cycle, and menopause, have not been incorporated into mental health theory or treatment. In response to these concerns, gender-sensitive therapists have attempted to help their clients become more aware of the extent to which their problems derive from external controls, female physiology, and inappropriate sex roles. They help them become more conscious of their own needs and goals and help them avoid passively accepting the status quo by developing a sense of pride in their womanhood (Williams, 1987).

The American Psychological Association (1978) provides several guidelines regarding the treatment of women in psychotherapy. For example, therapy should be free of constrictions based on gender-defined roles, and the options explored between client and practitioner should be free of gender role stereotypes. Therapists should recognize the reality, variety, and implications of sex-discriminatory practices in society and should facilitate client examination of options in dealing with such practices. They should not only be knowledgeable about current empirical findings on sex roles, sexism, and individual differences resulting from the client's gender-defined identity, their theoretical concepts should be free of sex bias and sex role stereotypes. A therapist' language should be free of derogatory labels involving men and women. If authoritarian processes are employed as a technique, the therapy should not have the effect of maintaining or reinforcing stereotypic dependency of women. The therapist whose female client is subjected to violence in the form of physical abuse or rape should recognize and acknowledge that the client is the victim of a crime.

THE DIFFERENTLY ABLED

Persons with disabilities face issues good counselors must be prepared to deal with. Like ethnic-minority clients, persons with disabilities often feel singled out and isolated from the general population. The basic skills and procedures that form the core of any helping relationship are integral to counseling these persons and, from this perspective, these clients are no different from the general population (Cristiani and Sommers, 1978; Hosie, 1979; Vandergriff and Hosie, 1979). However, from the psychosocial point of view, there are a number of factors that make them exceptional (Perlman & Kirk, 1991).

Differently abled persons are challenged by at least three significant hurdles: (1) the physical conditions that render them exceptional in the first place, (2) the unreal perception that many have of them because of their disabilities, and (3) the impact of these interpersonal responses—their own physical condition and the public perception of them—on their own self-perceptions. These combined factors expose the differently abled person to stressors most of the general population cannot comprehend (Rusalem and Cohen, 1975; Van Hasseld, Strain, & Hersen, 1988).

Counselors are typically unaware of the complexity of being differently abled. They are too often ill prepared to provide effective services for the differently abled because they carry biases, prejudices, and values regarding handicapping conditions (Filer, 1982; Nathanson, 1979). Counselors, therefore, should not only be familiar with the psychosocial needs of differently abled individuals, they should be informed of specific counseling strategies to deal with such special needs as self-concept, body image, frustration, anger, dependency, and motivation (McDowell, Coven, and Eash, 1979).

Not every counselor should be able to work with the physically or developmentally challenged client. State and federal regulations are constantly changing and those therapists who specialize in this population are most apt to be current in the field and so better prepared to do this work. However, every counselor-in-training should be aware of some basic guidelines and factors in working with differently abled clients (Hosie, 1979). For example, counselors must be aware of the rights of differently abled children and their parents and have the skills necessary to advise parents on how to exercise those rights. The growth and development process, characteristics, and impediments of the differently abled must be understood and the counselor must be able to relate this knowledge to developmental learning tasks and strategies. Of course, the characteristics and development of the learning disabled must also be understood, and counselors need the skills to diagnose why the individual is failing tasks. Sensory impairments, speech disorders, and communication deficits must be understood along with their effects on diagnosis and remediation; counselors will need to be able to overcome or lessen these effects in learning and counseling settings.

> It is a high privilege to be able to share the experiences of so many different people; counselors are in an enviable role because they are able to interact with a very wide range of unique individuals.
>
> —Susan K. Gilmore

Contemporary counselors must understand the characteristics of differently abled persons related to employment skills, training programs, and potential occupational and educational opportunities and have the skills necessary to assist the individual in career decision making and development (Parrott & Parrott, 1995). This is accomplished, in part, by knowing the abilities, learning rates, and modes of learning of the differently abled and being able to utilize these factors in recommending educational placements, environments, and support groups (see Sidebar 4-2).

Sidebar 4-2

SUPPORT GROUPS

Charles Leerhsen with Shawn D. Lewis in Detroit and Los Angeles, Stephen Pomper in New York, Lynn Davenport in Boston and Margaret Nelson in Minneapolis

All of a sudden, people are pouring back into churches and synagogues with a fervor that hasn't been seen since the '50s. It appears that a great religious revival is sweeping the land—until you examine the situation a little more closely. Then you'll notice the biggest crowds today often arrive in midweek. And instead of filing into the pews, these people head for the basement, where they immediately sit down and begin talking about their deepest secrets, darkest fears and strangest cravings.

Alcoholics? Third door to the right.

Sex addicts? They meet on Tuesday.

Overweight men who have a problem with compulsive shopping? Pull up a folding chair, buddy. You're in the right place.

Where you are, specifically, is at a support-group meeting—one of about 500,000 that will be attended by some 15 million Americans this week. In the last 10 years, the number of these self-help organizations has quadrupled, and the topics they cover have been expanded to include everything from abused wives of doctors to zoologists who love too much. Alcoholics Anonymous, once heavily male and middle class, has experienced a huge influx of female and low-income members. Men, meanwhile, are streaming into the self-help movement at what is—considering the usual male reluctance to discuss intimate feelings—an absolutely astonishing rate.

Why is this happening? Because people have discovered that talking and listening to their fellow sufferers has a soothing effect on the psyche, sometimes more so than doing the same thing in the presence of a therapist. Support groups—a rather high-falutin name for what's usually nothing more than loosely structured gab sessions—salve psychological wounds, help destroy addictions and even extend the lives of people suffering from cancer and other physical afflictions.

And how do they do all this? Well, let us first acknowledge that there are some doctors, psychiatrists and others who say that support groups do nothing of the sort—that they in fact represent a dangerous do-it-yourself approach to problems of the mind, body and spirit. Yet most professionals and, of course, support-group members themselves, see the meetings as an amazingly effective antidote to aloneness—something that, apart from being a problem in its own right, compounds every known condition brought on by late 20th-century living, from compulsive hand-washing to AIDS. Though no academicians or researchers have yet studied the self-help movement, there seems to be

---

Continued.

something at once common-sensical and utterly mysterious about how the meetings work. "Just the sight of your fellow sufferers," says one self-help group organizer, "tends to make your pain a little more bearable."

And so there is a group for every season. Got the midwinter blues? (Call Depressives Anonymous.) Are you obese? (Overeaters Anonymous or the National Association to Aid Fat Americans.) A gay Episcopalian? (Integrity.) Consider yourself asexual? (Finding Our Own Way.) Feel certain that aliens are trying to transform you into George Jessel? (National Organization of Rare Disorders.) *Wish* that aliens would transform you into George Jessel? (True Potential Toastmasters.)

Cultural Upheaval
You could call this a trend, of course. But when there is a group for women whose daughters won't talk to them meeting weekly in Westchester County, N.Y.—and when the New York City Self-Help Clearinghouse has had several callers ask if there were meetings for people who, to quote a spokesperson, "drink a little too much but not way too much Coca-Cola"—then what you have, really, is a sea change, the kind of cultural upheaval that makes the fax machine look like mood rings, break-dancing or some other fleeting fad.

Through it all, though—as the national registry of support groups has grown to include Compulsive Shoppers, Pedestrians First, the Trichotillomania Support Network (for people who pull their hair out, strand by strand), Hot Flashes ("support for women with menopausal problems") and numerous bereavement groups—two basic conditions have endured. The first is that participation in a true self-help meeting is limited to peers. That means there is no professional moderator to make Wise Pronouncements based on a purely academic understanding of the subject matter, to sell books or to collect fees. While some groups designate a leader who might be charged with making announcements or recognizing members who want to "share" an experience or observation, no true self-help organization can have a hierarchy, especially one headed by someone who doesn't share the members' problems. To include such a person transforms the support-group meeting into group therapy, a standard psychiatric technique which tends, the self-help people say, to take the burden of recovery off the group member. "As soon as you have a therapist or someone like that running the meeting," says Marilyn Ng-A-Qui, director of the New York City Self-Help Clearinghouse, "the group members tend to dump their problems on the so-called expert. Their attitude becomes 'Here I am—fix me.' In a support group, though, the members know they can't be lazy. The responsibility for getting better is in each member's hands."

The second common trait among support groups is that they engender a near-religious fervor. Listen to a member of Schizophrenics Anonymous in Southfield, Mich.: "If I don't come to a meeting and I'm by myself for three or four days, I'll start getting weirder than I am now. I have to realize that I can't do it alone." Many members of Alcoholics Anonymous—the oldest and by far the largest support group, with an estimated membership of 1.73 million worldwide—strongly suggest that newcomers attend 90 meetings in as many days in order to break their bonds with the past.

Traditional "couch" therapy has certainly helped a lot of people, offering as it does the advantage of a professional caregiver and a greater focus on the individual patient. But even those who can afford the high cost of psychotherapy have sometimes grown dissatisfied with the open-ended nature of the process, and suspicious of advice that comes from someone who has never sparred with their particular demons. For those people, the only viable option is frequent support-group sessions.

It was the women's consciousness-raising movement that first extended the self-help concept beyond alcoholism. For the most part, these oh-so-'60s "organizations" engaged in unstructured discussions that were as likely to concern drinking or drugs as they were sexual harassment, the military-industrial complex, lower-back pain, Vietnam or anything else that wasn't groovy. What the get-togethers were mostly about, though, was getting together. The consciousness-raising groups set the tone for the self-help revolution of today, by giving people a chance to come out and see others who—despite having some very recognizable flaws and problems—were surviving, thriving and even smiling.

Support groups in the past few years seem to have sorted themselves into four basic categories: those that address problems of addictive behavior (Compulsive Shoppers, Workaholics and others that often follow a slight variation on AA's 12 steps); those for physical and mental illness (Parkinson's Support Group, Recovery, Inc.); those for dealing with a transition or some other crisis (Widowed Persons Service, Recently Divorced Catholics), and those for friends and relatives of people with a problem (Adult Children of Alcoholics, Parents of Agoraphobic Teenagers). Though it sounds sacrilegious, Borck Jameson and others think that a support group can be a better place to seek help than the traditional family. A dysfunctional family, after all, is often what brings people to support groups in the first place. Among strangers, people can be brutally honest. At one recent meeting of Batterers Anonymous (sometimes

called Forte) in Los Angeles, a member posed the rhetorical question, "Man, what am I supposed to do when my old lady tried to block my way out of the door? There's nothing left to do but remove her with my fist." Moments later, another member explained that being arrested for beating his wife only fueled his anger. "The last time we had a fight, I pulled a shotgun on her and it jammed," he said. "That's the only reason I'm here today. If it hadn't jammed, I'd be doing time."

The relationship between support groups and health-care professionals is improving. There are, for example, few, if any, alcohol treatment centers in the United States that do not funnel their outpatients into AA. At the same time, says Marion K. Jacobs, adjunct professor of psychology at UCLA and codirector of the California Self-Help Center, "there is still a huge amount of resistance in medicine to incorporating self-help as part of health care." Though there are probably more people involved in self-help than in any other single form of therapy, psychiatrists have "scant" training in support groups, according to Dr. Frederick E. Miller, director of the Adult Inpatient Psychiatry Unit at the University of Chicago. "It's a neglected area," he says. Professionals don't like the idea of self-help groups for two seemingly unassailable reasons: a little knowledge is a dangerous thing, and he who treats himself has a fool for a patient.

It's probably time, though, to stop relying on the kind of wisdom that comes from fortune cookies. It used to be accepted without question, before AA, that the blind couldn't lead the blind. Of course, some people will overdo anything. Frank Riessman says he's heard talk recently that there's a group forming for people who go to support groups too much. Oh, well, let them come in and sit down. To find oneself in an imperfect situation is human. To learn that you are not alone, divine.

From: *Newsweek*, February 5, 1990, pp. 50–55.

RELIGIOUS CLIENTS

In a recent poll, it was shown that two thirds of the population of the United States consider religion to be "important" or "very important" in their lives. And people seeking help from psychotherapists are increasingly presenting problems that involve spiritual and religious issues and overtones (Butler, 1990; Shafranske, 1996; *Religion in America,* 1985). As a result, counselors are being confronted with calls for help in areas that were formerly the primary domain of the clergy. The challenge is how to handle the spiritual and religious issues in a way that assures ethical integrity for the therapist as well as the client.

"The possibility for greater empathy with religious clients," says Bergin (1991, p. 396), "is suggested by the substantial but professionally unexpressed religiosity that exists among therapists." Bergin is talking about the unexpected personal investment psychotherapists have in religion. Almost half of the professional counseling community agrees with the statement, "My whole approach to life is based on my religion," and almost 80% agree with the statement, "I try hard to live by my religious beliefs."

Given the value that both clients and therapists place on spirituality and religion, it is surprising that these issues are only recently showing up in the counseling room as major themes of concern. For most of counseling's history, religion has been seen as irrational and equivalent to emotional disturbance (Ellis, 1980; Freud, 1927). Gladding (1992), however, points to three events that brought spirituality more to the forefront of professional contemporary counseling. First were the spiritual factors incorporated in Alcoholics Anonymous and other 12-step programs. Another was the writings of M. Scott Peck, whose book, *The Road Less Traveled,* bridged the gap between traditional psychotherapy and religion. The final event Gladding cited for the increase in spiritual awareness was the series of interviews Bill Moyers had with Joseph Campbell, who "gave respectability to the spiritual–psychological quest itself, even in modern-times" (Butler, 1990, p. 30).

> Wisdom lies neither in fixity nor in change, but in the dialectic between the two.
>
> —Octavio Paz

Perhaps another contributing factor has been the growing success of professional organizations devoted to religion and psychology. The Association for Religious and Value Issues in Counseling (ARVIC) is one of the fastest growing divisions within the American Counseling Association. The same is true for Psychology of Religion, Division 36 of the American Psychological Association. In 1992, the American Association of Christian Counselors began with fewer than 300 members and its membership in 1995 was over 19,000. Professionals associated with organizations similar to these are providing the counseling community with descriptive evidence of the usefulness of spiritual dimensions for enhancing change (e.g., Bradford & Spero, 1990; Collins, 1993; Malony, 1988; Stern, 1985; Tan, 1993; Worthington, 1989). In addition, there are now professional schools of psychology that are fully accredited and teaching students to integrate their faith seriously with the practice of psychotherapy. The Fuller

Fuller Graduate School of Psychology in Pasadena, California.
(Courtesy of Fuller Graduate School of Psychology)

Graduate School of Psychology in Pasadena, California and The Rosemead
Graduate School of Psychology in La Mirada, California are two of the most
visible and influential.

Regardless of the causes, the issue of religiousness in the contemporary
counseling office cannot be ignored. The religious client must be taken seriously and, as Richards (1991) cautions, counselors need to avoid stereotypical
assumptions that religiously devout clients are more emotionally disturbed
than other clients. Spiritual and religious issues are expressed in beliefs and behavior. Because they are part of the client's total functioning, religious feelings
and values should be considered as part of therapeutic treatment for religious
and spiritual persons (Browning, Jobe, & Evison, 1990; Tan, 1996).

AIDS

No disease in modern times has received more attention or produced such concern as AIDS (acquired immunodeficiency syndrome). It is a disease that results
in the body's immune system breaking down and is caused by the human immunodeficiency virus (HIV). People infected with HIV may appear completely
healthy, but they may also develop many health problems that signal the onset
of AIDS, including extreme weight loss, severe pneumonia, a form of cancer
(Kaposi's sarcoma), and damage to the nervous system. The AIDS epidemic

constitutes a worldwide public health threat whose magnitude is growing rapidly. In some areas of the United States, it is the number one cause of premature death (Hearst & Hulley, 1988) and it is nearly impossible for contemporary counselors to avoid clients whose lives have not been touched, directly or indirectly, by AIDS (Newman, Durrance, & Fell, 1993).

Although thousands of researchers are involved in an unprecedented, worldwide effort to understand and ultimately cure or prevent AIDS, a committee of knowledgeable scientists commissioned by the National Research Council has predicted that the AIDS virus will be around well into the next century (Byrne, 1989). Today's counselors, therefore, cannot afford to neglect understanding this disease and its relationship to counseling. To begin with, counselors must be prepared with practical information about when, where, and why a client should obtain testing for HIV. The disease, of course, restricts personal freedom, subdues pleasure with fear, and calls for discipline of desires. As a result, counselors will face some belligerence, from time to time, when dealing with clients who are filled with denial and expressing anger and confusion toward this dreadful disease (Albers, 1990). However, if today's counselors do not break through this hardened emotional shell, these clients will suffer and others may lose their lives.

> You could not step twice into the same river; for other waters are ever flowing on to you.
>
> —Heraclitus

On the other hand, some clients will be overly concerned about whether they should be tested for AIDS. Sexual contacts before 1980, casual contact with possible AIDS patients, excessive fears of HIV in the environment, and many other irrational reasons for asking for testing are often given. Counselors should always listen to these concerns and acknowledge them as real, but not everyone need be recommended for medical consultation and HIV testing. Once the client is educated about the virus, if he or she shows unrealistic concern that will not be dissuaded with education or indicates need for absolute confirmation with a negative test, then counselors should be firm in suggesting the patient have his or her blood tested. The fear of knowing one's HIV status is greatly outweighed by the benefits of testing, no matter what the end result is, and blood testing for HIV is now very common and inexpensive, under $50 per test.

Anticipatory counseling can benefit the client who is at risk for HIV and about to be tested. Dealing with their present emotional state—the fears, guilts, anxieties, and relationships—helps them sort through these confused reactions to their devastating predicament. Personal and psychological ramifications of both a negative test and the dreaded positive test can be explored. When a patient learns he or she is HIV positive, group counseling has proved to be quite effective, and also as the disease progresses (Sorenson, London, Heitzmann, & Gibson, 1994). Participants in one program, for example, have six sessions, each focusing on one right that is felt necessary by dying people: to be in control, to reminisce, to laugh, to feel connected to a family, to have a sense of purpose, and to feel religious or spiritual (Smith, 1994).

AIDS counseling.
(Rhoda Sidney/Monkmeyer)

Of course, many clients also need counseling for staying free from AIDS. Often a crisis fear of HIV brings a client to counseling and education as well as support is needed to keep the client from making the same, risky mistakes again and again. Counselors today must also be prepared to counsel the families of AIDS patients. Besides the emotional support families can provide clients, they are also the most important source of prevention of AIDS. Families, for example, are becoming involved in educational programs designed to equip young people with the skills to avoid getting involved in high-risk behavior, and the counselor can enlist their help in these efforts (Beckerman, 1994).

Another important consideration in AIDS counseling is confidentiality. When a client infected with HIV is sexually irresponsible, threatening others with infection, counselors are placed in a dilemma of preserving the right of confidentiality of the client or taking action to protect unsuspecting sexual partners from potential harm. The issue is never clear-cut, but measures of action must be taken by the competent counselor to assure that the HIV virus is not spread to unsuspecting persons (Erickson, 1993; Friedman & Hughes, 1994).

In summary, dispelling the myths about this deadly disease becomes the job of every contemporary counselor. A great deal of anxiety in some clients can be relieved simply with accurate information about AIDS. Magazines, tabloids, and broadcasts, to say nothing of the person on the street, add to the general rumor mill creating hundreds of pieces of misinformation about this disease (Trezza, 1994). Fears create rumors that foster ignorance that creates more fear. Even though the disease is dangerous, people's perceptions of their personal risk are often blown out of proportion and counselors can ease this anxiety with factual information (Batchelor, 1988); a concise summary of this information appears in Sidebar 4-3.

Sidebar 4-3

FACTS ON AIDS: ACQUIRED IMMUNE DEFICIENCY SYNDROME

On June 5, 1981 the United States Centers for Disease Control issued a brief report describing five gay men in Los Angeles with a rare form of pneumonia; in time, this pneumonia was determined to be one symptom of AIDS. Today, more than 250,000 Americans have died from AIDS and it has spread to over 130 countries and has resulted in a global total of more than 1.5 million cases. Here are some of the frequently asked questions about AIDS:

What Does HIV Positive Mean?
Being HIV positive means that one has been exposed to HIV (human immunodeficiency virus) but may actually be symptom-free. After initial exposure, the virus may lie dormant for an average of 7 to 8 years before being reactivated. Once active, the virus progressively destroys the immune system, making the patient vulnerable to life-threatening infections and diseases. Once the symptoms of AIDS are diagnosed, a person has an average life expectancy of about 1 year.

What Are the Symptoms of AIDS?
The symptoms vary with the types of infections that inflict an AIDS virus victim but commonly include fevers, night sweats, weight loss, loss of appetite, fatigue, swollen lymph nodes, diarrhea, atypical bruising or bleeding, skin rashes, headache, chronic cough, and a whitish coating on the tongue or throat.

How Is AIDS Transmitted?
The HIV virus survives best in blood tissues and some bodily fluids, such as semen and vaginal fluids. Thus, AIDS is transmitted through sexual contact; by sharing needles for drugs, tattooing, or ear piercing; by having had a blood transfusion before 1985 (when a test was developed to detect the HIV virus); or from an infected mother to her unborn child. The most common age group for full-blown AIDS is 20–39 years. Most affected people were infected with the virus several years before they became sick (Konins, Hein, & Futterman, 1993).

How Does One Protect Against Getting AIDS?
There are two primary means of protecting oneself against AIDS. First, one should steer clear of injecting drugs because AIDS is commonly spread by sharing needles. Second, because AIDS can be spread through sexual contact, the surest way to avoid it is to abstain from sex. For the non-celibate, a monogamous relationship with a person whose HIV status is negative is the only other sure way of protection. Using latex condoms can decrease the chances of contracting AIDS, but condoms are not guaranteed protection from the disease—they simply decrease the chances.

What Is the Treatment for AIDS?
As of this writing, there is no cure for AIDS. Several drugs, such as AZT, appear to slow the progression of AIDS and extend patients' lives.

OLDER ADULTS

The population of the United States is becoming increasingly elderly. In 1981, 11% of the population was 65 years of age or older. In 1900 that percentage was only four. For the most part, this change is due to a declining birth rate accompanied by an increase in life expectancy. In 1900 the average life expectancy was about 48 years. Today it has risen to about 73 years

> Among all my patients in the second half of life—that is to say, over thirty-five, there has not been one whose problem in the last resort was not that of finding a religious outlook on life. It is safe to say that every one of them fell ill because he had lost that which the living religions of every age have given to their followers and none of them has been really healed who did not regain his religious outlook.
>
> —Carl Gustave Jung

(Butler & Lewis, 1982). It is estimated that in the year 2000, over half of the U.S. population will be over 50 years of age and 44% of older persons will be over 75. The American Association of Retired Persons (AARP) currently has a membership of over 27 million persons. Whereas it was originally formed to promote life insurance and other group benefits, AARP has developed into a powerful political force (Hess, 1991). In spite of this impressive statistical growth among the aged—the "graying of America" as it is called—professional counselors have yet to devote adequate attention to this overlooked segment in society (Myers, 1989, 1990).

The therapeutic treatment of problems associated with later life starts with an understanding of this segment in the lifespan. Well-known developmental psychologist Erik Erikson has identified the primary developmental task of older persons as "integrity vs. despair" (p. 12). The positive resolution of this task results in wisdom, which Erikson defines as "informed and detached concern with life itself in the face of death itself" (1987, p. 52). The negative counterpart of wisdom is despair and disdain, which is basically a bitter rejection of one's place in life—a rejection of the self as finished and helpless. It is in this despair that counseling can help lift the older adult and help them adjust to life's losses and changes.

The transitions and role losses in old age greatly affect the vulnerability of the elderly adult. Typical transitional difficulties include relocation, employers' ageist attitudes toward older workers, terminal illness, sexuality, widower- and widowhood, grief, loneliness, depression, isolation, and chronic health problems (Glass and Grant, 1983; Lombana, 1976; Simonton, 1990).

The American pioneer in geriatric counseling was Lillien J. Martin. In 1929 she founded the San Francisco Old Age Counseling Center. For the next 15 years she developed her own techniques. The Martin method involved a s⸢ ⸣es of structured interviews emphasizing a directive approach of specific ⸢ tions. Although the Martin Clinic appeared to be successful, her i⸢ geriatrics never extended to the mainstream of social work or p⸢ Today, however, that is changing. The contemporary counseli⸢ being equipped to cope with a wide range of elderly stru⸢ problems associated with aging can be mediated and s⸢ postponed through counseling (Afresti, 1992). Preretir⸢ ample, can help the retiree plan more effectively fo⸢

good physical and mental health. Family counseling services can enable better communication among family members and it can promote acceptance of the adjustment required by the aging process for all involved (Lombana, 1976).

A SUMMARY WORD

Counseling and cultural differences, gender differences, the differently abled, religious clients, AIDS, and older adults—each area presents a unique set of issues and special needs. But all are calling to the contemporary counselor for help, and it is the responsibility of today's counselors to wake up and answer the call. It is also the responsibility of counselors-in-training to help the field of counseling respond professionally to these contemporary concerns. The future of counseling depends on it.

REFERENCES

Afresti, A. A. (1992). Counselor training and ethical issues with older clients. *Counselor Education & Supervision, 31,* 43–50.

Albers, G. R. (1990). *Counseling and AIDS.* Waco, TX: Word.

American Psychological Association. (1975). Report on the task force on sex bias and sex-role stereotyping in psychotherapeutic practice. *American Psychologist, 30,* 1169–1175.

American Psychological Association. (1978). Guidelines for therapy with women. *American Psychologist, 33,* 1122–1123.

Antill, J. K., & Cotton, S. (1986). Self-disclosure between husbands and wives: Its relationship to sex roles and marital happiness. *Australian Journal of Psychology, 39,* 11–24.

Aponte, H. J. (1990). Ethnicity dynamic, important in therapeutic relationships. *Family Therapy News, 21,* 3.

Asher, J. (1975, April). Sex bias found in therapy. *APA Monitor, 1,* 5.

Atkinson, D. R., Morten, G., & Sue, D. W. (1989). *Counseling American minorities: A cross cultural perspective* (3rd ed.). Dubuque, IA: Wm. C. Brown.

Batchelor, W. (1988). The science and the limits of science. *American Psychologist, 43,* 853.

Beckerman, N. L. (1994). Psychosocial tasks facing parents whose adult child has AIDS. *Family Therapy, 21,* 209–216.

Bergin, A. E. (1991). Values and religious issues in psychotherapy and mental health. *American Psychologist, 46,* 394–403.

Bradford, D. T., & Spero, M. H. (Eds.). (1990). Psychotherapy and religion [Special issue]. *Psychotherapy, 27* (1).

Broverman, I. K., Broverman, D. M., Clarkson, F. E., Rosenkrantz, P., & Vogel, S. R. (1970). Sex role stereotypes and clinical judgments of mental health. *Journal of Consulting and Clinical Psychology, 34,* 1–7.

Browning, D. S., Jobe, T., & Evison, I. S. (1990). *Religious and ethical factors in psychiatric practice.* Chicago: Nelson-Hall.

✓   1990). Spirituality reconsidered. *Family Therapy Networker, 14,* 226–37.

Butler, R. N., & Lewis, M. I. (1982). *Aging and mental health* (3rd ed.). NY: Macmillan.

Byrne, G. (1989). AIDS panel urges new focus. *Science, 243,* 887.

Carter, R. T. (1991). Cultural values: A review of empirical research and implications for counseling. *Journal of Counseling and Development, 70,* 164–173.

Collins, G. R. (1993). *The Biblical basis of Christian counsing for people helpers.* Colorado Springs: NavPress.

Cristiani, T. S., & Sommers, P. (1978). The counselor's role in mainstreaming the handicapped. *Viewpoints in Teaching and Learning, 54,* 20–28.

DeForest, C. & Stone, G. L. (1980). Effects of sex and intimacy on self-disclosure. *Journal of Counseling Psychology, 27,* 93–96.

Devore, W., & Schlesinger, E. G. (1991). *Ethnic-sensitive social work practice* (3rd ed.). New York: Macmillan.

Ellis, A. (1980). Psychotherapy and atheistic values: A response to A. E. Bergin's "Psychotherapy and religious values." *Journal of Consulting and Clinical Psychology, 48,* 635–639.

English, A. (1991). Runaway and street youth at risk for HIV infection: Legal and ethical issues in access to care. *Journal of Adolescent Health, 12,* 504–510.

Erickson, S. H. (1993). Ethics and confidentiality in AIDS counseling: A professional dilemma. *Journal of Mental Health Counseling, 15,* 118–131.

Erikson, E. H. (1987). *A way of looking at things: Selected papers from 1930 to 1980.* New York: Norton.

Filer, P. (1982). Counselor trainees' attitudes toward mainstreaming the handicapped. *Counselor Education and Supervision, 22,* 61–69.

Freud, S. (1927). The future of an illusion. *Standard Edition, 21,* 5–56.

Friedman, A. L., & Hughes, R. B. (1994). AIDS: Legal tools helpful for mental health counseling interventions. *Journal of Mental Health Counseling, 16,* 291–303.

Gladding, S. T. (1992). *Counseling: A comprehensive profession* (2nd ed.). New York: Merrill.

Glass, J., & Grant, K. (1983). Counseling in the later years: A growing need. *Personnel and Guidance Journal, 62,* 210–213.

Goldrick, M., Pearce, J. K., & Giordano, J. (1982). *Ethnicity & family therapy.* New York: Guilford Press.

Good, G. E., Gilbert, L. A., & Scher, M. (1990). Gender aware therapy: A synthesis of feminist therapy and knowledge about gender. *Journal of Counseling and Development, 68,* 376–380.

Gove, W. R., & Tudor, J. F. (1973). Adult sex roles and mental illness. In J. Huber (Ed.), *Changing women in a changing society* (pp. 50–73). Chicago: University of Chicago Press.

Greenblatt, L., Hasenauer, J. E., & Freimuth, V. G. (1980). Psychological sex type and androgyny in the study of communication variables: Self-disclosure and communication apprehension. *Human Communication Research, 6,* 117–129.

Hackney, H., & Wrenn, C. G. (1990). The contemporary counselor in a changed world. In H. Hackney (Ed.), *Changing contexts for counselor preparation 1990s* (pp. 1–20). Alexandria, VA: Association for Counselor Educa' Supervision.

Hare-Mustin, R. T. (1983). An appraisal of the relationship between w chotherapy: 80 years after the case of Dora. *American Psychologis'*

Hearst, N., & Hulley, S. (1988). Preventing the heterosexual spread *American Medical Association, 259,* 2428–2432.

Hendrick, S. S. (1981). Self-disclosure and marital satisfa *and Social Psychology, 40,* 1150–1159.

Hess, B. B. (1991). Growing old in the 1990s. In B. B. Hess & E. W. Markson (Eds.), *Growing old in America* (4th ed., pp. 5–22). New Brunswick, NJ: Transaction Books.

Hosie, T. (1979). Preparing counselors to meet the needs of the handicapped. *Personnel and Guidance Journal, 58,* 271–275.

Hubbard, M. G. (1992). *Women: The misunderstood majority.* Waco, TX: Word.

Kelly, E. W. (1995). *Spirituality and religion in counseling and psychotherapy: diversity in theory and practice.* Alexandria, VA: American Counseling Association.

Kunins, H., Hein, K, & Futterman, D. (1993). Guide to adolescent HIV/AIDS program development. *Journal of Adolescent Health, 14,* 140.

Lee, C. C., & Richardson, B. L. (1991). *Multicultural issues in counseling.* Alexandria, VA: American Association for Counseling and Development.

Lombana, J. H. (1976). Counseling the elderly: Remediation plus prevention. *Personnel and Guidance Journal, 55,* 143–144.

Lopez, R., Lopez, A., and Fong, K., (1991). Mexican Americans' initial preferences for counselors: The role of ethnic factors. *Journal of Counseling Psychology, 38,* 487–496.

Malony, H. N. (1988). The clinical assessment of optimal religious functioning. *Review of Religious Research, 30,* 3–17.

McDowell, W., Coven, A., & Eash, U. (1979). The handicapped: Special needs and strategies for counseling. *Personnel and Guidance Journal, 58,* 228–232.

Myers, J. E. (1989). *Infusing gerontological counseling into counselor preparation.* Alexandria, VA: American Association for Counseling and Development.

Myers, J. E. (1990). Aging: An overview for mental health counselors. *Journal of Mental Health Counseling, 12,* 245–259.

Nathanson, R. (1979). Counseling parents with disabilities: Are the feelings, thoughts, and behaviors of helping professionals helpful? *Personnel and Guidance Journal, 58,* 233–237.

Newman, S., Durrance, P., & Fell, M. (1993). Counseling in HIV and AIDS. *British Journal of Clinical Psychology, 32,* 117–119.

O'Brien, M. (1988). Men and fathers in therapy. *Journal of Family Therapy, 10,* 109–123.

Parrott, L., & Parrott, L. (1995). *The career counselor.* Dallas: Word.

Peck, M. S. (1978). *The road less traveled.* New York: Simon & Schuster.

Pederson, P. B., (Ed.). (1994). *Handbook of cross-cultural counseling and therapy.* Westport, CT: Greenwood Publishing Group.

Perlman, L. G., & Kirk, F. S. (1991). Key disability and rehabilitation legislation. *Journal of Applied Rehabilitation Counseling, 22,* 21–27.

Ponterotto, J. G., Casas, J. M., Suzuki, L. A., & Alexander, C. M. (1995). *Handbook of multicultural counseling.* Thousand Oaks, CA: Sage Publications.

Religion in America. (1985). Report No. 236. Princeton, NJ: Gallup Organization.

Richards, P. S. (1991). Religious devoutness in college students: Relations with emotional adjustment and psychological separation from parents. *Journal of Counseling Psychology, 38,* 189–196.

Ridley, C. R. (1995). *Overcoming unintentional racism in counseling and therapy: A practitioner's guide to intentional intervention.* Thousand Oaks, CA: Sage Publications.

Rusalem, H., & Cohen, J. (1975). Guidance of the exceptional student. In William M. Cruickshank & G. Orville Johnson (Eds), *Education of exceptional children and youth* (pp. 613–622). Englewood Cliffs, NJ: Prentice-Hall.

Scher, M., & Good, G. E. (1990). Gender and counseling in the twenty-first century: What [do]es the future hold? *Journal of Counseling & Development, 68,* 388–391.

Schlossberg, N. K., & Pietrofesa, J. J. (1973). Perspectives on counseling bias: Implications for counselor education. *Counseling Psychologist, 4,* 44–54.

Shafranske, E. (Ed.) (1996). *Religion and the clinical practices of psychology,* Washington, DC: American Psychological Association.

Simonton, D. K. (1990). Creativity in the later years: Optimistic prospects for achievement. *The Gerontologist, 30,* 626–631.

Smith, D. C. (1994). A "last rights" group for people with AIDS. *Journal for Specialists in Group Work, 19,* 17–21.

Sorenson, J. L., London, J., Heitzmann, C., & Gibson, D. R. (1994). Psychoeducational group approach: HIV risk reduction in drug users. *AIDS Education and Prevention, 6,* 95–112.

Stern, E. M. (Ed.). (1985). *Psychotherapy and the religiously committed patient.* New York: Haworth Press.

Sue, D. W. (1977). Counseling the culturally different: A conceptual analysis. *Personnel and Guidance Journal, 55,* 422–425.

Sue, D. W., Arredondo, P., & McDavis, R. J. (1992). Multicultural counseling competencies and standards: A call to the profession. *Journal of Counseling and Development, 70,* 477–486.

Sue, D. W., & Sue, D. (1990). *Counseling the culturally different: Theory & practice* (2nd ed.). New York: Wiley.

Sue, S., Fujino, D. C., Hu, L., Takeuchi, D. T., & Zane, N. W. S. (1991). Community mental health services for ethnic minority groups: A test of the cultural responsiveness hypothesis. *Journal of Consulting and Clinical Psychology, 59,* 533–540.

Sue, S., & McKinney, H. (1975). Asian Americans in the community mental health care system. *American Journal of Orthopsychiatry, 45,* 111–118.

Sue, S., McKinney, H., Allen, D., & Hall, J. (1974). Delivery of community mental health services to black and white clients. *Journal of Consulting and Clinical Psychology, 42,* 794–801.

Tan, S. Y. (1993). *Training in professional psychology: Diversity includes religion.* Paper presented at the National Council of Schools of Professional Psychology. Midwinter conference, January 19–23, 1993, LaJolla, CA.

Tan, S. Y. (1996). Religion in clinical practice: implicit and explicit integration. In E. Shafranske (Ed.). *Religion and the clinical practice of psychology.* (pp. 365–387). Washington, DC: American Psychology Association.

Trezza, G. R. (1994). HIV knowledge and stigmatization of persons with AIDS: Implications for the development of HIV education for young adults. *Professional Psychology Research and Practice, 25,* 141–148.

Vandergriff, A., & Hosie, T. (1979). PL 94-142: A role change for counselors or just an extension of present role? *Journal of Counseling Services, 3,* 6–11.

Van Hasselt, V. B., Strain, P. S., & Hersen, M. (1988). *Handbook of developmental and physical disabilities.* New York: Pergamon Press.

Vontress, C. E. (1971). Racial differences: Impediments to rapport. *Journal of Coun   Psychology, 18,* 7–13.

Wade, P., & Bernstein, B. L. (1991). Culture sensitivity training and counsel fects on Black female clients' perceptions and attrition. *Journal of chology, 38,* 9–15.

Williams, J. H. (1987). *Psychology of women: Behavior in a biosocial York: W. W. Norton.

Williams, M. H. (1992). Exploitation and inference: Mapping patient sexual involvement. *American Psychologist, 4*

Worell, J., & Remer, P. (1992). *Feminist perspectives in therapy: An empowerment model for women.* New York: Wiley.

Worthington, E. L. (1989). Religious faith across the life span: Implications for counseling and research. *The Counseling Psychologist, 17,* 555–612.

Wrenn, C. G. (1958). Psychology, religion, and values for the counselor, Part III, in the symposium, the counselor and his religion. *Personnel and Guidance Journal, 36,* 326–334.

PART TWO

Major Therapeutic Theories

CHAPTER 5

Introduction:

Your Personal Theory of Therapy

Chapter Outline

Why Study Theories?
Discovering the Theory Within You
An Overview of the Chapters

In 585 B.C., a mathematician named Thales of Miletus had a theory about solar activity and as a result successfully predicted a solar eclipse—but only after he had made an embarrassing mistake. While contemplating the stars, it seems, Thales lost his footing and fell head over heels into a deep hole. And although his amazing prediction won popular acclaim, he was also remembered as an absent-minded, bumbling theorist. Someone reportedly asked him: "How can thou knowest what is doing in the heavens, when thou seest not what is at thy feet?" That's a good question. There is danger in lofty and speculative theorizing. But a good theory, on the other hand, can reveal truth and lead to valuable benefits—especially good theories about how to practice psychotherapy.

Aristotle was the first to make a distinction between theory and practice. His terms were *theoria* and *praxis*. According to Aristotle, praxis follows analysis and has to do with *doing*. Praxis is the application of theoretical knowledge. Each of the theories in this book is designed to lead eventually to praxis. For this reason, they are practical theories, tested in the comprehensive laboratories of counseling, and have been confirmed as social scientists have thrown out parts of theories that have not continued to make sense over time while retaining those that do. In the words of Kurt Lewin, "There is nothing so practical as a good theory" (Lewin quoted by Marrow, 1969, p. viii).

The theories covered in this text—the theories of Freud, Adler, Rogers, and all the rest—have been studied, evaluated, critiqued, compared, and scrutinized. Yet they continue to stand tall. Some are more popular than others, but each offers significant insight and salient strategies for the helping profession.

79

It is not the goal of this text to convert anyone to a specific theory of psychotherapy. Neither is it the purpose of this text to guide students into choosing and committing themselves henceforth to the assumptions and techniques of any one theory. The goal of this text, however, is to make you, as a prospective counselor, aware of the most important approaches to psychotherapy. Truth be known, few counselors today are theoretical purists, putting all their eggs in one basket. Human pain and suffering in contemporary society is far too complex for universal and strict formulas broadly applied. For this reason, a pragmatic rather than a dogmatic approach to counseling is affirmed throughout this text. Each theory in this book has been carefully selected to undergird your future counseling with professional knowledge, human understanding, and the application of useful techniques for the counseling relationship.

After you study the various theories, you may find yourself gravitating toward one or two theories in particular, dedicating your focus to them exclusively. Or perhaps, like many, you will view the successive presentation of these theories more as a smorgasbord from which to choose main entrees and side dishes that will please the pallates of hurting people. Whatever the result, it is important that you become knowledgeable in each of these theories, which hold historical, conceptual, and pragmatic significance to the entire field of counseling.

WHY STUDY THEORIES?

"The way we think about problems determines to a large degree what we will do about them," says Krumboltz (1966, p.4). Therefore, it is important for therapists (1) to know how their decision-making process functions in *analyzing* human problems, (2) to understand what *assumptions* about counseling they believe are really true, and (3) to discover what they see as the best features in the theories they tend to *accept* as good. "Analyze," "assume," and "accept"—the triple A's—are three important verbs counselors must think about in the development of their personal approach to therapy. Our thinking, our assumptions, and our beliefs form the foundation of what we do as counselors.

It is safe to assume that every counselor believes a therapeutic intervention has the potential to help a client. Therapists believe that therapy is a worthy enterprise. Moving beyond this fundamental and essential assumption, there are a great many hypotheses or questions about the helping process. And each and every question requires its own answer. Throughout the chapters in this section, you will encounter a number of questions requiring reflection and personal exploration (Brammer, 1973). Questions such as:

- How is human personality structured?
- What is my responsibility to others?
- What motivates people to behave as they do?
- How do people get the way they are?
- How do people change?
- How does thinking influence behavior?

- What are the relationships among thinking, feeling, and behaving?
- Where do our values come from?
- How do people make choices?
- How do people learn?
- How can I facilitate change?
- Does our personality influence the environment or is it the other way around?

Theories help answer these and many other questions. They help us formulate beliefs and values. Historically, many counselors took refuge in the comforting notion that a counselor's values could and should be kept out of the therapeutic relationship. However, in the late 1950s and early 1960s, therapists began to express the philosophy that counselors, instead of remaining neutral,

The prospect of preparing an overview of psychotherapy in America today is enough to make the most stout-hearted quail.

—Jerome D. Frank

should bring goals and techniques into the counseling relationship that are products of their personal values. For instance, theorists such as Lowe (1976) described the counselor as one who provides the client with a moral meaning and direction for life. Patterson (1959) found a direct relationship between the counselor's values and his or her style of counseling. For this reason it is imperative that you as a counselor-in-training explore a variety of theories—theories that will help you discover your own approach to psychotherapy.

DISCOVERING THE THEORY WITHIN YOU

Michelangelo attempted 44 statues in his life, but finished only 14 of them. They include such masterpieces as David in the Piazza of Florence, the Pieta in the Vatican basilica, and Moses in another of Rome's great churches. Michelangelo's 30 unfinished sculptures, however, are, in their own way, just as interesting as those that have become classics. They are preserved in one of Italy's many museums. Each is a huge chunk of marble from which Michelangelo sculpted only an elbow or the beginning of a wrist. One mass of marble reveals a leg, thigh, knee, calf, and foot. The rest of the body is locked forever into the stone. The person Michelangelo had in mind will never step forth.

The following brief questionnaire is designed to help chip away at the theory of therapy developing inside you. Every potential counselor holds beliefs and values, still under construction, which will one day meld into a personal theory about the human condition and how best to help it. Take time to reflect and respond thoughtfully to these questions. It is a simple step you can take in revealing your values and sculpting your own theory of counseling.

T F **1.** Therapists should work only with clients whom they really like and care for.

T F **2.** My values should be kept out of the therapy process.

T   F   **3.** Giving advice is possibly the most important function of a therapist.

T   F   **4.** Confidentiality is an absolute, and I would never disclose anything a client revealed during therapy.

T   F   **5.** My own mental health is probably the most important variable that determines the success or failure of counseling.

T   F   **6.** Counseling is basically for people who are not coping with life very well.

T   F   **7.** I should be completely open, honest, and transparent with my clients.

T   F   **8.** It is essential to know the origin and causes of a problem before a person can truly change.

T   F   **9.** To be effective as a counselor I need to have an attitude of total acceptance toward my client.

T   F   **10.** Intellectual insight is necessary for a person to change.

T   F   **11.** Asking questions is generally helpful as a therapeutic technique.

T   F   **12.** A therapist should rarely allow long moments of uncomfortable silence to occur.

T   F   **13.** As a counselor my job is basically that of a teacher—I am reeducating clients with better coping skills.

T   F   **14.** Confrontation generally causes great pain or discomfort and it is better to let clients confront themselves when they are ready.

T   F   **15.** In a counseling session, my needs as a counselor are not important.

T   F   **16.** To be effective in counseling, one must be fairly good at persuasion.

T   F   **17.** A good therapist is born, not made.

T   F   **18.** One of the most valuable gifts a client can receive is a word of solid advice.

T   F   **19.** Counseling should focus on the present more than the past.

T   F   **20.** The primary purpose of counseling is to provide solutions to problems.

T   F   **21.** The primary purpose of counseling is to change behavior.

T   F   **22.** The primary purpose of counseling is help people think rationally.

T   F   **23.** The most effective therapy is done over a long period of time.

T   F   **24.** To be a good counselor, one needs to be undergoing therapy.

T   F   **25.** It is generally best to go with one's instincts as a counselor—one's perception of a client's situation is probably correct.

For now, do not seek to "score" this questionnaire. It was not designed to have a right or wrong answer for every question. Its sole purpose is to help you begin thinking about how you already approach the practice of psychotherapy. However, after you have studied each of the theories in this book, you may find it quite helpful to come back to these questions and attempt to answer them the way a particular theorist would. For example, after reading the chapter "Psychoanalytic Therapy," try to answer the question in the way that you believe Freud would and then compare your responses to his. This exercise will help you better internalize Freud's theoretical approach and it will help you sharpen your personal theory as well.

AN OVERVIEW OF THE CHAPTERS

Your journey through the theories of the following chapters is much like navigating a river. Knowing where the rocks are, estimating strength in the rolls of water off big boulders, determining the power and momentum of the current, and identifying the sink holes that threaten the destruction of the boat are, figuratively, the pieces of information each counselor needs in developing his or her own strategic approach—before he or she launches into the whitewater rapids of a counseling relationship. To eliminate unexpected turns and to make the trip more pleasurable, each chapter features a consistent structure. Sidebars are also used at various points in the text to enhance your journey. But the basic outline in the chapters remains constant: brief biography, historical development, view of human nature, development of maladaptive behavior, function of the therapist, goals of therapy, major methods and techniques, application, critical analysis, current status, key terms, chapter summary, recommended reading.

In order to understand anything well, you need at least three good theories.

—William Perry

Brief Biography

It is difficult to separate the theory from the theorist. Serious students of psychotherapeutic theories will enhance and expand their understanding of a particular theory by studying the life of the theorist. Even a brief look into the background of a founding theorist can cast light and shadows onto their theory and provide a deeper understanding of their therapeutic perspective.

Historical Development

"The main thing is to make history, not to write it," wrote Otto von Bismarck. While many of the theorists covered in this book did not "write" the history of their ideas, the historical development of their thinking cannot be overlooked. Marcus Tullius Cicero, the great Roman statesman, declared, "To be ignorant of what occurred before you were born is to remain always a child." In the spirit of this aphorism, the origins and development of major concepts and hypotheses of each theory are explored. In this way, the chapters provide historical hooks on which to hang theoretical concepts.

View of Human Nature

Each of us, knowingly or not, holds personal thoughts on what human beings are really like. And each theorist also holds a concept of the nature of being human. From Freud's determinism to Rogers' humanism, each theory reveals the theorist's view of human nature. Thoughtful students of therapeutic theory will delve into this aspect of a particular approach to discover its vital importance. For as Mark Twain said, "There is a great deal of human nature in people."

Development of Maladaptive Behavior

The biblical story of King Saul shows how he suffered from episodes of extreme melancholy followed by outbursts of mania. Today his condition is known as bipolar mood disorder. But although maladaptive behavior has been around since ancient days, our understanding of why it occurs still is not complete. Hippocrates argued that it was not caused by divine intervention, as was commonly believed, but by disturbances in the brain. Thousands of years later, modern scientists study and debate his claim. Each of the theorists in these chapters also has a unique perspective on how and why maladaptive behavior develops. Many of their views may surprise you.

The only therapy is life.

—Otto Rank

Function of the Therapist

Each theorist assigns specific and unique duties to the counselors who join their camp. Some require active involvement, whereas others urge contemplative and minimal interaction with their clients. Some prescribe explicit values, whereas others assign a counselor role wherein values are left to personal style. In each chapter, the role and function of the therapist is explored.

Goals of Therapy

Jean de La Fontaine said, "In everything we ought to look to the end." The theorists in this book have certainly taken his advice. Each theory calls for outcomes or clearly conceived ends. For some the goal of therapy is decidedly specific: to change irrational thinking, for example. Other goals, when voiced, seem vague and obscure: to experience one's experience as real. Still others aim to reconstruct a person's entire personality. Regardless of its goals, each theory is dedicated to making outcomes a reality. In the following chapters these goals will be laid out for thorough examination.

Major Methods and Techniques

Eventually, after discussing the ideas of therapeutic intervention, every theory comes to a place of action. In their own ways, each theory echoes the words of another great artist, William Wordsworth, when he said, "Thought and theory must precede all salutary action; yet action is nobler in itself than either thought or theory." In these chapters, each theory will be identified with a series of customary therapeutic actions that are appropriate to their outcomes. Each theory packs a therapeutic bag of methods and techniques for healing the human psyche.

Application

There is perhaps no better way of understanding the heart of a particular therapeutic theory than to see it demonstrated. Each chapter provides you with examples of how and where the theory is applied and of exactly how it works through excerpts from actual counseling cases. Many times, these cases come directly from the files of the founding theorist.

Critical Analysis

Once a thorough exploration of the theory has taken place, you will be challenged to think through what each approach has to offer. What are its major contributions to the field of counseling? Where does it miss the mark? A critique of each theory will be offered as a catalyst to further critique by you. This subsection, by the way, gives special attention to the pluses and minuses of the approach to cross-cultural counseling issues.

Current Status

After exploring the inner corridors of a theory, the chapter will turn briefly to its current status among contemporary counselors. The chapter notes the professional organizations, associations, and publications that keep the theory alive and suggests sources to which students may turn for more information.

Key Terms

Every field of study has its own professional language. Depending on your previous knowledge of psychology, you may already be familiar with some of the terminology in these chapters. Regardless, a glossary of terms that is specific to that theory is located at the end of each chapter.

Chapter Summary

To help you conceptualize and internalize the components of each theory, a chapter summary is offered. Its purpose is in no way to substitute for a thorough study of the chapter itself. It is meant simply to help you refresh your reading by highlighting many of the specific theory's features.

Near the beginning of the nineteenth century, the philosopher Immanuel Kant wrote an essay entitled, "On the Old Saw: It May Work in Theory, But It

Won't Work in Practice." The theories that make up this section have all been shown to "work" to some degree or another. But ultimately, the effectiveness of any one of them must be up to you, the counselor.

REFERENCES

Brammer, L. (1973). *The helping relationship: Process and skills.* Englewood Cliffs, NJ: Prentice-Hall.

Krumboltz, J. D. (1966). Promoting adaptive behavior: Behavioral approach. In J. Krumboltz (Ed.), *Revolution in counseling.* Boston: Houghton Mifflin.

Lowe, C. M. (1976). *Value orientations in counseling and psychotherapy: The meanings of mental health.* Cranston, RI: Carroll Press.

Marrow, A. J. (1969). *The practical theorist: The life and work of Kurt Lewin.* New York: Basic Books.

Patterson, C. H. (1959). The place of values in counseling and psychotherapy. *Journal of Counseling Psychology, 5,* 216–223.

CHAPTER 6

Psychoanalytic Therapy

Chapter Outline

Introduction
Brief Biography
Historical Development
View of Human Nature
Development of Maladaptive Behavior
Goals of Therapy
Function of the Therapist
Major Methods and Techniques
Application
Critical Analysis
Current Status
Chapter Summary
Key Terms
Suggested Reading

INTRODUCTION

Throughout history, scientists have rewritten humanity's place in the universe three times over. Nicolaus Copernicus proved the Earth is not the center of the universe, but merely one of several planets revolving around the sun. Charles Darwin added insult to injury when he convinced much of the Western world that humans are not a uniquely created life form, but one of the many species that have evolved over millions of years. And according to Sigmund Freud, we are masters not even of our own minds, but victims of powerful unconscious motives, seldom recognized and less often understood.

Each of these scientists, Copernicus, Darwin, and Freud, changed the paradigms by which we think. But for the counselor none is more important than

Sigmund Freud, an intellectual revolutionary who developed a psychoanalytic theory that sought to help troubled people come to grips with their demons. Freud's explorations led him into previously uncharted territory and allowed him to draw a new map of the human mind. Most social scientists agree that Freud's theory is the "most comprehensive and far-reaching conceptualization of personality, psychopathology, and psychotherapy in existence" (Korchin, 1976, p. 332).

The pervasiveness of psychoanalysis can be seen in nearly every academic discipline, and its direct and indirect influence on the larger public consciousness can hardly be overestimated (Arlow & Brenner, 1988; Jones & Wilson, 1987; Runyan, 1988; Sampson, 1990). Freud's influence is reflected in art, literature, and music, and even in Hollywood, where the Freudian concepts of sex and agression are taken as basic not only to the nature of human beings but to the film industry as well. Along with others who changed the world, Freud stands with Plato, Marx, and Einstein.

BRIEF BIOGRAPHY

Sigmund Freud was born on May 6, 1856, in a German-speaking territory that is now Czechoslovakia. Freud's father, Jakob, a wool merchant, was married the third time to Amalie, who favored Sigmund, calling him her "golden Sigi." She entertained higher hopes for Freud than for her five daughters and two sons born after him. Freud's great grandfather was a rabbi, and Freud himself was raised in the traditions and beliefs of the Jewish religion.

When Freud was 3 years old his father moved the family to Vienna, where Freud lived most of his life. A brilliant student, graduating from high school with honors, Freud loved literature, especially Shakespeare, and was proficient

Freud—the Darwin of the mind.

—Ernest Jones

in German, French, English, Italian, Spanish, Hebrew, Latin, and Greek (Jones, 1953). Although he dreamed of becoming a Napoleon or a minister of state like Oliver Cromwell, a Jewish boy's choices were limited in late nineteenth-century Vienna. He considered a career in law, but eventually chose medicine. After receiving his medical degree from the University of Vienna at age 25, he practiced medicine at Vienna's General Hospital, where he continued his studies in organic diseases of the nervous system.

In 1886 Freud married Martha Bernays, to whom he had been engaged for 4 years. They had six children, three boys and three girls, the youngest of whom, Anna, became famous in her own right as a psychoanalyst specializing in the treatment of children.

Freud supported his family through his private practice in psychiatry, specializing in nervous diseases. At first he employed the conventional treatments of his day: baths, massage, electrotherapy, and rest cures. But gradually Freud's interests moved away from the physical aspects of the nervous system and more toward the psychological factors—a move that may have been prompted, as some have suggested, by a need to escape the anti-Semitic medical commu-

Sigmund Freud at work on the outline of *Psychoanalysis,*
his last sustained effort, in the summer of 1938.
(Archiv/Photo Researchers)

nity of Vienna. This shift in focus intensified with each year and resulted in full-
time study of the psychological origins of neuroses (Gay, 1988). Eventually acclaim came his way, as did popular attention. (He was even offered a job writing an advice column for the lovelorn in *Cosmopolitan* [Clark, 1980].)

During the last 16 years of his life, Freud was afflicted with a painful cancer of the mouth and jaw, requiring no fewer than 33 operations. Often smoking as many as 20 cigars daily, as a physician Freud was well aware of the risks
he took, and many times tried desperately to stop. A tragic prototype of a tobacco addict, even after his cancer was diagnosed he continued to smoke.
"Don't try to live forever," he often said, quoting George Bernard Shaw. "You
will not be successful" (Brecher, 1972, p. 67).

Having abandoned his long-time home in Vienna in 1938 to escape Nazi
persecution, Freud died at his son's home in London a year later at age 83.
Never lamenting his persecution and illness, Freud waited for death. "It is
tragic when a man outlives his body," was his only complaint.

A lucid and prolific writer, Freud continued to publish well into his 70s. On
a typical day he was up by 8 a.m., saw patients until 7 and often wrote until 1
in the morning. More than half a century after his death, many of his 23 books
are still in print, among them *The Interpretation of Dreams* (1900/1957), *The Psychopathology of Everyday Life* (1901), *Beyond the Pleasure Principle* (1920), *The Ego*

and the Id (1923), and *Civilization and Its Discontents* (1930). Sigmund Freud's life has been chronicled and analyzed by many; especially valuable are those by his official biographer, Ernest Jones, who wrote the definitive three-volume work (1953, 1955, 1957) and, more recently, those by Ronald W. Clark (1980) and Peter Gay (1988).

HISTORICAL DEVELOPMENT

Although the beginnings of psychoanalysis cannot be restricted to a specific year, its origins are identified with the early 1880s, at the height of the industrial revolution. People swarmed to the cities, where sweat shops brutalized the disenfranchised, usually children, women, and immigrants. On both sides of the Atlantic, the Victorian Age set the moral climate of Europe and America, leaving many people torn between behavioral norms and their own inner feelings. Few had addressed the psychological suffering during this troubled era.

The Talking Cure

In late nineteenth-century Vienna, Josef Breuer, the neurologist known as the "doctor with the golden touch," was especially successful in treating hysteria. Freud described him as having a striking intelligence. "We [shared] all our scientific interests with each other," Freud recalled. "In this relationship the gain was naturally mine" (1935, p. 33).

The seeds of psychoanalysis were sown by Dr. Breuer's patient, Bertha Pappenheim or, as she later came to be known, Anna O. She was a bright young woman who presented a variety of hysterical symptoms including a nervous cough, anorexia, paralyses, a double personality, and, despite an inability to speak her native German, a proficiency in English. Not surprisingly, Breuer was fascinated by Miss Pappenheim and devoted much of his time to treating her. Each evening they explored the ties between her memories and her symptoms. The paralysis of her arm, for example, first appeared when she hallucinated a large, black snake in her father's bed. She tried to ward the snake off with her arm, but it would not move, and from that time her arm had been paralyzed. Although such recollections were intensely emotional, afterwards she felt cheerful and calm—so calm, in fact, that Breuer spoke of this release of tension as a "catharsis." The effects of this catharsis were welcomed but not expected by Breuer. He began describing his treatment of Bertha Pappenheim as the "talking cure" (Freud, 1935).

Breuer devoted a disproportionate amount of time to his treatment of Bertha, often seeing her twice a day. In time, Breuer's wife became concerned about their relationship and insisted that he end his treatment. Bertha went on to a successful career as Germany's first social worker and was a zealous champion of women's rights.

> A man who has been the indisputable favorite of his mother keeps for life the feeling of a conqueror.
>
> —Sigmund Freud

The Birth of Psychoanalysis

Breuer exchanged his views on the case with the 26-year-old Freud, and they eventually coauthored the landmark *Studies on Hysteria* (Freud & Breuer, 1895). To respect Bertha Pappenheim's privacy, Breuer would refer to her as Fräulein Anna O. It was this woman, the "best-known of all psychotherapy patients" (Hollender, 1980, p. 797), who played an important role in Freud's formulation of psychoanalysis.

In 1885 Freud was awarded a grant that allowed him to study hysteria in Paris with the famous French neurologist Jean Charcot. Under hypnosis, Charcot found that some hysterical patients relinquished their symptoms and recalled the traumatic experiences that had generated them. Impressed by Charcot's techniques, Freud quickly recognized the connection to Breuer's work.

After returning from his sojourn in Paris, Freud lost no time in explaining his discoveries to his circle of physicians in Vienna. His advocacy of hypnotic techniques was met with skepticism, but this did not deter him from incorporating it into his treatment of nervous disorders (Jones, 1953).

Together with his interest in Anna O., Freud's work with Charcot lay the groundwork for a revolutionary theory. It was a theory that Freud first referred to as "Breuer's method," then as "psychical analysis," and finally as "psychoanalysis" (Freeman, 1972). Freud first used the term "psychoanalysis" in 1896 (Gay, 1988). Although it was only in crude form and far from its ultimate shape, the basic outline of psychoanalysis was in hand, and a view of humans and how to treat them eventually emerged.

VIEW OF HUMAN NATURE

Sigmund Freud painted a vivid portrait of human nature. He believed people were dominated by instinctual, unconscious, and irrational forces, leaving people at war internally and externally. But chief among these drives was aggression and sex, housed within an inner core dominated by the super-ego. Everyone was highly sexual, he believed, even during years of "childhood innocence."

For Freud, personality was determined entirely by conditions and events beyond personal control. Lying behind every human thought or action was a cause, Freud believed. Thoughts, feelings, and actions did not occur by chance. They were not accidents. Reading the word "breast" when the text says "beast," for example, forgetting a relative's name, or losing a borrowed book may not be in conscious awareness, but each is the hidden expression of a feeling or impulse buried in the mind. Freud believed that these causes could be identified and that undesirable personality traits, their distorted outcomes, could be treated. One need only explore the unconscious to trace and uncover these hidden causes (Pine, 1990).

The Unconscious

At the epicenter of this revolutionary theory is the unconscious. "If Freud's discovery had to be summed up in a single word, that word would without a doubt have to be 'unconscious'" (Laplanche and Pontailies, 1973, p. 474). Freud believed a revelation of the unconscious could explain all human thought, feeling, and action. Like woolly mammoths, perfectly preserved in the Arctic tundra, Freud wrote, once the layers of resistence have been laid bare, our past, our memories, still retain their freshness (Wachtel, 1977, p. 28).

Freud's focus on the unconscious, however, was not in the mainstream of turn-of-the-century medical practice. Physicians were, by and large, not attempting to deal with the psychology of disease; few considered the unconscious self a subject deserving of critical scientific study and analysis. At the time the field of psychology was primarily concerned with the perception of objects and other such states of consciousness.

Freud, in contrast, viewed consciousness as only a small part of the total psyche, the proverbial tip of the iceberg. In traditional psychoanalytic theory there are, in fact, three levels of personality: the visible *consciousness*, which consists of everything within cognitive awareness; the *preconscious*, made up of material that is fairly accessible, but not immediately within the person's awareness; and then the underlying *unconscious*, which consists of every aspect in human personality of which we are unaware. And it was here, in the powerful unconscious drive, that Freud found the most fruitful place to look for explanations of human motivation.

The great question that has never been answered...is "What does a woman want?"

—Sigmund Freud

Structure of Personality

Freud (1901, 1924) divided personality, which he called the "scaffold of the mind," into three components: the *id*, which represents the biological self in personality; the *ego*, the partially unconscious drive or psychological center of personality; and the *superego*, the governor, the social controller in the tower, which brings behavior within culturally acceptable limits.

These three aspects, or factors, are not physical parts of the personality. They cannot be located and photographed. They are unseen, but nonetheless real, psychological processes of the mind. They interact with one another in dynamic ways that change and influence personality. The id, ego, and superego are in unrelenting contention, each driven to dominate the personality at the expense of the other.

The Id   The id—literally the "it"—is the most basic of the three systems. A reservoir of instincts, needs, and wishes, it is entirely unconscious, being "the dark inaccessible part of personality . . . a cauldron full of seething excitations" (Freud, 1933, p. 73). The id engages in *primary process thinking*, which is as primitive and illogical as a newborn baby instinctually grasping, crying for milk, sleeping, sucking, urinating, and so on. Preoccupied with its own needs and desires, the id is entirely self-centered and selfish. By nature it does nothing for anyone else. Biological in nature and oriented toward the past, the behavior of the id is determined by what Freud called the *pleasure principle,* whose aim is self-gratification.

Freud identified two instincts fundamental to the id, both of them wholly illogical and amoral: life and death. Instincts toward life, called *eros,* represent energy for preserving oneself and others. The most important aspect of eros is *libido,* a generalized pleasure drive. Clinical observation of patients who suffered traumatic experiences during World War I led Freud to add to his recognizable drives the instinct toward death, *thanatos,* a negative force propelling people toward aggressive and destructive behaviors. This primitive urge to obey the law of entropy, to return to an inorganic state, seemed to Freud to be a primitive urge common to all living things. These life and death instincts, Freud believed, may fuse together or work against each other.

Although in Freud's model the ego and superego operate at all three levels of awareness—the conscious, the preconscious, and the unconscious—the id is entirely unconscious, expressing its urges at a conscious level through the ego.

The Ego   Beginning at about age 6 to 8 months, the ego, literally the "I," develops for the purpose of helping the id satisfy its physical and social needs in ways that do not impinge upon others. According to Freud, the ego is "a kind of facade of the id . . . an external, cortical layer of it" (Freud, 1926, p. 18). Unlike the id, the reservoir of desires and wishes, the ego spans the conscious, preconscious, and unconscious aspects of the mind. Rational, capable of forming realistic plans of action, the ego serves as a liaison between the real world and the hidden world of the id. Psychological in nature and oriented toward the present, the behavior of the ego is guided by reality, and it seeks out the safety of the self.

Although the ego has a bent toward pleasure, it can suspend the pleasure drive in favor of the *reality principle.* Whereas the id is subjective, directed internally toward its own wants and needs, the ego is objective, focused outside itself. The ego counsels with reality to determine whether or not it can satisfy the pleasures that the id seeks to express without harming itself or others. The ego works to tame the unbridled desires of the id by delaying gratification for a more appropriate time and place. "Like a man on horseback, [the ego] has to hold in check the superior strength of the horse" (Freud, 1923, p. 15).

In the long run, however, the ego seeks to maximize gratification, as does the id. But the ego engages in realistic *secondary process thinking,* which is oriented toward problem solving and self-preservation. The highest function of the ego is decision making, which holds in check the passions of the id or which, in reasonable circumstances, ordains them as realistic. "Such decisions," wrote Freud, "make up the whole essence of worldly wisdom" (1926, p. 27).

Anxiety is caused by the ego's reaction to threatening or destructive urges from the id. To minimize this unpleasant emotional state, which may run from mild to extreme, the ego recruits a variety of internal *defense mechanisms,* which protect the person by blocking unacceptable urges or propositions from ever reaching conscious awareness. These unconscious, involuntary strategies for coping with the threatening instincts of the id serve as a kind of pain reliever to the psychological system. Because all of these defenses not only operate at an unconscious level but also distort one's perception of reality (see Sidebar 6-1), they reduce the dark sense of anxiety (Freud, 1966).

The Superego   The third component in personality formation, according to Freud, is the superego, which operates according to the *morality principle.* It represents society's views of right and wrong. But, unlike the ego, it is irrational, directing all of its energy toward extinguishing the id's unacceptable expression of sexual and aggressive instincts. Social in nature and oriented toward the past, then, the behavior of the superego is guided by morality, and it seeks perfection.

The content of each person's superego results from *introjection*—a process of incorporating the norms and standards of culture into personality by identifying with significant adults during childhood, when the ego is especially sensitive to potential losses of love. Although these significant role figures may include uncles and aunts, neighbors, clergy, and teachers, it is parents, of course, who are the primary interpreters of society's rules for most people. It is parents and other primary caregivers especially who convey their values to their children by offering love when they are "good" and, when these standards are not followed, by punishing them when they are "bad." A punished child may or may not be guided toward better behavior, but he or she is certainly pushed toward debilitating feelings of rejection.

Freud's greatest achievement probably consisted in taking neurotic patients seriously.

—Carl Jung

The superego is a significant force that the ego must contend with in its struggle to ameliorate the id. Like an inner master, the superego can become an independent and dominant force in one's personality, which is when and how neuroses develop. The superego can work against both the id and the ego by pushing the personality toward excessive and sometimes irrational conformity to internalized norms. Given free rein, it can lock a person into rigid moral patterns, unrelentingly seeking total perfection in everything it does (Leak & Christopher, 1982). It can take the ego to task, give orders, lay blame, induce guilt, and make threats. On the other hand, when its standards, its *ego ideal,* are met, the superego can offer the personality positive emotional experiences, reinforcing a sense of self-respect.

Development of Personality

Since Freud believed adult personality was established by about the age of 5 years, the importance of early childhood development is a cornerstone in his theory. Freud theorized that personality development follows a more or less set course from birth, a series of discrete stages defined by *erogenous zones*—those parts of the body that are sensitive to sexual stimulation: the mouth, anus, penis, clitoris, and vagina. Defined broadly, this "sexual" activity encompasses

MAJOR DEFENSE MECHANISMS

Denial

"Elvis is dead!" "No way!" When circumstances of reality frustrate an id impulse, denial intervenes to protect the ego from the frustration of the real situation. It protects the self from unpleasant reality by refusing to perceive it.

Displacement

Displacement replaces the object of an impulse with a substitute object. Here's an example: A researcher's grant proposal is rejected for funding. She tells her lab assistant he's been goofing off, who tells his wife she's been ignoring the kids, who tells their 6-year-old to pick up his toys, who throws a shoe at the dog, which pees on the kitchen floor.

Intellectualization

Intellectualization involves escaping one's emotions through a focus on intellectual concepts, abstract and insignificant details, or rational explanation devoid of personal significance. This may be seen in the example of a person who, having suffered a major career setback, discusses with apparent detachment all the ways his debacle could have been more devastating.

Projection

Projection is the process of unconsciously attributing one's own unacceptable impulses, attitudes, and behaviors to other people. Projection enables us to blame someone else for our shortcomings. A student who blames his poor grade on a professor who "can't teach" is an example. A favorite projection of young men who are not admitting their desires is, "She wants me."

Rationalization

Sometimes referred to as "sour grapes," rationalization is typified by the famous Aesop fable of the fox who tried repeatedly without success to reach a bunch of grapes. The fox finally gave up his attempts, rationalizing that the grapes looked sour anyway. Rationalization allows a person to defend the self's real feeling by creating false motives.

Reaction Formation

Sometimes the ego can control or defend against the expression of a forbidden impulse by consciously expressing its opposite. Reaction formation operates in two steps: first, the unacceptable impulse is repressed; next, the opposite is expressed on a conscious level. For example, this process may cover repressed hostility with an overwhelming show of kindness, unconscious desires for sexual promiscuity with celibacy or great moral restraint.

Regression

Regression is a way of alleviating anxiety by retreating to an earlier period of life that has been more secure and pleasant. Losing one's temper, pouting, sulking, talking baby talk, rebelling against authority, and other childish behaviors are forms of regression. When ex–television evangelist Jim Bakker's illegal dealings were discovered, he clearly demonstrated an extreme form of regression. He was found under his attorney's desk in the fetal position.

Repression

Threatening instinctual impulses from the id are removed from consciousness in repression. Visual or auditory perceptions may be distorted, or memories associated with painful events may be obliterated completely. For example, an adult may have suffered a terrible act of child abuse in early years. If anger over this toward the abusing person is fully repressed, leaving no conscious memory of the event or feelings surrounding it, it may seek conscious expression through anger toward some authority or parentlike figure.

Sublimation

According to Freud, sublimation is the only healthy way to deal with objectionable impulses because it allows the ego to convert them into socially acceptable forms of expression. A person with a great deal of unrecognized hostility, for example, may sublimate by taking up karate.

any pleasurable feelings associated with stimulation of the erogenous zones, whether or not the stimulation is directed toward genital sex. (One Freudian example of libidinous satisfaction is the release of tension associated with urination.) Nothing Freud wrote shocked Victorian culture more than his exploration of this mysterious drive. At the turn of the century public discussion of sexuality was abhorrent, but attributing sexual impulses to children seemed monstrous.

According to Freud, every human being experiences the resulting five sequential stages of *psychosexual development:* oral, anal, phallic, latency, and genital.

The Oral Stage   During the first year of life oral functions such as sucking, eating, biting, cooing, and crying are the primary means of a baby's gratification. Mothers have long observed that a baby's gateway to the world is the mouth, through which almost everything that enters the field of consciousness passes.

At about 8 months, weaning begins, the breast is withdrawn, and other foods are offered. This shift can be traumatic, especially if it is abrupt or uncaring. If such is the case, vestiges of the oral period may stay with the person throughout life. The more difficult it is for the child to leave the mother's breast (or bottle), the more the libido is *fixated* at the oral stage: that is, the more likely it is that the libido becomes developmentally arrested or halted at a particular stage because of excessive satisfaction, frustration, or anxiety. At the oral stage fixation is characterized by excessive concern with eating, drinking, smoking, kissing, and so on.

Psychoanalytic literature identifies two modes of oral expression: receptive (taking in) and aggressive (spitting out). According to Freud, infants who are overindulged will grow up with an *oral-receptive trait,* relying on other people for gratification of their needs. As adults they become dependent on others and overly gullible, swallowing anything they are told. They will also be interested in receiving information and acquiring material goods. The *oral-aggressive trait* is also derived from childhood pleasure associated with the mouth. Chewing, crunching, biting, and use of teeth are dominant expressions of this trait. People of this character type are expected to favor hard candy to soft, hard-stemmed pipes to cigarettes. They chomp the ice in their drinks and chew the end of their pencil. The orally aggressive character is sarcastic and argumentative, making "biting" remarks.

Freud would often say three things were impossible to fulfill completely: Healing, educating, governing. He limited his goals in analytic treatment to bringing a patient to the point where he could work for a living, and learn to love.

—Theodore Reich

The Anal Stage   Around the age of 2 or 3 years the child moves into the anal stage, when libidinal gratifications are met through the region of the anus. Here the child derives sexual gratification in two ways: *eliminating* feces and *retaining* them. Toilet training is the highlight of the anal period. From the parent's perspective, the issue is social control. Some parents are rigid and demanding with their 2-year-old, which reaps *rebellion* or *passive acceptance* in the toddler.

An adverse reaction to parental demands takes some form of rebellion, whereas the child who responds positively exhibits cooperation. Some parents are highly permissive in accepting their child's preferences and schedule.

Fixation at the anal stage produces either the anal-retentive or anal-expulsive personality. *Anal-retentive* people delay satisfactions until the last possible moment, "saving" dessert, for example, to eat after others have finished theirs. They are orderly, stingy, or stubborn. In contrast, children who discover social control by means of direct opposition develop an *anal-expulsive* personality. They are expected to express anger by becoming wasteful, disorderly, or messy. Their room, office, or car tends to be unkempt. Good grooming or well-organized plans run against the grain in the personality of the anal-expulsive individual.

The Phallic Stage   Around 4 or 5 years of age, the child enters the phallic stage, when satisfaction is gained primarily through stimulation of the penis or clitoris. The phallic stage is dominated by the realization that boys have penises whereas girls do not. Freud maintained that this realization is startling to both boys and girls because of their assumption that all persons are supposed to have penises. This discovery, according to Freud, causes *castration anxiety* in boys and *penis envy* in girls. In other words, boys fear losing their highly prized organ of pleasure and girls wish to someday overcome feelings of inferiority by obtaining a penis of their own (but see Sidebar 6-2).

This last and most crucial childhood conflict involves the child's unconscious wish to possess the parent of the opposite sex and, at the same time, to eliminate the parent of the same sex. Up to this stage of development, Freud theorized, boys love their mothers and see their fathers as rivals. Well read in classical mythology, Freud termed this dynamic the *Oedipus complex,* in memory of Oedipus, who killed his father and married his mother (Glenn, 1987). The reverse dynamic for girls, the love of the father and hatred of the mother, was termed the *Electra complex* by Carl Jung.

The Latency Stage   Freud's fourth stage of psychosexual development is notable for its absence of dominant erogenous zones and readily visible events or outcomes. The time between 6 and 12 years of age is marked by repression of sexual impulses and a curbing of oral, anal, and phallic activities that provide pleasure. As its name implies, latency is a quiet period of transition from pre-genital to genital stages. Incidentally, an assumption of a decrease in sexual urges and interest during the ages of 6 through 13 might have suited Victorian European children, but it does not fit observations of children in other cultures. A more plausible assumption, and one more difficult to test, is that there are no new developments during this stage in terms of the ways in which children gratify their instincts.

The Genital Stage   With the onset of puberty the child emerges from latency and enters Freud's final stage of development, the genital stage, characterized by pleasure provided through the genitals in the course of heterosexual activity. The greater a person's success in reaching the genital stage without large

WOMB ENVY

The male bias in Freud's theory was questioned by later psychoanalysts, who proposed revisions of his ideas (e.g.,

Karen Horney (1885–1952).
(UPI/Corbis-Bettmann)

Horney, 1926; Thompson, 1943). Karen Horney (pronounced HORN-eye) challenged Freud's use of penis envy to explain feminine inferiority and disputed Freud's claim that motherhood's greatest psychological importance for women was as a means of compensating for that inferiority. Horney believed that Freud's image of women was distorted and biased because he based it exclusively on observations of neurotic women.

Most see the origins of Freud's concept of penis envy coming out of social rather than anatomical factors. In other words, revisionists see penis envy as a symbolic reflection of men's greater cultural and economic advantages. But anthropologist Margaret Mead (1974) took it even further by offering a parallel, female-oriented concept of *womb envy*. Mead hypothesized that as boys begin to accept the fact they cannot bear children, they compensate for this inferiority by learning to place a high value on achievement. More recent psychoanalysts echo Mead's complementary concept and emphasize the fascination boys have with childbirth and their mothers' ability to have children (Buie, 1989).

amounts of libido fixated in pregenital stages, the greater will be the person's capacity to lead a "normal" life, free of neurosis.

The genital stage differs from the first three stages by being less selfish and more altruistic. Its energies are directed toward psychoanalytic ideals of personal maturity: love and work. The pursuit of these goals contributes to the fulfillment of eros' instinctual aim of preserving the self and the species. According to psychoanalytic theory persons unable to make psychological attachments during adolescence and young adulthood will show abnormal personality patterns.

DEVELOPMENT OF MALADAPTIVE BEHAVIOR

According to psychoanalytic thought, we are all "a little neurotic" (Freud, 1901). Maladaptive behavior is universal and inevitable in this model because conflicts and fixations in our formative years are unavoidable. Nobody proceeds through early developmental stages without problems. Specific symptoms of abnormality vary, however, depending upon the psychosexual stage in which the conflicts and fixations have first developed, and upon the manner in which defense mechanisms are used to deal with the resulting anxiety (Fromm, 1991; Munroe, 1955).

Operating largely at the unconscious level, anxiety is at the core of all psychopathology. The degree of anxiety depends on the leadership of the ego. When effective, the ego sublimates or blocks dangerous id impulses. It heeds the moral dictates of the superego, but checks a conscience that speaks too loudly or an *ego ideal* that becomes overly perfectionistic.

A weakened ego spends excessive amounts of psychic energy wrestling with the id and superego. Life's inevitable frustrations give the id and superego renewed power, whereas the weak ego is unable to cope. It may allow more libido to regress to earlier points of fixation, resulting in childishness, narcissism, or immorality and destructiveness.

The weak ego may be dominated by a stern superego enforcing rigid defenses that deprive the person of pleasures most people consider socially acceptable. A person is rarely aware of how events are affecting underlying impulses or unresolved conflicts and fixations. As anxiety intrudes on consciousness, the person tends to panic and the full spectrum of psychopathology takes shape.

GOALS OF THERAPY

Freud made rather modest claims for his therapy. He never presented it as a panacea for all psychic ills. He never guaranteed that healing gained through psychoanalysis was permanent or irreversible. Psychoanalysis offers help to those who are willing and able to endure a lengthy, arduous, and often painful process to achieve a resolution for intrapsychic conflicts that will enable them to handle life's other conflicts in a healthier way.

The ultimate goal of psychoanalysis is not the removal of symptoms. Rather, it is the total reconstruction of personality. What Freud tried to accomplish in therapy was a general strengthening of a person's ego so that instinctual aggressive and sexual impulses could be brought under control. Designed to reintegrate previously repressed experiences into the total personality structure, psychoanalysis attempts to make unconscious material accessible to consciousness by identifying and overcoming resistances to its awareness. However, Freud recognized this was an impossible ideal. He believed that a more realistic aim of treatment was the recovery of the patient's "ability and capacity for enjoyment and an active life" (1963, p. 60). Of course, this does not happen quickly. As a consequence, psychoanalysis is a long, intense, and expensive process (Harper, 1975; Nye, 1992).

> *By words one can give to another the greatest happiness or bring about utter despair.*
>
> —Sigmund Freud

FUNCTION OF THE THERAPIST

Freud consistently asserted that compassionate neutrality was the proper mindset for the analyst during the psychoanalytic session. Although attentive, accepting, and nonjudgmental, the analyst is a neutral observer of the therapeutic process, intervening only occasionally to offer interpretations of the client's past experiences.

Typically, the analyst is viewed as extremely passive and detached, repeatedly responding with the famous "Um hum." Although it is important to recognize that modern psychoanalytic views which see the analyst as being more active have modified the classical conception of the role of the emotionally neutral psychoanalyst (Strupp & Binder, 1984), the traditional analyst neither offers advice nor extends sympathy, but encourages clients to talk about whatever comes to mind, especially about childhood experiences (Meissner, 1985). To allow patients to talk freely, psychoanalysts often have clients recline on a couch while the analyst sits out of view in a chair behind the client's head.

In classical psychoanalysis the analyst fosters a transference by allowing the client to project unresolved conflicts, feelings, and experiences onto the analyst. Pure Freudian analysts believe that saying little about themselves and rarely sharing their personal reactions leads the client to project on them the

Freud's famous analytic couch.
(AP/Wide World)

feelings they have had toward significant figures in their past. This transference of the client's inaccurate perceptions to the analyst is of central importance in classical psychoanalysis.

Analytically oriented therapists, not pure Freudians, often dispense with the couch and sit in a chair, face to face with the patient, and develop a less neutral relationship with their clients. They view transference as important but place a greater focus on outside events in the client's life (Blanck & Blanck, 1968; Meares, 1992). They may use psychoanalytic understandings simply as a flexible guide for the therapeutic process, but not as binding law. Whereas a classic psychoanalyst is more concerned with lifting repressions of deeply unconscious material from the past, for example, today's analytical therapist may concentrate on the conflicts in the present.

Some of the most vocal reformers of traditional psychoanalysis are Franz Alexander and Thomas French (1946), who have argued that Freud fit the client's problems to analytic techniques rather than the techniques to the client's problems. They encouraged the use of nonanalytic techniques and made a distinction between *uncovering therapy* and *supportive therapy*. Uncovering therapy, also called *insight therapy,* is aimed at permanently changing the ego through the insight gained in the emotional resolution of transference.

| *Where id was, let ego be.*
—Sigmund Freud

Supportive therapy is not aimed at changing the ego; instead, the therapist encourages the client's ego to respond maturely to life's demands. Alexander and French argued that the practice of contemporary psychoanalysis called for both uncovering and supportive methods. But such alternate forms of psychotherapy only contaminate the psychoanalytic orthodoxy of "pure" analysts. Contemporary psychoanalysts remain divided on the precise function of the therapist (Nemiah, 1984).

MAJOR METHODS AND TECHNIQUES

Psychoanalysts and other contemporary therapists have introduced many treatment variations on the early techniques: *free association, dream analysis, analysis of transference,* and *analysis of resistance* still endure.

Free Association

The cardinal technique of psychoanalysis is to allow the client to say anything and everything that comes to mind—no matter how illogical, silly, painful, or trivial. This "free association has the priority over all other means of producing material in the analytic situation" (Greenson, 1967, p. 32). Through free association the client abandons normal ways of censoring or editing thoughts, although, in harmony with Freud's deterministic position, a client's "free" associations are, of course, not really free at all. Free association is predicated on the assumption that one association leads to another that is deeper in the unconscious (Laplanche & Pontailis, 1973). Freud felt such insights into the true nature of a person's problems could only be discovered through this verbal stream of consciousness, a technique that he labelled *catharsis,* from the Greek word meaning *purification.*

In free association, nothing the client says is taken at face value. Even a slip of the tongue can reveal hidden wishes. Freud demonstrated how the repressed content of the unconscious inadvertently slips into the spoken word—a woman talking with her therapist about flying home to see her parents, for example, says "I haven't bought my pain [instead of *plane*] ticket yet"—resulting in what is now known as a "Freudian slip."

Dream Analysis

In both classical and modern analysis dreams, which Freud referred to as "the royal road to the unconscious," play a central role. When a person sleeps, the ego relaxes its control over unconscious material. As a result, because wishes that are unacceptable to the conscious mind are uncovered, dreams become a window into the unconscious (Abrams, 1992; Lipschitz, 1990).

Analysts encourage clients to report their dreams and free-associate about them. The analyst may also discuss or interpret the meaning of dreams, which are said to contain surface material called the *manifest content* and then the deeper, hidden meaning, the *latent content.* The analyst's job is to discover and interpret the latent dream content.

Freud's attempts to interpret dreams resulted in his monumental study, *The Interpretation of Dreams* (1900/1957). Over the course of his work with patients, Freud found consistent symbols in dreams that signified the same thing for nearly everyone. For example, he said that steps, ladders, and staircases represented sexual intercourse; candles, snakes, and tree trunks stood for the penis. In spite of apparent universality of certain symbols, Freud warned that they still have to be interpreted within the context of the individual's life.

Interpretation of Transference

Originally Freud considered transference, which occurs when the client responds to the analyst as a significant authority person out of his or her life, an obstacle to treatment. Eventually, however, he realized it was the phenomenon of transference that made the treatment and the cure possible. Only when the analyst serves as a surrogate, allowing old reactions and conflicts to be relived, is the nature of childhood difficulties revealed.

Both positive and negative feelings can be transferred. Statements of admiration, anger, or dislike are categories of transference. Because clients' reactions indicate the presence of emotional residues from their past, they are unaware of their functional importance. The therapist, not interpreting the transference immediately, encourages its development to enhance insight into the client's ways of perceiving, feeling, and reacting to significant figures from early life. Orthodox psychoanalysts regard analysis of transference as absolutely vital to the therapeutic process (Winnicott, 1956).

As clients become gradually aware of the true meaning of their transference relationship with the analyst, they gain insight into their past and present experiences. A therapist, however, must be keenly aware of the transference and not take it personally. When the therapist does react personally, it is called *countertransference.* A certain client may inadvertently touch on issues in a therapist's life that have not been resolved. Dealing with the complexities of countertransference can be difficult and sometimes requires professional outside consultation.

Interpretation of Resistance

As a client's unconscious mind is stirred, resistance arises. Despite consciously desiring to change, a client may unconsciously resist efforts to help eliminate old behavior patterns. Resistance is a means of keeping the unconscious conflict intact, thereby impeding any attempts to probe into the real sources of personality problems.

Resistance can be expressed in many ways—"forgotten" counseling appointments, difficulty in free association, dismissal of interpretations, and so on. Another form of resistance is talking about topics unrelated to the real work

The dream is a disguised fulfillment of a repressed wish.

—Sigmund Freud

of therapy. A client, for example, may talk at length about the economy, the weather, or anything else that is not related to his or her personal issues. The ultimate form of resistance, of course, is for the client to discontinue therapy prematurely. When resistance begins to interfere with the therapeutic process, however, a psychoanalytic therapist will skillfully interpret it, bringing repressed conflicts into the open and ridding the client of unconscious defenses (Hornstein, 1992).

Each of the previous therapeutic techniques—free association, dream analysis, interpretation, analysis of transference and resistance—is designed to make the unconscious conscious and help people achieve greater insight into the causes of their distress. Insight alone, however, is not a sufficient condition for behavioral change in the client. In the final stages of treatment, analysts encourage patients to convert their newly discovered insights into their everyday living experiences. This is sometimes called *emotional reeducation.* The whole point is to think, perceive, feel, and behave differently.

APPLICATION

Freud discovered that patients did not always willingly provide free associations or obediently present their dreams for interpretation. They often "resisted" the very methods the analyst assured them would be the way to relief. Why was this so, and how did Freud achieve insight into the explanation that was to serve as a basic credo in psychoanalysis? A brief description of the following case will illustrate Freud's therapeutic work as well as how he came to some of his conclusions (Freud, 1957).

"Dora" was 18 years old. She had threatened suicide and also manifested several hysterical symptoms. She was referred to Freud by her father. At first, everything went very well. Dora was bright and took readily to free association. Although she showed quick improvement following Freud's interpretations regarding her infantile sexuality problems, soon after she terminated therapy.

Why did she leave when everything seemed to be going so well? To answer this question, Freud carried out a retrospective analysis of the case and, to his own satisfaction, discovered the reasons. Although Dora's father was often ill, his wife's major preoccupation seemed to be keeping the house clean. She had little time for either Dora or her husband. As a result, nursing care for Dora's father fell increasingly to Ms. K, a neighbor who, along with her husband, was a close friend of Dora's parents. Later Dora realized that Ms. K had become not just a nurse but also her father's mistress. For a variety of reasons, Mr. K seemed to sanction the affair. As Dora began to turn into an attractive young woman, she caught the eye of Mr. K, and he began to buy her gifts (including a jewelry box). He also made several amorous advances. Later, Dora remarked in therapy how much she hated the tobacco smell on his breath.

> *Innocent dreams...are wolves in sheep's clothing. They turn out to be quite the reverse when we take the trouble to analyze them.*
>
> —Sigmund Freud

During a summer vacation when Dora, her parents, and Mr. and Ms. K shared a house, Dora and Mr. K were taking a walk when Mr. K complained that his wife "gave him nothing." Dora did not tell her parents about this direct sexual suggestion on the part of Mr. K., but for 2 weeks afterwards she experienced an unpleasant dream. At that point, she insisted to her parents that she could no longer remain in the vacation house. As a result, she accompanied her father on a business trip and told him about her difficulties with Mr. K. Although her vivid dreams ceased, several hysterical problems arose to take their place. It was at this point that her father had referred her to Freud.

During the analysis Dora's dreams came back: "A house was on fire. My father was standing beside my bed and woke me up. I dressed myself quickly. Mother wanted to stop and save her jewel-case; but father said: I refuse to let myself and my two children be burnt for the sake of your jewel-case. We hurried downstairs, and as soon as I was outside I woke up" (Freud, 1953, p. 64).

Some of the hidden elements of the dream became apparent in Dora's free associations. Represented by the jewel case and the fire, suggesting the smell of tobacco, Mr. K's presence was obvious to Freud. The dream also prompted Dora to recall that at the vacation house she slept in a hallway, which necessitated her dressing hurriedly so that Mr. K would not see her in her nightdress. Freud also deduced that the fire symbolized some of Dora's developing sexual urges. From all this, Freud concluded that Dora was experiencing the conflicting sensations of being attracted to Mr. K while at the same time being fearful of him.

The meaning of the dream was clear to Freud: it signified not only her present, conflict-ridden attraction toward Mr. K but also her earlier attraction for her father during the Oedipal period.

But if this were true, why did Dora flee from therapy? And why did the dream recur during therapy? After further analysis, Freud concluded that his original analysis of the dream had been incomplete. He realized that the dream did not simply revolve around Dora's feelings toward Mr. K. After all, Mr. K was no longer a part of her life. Whereas the original dream had signified something about Mr. K, the recurrence of the dream signified something about Freud himself. Freud smoked many cigars and often discussed a variety of sexual matters with Dora, which could have stirred up numerous threatening urges. Just as before, Dora was fleeing from a relationship with another man who had tobacco on his breath, this time not from a vacation house but from a therapy room.

According to Freud the case of Dora clearly revealed both resistance and transference. Not only did Dora resist confronting her basic conflicts, she also transferred onto Freud some of the chief motives and characteristics of significant people from her past. Of course, Dora is one of Freud's exemplary case studies. The elements of resistance and transference are not always so plain, and the analysis is not always dramatic. See the box, "A Modern-Day Psychoanalytic Therapy Session," for an example of what the daily work of a psychoanalyst might involve.

CRITICAL ANALYSIS

In the entire field of psychology there is perhaps no ongoing issue more controversial than the value of psychoanalytic treatment. The psychiatric literature contains many testimonials to the insights and personality changes achieved through psychoanalysis. But from other quarters, the value of psychoanalytic therapy has been sharply criticized. The contributions and oppositions of psychoanalysis must be weighed carefully.

To begin with, Freud's theory is very comprehensive. The range and diversity of issues Freud sought to understand included more than the treatment of emotional and behavioral disorders. He explored and explained issues related to war, death, humor, marriage, friendship, societal mores, creativity, competition, fairy tales, and absentmindedness. Few scholars would disagree that Freud's thinking led to an extraordinarily comprehensive conceptual system of human understanding.

Whereas Freud's theory is comprehensive, however, its explanatory scheme is highly restricted in nature: sex and aggression are the sole determinants of behavior. Thus, the motivational base of the theory is limited and does not allow for different and more adequate explanations of behavior. Its pessimistic perspective views people as essentially irrational and controlled by amoral forces. Similarly, the structure of personality is divided into only three components, and the interactions among them are presumed to account for all underlying conflicts that hinder a person's functioning. So while his theory is comprehensive, its explanatory scheme is restricted.

Another problem with psychoanalysis is the relative vagueness of its concepts and the difficulties it presents in deriving clear and verifiable hypotheses.

A Modern-Day Psychoanalytic Therapy Session

The following brief excerpt from a post-Freudian analytic session illustrates the type of verbal interchange that takes place between patient and analyst. The patient is a 34-year-old woman.

PATIENT: I feel uneasy . . . like I'm out of balance or something . . . I don't really know what to say about it. (18-second pause)

PATIENT: Well, I just feel torn apart. If I lose any more control I don't know what would happen. (12-second pause)

PATIENT: Of course, I may be exaggerating things. My imagination . . . well, the worst things rarely happen. (30-second pause)

PATIENT: Sometimes . . . Sometimes, like right now, I feel as though there is nothing for me to say. (8-second pause)

PATIENT: I just, um . . . feel like I'm just making up stuff to try and fit into the conversation . . . but I'm at a total loss (12-second pause)

PATIENT: It's like a big game of charades or something (laughs). (15-second pause)

ANALYST: You know what kind of charade you would play?

PATIENT: Not really. (8-second pause)

PATIENT: I could just let go, I suppose, and do what comes naturally . . . whatever comes to mind. I have some pretty wild feelings, come to think of it.

ANALYST: Hmm-mm.

PATIENT: Is that it? Should I just let go and dance and scream if I want to?

ANALYST: I'm not asking you to do anything.

PATIENT: No, I know you're not. . . . But do you feel that I have unnatural control?

ANALYST: You have some doubt about that?

PATIENT: No. I just wanted to hear you say so.

There is nothing terribly striking about this excerpt. The patient says nothing extraordinary and the therapist makes no monumental interpretations. Uncovering the roots of the patient's problems is a long, slow process. The excerpt, however, as mundane as it might appear, is typical. Major breakthroughs come infrequently. The patient does most of the talking, mainly in the form of free association. There are many pauses. After listening to the patient, the analyst interprets what the patient has said. The patient then uses the interpretations to begin to gain insight about his or her feelings.

Much of the theory is presented in terms that do not lend themselves to precise scientific testing—the life and death instincts, for example. The universal conclusions that Freud drew about human behavior on the basis of extensive observations of a few patients seem naive. Recently, some historians assert that Freud even distorted facts that contradicted his theory (Raymond, 1991; Silverstein, 1989; Storr, 1989). Whatever the reason, it has become plain to see that, when psychoanalytic theory is put to the empirical test, gaps quickly emerge.

Eysenck (1952), for instance, conducted an early massive review of the clinical literature to assess the effectiveness of psychoanalysis in curing people. After examining more than 7000 case histories of patients, he concluded that psychoanalytic therapy did not significantly facilitate the recovery of neurotic patients. Although 66% of patients treated to completion by means of psychoanalysis were much improved or cured, Eysenck found that 72% of patients who were not treated by means of any formal therapy were also much improved or cured within 2 years of the onset of their illnesses. Thus, approximately two thirds of patients recovered or improved to a marked extent whether they were treated psychoanalytically or not. Although numerous critics have attacked Eysenck's conclusions, reviews of all the evidence show that Eysenck's argument is still essentially valid today (Erwin, 1980; Franks, Wilson, Kendall, & Foreyt, 1990; Rachman, 1971; Stunkard, 1991).

> *Just as for the individual, so also for all mankind, life is hard to bear.*
>
> —Sigmund Freud

Research exploring the connection between psychoanalytic insight and personal change also raises some questions. The Menninger Foundation conducted an intensive longitudinal study of the psychodynamic therapy of 42 patients beginning in 1952 and following them for 30 years (Wallerstein, 1989). To the researchers' surprise, they found that many patients achieved significant personal change even though they had not achieved a comparable degree of psychoanalytic insight into their problems. What was particularly surprising was that changes persisted, suggesting that other mechanisms in therapy, such as attempts to change interpersonal behavior directly and changes initiated to please the therapist, may be as important as insight.

There has always been a question as to how valid certain aspects of psychoanalytic thought are when applied to women. In many ways it views women as more vain, sensitive, submissive, and dependent than men. These attributes have been seen as part of the biology of being female. Quite bluntly, in Freud's view, women were inferior to men. He believed that the part of their personality that was different from men's came from defending against and overcompensating for their inferiority. Exception to the psychoanalytic implications that "biology is destiny" was voiced early on by analyst Karen Horney. She questioned many of Freud's views concerning women and feminine sexuality and, more than anyone, made room for female figures within its ranks (e.g., Anna Freud, Helene Deutsch, Greta Bibring, Margaret Mahler, Clara Thompson, and Frieda Fromm-Reichman). Freud clearly did not consider cultural factors in his understanding of women, and psychoanalysis is clearly biased as a result (Caplan, 1984). Sidebar 6-3 amplifies on some of these concerns.

Psychoanalysis also presents limitations when applied to multicultural counseling. Since the time and money that psychoanalysis requires rules out most people who are not wealthy, it is generally perceived as being based on upper- and middle-class values. In addition, its focus on personality restructuring conflicts with the more fundamental socioeconomic issues of survival and security. Finding resources to solve immediate and pressing problems is not the primary focus. It is not a practical theory for minority clients, who

Sidebar 6-3

FEMINIST FREUDIANS?

The women who came together in the feminist movement of the 1970s were an . . . assorted lot with often sharply clashing views. But on one issue, they were as solid as an upraised fist: they had seen the enemy, and he was Freud. It was Sigmund Freud, they agreed, who had helped institutionalize the oppression of women by ratifying the notion that they were innately inferior to men. It was Freud who had suggested that their very development as women, and their demand for equality, were driven mainly by their need to compensate for the lack of a penis. . . .

In recent years some feminists have been advocating not precisely forgiveness but a new circumspection about the man who once described women as "maimed"

Excerpted from: "A Fresh Take on Freud," by David Gelman, *Newsweek*, October 29, 1990, p. 47.

little creatures lacking "the only proper genital organ." In a stream of books and articles reappraising Freudian texts, they are suggesting that the father of psychoanalysis may have had something useful to say about women after all. Observes Wesleyan College humanities professor Elisabeth Young-Bruehl: "This whole new feminist appropriation of Freud reads him as saying, not 'Women are inferior,' but 'Women *feel* inferior'" in social structures established by men.

Young-Bruehl, who teaches a popular course on the history of psychoanalysis at the Connecticut school, is one of the women cautiously nudging Freud back into the feminist fold by finding new meaning in his writings. In "Freud On Women,". . . she suggests that rather than simply passing judgment on women, Freud was attempting to describe the convoluted course by which their femininity develops.

---

might benefit from personality reconstruction only after more pressing issues have been resolved. On the other hand, a strength of psychoanalytic theory is its awareness of countertransference. The value it places on intensive psychotherapy as part of the training of therapists helps therapists of all ethnic and racial backgrounds become aware of their own biases and prejudices (Comas-Diaz & Minrath, 1985).

Freudian thought has come under fire from many sectors: "from the academic psychologist for being unscientific, from humanistic and theistic psychology for being too reductionistic, and from the behaviourists for not being reductionistic enough" (Hurding, 1985, p. 70). Still, despite its critics, psychoanalysis' seminal contributions to therapy have been an inspiration, in some form, to nearly all other theories of therapy. It is a stimulating theory that has left a permanent imprint not only on psychology, but on literature, art, sociology, history, anthropology, religion, philosophy, and political science as well. Freud's ideas reverberate throughout all of contemporary culture.

What progress we are making. In the Middle Ages they would have burnt me; nowadays they are content with burning my books.

—Sigmund Freud

CURRENT STATUS

Although psychoanalytic purists do exist, contemporary analytic psychotherapies have evolved substantially beyond orthodox analytic thought. Most typically, psychoanalytic therapists take aspects of Freud's work and shape it to
their own particular ends (Sampson, 1990; Zucker, 1993).

Psychoanalysts have proposed several variations of Freud's original theory
(Liff, 1992). A major issue on which many contemporary analysts differ is the
extent to which they adopt Freud's assumption that the infant (as well as adult)
is primarily motivated by pleasure seeking. The theories range from those
building on traditional Freudian theory (e.g., Kernberg, 1975, 1976; Mahler,
1968) to those replacing it with a whole new view of development (e.g.,
Fairbairn, 1952; Guntrip, 1969; Klein, 1976; Kohut, 1977, 1984). There are also
theories that accept Freudian theory with modifications (e.g., Modell, 1975).

Contemporary psychoanalytic thinking can be divided into three major
camps (Pine, 1988): *ego psychology, object-relations theories,* and *self-psychology.*

Ego Psychology

Since the death of Freud in 1939, ego psychology, sometimes dubbed the
"American school," arose to give more attention to the conscious adaptive and
controlling functions of the ego. It also stressed development of the personality
across the lifespan. In reaction to what is perceived as Freud's excessive attention to the unconscious and the id, in ego psychology the patient and therapist
sit face to face and free association may or may not be invoked. The client's talk
is much more reality based and present oriented (Blanck & Blanck, 1968). The
therapist's job is to create an atmosphere in which the client feels free to delve
into feelings of anxiety, guilt, and shame. The goal is to help clients know themselves more fully, understand their inner conflicts, and become more aware of
ways to respond differently in the future. Beyond the tensions surrounding sex
and aggression, issues of identity, intimacy, and integrity become especially
salient in this tradition. Heinz Hartman, René Spitz, Margaret Mahler, Anna
Freud, Erik Erikson, and David Rapaport are among the major theoreticians in
this tradition (Prochaska, 1984).

Object Relations

Object relations theorists from the "the British school," such as W. R. D.
Fairbairn, Otto Kernberg, and Melanie Klein (1975), have identified more
clearly than Freudians how past childhood experience is reflected unconsciously in *object relations,* a technical term roughly translated as "past interpersonal relationships." (Although the term *object* primarily refers to persons,
it may also include things.) These theorists point out that we develop our patterns of living from our early relations, particularly with parents—internalized
"objects" (St. Clair, 1986). Experiences and relationships in early years leave im-
pressions on the personality that profoundly influence behavior and thought

Freud and daughter Anna, on the train
taking them to France and freedom in 1938.
(Mary Evans/Sigmund Freud Copyrights)

over a lifespan. These internal objects replace the id, ego, and superego as the structure of personality, so that drives are seen as relational rather than sexual or aggressive. The goal of object relations therapy is to understand how these childhood patterns are repeated in adult life (Edkins, 1985).

Self-Psychology

Heinz Kohut (1985) developed self-psychology based on the construct of the self. Originating in infancy, the self integrates and develops incrementally to produce either healthy relationships or the opposite, the full range of adult psychopathologies. If early relationships are healthy and nurturing, a stable or "true" self will develop that is capable of mature relationships. If the early environment is characterized by emotional deprivation, however, the resulting "false" self remains limited in its capacity for relationship (Tobin, 1990).

Kohut asserted that the id, ego, and superego, as well as the Oedipus conflict and penis envy, are inadequate to describe the basic infant psyche. The self is the sum of all these entities plus an unnamed integrating function. Kohut's work is presented in two volumes, *The Analysis of the Self* (1971) and *The Restoration of the Self* (1977).

A summary word on Freudian adaptations: (1) Classical psychoanalysis believes that people who *understand* their problems through interpretation will be able to overcome them. (2) Modern psychoanalysis is concerned with helping people meet unmet maturational needs. Greenberg and Mitchell (1983) point out that the three contemporary traditions also view cognitive processes and interpersonal relationships as the building blocks of personality. (3) The ego psychologists modify the classic id-drive model by emphasizing early, formative relationships. (4) A more radical strategy, adopted by the object-relations theorists, requires complete replacement of Freud's drive concept with a strong interpersonal model. (5) Self-psychology has adopted drive-model concepts and mixed them with the relational model.

Whether we are Freudians or not, as I am not, we are surely all post-Freudians.

—Rollo May

During World War II a number of European analysts moved to the United States, making it the country with the largest number of psychoanalytic adherents. Most of today's analysts are located in large urban settings near psychoanalytic institutes in such cities as New York, Los Angeles, Boston, and Chicago (Nye, 1992). It is in these institutes that the next generation of analysts is being trained.

Despite the criticisms of traditional analysts, who claim that psychoanalysis is being watered down by those who deviate from Freud's basic theory, changes seem inevitable (Cooper, 1987). And it may very well be these changes that prevent psychoanalysis from becoming a relic of times past. These updated forms of psychoanalysis are contributing to its good health, as evidenced by the bulk of material being published on the subject (Fine, 1990). Although it has been a century since Breuer and Freud developed the structure of psychoanalysis, it sustains a promising future (Gay, 1989).

Many today still echo the sentiments of W. H. Auden's poetic tribute to the Viennese master, which he wrote a few months after Freud's death in 1939:

If often he was wrong and at times absurd,
To us he is no more a person now
But a whole climate of opinion
Under whom we conduct our differing lives.

CHAPTER SUMMARY

1. *Biography.* Freud (1856–1939) spent nearly all of his life in Vienna. He was an excellent student but his career choices were restricted because of his Jewish heritage. He settled on medicine and at the age of 26 attained a position at the

University of Vienna. By exploring the meaning of his own dreams, he gained insights into the dynamics of personality and he formulated his clinical theory as he observed the work of his patients in analysis. He had very little tolerance for colleagues who diverged from his psychoanalytic doctrines. He died of cancer of the jaw in London.

2. *Historical Development.* The origins of psychoanalysis are identified with the early 1880s. During this time, Josef Breuer's treatment of hysteria (specifically with Anna O.) influenced Freud's thinking. Freud studied under Jean Charcot, where he explored the use of hypnotic techniques. These two experiences, among others, led to Freud first using the term *psychoanalysis* in 1896.

3. *View of Human Nature.* Freud viewed people as being dominated by the instinctual, unconscious, and irrational forces of sex and aggression. For Freud, personality was determined entirely by conditions and events beyond personal control. He viewed consciousness as only a small part of the total psyche. Freud divided personality into three components: id (present at birth, entirely unconscious, and including all innate instincts), ego (developing out of the id at about 6–8 months to help the id gain its ends), and superego (developing out of the ego at about age 3–5 years and including the ego ideal and the conscience). Furthermore, Freud believed adult personality was established by about age 5, following a more or less set course through a series of psychosexual stages: oral, anal, phallic, latency, and genital.

4. *Development of Maladaptive Behavior.* Symptoms of abnormality vary in psychoanalytic thought depending upon the psychosexual stage in which conflicts and fixations have first developed and the manner in which defense mechanisms are used to deal with the resulting anxiety. The fixation of excessive amounts of libido at pregenital stages generally results in various character patterns and psychopathology. Libido may also regress to a previous psychosexual stage or to an earlier object choice long since abandoned, usually one that was strongly fixated. Anxiety, operating largely at the unconscious level, is at the core of all psychopathology. The degree of anxiety depends on the leadership of the ego. A weakened ego spends excessive amounts of psychic energy wrestling with the id and superego, resulting in maladaptive behavior.

5. *Goals of Therapy.* The ultimate goal of psychoanalysis is not the removal of symptoms. Instead, it is the total reconstruction of personality through making the unconscious conscious. The person's ego is to be strengthened so that aggressive and sexual impulses can be brought under control. It is designed to reintegrate previously repressed experiences in the total personality structure.

6. *Function of the Therapist.* The analyst neither offers advice nor extends sympathy, but encourages clients to talk about whatever comes to mind, especially about childhood experiences. In classical psychoanalysis the analyst fosters a transference by allowing the client to project unresolved conflicts, feelings, and experiences onto the analyst. This classical conception of the role of the psychoanalyst as an emotionally neutral figure, however, has been modified by modern psychoanalytic views that see the analyst as being more active.

7. *Major Methods and Techniques.* The most enduring therapeutic techniques of psychoanalysis are free association (the cardinal technique of allowing the client to say whatever comes to mind, no matter how illogical or trivial), dream analysis (interpreting the latent content of the dream primarily through the use of consistent symbols that signify the same thing for nearly everyone), analysis of transference (when the client responds to the analyst as to a significant authority person from his or her life, thus revealing the nature of childhood difficulties), and analysis of resistance (the unconscious resisting of efforts to help eliminate old behavior patterns, thereby impeding any attempts to probe into the real sources of personality problems).

8. *Application.* Freud leaned heavily on case studies in the formulation of his theory. The case of "Dora" is one example that illustrated how Freud used resistance and transference to bring about psychological insight. Since the therapeutic goals are so high and difficult to obtain, and the self-defeating patterns so deeply established with the client, it is inevitable that psychoanalytic treatment be intensive and long term. A modern-day excerpt from an analytic session is also given in the chapter.

9. *Critical Analysis.* Psychoanalysis has both devoted admirers and strong critics. Among its strengths are its comprehensive nature and its monumental value to spurring on other therapeutic theories. Among its shortcomings are methodological problems, an overemphasis on biological determinants of personality, relative vagueness of concepts, and male chauvinism.

10. *Current Status.* Contemporary analytic psychotherapies have evolved substantially beyond orthodox analytic thought. A major issue on which many contemporary analyst differ is the extent to which they adopt Freud's assumption that the infant (as well as the adult) is primarily motivated by pleasure seeking. Contemporary psychoanalytic thinking can be divided into ego psychology (present oriented and reality based, focusing on issues of identity, intimacy, and integrity), object-relations theories (focusing on early relations and rational drives), and self-psychology (focusing on the construct of the self originating in infancy and its integrating function).

KEY TERMS

Anal Stage   The second of Freud's psychosexual stages, during which gratification comes primarily from the elimination process.
Anxiety   A feeling of fear and dread without an obvious cause.
Castration Anxiety   A boy's fear during the Oedipal period that his penis will be cut off.
Catharsis   The expression of emotions that is expected to lead to their reduction.
Conscious   A component of the superego containing behaviors for which the child has been punished.

Countertransference   The phenomenon of the therapist's transferring feelings, fantasies, and behaviors from a previous relationship onto the client and thus creating an inappropriate therapeutic relationship.

Defense Mechanisms   A strategy of distorting reality used by the ego to defend itself against the anxiety provoked by the conflicts of everyday life.

Dream Analysis   A technique involving the interpretation of dreams to uncover unconscious conflicts.

Ego   The rational aspect of the personality, responsible for directing and controlling instincts.

Ego Ideal   A component of the superego containing the moral or ideal behaviors for which a person should strive.

Electra Complex   The unconscious desire of girls during the phallic stage of psychosexual development for their fathers, accompanied by a desire to replace or destroy their mothers.

Fixation   The state in which a portion of the libido remains invested in one of the psychosexual stages because of excessive frustration or gratification.

Free Association   A technique in which the client says whatever comes to mind; a kind of daydreaming out loud.

Freudian Slip   A slip of the tongue, revealing unconscious material that has slipped out.

Genital Stage   The fifth and final stage in Freud's psychosexual stages, during which a person learns socially appropriate channels for the expression of sexual impulses.

Id   The aspect of personality operating according to the pleasure principle and allied with drives.

Latent Content   The symbolic meaning of events in a dream.

Latency Stage   The fourth stage of Freud's psychosexual stages, during which satisfaction is gained primarily through exploration of the environment and development of skills and interests.

Libido   The form of psychic energy manifested by the life instincts that drive a person toward pleasurable behaviors and thoughts.

Manifest Content   The actual events in a dream.

Oedipus Complex   The unconscious desire of boys during the phallic stage of psychosexual development for their mothers, accompanied by a desire to replace or destroy their fathers.

Oral Stage   The first and most primitive of Freud's psychosexual stages, during which the mouth region is the primary source of gratification.

Penis Envy   The envy females feel toward males because they possess a penis, accompanied by a sense of loss because females do not have one.

Phallic Stage   The third of Freud's psychosexual stages during which satisfaction is gained primarily through genital manipulation and exploration.

Pleasure Principle   Principle on which the id functions to avoid pain and to maximize pleasure.

Preconscious   Memory accessible to consciousness only after something calls one's attention to it.

Primary Process Childlike thinking by which the id attempts to satisfy the instinctual drives.

Psychoanalysis Sigmund Freud's system of therapy.

Psychosexual Stages The stages through which children pass and in which instinctual gratification depends on the stimulation of a corresponding area of the body.

Reality Principle Principle on which the ego functions to provide appropriate constraints on the expression of the id instincts.

Resistance A blockage or refusal to disclose painful memories in free association.

Secondary Process Mature thought processes needed to deal rationally with the external world.

Superego The moral aspect of personality, which has internalized parental and societal values and standards.

Thanatos The unconscious drive toward decay, destruction, and aggression.

Transference The phenomenon of clients placing their unconscious material onto the therapist and experiencing the therapist as if they were another previously encountered person.

Unconscious The domain of the psyche that stores repressed urges and primitive impulses.

Womb Envy The inferiority experienced by boys in discovering they cannot bear children.

SUGGESTED READING

Translations of Freud's writing are found in many forms put out by various publishers. Hogarth Press of London has published a complete Standard Edition of his works, consisting of 24 volumes. Other paperbound editions of Freud's works can be found in most bookstores. They include the following:

An outline of psychoanalysis. New York: W. W. Norton.

Beyond the pleasure principle. New York: Bantam Books.

Civilization and its discontents. New York: W. W. Norton.

The ego and the id. New York: W. W. Norton.

The interpretation of dreams. New York: Avon Books.

In addition to Freud's own writings there are many helpful books about psychoanalysis:

Brenner, C. (1974). *An elementary textbook of psychoanalysis* (Rev ed.). Garden City, NY: Doubleday (Anchor).

Gay, P. (1988). *Freud: A life for our time.* New York: W. W. Norton.

Jones, E. (1961). *The life and work of Sigmund Freud* (abridged ed.). New York: Basic Books.

Kline, P. (1984). *Psychology and Freudian theory.* New York: Methuen.

St. Clair, M. (1986). *Objects relations and self psychology: An introduction.* Pacific Grove, CA: Brooks/Cole.

REFERENCES

Abrams, D. (1992). The dream's mirror of reality. *Contemporary Psychoanalysis, 28,* 50–71.

Alexander, F., & French, T. (1946). *Psychoanalytic therapy.* New York: Ronald Press.

Arlow, J. A., & Brenner, C. (1988). The future of psychoanalysis. *Psychoanalytic Quarterly, 57,* 1–14.

Blanck, G., & Blanck, R. (1968). *Ego psychology: Theory and practice.* New York: Columbia University Press.

Brecher, E. M. (1972). *Licit and illicit drugs.* New York: Consumers Union.

Buie, J. (1989, January). Traditional analysis may be changing. *APA Monitor,* p. 19.

Caplan, P. J. (1984). The myth of women's masochism. *American Psychologist, 39,* 130–139.

Clark, R. W. (1980). *Freud: The man and the cause.* New York: Random House.

Comas-Diaz, L., & Minrath, M. (1985). Psychotherapy with ethnic minority borderline clients. *Psychotherapy, 22,* 418–426.

Cooper, A. M. (1987). Changes in psychoanalytic ideas: Transference interpretation. *Journal of the American Psychoanalytic Association, 35,* 77–98.

Edkins, W. (1985). Object relations theory. In D. Benner (Ed.), *Baker encyclopedia of psychology* (pp. 771–796). Grand Rapids, MI: Baker Books.

Erwin, E. (1980). Psychoanalytic therapy: The Eysenck argument. *American Psychologist, 35,* 435–443.

Eysenck, H. J. (1952). The effects of psychotherapy: An evaluation. *Journal of Consulting Psychology, 16,* 319–324.

Fairbairn, W. R. D. (1952). *Psychoanalytic studies of the personality.* London: Tavistock Publications and Routledge & Kegan Paul.

Fine, R. (1990). Freud and psychoanalysis. *Contemporary Psychology, 35,* 775–776.

Franks, C. M., Wilson, G. T., Kendall, P. C., & Foreyt, J. P. (1990). *Review of behavior theory: Theory and practice* (Vol. 12). New York: Guilford Press.

Freeman, L. (1972). *The story of Anna O.* New York: Walker.

Freud, A. (1966). *The ego and the mechanism of defense* (Rev. ed.). New York: International Universities Press.

Freud, S. (1901). *The psychopathology of everyday life.* London: Hogarth Press.

Freud, S. (1920). *Beyond the pleasure principle* (Std. ed., Vol. 18) London: Hogarth Press.

Freud, S. (1923). *The ego and the id.* London: Hogarth Press.

Freud, S. (1924). *A general introduction to psychoanalysis.* New York: Boni and Liveright.

Freud, S. (1926). *Inhibitions, symptoms, and anxiety.* London: Hogarth Press.

Freud, S. (1930). *Civilization and its discontents.* London: Hogarth Press.

Freud, S. (1933). *New introductory lectures on psychoanalysis.* London: Hogarth Press.

Freud, S. (1935). *An autobiographical study.* J. Strachey (Trans.). London: Hogarth Press.

Freud, S. (1957). The interpretation of dreams. In J. Strachey (Ed.), *The standard edition of the complete psychological works of Sigmund Freud,* Vol. 12. London: Hogarth. (Originally published 1900)

Freud, S. (1963). *Sigmund Freud: Therapy and technique.* New York: Collier Books.

Freud, S., & Breuer, J. (1895). *Studies on hysteria.* London: Hogarth Press.

Fromm, E. (1991). Causes for the patient's change in analytic treatment. *Contemporary Psychoanalysis, 27,* 581–602.

Gay, P. (1988). *Freud: A life for our time.* New York: W. W. Norton.

Gay, P. (1989). *The Freud reader.* New York: W. W. Norton.

Glenn, J. (1987). Freud, Virgil, and Aeneas: An unnoticed classical influence on Freud. *American Journal of Psychoanalysis, 47* (3), (279–281).

Greenberg, J., & Mitchell, S. (1983). *Object-relations in psychoanalytic theory*. Cambridge, MA: Harvard University Press.

Greenson, R. R. (1967). *The technique and practice of psychoanalysis* (Vol. 1). New York: International Universities Press.

Guntrip, H. (1969). *Schizoid phenomena, object relations and the self*. New York: International Universities Press.

Harper, R. (1975). *The new psychotherapies*. Englewood Cliffs, NJ: Prentice-Hall.

Hollender, M. H. (1980). The case of Anna O.: A reformulation. *American Journal of Psychiatry, 137*, 787–800.

Horney, K. (1926). The flight from womanhood: The masculinity complex in women as viewed by man and by women. *International Journal of Psychoanalysis, 7*, 324–329.

Hornstein, G. (1992). The return of the repressed: Psychology's problematic relations with psychoanalysis, 1906-1960. *American Psychologist, 47*(2), 245–263.

Hurding, R. (1985). *Roots and shoots*. London: Hodder and Stoughton.

Jones, E. (1953). *The life and work of Sigmund Freud* (Vol. 1). New York: Basic Books.

Jones, E. (1955). *The life and work of Sigmund Freud* (Vol. 2). New York: Basic Books.

Jones, E. (1957). *The life and work of Sigmund Freud* (Vol. 3). New York: Basic Books.

Jones, J., & Wilson, W. (1987). *An incomplete education*. New York: Ballantine Books.

Kanzer, M., & Glenn, J. (1980). *Freud and his patients*. New York: Jason Aronson.

Kernberg, O. (1975). *Borderline conditions and pathological narcissism*. New York: Jason Aronson.

Kernberg, O. (1976). *Object-relations theory and clinical psychoanalysis*. New York: Jason Aronson.

Klein, G. S. (1976). *Psychoanalytic theory: An exploration of essentials*. New York: International Universities Press.

Klein, M. (1975). *Envy and gratitude and other works, 1946-1963*. London, Hogarth Press.

Kohut, H. (1971). The analysis of the self. *Monograph series of the psychoanalytic study of the child (4)*. New York: International Universities Press.

Kohut, H. (1977). *The restoration of the self*. New York: International Universities Press.

Kohut, H. (1984). *How does analysis cure?* Chicago: University of Chicago Press.

Kohut, H. (1985). *Self psychology and the humanities: Reflections on a new psychoanalytic approach*. New York: W. W. Norton.

Korchin, S. (1976). *Modern clinical psychology*. New York: Basic Books.

Laplanche, J., & Pontailis, J. (1973). *The language of psychoanalysis*. New York: W. W. Norton.

Leak, G. K., & Christopher, S. B. (1982). Freudian psychoanalysis and sociobiology. *American Psychologist, 37*, 313–322.

Liff, Z. A. (1992). Psychoanalysis and dynamic techniques. In D. K. Feedheim (Ed.), *History of psychotherapy: A century of change* (pp. 571–586). Washington, DC: American Psychological Association.

Lipschitz, F. (1990). The dream within a dream: Profliction vs. reflection. *Contemporary Psychoanalysis, 26*, 716–731.

Mahler, M. (1968). *On human symbiosis and the vicissitudes of individuation: Infantile psychosis* (Vol. 1). New York: International Universities Press.

Mead, M. (1974). On Freud's view of female psychology. In J. Strouse (Ed.), *Women and analysis: Dialogues on psychoanalytic views of femininity* (pp. 95–106). New York: Grossman.

Meares, R. (1992). Transference and the play space: Towards a new basic metaphor. *Contemporary Psychoanlysis, 28*, 32–49.

Meissner, W. (1985). Theories of personality and psychopathology: Classical psycho-analysis. In H.I. Kaplan and B. J. Sadock (Eds.), *Comprehensive textbook of psychiatry* (Vol. 4, pp. 337–418). Baltimore, MD: Williams & Wilkins.

Modell, A. (1975). The ego and the id: 50 years later. *International Journal of Psychoanalysis, 56,* 57–68.

Munroe, R. (1955). *Schools of psychoanalytic thought.* New York: Holt, Rinehart and Winston.

Nemiah, J. C. (1984). Psychoanalysis and individual psychotherapy. In T. B. Karasu (Ed.), *The psychiatric therapies* (pp. 321–346). Washington, DC: American Psychiatric Association.

Nye, R. D. (1992). *Three psychologies: Perspectives from Freud, Skinner, and Rogers* (4th ed.). Monterey, CA: Brooks/Cole

Pine, F. (1988). The four psychologies of psychoanalysis and their place in clinical work. *Journal of the American Psychoanalytic Association, 36,* 571–596.

Pine, F. (1990). *Drive, ego, object and self.* New York: Basic Books.

Prochaska, J. (1984). *Systems of psychotherapy* (2nd ed.). Chicago: Dorsey Press.

Rachman, S. (1971). *The effects of psychotherapy.* Oxford, U.K.: Pergamon Press.

Raymond, C. (1991). Study of patient histories suggest Freud suppressed or distorted facts that contradicted his theories. *Chonicle of Higher Education, 37,* A4–A6.

Runyan, W. McK. (Ed.). (1988). *Psychology and historical interpretation.* New York: Oxford University Press.

Sampson, H. (1990). The problem of adaptation to reality in psychoanalytic theory. *Contemporary Psychoanalysis, 26,* 677–691.

Silverstein, S. (1989). Freud's dualistic mind-body interactionism: Implications for the development of his psychology. *Psychological Reports, 64,* 1091–1097.

St. Clair, M. (1986). *Object relations and self psychology.* Belmont, CA: Wadsworth.

Storr, A. (1989). *Freud.* New York: Oxford University Press.

Strupp, H. H., & Binder, J. L. (1984). *Psychotherapy in a new key.* New York: Basic Books.

Stunkard, A. J. (1991). Review of Schwartz, H. J. (Ed.), Bulimia: Psychoanalytic treatment and theory. Madison, CT: International Universities Press, 1988. *Psychiatric Annals, 19,* 279.

Thompson, C. (1943). "Penis envy" in women. *Psychiatry, 6,* 123–125.

Tobin, S. A. (1990). Self psychology as a bridge between existential-humanistic psychology and psychoanalysis. *Journal of Humanistic Psychology, 30,* 14–63.

Wachtel, P. L. (1977). *Psychoanalysis and behavior therapy: Toward an integration.* New York: Basic Books.

Wallerstein, R. S. (1989). The psychotherapy research project of the Menninger Foundation: An overview. *Journal of Consulting and Clinical Psychology, 57,* 195–205.

Winnicott, D. W. (1956). On transference. *International Journal of Psycho-Analysis, 37,* 386–388.

Zucker, H. (1993). Reality: Can it be only yours or mine? Conference of the Westchester Center for the Study of Psychoanalysis and Psychotherapy. *Contemporary Psychoanalysis, 29,* 479–486.

CHAPTER 7

Adlerian Therapy

Chapter Outline

Introduction
Brief Biography
Historical Development
View of Human Nature
Development of Maladaptive Behavior
Function of the Therapist
Goals of Therapy
Major Methods and Techniques
Application
Critical Analysis
Current Status
Chapter Summary
Key Terms
Suggested Reading

INTRODUCTION

So influential is Alfred Adler, the first of the Viennese psychoanalysts to break with Freud, that he has been called the "true father of modern psychotherapy" (Ellis, 1970). Their separation occurred in 1911, when it became apparent that their thinking was irreconcilably at odds. Unfortunately, the professional dispute became personal when Freud, who accused the "defector" of being too proud to live in the shadow of a giant, forbade his followers to attend any of Adler's conferences. Undaunted, Adler went on to develop a new society, a new journal, and a new therapeutic approach called *individual psychology*.

Adler holds a significant place in psychology. He influenced neo-Freudians such as Karen Horney and Erich Fromm (although some argue they should be

119

called neo-Adlerians) as well as more modern theorists such as Carl Rogers and Albert Ellis (Corsini & Wedding, 1989). Some of these contributions are indicated in Sidebar 7-1. Not only did he shift the Freudian emphasis on the libido to the ego's striving for power, he also developed a personality model, a theory of psychopathology, the concept of the *inferiority complex*, and a treatment method (Parrott, 1992).

According to Adler, individuals are victims neither of their genetic endowment nor of their social conditioning. Rather, they are responsible for themselves and learn to respond in adaptive, creative ways to their surroundings. Even early in life, individuals strive toward an ideal, which runs as a major theme throughout their lives (Adler, 1959).

Surprisingly, Adler's influence remains largely unrecognized (Mosak, 1973). "It would not be easy," writes Ellenberger, "to find another author from which so much has been borrowed from all sides without acknowledgment, than Adler" (1970, p. 645). Wilder, in his introduction to *Essays in Individual Psychology*, writes, "Most observations and ideas of Alfred Adler have subtly and quietly permeated modern psychological thinking to such a degree that the proper question is not whether one is Adlerian but how much of an Adlerian one is" (Adler & Deutsch, 1959, p. xv).

Sidebar 7-1

**ADLER'S CONTRIBUTION
TO MODERN PSYCHOLOGY**

Adlerian Concept	*Modern Counterpart*
• Emphasis on the social rather than the sexual aspects of the person	• Socially oriented theories of Fromm, Horney, and Sullivan
• Emphasis on the ego	• Ego psychology of Erikson, Hartmann, and others
• Importance of personal choices and courage in living	• Existential perspective of "being-in-the-world," and facing the fear of nothingness
• Importance of self-esteem and equality in therapy	• Rogers' emphasis on self-esteem and positive regard
• Use of physical movements to reveal a style of life	• Body language; Allport's study of expressive behavior
• Equality of women	• Feminist movement
• Self-created style of life	• Kelly's psychology of personal constructs
• Social interest	• A criteria of mental health in Maslow's theory
• Treating children in the company of their parents and establishing child guidance clinics	• Family therapy, group therapy, community psychology
• Face-to-face weekly interviews in psychotherapy	• Almost all modern forms of psychotherapy

---

BRIEF BIOGRAPHY

Born on February 7, 1870 in a suburb of Vienna, Alfred Adler was the second of six children. He grew up in the shadow of a gifted and successful older brother. One of his earliest childhood memories was of sitting on a bench, bandaged and incapacitated by rickets, while his athletic older brother played vigorously. As a young student, Adler tasted early failure. He could not draw well and repeated an arithmetic class. One teacher told his father that the boy should be apprenticed to a shoemaker because he was unfit for anything else.

A grain merchant, Adler's father provided the family with a comfortable life even though they faced financial difficulties. Whereas Adler's mother—gloomy, rejecting, and self-sacrificing—embodied what her son later called the martyr complex, his father was cheerful and self-confident, and Adler identified with him. Understandably, he would later reject Freud's Oedipus complex, so foreign to his own childhood experience. And, whereas Freud, raised in a Jewish ghetto, was at times self-conscious about his minority status, Adler knew few Jewish children. In fact, Adler was so much more immersed in Viennese culture than in his Jewish heritage that at the age of 34 he converted from Judaism to Christianity.

Alfred Adler (1870–1937).
(AP/Wide World)

Adler described his childhood as unhappy. There were close encounters with disease and death. At 3 years he witnessed the death of a younger brother in the bed next to his. When he was 5 years old, he barely survived pneumonia. When he heard the doctor say to his father, "Your boy is lost," he decided to become a doctor himself (Orgler, 1963, p. 16). Twice he was injured in serious street accidents.

Despite these personal and family setbacks, in 1895 at age 25 years Adler received a medical degree from the University of Vienna. Ironically, he never attended any of the lectures on hysteria given there by a relatively unknown physician, Sigmund Freud. His field of specialization was ophthalmology; his interest in psychiatry would bloom later.

From his clinic in a lower-middle-class neighborhood, Adler worked with a broad range of patients and diseases. Because his office was near an amusement park, his patients were often performers and artists, including acrobats, many of whom, Adler learned, had developed their abilities in reaction to childhood weaknesses or accidents (Furtmuller, 1964). These early investigations first suggested to Adler that the organic and psychological dimensions of disease were not separate, that many high-achieving people with great mental or physical abilities were overcompensating for childhood inferiorities.

Perhaps there are so few Adlerians because we are all Adlerians.

—Joseph F. Burke

At a political rally Adler met his strong-willed future wife, Raissa Epstein, who would shape her husband's views on the equality of women. The daughter of Russian intelligentsia, she had come to Vienna to complete her education. After she returned home, Adler scraped together enough money to visit her in Russia, where they were married in 1897. They had four children, three daughters and a son, two of whom became psychiatrists themselves.

After World War I Adler was given the task of establishing guidance clinics for the Vienna school system. Every child from 6 to 14 years old was screened in order to refer for counseling those with learning disabilities, emotional disturbances, or behavioral problems. This project reduced delinquency in a city where it might have been expected to be rampant. More importantly, this work so convinced Adler of the importance of child-rearing practices that his subsequent theories about parent–child relationships would have a lasting effect on modern educational theory and practice.

A short man, inclined to an unpretentious, sometimes slovenly, appearance, Adler was markedly less handsome or charismatic than Freud. Adler first heard Freud lecture in 1899, and he was invited to join Freud's discussion group in 1902. Although Adler was never psychoanalyzed himself, as were other members of the inner circle, he won the respect of his colleagues and was selected as the editor of their journal. In 1910 Adler was elected president of the Vienna Psychoanalytic Society, an honor previously held by Freud, and he came to impress people as a witty and inspiring lecturer.

Adler never considered himself a disciple of Freud, however, and his intellectual independence led to a widening rift between them. "Do you think it gives me such great pleasure to stand in your shadow my whole life long?" he once remarked to Freud (Freud, 1914, p. 51). Seemingly in response, Freud wrote in a letter to Carl Jung that Adler "is always . . . complaining that he is disappearing under my shadow, and forcing me into the unwelcome role of the aging despot who prevents young men from getting ahead" (McGuire, 1974, p. 373). He called Adler a "pygmy," and with equal bitterness, Adler called Freud's psychoanalysis "filth" (Roazen, 1975, p. 210). Their breakup was precipitated by the primacy Freud assigned to sexuality. Although Adler acknowledged the significance of sexual conflicts, he felt that people's problems stemmed from a variety of social sources. So, whereas Freud argued that women find themselves inferior because they lack male genitals, Adler looked, not to women's anatomy, but to their interactions with society to find the source of their perceptions. Toward the end of their relationship, Freud and Adler had little more in common than their mutual appreciation for cigars (Stepansky, 1983).

Early in 1911 Adler delivered to Viennese society three lectures that elaborated the differences that distinguished his work from Freud's. This resulted in the formation of the Society for Free Psychoanalysis, which later became known as the Society for Individual Psychology (Orgler, 1963). In 1926 Adler visited the United States for the first time, accepting appointments at Columbia University and later at Long Island College of Medicine. Adler made the United States his permanent home in 1934 in order to flee Nazi Germany, and 3 years later he died of a heart attack, in the midst of a strenuous European lecture tour, at the University of Aberdeen in Scotland.

HISTORICAL DEVELOPMENT

The Bible and the Stoic philosophers were among the many influences on Adler's thinking. He drew from such writers as Dostoevsky, Goethe, and Shakespeare, and from Karl Marx, Friederich Nietzsche, Henri Bergson, and Immanuel Kant as well. His theory was informed by such Americans as G. Stanley Hall, John Dewey, and William James (Ansbacher, 1983). However, the primary influence on Adler's views came from the philosopher Hans Vaihinger (1924), who taught that none of us can know truth completely. We formulate approximations of reality, Vaihinger wrote, and then live by these constructions as if they were true. Vaihinger's (1935) book, *The Psychology of "As If,"* proposed that people live in accordance with fictional goals they set for themselves. Adler seized upon this notion to develop his own concept of a *life style:* the particular arrangement of convictions or conclusions about self, others, and reality that we establish early in life. Significantly, Vaihinger's work provided Adler with the grounds for his reaction against Freud's strict determinism. According to Adler, people are motivated not so much by their past experiences as by their future goals, an explanation called *teleology.* Although people are usually unaware of these goals, according to Adler they are the keys to their unconscious, guiding their striving for superiority.

Others influenced Adler's thinking as well: Pierre Marie Félix Janet, who believed that a sense of inferiority is the general cause of neurosis; Nietzsche, whose emphasis on both the importance of the individual and the striving for perfection lay behind much of Adler's concept of the striving for superiority; and Marx, who identified social forces as the prime determinants of human behavior and who urged reforms promoting equal opportunity regardless of birth or gender. It was Marx who allowed Adler to formulate his concern for *social interest* (Brink, 1985). And it was Vaihinger's contention that people are motivated not by reality, but by fictions, by goals and interpretations, that inspired Adler's concepts of *guiding fiction* and the subjective *as if.*

But the greatest contemporary influence on Adler's individual psychology was, of course, Sigmund Freud, with whom Adler collaborated for almost a decade (1902–1911). Freud's emphasis on the importance of early childhood and parental factors was adopted by Adler, as well as his psychoanalytic perspective that all behavior resulted from and reflected the underlying personality. However, Adler disputed the claim that neither hereditary nor environmental forces completely determined an individual's personality.

Six years before his death, Adler published a paper that elaborated the differences between Freud's approach to psychoanalysis and his own approach to individual psychology. Unlike Freud, Adler spoke of neither instincts, such as eros or thanatos, nor of entities of the mind, such as the id, ego, or superego.

A psychological system has an inseparable connection with the life philosophy of its formulator.

—Alfred Adler

Neither did Adler distinguish between the conscious and unconscious, although he used both concepts. Not only was Adler less inclined than Freud to attribute problems to human sexuality, he was also less systematic in his theorizing—his constructs are not particularly well integrated, and there are fewer of them—and he was less methodical in laying out a plan for treatment. Adler placed much more emphasis than Freud on defensive mechanisms and on family relationships, on environment, and on learning. And, whereas Freud spoke of the internal drive of the instincts, Adler emphasized the many different goals that motivate human behavior.

VIEW OF HUMAN NATURE

Central to Adler's program is the premise that human beings are irreducibly whole. In fact, so fundamental to Adler's work is this premise, that he called his system of psychotherapy *individual psychology,* after the Latin term *individuum:* indivisible, complete, whole. Unlike Freud, Adler saw human nature not in reductionistic, but in holistic terms. In other words, the way individuals organize themselves largely determines their response to the outside world (Dinkmeyer, Pew, & Dinkmeyer, 1979).

Inferiority

In *The Neurotic Constitution,* one of Adler's earliest and most influential works, he considered the problem of *organ inferiority,* that is, the role of physical abnormalities or personality deficits that contribute to the development of neurosis (1926). "A body which is ill-suited to the environment," wrote Adler, "will usually be felt by the mind as a burden" (1931, pp. 34). Adler believed that the resulting sense of inferiority is the source of human striving, the driving force that motivates behavior. All individual progress, growth, and development result from the attempt to *compensate* for our inferiorities, be they imagined or real.

In one of his earliest papers, Adler investigated the issue of inferiority and compensation (1907/1964). It was well-known that disease often attacks weaker organs in the body, but Adler observed that disease was not the inevitable consequence of a weak organ. Under some circumstances, such as when a broken bone heals even stronger at its fracture line, the body compensates for this weakness and develops an offsetting strength, either by rebuilding its organ or by increasing its capacity to function in spite of its disability. Adler held that this compensation is achieved because the organic inferiority stimulates the process of rebuilding the affected organ.

Adler, who was an optimist, believed that people could find personal happiness by similarly compensating for emotional inferiority. Studying the functional tendencies of the body to unravel the secrets of the mind, Adler turned to history and literature for illustrations of how inferiority could be turned to superiority under favorable environmental conditions. Teddy Roosevelt, for example, a weakling as a child, developed into a hearty and robust adult who led the charge up San Juan Hill. He launched the National Park Service, led legislative initiatives to protect the environment, broke up such ruthless corporations as Standard Oil, popularized the slogan "Speak softly but carry a big stick," and, significantly, coined the term "rugged individualism."

Adlerian counseling assumes that individuals are motivated by a striving for superiority. Because all children feel inferior by virtue of their size and lesser capabilities, Adler believed that the longing for significance, for self-esteem, emerges early. Individuals crave a sense of mastery, purposefulness, and meaning, and this *striving for superiority* is what drives adult life (Adler, 1930). By "striving for superiority" Adler of course meant not human tendencies toward domination or arrogance, but the human capacity to turn a deficiency into an advantage. As a synonym for *superiority,* he occasionally used the word *perfection,* in the sense of wholeness and completion, from the Latin *perficere,* "to complete" or "to finish."

Finalism

Whereas Freud believed that human behavior is pushed by the past, Adler believed it is pulled by the future. Thus, whereas Freud considered behavior to be rigidly determined by physiological instincts and experiences of childhood, Adler believed that expectations and goals for the future motivated human activity. It is this final goal of superiority or perfection that explains human motivations. And it is this *finalism,* as Adler termed it, this belief in an ultimate goal, a final state of being, that accounts for our ever-present tendency or necessity to move in that direction. What is intriguing about personal goals, according to Adler, is that they do not exist as actualities but as potentialities. We strive for unfulfilled ideals, for the belief, for instance, that people are created equal or that people are basically good. To this notion that such ideals guide the way we perceive and interact with those around us, Adler gave the term *fictional finalism*.

Social Interest

From earliest times, people have congregated in communities, in families, tribes, and nations, for survival and protection. It has always been necessary for people to cooperate. Adler believed that people were inherently concerned with the welfare of others, a capacity that he labeled *Gemeinschaftsgefuhl* or *social interest* (O'Connell, 1965). People need to cooperate with and contribute to society in order to realize personal as well as social goals. Social interest is the engine, then, that drives empathy and altruism. Originally Adler regarded social interest as a force that opposed a striving for superiority, that prevented people from being ruthlessly selfish; but he later combined the two concepts. The enhancement of social interest, Adler came to believe, was the most important goal toward which people strive (Ansbacher, 1983).

In contrast to Freud, who believed that the individual and society were in conflict, Adler believed that the relationship between people and their larger world was harmonious (Adler, 1931, 1959). In fact, Adler's concept of social interest encompasses the whole of human actions, thoughts, and emotions (Mosak, 1991; O'Connell, 1965). Included among behaviors associated with social interest are, for example, those that encourage individuals to help and to respect one another; to share, cooperate, and compromise with one another; to encourage one another; and to empathize with another's thoughts and emotions. But it was not only behaviors that emerged from out of this social interest, Adler argued. A feeling of ease or communality; a sense of belonging, of being "at home"; a faith in others; a spirit of optimism; the courage to be "imperfect," recognizing that making mistakes is a natural part of being human; even a broader sense of "being human," that is, of feeling a part of humanity, especially in an existential sense—all of these emotions, Adler proposed, grew from out of people's need to cooperate with one another, to contribute to the social good. All of these emotions grow out of social interest (Kaplan, 1986; Moschetta, 1993).

> To be human means to feel inferior. At the beginning of every psychological life there is a deep inferiority feeling.
>
> —Alfred Adler

As a result Adler's criteria for mental health include an intrinsic concern for others. "Social interest is the barometer of the child's normality" (Ansbacher & Ansbacher, 1956, p. 154). The degree to which people successfully contribute to the common good is an indicator of their maturity and psychological health. Without such an interest in the social welfare, maladaptive behavior is inevitable.

DEVELOPMENT OF MALADAPTIVE BEHAVIOR

According to Adler, maladaptive behavior results from discouraging or disappointing circumstances. When people lose the courage to face life's demands directly, when they seem insignificant to themselves, they move from a sense of inferiority to an inferiority complex. Unconsciously convinced of their inferiority, people in this disillusioned state develop abnormal behavior to divert attention from their troubles (Ansbacher, 1992).

The seeds for such pathological behavior were planted early in life. Ideally, the child's potential for social interest was brought to fruition by the mother. It is she who administered the initial lesson in cooperation by nursing the baby at her breast, thereby serving as the child's first bridge to social life (Adler, 1964a). And it was she who later helped the child extend relationships to the father and to others. If the mother was clumsy, uncooperative, or untrustworthy, however, the child would learn to resist rather than strive to develop social interest.

The father's role was to instill within the child courage and self-reliance and to stress the need for choosing a satisfying and worthwhile occupation. To Adler, too many parents were poorly prepared for the challenging task of raising their children. Too many parents, Adler believed, showered their children with excessive attention, protection, and assistance. Such *pampering,* the most serious of parental errors, robs children of their independence and initiative, shatters their self-confidence, and creates the impression that the world will not hold them accountable for rules that apply to others (Adler, 1964b).

It is these pampered children who develop inferiority complexes, a pathological condition that often remains concealed until life passes the inevitable milestones of stress and disappointment. Having never learned self-reliance, such people try to resolve their problems by making unrealistic demands on other people and by expecting everyone to treat their wishes as law. Rather than focusing on the need for social or human cooperation, as adults they approach work and marriage with the same self-centered orientation (Stone, 1993).

On the other hand, when parents fail to provide sufficient care for and attention to their children, they collapse into the opposite error of *neglect,* creating the impression that the world is cold and unsympathetic. Unable to see the need to win affection and esteem by socially approved behavior, children with this mindset regard life, and especially other adults, as the enemy. The resulting inferiority complex is expressed through suspicion, isolation, stubbornness, and maliciousness (Adler, 1931).

Parents contribute to the development of maladaptive behavior in their children in other ways as well: by failing to show them tenderness, for instance, by stigmatizing sentimentality as being ridiculous, or by establishing unattainable standards. Resorting to harsh, nonrehabilitating punishment, which exaggerates the child's helplessness, is just as likely to precipitate an inferiority complex. In fact, Adler was the first to emphasize that any praise or blame of a child should be directed, not toward the person, but toward his or her behavior (Adler, 1931; Nikelly, 1971).

In addition to parenting errors, a significant physical deficiency or severe illness may also trigger strong psychological feelings of helplessness (Adler, 1907/1964). Although inferiority need not result in psychopathology, it often presents substantial difficulties, which concerned parents are likely to exacerbate by pampering—by misguided help that only fuels the development of an inferiority complex. If a child is unable to compensate adequately for inferiority, whether brought on by pampering, neglect, or disability, a sense of helplessness becomes more intense and a long-term inferiority complex develops. Adler saw the consequence as "an inability to solve life's problems" (Orgler, 1963, p. 63).

Alternatively, people may attempt to compensate for their sense of inferiority by developing what Adler called a *superiority complex*, that is, by developing an exaggerated opinion of their own abilities and accomplishments, or by finding no need to back up their sense of superiority with accomplishments. In either case their behavior is characterized by boasting, banality, self-centeredness, and a tendency to denigrate others. It should be noted, however, that as a means of compensating for their inferiority, some people become extremely successful.

In summary, abnormal behavior characterizes individuals who develop such a massive sense of inferiority in early childhood that they become discouraged about life. To compensate, children develop inappropriate patterns of behavior, frequently manifesting an unrealistic striving for personal superior-

Denigrating others indicates a *superiority complex.*
(Richard Hutchings/Photo Researchers)

ity. This compensatory, self-centered, self-protective behavior precludes any chance of fulfilling social interest. In and of themselves, such feelings of inferiority are not abnormal. It is only when individuals *act as if* they were inferior that an inferiority complex becomes operative.

FUNCTION OF THE THERAPIST

Identifying and building on strengths the client already demonstrates, Adlerian therapists often function as educators or tutors. They encourage their clients to use their talents for the benefit of others. From the initial contact, Adlerians work to establish and maintain an accepting, caring, cooperative relationship with their clients. Convinced that clients are discouraged when they enter therapy, counselors work to develop a supportive and encouraging relationship. By being humorous rather than anxious, unimpressed by their own mistakes rather than perfectionistic, and curious rather than defensive, they model the behavior they desire for their clients. As educators, they realize that much of what clients take with them from the counseling relationship will be caught rather than taught. Adlerian therapists are seldom impassive, sphinxlike persons. They are more likely to be active and talkative.

| *To live is to feel inferior.*
—Alfred Adler

Nevertheless, whereas qualities of empathy, warmth, and genuiness are important to Adlerian therapists, the focus is on action-oriented behaviors such as interpretation, confrontation, and concreteness. In addition, Adlerian counselors must be fully aware of their own beliefs and emotions, of their role as models for the client, and of conditions that are essential to the client's development.

Adlerian practitioners view therapy as a collaborative effort. The counselor and client are partners who work toward goals that are mutually agreed upon and clearly identified. They focus not on the conditions that have made the clients what they are, but on what it is that they may become. At times the therapy strategy is spelled out in a written contract, which specifies the goals of the process and the responsibilities of each partner. The counselor then uses the plan as a means of support—as a means of maximizing assets and minimizing deficits. In short, the counselor's energy is invested not in analysis, but in encouragement.

Since Adlerian therapists view their clients' lives as personal constructs built out of perceptions, beliefs, and feelings, they strive to develop and deepen their understanding of these *life styles*. Once counselors understand the life style, they can help their clients understand how their life styles have been influenced by their basic beliefs and perceptions. Since Adler held that beliefs influence emotions, not vice versa, counselors discuss the beliefs that underlie emotions rather than simply reflecting on the emotions themselves. This is, of course, a crucial distinction between Freud and Adler.

Although Adlerian counselors are empathic and accepting, they also confront clients with their basic mistakes, misplaced goals, self-defeating behaviors, and restrictive beliefs. These confrontations help clients to resolve apparent contradictions and realign mistaken goals.

Another important function of Adlerian therapists is to help translate insight into action. Therapists encourage their clients to act upon new alternatives for reaching specific goals. The counselor and counselee "work together to consider alternative attitudes, beliefs, and actions" (Dinkmeyer et al., 1979, p. 98).

GOALS OF THERAPY

Adlerians believe that most people seek therapy because they have low social interest. In these instances, the primary goal of therapy is to increase the clients' social interest, or sense of commonality with all fellow humans. By virtue of our limitations, human solidarity is a universal necessity. We need one another's cooperation in order to live.

In addition to fostering social interest, Adlerian therapy also seeks to decrease a sense of inferiority in the clients to help them overcome discouragement, and to allow them to recognize and use their resources. By helping people to contribute, by altering faulty motivations that underlie even acceptable behavior, by encouraging equality—in all these ways, Adlerians seek to change the life styles, the perceptions and goals, of their clients (Dreikurs, 1971; Mosak, 1989; Kottman & Warlick, 1990; Mosak & Dreikurs, 1973).

Adlerian therapy seeks to develop courageous people who view a task or situation not in terms of potential threats and dangers, but in terms of possible actions and solutions. For the Adlerian, courage is comprised of self-confidence and the conviction that solutions can be found to cope with life's situations. Courageous people do not feel defeated or inferior (Dinkmeyer & Dreikurs, 1963). It rarely takes longer than a year for a therapeutic relationship to achieve such goals; most clients are expected to show at least partial improvement by their third month of treatment (Adler, 1959; Ellenberger, 1970).

MAJOR METHODS AND TECHNIQUES

Adlerians apply a wide variety of therapeutic techniques. After beginning by establishing a warm, caring empathic relationship between the client and the therapist, the therapist will assess the client's goals and life style, generate insight into the client's mistaken thoughts and the resulting maladaptive behaviors, and, finally, effect change in the behavior by reeducating the client and by encouraging the client to act on alternative ways of thinking.

Initiating the Therapeutic Relationship

Establishing rapport between clients and practitioners is a process characterized by mutually determined goals, confidentiality, and respect for the clients' ability ultimately to direct their own lives (Dinkmeyer et al., 1979). A warm and trusting counseling relationship, enhanced by a number of professional techniques, is crucial to effective Adlerian therapy.

Encouragement remains the bedrock of Adlerian intervention, especially in establishing a therapeutic relationship (Dinkmeyer & Losoncy, 1980). Adlerian practice is built on the assumption that clients feel powerless and discouraged. Only when clients change their attitude toward themselves will their behavior change. It is crucial, therefore, to encourage, to accept clients as they are, and to focus on clients' assets rather than their liabilities. The ultimate goal of such encouragement is to share and analyze the private logic of the clients, and to persuade them to accept responsibility for living as well as to change their self-defeating behaviors (Nikelly & Dinkmeyer, 1972).

A common pitfall in such a therapeutic relationship is that clients often expect their therapists to respond to them as do other people in their lives. If clients feel misunderstood or unloved by others, for example, they may expect the therapist to behave in the same way. They may even create situations that unconsciously invite the therapist to respond negatively. Aware of subtle sabotages, Adlerian therapists use them to better understand how their clients typically elicit responses from others.

On yet other occasions clients may attempt to make the counselor more powerful than themselves. They may want to relinquish symptoms but not the underlying causes of those symptoms. Or they may look to the counselor to perform a "miracle." The Adlerian therapist understands, however, that an effective relationship can be built only if the counselor refuses to be caught by the vanity of believing that miracles can be performed (Dinkmeyer, Dinkmeyer, & Sperry, 1987).

Lifestyle Investigation

Since Adler believed that our ultimate goal is superiority or perfection, he uncovered ways for individuals to strive for that goal. Each of us develops a unique pattern of behavior, characteristics, and habits that help us reach our goal. In other words, every person develops a distinctive *life style*—a basic orientation toward life, a psychological map, that becomes a guide for action. Our psychological life styles are a repertoire of specific behaviors that help us to deal with the demands of living (Mosak, 1972; Mullis, Kern, & Curlette, 1987). All of us, according to Adler, have unique life styles that enable us to compensate for inferiority feelings and strive toward superiority (see Sidebar 7-2). Like two pine trees, one growing in a valley, another on a mountain top, each of us develops distinctively. Although both are the same kind of tree, each shows a distinct style of life, with adaptation "expressing itself and molding itself in an environment" (Adler, 1959, p. 173).

Parents who most need advice are the [ones] who never come for it.
—Alfred Adler

Adler's concept of life style is composed of four elements: the *self-concept*, or view of the self "as is"; the *self-ideal*, or self as one would like to be; the *picture*

WHAT'S YOUR LIFE STYLE?

Everyone achieves meaning out of life by interpreting his or her existence. A person's *life style,* according to Adler, is the platform from which these interpretations are made. A person's life style is his or her basic orientation to life. It is the cognitive framework from which people select the specific behaviors that enable them to cope with life. It includes the individual's unique views on how security, belonging, superiority, perfection, or completion can be achieved. All behavior is understandable if seen in the light of the individual's *private logic* — the key to that individual's life style (Dinkmeyer et al, 1979). By age 4 or 5 years, the life style is pretty well in place, and new experiences are fitted into it rather than used to form it. It remains essentially unchanged throughout life, unless challenged by some overwhelming experience or adjusted through therapy. Mosak (1971, pp. 78–80) has identified 14 probable behaviors associated with commonly observed life styles:

1. The *getter* exploits and manipulates life and others by actively or passively putting others into his or her service. The getter may use charm, shyness, temper, or intimidation as methods of operation.
2. The *driver* is the person in motion: overconscientiousness and dedication to goals rarely permit rest. Underneath, such a person nurses a fear that she or he is a "zero."
3. The *controller* is either a person who wishes to control life or one who wishes to ensure that life will not control him or her. He or she generally dislikes surprises, controls spontaneity, and hides feelings because all of these may lessen his or her control. As substitutes, such people favor intellectualization, rightness, orderliness, and neatness.

4. Persons who need to be *right* elevate themselves over others, whom they manage to see as wrong. They scrupulously avoid error. Should they be caught in an error, they rationalize that others are more wrong than they.
5. The person who needs to be *superior* may refuse to participate in any activity which he or she cannot "win."
6. The person who needs to be *liked* tries to please everyone all the time. Particularly sensitive to criticism, such people are crushed when they do not receive universal and constant approval. They see the evaluations of others as the measure of their worth.
7. The person who needs to be *good* prefers to live by higher moral standards than anyone else's. Sometimes these standards are higher than God's, because these persons sometimes expect God to forgive "sins" in them that they cannot forgive in others.
8. The oppositional person *opposes* everything, especially life's demands of him or her.
9. Everything happens to the *victim,* who may be characterized by feelings of nobility, self-pity, or resignation.
10. The *martyr* is similar to the victim except that whereas the victim merely "dies," the martyr "dies" for a cause. The martyr's goal is nobility and his or her vocation is injustice collector.
11. The *baby* finds a place in life through charm, cuteness, and exploitation of others.
12. The *inadequate* person acts as though he or she cannot do anything right. Through this default, he or she binds others as servants.
13. People who *avoid feelings* may fear their own spontaneity because it may move them in directions they have not thoroughly planned.
14. The *excitement seeker* despises routine and repetitive activities, seeks novel experiences, and revels in commotion.

of the world, one's model or "myth" about why things work as they do outside of oneself; and one's *ethical convictions.* Since this map determines the choices we make, it determines who we are (Mosak, 1989). Unless challenged to change, clients may persist in reading an inappropriate map—in always trying to please others, for example. Adlerians systematically explore their clients' life styles and unravel their secrets by focusing on the "three entrance gates to mental life": *birth order, early memories,* and *dreams.*

Birth Order   Although no two children are born into the same environment, the position of the child within the family, as well as the atmosphere of the family, plays a significant role in the client's development and behavior (Bohmer & Sitton, 1993; Curtis & Cowell, 1993; Gates, Lineberger, Crockett, & Hubbard, 1988; Shulman & Nikelly, 1972). The family constellation includes more than a list of family members. It also includes descriptions of each person in the family, their respective personalities, their relationships with each other, and the family's dynamics of interpersonal power and influence (Adler, 1937).

Birth order, the sequence of siblings, is part of the family constellation and a major influence on the creation of a person's style of life. Adlerians know that siblings, although living in the same house with the same parents, do not have identical social environments. Being older or younger than one's siblings and being exposed to parental attitudes that have evolved as a result of the arrival of each additional child create different conditions that greatly influence one's personality (Claxton, 1994; Narayan, 1990; Perlin & Grater, 1984; Shulman & Mosak, 1977; Forer, 1977).

Because parents typically devote a considerable amount of time and attention to their first child, the *first-born* is in a unique and enviable situation. Often the first-born has a happy, secure existence—until, that is, the appearance of the second child. Suddenly she or he is no longer the primary focus of attention, and the child, in Adler's terms, becomes *dethroned.* No matter how hard the first-born tries, things will never be the same. Although all first-born feel this shock, this altered position in the family, those who are younger or who have been pampered will experience an even greater loss.

> *There is no greater evil than the pampering of children.*
>
> —Alfred Adler

Adler found that oldest children are often oriented toward the past, locked in nostalgia, and pessimistic about the future. Having learned at one time the advantages of power, they remain concerned to gain power all their lives. As a result, first-born children become conscientious and scrupulous, and long for positions of authority. Adler viewed the only child, in essence, as a first-born who never forfeits the priesthood (Byrd, DeRosa, & Craig, 1993).

By the time the *second-born* child arrives, the element of novelty is greatly reduced, and parents are typically less anxious and more relaxed in their child rearing. From the beginning, the second-born finds in the older sibling a pace-setter: a model or a threat against which to compete. So significant is this competitive spur, that the second child usually begins speaking at an earlier age than the older child. Adler also found that second-borns are not only more competitive and ambitious but more optimistic about the future as well. If, however, the older sibling excels in everything, the second-born may fail to incorporate competitiveness into his or her life style and may eventually give up trying to succeed.

The youngest or *last-born* child never faces the shock of dethronement. Spurred on by the need to surpass older siblings, last-borns often develop remarkably fast, turning into high achievers in whatever work they undertake as adults. If the youngest child remains the baby of the family, however, and is spoiled or pampered, the opposite may take place. Unaccustomed to striving and struggling, this pampered youngster may find it difficult to cope as an adult (Barry & Blane, 1977; Miller & Maruyama, 1976).

Without attempting to force a client rigidly into one of these birth order positions, Adlerian therapists simply consider the likelihood of certain styles of life developing as a result of the client's position within the family. But they do not expect that clients' life styles automatically result from their place in the family constellation (Dewey, 1972; Dinkmeyer et al., 1979).

Early Recollections   From early childhood most adults carry memories that appear to have little importance. According to Adler, however, these seemingly insignificant recollections are an excellent guide to uncovering people's life styles. To Adlerians, *early recollections* encapsulate our present philosophy of life. People remember particular, presumably inconsequential events from childhood because these memories reinforce their basic view of life (Bishop, 1993). Whether these early recollections are of real events or fantasies makes little difference; in either case, our adult lives revolve around what has been perceived in these remembered incidents (see Sidebar 7-3).

Adler contended that people remember those events from their childhood that are consistent with their present views of life (1931). Early memories are extraordinarily significant, then, because they have been preserved for years and thus reveal personality and life style. For Adlerians these memories are "an X-ray into the human mind" (Manaster & Corsini, 1982, p. 188).

Adlerian therapists obtain these early recollections by saying, for example, "Think as far back as you can and tell me your earliest memory from your childhood years." If this fails to elicit a recollection, the therapist may ask clients to close their eyes, think back to their childhood, and describe what they see. Clients may even be coached by being asked to recollect their friends, their school days, or holidays (Nikelly & Verger, 1973). The therapist looks, not for general memories, but for actual recollections: not for, "We used to go to the beach a lot every summer when I was a child"; but for, "I remember traveling across a bridge with my family in a new station wagon."

Since I cannot prove a lover . . . I am determined to prove a villain.
             —Shakespeare

Although Adler insisted that these recollections must be interpreted within the context of each client's life, he found some commonalties. Memories of danger or punishment, for example, might suggest a tendency toward hostility, whereas memories of the birth of a sibling indicate a continued sense of

Sidebar 7-3

VOICES, GLANCES, FLASHBACKS:

OUR FIRST MEMORIES

Patrick Huyghe

The earliest memory that I have is of waking up one morning with blood on my pillow and being extremely frightened."

"I don't remember how old I was, but I distinctly remember the joy of digging both hands into the dirt and stuffing it into my mouth."

"My first memory is of a chocolate birthday cake with white frosting and pink trim, and a little wooden train chugging around it."

Think back, for a moment, to your earliest memory. It is probably not your doctor's hands in the delivery room, or even your precarious first step. More likely, the tantalizing event occurred several years later. Perhaps you recall the birth of a sibling or the death of a family member or pet. Many first memories are of mundane events or images: sitting on the stairs, having a picture taken, eating a bowl of cereal.

That first childhood memory is notoriously hard to pin down. To be certain that you are in fact remembering, you must avoid the influence of family photographs and stories, which you may unintentionally substitute for true memories. While the distinction between memory and memento is easy to understand, in practice it is often hard to make. And even when you do manage to summon up an early experience, you may find it difficult to date accurately.

Or it may not have happened at all. Child psychologist Jean Piaget used to tell of a memory at the age of 2 in which he was nearly kidnapped as his nurse was wheeling him down the street in Paris. His recollection included the fact that the nurse's face was scratched by the kidnap-

pers during the fracas. But when he was in his teens, the nurse confessed that she had fabricated the entire story.

Our earliest childhood memories have a magical quality about them, if for no other reason than their being the apparent beginnings of our conscious lives. These "islands in the sea of oblivion," as the novelist Esther Salaman called them, have fascinated psychologists for more than a century, and their studies of the phenomenon indicate that most people's early memories are remarkably similar on the surface.

"Almost all of our earliest memories are located in the fourth year of life, between the third and fourth birthdays" [italics added], psychologist John Kihlstrom of the University of Wisconsin says. His survey of 314 high school and college students, conducted with Columbia University psychologist Judith Harackiewicz, found that *most early recollections are visual, many in color.* [italics added] Their content, however, varies widely, and seems to fall into three broad categories: trauma, transition and trivia. Other studies have shown that the *first memories of women appear to date back somewhat further than those of men, but the difference, which is no more than a few months, may be due to earlier brain development among girls.* [italics added]

The pioneers of psychoanalysis attached great significance to first memories. Freud believed that they could open the secret chambers of a person's inner life. Alfred Adler, originator of the Individual Psychology school, said, "The first memory will show the individual's fundamental view of life." *Adler believed that childhood memories have a great diagnostic value, regardless of whether they are real or imaginary, because of their unique capacity for revealing a person's attitude toward self, others and life in general.* [italics added]

Continued.

Interestingly, Adler, who conceived of the inferiority complex, had a vivid first memory of sitting on a bench, sidelined by disease, watching his brother play.

In their autobiographies, various public figures show their tendency to fasten onto early experiences that are important to them. Golda Meir's earliest recollection, which she thought might have been a dream, was of a group of Jews being trampled by cossack horses in czarist Russia. The earliest memories of Seymour Papert, the creator of the LOGO computer language for children, center on wheels, mechanical devices and figuring out what things do and how they work. *Albert Einstein remembered receiving a magnetic compass at about the age of 4 or 5 and being awed by the needle's urge to point north.* [italic added]

"Some people think that these early experiences may somehow form personality, and that's why they get remembered," Kihlstrom says, "but I don't think that's right." Do our memories make us, or do we make our memories? "I think that personality leads to selectivity of memory," Kihlstrom says. "People remember things that are consistent with the concept they have of themselves."

Considering the novelty and richness of the first several years of life, it is perhaps surprising that adults have so few early recollections. This apparent amnesia has been a puzzle to psychologists ever since Freud observed it in his patients at the turn of the century.

The phenomenon, which he labeled infantile or childhood amnesia, applies only to our memories about the self, not to our memory for words or recognizable objects and people. Freud believed that we lose contact with most of our autobiographical memories from the first six years because as children, during the Oedipal phase, we repress anxiety-evoking memories of sexuality and aggression. All that remains, he noted, are "screen memories," memories that are totally lacking in feeling.

"Childhood amnesia does exist, but it's not necessarily Oedipal," contends Emory University psychology professor Ulric Neisser. "The child forgets everything about the self, not just sexual or aggressive memories. We begin to remember our life pretty well only from about the age of 5 or 6 because that's when we go to school and develop an organized structure for our lives."

But if schooling does allow children to better encode episodes for later retrieval, it would seem to follow that children who attend nursery school or other prekindergarten schools should have more early memories than those who did not. So far there haven't been any studies, however, to confirm this intriguing hypothesis.

"The evidence that the phenomenon of childhood amnesia even exists is mostly anecdotal," Kihlstrom says. Some people claim to have memories that date back before the age of 3, and most surveys of childhood memories indicate that there is no age when continuous, uninterrupted memories consistently begin. We are simply less likely to retain a memory as more time elapses from the event.

So perhaps what we call childhood amnesia is really no different from normal forgetting. "After all," says David Rubin, a researcher in human memory at Duke University, "childhood was a long time ago, and perhaps the reason we don't remember much of it is because we have just normally forgotten it."

People often assume that they cannot remember anything before about age 3, not because they have forgotten, but because they were incapable of storing memories in the first place. The evidence for this is conflicting. "If you look at a 3- or 4-year-old in action," Neisser says, "you will see a person who remembers quite a lot, in the sense that you can ask a 4-year-old about things that happened the year before and get very intelligent answers. It's not that they have no memory, but when they become 10 or 12 or 20, they don't remember those things much anymore."

Psychologist Marion Perlmutter and her associates at the University of Michigan have been assessing the mnemonic abilities of preschool children in both experimental and naturalistic settings since the mid 1970s. In one study, she and psychologist Christine Todd examined the conversations between young children and adults to determine, among other things, the length of time children could retain information. They found that children between 35 months and 38 months old could remember events that had occurred more than seven-and-a-half months previously. The older children, those between 45 months and 54 months old, recalled episodes that had occurred as much as 14 1/2 months ago.

Perlmutter was particularly impressed by the fact that in some cases the children "demonstrated a verbal recall for events that occurred prior to the time that they were speaking extensively." Her findings contradict some psychologists' long-held notion that children's autobiographical memory develops with language ability.

The study of memory in children who aren't yet speaking relies on the evidence of habituation and other forms of conditioned learning. In a study with psychologist Daniel Ashmead, Perlmutter asked parents to keep a diary recording the actions of their 7-, 9- and 11-month-old infants that revealed the use of memory. "Albert eating lunch," one typical entry reads. "Handed Dorine [the babysitter] his glass. Dorine saw it was empty and filled it. He did the same for me several days ago. Twice during one meal he handed me his glass. Each time it was empty. Each time I filled it."

While all the infants in the study showed some spontaneous memory, such episodes were less frequent among the youngest infants. Perlmutter also found that older infants were more likely to reveal actual memory, rather than to just respond to a familiar environmental cue. "We think that this is evidence of something like recall memory beginning to appear in the older infants," she says.

When a child is between 8 and 12 months old, a change does seem to occur in memory abilities. Some psychologists see the change as a transition from conditioned recognition and response to recall memory, but others, such as Daniel Schacter and Morris Moscovitch of the University of Toronto, suggest that two different memory systems are at work. They refer to these systems as early and late memories.

Schacter and Moscovitch compared the performance of two groups: amnesiacs, who have an impaired memory system, and very young infants, who have not yet fully developed a memory system. They used a simple task that Piaget made famous in 1954. Piaget had observed that 7- to 8-month-old infants can easily find an object when it is hidden at the same location all the time. But after several successful searches at that location, many infants continue to search there even after seeing the object hidden someplace else.

"The amnesiac remembers where you put the object in the first place," Schacter says, "but then gets tripped up when you switch locations, just like the infant." But while amnesiacs continue to make the

Continued.

error, infants stop making it as they approach their first birthday. Schacter thinks that the appearance of a late memory system may explain this improvement. "The neural machinery that underlies the ability to remember the past may be in place within a year of birth. Any further developments in memory are probably the result of building up the knowledge base and integrating this machinery with other cognitive functions."

Studies of visual and auditory memory have shown that even the youngest of infants are consistently more responsive to novel stimuli than to familiar stimuli. These observations have led many psychologists to conclude that infants have a memory capacity from birth.

"Infants are able to encode and retain some information about their visual world from the first hours of life," Perlmutter says. Other researchers have shown that premature infants, with an average gestational age of 35 weeks, can discriminate between novel and familiar stimuli.

Despite evidence for early infant memory, psychologists have been reluctant to date the origins of memory before birth. Prebirth memory remains largely uncharted territory, and even those who willingly concede the possibility that the fetus has the rudimentary capacity to encode experience will cry foul at the claims for prebirth memories.

"On one level the subject is very, very controversial," Rubin explains, "but on another level it's totally dull. Why should the act of birth increase your learning abilities?"

Research by Anthony DeCasper at the University of North Carolina at Greensboro strongly implies the existence of prebirth memory. In his study, a newborn infant could choose to hear a recording of its mother's voice or that of another woman by sucking on a nipple in a particular way.

Infants as young as 30 hours consistently chose their mothers' voices.

It is very likely that they recognized their mothers' voices from what they heard in the womb. As Rubin points out, "The acoustics are there. There are studies in which microphones have been placed in the uterus of sheep and the sound is not muffled as much as you might think."

But in general, claims for birth and prebirth memories are regarded with suspicion by psychologists, most of whom tread more traditional ground in trying to answer the question, "When does autobiographical memory begin?"

Katherine Nelson, a developmental psychologist at the Graduate School of the City University of New York, has studied the question of early memories in connection with "scripts" that children have for familiar events. These scripts refer to the way children have organized their acquired knowledge in terms of general events. According to her theory, children have scripts for such familiar routines as eating dinner at home and going to the supermarket. This script-building appears by age 1, or earlier.

"The drive to build up these scripts seems to come out of a biological need to understand what is going on," Nelson says. "So the child doesn't need language or anything else; all that is needed is the background of experience."

While these scripts help children remember general events, they can also block or override memories of specific experiences. Nelson found that while 3- and 4-year-old children can produce reasonably good general accounts of dinner at home, they have difficulties producing an account of a specific dinner. They will speak about "what happens" rather than "what happened." Perhaps this explains why children insist upon routines, she says.

Nelson speculates that certain memories are lost as children enter specific experiences into their more general scripts. Unique events, like going to the circus, may be more memorable because they haven't been repeated or overridden by other similar experiences. "But after a while, if you don't go to the circus, you will forget about it, because it's not adaptive to hold onto that memory if it's not going to tell you anything about the future," Nelson says.

By the time children are 2 or 3, speech has developed and memory begins to show signs of social construction. "Children are also taught to remember by their parents," Nelson says, "when they say such things as 'Do you remember when we went to the store last week and you said such and such?' So their memory becomes at least partially formulated in terms of language. *At about the age of 3, sig-*

From: *Psychology Today,* September 1985, pp. 48–52.

nificant variations of emotionally involving events begin to create a memory string that is uniquely human and social. That's when auto-biographical memory begins.'' [italics added]

Although Nelson's view of early memory development does not pretend to explain the multitude of phenomena involved in memory, it certainly ties up a lot of loose ends regarding autobiographical memory. If, as she says, memory proceeds from the accumulation of single novel experiences, repeated and built into scripts, and then to unique events capable of being shared, it should be easy to see why we, as adults, cannot remember specific autobiographical memories before about the fourth year of life. Such memories could not form until a significant general base of event knowledge had been established. And this, of course, would take a number of years to build up. The reason that early memories are so elusive may be that the process of gaining autobiographical memories is like other developmental processes, something learned with time.

dethronement. Once Adler asked more than 100 physicians for their early recollections. A majority of them recalled either an illness or a death in the family—most likely a factor that helped to lead them into a career of combating sickness.

The process of collecting early recollections is simple and generally nonthreatening to clients. Most often, clients freely give the therapist as many memories as desired, typically about six. The therapist writes down the recollections and begins to look for specific details and themes connecting each of the memories, especially themes that might illuminate the client's perspective on life (Nikelly & Verger, 1972; Watkins, 1985). Although Adler never suggested that such early memories were the sole determinants of behavior, he found that they provided glimpses into events that helped shape clients' beliefs about life and its demands.

Dreams   Whereas Freud interpreted dreams as wish fulfillments, Adler believed that clients used dreams to rehearse how they might deal with problems in the future. Pointing out that people often could not recall the specific events of a dream but did remember its mood, Adler further suggested that the moods experienced in a dream might set the stage for the next day's activities (Mosak & Dreikurs, 1973). Adler also used dreams as an indicator of therapeutic progress. Whereas brief dreams with little action may reflect a passive approach to dealing with problems, dreams seem to become increasingly active as treatment proceeds and as patients begin to experiment with a more active life style. In fact, some Adlerians use the clients' dreams to guide them in deciding when to terminate therapy (Rosenthal, 1959).

Although Adlerians often use dreams as a therapeutic strategy, they usually use them to confirm observations that have already been made concerning the family constellation and early recollections (Manaster & Corsini, 1982). Because dreams are a manifestation of people's life styles, Adler insisted that they never be interpreted in isolation.

Developing Self-understanding

By asking open-ended questions that allow clients to explore patterns in their lives that have previously gone unnoticed, Adlerian counselors try to help clients develop insight. Since interpreting the answers often takes the form of intuitive guesses, the ability to empathize is especially important. The counselor must be able to sympathize with clients before discovering the reasons for their behavior. At other times, interpretations are based on the counselor's knowledge of ordinal position in the family constellation. However, the Adlerian counselor never puts clients in a position that requires them to accept the therapist's interpretation. The counselor's respect for the clients is never compromised.

I should compare [the pathological person] to a man who tries to put a horse's collar on from the tail end. It is not a sin, but it is a mistaken method.

—Alfred Adler

Through Adlerian counseling, clients come to recognize that faulty ways of thinking have resulted in unrealistic goals and that actions directed toward attaining these goals are self-defeating (Dinkmeyer et al., 1979). Such insight requires both encouragement and confrontation. It is the general tone of encouragement set during the rapport-building stage of therapy that allows the practitioner to confront the clients about their goals and behavior. Only as a result of this confrontation are patients able to gain insight that leads to behavioral change (Dreyfus & Nikelly, 1972).

Reorientation

Adlerian interventions, or helping techniques, are fundamentally action oriented. In early stages of the intervention, the practitioner identifies with and reveals the counselees' failed patterns of thinking, feeling, and acting. Once clients decide on the kind of person they want to become and the kinds of relationships they wish to establish, they can begin to shift from insight to practice. Old patterns of behavior are shed while they become oriented to new, more active ways of being that are especially encouraged in this final phase of therapy. With the help of the practitioner, clients decide what behaviors will help them reach their goals. Often the therapist employs a number of specific techniques that help clients translate their goals into actions.

Asking "The Question"   As one technique the counselor asks, *"What would be different if you were well?"* This question allows clients to cut to the heart of how they want to change. For example, a client might respond by saying, "I would be a husband who doesn't complain as much," "I would quit my job and start a business of my own," or "I would be able to accept my son despite what he has done." Clients are often asked "the question" during the initial stages of therapy, but it is appropriate to ask it at any time.

Paradoxical Intention   Using *paradoxical intention*, therapists encourage their clients to exaggerate, practice, or perform the symptoms or behaviors they are attempting to avoid or overcome. Clients who complain of being unable to sleep, for example, may be instructed to stop trying and to concentrate on remaining awake, and constant nail biters may be instructed to stop once every 2 hours during the day and bite their nails intentionally. Each evening they may be asked to spend at least 3 minutes biting their nails in front of a mirror.

Acting "As If"   Sometimes clients claim they would do thus and so if they had a certain quality or trait. When this occurs, Adlerians often instruct their clients to act *as if* they possess that desired quality, *as if* they were the ideal persons they see in their dreams (Gold, 1979). They may be asked to role-play a situation and act *as if* they are the person they want to become. If clients want to overcome shyness and be more assertive, for example, the counselor might assign them to "act" assertively for 1 day next week. This technique is based on the assumption that clients change behavior when they are able to elicit different responses from others. They learn that change is less hazardous than they have thought and that it may be rewarding.

Spitting in the Client's Soup   Adler borrowed the concept of *spitting in the client's soup* from a dirty practice he witnessed in a private school dining hall. By spitting in their neighbor's soup, boys would obtain a second helping for themselves. In a similar way, this therapeutic strategy involves identifying a certain client behavior and, in doing so, ruining the payoff of the behavior for the client—it is a way of besmirching a clean conscience. For example, a mother who always acts superior to her daughter by undercutting her may continue to do so after the behavior is pointed out, but the reward for doing so has disappeared. Like the boys in the dining hall, clients may continue to eat the soup, but it will never taste the same and they can never enjoy it as much.

Catching Oneself   Another technique, *catching oneself*, allows clients to become aware of self-destructive behaviors or thoughts without guilt. Often, despite people's strong desire to change a behavior, they may revert to old patterns out of sheer habit. Catching oneself allows clients to pause for a moment and consider other ways of responding. At first the counselor may help in the process, but eventually clients take over this responsibility. With practice, clients catch themselves before they fall into self-defeating behavior.

Push Button   The so-called *push-button* technique encourages clients to realize they have choices in responding or reacting to stimuli in their lives. More specifically, it teaches clients they can create desired feelings by choosing what to think about. In this technique, clients picture alternately pleasant and unpleasant experiences and then notice the emotions accompanying these experiences. By concentrating on their thoughts, they recognize that they can create the feelings they desire. The technique is like pushing a mental button because clients can choose to remember negative or positive experiences. Clients leave the session realizing they can push buttons that will either depress or elate them. They are in control (Mosak, 1989).

APPLICATION

Adlerians function in a variety of settings (private practice, in- and outpatient settings, schools) and in a variety of modalities (e.g., one on one, groups, families). The case of "Pablo," cited by Garfinkle, Massey, and Mendel (1986), illustrates many of the most common Adlerian strategies in working with children.

Pablo, 9 years of age and a middle child, had a well-behaved older sister and a very bright younger brother. Pablo's parents were separated and his mother saw in Pablo many aspects of her estranged husband. Her behavior toward Pablo was, needless to say, quite ambivalent, sometimes provocatively loving and at other times very punitive.

From an Adlerian perspective, every child will strive for belonging in a family in the child's own unique way. Pablo's style was to reinforce the identification with his father, since he could not compete with his sister's good behavior or his brother's academic excellence. He tried to find his place by continuously misbehaving at home and in school. He also tried to gain recognition by having headaches, through fears of being alone at night, and by crying frequently. He had no friends because he teased the other children, yet he often felt that they had wronged him. Pablo's life style is one of discouragement about wanting to belong in a socially useful way, so he drifts toward the useless side of life. His basic mistaken conviction is: "Only if I misbehave or am sick will I be noticed and can find my place."

> The Bible gives us many marvelous psychological hints, and the typical second child is beautifully portrayed in the story of Jacob.
>
> —Alfred Adler

Pablo's behavior and his mother's reaction to it were examined in the exploration and interpretation phases of Adlerian counseling. The counselor formed several hypotheses about the reason for Pablo's behavior and presented them to him: "Could it be that you like the extra attention when you have headaches?" Pablo showed little reaction. "Could it be that you get your headaches when you think the work is hard and you're not sure if you can do it?" Pablo smiled with recognition.

Recognizing this nonverbal cue gave the counselor some tentative ideas about the client's private logic. Later in counseling, in the reorientation stage, the counselor suggested that Pablo's mother focus on her son's strengths and assets rather than berate him for his misbehavior. It was reemphasized that Pablo was a discouraged child who needed encouragement to overcome his feelings of inadequacy and, instead of punishing Pablo, she should allow the natural logical consequences of his behavior to flow. For example, if he deliberately sprayed her perfume over the room and spilled her cosmetic lotion, instead of beating him for it, she should teach him how to clean it up and encourage him to replace what had been broken. She could thereby teach Pablo social interest and consideration for others.

A great deal of time was spent discussing alternatives to his having headaches in order to avoid difficult matters. Together with his teacher, the counselor worked out a mutual tutoring program in which he would receive help in reading from a child who would in turn get help from him in math. The teacher also agreed not to call Pablo's mother when he ran out of the room, since that would give him extra attention and would reinforce his attention-getting behavior. As an alternative, she would try to encourage him to cope with his difficulties within the classroom. Pablo was encouraged to stop teasing his classmates and to make new friends. This was illustrated to him through role-playing with the counselor. The focus in the counseling session was on helping Pablo to belong to a peer group through improved social interactions and concern for others.

CRITICAL ANALYSIS

Few theories are more versatile than Adler's. Its strategies have proved useful in working with children, adolescents, parents, entire families, teacher groups, and other segments of society (Kottman & Warlick, 1990; Purkey & Schmidt, 1987). The Adlerian approach has shown promise in treating conduct disorders, antisocial disorders, anxiety disorders, personality disorders, and some affective disorders (Seligman, 1986). The theory's versatility is also seen in its adaptation to other helping theories and to the public's knowledge and understanding of human interaction. Such concepts as freedom, phenomenology, interpretation of events, life scripts, and personal responsibility are found in existential, Gestalt, rational-emotive, transactional analysis, person-centered therapy, and reality counseling or therapy. Adlerian terms, such as *inferiority complex*, have also become a part of the public's vocabulary.

Another strength of Adlerian therapy is the egalitarian prosocial atmosphere it fosters. Of course, Adler shares the stage with Freud in this regard, since Freud also understood the role of narcissism in neurosis. The critical difference, however, is Adler's challenge to battle self-centeredness by choosing to do something for society, choosing to display social interest. In his last book, *Social Interest*, long before World War II and the atom bomb, Adler said that humankind might be doomed unless it developed more social feelings, nationally and internationally, and he warned: "The belief that the cosmos ought to have an interest in the preservation of life is scarcely more than a pious wish" (1964a, p. 272).

Few classical theorists have affirmed the importance of understanding diversity within the context of counseling more than Adler. His schema, for example, serves counselors who integrate multicultural perspectives into a single comprehensive theoretical approach (Nicoll, 1993). And Adler's constructs have been shown to have acculturative power among diverse cultural loyalties (Miranda & White, 1993). Adler strove to bring understanding to an important component of people's heritage as individuals. The extensive convergence of social interest with dominant worldviews suggests that he succeeded (Leak, Gardner, & Pounds, 1992). Along these lines, Adler also viewed religious and spiritual values as a part of the global elements of culture. He proposed that counselors who fail to assess their client's diverse religious values risk overlooking potentially important aspects of the client's cultural background and experience (Bishop, 1992).

Adler's theories continue to impact contemporary clinical issues. For example, how a client might cope with physical disability can be understood within an Adlerian framework. The counselor focuses on how the client's lifestyle notions and goals (how the client's personal meaning is attached to the disability) are contributing to or undermining the acceptance of and adjustment to the disability (Rule, 1984, 1987).

Adlerian psychology's strengths continue to impact today's counselors and, in a sense, Adler's theories are still ahead of their time (Evans, 1991). But, like all theorists of psychotherapy, Adler is not without his critics. Prochaska (1979), for example, questions the very name of Adlerian theory: "It is ironic that Adler called his approach individual psychology when in fact he ultimately values social interests over the interests of the individual" (p. 196).

Adler placed emphasis on practice and teaching instead of on theoretical definitions and organization. As a result, a major difficulty with Adler's work is the lack of systematization in his writings and the vagueness that clouds his constructs. In addition, because he presents so few constructs to explain complex behavior, the application of those constructs, of necessity, is troubled by generalities. Perhaps the vaguest, and therefore most difficult, Adlerian construct to understand is that of the *creative self* or the *creative power*. Although at times it appears to add freedom of choice to the style of life, on other occasions it seems to take on a mystical quality of free will that is totally independent of any prior experiences. The source of this power is unclear. In other words, although Adler's position on the individual's freedom to choose is clear, his explanation of the individual's creative power that permits this freedom is not.

| *There are no "chance memories."*
                   —Alfred Adler

Another limitation of the Adlerian approach to therapy is its lack of a firm research base. For decades, Adlerian therapy has attracted few researchers, the result of which has been a scarcity of empirical studies of either the theory or its effectiveness (Wallace, 1986). In fairness, however, a recent comparison of research about Adlerian therapy between 1982 and 1990 with research reported between 1970 and 1981 shows that research on Adlerian therapy has increased significantly. A number of these studies have served to validate many of Adler's constructs (Wittmer, 1989). For example, research about early recollections, birth order, social interest, and other studies continues to grow (Watkins, 1992). Also, journals devoted to the Adlerian viewpoint, such as the *Journal of Individual Psychology,* are doing much to rectify the need for a sturdier research base.

CURRENT STATUS

Although Adler's approach to counseling is as venerable as psychoanalysis itself, it remains entirely contemporary. Its vitality is not demonstrated by the number of "Adlerian" practitioners, however. A 1982 survey of over 400 clinical and counseling psychologists found that fewer than 3% described themselves as "Adlerians" (Smith, 1982). Nevertheless, Adler's approach to therapy hovers over counseling rooms: his ideas and techniques have been integrated wholesale into other approaches to counseling, and contemporary eclectic practitioners shamelessly incorporate his techniques in their work (Burk, 1989).

Freud's ideas may be the most remembered, but Adler's counseling techniques have been the most practiced. Ironically, upon Freud's death an obituary in the London *Times* gave him credit for the term "inferiority complex," and when Carl Jung died the *New York Times* credited *him* with the term. However, it was neither Freud nor Jung, but Adler who originated the concept and coined the term (Kaufmann, 1980).

Adler greatly influenced humanistic and existential psychology (Frankl, 1970; Maslow, 1970). Abraham Maslow was influenced by Adler's stress on the creative power of the individual in shaping his or her own life, and by his insistence that future goals were more important than past events. "Alfred Adler becomes more and more correct year by year," Maslow once said (1970, p. 13). And existentialists have stressed the importance that Adler gave to an individual's uniqueness (Ansbacher, 1990; Duncan, 1993).

Carl Roger's emphasis on empathy is likewise an outgrowth of Adlerian therapy. The cognitive approaches to behavior therapy also acknowledge a debt to Adler's pioneering work (Elliott, 1992; Ellis, 1970, 1971). And the Adlerian duty of making a contribution to the whole and his emphasis on the role of social interest in countering self-centeredness parallels Erik Fromm's idea of the productive character.

As suggested at the beginning of this chapter, the question is no longer whether one is an Adlerian, but how much of an Adlerian one is (Wilder, 1959). Before Adler's death in 1937, individual psychology had become an international movement with local societies in three dozen nations. Today Adlerian psychology is promoted in America through The North American Society of

Adlerian Psychology (NASAP), a membership society that publishes a quarterly journal and a monthly newsletter and that sponsors an annual convention:

The North American Society of Adlerian Psychology
65 East Wacker Place, Suite 400
Chicago, Illinois 60601-7203
(312) 629-8801

The Adler School of Professional Psychology is an accredited graduate school, offering a Master's in Counseling and a Doctorate in Psychology. A clearing house of Adlerian books and publications, it also provides a mail-order service:

The Adler School of Professional Psychology
656 East Wacker Place, Suite 2100
Chicago, Illinois 60601-7201
(312) 201-5900

The Americas Institute of Adlerian Studies (AIAS) is the postgraduate, professional continuing education provider for counselors:

The Americas Institute of Adlerian Studies (AIAS)
600 North McClurg Court
Suite 2502-A
Chicago, Illinois 60611
(312) 337-5066

AIAS San Diego County
486 Hillway Drive
Vista, California 92084
(619) 758-4658

The AIAS offers three brief courses each year. By completing all three courses along with course requirements, students receive the institute's certification.

CHAPTER SUMMARY

1. *Biography.* Adler (1870–1937) described his childhood as unhappy, growing up with physical and family set backs. At age 25, he received his medical degree from the University of Vienna and soon worked in a neighborhood clinic. After World War I, Adler established guidance clinics for the Vienna school system, where he became convinced of the importance of child-rearing practices. In 1902 Adler was invited to join Freud's discussion group. Adler, however, never considered himself a disciple of Freud, and the two men eventually drifted apart as Adler spoke openly about their differences. Adler, in fact, formed the Society for Individual Psychology and established his own theory of psychotherapy.

2. *Historical Development.* Adler's thinking was influenced greatly by Hans Vaihinger's "as if" principle. Janet also influenced his thinking on the power of

inferiority, while the Nietzschean theory of striving for perfection helped Adler shape his concept of the striving for superiority. And, of course, the greatest influence of Adler's thinking was Sigmund Freud, with whom he collaborated for nearly a decade (1902–1911).

3. *View of Human Nature.* Adler viewed a person as an irreducible whole, thus the term *individual* psychology. Individuals, according to Adler, experience a sense of inferiority and strive to overcome it. This striving for superiority is what turns a deficiency into an advantage. Adler also believed that expectations and goals for the future motivated human activity and provided the capacity for social interest (an intrinsic concern for others), the most important goal toward which people strive.

4. *Development of Maladaptive Behavior.* According to Adler, maladaptive behavior results from discouraging or disappointing circumstances. When people lose the courage to face life's demands directly, they move from a sense of inferiority to an inferiority complex. Pathological behavior, although not always evident until later years, originates in childhood as a result of the family of origin relationships. Being pampered or neglected as a child, for example, contributes to maladaptive behavior because the child will compensate for either error by manifesting unrealistic striving for personal superiority.

5. *Function of the Therapist.* Adlerian therapists often function as educators who attempt to build on strengths the client already demonstrates. Encouragement is critical as the therapist works to establish and maintain an accepting, caring, cooperative relationship with the client. The work of therapy is viewed as collaborative, where the client and the counselor are partners, working toward mutually agreed-upon and clearly identified goals. In short, the Adlerian counselor's energy is invested not in analysis, but in encouragement.

6. *Goals of Therapy.* Adlerian therapy seeks to decrease a sense of inferiority in clients and help them encase their social interest. By helping people to contribute, by altering faulty motivations that underlie even acceptable behavior, by encouraging equality, Adlerians seek to change the life styles, the perceptions, and the goals of their clients.

7. *Major Methods and Techniques.* The most common therapeutic techniques of Adlerian therapy include investigating the client's life style (basic orientation toward life). This is done systematically by exploring "three entrance gates to mental life." The first of these is birth order, which examines one's position within the family and the expectations and roles that typically result from it. The second is early recollections, which encapsulate one's present philosophy of life. And the third is dreams, which, in Adler's view, serve to rehearse how one might deal with problems in the future.

8. *Application.* Many of the most common Adlerian strategies can be seen clearly when working with children. The case of "Pablo," a 9-year-old middle child, is such an example. Together with Pablo's teacher, the counselor worked

to focus the counseling session on helping Pablo to belong to a peer group through improved social interactions and concern for others.

9. *Critical Analysis.* Adlerian therapy's versatility is evident. It has been proved to work with a wide variety of populations. Its impact on other counseling approaches is also very noteworthy. Its emphasis on egalitarian, prosocial ideals is another plus. Few classical theorists have affirmed the importance of understanding diversity within the context of counseling more than Adler. However, Adlerian theory has been criticized for placing practice and teaching over definition and organization. As a result, a major difficulty with Adler's theory is the lack of systematization in his writings and the vagueness that clouds his constructs. Another limitation is its lack of a firm research base.

10. *Current Status.* Although the number of "Adlerian" practitioners is not staggering, this approach to therapy is integrated to some degree or another into many of today's counseling approaches. Adler has had a tremendous impact on today's counselors and specialized centers of learning continue to promote his methods and strategies with upcoming practitioners.

KEY TERMS

Birth Order   One's position in the family constellation (first-born, second-born, etc.). To Adler, it was a major factor in the development of personality.

Compensation   A motivation to overcome real or imagined inferiority, to strive for higher levels of development through effort and practice.

Creative Power of the Self   The ability of the individual to create an appropriate style of life.

Early Recollections   A therapeutic assessment technique in which a person's earliest memories are assumed to reveal the individual's primary interest in life.

Fictional Finalism   The idea that there is an imagined or potential goal that guides an individual's behavior because he or she act "as if" it were true.

Individual Psychology   The theory of counseling and method of diagnosis and treatment formulated by Alfred Adler.

Inferiority Complex   A condition that develops when an individual is unable to compensate for normal inferiority feelings. It is characterized by exaggerated feelings of weakness, including the belief that one cannot overcome one's difficulties through appropriate effort.

Inferiority Feelings   The source of human striving that is the normal condition of all people.

Life Style   A unique character structure, or a pattern of personal behaviors and characteristics, by which an individual strives for perfection. Four basic styles of life are the dominant, getting, avoiding, and socially useful types.

Masculine Protest   Behavior motivated by objections to the belief that society regards men as superior to women. It may occur in males or females.

Neglect   Failing to give a child sufficient care and attention, thereby creating the belief that the world is a cold and unfriendly place.

Organ Inferiority   A significant physiological defect, usually of unknown cause, that can trigger strong feelings of inferiority.

Pampering   Also known as "spoiling," pampering is giving a child excessive attention and protection, thereby preventing the development of initiative and independence and creating the impression that the world owes one a living.

Social Interest   The innate potential of all individuals to cooperate with other people to achieve personal and societal goals.

Striving for Superiority   The urge toward perfection or completion, the ultimate goal that motivates the individual. Healthy strivings are guided by social interest, whereas pathological strivings ignore the welfare of others.

Superiority Complex   A condition that develops when an individual overcompensates for normal inferiority feelings. It is a false feeling of power and security that invariably concerns an underlying inferiority complex

Teleological   From the Greek *tele,* meaning *far* or *distant,* an adjective indicating the goal-directedness of human behavior.

SUGGESTED READING

Dinkmeyer, D., Pew, W., & Dinkmeyer, D. (1979). *Adlerian counseling and psychotherapy.* Belmont, CA: Wadsworth.

Orgler, H. (1963). *Alfred Adler, the man and his work: Triumph over the inferiority complex.* New York: Horace Liveright.

Stepansky, P. E. (1983). *In Freud's shadow: Adler in context.* New York: Analytic Press.

Sperber, M. (1974). *Masks of loneliness: Alfred Adler in perspective.* New York: Macmillan.

Sweeney, T. (1981). *Adlerian counseling, proven concepts and strategies* (2nd ed.). Muncie, IN: Accelerated Development.

REFERENCES

Adler, A. (1907/1964). Organic inferiority and its compensation. In H. L. Ansbacher & R. R. Ansbacher (Eds.), *The individual psychology of Alfred Adler.* New York: Harper.

Adler, A. (1926). *The Neurotic Constitution.* Freeport: Books for Libraries Press.

Adler, A. (1930) Individual Psychology. In C. Murchison (Ed.). *Psychologies of 1930.* Worcester: Clark University Press.

Adler, A. (1931). *What life should mean to you.* Boston: Little Brown.

Adler, A. (1937). Position in family constellation influences life style. *International Journal of Individual Psychology, 3,* 211–227.

Adler, A. (1959). *The practice and theory of individual psychology.* Totowa, NJ: Littlefield-Adams.

Adler, A. (1964a). *Social interest: A challenge to mankind.* New York: Capricorn.

Adler, A. (1964b). *Problems of neurosis.* New York: Harper & Row.

Adler, A., & Deutsch, D. (1959) *Essays in individual psychology*. New York: Grove Press.

Ansbacher, H. L. (1983). Individual psychology. In R. J. Corsini & A. J. Marsella (Eds.), *Personality theories, research and assessment*. Itasca, IL.: F.E. Peacock.

Ansbacher, H. L. (1990). Alfred Adler's influence on the three leading cofounders of humanistic psychology. *Journal of Humanistic Psychology, 30,* 45–53.

Ansbacher, H. L. (1992). Alfred Adler, pioneer in prevention of mental disorders. *Individual Psychology: Journal of Adlerian Theory, Research and Practice, 48,* 3–34.

Ansbacher, H. L., & Ansbacher, R. (Eds.). (1956). *The individual psychology of Alfred Adler*. New York: Basic Books.

Barry, H., & Blane, H. T. (1977). Birth order of alcoholics. *Journal of Individual Psychology, 62,* 62–79.

Bishop, D. R. (1992). Religious values as cross-cultural issues in counseling. *Counseling and Values, 36,* 179–191.

Bishop, D. R. (1993). Applying psychometric principles to the clinical use of early recollections. *Individual Psychology: Journal of Adlerian Theory, Research and Practice, 49,* 153–165.

Bohmer, P., & Sitton, S. (1993). The influence of birth order and family size on notable American women's selection of careers. *The Psychological Record, 43,* 375–380.

Brink, T. (1985). Individual psychology. In D. Benner (Ed.), *Baker encyclopedia of psychology* (pp. 568–573). Grand Rapids, MI: Baker Books.

Burk, J. F. (1989). *Contemporary approaches to psychotherapy and counseling: The self-regulation and maturity model*. Pacific Grove, CA: Brooks/Cole.

Byrd, B., DeRosa, A. P., & Craig, S. S. (1993). The adult who is an only child: Achieving separation or individuation. *Psychological Reports, 73,* 171–177.

Claxton, R. P. (1994). Empirical relationships between birth order and two types of parental feedback. *The Psychological Record, 44,* 475–487.

Corsini, R. J., & Wedding, D. (1989). *Current psychotherapies* (4th ed.). Itasca, IL: F. E. Peacock.

Curtis, J. M., & Cowell, D. R. (1993). Relation of birth order and scores on measures of pathological narcissism. *Psychological Reports, 72,* 311–315.

Dewey, E. A. (1972). Family atmosphere. In A. G. Nikelly (Ed.), *Techniques for behavior change* (pp. 41–48). Springfield, IL: Charles C Thomas.

Dinkmeyer, D., Dinkmeyer, D., Jr., & Sperry, L. (1987). *Adlerian counseling and psychotherapy* (2nd ed.). Columbus, OH: Charles Merrill.

Dinkmeyer, D., & Dreikurs, R. (1963). *Encouraging children to learn*. New York: Hawthorn Books.

Dinkmeyer, D., & Losoncy, L. E. (1980). *The encouragement book: Becoming a positive person*. Englewood Cliffs, NJ: Prentice-Hall.

Dinkmeyer, D., Pew, W., & Dinkmeyer, D. (1979). *Adlerian counseling and psychotherapy*. Monterey, CA: Wadsworth.

Dreikurs, R. (1971). *Social equality: The challenge of today*. Chicago: Henry Regnery.

Dreyfus, E. A. & Nikelly, A. G. (1972). Existential–humanism in Adlerian psychotherapy. In A. G. Nikelly (Ed.), *Techniques for behavior change* (pp. 13–20). Springfield, IL: Charles C Thomas.

Duncan, L. (1993). A contextual theory of counseling. *TCA Journal, 21,* 55–68.

Ellenberger, H. (1970). *The discovery of the unconscious: The history and evolution of dynamic psychiatry*. New York: Basic Books.

Elliott, J. E. (1992). Compensatory buffers, depression, and irrational beliefs. *Journal of Cognitive Psychotherapy, 6,* 175–184.

Ellis, A. (1970). Tribute to Alfred Adler. *Journal of Individual Psychology, 26,* 11–12.

Ellis, A. (1971). Reason and emotion in the individual psychology of Adler. *Journal of Individual Psychology, 27*, 50–64.

Evans, T. D. (1991). How far can you go and still be Adlerian? *Individual Psychology: Journal of Adlerian Theory, Research and Practice, 47*, 541–547.

Forer, L. (1977). Bibliography of birth order literature in the '70s. *Journal of Individual Psychology, 33*, 122–141.

Frankl, V. E. (1970). Fore-runner to existential psychiatry. *Journal of Individual Psychology, 26*, 38.

Freud, S. (1914). *On narcissism: An introduction.* London: Hogarth Press.

Furtmuller, C. (1964). Alfred Adler: A biographical essay. In H. L. Ansbacher & R. R. Ansbacher (Eds.), *Superiority and social interest* (pp. 177–181). Evanston, IL: Northwestern University Press.

Garfinkle, M. I., Massey, R. F., & Mendel, E. (1987). Two cases in Adlerian child therapy. In G. S. Belkin (Ed.), *Contemporary Psychotherapies*, (2nd ed.). Monterey, CA: Brooks/Cole.

Gates, L., Lineberger, M. R., Crockett, J, & Hubbard, J. (1988). Birth order and its relationship to depression, anxiety, and self-concept test scores in children. *Journal of Genetic Psychology, 149*, 29–34.

Gold, L. (1979). Adler's theory of dreams: An holistic approach to interpretation. In B. B. Wolman (Ed.), *Handbook of dreams: Research, theories, and applications* (pp. 91–103). New York: Litton.

Kaplan, H. B. (1986). A guide for explaining social interest to laypersons. *Journal of Individual Psychology.*

Kaufman, W. (1980). *Discovering the mind: Vol. 3. Freud versus Adler and Jung.* New York: McGraw-Hill.

Kottman, T., & Warlick, J. (1990). Adlerian play therapy. *Journal of Humanistic Education and Development, 28*, 125–132.

Leak, G. K., Gardner, L. E., & Pounds, B. (1992). A comparison of Eastern religion, Christianity, and social interest. *Individual Psychology: Journal of Adlerian Theory, Research and Practice, 48*, 53–64.

Manaster, G. J., & Corsini, R. J. (1982). *Individual psychology: Theory and practice.* Itasca, IL: F. E. Peacock.

Maslow, A. (1970). Tribute to Alfred Adler. *Journal of Individual Psychology, 26*, 13.

McGuire, W. (Ed.). (1974). *The Freud/Jung letters.* Princeton, NJ: Princeton University Press.

Miller, N., & Maruyama, G. (1976). Ordinal position and peer popularity. *Journal of Personality and Social Psychology, 33*, 123–131.

Miranda, A. O., & White, P. E. (1993). The relationship between acculturation level and social interest among Hispanic adults. *Individual Psychology: Journal of Adlerian Theory, Research and Practice, 49*, 76–85.

Mosak, H. (1971). Lifestyle. In A. G. Nikelly (Ed.), *Techniques for behavior change* (pp. 77–81). Springfield, IL: Charles C Thomas.

Mosak, H. (Ed.) (1973). *Alfred Adler: His influence on psychology today.* Park Ridge, NJ: Noyes Press.

Mosak, H. (1989). Adlerian psychotherapy. In R. Corsini (Ed.), *Current psychotherapies* (3rd, ed.), (pp. 65–116). Itasca, IL: F. E. Peacock.

Mosak, H. (1991). "I don't have social interest": Social interest as construct. *Individual Psychology: Journal of Adlerian Theory, Research and Practice, 47*, 309–320.

Mosak, H., & Dreikurs, R. (1973). Adlerian psychotherapy. In R. Corsini (Ed.), *Current psychotherapies* (pp. 35–83). Itasca, IL: F. E. Peacock.

Moschetta, P. V. (1993). Encouraging social interest between married partners. *Individual Psychology: Journal of Adlerian Theory, Research and Practice, 49*, 399–405.

Mullis, F. J., Kern, R. M., & Curlette, W. L. (1987). Life-style themes and social interest: A further factor analytic study. *Individual Psychology, 43*, 339–352.

Narayan, C. (1990). Birth order and narcissism. *Psychological Reports, 67*, 1184–1186.

Nicoll, W. G. (1993). Multiple Systems Counseling: An integrative and extension of Adlerian and systems theories. *Individual Psychology: Journal of Adlerian Theory, Research and Practice, 49*, 132–152.

Nikelly, A. G. (1971). Fundamental concepts of maladjustment. In A. G. Nikelly (Ed.), *Techniques for behavior change* (pp. 27-32). Springfield, IL: Charles C Thomas.

Nikelly, A. G., & Dinkmeyer, D. (1972). The process of encouragement. In A. G. Nikelly (Ed.), *Techniques for behavior change* (pp. 97–101). Springfield, IL: Charles C Thomas.

Nikelly, A. G., & Verger, G. (1973). Current Adlerian Therapies. *Comprehensive Psychiatry.* (Vol. 14) (pp. 41–48).

O'Connell, W. E. (1965). Humanistic identification: A new translation for Gemeinschaftsgefuhl. *Journal of Individual Psychology, 21*, 44–47.

Orgler, H. (1963). *Alfred Adler, the man and his work: Triumph over the inferiority complex.* New York: Horace Liveright.

Parrott, L. (1992). Earliest recollections and birth order: Two Adlerian exercises. *Teaching of Psychology, 19(1)*, 40–42.

Perlin, M., & Grater, H. (1984). The relationship between birth order and reported interpersonal behavior. *Journal of Individual Psychology, 40*, 22–28.

Prochaska, J. O. (1979). *Systems of psychotherapy: A transtheoretical analysis.* Homewood, IL: Dorsey Press.

Purkey, W. W., & Schmidt, J. J. (1987). *The inviting relationship.* Englewood Cliffs, NJ: Prentice-Hall.

Roazen, P. (1975). *Freud and his followers.* New York: Alfred Knopf.

Rosenthal, H. R. (1959). The final dream: A criterion for the termination of therapy. In A. Adler & D. Deutsch (Eds.), *Essays in individual psychology* (pp. 400–409). New York: Grove Press.

Rule, W. (Ed.). (1984). *Lifestyle counseling for adjustment to disability.* Rockville, MD: Aspen Systems.

Rule, W. R. (1987). Acceptance and adjustment to disability: An Adlerian orientation. In G. L. Gandy, E. D. Mertin, R. E. Hardy, & J. G. Cull (Eds.), *Rehabilitation counseling and services: Profession and process* (pp. 219–233). Springfield, IL: Charles C Thomas.

Seligman, L. (1986). *Diagnosis and treatment planning in counseling.* New York: Human Sciences Press.

Shulman, B. H., & Mosak, H. M. (1977). Birth order and ordinal position: Two Adlerian views. *Journal of Individual Psychology, 33*, 114–121.

Shulman, B. H., & Nikelly, A. G. (1972). Family constellation. In A. G. Kikelly (Ed.), *Techniques for behavior change* (pp. 35–40). Springfield, IL: Charles C Thomas.

Smith, D. (1982). Trends in counseling and psychotherapy. *American Psychologist, 37*, 802–809.

Stepansky, P. E. (1983). *In Freud's shadow: Adler in context.* New York: Analytic Press.

Stone, M. (1993). Balancing the self with the marital system. *Individual Psychology: Journal of Adlerian Theory, Research and Practice, 49*, 392–398.

Vaihinger, H. (1935). *The psychology of "as if": A system of the theoretical, practical and religious fictions of mankind.* New York: Harcourt, Brace & World.

Wallace, W. A. (1986). *Theories of counseling and psychotherapy.* Boston: Allyn & Bacon.

Watkins, C. E., Jr. (1985). Early recollections as a projective technique in counseling: An Adlerian view. *American Mental Health Counselors Association Journal, 7*, 32–40.

Watkins, C. E., Jr. (1992). Research activity with Adler's theory. *Individual Psychology: Journal of Adlerian Theory, Research and Practice, 48*, 107–108.

Wilder J. (1959). Alfred Adler's influence. In K. Adler, & D. Deutsch (Eds.), *Essays in individual psychology.* New York: Grove Press.

Wittmer, J. M. (1989). Reaching toward wholeness. In Sweeney, T. J. (Ed.), *Adlerian counseling: A practical approach for a new decade* (3rd ed.) (pp. 32–40). Muncie, IN: Accelerated Development.

CHAPTER 8

Existential Therapy

Chapter Outline

Introduction
Brief Biography
Historical Development
View of Human Nature
Development of Maladaptive Behavior
Function of the Therapist
Goals of Therapy
Major Methods and Techniques
Application
Critical Analysis
Current Status
Chapter Summary
Key Terms
Suggested Reading

INTRODUCTION

Midway through the 20th century, psychotherapy encountered a puzzling phenomenon. Although social mores had become more permissive than those of the Victorian era, this new liberalism did not seem to alleviate conflicts between the id and superego. Supposedly liberated by the sexual revolution, people were entering psychotherapy in increasing numbers. Suffering from the inability to enjoy their new freedom and self-expression, they were struck with a sense of alienation, emptiness, and self-estrangement. They yearned for meaning and purpose, and sought solutions in the offices of their therapists.

Existentialism, which concerned itself with the essence of inner being— with *ontology*, the science of being—promised an answer. Moving away from attempts to recover an unconscious personal past (May & Yalom, 1995), it gave focus to living productively in the present and held out hope for a spiritual awakening, a restoration of the meaning of life (Becker, 1973; Bugental, 1978).

On the other hand, existential therapy is said to be "plagued by a lack of consistency, coherency, and scrutiny" (Norcross, 1987, p. 41) Since existentialists cannot agree on a theory that fully articulates their ideas, existential thera-

pists approach their profession in a variety of ways. And, in fact, existentialism does not lend itself to neatly defined models of personality, causes of maladaptive behavior, or treatment strategies. In addition to this criticism, Yalom notes that existential

The meaning of life always changes but it never ceases to be.

—Victor Frankl

therapy is like "a homeless waif who was not permitted into the better academic neighborhoods" (1980, p. 14). Despite outward diversity and the resistance of academia, existential therapists continue to influence many systems of counseling.

BRIEF BIOGRAPHY

Today the existential approach to counseling is represented by a number of different theorists (e.g., Boss, 1963; Kaam, 1967; Sartre, 1953, 1956), but it began with the work of Ludwig Binswanger (1958), a Swiss psychiatrist. Although Binswanger was the first to realize the possibilities of applying the philosophy of existentialism to his day-to-day counseling practice, it was Rollo May, another theorist, who enlarged upon and popularized the work of his predecessor.

Born on April 21, 1909, May was the eldest son of Earl and Matie May, who named him after Little Rollo, a character in a series of 19th-century children's books. Growing up in the small town of Ada, Ohio, May grew to detest the name. Throughout his childhood, Little Rollo's exploits in literature were presented to May as the model for proper conduct in life. It was no accident that his father, who valued exercise, subjected his son to a strict regimen of swimming and character building. May's intense dislike for his name remained with him until, as a young adult living in Europe, he learned about a medieval Norman ruler named Rollo the Conqueror (Rabinowitz, Good, & Cozad, 1989).

Since his father was a field secretary for the YMCA, May's family moved from Ohio to Michigan, and it was here that May enrolled at Michigan State College in East Lansing. He and a friend founded a campus magazine, *The Student*, and published an editorial charging the state legislature with using the college to conceal unscrupulous methods for gaining profit. Anticipating dismissal, May left Michigan State and set out for Oberlin College in Ohio. After a brief conference with Oberlin's dean, May was admitted without formal application. With a major in English and minor in Greek history and literature, May received his B.A. degree in 1930.

Despite his lack of proficiency in Greek, May was offered a teaching position at Anatolia College in Salonika, Greece. He accepted the appointment and

Rollo May (1909–1994).
(Bernard Gotfryd/Woodfin Camp & Associates)

held the post for 3 years. During two summer vacations May visited Vienna, where he worked as a secretary for the International School of Art, studied painting in his free time, and—more significantly for our purposes—enrolled in seminars conducted by Alfred Adler. It was these summer visits to Vienna that marked the beginning of May's interest in psychotherapy.

In 1933 May returned to the United States and enrolled in Union Theological Seminary in New York in order to enter the ministry. Following the divorce of his parents, he withdrew from seminary after his first year to support his younger brothers and sisters in Michigan. Eventually returning to Union, he completed his studies under the German philosopher Paul Tillich, who, like Adler, strongly influenced May's thinking. In 1938 May graduated *cum laude* with a Bachelor of Divinity degree.

May began his ministry in a Congregational parish in Verona, New Jersey. His 2 years as pastor were disappointing, and he soon enrolled in Columbia

University to major in clinical psychology. His studies were cut short, however, by a bout with tuberculosis. Faced with an even chance of surviving, May entered a sanitarium on Saranac Lake in upstate New York, where he remained for 18 months, and it was here that his struggle with the realities of death reinforced his existential leanings. He was especially impressed with Kierkegaard's explanation of anxiety as the result of a threat to one's being. He learned from this experience that he alone had to decide whether he lived or died.

Although not fully recovered, May completed his Ph.D. at Columbia in 1949 at the age of 40 years. May's doctoral dissertation, "The Meaning of Anxiety," was a prophetic work. After comparing and synthesizing the existing theories of anxiety, May challenged the popular view that life without anxiety is healthy and argued that anxiety is not only normal but essential to the human condition. His dissertation was published in 1950, and 5 years later the New York Society of Clinical Psychology recognized his distinguished contribution to the profession and science of psychology. Throughout his career May published, among other works, *Existential Psychology* (1961), *Psychology and the Human Dilemma* (1966), *Man's Search for Himself* (1967a), *Love and Will* (1969), *Power and Innocence* (1972), and *The Courage to Create* (1975). He was a visiting professor at Harvard (1965), Princeton (1967), and Yale (1972), and lived out his later years in the San Francisco area, where he wrote about the meaning of myths for modern society. May died of congestive heart failure in October of 1994 in his home.

An achievement is a bondage. It obliges one to a higher achievement.
—Albert Camus

HISTORICAL DEVELOPMENT

As a philosophical movement, existentialism developed in continental Europe during the 19th century from the work of the philosophers Søren Kierkegaard and Friedrich Nietzsche. Although its roots are philosophical, its tenor is often poetic. "Some vision of the good, the true, and the beautiful is essential to a meaningful personal life and a humanistic society" (Partenheimer, 1990, p. 44).

Søren Kierkegaard (1813–1855) lived almost his entire life in Copenhagen. When he was 22, Kierkegaard learned to his dismay that his father had not only cursed God but had seduced his mother before marrying her as well. So deeply did these revelations disturb Kierkegaard, that he referred to them in his writings as "the great earthquake."

Partially in response to this crisis, Kierkegaard's many books came to explore the very nature of religious faith—more specifically, the very meaning of Christianity. Arguing that religious beliefs could not be supported by rational argument, Kierkegaard believed that true faith was essentially irrational. At its heart, Christianity demands that the believer accept the "absurd": the logical impossibility of God, who is infinite and immortal, being born on earth in Jesus Christ, who was finite and mortal. Religious faith could not be achieved by an objective examination of the evidence, Kierkegaard argued, but only by a subjective choice, by a so-called "leap of faith." God wants us not to argue *for* Him, but to be obedient *to* Him. Kierkegaard also stressed the virtues of individuality, freedom, responsibility, honesty, and commitment.

Kierkegaard's emphasis on such a subjective commitment provided a provocative stimulus for later counseling theorists (Dopson & Gade, 1981). Although Kierkegaard did not call his philosophy "existentialism"—the term would be applied to his work only some years after his death—he did insist that each person carves out his or her own destiny and that being is the product of action. When existentialism finally took hold as a distinct philosophical movement some 70 years after his death, it was on this framework that all later existentialist thinking was built.

The son and grandson of Protestant ministers, the German philosopher Friedrich Nietzsche (1844–1900) was nevertheless highly skeptical of religion. In *Thus Spake Zarathustra* he proclaimed, "God is dead," which became a popular theological slogan of the 1960s after an Episcopalian bishop wrote a book by that title. Unlike Kierkegaard, Nietzsche believed religion had lost its hold upon people and could no longer serve as the reference point for moral values. The time had come, he said, for people to examine critically their traditional values, which were based on fear and resentment. Associating these values with the Judeo-Christian tradition, Nietzsche repeatedly criticized Christianity in his book *The Antichrist* (1895).

Soren Kierkegaard (1813–1855).
(Corbis-Bettmann)

Friedrich Nietzsche (1844–1900).
(Corbis-Bettmann)

Nietzsche boasted that he was one of the few philosophers who was also a psychologist. His goal and ideal was the passionate individual who learned to control unruly passions and use them in art or in other creative endeavors. So completely should such people accept and love their own lives, Nietzsche believed, that they would choose to relive them, with all of their joys and sufferings, an infinite number of times. In 1889 Nietzsche suffered a mental breakdown from which he never recovered.

Kierkegaard and Nietzsche introduced existential thought to Western Europe. It was their work that established the footing for several influential philosophers, including the French writers Albert Camus, Jean-Paul Sartre, and Gabriel Marcel; the German philosophers Karl Jaspers and Martin Heidegger; the Russian religious and political thinker Nicolas Berdyaev; and the Jewish philosopher Martin Buber (see Sidebar 8-1).

Sidebar 8-1

I AND THOU

In his mid-20s, Martin Buber (1878–1965) began to study Hasidism and wrote prolifically on the philosophy of dialogue and human interaction. *I and Thou* became the title of his best known book, which was originally published in 1923. In this work, and as further developed and amplified

Martin Buber (1878–1965).
(AP/Wide World)

in his later writings, Buber distinguishes between the I–Thou and I–It relationships. The I–Thou relationship is one of mutuality and openness between being and being. The I–It is the contrasting concept, which refers to relations in which ingenuine dialogue takes place and another person is used to satisfy one's own needs.

In therapeutic relations Buber's account of I–Thou allows the greatest opportunity for profound psychological transformation. When one allows the I–Thou relationship to occur, it can have a pervasive influence in one's life: an "air" of continuous conversation develops; freedom for otherness and difference emerges; one has a sense of the limits of autonomy and identity; one trusts communication and experiences freedom from the ultimate claims of possessions. No matter how alienated one feels in the immediate environment, nonalienated trust moves one's soul.

Buber's description of I–Thou means that the psyche is founded in a nonpersonal relatedness that is religious in meaning and that creates psychological well-being through a decentering of the self.

VIEW OF HUMAN NATURE

As the radically divergent approaches of even Kierkegaard and Nietzsche suggest, existentialism is alternately religious, atheistic, and antireligious. It emphasizes hope and optimism, as well as despair and nothingness. Whereas some of its practitioners revel in its philosophical roots, still others are compelled by the therapeutic outcomes of clinical cases (Pervin, 1960). In short, existentialists do not agree on a basic view of human nature (Cogswell, 1993; Kobasa & Maddi, 1977; Maddi, 1980; Pervin, 1960). Despite its diverse interpretations, however, common threads run throughout all existential perspectives on counseling.

The central focus of existentialism is on the essence of *existence*—on the phenomena that are inherent in the very nature of being alive. Almost every existentialist believes we face important and difficult decisions, and that the quality of these decisions is limited by our knowledge and by the frames of reference in which these decisions are made (May, 1991). It is this existential predicament that lies at the heart of the human condition. Existentialists believe that life is either fulfilled or constricted by a series of decisions that we make, with no way of knowing conclusively what the correct choices are. Continually we must decide what is true and what is false, what is right and what is wrong, which beliefs to accept and which to reject, what to do and what not to do (Kaam, 1969, Tillich, 1952).

I don't like religion much, and I am glad that in the Bible the word is not to be found.

—Martin Buber

Despite the importance of these decisions, existentialists believe there are no objective standards or rules to guide us in making decisions. Because different sources supply conflicting advice, we cannot turn to any specific source for direction. Although each of us, as a result, must decide which standards to accept and which to reject, from another point of view each of us has the need and the ability to make crucial choices. "I prefer to live in a world in which man has the right to make choices, even if they are wrong choices," Frankl writes, "rather than in a world in which no choice at all is left to him" (1967a, p. 13).

In the absence of external standards, laws, ethical rules, or traditions, existentialists believe these choices must be made. From the point of view of the so-called *phenomenological* or "here-and-now" perspective, such human choice is wholly subjective. Existentialists, then, emphasize experience as the primary phenomenon in the study of human nature. Both theoretical explanations and overt behavior are secondary to experience itself and its meaning to the person (Owen, 1992).

Only when individuals have learned to make choices and to live with the consequences are they truly free. But, because they freely choose, individuals are also fully *responsible* for their choices. Responsibility is the mirror image of such freedom, the opposite side of the coin. Forced to make choices for themselves, individuals have both freedom and congruent responsibility thrust upon them. As a result they are, in the words of Jean Paul Sartre (1953), "condemned to be free."

Responsibility is the burden that freedom bears. When individuals realize they are completely responsible for their decisions, actions, and beliefs, they are overcome by anxiety. By ignoring or denying their freedom to escape the concomitant responsibility, they attempt to escape this anxiety. But since this rejection actually denies their circumstance, they succeed only in self-deception. Fugitives from freedom are not free, only self-deceived. Existentialists insist that individuals must accept full responsibility for their behavior, no matter how difficult. If people are to live meaningfully and authentically, they must become fully aware of the reality of the human situation and courageously accept it. They must come to terms with being not only of the world but with "being-in-the-world."

"Being human means being engaged and entangled in a situation," writes Frankl. "'Being-in-the-world' is to be confronted with a world whose objectivity and reality is in no way diminished by the subjectivity of that 'being' who is in the world" (1967b, p. 138). In short, the objectivity of the world does not impinge on the subjective nature of humankind.

Death, or nonbeing, is also significant to an existential understanding of human nature, for we live on two levels: in a state of forgetfulness of being and in a state of mindfulness of being (Heidegger, 1962). To live in the former state is to live in continual distraction and diversion and thus to be wholly unaware of oneself. It is to be preoccupied with things, abstractions, and diversions. In the latter state, however, individuals are continually aware of being—continually in touch with existence and the world of being. Although this living in awareness of being produces authenticity, it is also fraught with anxiety, which increases when individuals confront the reality of nonbeing or death. An extraordinary sense of accountability is initiated with the realization of death, which urges them on to greater fulfillment or authenticity. In fact, in many ways any experience that diminishes individuality or identity is an anticipation of death, which in turn challenges people to live a fuller, more authentic existence.

Rejecting the concept of causality, Ludwig Binswanger (1963) and Medard Boss (1963, 1977) represent many existentialists' further concentration on *Dasein*—"being there." In a so-called *Daseinsanalysis*—that is, the analysis of our immediate experience—the existentialist therapist will focus on the three levels in which we exist: the *Umwelt*, the physical environment of animate and inanimate objects; the *Mitwelt*, the social environment; and finally the *Eigenwelt*, the inner feelings or our "own world." Together these three levels of existence constitute *Dasein*.

In other words, the existential therapist does not analyze human motivation in terms of past events. It is *Dasein* that motivates us, that offers us possibilities which draw us forward. If we are truly authentic, we take responsibility, make choices, free ourselves from domination, and approach our ultimate potential. Failure to be free causes anxiety, and our *Dasein* contracts. Although existentialists do not talk about stages of development, they do believe that *Dasein* develops over time: they do believe that we become free of the influence of others. This is what brings us to true existence.

Rollo May (1961) has proposed six essential characteristics that constitute the nature of an authentic person:

1. Humans are centered in themselves. Anxiety is only one method the individual uses to protect his or her own center of existence.
2. Humans are typically in a state of anxiety, in a struggle against that which would destroy their being.
3. Humans are self-affirming; they need to preserve their centers. The preservation of this center requires will.
4. Humans can move from centeredness to participation with other beings, but this movement involves risk.
5. Awareness lies on the subjective side of centeredness. Persons are able to be subjectively aware of that with which they are in contact.
6. Self-consciousness is a form of awareness, of knowledge of external dangers and threats, that is unique to human beings. Consciousness has to do with our experience with ourselves as subjects who have a world (1961).

And Frankl (1963) adds a seventh characteristic to May's description of the "existing person":

7. The primary force in our lives is a search for meaning. Each person must have a unique and specific meaning, one that can be fulfilled by that person alone. Our striving toward existence requires will (see Sidebar 8-2).

DEVELOPMENT OF MALADAPTIVE BEHAVIOR

The existential therapist believes that if we fail to live in a state of awareness of our being, even at the risk of anxiety, we will inevitably collapse into maladaptive behavior. But instead of directly confronting and dealing with anxiety, we sometimes lie to ourselves (Stevens, Pfost, & Potts, 1990). We don't want to believe the nature of our predicament, and we attempt to manipulate others into supporting our self-deception. When this occurs, the result is maladaptive behavior (Westman, 1992).

From the point of view of existential psychologists, then, psychopathology is a difference not in degree but in kind, and they consider traditional nomenclature, including diagnostic labels, to be alienating and depersonalizing. From an existential perspective, healthy people enjoy a strong *Dasein* and live actively and purposefully in the three levels of existence, *Umwelt, Mitwelt,* and *Eigenwelt.* Maladaptive individuals, in contrast, lack "authenticity"; that is, they lack meaning and a sense of being-in-the-world. All psychological symptoms, according to the existential therapist, result at some level from decisions that compromise this authenticity.

| *I am my choices.*
    —Jean-Paul Sartre

Individuals may reject interpersonal relationships *(Miltwelt)*, for example, as irreconcilable with their own needs and values *(Eigenwelt).* Or, vice versa,

Sidebar 8-2

VICTOR FRANKL'S SEARCH FOR MEANING

Victor Frankl is best known through his compelling book *Man's Search for Meaning* (1959). In this small volume, Frankl describes his imprisonment in Nazi concentration camps at Auschwitz and Dachau during World War II (1942–1945). Whereas Frankl gives attention to the horrors of the concentration camp, the book is more a testimony to the power of the human spirit and its ability to survive.

Following are some illustrative quotations from Frankl's famous book.

The most ghastly moment of the twenty-four hours of camp life was the awakening, when at a still nocturnal hour, the three shrill blows of a whistle tore us pitilessly from our exhausted sleep and from the longings in our dreams. We then began the tussle with our wet shoes, into which we could scarcely force our feet, which were sore and swollen with edema. And there were the usual moans and groans about petty troubles, such as the snapping of wires which replaced shoelaces. One morning I heard someone, who I knew to be brave and dignified, cry like a child because he finally had to go to the snowy marching grounds in his bare feet, as his shoes were too shrunken for him to wear. In those ghastly minutes, I found a little bit of comfort; a small piece of bread which I drew out of my pocket and munched with absorbed delight. (p. 50)

We stumbled on in the darkness, over big stones and through large puddles, along the one road leading from the camp. The accompanying guards kept shouting at us and driving us with the butts of their rifles. Anyone with very sore feet supported himself on his neighbor's arm. Hardly a word was spoken; the icy wind did not encourage talk. Hiding his mouth behind his upturned collar, the man marching next to me whispered suddenly: "If our wives could see us now! I do hope they are better off in their camps and don't know what is happening to us."

That brought thoughts of my own wife to mind. And as we stumbled on for miles,

slopping on icy spots, supporting each other time and again, dragging one another up and onward, nothing was said, but we both knew: each of us was thinking of his wife. Occasionally I looked at the sky, where the stars were fading and the pink light of morning was beginning to spread behind a dark bank of clouds. But my mind clung to my wife's image, imagining it with an uncanny acuteness. I heard her answering me, saw her smile, her frank and encouraging look. Real or not, her look was then more luminous than the sun which was beginning to rise.

A thought transfixed me: for the first time in my life I saw the truth as it is set into song by so many poets, proclaimed as the final wisdom by so many thinkers. The truth—that love is the ultimate and the highest goal to which man can aspire. Then I grasped the meaning of the greatest secret that human poetry and human thought and belief have to impart: The salvation of man is through love and in love. I understood how a man who has nothing left in this world still may know bliss, be it only for a brief moment, in the contemplation of his beloved.

In front of me a man stumbled and those following him fell on top of him. The guard rushed over and used his whip on them all. Thus my thoughts were interrupted for a few minutes. But soon my soul found its way back from the prisoner's existence to another world, and I resumed talk with my loved one: I asked her questions, and she answered; she questioned me in return, and I answered. (Frankl, 1959, pp. 58–60)

Frankl maintained a sane response in an insane situation. He paid attention to a crust of bread, he secretly worked on a book, but most of all he thought of his wife. At a more basic level, Frankl found meaning outside the horror of the immediate situation that gave him strength to cope with life's difficult reality. It was here that he found the essence of life and developed logotherapy.

Continued.

Although Frankl was a student of Freud, he became interested in existentialism in the 1930s through reading such philosophers as Martin Heidegger and Max Scheler. He began formulating his ideas about an existentialist approach to counseling before his death camp experi-ences, having used the term *logotherapy* as early as 1938. The impact of the concentration camps, however, crystallized Frankl's thoughts about the meaning of life and suffering, and it was partly his determination to share his beliefs that kept him alive.

Victor Frankl (1905–   ).
(Kovesdi Presse Agentur)

Emaciated survivors of a
Nazi concentration camp in 1945.
(Corbis-Bettmann)

constantly attempting to adapt to the wishes of others, maladaptive people may become social chameleons, sacrificing *Eigenwelt* to *Mitwelt*. Alternatively, *Mitwelt* or *Eigenwelt* may be consistently ignored in favor of their biological needs *(Umwelt)*. On the other hand, sufferers may deny their sexuality *(Umwelt)* in order to conform to parental demands. Whatever the form, such a constriction or loss of *Dasein* ultimately results in self-estrangement, apathy, and an inability to experience existence as real. "The fundamental neurotic process in our day," writes May (1969, p. 75), "is the repression of the ontological sense, the loss of [one's] sense of being."

In *The Divided Self*, R. D. Laing (1959) provides a phenomenological account of a schizoid individual who experiences what he calls a basic "ontological insecurity": a split between the relation with the world and the self. The individual lacks a firm sense of self or identity. Although most people experience similar feelings of uncertainty at times, the maladaptive individual's experience of ontological insecurity is intense and pervasive.

For the existentialist, such maladaptive behavior is fundamentally the result of meaninglessness, of an "existential vacuum," according to Frankl (1967a). Substance abuse, marital and family discord, depression, confusion, and self-defeating activity can all develop as a result of perceived meaninglessness (Lantz and Pegram, 1989). Maladaptive behavior is the result of not embracing our freedom and responsibility, of disregarding our true self, and of forsaking genuine meaning in life.

FUNCTION OF THE THERAPIST

Regardless of the strategy, the linchpin of existential therapy is the therapist. Helping clients restore meaning in their lives, the therapist may use advocacy, empathy, concern, sincere personal interest, reflection, action, environmental modification, or support. And restoration of meaning can occur through work with individuals, families, or even groups (Greenlee, 1990; Lantz and Pegram, 1989; Schwartzberg, 1993).

According to Arbuckle (1975), counselors who view the predicament of individuals from the existential perspective are distinguished by an intellectual flexibility that is not threatened by the ideas and beliefs of others and that does not adhere stubbornly to any one intellectual system, theory, or ideology; by a personality that exemplifies freedom and integrity, which can provide strength to a struggling counselee; and by a recognition that beliefs are ideas that cannot be proven right or wrong but are expressions of faith.

| *Man is condemned to be free.*
| —Jean-Paul Sartre

The existential therapist expects the therapeutic responsibility to rest squarely on the clients. Therapy is not imposed. Neither are the clients viewed as objects to be evaluated, assessed, reported about, programmed for change, or modified. Starting therapy, ending therapy, taking each step in the therapeutic process—all of this is determined in large part, not by the therapist, but by the client.

The existential therapist, however, is grounded in the immediate, subjective experience of encountering the client. The emphasis is on a sensitive presence that puts personal needs aside and centers exclusively on the client, on "one existence communicating with another" (May, Angel, & Ellenberger, 1958). To use Martin Buber's well-known phrase, the therapeutic relationship must be an "I–Thou" encounter—an encounter built on honesty, in which counselors expose their true selves. The counselor's ability to be genuinely human enables clients to become aware of similar qualities in themselves. Through this encounter individuals recognize their potentials. "Encounter is always a potentially creative experience; it normally ensues in the expanding of consciousness, the enrichment of the self" (May, 1953, p. 22). Nor is this genuine encounter an isolated pocket of intimacy. According to Irvin Yalom, "it exists in one's inner world as a permanent reference point: a reminder of one's potential for intimacy" (1980, p. 404).

Most existential counselors do not believe that individuals are divided into conscious and unconscious dimensions. Too often the so-called unconscious is used to rationalize behavior and evade responsibility, the existential therapist believes, thus avoiding the realities of one's existence. Only when clients embrace this responsibility can therapeutic change occur. Usually an existential therapist views the process of this change from six perspectives or angles.

First, clients can change as a result of insight, by understanding personal modes of existing in concert with a developing sense of choice, freedom, and responsibility. The process provides opportunity for seeing and grasping their own potential for existing and exercising choice for, or declining, this way of "being-in-the-world."

Second, change occurs through a process of therapeutic encountering between therapists and clients, a genuine meeting of persons, an open confrontation, a full "being-with-one-another." It is this risk of an existential clash that culminates in transformation and existential growth.

Third, change occurs when clients carry forward their own potential for existing. This is a process of opening up, of actualization, of being, existing, and experiencing one's own potentials.

Fourth, change occurs by means of an internal process of therapeutic encountering between the person and his or her own deeper potentials for existing. It is this internal encounter that risks existential clashes and that culminates in an integrative meeting, in a welcoming, touching intimacy between patients and their inner potentials.

Fifth, change occurs when clients completely disengage from their own personality structure, identity, or self, and when they enter wholly into a deeper existence or mode of being, into deeper experiencing. In this process of existential death and rebirth, the innermost core of the person undergoes radical transformation into a new and authentic being.

And, finally, change occurs when clients open up new worlds, when they construct new and changing life situations, when they risk actual new and changing ways of being in worlds of their own construction.

GOALS OF THERAPY

Because the goals of existential therapy emerge from the therapeutic process, they often seem vague and obscure. For example, May asserts, "The aim of therapy is that the patient *experience his existence as real*" (May et al., 1958, p. 85). Corlis and Rabe maintain that the therapist's goals are "to stimulate the patient's willingness to work through pain, to offer help without the jeopardy of undercutting the other's own effort, to offer him strength without dependence" (1969, p. 13). The ultimate goal of existential psychotherapy, according to Phares, is "to help the individual reach a point at which awareness and decision making can be exercised responsibly" (1988, p. 417). With an

Our enemy is as necessary for us as is our friend. Both together are part of authentic community.

—Rollo May

equally broad stroke, Frey and Heslett say "existential counselors agree with the general goals of most other approaches to counseling and psychotherapy, but seek to embellish these general goals with existential points of view" (1975, p. 43).

Although therapists debate the various goals of existential therapy, most would agree that its overarching purpose is to help their clients find purpose and meaning in life. According to Frankl (1963), meaning can be uncovered in three ways: by doing a deed *(creative values)*, by experiencing a value *(experiential values)*, and by suffering *(attitudinal values)*.

Whereas there is value in each of these three paths to meaning, the first two can lead to difficulty. The problem with creative values comes, for example, in seeking all of life's meaning through work. Faced with retirement, illness, or economic recession, maladjusted individuals often lose their elusive sense of meaning. Similarly, people may realize experiential values through a symphony or the intimacy of a friendship, but if they become deaf or their friends move away, meaning becomes a mirage.

As a result, Frankl emphasized attitudinal values, for good reason. Unlike creative and experiential values, attitudinal values allow individuals to adjust to things beyond their control so that they are able to respond to whatever circumstances life brings. The capacity to respond to life's circumstances—even to undeserved suffering—knows no limit. "In the realization of attitudinal values [the individual] is free," writes Frankl. "This freedom knows no conditions, it is a freedom 'under all circumstances' and until the last breath" (1963, p. 48).

Cunningham and Peters assign six more specific aims to the process of existential therapy: (1) to make the clients more aware of their own existence, (2) to elucidate their uniqueness, (3) to improve client's encounters with others, (4) to foster freedom, (5) to foster responsibility, and (6) to help clients establish their "will to meaning" (1973, p. 71).

From the point of view of the existential therapist, clients have the capacity for change, which can occur on the twin axes of actualization and integration. The critical word here is "capacity," for existential psychologists do not believe that human beings are the packages of innate drives and desires that characterize most other theories of therapy. There is no biological or biopsychological sequence of growth or development; no force toward becoming mature; no constitutional wellspring, pushing or pulling us toward authenticity, spirituality, social consciousness, normality, or health. At the same time, however, the existential therapist recognizes that each person still has the potential to move in the direction of ever-increasing actualization and integration (DeCarvalho, 1990).

MAJOR METHODS AND TECHNIQUES

Existential therapists are not known for their repertoire of techniques. In fact, some practitioners regard it not so much as a distinct approach to therapy, but as a philosophy of therapy (LeVine, 1993; Osipow, Walsh, & Tosi, 1984; Wallace,

1986). Kemp points out that in existential counseling "technique follows understanding" (1971, p. 18). "Approaching human beings merely in terms of techniques necessarily implies manipulating them," writes Frankl. "Approaching them merely in terms of dynamics implies reifying them, making human beings into mere things" (1967b, p. 139). Nor are existential therapists, in general, particularly concerned with issues of transference, countertransference, personal distortions, or defense mechanisms. Far more basic existential issues are freedom, meaning, spirituality, and responsibility (Bylski & Westman, 1991; Payne, Bergin, & Loftus, 1992).

As might be expected, then, the methods used by existential counselors tend to be as varied as the number of practitioners (Osipow & Walsh, 1970). Perhaps more so than any other counselor, the existential therapist will rely on those techniques that are most compatible with his or her personality. In addition, the behavior of counselors can vary considerably during the counseling interview simply because the client and counselor differ at any given moment. And, of course, the training of existential counselors influences the intervention strategies they incorporate into their practice. Those trained in the Freudian approach, for example, may rely heavily on interpretation, whereas those with a client-centered background will verbally engage their clients.

Truth, like light, blinds. Falsehood, on the contrary, is a beautiful twilight that enhances every object.
—Albert Camus

There are, however, some identifiable characteristics in the practice of existential psychotherapy. Recognizing that the "being" of the counselor is the most dynamic force in the counseling process, the following components of existential therapy are noteworthy.

Course of Therapy

Like those that follow, the initial therapy session begins with the client's circumstances at the moment and moves on from there. Because this first session can be frightening for the client who does not know what to expect from therapy, it is important that the therapist explore the client's expectations. In response to clients who enter therapy passively, expecting a quick and painless cure, the therapist may begin by expressing his or her inability to provide simple answers or quick solutions to the inherently difficult facts and possibilities of existence. Rather, existential therapy will entail the painful work of self-discipline and the will to act. This kind of structuring communicates the therapist's faith in the client's abilities and serves to give the client hope.

Confrontation of Life Issues

In the world of the existentialist, at least three polarities are fundamental to the human condition: (1) dependence versus independence, (2) rationality versus irrationality, and (3) freedom versus determinism. Knowing that the client who avoids these issues may eventually collapse into an existential crisis (i.e., despair, anxiety, guilt, and nothingness), the existential therapist will confront these philosophical alternatives head-on. The resolution of these dilemmas, on the other hand, helps establish purpose and meaning in life. In short, it is the goal of the existential therapist to move the client from a psychological to a spiritual plane. For this reason, the most important attribute that a therapist can bring to his or her clients is a "philosophy of life" (Bugental, 1965; Yalom, 1980).

Focusing

Although not exclusively existential, Eugene Gendlin developed an approach, known as *focusing,* that is often used by existential counselors (1981). This practical method derives from the accidental finding that the difference between successful and unsuccessful therapeutic outcomes is not so much a result of what is achieved by the therapist, but of what is achieved by the client. The crucial difference lies in the client's attitude toward a specific problem—in focusing on and changing one's deepest feelings by discovering what Gendlin calls the "felt sense." "What happens," according to Gendlin, "is that from discovering this felt sense, new and changed feelings and aspects of experience emerge and the problem changes." (1981, p. 11). Focusing is not facing painful emotions, nor is it an intellectual or analytical process. "When you learn how to focus," writes Gendlin, "you will discover the body finding its own way provides its own answers to many of your problems" (1981, p. 11). One's "felt sense" is actually discovered, then, through awareness of one's body (see Sidebar 8-3).

Sidebar 8-3

AN EXISTENTIAL FOCUSING EXERCISE

Eugene T. Gendlin

Helping a Felt Sense Form
It is possible for a person to focus a little between one communication and the next. Having made a point, and being understood, the person can focus before saying the next thing.

Most people don't do that. They run on from point to point, only talking.

How can you help people stop, and get the felt sense of what they have just said?

This is the second focusing movement. Finding the felt sense is like saying to oneself, "That, right there, *that's* what's confused," and *then feeling it there.*

The focuser must keep quiet, not only outwardly but also inside, so that a felt sense can form. It takes as long as a minute.

Some people talk all the time, either out loud or at themselves inside. Then nothing directly felt can form, and everything stays a painful mass of confusion and tightness.

When a felt sense forms, the focuser feels relief. It's as if all the bad feeling goes into one spot, right there, and the rest of the body feels freer.

Once a felt sense forms, people can relate to it. They can wonder what's *in* it, can feel around it and into it.

When to help people let a felt sense form
When people have said all that they can say clearly, and from there on it is confusing, or a tight unresolved mess, and they don't know how to go on.

Continued.

When there is a certain spot that you sense could be gone into further.

When people talk round and round a subject and never go down into their feelings of it. They may start to say things that are obviously personal and meaningful, but then go on to something else. They tell you nothing meaningful, but seem to want to. In this very common situation, you can interrupt the focuser and gently point out the way into deeper levels of feeling.

FOCUSER: "I've been doing nothing but taking care of Karen since she's back from the hospital. I haven't been with me at all. And when I do get time now, I just want to run out and do another chore."

This section originally appeared in *Focusing*. New York: Bantum Books, 1981. Reprinted by permission.

LISTENER: "You haven't been able to be with yourself for so long, and even when you can now, you don't."

FOCUSER: "She needs this and she needs that and no matter what I do for her it isn't enough. All her family are like that. It makes me angry. Her father was like that, too, when he was sick which went on for years. They're always negative and grumpy and down on each other."

LISTENER: "It makes you angry the way she is, the way they are."

FOCUSER: "Yes. I'm angry. Damn right. It's a poor climate. Living in a poor climate. Always gray. Always down on something. The other day, when I. ..."

LISTENER: (interrupts:) "Wait. Be a minute with your angry feeling. Just feel it for a minute. See what more is in it. Don't think anything. ...."

Logotherapy

Victor Frankl first set forth his ideas of "logotherapy," a term derived from the Greek words *logos* (word or meaning) and *therapeia* (healing), in *The Doctor and the Soul* (1955). Logotherapy, then, is a means of providing or experiencing healing through meaning. Responding to people whose "will to meaning" is so frustrated that they develop a sense of "meaninglessness," Frankl designed logotherapy to help clients overcome this existential "void" and find purpose in their lives. This approach seeks to establish responsibility, meaning, and purpose within the context of the I–Thou relationship.

In contrast to Freud's "will to pleasure" and Adler's "will to power," Frankl characterizes his approach as the "will to meaning." Frankl views human beings as self-determining and self-actualizing. Because of a spiritual freedom that distinguishes us from the animal world, we possess the innate capacity to transcend environmental factors, whether biological, psychological, or sociological. This spiritual freedom is not so much freedom from oppressive forces as it is the potential for discovering, deciding, and actualizing one's existence. Such freedom cannot be taken from us, and it is this dimension that makes life meaningful and purposeful.

Unlike other existential approaches, however, logotherapy uses several distinctive "techniques," including *paradoxical intention, dereflection,* and *modification of attitudes* (Lukas, 1984).

Like Adler, Frankl found great value in *paradoxical intention,* which requires clients to act against their anticipation of fear (Frankl, 1963). The individual who has difficulty sleeping, for example, may be asked to practice staying awake; a client who complains of blushing when speaking before a group would be instructed to try to blush on such occasions. This is a reversal of the client's attitude toward the situation, especially if it is carried out in as humorous a fashion as possible. Paradoxically, she or he will usually be unable to blush when she or he tries to do so. Frankl provides an example of a client, fearful of trembling before his instructor, who was instructed to say to himself: "Oh, here is the instructor! Now I'll show him what a good trembler I am—I'll really show him how nicely I can tremble" (1955, p. 226). Such a reversal brings a change of attitude toward the symptom, enabling the client to gain some distance from the symptom and view the troubling situation with a degree of detachment (Ascher & Turner, 1979; Solyom, Garza-Perez, Ledwidge, & Solyom, 1972).

Dereflection, the second of these logotherapeutic techniques, is an approach to treating excessive self-observation, obsession, or self-attention. It is a strategy that encourages clients to ignore the problem and direct awareness toward something favorable and pleasant. The clients focus attention away from themselves and onto the real meanings of their existence and the actions that a commitment to those meanings demands. Frankl gives the example of a depressed survivor of the concentration camps who could find no meaning in his suffering or in his life: He had lost his wife and many children to the Nazi ovens and gas chambers. Frankl tentatively asked whether it were possible that his suffering might be meant to allow the client "to become worthy of joining them [his family] in heaven" (1955, p. 190). He reported that the individual subsequently dereflected his negative self-obsession and became better able to bear his grief.

> The most common lie is that with which one lies to oneself: lying to others is relatively an exception.
>
> —Friedrich Nietzsche

A third logotherapeutic approach is to *modify the clients' attitudes,* to change the way they think about their situation, to put new meaning into their predicament. In spite of many positive realities, for example, clients may be pessimistic and negative about their lives. Or perhaps the situation is truly horrific—they may have been terribly burned, for instance—and there is little that can be done to improve the circumstances. In either case, the goal is to help clients change perspective. "This modification of attitudes is most often conducted in a rather direct approach through sharing one's opinions, arguing with the client, or positive suggestions" (Ivey, Ivey, & Simek-Downing, 1987, p. 291). The point is that the clients can often do nothing to repair the past or present, but they *can* change the way they think about it. One can find meaning in spite of one's circumstances—even in a concentration camp.

Today, traces of these three central techniques—paradoxical intention, dereflection, and change of attitudes—are components of current popular strategies, including cognitive-behavioral therapy, rational-emotive therapy, and family systems theories (Ivey et al., 1987; Lukas, 1984). "Paradoxical intention," according to Ivey et al., "is one of the key 'new' methods that can be used to produce rapid change, yet it was used by Frankl as early as 1929" (1987, p. 290).

APPLICATION

In rehearsing the case of Mrs. Hutchens, Rollo May illustrates many of the assumptions and principles that have guided him and other existential therapists. A suburban woman in her mid-30s, Mrs. Hutchens suffered from a hysterical tenseness of the larynx so severe that she spoke only with a perpetual hoarseness. May found that the woman believed that if she spoke her mind to people, to her parents in particular, she would be rejected. It was safer to be quiet, she concluded. Whereas May believed that he understood the childhood origins of her problem—her need to protect herself against the belittling remarks of her mother and grand-mother—he felt that the most important part of the therapy was not his interpretation but rather the client now "existing, becoming, emerging . . . in the room with [him]" (1983, p. 25). May soon realized that his patient, like every human being, was *centered* in herself, that she was making an attempt to preserve her existence, to protect herself by being excessively in control, by being proper in her behavior, and, most remarkably, by speaking in a hoarse voice.

He who has a why to live for can bear with almost any how.
—Friedrich Nietzsche

In the course of therapy, Mrs. Hutchens revealed that she had dreamed that she was searching room by room for a baby in an unfinished house at an airport. When she found the baby, she placed it in a pocket of her robe, only to be seized by anxiety, lest it be smothered. Much to her joy, she found that the baby was still alive. Then she had a terrifying thought: "Shall I kill it?"

Analysis revealed that the house was located near an airport where she had learned to fly solo at the age of 20, an act that asserted her independence from her parents. The baby was her youngest son, with whom she so closely identified that the infant was, in effect, herself—a symbol, that is, of her emerging consciousness, which she considered killing in her dream.

Moreover, approximately 6 years before Mrs. Hutchens entered therapy, she had abandoned the religious faith of her parents, only to join another denomination that she dared not reveal to her authoritarian parents. During therapy she considered telling them, but whenever May brought up the topic, she became faint. She would report feeling empty inside and would have to lie down on the couch for a few minutes. Finally, she wrote to her parents about her change in religious faith and told them it would accomplish nothing if they tried to change her mind. In the next therapeutic session she told May that she felt tremendous anxiety and wondered whether she might become psychotic. May said that he thought this outcome was highly unlikely.

May interpreted her fainting and attacks of anxiety as attempts to kill her emerging consciousness. She was struggling to accept her hatred of her mother and her mother's hatred of her, to free herself from her mother's painful domination, and to accept responsibility for her own actions and choices, even though they might not always have the best consequences. In brief, Mrs. Hutchens was actively confronting herself in these areas. The result was the opportunity for fuller independence, positive growth, and the development of a healthier life.

CRITICAL ANALYSIS

Few can discount the breadth of existential theory, for it encompasses many of the great philosophical questions of our age. It is an approach that wastes no time on lesser issues; its concepts are all-encompassing, sometimes ambiguous or even paradoxical, but always meaningful.

Reaching into the innermost recesses of human experience, existential psychotherapy has explored aspects of humanity not examined by other theorists. It is a position that has proved highly stimulating to humanistic investigators as well as to members of the general public (McLeod & Ryan, 1993; Tobin, 1990). And although the existential approach has been criticized for being cumbersome or excessively conceptual, it is nonetheless persevering. May's writings, for example, may at times be somewhat awkward, but to his credit he confronts complex issues and does not attempt to oversimplify human personality.

Existential concepts such as being-in-the-world have given practitioners new ways to conceptualize human personality. The existentialists' emphasis on our repressed fear of death and on our sense of alienation and meaninglessness has furthered our understanding of psychopathology and treatment. Existentialists have helped the professional community recognize that humans need and seek meaning, that they are lost without it; that exercising choices brings growth, whereas attempting to escape freedom is debilitating; that humans differ in the experiences they seek and in their interpretations of these experiences (Allman, de la Rocha, Elkins, & Weathers, 1992). For many, the existential approach has breathed new life into psychology.

With its particular focus on personal choice and freedom, existential therapy can be especially useful in helping minority clients deal with multicultural issues. It provides for "cultural relativity," for the ability to understand one's own cultural heritage and world views within the context of still other perspectives (Ibrahim, 1985, 1991). With this in mind, ethnic-minority clients facing social limitations, for example, can be encouraged to look at the price they are paying for personal decisions. Through the existential approach some clients, while still recognizing actual discrimination, can be challenged to separate themselves more objectively from their contexts and move beyond imagined limits. They can come to recognize that they are more than victims of circumstances; that they are human beings with choices, who can transcend culturally learned assumptions. In other words, while accepting some environmental and personal limitations, clients can use the existential approach to exercise some degree of freedom.

Although rich in appreciation of the human condition, existentialism provides no systematic presentation of procedure, methodology, or empirical validation of its therapeutic approach. The concepts, which are often highly provocative, are imprecise and hence difficult to define, learn, teach, or research. A variety of definitions are offered for such concepts as anxiety, guilt, intentionality, will, and destiny; and none is operationally defined. Of course,

> *If a man hasn't discovered something that he will die for, he isn't fit to live.*
> —Martin Luther King, Jr.

such difficulties and, in fact, existentialism's fundamental lack of coherence, lie in the very origins of the approach. Nietzsche and Kierkegaard were both influential in articulating the characteristics of existentialism, but even in the conception there were significant differences between them: whereas Nietzsche's Zarathustra declared that "God is dead," emphasizing that humankind is ultimately alone, Kierkegaard excoriated those who supposed it possible to generate meaning through observation and reason, and he insisted that all sense and meaning must begin with an initial "leap of faith." And whereas Jean-Paul Sartre sought to reconcile his existentialist views with Marxism, it was Albert Camus who scathingly denounced Marxist efforts to represent human behavior as deterministic.

Attempts to account for human behavior by means of explanatory generalizations are not welcomed by staunch existentialists; such explanations are possible only for objects and events that are determined, not for those that are free. Attempts to use statistical analyses of human behavior cannot unravel causal effects; they can only make things appear to be determined, after the fact. To the thoroughgoing existentialist, such exercises are not scientific, they are merely scholastic. Some radical existentialists can even be antiintellectual, believing that such intellectual schema victimize the very people who should be responsible for their own freedom, for constructing their own universe, and for engineering their own development. According to existentialists, what is crucial is not science but experience. Staunchly defending his psychology against the charge of being antiintellectual or antiscientific, however, Rollo May points to the sterility of conventional scientific methods and their inability to unlock the ontological character of willing, caring, and acting human beings.

A final noteworthy critique of the existential approach is its lack of educational and training programs. Although there may be some validity to the proposition that each existential practitioner is unique, it clearly prohibits the systematic teaching of theory. Under these circumstances, Wallace (1986) wonders whether May's existential approach will last.

CURRENT STATUS

A mere 4% of the psychotherapists in America endorse existentialism as their primary orientation (Prochaska and Norcross, 1983); however, this approach has been a powerful force in changing the face of contemporary psychotherapy.

Except perhaps for the classic forms of behavior therapy, existential therapy has been wedded to nearly all major traditions (Norcross, 1987). Thus, most existential therapists are "existential–psychodynamic," "existential family systems," and so forth. World congresses of logotherapy have been held since 1980, and institutes of logotherapy are gradually developing around the world as therapists on an international scale are adding logotherapeutic insights to their practices. Although few, if any, counseling psychologists would advertise themselves as "logotherapists" or "existentialists," even fewer clients today enter therapy without exposing themselves to the assumptions and approaches of existentialism.

CHAPTER SUMMARY

1. *Biography.* May (1909–1994) grew up in the midwestern United States. He attended Michigan State and graduated from Oberlin College in Ohio with a B.A. in English. Shortly after graduation he taught in Salonika, Greece, and spent two summers in Vienna, where he enrolled in seminars conducted by Alfred Adler. After 3 years abroad, May returned to the United States and enrolled in Union Theological Seminary in preparation for the ministry. May's first 2 years as a pastor after graduation were disappointing, and he soon enrolled in Columbia University to major in clinical psychology. His studies were cut short by a bout with tuberculosis, but it was during this illness that he read Kierkegaard's works and became interested in existentialism. He eventually completed his Ph.D. and went on to write extensively on existential theory.

2. *Historical Development.* Existential psychotherapy is rooted in the philosophical writings of Kierkegaard and Nietzsche. They introduced existential thought to Western Europe, and it was their work that established the footing for several influential philosophers, including Albert Camus, Jean-Paul Sartre, Martin Heidegger, and Martin Buber.

3. *View of Human Nature.* Existentialism is alternately religious, atheistic, and antireligious. It emphasizes hope and optimism, as well as despair and nothingness. In short, existentialists do not agree on a basic view of human nature. Despite its diversity, however, all agree on the importance of existence and on the phenomena that are inherent in the very nature of being alive. Existentialists believe that life is either fulfilled or constricted by a series of decisions that we make, with no way of knowing conclusively what the correct choices are. Existentialists emphasize experience as the primary phenomenon in the study of human nature. Both theoretical explanations and overt behavior are secondary to experience itself and its meaning to the person.

4. *Development of Maladaptive Behavior.* If we fail to live in a state of awareness of our being, according to existential thought, we inevitably develop psychopathology. Of course, this state of being has the potential for great anxiety,

which can lead to self-deception and ever greater maladaptive behavior. The bottom line is that such maladaptive behavior is fundamentally the result of meaninglessness; maladaptive behavior is the result of not embracing our freedom and responsibility, or of disregarding our true self, of forsaking genuine meaning in life.

5. *Goals of Therapy.* The overarching purpose of the existential approach is to help clients find purpose and meaning in life. More specifically, existentialism attempts to make clients more aware of their existence, elucidate their uniqueness, improve encounters with others, and foster freedom and responsibility. The existential approach strives to help persons move in the direction of ever-increasing actualization and integration.

6. *Function of the Therapist.* The existential therapist is grounded in the immediate, subjective experience of encountering the client. In an effort to restore personal meaning in the life of a client, existential therapists may use advocacy, empathy, concern, reflection, action, environmental modification, or support. They have a kind of intellectual flexibility that is not threatened by the ideas and beliefs of others and does not adhere stubbornly to any one intellectual system, theory, or ideology.

7. *Major Methods and Techniques.* The methods used by existential counselors are varied. However, the typical course of therapy begins with the client's circumstances at the moment. Paradoxical intention, which requires clients to act against their anticipation of fear, is sometimes used. Dereflection is an approach to treating excessive self-observation, obsession, or self-attention. It encourages clients to ignore the problem and direct awareness toward something favorable and pleasant. Modifying one's attitude, changing the way one thinks about a situation, is also a commonly used existential method.

8. *Application.* The case of Mrs. Hutchens illustrates a number of the principles Rollo May applied to counseling. This suburban woman in her mid-30s suffered from a hysterical tenseness of the larynx. May found that the woman believed that if she spoke her mind to people, she would be rejected; it was safer to keep quiet. May also observed the patient's fainting spells and anxiety attacks and he interpreted them as attempts to kill her emerging consciousness. In the end, Mrs. Hutchens was left only to confront herself and the result was an opportunity for greater independence, positive growth, and the development of a healthier life.

9. *Critical Analysis.* Existential therapy must be commended for its breadth as well as its focus on issues other approaches have avoided. It is a position that has proved to be highly stimulating and rewarding. The existentialists' emphasis on our repressed fear of death and on our sense of alienation and meaninglessness has furthered our understanding of psychopathology and treatment. Existentialists have helped the professional community recognize that humans need and seek meaning. It is an approach that also lends itself to working with ethnic-minority clients. It provides cultural relativity by helping to understand

one's own cultural heritage within the context of other perspectives. Still, existentialism provides no systematic presentation of procedure, methodology, or empirical validation of its therapeutic approach.

10. *Current Status.* Although only a very small percentage of today's counselors label themselves primarily as existentialists, this approach has been a powerful force in changing the face of contemporary psychotherapy. It has been incorporated in almost every major therapeutic tradition.

KEY TERMS

Anxiety   Apprenhension caused by a threat to some value deemed essential to the existence of one's personality. Since death is an absolute and inevitable aspect of existence, a certain amount of anxiety is a natural characteristic of being human.

Dasein   A conscious and unconscious sense of oneself as a distinct, autonomous, and responsible entity existing in the world of physiological and physical surroundings *(Umwelt)*, other people *(Mitwelt)*, and one's own self *(Eigenwelt)*. A strong *Dasein* is essential to the healthy personality.

Daseinsanalysis   A method of existential psychotherapy, developed by Medard Boss, that focuses on the individual's existence or his or her specific way of "being-in-the-world."

Dereflection   A technique of counteracting obsessive ideation or hyperreflection by helping the client stop thinking about the problem.

Eigenwelt   The world of relationship to oneself, and to one's own potentials and values. One of the three simultaneous and interrelated modes of being-in-the-world.

Focusing   A technique for introspection and change that identifies how a client talks about his or her experiencing.

Guilt   Regret resulting from the impossibility of fulfilling all of one's innate potentials (a denial of *Eigenwelt*), of relating perfectly to others (a denial of *Mitwelt*), and of always recognizing our communion with nature (a denial of *Umwelt*).

Intentionality   The capacity of human beings to have a conscious and unconscious sense of purpose and to behave teleologically.

Logotherapy   An existential approach to psychotherapy developed by Victor Frankl shortly after World War II. It accents the capacity of each person to exercise the power of choice and experience healing through meaning.

Love   A delight in the presence of another person and a readiness to affirm that person's values and development as much as one's own.

Mitwelt   The world of relationship to other people. One of the three simultaneous and interrelated modes of being-in-the-world.

Ontological Characteristics   Those qualities that are distinctively and definitively human, including *Dasein*, anxiety, guilt, intentionality, love, and care.

Ontology   The science of existence or being.

Paradoxical Intention   A technique for directing a client to do something contrary to one's actual instructions; the success of the directive is a result of not being able to force that which is involuntary.

Phenomenological   An attitude of respect for the dignity and integrity of each person's experience and an approach or methodology for studying the personal meanings of experience.

Teleology   The philosophical study of purpose, believing that natural processes are determined not by mechanism but by their utility in an overall natural design.

Umwelt   The world of internal and external objects, which forms our physiological and physical environment. One of the three simultaneous and interrelated modes of being-in-the-world.

Will   The conscious capacity to move toward one's self-selected goals. It is the more self-evident aspect of intentionality.

SUGGESTED READING

Becker, E. (1973). *The denial of death.* New York: Free Press.
Frankl, V. E. (1963). *Man's search for meaning.* Boston: Beacon Press.
May, R. (1981). *Freedom and destiny.* New York: W. W. Norton.
May, R. (1991). *The cry for myth.* New York: W. W. Norton.
Reeves, C. (1977). *The psychology of Rollo May.* San Francisco: Jossey-Bass.
Yalom, E. D. (1980). *Existential psychotherapy.* New York: Basic Books.

REFERENCES

Allman, L.S., de la Rocha, O., Elkins, D., & Weathers, R. S. (1992). Psychotherapists' attitudes toward clients reporting mystical experiences. *Psychotherapy, 29,* 564–569.
Arbuckle, D. S. (1975). *Counseling and psychotherapy.* Boston: Allyn & Bacon.
Ascher, L. M., & Turner, R. M. (1979). Controlled comparison of progressive relaxation, stimulus control, and paradoxical intention therapies for insomnia. *Journal of Consulting and Clinical Psychology, 47,* 500–508.
Becker, E. (1973). *The denial of death.* New York: Free Press.
Binswanger, L. (1958). The case of Ellen West. In R. May, E. Angel, & H. Ellenberger (Eds.), *Existence: A new dimension in psychology and psychiatry* (pp. 237–364). New York: Basic Books.
Binswanger, L. (1963). *Being-in-the-world.* New York: Basic Books.
Boss, M. (1963). *Psychoanalysis and Daseinsanalysis.* New York: Basic Books.
Boss, M. (1977). *Existential foundations of medicine and psychology.* New York: Aronson.
Bugental, J. F. T. (1965). *The search for authenticity.* New York: Holt, Rinehart and Winston.
Bugental, J. F. T. (1978). *Psychotherapy and process: The fundamentals of an existential-humanistic approach.* Reading, MA: Addison-Wesley.
Bylski, N. C., & Westman, A. S. (1991). Relationships among defense style, existential anxiety, and religiosity. *Psychological Reports, 68,* 1389–1390.

Cogswell, J. F. (1993). Walking in your shoes: Toward integrating sense of self with sense of oneness. *Journal of Humanistic Psychology, 33,* 99–111.

Corlis, R. B., & Rabe, P. (1969). *Psychotherapy from the center: A humanistic view of change and of growth.* Scranton, PA: International Textbook.

Cunningham, L. M., & Peters H. J. (1973). *Counseling theories.* Columbus, OH: Charles E. Merrill.

DeCarvalho, R. J. (1990). The growth hypothesis and self-actualization: An existential alternative. *Humanistic Psychologist, 18,* 252–258.

Dopson, L., & Gade, E. (1981). Kierkegaard's philosophy: Implications for counseling. *Personnel and Guidance Journal, 60,* 148–152.

Frankl, V. E. (1955). *The doctor and the soul: An introduction to Logotherapy.* New York: Alfred A. Knopf.

Frankl, V. E. (1963). *Man's search for meaning.* Boston: Beacon Press.

Frankl, V. E. (1967a). *Psychotherapy and existentialism: Selected papers on Logotherapy.* New York: Simon & Schuster.

Frankl, V. E. (1967b). Logotherapy and existentialism. *Psychotherapy: Theory, research and practice, 4,* 138–142.

Frey, D. H., & Heslett, F. E. (1975). *Existential theory for counselors.* Boston: Houghton Mifflin.

Gendlin, E. (1981). *Focusing.* New York: Bantam Books.

Greenlee, R. W. (1990). The unemployed Appalachian coal miner's search for meaning. *International Forum for Logotherapy, 13,* 71–75.

Heidegger, M. (1962). *Being and time.* New York: Harper & Row.

Ibrahim, F. A. (1985). Effective cross-cultural counseling and psychotherapy: A framework. *The Counseling Psychologist, 13,* 625–638.

Ibrahim, F. A. (1991). Contribution of cultural worldview to generic counseling and development. *Journal of Counseling and Development, 70,* 13–19.

Ivey, A. E., Ivey, M. B., & Simek-Downing, L. (1987). *Counseling and psychotherapy* (2nd ed.). Englewood Cliffs, NJ: Prentice-Hall.

Kaam, A. L. Van (1967). Counseling and psychotherapy from the viewpoint of existential psychology. In D. S. Arbuckle (Ed.), *Counseling and psychotherapy: An overview.* New York: McGraw-Hill.

Kaam, A. L. Van (1969). *Existential foundations of psychology.* New York: Doubleday.

Kemp, C. G. (1971). Existential counseling. *The Counseling Psychologist, 2,* 2–30.

Kobasa, S. C., & Maddi, S. R. (1977). Existential personality theory. In R. J. Corsini (Ed.), *Current personality theories.* Itasca, IL: F. E. Peacock.

Laing, R. D. (1959). *The divided self.* London: Tavistock.

Lantz J., & Pegram, M. (1989). Casework and the restoration of meaning. *Social Casework: The Journal of Contemporary Social Work,* 549–555.

LeVine, P. (1993). Morita therapy and its divergence form existential psychotherapy: A proposal for adopting a Morita-based philosophy for use in counseling and psychotherapy. *International Bulletin of Morita Therapy, 6,* 47–58.

Lukas, E. (1984). *Meaningful living.* Cambridge, MA: Schenkman.

Maddi, S. R. (1980). *Personality theories: A comparative analysis* (4th ed.). Chicago: Dorsey Press.

May, R. (1961). *Existential psychology.* New York: Random House.

May, R. (1966). *Psychology and the human dilemma.* New York: W. W. Norton.

May, R. (1967a). *Man's search for himself.* New York: The American Library.

May, R. (1967b). *The art of counseling.* Nashville, TN: Abington.

May, R. (1969). *Love and will*. New York: Dell.

May, R. (1972). *Power and innocence*. New York: Dell.

May, R. (1975). *The courage to create*. New York: W. W. Norton.

May, R. (1977). *The meaning of anxiety* (rev. ed.). New York: W. W. Norton.

May, R. (1983). The case of Mrs. Hutchens. In *The discovery of being: Writings in existential psychology* (pp. 24–34). New York: W. W. Norton and Co.

May, R. (1991). *The cry for myth*. New York: W. W. Norton.

May, R., Angel, E., & Ellenberger, H. (Eds.). (1958). *Existence*. New York: Simon & Schuster.

May, R., & Yalom, I. D. (1995). Existential psychotherapy. In R. J. Corsini & D. Wedding (Eds.), *Current psychotherapies* (5th ed., pp. 262–292). Itasca, IL: F. E. Peacock.

McLeod, J., & Ryan, A. (1993). Therapeutic factors experienced by members of an outpatient therapy group for older women. *British Journal of Guidance and Counseling, 21*, 64–72.

Nietzsche, F. (1971) *Thus spoke Zarathustra: A book for all and some* (T. Common, Trans.). New York: Gordon Press. (Original work published in 1883.)

Nietzsche, F. (1972). *The antichrist*. Salem, NH: Ayer. (Reprint of 1930 ed.)

Norcross, J. (1987). A rational and empirical analysis of existential psychotherapy. *Journal of Humanistic Psychology, 27*, 41–68.

Osipow, S. H., & Walsh, W. B. (1970). *Strategies in counseling for behavior change*. Englewood Cliffs, NJ: Prentice-Hall.

Osipow, S. H., Walsh, W. B., & Tosi, D. J. (1984). *A survey of counseling methods*. Homewood, IL: Dorsey Press.

Owen, I. R. (1992). Applying social constructionism to psychotherapy. *Counseling Psychology Quarterly, 5*, 385–402.

Partenheimer, D. (1990). Teaching literature toward a humanistic society. *Journal of Humanistic Education and Development, 29*, 40–44.

Payne, I., Bergin, A. E., & Loftus, P. E. (1992). A review of attempts to integrate spiritual and standard psychotherapy techniques. *Journal of Psychotherapy Integration, 2*, 171–192.

Pervin, L. A. (1960). Existentialism, psychology, and psychotherapy. *American Psychologist, 15*, 305–309.

Phares, E. J. (1988). *Clinical psychology: Concepts, methods, and profession* (3rd ed.). Pacific Grove, CA: Brooks/Cole.

Prochaska, J. O., & Norcross, J. C. (1983). Contemporary psychotherapists: Characteristics, practices, theories, and attitudes. *Psychotherapy: Theory, Research and Practice, 20*, 620–627.

Rabinowitz, F. E., Good, G., & Cozad, L. (1989). Rollo May: A man of meaning and myth. *Journal of Counseling and Development, 67*, 436–441.

Sartre, J. P. (1953). *Existential psychoanalysis*. Chicago: Gateway.

Sartre, J. P. (1956). *Being and nothingness*. New York: Philosophical Library.

Schwartzberg, S. (1993). Struggling for meaning: How HIV-positive gay men make sense of AIDS. *Professional Psychology Research and Practice, 24*, 483–490.

Solyom, L., Garza-Perez, J., Ledwidge, B. L., & Solyom, C. (1972). Paradoxical intention in the treatment of obsessive thoughts: A pilot study. *Comprehensive Psychiatry, 13*, 291–297.

Stevens, M. J., Pfost, K. S., & Potts, M. K. (1990). Sex-role orientation and the willingness to confront existential issues. *Journal of Counseling and Development, 68*, 414–416.

Tillich, P. (1952). *The courage to be*. New Haven, CT: Yale University Press.

Tobin, S. A. (1990). Self psychology as a bridge between existential-humanistic psychology and psychoanalysis. *Journal of Humanistic Psychology, 30,* 14–63.

Wallace, W. A. (1986). *Theories of counseling and psychotherapy: A basic issues approach.* Boston: Allyn & Bacon.

Westman, A. S. (1992). Existential anxiety as related to conceptualization of self and of death, denial of death, and religiosity. *Psychological Reports, 71,* 1064–1066.

Yalom, E. D. (1980). *Existential psychotherapy.* New York: Basic Books.

CHAPTER 9

Person-Centered Therapy

Chapter Outline

Introduction
Brief Biography
Historical Development
View of Human Nature
Development of Maladaptive Behavior
Function of the Therapist
Goals of Therapy
Major Methods and Techniques
Application
Critical Analysis
Current Status
Chapter Summary
Key Terms
Suggested Reading

INTRODUCTION

By the middle of the 20th century, two major psychological views of humanity had emerged: the Freudian perspective, which viewed people as victims of repressed sexual and aggressive instincts; and the behavioristic perspective, which derived personality from the stimulus–response mechanism in human behavior. Taken to an extreme, behaviorists thought of individuals as little more than complex laboratory animals responding to their environment.

Many psychologists found it difficult to accept either of these explanations of human nature, for neither made any allowance for free will, human dignity, or cognitive processes. Behavior was controlled, not by personal choices, but by the impulses of the id or by learning histories. In response to these concerns, a third approach to understanding human behavior began to develop: the *humanistic* approach. Unlike other counseling theories, this approach assumes that we are largely responsible for our own actions, that we have the power to determine our own destiny. At almost any given moment, we can choose our actions because we have free will.

During the 1960s and 1970s the cultural preoccupation with individuality and personal expression provided fertile soil for the growth of this humanistic perspective. As a result this "third force" in American psychology caught on rapidly among many psychotherapists and with the public. People began talking about "getting in touch with feelings," "letting it all hang out," and "tuning in." Whereas this "psychedelic" terminology may have advanced the growth of the humanistic approach in popular culture, it was Carl Rogers who planted the seeds of this movement.

Brief Biography

Born January 8, 1902, in a suburb of Chicago, Carl Ransom Rogers was the product of midwestern America. He grew up in a close-knit, pragmatic, Protestant family dedicated to Christian principles and the virtues of hard work—so dedicated, in fact, that Dr. Rogers would later recall his feelings of guilt and "wickedness" while drinking his first bottle of soda pop (Kirschenbaum, 1979). A precocious child, Rogers "read incessantly" (Rogers, 1961a, p. 6). He loved reading the Bible and adventure stories; the *Encyclopedia Britannica* taught him to play chess. When he entered school, young Rogers was promptly advanced to the second grade.

Carl Rogers (1902–1987).
(Corbis-Bettmann)

The Rogers family was well off. Their 300-acre farm featured a house with a slate roof, tile floors, eight bedrooms, five baths, and a clay tennis court (Kirschenbaum, 1979, p. 10). Carl's father, a contractor and civil engineer, employed a manager to implement the latest scientific farming methods. It was here that Rogers began exploring science, studying books on agriculture, for instance, and breeding night-flying moths. Familiar with the scientific method by the age of 14 years, he read volumes about testing the effectiveness of various fertilizers and animal feeds. Rogers learned how to design experiments and how to conduct statistical tests of his own hypotheses (Rogers, 1961a), and thus he developed an abiding respect for the scientific method.

As an undergraduate at the University of Wisconsin, which his mother, father, two older brothers, and sister had attended, Rogers majored in agriculture and history. During this time he became involved with student religious groups, and when he "heard the call" during his sophomore year he committed himself to Christian ministry (Roberts, 1985). A year later he was one of 12 American students who traveled to Peking, China, for the World Student Christian Federation Conference. In 1924 he graduated from college.

Carl Rogers married Helen Elliott, an art major who was gentle, straightforward, and open-minded. Rogers later credited their two children, David and Natalie, with "teaching me far more about individuals, their development, and their relationships, than I could ever have learned professionally" (Rogers, 1961b, p. 12). David later became an administrator in a medical center, and Natalie worked with her father as a cotherapist in encounter groups.

Although his father offered to pay all expenses if Rogers would go to Princeton, his son declared his independence and moved to the more liberal Union Theological Seminary in New York, where he enrolled in the usual courses in scripture and theology. A turning point for his life, however, was a course in Working with Individuals, in which the professor brought in psychologists and psychiatrists as guest lecturers. For the first time, Rogers considered helping people not as an ordained minister, but as a psychologist. After 2 years at Union, he transferred across the street to Columbia University Teachers College, where he earned his Ph.D. in clinical and educational psychology in 1931.

> *Freud fails to do justice to the positive aspect of life. He only knows the lust of release, not the pleasure of tension.*
>
> —Kurt Goldstein

For 12 years after leaving Columbia, Rogers immersed himself in practical clinical work with the Society for the Prevention of Cruelty to Children in Rochester, New York. During the summers he taught courses at Columbia and the University of Rochester. His first book, *Clinical Treatment of the Problem Child* (1939), finally brought Carl Rogers to the attention of a search committee at Ohio State University, which appointed him full professor in 1940.

Although Rogers had absorbed the views of Freud, his own clinical experience and experimental research failed to confirm these views, and he gradually began to rely less on traditional psychoanalysis and more on his own thinking. His ideas on counseling were published in *Counseling and Psychotherapy* (1942a). During subsequent years Rogers held teaching and administrative positions at the University of Chicago (1945–1957) and the University of Wisconsin (1957–1962). In 1964 he became a resident fellow at the Western Behavioral Sciences Institute. In 1968 he helped found the Center for Studies of the Person in La Jolla, California, an experimental "psychological community" in which social and behavioral scientists and others undertook a variety of training, research, and social projects (Meador & Rogers, 1984). Here Rogers remained until, following surgery for a broken hip, he died at the age of 85 on February 4, 1987.

Among Rogers' most noteworthy works is "Client-Centered Therapy" (1951), which thrust him into the professional spotlight and gave him uncontested prominence in the field of human understanding. His *On Becoming a Person* (1961b), which he wrote in 3 weeks, further solidified his professional stature. Until the end of his life, Rogers continued to be a productive writer. He authored several books after the age of 65, including *Freedom To Learn* (1969), *Carl Rogers on Encounter Groups* (1970), *Becoming Partners: Marriage and Its Alternatives* (1972), *Carl Rogers on Personal Power* (1977), *A Way of Being* (1980a), and *Freedom to Learn for the 80's* (1983).

HISTORICAL DEVELOPMENT

"It would seem quite absurd to suppose that one could name a day on which client-centered therapy was born," Carl Rogers has said. "Yet I feel it is possible to name that day and it was December 11, 1940" (Kirschenbaum, 1979, p. 112). On this date Rogers, then a professor at Ohio State University, delivered a speech at the University of Minnesota on "Newer Concepts in Psychotherapy." In his address, Rogers described the pitfalls of traditional approaches to counseling, especially their heavy reliance on advice, exhortation, suggestion, ordering, forbidding, and intellectualized interpretation. Having criticized the older methods, many of which were still in practice by members of his audience, Rogers went on to describe the "newer practices."

"The aim of this newer therapy," he said, "is not to solve one particular problem, but to assist the individual to grow, so that he can cope with the present problem and with later problems in a better integrated fashion." In response Rogers was both praised and criticized by the puzzled professionals in his audience. "I was totally unprepared for the furor the talk aroused," he said afterwards. In the ensuing clamor, Rogers realized he had delivered an address that was radical and significantly original.

Shortly thereafter, Rogers presented his thoughts to a larger audience in *Counseling and Psychotherapy: Newer Concepts in Practice* (1942a). Actually Houghton Mifflin, which had published his previous *Clinical Treatment of the Problem Child* (1939), was reluctant to publish the second, fearing that they would be unable to recoup their investment. Only after Rogers threatened to take his manuscript elsewhere did they reluctantly agree to publish it. Selling well over 100,000 copies in English and having been translated into numerous languages, *Counseling and Psychotherapy* has had a major, if not revolutionary, effect on the field of psychotherapy.

The Rogers methods and perspective were a reaction to what he has often labeled "counselor-centered therapy," in which the therapist administers tests, asks questions, makes a diagnosis, and suggests courses of action for the so-called patients to follow. The greater the responsibility that clients—as he came to call them—could take for their healing, both in and out of therapy, the more effective and long-lasting the therapy would be, Rogers believed. In Farson's (1975) words, Rogers' assertions made him "a quiet revolutionary" (p. xxviii).

One of the changes Rogers urged upon his colleagues may appear rather inconsequential on the surface but connotes the heart of his new therapy. Rogers used the term *client* instead of the traditional *patient*, which seemed to him to indicate a "sick" person who expects a cure from the doctor. Since psychiatry had emerged from the medical profession, the term *patient* had been accepted without much thought or question. To Rogers, however, the term *client* implied a different locus of control. Clients, he believed, might consult a professional who has helping skills, but the control remains with them. They make their own decisions.

Initially termed *nondirective counseling*, this new therapeutic approach was named *client-centered counseling* in 1951 as a means of emphasizing Rogers' positive focus on human capacities (Rogers, 1951, 1967). Although Rogers realized, of course, that it was impossible for anyone to be absolutely nondirective, it was during this period that he emphasized the importance of the clients' world as they saw it (Zimring and Raskin, 1992). "The individual," wrote Rogers, "exists in a continually changing world of experience of which he is the center" (Rogers, 1951, p. 483). In other words, how the client sees reality is more important than the reality itself; perception, more important than fact. This manner of thinking was rooted in applied *phenomenology* (Rychalk, 1973), which contends that what we are and what we do reflect our subjective experience of the world and ourselves. External reality can be known only through the inner reality of personal experience (Jones & Butman, 1991). With a profound respect for the client's perception of reality, Rogers focused on experience as the ultimate authority in understanding life: "It is to experience that I must return again and again; to discover a closer approximation to truth as it is in the process of becoming in me. Neither the Bible nor the prophets—neither Freud nor research—neither the revelations of God nor man—can take precedence over my own direct experience" (Rogers, 1961b, pp. 23–24). In fact, it was this emphasis on experience that led some to develop techniques such as focusing (Gendlin, 1981), which helps people "get in touch" with their experience.

A musician must make music, an artist must paint, a poet must write if he is to be ultimately at peace with himself.

—Abraham Maslow

In 1974 the name of Rogers' program was once again changed to "person-centered counseling" (Meador and Rogers, 1984), marking the beginning of yet another historic period in the development of this theory. During this period Rogerian principles found a broad range of applications in teaching, administration, organizational behavior, marriage, parenting, and interpersonal relations. In his own classroom at the University of Chicago, for example, Rogers began to shift the responsibility for learning and grading to his students. He simply offered himself as a learning resource. "I ceased to be a teacher," wrote Rogers. "It wasn't easy. It happened rather gradually, but as I began to trust students, I found they did incredible things..." (1983, p. 26). In *Freedom To Learn*, Rogers applied this approach to a "person-centered" education to all educational levels.

Reluctant to turn his students into "Rogerians" (Cain, 1987) and wanting to facilitate the process of becoming more self-directed, until 1980 Rogers discouraged the institutionalization of person-centered therapy. In the late 1970s, however, Rogers surrendered to international pressure and officially organized. In the first issue of the *Person-Centered Review,* he explained his rationale for becoming more institutionalized as a counseling movement: "There has . . . developed a large number of people in many nations—therapists, teachers, business people, doctors, social workers, researchers, lay people, pastors—who have a strong interest in the continuing development of a client-centered/person-centered approach" (Rogers, 1986, p. 4).

VIEW OF HUMAN NATURE

Person-centered therapy holds an optimistic view of human personality and focuses on present rather than past experience. Focusing on the inner experience of persons rather than on observable behavior, it holds that behavioral change evolves from within the person rather than through the manipulation of the environment. Unlike the Freudian approach, person-centered therapy views people as basically good and trustworthy.

Rogers emphasized an inherent tendency of people to grow and move in healthy directions, to develop their capacities to the fullest. He defined this directional learning, this *actualizing tendency,* as "the inherent tendency of the organism to develop all its capacities in ways which serve to maintain or enhance the organism" (1959, p. 196). Because this actualizing tendency creates the inner urge for fulfillment, it is the primary motivating force of every human being.

The actualizing tendency is guided by what Rogers called the *organismic valuing process,* an inherent capacity to choose that which will enhance us and reject that which does not. This innate drive serves as a pathfinder. Presumed to be an infallible and instinctive compass for guiding choice and action, the organismic valuing process determines or reveals that which will provide inner fulfillment.

An avid gardener, Rogers often suggested that, in the same way that plants grow well when conditions are favorable, so persons have a tendency to flourish when their circumstances support growth. Rogers believed that human beings possess this guiding tendency to actualize themselves and the capacity to do so. Given the proper conditions, the capacities for normal growth and development could be released in every human being. Rogers' counseling theory simply attempts to specify the conditions that allow this developmental process to occur.

Rogers recognized, of course, that human beings were capable of great evil—that they were capable of deceit, hatred, and cruelty—but he believed that these propensities were the result of negative "conditions of worth" imposed on children by family and society (Moreira, 1993). This negative side of the personality, which is not inborn but acquired, is a defensive reaction to an environment that is perceived as dangerous and threatening. Given the opportunity, this defensiveness would diminish, Rogers believed, and individuals would behave in ways that were trustworthy, reliable, constructive, and good. When this defensive reaction overwhelms individuals, however, they are alienated from their own inherent goodness, and it is this negative reaction to environment that leads to maladaptive behavior.

> I had expressed an idea whose time had come.
>
> —Carl Rogers

DEVELOPMENT OF MALADAPTIVE BEHAVIOR

Blessed with a drive toward actualization and an inerrant organismic valuing process to guide them, children still need acceptance and positive regard from others. If this need for acceptance is met, according to Rogers, children begin to define their sense of self in accordance with their own experience, rather than in terms of how others see or expect them to be (Rogers, 1931). Unpolluted by distortions caused by other persons' judgments, a self-concept allows the organismic valuing process to continue to function as a trustworthy guide. Well-being, then, is seen as congruence between what one wants to become, what one perceives one's self to be, and what one actually is.

Unfortunately, the emotional climate and healthy progression Rogers idealizes is an uncommon commodity in American families; few individuals escape childhood without some kind of abuse that distorts the self-concept. Even with good parents, most of us experience limited conditions of worth; we are loved conditionally, not unconditionally. We allow the expectations of parents or significant others to mold our ideal selves, and we develop a self-concept based on how well our experiences match those expectations. Children learn to falsify their perceived selves in order to maintain parental love and protection. Without fail, this leads to a distorted self-concept that quickly warps the organismic valuing process and leads to "problems in living" (Rogers, 1942a).

Rogers suggested that a number of values, learned at school, church, or home, may be incompatible with organismic experiencing: that sexuality is wrong, for instance, that unquestioning obedience to authority is good, that making money is important, that unstructured learning is a waste of time, that it is improper for men to cry or hug each other, and that women should not be independent or assertive (Nye, 1992). Such thoughts, feelings, and behaviors approved by significant others may vary so radically from the experiences approved by the person's own organismic valuing process that an almost complete dissociation develops. Initially this unhealthy development results in anxiety; eventually it causes people to collapse into maladaptive behavior.

In summary, maladaptive behavior results when persons become more externally than internally oriented. When our passion becomes whatever will gain us acceptance from others, we are tempted to distort our feelings to match the expectations of others. We ask "How *should* I be feeling?" rather than "How do I actually feel?" and it is this incongruity between what we really are and what we are trying to be, that gives birth to psychological pain and maladjustment (see Figure 9-1).

FUNCTION OF THE THERAPIST

Since the person-centered therapist's role is rooted in *being*, not *doing* (McLeod & McLeod, 1993), the major task of the therapist is to provide a climate of safety and trust, which will encourage clients to reintegrate their self-actualizing and self-valuing processes. This the therapist accomplishes by encouraging the psychotherapeutic conditions—the so-called therapeutic triad—of accurate empathic understanding, congruence, and unconditional positive regard. These are discussed in detail in a later section of this chapter.

Rogerians believe that each of these qualities is rooted in the personhood of the therapist (Levant and Shlien, 1984). Although they can be learned as counseling skills, they must spring from the very being of the counselor to be used effectively. Seldom, if ever, does the Rogerian counselor give advice, interpret, or teach the client. Based on a fundamental disrespect of others, such strategies, it is argued, foster dependency and thwart the development of any meaningful sense of autonomy. Unlike therapists who "do something to" the client, the person-centered therapist cultivates the soil in which the client's hidden drive to grow and develop can be nurtured and released. Only through the proper characteristics and competencies of the therapist, then, can the client move toward greater congruence.

As a result, the person-centered therapist is nonauthoritarian, and formal assessment of the client's problems in the form of psychological testing is considered to be inappropriate and unnecessary. Techniques, of which there are few in person-centered therapy, are secondary to the therapist's attitudes, sensitivities and skills.

FIGURE 9-1   Congruity and incongruity depend on the relationship between the real self and the ideal self.

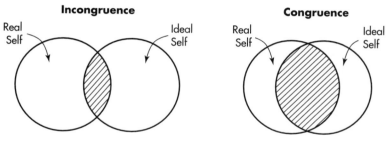

GOALS OF THERAPY

"To be that self which one truly is," a phrase Rogers borrowed from the Danish philosopher–theologian Søren Kierkegaard, is the singular goal of our lives. It is the goal of person-centered therapy to facilitate this process. Habitual modes of impressing others, lying to ourselves, and distorting our perceptions all cause us to lose contact with our true selves. Person-centered therapy strives to create an environment safe enough to eliminate the need for these facades.

The aim of person-centered therapy, then, is not so much to solve problems (Rogers, 1977) as to assist clients in their growth process, so they are equipped as human beings who are *fully functioning,* and who are able to cope effectively with current and future problems. They live in a way that most fully expresses and develops their potential as human beings while mutually supporting growth in others. According to Rogers (1980a, p. 117), fully functioning persons are increasingly open to experience, increasingly accepting of their own feelings, and capable of living in the present from moment to moment. Since they are increasingly free to make choices and act on them spontaneously, they are trusting of self and of human nature and are capable of balanced and realistic expressions of affection and aggression. Increasingly, they are active and non-conformist.

The goals of person-centered therapy can be thought of as two processes that occur concurrently: first, moving away from the self one is not; and, second, moving toward one's true self.

Moving Away from the Self One Is Not

Person-centered therapy initially strives to help clients relinquish self-concealment and phoniness, in order that they may gradually dismantle their false selves. The therapist seeks to emancipate individuals from "oughts" and "shoulds" that imprison them in behaviors designed to meet the expectations of others: the father who wants his son to grow up to take over the family business, the mother who would be proud to have her son become a doctor, the teacher who labels a young person a daydreamer. Whatever the source of these expectations, most of us unwittingly adopt external specifications for the kind of person we "ought" to be or "should" become. Our need for acceptance and love, from a parent or a peer group, locks us into a pattern of behavior that we mistakenly come to accept as our own true self. Person-centered therapy gradually chips away at the "oughts" and "shoulds" that form the artificial self.

> *Call a client a patient, and he is liable to act like one.*
>
> —Carl Rogers

To help clients move away from their phony selves, person-centered therapy fosters a nonconformist way of being. The therapist allows clients to ignore the pressures not only of parents, teachers, and friends but also of the surrounding culture, which defines what a beautiful person wears, what a popular person drives, and so on. Fully functioning persons resist the attempts of Madison Avenue and mass culture to dictate what they should buy and who they should become. Therapy attempts to release people from such cultural imprisonment, so that they might use their own minds.

Person-centered therapy tries to eliminate the unhealthy need to please others. This false sense of self begins to develop in children when youngsters become obsessed with pleasing their mother and father, and for some this urge to please becomes a characteristic way of relating to others throughout life. Of course, it can't be done, and as people escalate their attempts to please everyone, the drive to please is self-defeating. In the process of moving away from their false selves, clients gradually give up trying to please the counselor and the significant others in their lives. They no longer allow themselves to be under bondage to persons who are not significant to their lives. This does not imply that fully functioning individuals are selfish. Whereas they will *do* things to please others, they will not *become* someone else just to please others. As healthy people, they are true to the essence of their own selves.

Moving Toward One's True Self

As clients discard their emotional armor, they open themselves to others and to the pleasures that come with being authentic. In fact, it is the goal of person-centered therapy to move not only away from what one is not, but also toward what one is meant to be—one's true self. The antithesis of defensiveness, this "openness" allows fully functioning people to be receptive to feelings that may have been denied for years. Openness allows us to be moved emotionally and experience reality more accurately, and it is this accurate perception of reality that is a universally accepted criterion of mental health.

As clients move toward their true selves, finally free of inhibitions and rationalizations, increasingly they come to trust their own experience. Comfortable with its impulses and intuitions, the true self is equally confident in its judgments and beliefs. Einstein, for example, must have known that his thinking represented a serious departure from traditional scientific assumptions, yet he trusted his own judgment more than that of his colleagues. This approach is not reserved for geniuses, however; according to Rogers, it is the goal of all who enter person-centered therapy (see Sidebar 9-1).

Sidebar 9-1

SELF-ACTUALIZATION

Central to Rogers' theory is the motive toward actualization (Bozarth & Brodley, 1991). People have an inherent need to enhance themselves by becoming the best selves their inherited natures will allow them to be. The term *self-actualization* was first introduced to psychology by Kurt Goldstein (1939), who studied brain-damaged soldiers following World War I. Goldstein was struck with the fact that these individuals, despite an injured nervous system, still had an integrity and wholeness about their personalities.

Rogers theorized that fully functioning people, guided by their organismic

---

Continued.

valuing processes, epitomize psychological health. Actually, the person Rogers
described is an ideal. However, some
individuals come close to the goal of
being fully functioning or self-actualizing.
Abraham Maslow (1968) is well known for
his contribution to self-actualization. He
identified several characteristics of self-
actualizing people. For example, he found
that they perceive reality accurately, accept themselves and others, have a continued freshness of appreciation, are spontaneous, discriminate between means and
ends, have a deep desire to help humankind, are creative, have a philosophical
sense of humor, and so on. Maslow also
made it clear that these individuals are not
perfect.

The following scale attempts to help
measure your own level of actualization.
For each of the following statements, indicate the extent to which the statement applies to you, using this four-point scale:

> 1=Disagree
> 2=Disagree somewhat
> 3=Agree somewhat
> 4=Agree

___ 1. I do not feel ashamed of any of my
emotions.

___ 2. I feel I must do what others expect
of me.

This test is a short form of a measure of self-
actualization developed by Jones and Crandall
(1986). Reprinted with permission.

___ 3. I believe that people are essentially
good and can be trusted.

___ 4. I feel free to be angry at those I
love.

___ 5. It is always necessary that others
approve of what I do.

___ 6. I don't accept my own weaknesses.

___ 7. I can like people without having to
approve of them.

___ 8. I fear failure.

___ 9. I avoid attempts to analyze and
simplify complex domains.

___ 10. It is better to be yourself than to be
popular.

___ 11. I have no mission in life to which I
feel especially dedicated.

___ 12. I can express my feelings even
when they may result in undesirable consequences.

___ 13. I do not feel responsible to help
anybody.

___ 14. I am bothered by fears of being inadequate.

___ 15. I am loved because I give love.

To calculate your score, first reverse
the values for items 2, 5, 6, 8, 9, 11, 13,
and 14. In other words, for those items:
1=4, 2=3, 3=2, 4=1. Next, add the values
for all 15 items. The higher the score, the
more "self-actualized" you are said to be
at this point in your life. The average
score for females is 46 and the average
score for males is 45 (both have a standard
deviation of 5).

People who are becoming fully functioning never "arrive." They are continually in process. The notion that we can someday reach a permanent state of
being that is free from unpleasantness is pure fantasy. Those who are moving
toward their real selves, who accept the complexity of human relationships,
who do not deny their ambivalent or contradictory feelings—these fully functioning human beings accept this perennial condition of flux. They accept the
fact that they will never "have it all together." Having abandoned the goal of
solving all their problems, they focus not on product but on process. According

to Rogers, these are the people who manage to weather the vicissitudes of life, who live with zest.

As a by-product of perceiving oneself not as being, but as becoming, fully functioning individuals accept others who also are in process. They do not criticize others for not being what they "ought" to be. Just as we do not fault the water for being wet, Rogers pointed out, borrowing an analogy from Abraham Maslow, so fully functioning persons do not judge others for being what they are.

MAJOR METHODS AND TECHNIQUES

The traditional counseling relationship was "coercive," as Rogers put it, and it was never more than superficially effective for him. As a therapist he recalled trying hundreds of different ways of curing his clients before realizing that, in order to help, he must begin by no longer doing anything *to* them. Instead of explaining the causes of their problems or prescrib-

There are as many "real worlds" as there are people!

—Carl Rogers

ing actions for them to take, Rogers discovered that clients improved when he simply accepted and appreciated them as valuable human beings. In other words, when he created a relationship built on unconditional acceptance, his clients seemed to find ways to help themselves. As a result, person-centered therapy boldly asserts that it is the client, not the therapist, who should be at the heart of psychotherapy, for it is only the client who has the resources for becoming more aware of the obstacles to personal growth. Once awareness dawns, light floods all the dark corners. All person-centered methods lead to this end.

Rogers' therapeutic work led him to identify three "necessary and sufficient" conditions for growth and change in personality (1957): *congruence, unconditional positive regard,* and *accurate empathic understanding.* These three conditions are interrelated and may be best understood as general attitudes conveyed toward a client. When these conditions are fully present, persons become fully functioning, showing optimal maturity and adjustment.

Congruence

For a client to grow, the therapist must be genuine and transparent (Rogers, 1980b), a state of realness which Rogers called *congruence* because he wanted to emphasize the perfect match between the therapist's inner experiences and their observable outward actions. Without playing the role of a counselor or trying to hide behind a facade of professionalism, the therapist must exhibit an openness to his or her own inner experiences during the therapy hour. "I am more effective when I can listen acceptantly to myself, and can be myself," said Rogers, without trying to act "as though I were something I am not" (1961a, pp. 16–17). If a client relates an experience that is depressing or that arouses sadness, for example, the therapist need not smile benignly to disguise his or her true feelings. Even an experienced therapist might admit to the client, "I find myself saddened because you are touching on feelings that remind me of my own life" (Rogers, 1959). Whereas the sharing of such feelings expresses genuiness and value to clients, the successful practitioner never becomes so spontaneous, of course, that clients are burdened with impulsively shared experiences that do not directly relate to creating the necessary conditions of change (Rogers, 1980b).

Neither does a person-centered therapist depend on a secret strategy; he or she is neither defensive nor evasive. These therapists are what they seem to be. If a therapist is uncomfortable with some aspect of the client relationship but does not admit it, the discomfort acts as a shield against authenticity and creates *incongruence*, which keeps the therapist from being fully present in the counseling relationship and hinders unconditional positive regard (see Sidebar 9-2).

Sidebar 9-2

THE Q-SORT TECHNIQUE

When psychotherapy is effective, the patient experiences a reduction in the incongruency between the real and the ideal selves, a reduction that can be assessed by means of the Q-sort technique. The Q-sort technique requires the client to sort a set of 100 or so statements descriptive of personality into a series of nine categories (piles) varying from "most descriptive" to "least descriptive" of the person. Each card in a Q-sort deck contains a statement such as the following:

Has a wide range of interests.

Is productive; gets things done.

Is self-dramatizing; is histrionic.

Is overreactive to minor frustrations; is irritable.

Seeks reassurance from others.

Appears to have a high degree of intellectual capacity.

Is basically anxious. (Block, 1961, pp. 132–136)

In sorting the statement-containing cards in a Q-sort deck, the respondent is directed to make his or her choices in such a way that a certain number of statements fall in each category and so the resulting frequency distribution of statements across categories has a predetermined shape, usually normal. To approximate a normal distribution for a Q-sort of 100 statements, Block (1961) recommends instructing sorters to place the following numbers of statements into categories. 1 through 9: 5, 8, 12, 16, 18, 16, 12, 8, 5. The response to each statement in a Q-sort instrument is assigned an integer ranging from 1 to 9, depending on the category assigned to the statement by the respondent. The results obtained from different sorts or sorters can then be related by computing correlation coefficients between different sorts.

To assess the changes in self-concept resulting from psychotherapy, clients make before-and-after Q-sorts of a series of statements describing their feelings and attitudes. In a series of studies conducted by Rogers and Dymond (1951), each person was directed to make a separate Q-sort according to his or her "real self" and "ideal self." The results showed that, compared with "no-therapy" groups, differences between the "real" and "ideal" self-sorts of clients who had undergone therapy decreased.

Unconditional Positive Regard

Everyone needs positive regard, and most of us receive it, but only *if* we measure up to what others want us to be. Only if we meet peoples' specific conditions of worth will they accept and value us. The emphasis lies on the word *if*, because positive regard involves a contingent: "If you do as I want you to do, then I will value you as important. If you don't, then I won't." Often, then, we avoid whatever is judged by others as "worthless" and seek out what others judge as more worthy. That is, we learn to act in ways that significant people in our lives value, even if this results in our distorting our personal experiences to conform to their pressure. All of this acting is the price that we are willing to pay to receive positive regard.

In person-centered therapy, however, the client's worth is not dependent on others' expectations. There are no conditions of worth that the client must meet to qualify for the therapist's acceptance: no expectations that clients should do the "right" thing or be what they "should" be, no distinction between those aspects of personality that are judged to be "more or less worthy of positive regard than any other" (Rogers, 1959, p. 208). Clients do not need to earn approval, since they are freely given *unconditional positive regard*, that is, the experience of receiving warmth, respect, sympathy, acceptance, caring, and trust from others simply for being who they are (Rogers, 1959). Unconditional positive regard is a kind of love, says Rogers, "providing we understand the word love as equivalent to the theologian's term *agape,* and not in its usual romantic and possessive meanings" (1962, p. 422). This allows clients to feel unconditionally prized, valued, accepted, worthwhile, and trusted, simply for being who they are.

The good life is a direction, not a destination.

—Carl Rogers

Unconditional positive regard for people means respecting them, regardless of the different values the counselor might place on certain behaviors. The therapist does not judge behavior as being positive or negative. Rather, regardless of their beliefs or behaviors, the clients find acceptance: *acceptance* being defined as a deep and genuine caring for the client as a person without reservations, conditions, judgments, or evaluations (Rogers 1961b, 1980a, 1964). This is not to suggest that everything people do or say needs to be approved. Rogers was careful to distinguish between the individual as a person and the individual's freely chosen values and behaviors. A therapist may disapprove of a client's alcoholism, for example, although accepting him or her as a person. Even though the therapist might wish the client would behave differently, the client is not rejected but accepted. Clients who experience such unconditional positive regard draw a profound conclusion: Since someone who knows all their faults cares about them despite those faults, they must be worth something.

Empathic Understanding

The third ingredient of person-centered therapy is *empathy,* the capacity to enter the place of other human beings and understand the world from their perspective. Practitioners are almost universally agreed that the use of empathy is vital to counseling (Cramer, 1993; Egan, 1994; Fielder, 1950; Gladstein, 1983; Hackney, 1978; Truax & Mitchell, 1971). Through *empathic understanding*, the therapist, while maintaining objectivity, adopts the client's internal frame of reference, viewing reality through the client's eyes. Delving beneath the surface of the client's words and actions, empathic understanding perceives inner feelings, attitudes, meanings, and motives. Although a counselor never fully understands what an individual is experiencing internally, the therapist attempts to understand all that is possible. It is as if the person-centered therapist were the client, although Rogers is quick to warn that the therapist must never lose sight of the *as if* quality in the relationship.

But empathy is not sympathy. The sympathetic therapist stands on the shore and throws out a lifeline to someone who is drowning. But the empathetic counselor plunges beneath the surface, dives into the water to help the person who is struggling, and concentrates on the emotional, not the intellectual, elements in the therapeutic relationship. Intellectually, we may know what needs to occur in our own lives, but because we are emotional beings knowledge does not ensure behavioral change. Although clients may talk about factual information, the person-centered counselor empathizes with and "listens" to the feelings beneath the surface: to the body language, the facial expressions, the fluctuations in the voice.

To facilitate this empathic understanding, the person-centered therapist feeds back or "reflects" to his or her clients, as accurately as possible, the feelings they are expressing. It is an attempt to let clients know that they are accepted as persons, that they have been heard and understood (Barrett-Lennard, 1988). Avoiding explanations, questions, and advice, the therapist has done more than listen to words. When the therapist responds to clients with accurate reflection, they are moved forward by the interaction; their world is changed by the very act of being heard (Gendlin, 1970). In this way, empathic understanding is the vehicle for both positive regard and congruence. Thus, empathy communicates to clients that they are worth understanding, that their inner hopes and private fears have value. When clients become convinced that another person values them, they begin to value themselves. Like congruence and unconditional positive regard, empathy gives them the freedom to become fully functioning human beings.

My garden supplies the same intriguing question I have been trying to meet all my professional life: What are the effective conditions for growth?

—Carl Rogers

APPLICATION

Even though Rogers was devoted to research throughout his career, the years he spent researching his therapeutic procedures at the University of Chicago were among his most productive. During this time he documented many case studies, including that of Mrs. Oak. In her late 30s, feeling unattractive, frustrated, and generally miserable, Mrs. Oak entered the Counseling Center at the University of Chicago. In addition to difficulties with her husband, Mrs. Oak was deeply disturbed by her relationship with her teenage daughter, blaming herself for her daughter's recent, serious illness. Mrs. Oak was a dependent, passive person who felt rejected both at home and in social groups.

During the early stages of therapy, she talked mostly of other people. When she spoke about herself, it was as if she were an object, someone burdened with problems and puzzled as to the causes of her unhappiness. Although she had unrealistically high aspirations and a strong need to be perfect in nearly everything she did, she felt at the same time uninteresting, rebellious, useless, and deeply conflicted over her sexual identity. Finding her to be shy, nondescript, and very nearly incoherent, her therapist wrote that she expressed herself in "jumbled analogies, half-sentences, and incomplete thought" (Rogers, 1954, p. 264). As therapy progressed, Mrs. Oak became less problem oriented, better able to express herself, and more self-confident.

Once she realized that the therapist cared for her, she began to experience herself in a more positive way. "She gradually became aware of the fact that, though she had searched in every corner of herself, there was nothing fundamentally bad but, rather at heart she was positive and sound" (Rogers, 1954, p. 263). At the end of 40 counseling sessions, Mrs. Oak had experienced considerable change in her self-concept. Although still in conflict over her sexuality, and still somewhat pessimistic and depressed, she seemed to herself to be more self-sufficient, less threatened by people, and more integrated or whole. Even in the absence of further psychotherapy, she was nevertheless confident that she would continue to make progress.

Mrs. Oak, however, did receive more psychotherapy. Seven months later she returned for follow-up testing and at that time decided to resume counseling in order to clear up a few matters. As Rogers (1951, p. 66) stated, "There is little likelihood that any therapy is…complete." Subsequently, Mrs. Oak received eight additional therapy sessions, after which she soon took a job and improved her relationship with her daughter. No longer striving to be perfect, she was content to relax and enjoy life.

Taping these conversations on a thin thread of wire, well in advance of modern recording tape, Rogers was among the first therapist–researchers to record the psychotherapeutic relationship. Along with the willingness to use this new technology, Rogers committed his therapeutic process to scientific scrutiny. Sidebar 9-3 shows fragments of two recorded counseling interviews with college students, printed side by side to facilitate direct comparisons. The left column contains the transcript of a "patient" and a therapist who view therapy as a structured, problem-centered activity under the direct control of the therapist. The right column contains the transcript of a similar interview between a "client" and a counselor who recognizes that the therapeutic process is very much person centered.

The differences between these two session excerpts are easily discernible. Any Rogerian would be quick to point out that, if the feelings of the client are mentioned at all in the left-hand transcript, they are talked about rather than

Sidebar 9-3

COUNSELOR: I noticed that you stated you enrolled in Psychology 411 [study-habits course] because you didn't know how to study well enough—uh—you're worried about low grades and poor memory and so on. How well did you do in high school?

STUDENT: Well, I was just an average student.

COUNSELOR: And what major did you take there?

STUDENT: Ah, you mean—

COUNSELOR: In high school, you took college preparatory or commercial?

STUDENT: It was an academic course. I took languages and English and history.

COUNSELOR: What course did you like the best? [Student presumably answers; later in session counselor summarizes:]

COUNSELOR: It seems to me that your problem is that you want to learn more about yourself. We'll be getting all these tests back, and there are those [study] projects, and the way we do, I see you each week at this time and you'll begin to get a little better picture—And then I'll help you check it and I'll tell you if it's right—(Laugh).

STUDENT: Mm-hm.

COUNSELOR: So we can work it out. I would suggest—I would more or less work this project out because you say you are having difficulties concentrating. . . .

Source: (From Rogers, 1942a, pp. 116–117)

STUDENT: I haven't written to my parents about this at all. In the past they haven't been of any help to me in this respect, and if I can keep it away from them as much as possible, I'll do so. But there's a slight matter of grades to explain, and they're not good, and I don't know how I'm going to explain without telling them about this. Would you advise me to tell them about it?

COUNSELOR: Suppose you tell me a little more about what you had thought about it.

STUDENT: Well, I think I'm compelled to, because—

COUNSELOR: It's a situation you've really got to face.

STUDENT: Yes, there's no use getting around it, even if they can't take it the way they should, because I've already flunked my gym course, I just haven't come. . . .

COUNSELOR: It will be fairly hard for you to tell them.

STUDENT: Yes. Oh, I don't know if they're going to sort of condemn me. I think so, because that's what they've done in the past. . . .

COUNSELOR: You feel that they'll be unsympathetic and they'll condemn you for your failures.

STUDENT: Well my—I'm pretty sure my father will. My mother might not. He hasn't been—he doesn't experience these things; he just doesn't know what it's like. . . .

COUNSELOR: You feel that he could never understand you?

Source: (From Rogers, 1942a, pp. 135–136)

genuinely experienced. In the second transcript, in the right-hand column, the client is encouraged to express feelings, and every reply of the counselor is an attempt to respond, not to the informational aspects of the situation, but to the emotional content of the client's statements.

According to Rogers, this person-centered approach need not be limited to individual counseling sessions. Its principles have been widely used in resolving many different kinds of potentially polarized relationships, such as play therapy, marriage and family counseling, human relations training with paraprofessional helpers, institutional change, labor–management disputes, race relations, and encounter groups, which Rogers was largely, although not solely, responsible for promoting (Raskin & Rogers 1995) (see also Sidebar 9-4).

CRITICAL ANALYSIS

Perhaps Rogers' greatest strength is his unequivocal respect for persons, his insistence on viewing people holistically and as purposeful, and his reliance on his clients. No theorist before Rogers had the confidence to step outside the role of expert and to place trust and responsibility in the hands of the counselee. But whereas Rogers is to be commended for emphasizing the person, any student of therapy will inevitably ask how it is that clients can supply accurate self-appraisals. Critics say Rogers is naively optimistic, but he insists that he does "not have a Pollyanna view of human nature" (1961a, p. 27). Rogers argues that therapists are making a mistake when they assume they know what clients are thinking or why they act a certain way. But there are times, even under good circumstances, when clients are unable or unwilling to provide the therapist with accurate information for these judgments. This leads to an even weightier critique of Rogers' basic assumption that people are fundamentally good and that we are the sole masters of our own destiny. Personal wholeness assumes primacy; it becomes a moral imperative, possibly at the expense of appreciation of our responsibilities to others. With the self assuming a position of supreme importance, Rogers' individualistic and relativistic philosophy can lead to inflated notions of the self. Although this is more a theological than an empirical question, many 20th-century Americans find the fundamental premise of this theory difficult to accept. In particular, it seems doubtful that as inherently peaceful and cooperative a species as Rogers would have us, would so frequently engage in war, crime, and other destructive behaviors solely because of introjected, pathological conditions of worth.

> *Personality is a process, not an onion.*
>
> —Paul Wachtel

On a more pragmatic and clinical level, many practitioners do not agree that it is preferable to dispense with interpretations and rely wholly on genuineness, empathy, and unconditional positive regard. Others warn that in some instances—telling a narcissistic but vulnerable client, for example, that constant self-preoccupation is provoking boredom and anger—such genuiness might well be damaging (Kahn, 1985, p. 901).

Sidebar 9-4

ENCOUNTER GROUPS

Rogers was largely responsible for the growth of the "the group movement." From the late 1960s to the middle 1970s, he all but abandoned individual counseling in favor of encounter groups, or T-groups. Rogers, with missionary zeal, wanted to bring enhanced psychological health to greater numbers of people, so he developed these groups where people could learn more about themselves and how they relate to, or encounter, one another.

The typical encounter group ranges in size from 8 to 15 persons, and meets for from 20 to 60 sessions. The group meets with no structure or agenda and no leader. The people who run encounter groups are called *facilitators*. Their job is to establish an atmosphere in which the group members can easily express themselves and thus achieve self-insight.

The evidence for the effectiveness of encounter groups is mostly anecdotal, in which people report that they feel better and more aware of their true natures (Rogers, 1970). A review of research on encounter groups showed they can lead to negative as well as positive psychological experiences (Hartley, Roback, & Abramowitz, 1976; Newman & Lovell, 1993). Encounter groups are no longer as popular as they were when Rogers first promoted them, but they are still used by some of his followers.

An "encounter group," popular in the late 1960s and early 1970s.
(Sepp Seitz/Woodfin Camp & Associates)

Despite these criticisms, most agree that Rogers has made significant strides toward creating a counseling theory with explicitly stated concepts and verifiable hypotheses. Although there are problems with measuring some of his concepts, Rogers has received the justifiable respect of many of his peers for stimulating serious research in the practice of psychotherapy. Rogers valued constructing an approach that was empirically based, and in fact no model of therapy has been more extensively researched than his own (Goodyear, 1987; Seligmen, 1986).

One need only consider the global impact of person-centered therapy and its significant contributions to cross-cultural counseling in order to find still further testimony as to the impact of his theory. "Our international family consists of millions of persons world-wide whose lives have been affected by Carl Rogers' writings and personal efforts as well as his many colleagues who have brought his and their own innovative thinking and programs to many corners of the earth," writes David Cain (1987, p. 149), summing up the influence of Rogers' approach to cultural diversity. In many respects person-centered psychotherapy provides an ideal foundation for working with ethnically diverse clients (Freeman, 1993; Hayashi, Kuno, Osawa, & Shimizu, 1992; Hill-Hain & Rogers, 1988; Patterson, 1985), and it has proved just as helpful in teaching constructive therapeutic behavior in diverse settings (Fink, 1990; Yau, Sue, & Hayden, 1992).

I have no methods, all I do is accept people.

—Paul Tournier

Despite these significant contributions, the limitations of person-centered therapy, marked mostly by its reductionist nature, have become equally obvious (Usher, 1989). In an attempt to ease racial tension and aggression, for example, Rogers discusses the possibility of reducing these tensions by engaging the concerned parties with each other under facilitative group conditions (Rogers, 1977). Yet these principles, which are used with troubled individuals in therapy, are no match for the more complex set of historical, political, economic, and cultural factors that have preserved the status quo. Whereas sensitive communication under facilitative conditions can be an important beginning in trying to resolve discrimination in the job market, a racial conflict, or any other factor keeping minority groups in bondage, it is clearly not enough. Person-centered therapy may be useful for working out certain kinds of problems in middle-class adjustment, but it is not wholly adequate for dealing with the myriad of serious psychological and social disturbances.

In treating clients with physical disabilities, person-centered therapy has similar strengths and weaknesses. As one might expect, advocates of Rogerian intervention argue that disabled individuals are psychologically affected, not by the disability per se, but by its subjective impact and the personal attitudes associated with it. Early in counseling, therefore, clients can profit from gaining insight into their perceptions and feelings of being disabled, and they can come to accept their disability emotionally without devaluing themselves or resorting to defensive maneuvers. Most experts would undoubtedly value the counselor's providing and communicating early facilitative conditions, such as personal warmth and empathic understanding, to assist their clients with a disability and to establish a more positive self-concept. But the later phases of such a counseling process require more active and direct involvement than the person-centered approach permits. Among its limitations in such rehabilitation settings are a reluctance to set specific goals, an aversion to diagnose and evaluate or even to give advice, a lack of concern with the external environment, an orientation toward process rather than an outcome, and a tendency to overlook client behavior or skill development (See, 1985).

CURRENT STATUS

Nevertheless, other than Freud and Adler, no single psychologist has more significantly influenced the actual practice of counseling and psychotherapy than Carl Rogers. Whether explicitly or implicitly, his strategies are integrated into the work of almost every contemporary practitioner. Beyond that, the language of professional caring that Rogers pioneered has become embedded in the vocabulary of everyday conversation. "Whole person," "awareness," "potentials," "growth," "self-concept," "realness," "spontaneity," and "process" have all become staples of the terminology we use to describe our condition. More than any other individual, Rogers is responsible for the popularity of such concepts.

Several generations of practitioners have observed Carl Rogers demonstrate person-centered therapy—his expression of genuineness, unconditional positive regard, and empathic understanding—in numerous filmed and videotaped presentations. Observing Rogers has led practitioners to what Burke (1989, p. 278) calls an "unfortunate confusion of style with substance," so that imitations of Rogers may have replaced the genuine practice of his theory. After all, to the untrained eye Rogers' therapeutic style, including his reflections and his "Mm-hms" and "Un-huhs," can seem passive and artificial. Taken to the extreme, these mannerisms can become the subject not so much of therapy as of parody.

Still, many counseling psychologists and many "eclectic" counselors today report being strongly influenced by person-centered therapy (Baradell, 1990; Miller & Foxworth, 1992; Warner, 1991; Watkins, 1993; Watkins, Lopez, Campbell, & Himmell, 1986). The person-centered approach is used in everything from career counseling (Miller, 1991) to treatment of breast cancer (Burton, Parker, & Wollner, 1991). Not surprisingly, Rogers is ranked at the top of most lists of psychologists who have made the greatest impact in the field of counseling and psychotherapy (Smith, 1982). Rogers' effect on counseling has been so pervasive that many of his ideas now seem to be self-evident truths. "They have become so ingrained in counseling," said Gelso and Fretz (1992, p. 267), "that many counselors forget they ever came from Rogers!"

When I accept myself as I am, then I change.
                    —Carl Rogers

Despite Rogers' watershed influence, however, most psychologists today do not claim person-centered therapy as their primary theoretical orientation.

Regarding it as necessary but not sufficient, counselors treat the Rogerian approach as a foundation upon which they must build other therapeutic skills (Cain, 1988). One of the reasons for this may be that Rogers himself opposed the formation of a person-centered "school" of counseling that would grant certificates and set standards for membership. He viewed this kind of institutionalization as leading to a narrow, dogmatic perspective, which would ultimately be counterproductive. During the 1980s, however, person-centered therapists took the initiative and developed the Association for the Development of the Person-Centered Approach, founded by David Cain, whose purpose is to foster innovation in therapy, education, and supervision. The association has over 250 members. Dedicated to promoting the work of Rogers and his pioneering spirit, *The Person-Centered Review,* the association's quarterly newsletter, features articles on the current state of theory applied to practice and reviews relevant research.

Since the person-centered approach takes a relatively short time to master and since it emphasizes listening skills, it is the basis for much of today's counselor training. David Cain (1990), however, believes that in order for person-centered therapy to be viable in the future, its practitioners will need to focus more directly on drug abuse, child abuse, divorce, and other contemporary issues.

CHAPTER SUMMARY

1. *Biography.* Rogers (1902–1987) grew up in a well-to-do, conservative, midwestern family. He read voraciously as a child and developed a precocious respect for the experimental method. Rogers majored in agriculture and history at the University of Wisconsin and as a sophomore he committed himself to Christian ministry. After 2 years at Union Theological Seminary, he transferred to Columbia, where he eventually earned his Ph.D. in clinical psychology. Rogers immersed himself in practical clinical work and, after publishing his first book, he was invited to teach at Ohio State University. Following professorships at the University of Chicago and the University of Wisconsin, in 1968 he founded the Center for Studies of the Person in La Jolla, California, where he died at age 85.

2. *Historical Development.* The origins of person-centered therapy can be found in reaction to what Rogers often called "counselor-centered therapy," in which the therapist administers tests, asks questions, and suggests courses of action for the client. Rogers' revolutionary approach took on such subtle changes as using the term *client* instead of *patient,* and it was he who first called his approach "nondirective counseling," later changing it to "person-centered counseling," as a means of emphasizing its positive focus on human capacities.

3. *View of Human Nature.* Rogers viewed people through an optimistic lens, seeing human nature as basically good. He emphasized an inherent tendency of people to grow and move in healthy directions. For Rogers, this actualizing

tendency was the primary motivating force of every human being. It is guided by what he called the organismic valuing process, an inherent capacity to choose that which will enhance one's self and reject that which will not. The actualization drive creates the inner urge for fulfillment, and the organismic valuing process determines or reveals what will provide that inner fulfillment. Given the proper conditions, Rogers believed the capacities for normal growth and development could be released in every human being.

4. *Development of Maladaptive Behavior.* Distortions in the self-concept quickly warp the organismic valuing process and lead to maladaptive behavior. Rogers suggested that learned values, thoughts, feelings, and behaviors may differ so radically from the experiences approved by the person's own organismic valuing process, that an almost complete dissociation develops. Ultimately, this leads to being more externally than internally oriented, and thus individuals contort feelings to match the expectations of others. It is this incongruity that gives birth to psychological pain and maladjustment.

5. *Goals of Therapy.* Person-centered therapy seeks not to solve problems, but to facilitate a process in which clients can know who they really are and become fully functioning human beings. It strives to eliminate the need for impressing others, lying to oneself, or distorting perceptions. Person-centered therapy tries to eliminate the unhealthy need to please others and to move toward increasingly trusting one's own experience.

6. *Function of the Therapist.* The role of the person-centered therapist is rooted, not in doing, but in being. The major task of the therapist is to provide a climate of safety and trust, which will encourage clients to reintegrate their self-actualizing and self-valuing processes. The therapist accomplishes this through accurate empathic understanding, congruence, and unconditional positive regard. Although these skills can be learned, to be effective, they must spring from the very being of the counselor. The person-centered therapist is nonauthoritarian, seldom, if ever, giving advice, making interpretations, or teaching his or her clients.

7. *Major Methods and Techniques.* Rogers' therapeutic work led him to identify three "necessary and sufficient" conditions for growth and change in personality: congruence (in which the therapist's inner experiences and their observable outward actions match), unconditional positive regard (the client's worth is not dependent on others' expectations and approval), and empathic understanding (the therapist enters the client's place and understands the world from his or her perspective, adopting the client's internal frame of reference).

8. *Application.* Rogers was the first to expose the practice of counseling to audio recording. He made great use of this technology and as a result developed thorough case studies during the formulation of his theory. The case of "Mrs. Oak" is one example that illustrates just how Rogers used the three essential ingredients to bring about a truer sense of one's self and greater autonomy. A

comparison of the Rogerian transcript with the transcript of a more problem-solving approach reveals the stark difference between counselor-centered and client-centered approaches to therapy.

9. *Critical Analysis.* The respect of person-centered therapy for the individual and its reliance on the client is most admirable. Trusting clients to be responsible has its advantages. However, this approach leads many to ask how clients can supply accurate self-appraisals, and the underlying philosophical assumption that people are fundamentally good raises many questions among critics. Few can argue with the global impact and contributions to cross-cultural counseling of person-centered therapy. Although it is not a complete answer to these circumstances (especially after the initial facilitation processes), it certainly provides a foundation for working with many ethnically diverse clients.

10. *Current Status.* Several generations of practitioners who have been trained in Rogerian strategies report being strongly influenced by the person-centered approach—especially eclectic counselors. Despite Rogers' significant influence, however, most psychologists do not claim person-centered therapy as their primary theoretical orientation. One of their reasons for regarding the approach as necessary, rather than sufficient, may be that Rogers opposed the formation of a person-centered "school" of counseling that would grant certificates and set standards for membership.

KEY TERMS

Actualizing Tendency   The inherent tendency of human beings to develop all of their potential, to become the best that their inherited natures will allow them to be.

Conditional Positive Regard   Accepting another person only if that individual meets one's own standards.

Congruence   A healthy state of unison between one's total organismic experience and a self-concept that is free of conditions of worth. It is one of the three basic conditions for therapeutic effectiveness.

Empathy   The state of accurately understanding the client's world from the client's perspective. It is one of the three basic conditions for therapeutic effectiveness.

Encounter Group   A small group of relatively well-adjusted individuals that, through intense interaction, allows the individuals to discover more about themselves and how they relate to others.

Experience   Everything, including thoughts, needs, and perceptions, going on within the individual that is presently within awareness.

Fully Functioning   Describes individuals who are using their capacities and talents, realizing their potential, and moving toward complete knowledge of themselves and their full range of experiences.

Genuineness   Being truly oneself in relationship with others. It is one of the three basic conditions for therapeutic effectiveness.

Ideal Self   The self-concept an individual would like to have (it includes aspirations, moral ideals, and values).

Incongruence   A schism between one's total organismic experience and a self-concept burdened by conditions of worth, resulting in a state of inner tension and confusion.

Internal Frame of Reference   The realm of experience that is available to the awareness of a person at a given moment.

Introjection   Incorporating the standards of another person within one's own personality.

Nondirective Therapy   Psychotherapy in which the client leads the way by expressing feelings, defining problems, and interpreting behavior, while the therapist cultivates a warm and accepting atmosphere in which the client can clarify his or her process instead of directing it.

Organismic Valuing Process   The inherent capacity to choose that which will enhance our well-being and reject that which does not.

Person-Centered Approach   The phrase Rogers later used in place of "nondirective" because it more accurately reflected his approach.

Phenomenology   An approach to understanding personality that emphasizes the importance of understanding the individual's subjective experiences, feelings, and private concepts.

Positive Regard   Giving selective attention to the client's verbal and behavioral assets.

Self-actualization   The tendency to actualize that portion of experience represented by the self-concept.

Self-concept   A collection of learned perceptions about one's abilities and characteristics.

Significant Other   An important source of positive regard, such as a parent.

Unconditional Positive Regard   The acceptance of another person without conditions of worth. One of the three essential characteristics of the successful therapeutic relationship.

Warmth   The primarily nonverbal (e.g., vocal tone, posture, facial expression, etc.) means of expressing care in a therapeutic relationship.

SUGGESTED READING

Kirschenbaum, H., & Land-Henderson, V. (Eds.). (1989b). *The Carl Rogers reader*. Boston: Houghton Mifflin.

Rogers, C. R. (1954). The case of Mrs. Oak: A research analysis: In C. R. Rogers and R. F. Dymond (Eds.), *Psychotherapy and personality change: Co-ordinated research studies in the client-centered approach* (pp. 259–348). Chicago: University of Chicago Press.

Rogers, C. R. (1961b). *On becoming a person*. Boston: Houghton Mifflin.

Rogers, C. R., & Dymond, R. F. (1951). *Psychotherapy and personality change*. Chicago: University Press.

REFERENCES

Baradell, J. G. (1990). Client-centered case consultation and single-case research design: Application to case management. *Archives of Psychiatric Nursing, 4,* 12–17.

Barrett-Lennard, G. T. (1988). Listening. *Person-Centered Review, 3,* 410–425.

Block, J. (1961). Techniques for Rogerian counseling Q-sort. In *Q-sort method in personality assessment and psychiatric research* (pp. 132-136). Springfield, IL: Thomas.

Bozarth, J. D., & Brodley, B. T. (1991). Actualization: A functional concept in client-centered therapy. *Journal of Social Behavior and Personality, 6,* 45–59.

Burke, J. F. (1989). *Contemporary approaches to psychotherapy and counseling: The self-regulation and maturity model.* Pacific Grove, CA: Brooks/Cole.

Burton, M. V., Parker, R. W., & Wollner, J. M. (1991). The psychotherapeutic value of a "chat": A verbal response modes study of a placebo attention control with breast cancer patients. *Psychotherapy Research, 1,* 39–61.

Cain, D. J. (1987). Carl R. Rogers: The man, his vision, his impact. *Person-Centered Review, 2,* 283–288.

Cain, D. J. (1988). Roundtable discussion: Why do you think there are so few person-centered practitioners or scholars considering that literally thousands of persons throughout the world attest to the enormous impact Carl Rogers has had on their personal and professional lives? *Person-Centered Review, 3,* 353–390.

Cain, D. J. (1990). Celebration, reflection and renewal: 50 years of client-centered therapy and beyond. *Person-Centered Review, 5,* 357–363.

Cramer, D. (1993). Therapeutic relationship and outcome seen by clients in first and third sessions of individual therapy. *Counseling Psychology Quarterly, 6,* 13–15.

Egan, G. (1994). *The skilled helper* (5th ed.). Pacific Grove, CA: Brooks/Cole.

Farson, R. (1975). Carl Rogers, quiet revolutionary. In R. I. Evans (Ed.), *Carl Rogers: The man and his ideas* (pp. xxviii–xliii). New York: E. P. Dutton.

Fielder, F. (1950). The concept of the ideal therapeutic relationship. *Journal of Consulting Psychology, 45,* 659–666.

Fink, J. (1990). Can psychotherapeutic competence be taught? 14th International Congress of Medical Psychotherapy: Training in medical psychotherapy: Cross-cultural diversity. *Psychotherapy and Psychosomatics, 53,* 64–67.

Freeman, S. C. (1993). Client-centered therapy with diverse populations: The universal within the specific. *Journal of Multicultural Counseling and Development, 21,* 248–254.

Gelso, C. J., & Fretz, B. R. (1992). *Counseling psychology.* Fort Worth, TX: Harcourt Brace Jovanovich.

Gendlin, E. T. (1970). A short summary and some long predictions. In J. Hart & T. Tomlinson (Eds.), *New Directions in Client-Centered Therapy.* Boston: Houghton-Mifflin.

Gendlin, E. T. (1981). *Focusing.* New York: Everest House.

Gendlin, E. T. (1988). Carl Rogers (1902-1987). *American Psychologist, 43,* 127–128.

Gladstein, G. A. (1983). Understanding empathy: Integrating counseling, developmental, and social psychology perspectives. *Journal of Counseling Psychology, 30,* 467–482.

Goldstein, K. (1939). *The organism.* New York: American Book Company.

Goodyear, R. K. (1987). In memory of Carl Ransom Rogers. *Journal of Counseling and Development, 65,* 523–524.

Hackney, H. (1978). The evolution of empathy. *Personnel and Guidance Journal, 57,* 35–38.

Hartley, D., Roback, H. B., & Abramowitz, S. I. (1976). Deterioration effects in encounter groups. *American Psychologist, 31,* 247–255.

Hayashi, S., Kuno, T., Osawa, M., & Shimizu, M. (1992). The client-centered therapy and person-centered approach in Japan: Historical development, current status, and perspectives. *Journal of Humanistic Psychology, 32,* 115–136.

Hill-Hain, A., & Rogers, C. (1988). Cross-cultural challenges of facilitating person-centered groups in South Africa. *Journal for Specialists in Group Work, 13,* 62–69.

Jones, A., & Crandall, R. (1986). Validation of a short index of self-actualization. *Personality and Social Psychology Bulletin, 12,* 63–73.

Jones, S. L., & Butman, R. E. (1991). *Modern psychotherapies.* Downers Grove, IL: Inter-Varsity Press.

Kahn, E. (1985). Heinz Kohut and Carl Rogers: A timely comparison. *American Psychologist, 40,* 893–904.

Kirschenbaum, H. (1979). *On becoming Carl Rogers.* New York: Delta.

Kirschenbaum, H., & Land-Henderson, V. (Eds.). (1989a). *Carl Rogers: Dialogues.* Boston: Houghton Mifflin.

Kirschenbaum, H., & Land-Henderson, V. (Eds.). (1989b). *The Carl Rogers reader.* Boston: Houghton Mifflin.

Levant, R., & Shlien, J. M. (Ed.). (1984). *Client-centered therapy and the person-centered approach: New directions in theory, research, and practice.* New York: Praeger.

Maslow, A. (1968). *Toward a psychology of being.* (2nd ed). Princeton: Van Nostrand.

McLeod, J., & McLeod, J. (1993). The relationship between personal philosophy and effectiveness in counselors. *Counseling Psychology Quarterly, 6,* 121–129.

Meador, B., & Rogers, C. (1984). Person-centered therapy. In Raymond J. Corsini (Ed.), *Current psychotherapies* (3rd ed.). Itasca, IL: F. E. Peacock.

Miller, M. J. (1991). A thought or two on the future of research in career counseling. *Journal of Employment Counseling, 28,* 4–7.

Miller, M. J., & Foxworth, C. L. (1992). Validating a subscale for assessing aspects of the person. *College Student Journal, 26,* 436–439.

Moreira, V. (1993). Beyond the person: Merleau-Ponty's concept of "flesh" as (re)defining Carl Rogers' person-centered theory. *Humanistic Psychologist, 21,* 138–157.

Newman, J., & Lovell, M. (1993). A description of a supervisory group for group counselors. *Counselor Education and Supervision, 33,* 22–31.

Nye, R. D. (1992). *Three psychologies: Perspectives from Freud, Skinner, and Rogers* (4th ed). Pacific Grove, CA: Brooks/Cole.

Patterson, C. H. (1985). *The therapeutic relationship: Foundations for an eclectic psychotherapy.* Pacific Grove, GA: Brooks/Cole.

Raskin, N. J., & Rogers, C. (1995). Person-centered therapy. In Raymond J. Corsini & Danny Wedding (Eds.), *Current psychotherapies* (5th ed.). Itasca, IL: F. E. Peacock.

Roberts, R. C. (1985). Carl Rogers and the Christian virtues. *Journal of Psychology and Theology, 13,* 263–273.

Rogers, C. R. (1931). *Measuring personality adjustment in children nine to thirteen years of age.* New York: Teachers College.

Rogers, C. R. (1939). *Clinical treatment of the problem child.* Boston: Houghton Mifflin.

Rogers, C. R. (1942a). *Counseling and psychotherapy.* Boston: Houghton Mifflin.

Rogers, C. R. (1942b). Some observations on the organization of personality. *American Psychologist, 2,* 358–368.

Rogers, C. R. (1951, November). "Client-centered" psychotherapy. *Scientific American,* 66–74.

Rogers, C. R. (1954). The case of Mrs. Oak: A research analysis. In C. R. Rogers & R. F. Dymond (Eds.), *Psychotherapy and personality change: Coordinated research studies in the client-centered approach* (pp. 259–348). Chicago: University of Chicago Press.

Rogers, C. R. (1957). The necessary and sufficient conditions of therapeutic personality change. *Journal of Consulting Psychology, 21,* 95–103.

Rogers, C. R. (1959). A theory of therapy, personality and inter-personal relationships, as developed in the client-centered framework. In S. Koch (Ed.), *Psychology: A study of a science* (Vol. 3, pp. 184–256). New York: McGraw-Hill.

Rogers, C. R. (1961a). Actualizing tendency in relation to "motives" and to consciousness. In M. R. Jones (Ed.), *Nebraska Symposium on Motivation* (pp. 1-24). Lincoln: University of Nebraska Press.

Rogers, C. R. (1961b) *On becoming a person.* Boston: Houghton Mifflin.

Rogers, C. R. (1962). The interpersonal relationship: The core of guidance. *Harvard Educational Review,* 416–429.

Rogers, C. R. (1964). Toward a science of the person. In T. W. Wann (Ed.), *Behaviorism and phenomenology* (pp. 109–140). Chicago: University of Chicago Press.

Rogers, C. R. (1965). Dealing with psychological tensions. *Journal of Applied Behavioral Science, 1,* 6–24.

Rogers, C. R. (1967). Autobiography. In E. G. Boring & G. Lindzey (Eds.), *A history of psychology in autobiography* (Vol. 5, pp. 343–384). New York: Appleton-Century-Crofts.

Rogers, C. R. (1969). *Freedom to learn: A view of what education might become.* Columbus, OH: Charles E. Merrill.

Rogers, C. R. (1970). *Carl Rogers on encounter groups.* New York: Harper & Row.

Rogers, C. R. (1972). *Becoming partners: Marriage and its alternatives.* New York: Delacorte Press.

Rogers, C. R. (1977). *Carl Rogers on personal power: Inner strength and its revolutionary impact.* New York: Delacorte Press.

Rogers, C. R. (1980a). *A way of being.* Boston: Houghton Mifflin.

Rogers, C. R. (1980b). Client-centered psychotherapy. In A. M. Freeman, H. I. Kapplan, & B. J. Sadock (Eds.), *Comprehensive textbook of psychiatry* (3rd ed.) (Vol. 2, pp. 2153–2167). Baltimore: Williams & Wilkins.

Rogers, C. R. (1983). *Freedom to learn for the 80's.* Columbus, OH: Charles E. Merrill.

Rogers, C. R. (1986). A commentary from Carl Rogers. *Person-Centered Review, 1,* 3–5. As quoted in D. K. Freedheim (Ed.), *History of psychotherapy: A century of change,* 1992, (p. 651). Washington, DC: American Psychological Association.

Rogers, C. R., & Dymond, R. F. (1951). *Psychotherapy and Personality change.* Chicago: University Press.

Rogers, C. R., Gendlin, E. T., Kiesler, D. J., & Truax, C. B. (1967). *The therapeutic relationship and its impact: A study of psychotherapy with schizophrenics.* Madison: University of Wisconsin Press.

Rogers, C. R., & Stevens, B. (1968). *Person to person: The problem of being human.* Lafayette, CA: Real People Press.

Rychalk, J. (1973). *Introduction to personality and psychotherapy.* Boston: Houghton Mifflin.

See, J. D. (1985). Person-centered perspective. *Journal of Applied Rehabilitation Counseling, 16,* 15–20.

Seligmen, L. (1986). *Diagnosis and treatment planning in counseling.* New York: Human Sciences Press.

Smith, D. (1982). Trends in counseling and psychotherapy. *American Psychologist, 37,* 802–809.

Truax, C. B., & Mitchell, K. M. (1971). Research on certain therapist interpersonal skills in relation to process and outcome. In A. E. Bergin & S. L. Garfield (Eds.), *Handbook of psychotherapy and behavior change: An empirical analysis.* New York: John Wiley.

Usher, C. H. (1989). Recognizing cultural bias in counseling theory and practice: The case of Rogers. *Journal of Multicultural Counseling and Development, 17,* 62–71.

Warner, R. E. (1991). A survey of theoretical orientations of Canadian clinical psychologists. *Canadian Psychology, 32,* 525–528.

Watkins, C. E. (1993). Person-centered theory and the contemporary practice of psychological testing. *Psychology Quarterly, 6,* 59–67.

Watkins, C. E., Lopez, F. G., Campbell, V. L., & Himmell, C. D. (1986). Contemporary counseling psychology: The results of a national survey. *Journal of Counseling Psychology, 33,* 301–309.

Yau, T., Sue, D., & Hayden, D. (1992). Counseling style preference of international students. *Journal of Counseling Psychology, 39,* 100–104.

Zimring, F. M., & Raskin, N. J. (1992). Carl Rogers and client/person-centered therapy. In D. K. Freedheim (Ed.), *History of psychotherapy.* Washington, DC: American Psychological Association.

CHAPTER 10

Gestalt Therapy

Chapter Outline

Introduction
Brief Biography
Historical Development
View of Human Nature
Development of Maladaptive Behavior
Function of the Therapist
Goals of Therapy
Major Methods and Techniques
Application
Critical Analysis
Current Status
Chapter Summary
Key Terms
Suggested Reading

INTRODUCTION

Even in some of life's most trivial tasks we seek resolution and closure. We want the incomplete to be completed, the unfinished to be finished. Tension is not released until "the case is closed." An unfinished line of a familiar song or musical score—the first four notes of Beethoven's Fifth Symphony, for instance—won't allow our mind to rest until the lost is found, until the next four notes have been played. Perhaps you may have noticed the same need for visual closure. Consider Figures 10-1 and 10-2. In Figure 10-1, at any given moment two faces or a vase can be seen, but not simultaneously. Although they can be perceived separately, the removal of one changes the perception of the other. Only together are they complete. Similarly, when we turn to Figure 10-2,

FIGURE 10-1 Two faces or a vase?

FIGURE 10-2 Organizing images to make sense.

our brain attempts to make sense out of the ink blotches on this page, to organize the black ink into images that make sense. Just as it works at filling in the gaps of a song, or filling in a blank space to complete an image, even so it works at assembling the pieces until a coherent picture is formed.

While dining in a German cafe, Kurt Lewin observed this phenomenon, this need for closure, in the way waiters went about their work. Although waiters could remember the details of a customer's bill for a considerable stretch of time, he noticed that once it had been paid, they were often unable to recall any of the data, or even the total. As long as the bill remained unsettled, the tension in the incomplete transaction facilitated recall. Payment completed the transaction, which brought about closure, thus dissipating the tension and erasing the memory.

Gestalt therapy is, in a very real sense, a Gestalt.

—E. W. L. Smith

Whether it is such a transaction, a song, or a visual image, our minds demand what the Germans call *Gestalt*—a complete and meaningful whole. The word *Gestalt* has no precise English equivalent, but such words as *form, structure, configuration, essence,* and *whole* begin to triangulate its meaning.

Gestalt therapy is built on this premise, on a theory of perception known as Gestalt psychology, which has proposed the radical hypothesis that the whole is psychologically greater than the sum of its parts. It maintains that psychological phenomena can be understood, not when broken down into primitive perceptual elements, but only when viewed as organized, structured wholes (Banks & Krajicek, 1991; Osborn, 1991). Even the stars in the sky are grouped into wholes, into constellations such as the Big Dipper and the Southern Cross, not simply because we enjoy painting pictures in the night sky, but because we possess this fundamental need to make things whole.

Even before the founder of this approach to therapy was born, Gestalt psychology sprang up in Berlin, initially as a theory of perception. The system of therapy that eventually grew out of Gestalt principles, such as closure, emphasizes working with the whole person (Graumann, 1989). The focus is phenomenologic, dealing with the present rather than the past, with process rather than product. There is very little analysis. To Gestaltists, analyzing is mere intellectualizing rather than action leading to change. These concepts and their application to counseling were pioneered by Frederick Perls, whose dramatic ways and inimitable character make him unique.

BRIEF BIOGRAPHY

Born in Berlin in 1893, Frederick Solomon "Fritz" Perls was the middle child and only son of middle-class Jewish parents. Although he remembered his childhood as happy, Frederick's parents often fought bitterly. He loved his mother but lost respect for his father, a traveling wine salesman who drank

Fritz Perls *(far right)* at Esalen.
(Michael Alexander/LIFE Magazine © TIME Inc.)

heavily and whose primary avocation, from Perls' viewpoint, was to become Grand Master of the Freemasons. He and his younger sister, Grete, were always close, but his dislike for his older sister, Elsie, grew so intense and long-lasting, that he experienced only minimal emotion when he learned she had died in a concentration camp (Perls, 1969a).

As a child Perls was unruly, misbehaving at home and causing trouble in school. However, he loved to read and was an excellent student. He earned his M.D. degree, with a specialization in psychology, from Frederick Wilhelm University in 1920—just in time to join the German army as a medic in World War I.

After the war Perls began psychoanalytic training at both the Vienna and the Berlin Institute of Psychoanalysis. He was especially influenced by his own analyst, Wilhelm Reich, but he also worked with Otto Fenichel and Karen Horney (Rice & Greenberg, 1992). He later took a position at the Institute for Brain Injured Soldiers in Frankfurt, where he worked with Kurt Goldstein, and it was here that Perls first learned to view humans, not as the sum of their separate parts, but as complete entities.

If you are in the now, you are creative, you have your eyes and ears open, like every small child, you find a solution.

—Fritz Perls

When Hitler's anti-Semitic policies in Germany during the 1930s became intolerable, Perls left for Amsterdam. Carrying only 100 Marks (about $25) hidden in his cigarette case, he crossed the German–Dutch border with his wife, Laura, and their two-year-old daughter. They lived for a year in Amsterdam in a small attic apartment under conditions, much like those of Anne Frank, that Perls (1969a) would remember as "utter misery."

Anticipating the rising tide of Facism in Europe, Perls fled Holland in 1934, barely ahead of the Nazis, and emigrated to South Africa where he established the South African Institute for Psychoanalysis. In Johannesburg he and his wife built a strong practice, and he served as director of this institute for about 10 years. As the first traditional, trained analyst in South Africa, his success provided an affluent lifestyle: servants, a nursemaid for the children, tennis courts, a swimming pool, an ice-skating rink, cars, even an airplane.

In 1936 Perls attended an international psychoanalytic congress in Czechoslovakia, where he finally met Freud. The long-awaited meeting lasted under 4 minutes, however, and took place entirely in the doorway to Freud's room, leaving Perls feeling neither welcomed nor appreciated. Thereafter, Perls dedicated himself to proving Freud and psychoanalysis wrong. Returning to South Africa from the congress, the humiliated Perls was convinced that he needed no one, either personally or professionally, to support him or his views. It was this return to Africa from Czechoslovakia that marked the emergence of Gestalt therapy (Litt, 1978).

With the rise of apartheid in 1946, Perls left South Africa to make his home in New York, where he joined his wife and Paul Goodman in founding the New York Institute for Gestalt Therapy. Eventually becoming dissatisfied with New York life in general and with life with Laura in particular, he separated from his wife, lived in several cities, and eventually became instrumental in the development of the Esalen Institute in Big Sur, California. An actor at heart, Perls loved to parade his ideas before the public. For the last 10 years of his life he conducted popular experimental workshops at Esalen and across the country.

In 1969, the year before his death, Perls founded a "Gestalt community" at Cowichan on Vancouver Island, British Columbia, as a center where therapists could study for several months at a time. In March, 1970, Perls died in a Chicago hospital, where a large crowd of anxious followers had gathered together for a 6-day vigil preceding his death. Because of their grief and intensity, a police guard was called to keep them at bay.

Perls recounted many of the more personal moments of his life in the autobiographical book *In and Out of the Garbage Pail* (1969a), a free-floating, poetic, often playful autobiography that provides hundreds of glimpses into his unique personal life.

HISTORICAL DEVELOPMENT

The distinguished roots of Gestalt therapy reach back into the 19th century, to the very beginning of psychology as a discipline. The German word *Gestalt* was first used in a psychological context in 1890 by the Austrian psychologist and philosopher Christian von Ehrenfels (1859–1932). He argued that there is a gestalt or quality of form, absent in any of the parts, but present in the whole of a structure (Rock & Palmer, 1990; Saariluoma, 1992).

In 1912 three young German psychologists who were particularly interested in human perception joined forces to found the Berlin Gestalt School. These three friends—Max Wertheimer (1880–1943), Kurt Koffka (1886–1941), and Wolfgang Köhler (1887–1967)—reacted against the stark behaviorism of Watson and the narrow framework of Wundt's introspective analysis. Out of their work came such precepts as the *principle of similarity* (see Figure 10-3), which causes us to group stimuli together, if they appear similar within our perceptual field; the *principle of proximity* (see Figure 10-4), which suggests that the relative distance of stimuli from each other within the perceptual field determines how they are seen; and the *principle of closure* (see Figure 10-5), which describes our need to complete unfinished figures.

Wertheimer, Koffka, and Köhler spent considerable time between World Wars I and II describing principles of behavior that helped explain how the human mind seeks to make sense of the vast array of stimuli that call for attention and, more broadly, how we perceive and thus how we learn (Sarris, 1989; Yontef, 1982). Most significantly, these three men reasoned that an individual should be understood as a *meaningful whole.*

Years later, when Perls sought to recover something of the original holism of these three Germans who had studied perception, he often returned to his favorite example of water, H_2O, which loses its *Gestalt*, which ceases to be water, once it is broken down into hydrogen and oxygen. He applied the various

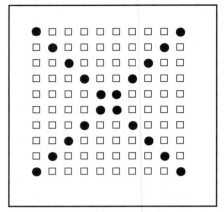

FIGURE 10-3 The principle of similarity. Why do you see an X?

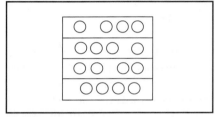

FIGURE 10-4 The principle of proximity. Why do you see groups of dots?

FIGURE 10-5 The principle of closure. What forms do you see here?

principles of Gestalt formation to the perception of one's own feelings, a contribution that subsequently blossomed into the birth of Gestalt therapy (Wallen, 1970).

Perls distinguished individuals' perceptions of themselves, of their feelings, of their relationships, and so on, in terms of the Gestalt dichotomy of figure and ground. Gestalt therapy seeks a smooth transition between those sets of experiences that are the *figure,* those that are immediately in the focus of awareness, and those that form the *ground*—the background. This is the basic premise of Gestalt psychology and an important contribution to Perls' Gestalt therapy.

Another important historical influence on Gestalt therapy was the existential movement in philosophy and psychology. Gestalt therapy's emphasis on such concepts as the expansion of awareness, freedom, the immediacy of experience, and the here and now all demonstrate its close relation to existentialism. Nowhere is this influence more clearly seen than in the controversial "Gestalt prayer":

I do my thing and you do your thing.
I am not in this world to live up to your expectations and you are not in this
    world to live up to mine.
You are you, and I am I, and if by chance we find each other, it's beautiful.
If not, it can't be helped. (Perls, 1969b, p. 4)

VIEW OF HUMAN NATURE

Perls believed that people develop in relation to their environment, and he distinguished three stages in this development. During the earliest, *social stage*, the
infant depends upon others for nearly everything; in general, this stage is characterized by an awareness of others but little awareness of self. During the *psychophysical stage*, we become more aware of what is
self and what is non-self, and it is during this stage
that the self and the self-image develop through the
process of adaptation, acknowledgment, and support. The third, or *spiritual stage*, is reached by very
few people. Kempler (1973) describes the spiritual stage as movement from
awareness that is sensory sensing to awareness that is extrasensory sensing. In
sum, the Gestalt view of human nature, which is further influenced by Eastern
philosophies, is existential and humanistic. The fundamental assumptions of
these several world views are evident in the basic assumptions that Gestalt theory makes about human nature.

> *Wherever we go we take a kind of*
> *world with us.*
>
> —Fritz Perls

Organism–Environment Field

People perceive their environment as a total unit of meaning, parts of which are
interpreted in one of two ways: as *figure*, where stimuli are attended to, and as
background, in which case the stimuli are not attended to. Since our most
pressing needs determine the figure that comes into focus, our foreground continually shifts as one foreground flows into another (Korb, Gorrell, & Van De
Riet, 1989). A healthy person focuses "sharply on one need (the figure) at a time
while relegating other needs to the background. When the need is met—or the
Gestalt is closed or completed—it is relegated to the background and a new
need comes into focus (becomes the figure)" (Thompson & Rudolph, 1988,
p. 66). This ceaseless, constantly changing flow of Gestalts or patterns is the basis of human experience. In any given situation what is foreground for one person may not be for another, making each of us unique. This idea of the figure
and the ground is the linchpin of Gestalt therapy.

Organismic Self-Regulation

The flow of individual experience is far from random. What becomes foreground for an individual is based upon his or her current needs. And

Gestaltists believe that what human beings need is wholeness and complete-
ness in life. When we are functioning freely, we make contact with the environment in ways that meet our needs.

Psychological Homeostasis

Given the environment we are in at any particular time, we attempt to meet these
personal needs as best we can. Just as living organisms seek a balance between
salt and water or between acid and alkali, so are we regulated by our own psychological rheostat that seeks homeostasis, an equilibrium or balance between
ourselves and our environment. When we become thirsty, getting a drink comes
into the foreground; when we become lonely, finding other people to be with
comes into the foreground. Through psychological homeostasis our most pressing needs come to the foreground to help us maintain balance in our lives.

Awareness

In order to achieve balance and satisfaction, we have the capacity to become
aware of our environment. This awareness, which determines what is "right for
us," is a vital part of our human nature. Awareness gives us a sense of direction
and motivation to become more fully who we are. It clarifies what our most
pressing need is and the options we have to meet that need. Only when we are
fully aware of our organism and our environment, do we have choice and freedom. With that choice and freedom we can contact, act on, or interact with our
environment to meet our needs. Without this awareness we would not form a
Gestalt, resulting in dissatisfaction.

There are other ways to conceptualize Gestalt therapy's understanding of
human nature. Passons (1975) lists several related or further assumptions about
the nature of humanity that form the framework for the Gestalt approach.
Gestalt therapists believe, for instance, that we are a composite whole made up
of interrelated parts, none of which—body, emotions, thoughts, sensations, and
perceptions—can be understood outside the context
of the whole person. At the same time, we are also
part of our own environments and cannot be understood apart from them. The implication is that
we are creatures of our environments, and that as
such, we are neither "good" nor "bad." Gestaltists further believe that we have
the potential to be fully aware of all sensations, thoughts, emotions, and perceptions, and we are capable of making choices because of this awareness. Only
when fully aware will we have the capacity to govern our own lives effectively—to choose how to respond to external and internal stimuli, for instance,
so that we are acting on our world, rather than reacting to it. Counselors trained
in Gestalt therapy also believe that we cannot truly experience the past and the
future; we can only experience ourselves in the present.

In short, Perls concluded that we are self-directed and that we must take responsibility for our own lives (see Sidebar 10-1). According to Perls, all needs

*Don't push the river; it flows by
itself.*

   —Fritz Perls

Sidebar 10-1

THE MORAL PRECEPTS OF GESTALT THERAPY

The "moral precepts" of Gestalt therapy have been described by several writers (Korb et al., 1989; Naranjo, 1970). The experience that underlies this set of injunctions is aliveness, "radiance" (Hycner, 1987), or "inspiration" (Jourard, 1964). The precepts are:

- Live now (i.e., be concerned not with the past or the future, but with the present).
- Live here (i.e., be concerned with that which is present and not with that which is absent).
- Accept yourself as you are.
- Stop imagining (i.e., experience only the real).

- Stop unnecessary thinking (i.e., be oriented toward hearing, seeing, smelling, tasting, and touching).
- Express directly—do not explain, judge, or manipulate.
- Be aware of both the pleasant and the unpleasant.
- Reject all "shoulds" and "oughts" that are not your own.
- Take complete responsibility for your actions, thoughts, and feelings.
- Surrender to being what you really are.
- Keep the memories of the past and the concern about the future in perspective.
- Be available to an open dialogue with the persons, ideas, things, and institutions in which your life is lived.
- Use the word *appropriate* as a touchstone for your choices.

---

stem from, and are grounded in, this basic need to actualize oneself, to become whole (Perls, 1969b). Gestaltists believe that a healthy personality is the result of a person's experiences forming a meaningful whole—a Gestalt. This occurs when there is a smooth transition between those sets of experiences that are immediately in the focus of awareness and those sets that are in the background.

DEVELOPMENT OF MALADAPTIVE BEHAVIOR

According to Gestalt theory, people develop psychological problems in several ways. They can either lose contact with the environment and the resources in it, or become so overinvolved with the environment that they lose touch with themselves. Some people fail to put aside unfulfilled needs or unexpressed feelings, whereas others may become fragmented or scattered in many directions. Others may experience what Perls labeled the conflict between the *top dog* (what one thinks one should do) and the *underdog* (what one wants to do). Still others may have difficulty handling the dichotomies of life such as love/hate and pleasure/pain. All of these difficulties keep us from being aware of who we really are.

Although Perls (1970) never developed a systematic or formal theory of maladaptive behavior, he identified five layers of neurosis that potentially interfere with our being authentically in touch with ourselves: the phony, the phobic, the impasse, the implosive, and the explosive. At the *phony layer* we pretend to be something we are not. We play a variety of games and act out various roles. Only when we become more aware of our game playing can we become more honest, open, and in touch with unpleasantness and pain. At the *phobic layer,* individuals attempt to avoid recognizing aspects of themselves they would prefer to deny. People who experience this layer of awareness are afraid that if they acknowledge who they really are and present it to others, they will be rejected. Below this phobic layer is the *impasse layer,* in which people are adrift in a sea of helplessness and dread with no sense of direction, leaving them to wonder how they are going to make it in the environment. The fourth and fifth layers, the *implosive* and *explosive,* often go together. At these layers people may frequently feel vulnerable to feelings. Yet, as they peel back the layers of defensiveness built up over the years, they become alive in an explosion of joy, sorrow, or pain that leads to being authentic. When a person reaches this point, the present can be experienced most fully.

Conflicts such as these are usually the result of an inability to bring together individual needs and environmental demands, so that one can be fully present in the now. Passons (1975) provides a Gestalt lens for viewing the styles of maladaptive behavior that can develop from the inability to reconcile the needs of the self with the demands of our environment. He divides the kinds of problems individuals experience into six areas. *Lack of awareness* is a problem for people with rigid personalities, who move though their daily lives with an uneasy feeling of nonfulfillment. Those who manipulate their environment rather than take charge of their own selves are said to exhibit a *lack of self-responsibility.*

Lose your mind and come to your senses.

—Fritz Perls

Or we can *lose contact with the environment* in one of two ways: either by becoming so rigid that no input from the environment is accepted, or by needing so much approval that the self becomes lost in trying to incorporate everything from the environment. Individuals can fail to complete necessary tasks in one of two ways as well: an *inability to complete unfinished business* prevents them from dealing with current situations, whereas a *denial of needs* causes them to lose the productive energy of the needs they disown. *Dichotomizing dimensions of the self* occurs when people perceive themselves at one end of a possible continuum, a self-perception that results in an internal conflict, leaving them divided.

Of course, when one is completely incapable of determining the boundaries between one's self and the environment, the result is an anxious state of temporal insecurity (Burke, 1989). "And now here comes the neurotic," wrote Perls in one of his last works (1976), "tied to the past and to outmoded ways of acting, fuzzy about the present because he sees it only through a glass darkly, tortured about the future because the present is out of his hands" (p. 44).

In short, from the point of view of the Gestalt therapist, people become maladjusted when they fail to utilize their own capacity for self-regulation and spend their energy on acting helpless, depending upon others, or manipulating the environment in countless other ways.

FUNCTION OF THE THERAPIST

In his section of the well-known film *Three Approaches to Psychotherapy,* which documents how Rogers, Ellis, and Perls treat a client named Gloria (Shostrom, 1965), Perls demonstrated the function of the Gestalt therapist. After a preliminary statement, in which Perls said that the therapist was "like an artist bringing something out which is hidden," he began the interview by stating that Gloria and he would be talking for a brief time. Gloria responded that she was very nervous and afraid of talking, to which Perls immediately replied, "You say you are afraid, but you are smiling." Launching into a series of confrontations with the client about the incompatibility of fear and smiling, not once did he ask Gloria what she would like to talk about. In this brief interview Perls demonstrated how Gestalt therapists provoke clients into awareness, on the premise that the clients who are aware will solve their own problems in their own time (Dolliver, 1991; Dolliver, Williams, & Gold, 1980; McClure, Merril, & Russo, 1994).

The role of the Gestalt therapist, then, is an extremely active one. Without taking the responsibility for change within the client, the therapist acts as a catalyst for change. As Perls says, "The therapist is a directive leader and orchestrates all aspects of the therapeutic interactions, with the advice and consent of the client who is working" (Perls, 1976, p. 86). In this context, the word *orchestrate* is especially interesting; Kempler (1973) compares the therapist to a "composing maestro" and the client to an "accomplished musician," both of whom meet to combine their talent and skill (p. 266).

One of the major functions of the Gestalt therapist is to frustrate the clients' demands for support and help, so that they are forced to rely on their own resources (Little, 1986). Perls calls this a "safe emergency." Of course, the clients may resist this transition from external to internal support, and it is at this point, when clients are unable to manipulate the counselor into solving their problems, that an impasse occurs. Because of the threatening prospect of relying only on themselves, the clients become immobilized and are unable to experience feelings (Harman, 1975; Zinker, 1978).

When such an impasse occurs, the therapist provides a *safe emergency,* which allows their clients to feel safe enough to work toward self-support. Since it is easier to keep things the way they are, most clients are reluctant to go beyond the impasse. To permit them to get in touch with and work through their patterns of frustration, it is therefore the goal of the therapist to compel clients to face and deal with this impasse (Fagan, 1970).

The Gestalt therapist views change, then, through a paradoxical lens. Gestalt theory holds that change and growth take place not when one tries to be what one is not, but when one becomes what one is. Gestalt therapy is about the process of "being what one is and not a process of striving to become" (Kempler, 1973, p. 262). As a result, change and growth occur in clients not as a result of coercion, persuasion, or interpretation, but only when they fully own what they are doing and the way they are doing it. Paradoxically, it is through standing still and becoming aware of ourselves, just as we are, that we grow and expand our boundaries. Significantly, this philosophy holds true for the therapist as well: To be authentic, the Gestalt therapist must try to be not a better therapist, but who he or she is at the moment (Tyson & Range, 1987). For these several reasons, Gestalt therapists do not make use of standardized assessment instruments such as psychological tests, nor do they diagnose their clients according to classification standards. They spend their time trying to be who they are and helping their clients to do the same.

GOALS OF THERAPY

One of the most significant goals of Gestalt therapy is helping individuals assume responsibility for themselves, rather than relying on others to make decisions for them. As Prochaska (1979) contends, the "ideal outcome of Gestalt therapy is the clients' discovery that they do not and never really did need a therapist" (p. 164). Gestalt therapy aims to challenge its clients to move from *environmental support* to *self-support*, in order to mobilize their own resources for dealing with the environment effectively and to make creative adjustments that permit the self to respond to environmental pressures as well as to inner needs.

Another goal of Gestalt therapy is that clients become complete and integrated, so that they function as a systematic whole that consists of both feelings, perceptions, and thoughts, and a physical body whose processes cannot be divorced from its more psychological components. Integration means bringing together all of the parts of a person that have been disowned. When our emotions and behavior match, little energy is wasted, and we are more capable of responding appropriately to meet our needs. This often comes about through what Köhler (1973) called the "Aha!" experience. Like Archimedes, whose discovery of the principle of the displacement of water by mass was so immediate that he dashed stark naked from his bath into the streets, crying out "Eureka!," we suddenly see and understand what has long eluded us in a climactic moment that is powerful and immediate. With such an "Aha!" experience, the energy that was previously directed toward the playing of roles is released for our self-regulating capabilities. This process of integration is ongoing. "Integration is never completed," Perls (1976) pointed out. "Maturation is never completed. It's an ongoing process forever and ever. . . . There's always something to be integrated; always something to be learned" (p. 64).

Very few people go in therapy to be cured, but rather to improve their neurosis.

　　　　　　　—Fritz Perls

Another basic goal of Gestalt therapy is to help clients become aware of the present, which Perls (1969a) viewed as both necessary and sufficient for change to occur. In fact, Perls claimed that "awareness per se—by and of itself—can be curative" (p. 16). Seeking to avoid the Scylla of what Perls referred to as "obsessive remembering of the past" and the Charybdis of the "anxious anticipation of the future," the counselor is always intent on cultivating awareness within clients. Latner (1973) maintains that "the point of therapy is not to make solutions, it is to make the problem-laden present more actual by increasing the patients' awareness" (p. 211).

Gestalt therapy helps clients become aware of what they do by letting the experience of *the now* flow through all of their senses. By fully experiencing the present moment, clients can eliminate self-manipulation, environmental control, and other factors that interfere with this natural self-regulating process and allow *organismic self-regulation* to take over. As a result, Gestalt therapy must focus on the *here-and-now*—not the there and then—the essence of which, according to Perls (1970), is summed up in the formula: Now = experience = awareness = reality. "The past is no more and the future not yet," Perls wrote. "Only the now exists" (p. 14). People become anxious, Perls suggested, because they leave the security of the present and become preoccupied with the future, frequently expecting things to go wrong.

Anxiety, for Gestaltists, is the gap between now and then, between the present and the past or the present and the future (Phares, 1988). Living with a focus on the future often results in failing to see what is at hand, and to focus on either the past or the future inevitably immobilizes us in the present. Our inclinations to daydream about better times to come or to worry about what might happen can only be dealt with by *presentizing* them into current awareness (Passons, 1975).

The Gestalt therapist also attempts to help clients identify and resolve *unfinished business:* earlier thoughts, feelings, and reactions that still affect their functioning. Unfinished business interferes with life in the present. Children, for example, may have been taught to deny and distort their own emotional reactions ("Wipe that scowl off your face and say you are sorry!"), causing them to lose touch with their *intuitive* instincts and to deny their needs. In these circumstances, the figure (needs) never clearly emerges from the background (all the competing needs), and thus we are left with the unfinished business of discovering our true emotions. As we begin to see everything incorrectly, this process weighs us down and keeps us from acting in accordance with our genuine feelings. It distorts the sensory-perceptual field and stimuli we receive in other contexts (Perls, 1969a). Very often, unfinished business takes the form of not forgiving our parents for a variety of reasons. This failure to attend to figure–ground relationships in the present can stem from a variety of other factors as well: our tendency to dwell upon incomplete experiences, for example, our tendency to return to and relive these experiences, or to carry around unresolved emotions regarding them.

Yontef and Simpkin (1984) describe three descriptive therapeutic principles that sum up the goals of Gestalt therapy. The *I and Thou* principle describes the horizontal relationship between client and therapist, which is characterized by addressing someone directly (even if absent) instead of talking about that person to the counselor. The *What and How* principle, which emphasizes clients' increasing awareness of what they do and how they do it, occurs through direct and immediate sharing of observations and through exercises and feedback. The *Here and Now* principle refers to the importance placed on present experience for both clients and therapists.

MAJOR METHODS AND TECHNIQUES

Gestalt therapy is not verbal, but primarily experiential; it is about doing rather than saying. Because the focus is on the here and now, Gestalt therapy is particularly intent on providing opportunities for *creative experimentation,* and some of counseling's most innovative techniques emerge from out of this therapeutic approach (Covin 1977; Perls, Hefferline, & Goodman, 1972). Few other major theories present such a diverse array of evocative techniques.

Gestalt therapy often begins with laying down the general "rules" of therapy (Levitsky & Perls, 1970). At the outset it is understood that communication is to be between equals—one talks with, rather than at—and it is in the present tense, since looking either backward or forward is discouraged. In fact, clients are to focus continually on immediate experience. To encourage acceptance of responsibility, clients use "I" rather than "it" language, and to encourage talking to rather than about someone, they are not permitted to engage in gossip.

The healthy person, with the present as reference-point, is free to look backwards or ahead as occasion warrants.

—Fritz Perls

Since questions are often covert means of stating opinions rather than seeking information, questions are similarly discouraged.

The steps in the Gestalt helping process are fourfold: expression, differentiation, affirmation, and choice and integration. Through *expression* clients are encouraged to tell who they are as fully as possible, even becoming aware of gestures, breathing and voice tone, and facial expressions. To keep them in the "now" and maintain responsibility, clients are urged to preface their expressions with the phrase, "Now I am aware...."

Once expression has begun, the gestalt therapist begins to experiment with techniques that lead to *differentiation,* so that clients can differentiate between the parts of their inner conflict. They might be encouraged, for example, to exaggerate their facial expression and in so doing they may become more aware of their "angry part."

The third, crucial stage in Gestalt therapy, *affirmation,* occurs when the client is encouraged to identify with "all the parts" that are emerging into awareness. It is here that the Gestalt therapist will allow clients to express fully their pent-up emotions.

In the final stage, *choice and integration,* the client comes to say, "I am responsible for my frustration and resentment." As Perls (1976, p. 79) put it, "responsibility is really response-ability, the ability to choose one's reactions," and it comes about only when we relinquish our defenses and allow ourselves to become aware of our true feelings and motivations. In this stage an internal integration brings a sense of peace and is a sign of a "completed gestalt" (see Sidebar 10-2).

Dream Work

Perls described dreams as "messages" that represent the person's place at a certain time (Bernard, 1986). Unlike psychoanalysts, however, Gestalt counselors

Sidebar 10-2

COMMON GESTALT TECHNIQUES

Gestalt counselors employ a wide assortment of powerful tools designed to increase client awareness and help them experience rather than intellectualize. The following list shows several common techniques, along with the client behavior each attempts to address (Passons, 1975).

Client Concern or Deficit	Gestalt Verbalization
• Ambivalence toward a situation	• Ask the client to omit such qualifiers as "may" or "possibly."
• Not listening to self	• Ask: "Are you listening to what you are saying?"
• Lack of experiencing own behavior	• Ask questions of "How" and "What" rather than "Why."
• Distorted messages through question asking	• Say: "Please change the question to a statement."
• Improper word usage	• Have client change the passive voice to the active voice; change "need" to "want"; change "have to" to "choose to"; change "can't" to "won't."
• Depersonalization of self	• Have client change "we" to "I"; change "it" to "I."
• Unaware of affect	• Say: "Stay with that feeling."
• Unaware of reactions of others or self	• Ask client to say: "I'm aware that I ____ ;" or "I'm aware that you ____ ."
• Unaware of *Now* experience or involvement	• Ask: "What are you aware of now?"

do not interpret dreams; dream work is experiential rather than analytical. Clients present dreams and are then directed to experience what it is like to be each part of the dream. Every image in a dream is believed to represent an alienated, disowned, discordant, or projected part of the self.

The therapist assists clients in understanding their dreams by drawing attention to the order in which the images are played, by helping clients deal with avoidance and resistance in playing the parts, and by suggesting when clients might relate the images and feelings of the dream to current life situations. Reporting the dream in the present tense, as though the dream were occurring now, allows clients to grow more in touch with the multiple aspects of the self and thus to reclaim and integrate the alienated parts of their personality. For example, the therapist might ask clients to "become" the automobile they are dreaming about. On the other hand, clients who experience repetitive dreams are encouraged to realize that unfinished business is being brought into awareness and that they need to take care of the message. In sum, the goal of Gestalt dream work is to help clients come into contact with, own, accept responsibility for, or empower themselves to interact in a different or similar way with the images in the dream—all of which is an attempt to heighten self-awareness and journey on the "royal road to integration," as Perls called it (1969b, p. 66).

Converting Questions to Statements

Perls found that questions, which seem to be helpful and supportive, frequently represent passivity, laziness, lack of personal involvement, manipulation, and cajoling. Often the therapist will ask clients to turn their questions into statements in order to help them take responsibility for their thoughts. Since clients can use questions to camouflage their real thoughts and keep the focus of attention off themselves, this technique heightens the effectiveness of communication. For example, the client who asks, "Do you really believe that?" is generally saying, "I don't think you believe that." Similarly, "Aren't you really saying something else?" more accurately means, "I believe you are saying something else." Forcing clients to convert their questions into statements like this helps them declare their own belief systems and forces them to take responsibility.

Use of Personal Pronouns

When clients are talking about themselves, the Gestalt therapist also encourages the use of *I* instead of such words as *it, you,* or *we.* Instead of saying, "It takes a long time to write a term paper," for example, the client is urged to say, "I take a long time to write a term paper." Such first-person expressions help clients to own and thus to control their behavior, which facilitates the perception of the self, not as a passive, acted-upon object, but as an active, dynamic agent.

Assuming Responsibility

Clients are also encouraged to conclude all expressions of feelings or beliefs with, "And I take responsibility for it." Sometimes clients are encouraged to assume responsibility by asking them to change *can't* to *won't* or by changing *but* to *and.* For example, the statement, "I want to go to graduate school but I haven't applied anywhere" sounds different when one coordinating conjunction is exchanged for another: "I want to go to graduate school and I haven't applied anywhere." By changing the *but* to *and,* the client is verbalizing responsibility. This assumption of responsibility helps clients see themselves as possessing internal strength, rather than relying on external controls.

Playing the Projection

When clients project something onto another person, the counselor will ask them to play the role of the other person. For example, when a client says to the counselor, "I have the feeling you don't really like me," the counselor may ask him or her to play the role of the therapist and to express what he or she believes the counselor is feeling. By entering into the world of others, by empathizing with them, by discovering that their projection may be off target, clients discover how much their images of others, and thus their self-images, are colored by their own insecurities. In this example, the client recognizes that his or her feelings toward the counselor are being projected in a way that affects what he or she believes the counselor is feeling.

Empty Chair

To help clients retrieve parts of themselves they are either unaware of or have denied, Gestalt therapists often give clients the opportunity to role-play the way they would like to behave toward another person (Greenberg, 1979). This is accomplished by asking them to picture that person sitting across from them in the empty chair. Clients are then asked to speak the part of the other person and, by moving back and forth from chair to chair, to carry on a dialogue with that person. In the case of a teenage boy who is upset with his mother, for instance, the counselor will ask him to respond from the perspective of his parent by physically moving to the designated chair, which contributes to his awareness that his mother may see things from a different perspective than he does. This technique can also be used when clients rehearse new roles that will be tried outside of the counseling session, in order to strengthen their belief that they can carry out the new behavior. This method is not recommended, however, for those who are severely emotionally disturbed (Bernard, 1986).

> *Don't worry about tomorrow; for tomorrow will worry about itself.*
> —Matthew 6:34

Making the Rounds

In group therapy Gestalt therapists often *make the rounds* of each member of the group, especially when a particular theme or feeling expressed by a client should be faced by every person. The client may say, for example, "Nobody understands me." The client is then encouraged to personalize this sentence by saying, "You don't understand me" to each person in the group, adding remarks about each group member as appropriate. This rounds exercise is very flexible and may include nonverbal and positive feelings as well. By participating in it, clients become more aware of inner feelings.

Exaggeration

By heightening unwitting movements or gestures, clients can become more aware of the inner meaning of their behaviors. For example, the therapist may notice that every time a woman mentions her male friend she agitates her right foot. She, in turn, will be prompted to move her foot even faster, exaggerating the movement as if the foot had a life and voice of its own. In doing this, the client may begin to realize that this particular mannerism points to her frustration with her friend's behavior toward her. Exaggeration may also be used when clients offer a significant statement in a casual or feeble manner, indicating a lack of awareness of its importance. If the client says mildly, "I'm angry with him," he or she would be asked to repeat the statement again and again with amplified movement, loudness, and emphasis. This helps clients achieve better contact with themselves.

Confrontation

At times the Gestalt therapist will point out incongruent behaviors and feelings to clients. For example, clients who report being happy about hearing seemingly satisfying personal news, but fail to smile while talking about it, are functioning incongruently. People who are happy typi-
cally express it, in part, through their smiles. Confrontation involves asking clients *what* and *how* questions, for example: "What is happening within you that keeps you from expressing your happiness with a smile?" *Why* questions are avoided because they lead to an avoidance of feeling, defensiveness, explanations, and intellectualization. According to Gestalt theory, trouble occurs because of an overde-
pendency on intellectual experience (Simkin, 1975).

> *In Gestalt therapy change is not planned, programmed, or coerced. It is allowed.*
>
> —William R. Passons

May I Feed You a Sentence?

Sometimes implicit attitudes or messages are implied in what the client is saying. In "May I feed you a sentence," the therapist asks if clients will repeat a certain sentence, given by the counselor, that attempts to make explicit their un-
derlying assumptions. In other words, the therapist proposes a sentence for clients "to try on for size." If the counselor is correct in interpreting the underlying message, clients will gain insight by rehearsing the sentence.

APPLICATION

Gestalt therapy, with adaptation to particular situations, can be used among a wide variety of clinical populations. The following excerpt, from the pages of *Gestalt Therapy Verbatim* (Perls, 1969b), provides one of the best first-hand accounts of how Perls applied his theory in a "dream work seminar" with Beverly. Pay particular attention to how Perls probes her to externalize her feelings, to center herself, and to get in touch with the games or gimmicks she is using to hide behind.

> BEVERLY: I guess I'm supposed to say something. I don't have any interesting dreams. Mine are sort of patent.
>
> PERLS: Are you aware that you're defensive? . . . I didn't ask you in only to bring dreams.
>
> BEVERLY: You asked for them last night and I was afraid that would disqualify me. If I could manufacture a few . . .
>
> PERLS: Now you have a very interesting posture. The left leg supports the right leg, the right leg supports the right hand, the right hand supports the left hand.

BEVERLY: Yeah. It gives me something to hang onto. And with a lot of people out there you kind of get some stage fright. There are so many of them.

PERLS: You have stage fright and there are people outside. In other words you're on stage.

BEVERLY: Yeah, I suppose I feel that way.

PERLS: Well, what about getting in touch with your audience?

BEVERLY: Well they look very good. They have wonderful faces.

PERLS: Tell this to them.

BEVERLY: You have very warm faces, very interested, very interesting . . . with—with a lot of warmth.

PERLS: So then shuttle back to your stage fright. What do you experience now?

BEVERLY: I don't have any more stage fright. But my husband doesn't look at me.

PERLS: So go back to your husband.

BEVERLY: You're the only one that looks self-conscious. Nobody else looks self-conscious at me. [Laughter] You sort of feel like you're up there don't you? Or sort of like your youngster's up there? . . . Now? [From audience, yells] Answer!

BEVERLY: [*As Husband*] She's the one who's up there, and she's trying to place me up there.

PERLS: [To husband] Yah. You've got to answer. [To Beverly] You have to know what I feel.

BEVERLY: Well, he doesn't usually answer. Did you want him out of character? [Much laughter]

PERLS: So, you are a clobberer.

BEVERLY: You need an ashtray.

PERLS: "I need an ashtray." [Perls holds up his ashtray.] She knows what *I* need. [Laughter]

BEVERLY: Oh, no—you have one. [Laughter]

PERLS: Now I get stage fright. [Laughter] I always have difficulties in dealing with "Jewish mothers." [Laughter]

BEVERLY: Don't you like "Jewish mothers"?

PERLS: Oh, I love them. Especially their matzoh-ball soup. [Laughter]

BEVERLY: I'm not a gastronomical Jewish mother, just a Jewish mother. [Chuckles] I don't like gefilte fish either. I guess I'm a pretty obvious Jewish mother. Well that's not bad to be. That's all right. Matter of fact, that's good to be.

PERLS: What are your hands doing?

BEVERLY: Well, my thumbnails are pulling at each other.

PERLS: What are they doing to each other?

BEVERLY: Just playing. I do this often. See, I don't smoke, so what else are you gonna do with your hands? I doesn't look good to suck your thumbs.

PERLS: That's also the Jewish mother. She has reasons for everything. [Laughter]

BEVERLY: [Jokingly] And if I don't have one I'll make one up. [Chuckles] The ordered universe. What's wrong with being a Jewish mother?

PERLS: Did I say there's something wrong with a Jewish mother? I only say I have difficulties in dealing with them.

There is a famous story of a man who was such an excellent swordsman that he could hit even a raindrop, and when it was raining he used his sword instead of an umbrella. [Laughter] Now there are also intellectual and behavioristic swordsmen, who in answer to every question, statement, or whatever, hit it back. So whatever you do, immediately you are castrated or knocked out with some kind of replay—playing stupid or poor-me or whatever the games are. She's perfect.

BEVERLY: I never realized that.

PERLS: You see? Again the word. Playing stupid. I want once more to restate what I said earlier. Maturation is the transcendence from environmental support to self-support. The neurotic, instead of mobilizing his own resources, puts all his energy into manipulating the environment for support. And what you do is again and again manipulate me, you manipulate your husband, you manipulate everybody to come to the rescue of the "damsel in distress."

BEVERLY: How did I manipulate you?

PERLS: You see, again. This question, for instance. This is very important for maturation—change your questions to statements. Every question is a hook, and I would say that the majority of your questions are inventions to torture yourself and torture others. But if you change the question to a statement, you open up a lot of your background. This is one of the best means to develop a good intelligence. So change your question to a statement.

BEVERLY: Well, th—that implies that, ah, there's a fault to me. Didn't you intend it so? . . .

PERLS: Put Fritz in that chair and ask him that question.

BEVERLY: Don't you like Jewish mothers? Did you have one that you didn't like?

PERLS: Well, I like them. They're just a very difficult lot to deal with.

BEVERLY: Well, what makes them so difficult?

PERLS: Well, they're very dogmatic and very opinionated and inflexible and the box that they construct for themselves to grow in is a little narrower than man. They're less easy to therapize.

BEVERLY: Does everybody have to be subject to your therapy?

PERLS: No. [Laughter]

BEVERLY: [To Perls] Did you ever switch chairs like this with yourself?

PERLS: [Laughing] Oh yes—Oh! Even I get sucked in! [Laughter]

BEVERLY: You said you had problems with Jewish mothers. [Laughter]

BEVERLY: [*As Husband*] Do you understand now why I didn't answer? [Laughter and applause]

PERLS: That's right, because you see how a Jewish mother doesn't say "You need an ashtray." [Laughter] Okay. Thank you (Perls, 1969b).

Traditionally, Gestalt therapy has been considered most effective with anxious, phobic perfectionists and with depressed clients, those who are "overly socialized, restrained, constricted individuals" (Shepherd, 1970, pp. 243-245). However, current practice of Gestalt therapy includes treatment of a much wider range of problems (e.g., Bryant, Kessler, & Shirar, 1992; Dolliver, 1981; Jessee & Guerney, 1981; Kastner & Neumann, 1986; Lawe & Smith, 1986; Tyson & Range, 1987). Gestalt therapy has also been used for crisis intervention, adults in poverty programs, school problems, psychosomatic disorders, psychotics, multiple personality disorders, couples, and almost any group imaginable. Unfortunately the literature, although providing examples, provides very little explication of necessary alteration in the focus of Gestalt therapy for these diverse settings.

CRITICAL ANALYSIS

One of the most appealing features of Gestalt therapy is its holistic emphasis on the integration of fragmented parts of the personality. By underscoring the importance of awareness, authenticity, confrontation, encounter, immediacy, personal responsibility, and risk taking, Gestalt therapy, more than any other approach, stresses the unity of mind, body, and feelings.

Exploring inconsistencies between what is said and what is done has similarly opened up many untapped therapeutic avenues and reveals Gestalt therapy's unusually insightful analysis of the games we play in our interpersonal relationships. The methods of confronting and directly encountering unfinished business also hold equal intuitive appeal. Although few therapists will go as far as does the Gestalt therapist to "frustrate the neurosis," they generally agree that "control issues" are central to the process of change and healing. Many of us would rather "confirm our neuroses," Perls correctly observed, than confront our inevitable tendency to deny, distort, or disown parts of ourselves.

A significant concern over Gestalt therapy, however, is its questionable outcomes. Perls argued that persons are essentially organisms with strong needs, and in any given day the primary task is to see to it that these organismic needs are met. Meeting one's own current organismic needs in a constructive, creative, and healthy fashion is the ultimate goal of Gestalt therapy. The problem, however, is that depending on one's perspective this way could result in either greater self-integration or in hedonism. That is, it is a matter of intense debate as to whether Gestalt therapy is capable of leading to more responsible ethical and moral behavior in the larger social context. Since it is the view of Gestalt therapy that our wants and needs assume a position of absolute primacy, our accountability to others is inevitably of secondary importance. The fully functioning person is the one who is fully alive and aware, who meets his or her

A Gestalt therapist does not use techniques; he applies himself in and to a situation with whatever professional skill and life experiences he has accumulated.

—Laura Perls

biological needs in an adult and responsible fashion, and who is not dependent on others to meet these needs. In short, the approach tends to glorify individuality, which can readily lead to a low estimation of the value of relationships. For the Gestalt therapist, self-sufficiency is the pre-eminent virtue.

Still others commonly raise questions, not about the games played by clients, but about those played by Gestalt therapists. Few counselors doubt that the techniques of Gestalt therapy are powerful tools, but they raise questions of possible misuse or abuse of these tools in a power game controlled by the therapist. The possibility for the counselor to enter into an unhealthy relationship of power with the clients or to avoid dealing with his or her own countertransference problems seems inevitable. To be fair, this is a concern in all therapeutic approaches. The issue seems more glaring in the Gestalt approach, however, and it reminds clinicians of the importance of timing, tact, and sensitivity, as well as personal and professional competencies (see Sidebar 10-3).

When Gestalt therapy turns its attention to the treatment of diverse populations, however, the approach does offer some beneficial elements. To begin with, any activity that helps clients become more integrative can be employed in Gestalt therapy. Since this approach is not limited to a few techniques, it is flexible enough to dismantle cross-cultural barriers. In other words, its techniques can be customized in ways that a client can perceive and interpret from a distinct culture.

Unfortunately, however, using Gestalt techniques with ethnic clients cannot be entered into without first considering the hazards that are bound to accompany its use. Some cultures, for example, are more emotionally reserved, and the intensity of Gestalt techniques is destined to lead, at best, to resistance and, at worst, to premature termination of therapy.

Permit yourself to express with full emotional force all the kicking, pounding and screaming of a child's tantrum.

—Fritz Perls

Also, in cultures that consider personal expression and public exposure to be not cathartic, but disgraceful, the Gestalt approach only increases a sense of shame and adds to an already heavy burden (McGoldrick, Pearce, & Giordano, 1982; Serok & Levi, 1993). The Gestalt approach, therefore, is only flexible within rather narrow parameters, which are defined by the confrontive role of the counselor, the intensity of the client's emotional experience in therapy, and the highly individualistic philosophy that the Gestalt approach encourages. Paradoxically, then, whereas the Gestalt therapist welcomes any techniques that heighten awareness and bring about wholeness, he or she may not appear to hold in contempt any social system or lifestyle that does not open itself to doing so.

In treating clients with physical disabilities, Gestalt therapy is particularly useful for those who are in the denial or hostility phases of adaptation. By mildly confronting and clarifying inconsistencies and discrepancies between verbal and nonverbal messages and behaviors, for example, counselors can engage clients who deny the permanence or severity of disabilities such as spinal cord injuries, for instance. With this approach, clients may also be asked to project into the future their difficulties related to their disability, thereby allowing

Sidebar 10-3

THE GESTALT WORKSHOP

Some Gestalt therapy and a good deal of training in Gestalt therapy is conducted in workshops, which are scheduled for a finite period, some for as short as one day. Weekend workshops may range from 10 to 20 or more hours. Longer work-shops range from a week through several months in duration. A typical weekend workshop membership consists of one

Role playing with an empty chair.
(Susan Rosenberg/Photo Researchers)

Gestalt therapist and 12 to 16 people. Given longer periods (ranging from one week up to a month or longer), as many as 20 people can be seen by one therapist. Usually if the group is larger than 16 participants, co-therapists are used.

Because workshops have a finite life and because limited hours are available to the participants, there is usually high motivation to "work." Sometimes, rules are established so that no one can work a second time until every other participant has had an opportunity to work once. At other times, no such rules are set. Thus, depending on their willingness, audacity, and drive, some people may get intense therapeutic attention several times during a workshop.

Although some workshops are arranged with established groups, most assemble people for the first time. As in ongoing groups, the ideal practice is to screen patients before the workshop. An unscreened workshop requires a clinician experienced with the range of severe pathology and careful protection for possibly vulnerable group members. Confrontive or charismatic Gestalt styles are particularly likely to exacerbate existing mental illness in some participants.

Source: Yontef, G. M, & Simkin, J. S. (1989). Gestalt therapy. In Corsini, R. J. & Wedding, D. (Eds.), *Current psychotherapies.* Itasca, IL: F. E. Peacock. Reprinted with permission.

them to deal with their denial in a less threatening and nonimmediate life context (Allen, 1985). For clients containing internalized anger, empty chair work or role playing can help them gain awareness of inner conflicts and of unfinished business, which may include a lost body part or function. Writing a farewell letter expressing grief, anger, and ambivalence toward the loss can also help clients to become more aware of inner conflicts and to assimilate and ultimately accept the new reality.

Like all approaches to therapy, Gestalt therapy has its advantages and disadvantages. But there is a further critique that needs to be addressed: Gestalt purists tend to be unconcerned with larger questions of meaning and purpose in life. Perhaps it is true that too many "why" questions, especially in the psychotherapeutic context, can be a means of avoiding more important issues, but this does not erase the fact that we have a compelling need to ask such questions. The ability to know, to understand properly, is at least as crucial as the imperative of Gestalt therapy to be fully alive, to living a life of integrity and value.

CURRENT STATUS

The impact of Gestalt therapy on the field of counseling has been significant. As an experiential therapy, it has provided a provocative challenge to earlier theoretical approaches such as psychoanalysis. The turbulence of the late 1960s and the early 1970s, with the focus of those years on "doing your own thing," welcomed Gestalt therapy with open arms, and the approach was propelled into widespread recognition. It can be said, however, that although Gestalt therapy captured the *Zeitgeist*, the spirit of the age, it failed to take hold.

Nevertheless, although seldom recognized by academic psychologists, the impact of Perls cannot be ignored. His contributions to the human growth and human potential movements in the United States cannot be denied. Thousands of people have participated in the workshops and seminars offered by more than 50 Gestalt training centers across the country. But the Perls era of Gestalt therapy is over, and few Gestalt "purists" remain. In a survey of a large sample of counseling psychologists (Watkins, Lopez, Campbell, & Himmell, 1986), for example, fewer than 5% of the participants claimed Gestalt therapy as either their primary or their secondary theoretical orientation. Some argue that Gestalt therapy's decline in popularity is due, in part, to its lack of a research base. Gestalt therapy has never truly been supported by empirical study. Few outcome studies have been conducted to support its effectiveness, and it has not received the respect of academicians (Epstein, 1988; Simkin, 1978). Cadwallader (1981) argues, for example, that Perls and his followers have accepted emotion and intuition in the place of intellect.

> *The dream is the royal road to awareness and integration.*
> —Fritz Perls

Despite the waning popularity of Gestalt therapy, the Gestalt approach continues to influence the field of counseling. Many therapists from different theoretical modes use the techniques created by Perls and other Gestaltists (Burke, 1989). There are over 60 Gestalt therapy institutes throughout the world, and the *Gestalt Journal* is devoted to publishing articles on Gestalt therapy. Although no national Gestalt therapy organization exists, the following institutes and training centers are among the most well known:

Gestalt Institute of Cleveland
1588 Hazel Drive
Cleveland, OH 44106

Gestalt Training Center
P.O. Box 2189
La Jolla, CA 92038

Gestalt Therapy Institute of Los Angeles
620 Venice Boulevard
Venice, CA 90291

Gestalt Institute of San Francisco
1790 Union Street
San Francisco, CA 94123

New York Institute for Gestalt Therapy
7 West 96th Street
New York, NY 10025

Gestalt Institute of the Southwest
7700 Alabama Street
El Paso, TX 79904

CHAPTER SUMMARY

1. *Biography.* Perls (1893–1970) grew up as the only son in a German family. He was an unruly child but loved to read and was an excellent student. He earned his M.D. degree from Frederick Wilhelm University in 1920 and soon joined the German army as a medic. After World War I, Perls began psychoanalytic training and eventually took a position in Frankfurt working with Kurt Goldstein, who taught him to view the human being as a complete entity, rather than the sum of its separate parts. During the 1930s Perls fled the Nazis, eventually emigrating to South Africa, where he and his wife, Laura, built a strong practice. But it was after a meeting with Freud in 1936 that Perls moved to New York, where he founded the Institute for Gestalt Therapy and dedicated himself to proving Freud wrong.

2. *Historical Development.* The origins of Gestalt therapy are found in three Germans whom Perls studied: Wertheimer, Koffka, and Köhler. Perls saw an individual's perceptions in terms of the Gestalt dichotomy of figure–ground and established his theory on that premise. Another important historical influence on Gestalt therapy was the existential movement in philosophy and psychology.

3. *View of Human Nature.* Perls believed that people developed in relation to their environment, and he divided this development into the social, psychophysical, and spiritual stages. His existential and humanistic perspective viewed people as self-directed; he believed they had to take responsibility for their own lives. Gestaltists believe that a healthy personality is the result of a person's experiences forming a meaningful whole (i.e., *Gestalt*). This occurs when there is a smooth transition between those sets of experiences that are immediately in the focus of awareness and those that lie in the background.

4. *Development of Maladaptive Behavior.* In Gestalt theory people develop maladaptive behavior, characterized by a lack of awareness, self-responsibility,

contact with environment, denial of needs, and so on, when they fail to utilize their own capacity for self-regulation and spend their energy on acting helpless, depending upon others, or manipulating the environment in countless ways. The result is an anxious state of temporal insecurity originating when the self is unable to determine the boundaries between the individual and the environment.

5. *Goals of Therapy.* Gestalt therapy tries to help individuals assume responsibility for themselves, rather than relying on others to make decisions for them. It tries to facilitate a process in which clients can become complete and integrated, functioning as a systematic whole that consists of feelings, perceptions, thoughts, and a physical body whose processes cannot be divorced from its more psychological components. This goal is often reached through an "Aha!" experience, in which we suddenly see and understand what has long eluded us.

6. *Function of the Therapist.* The role of the Gestalt therapist is to serve as a catalyst for change without assuming the responsibility for change within the clients. As a result, the Gestalt therapist plays an active role that often frustrates the clients' demands for support and help, forcing them to rely on their own resources. The Gestalt therapist also views change through a paradoxical lens, holding that change takes place, not when one tries to be what one is not, but when one becomes what one is. Thus, to be authentic, the Gestalt therapist must not try to be a better therapist, but to be who he or she is at the moment.

7. *Major Methods and Techniques.* Perls' work led him to identify many therapeutic techniques, all of which are experiential rather than verbal. Gestalt therapy is about doing rather than saying. After laying a foundation of general "rules" of therapy (e.g., communication is to be between equals in the present tense), a therapist may choose from a smorgasbord of methods: dream work, converting questions to statements, using personal pronouns, assuming responsibility, playing the projection, the empty chair, making the rounds, exaggeration, confrontation, and so on.

8. *Application.* Perls often demonstrated his therapeutic approach in open workshop settings. In his work *Gestalt Therapy Verbatim*, he provides many firsthand accounts of how Gestalt therapy can be applied to a variety of situations. The case of "Beverly" is one example that illustrates just how Perls probed a client to encourage her to externalize feelings, to center herself, and to get in touch with the games or gimmicks behind which she was hiding.

9. *Critical Analysis.* Gestalt therapy features a holistic emphasis on the integration of fragmented parts of the personality. More than any other theory, it stresses the unity of mind, body, and feelings. It has enormous intuitive appeal, but its intended outcomes raise questions. With its strong emphasis on individuality, relationships are in danger of being relegated to a secondary status.

The pre-eminent virtue is self-sufficiency. The Gestalt approach offers some benefits to cross-cultural counseling (e.g., its techniques can help dismantle some cross-cultural barriers) but also has many limitations (e.g., it can lead to resistance or greater shame). Nevertheless, in treating people with physical disabilities, Gestalt therapy has been found quite useful.

10. *Current Status.* As an experiential approach, Gestalt therapy has provided a provocative challenge to other theoretical approaches, but is it seldom recognized by academic psychology. In many respects, the Perls era of Gestalt therapy is over. In part because of its lack of a research base, there are few Gestalt purists. Despite its waning popularity, however, the Gestalt approach continues to influence the field of counseling as its strategies are integrated into other approaches.

KEY TERMS

Acknowledgment   Individuals discover themselves and develop a sense of self and appreciation through acknowledgment.

Adaptation   In this process the individual discovers personal boundaries and differentiates self from non-self.

Agression   The organism's means of contacting its environment to satisfy its needs and of meeting resistance to the satisfaction of its needs. Its purpose is not destruction, but simply overcoming resistance.

Approbation   A process through which people develop splits in their personalities and create a self-image (a notion of self based on external standards). Approbation interferes with the development of a sound and healthy notion of self.

Awareness   The process of observing and attending to your thoughts, feelings, and actions, including body sensations as well as visual and auditory perceptions. It is seen as a flowing panorama that constitutes your "now" experience.

Closure   The Gestalt concept that the mind synthesizes the missing parts of a perceived image and, in effect, closes the gap between the reality and the desired "picture."

Figure   That which occupies the center of a person's attentive awareness; what the person is now paying attention to.

Gestalt   German word meaning shape, figure, configuration, totality, or whole.

Gestalt Psychology   An approach that focuses on the dynamic organization of experience into patterns of configurations. This viewpoint came into prominence as a revolt against structuralism, which analyzed experience into static, atomistic sensations, and also against the equally atomistic approach of behaviorism, which dissected complex behavior into elementary conditioned reflexes.

Ground   The part of the perceptual field that is not "figure" is identified as ground. Taken together, figure and ground constitute a Gestalt.

Here and Now   An emphasis on understanding present feelings as they occur in an ongoing treatment, with little or no emphasis on past experience.

Homeostasis   The tendency for living organisms to find equilibrium or balance between themselves and their surrounding environment.

Impasse   The situation in which progress in the treatment process has ceased, and failure is imminent. This situation occurs when further insight is not forthcoming, or when the process is blocked by extreme resistance.

Introjection   The uncritical acceptance of other people's concepts, standards of behavior, and values. The person who habitually introjects does not develop his or her own personality.

Organismic Self-Regulation   The process by which an individual, confronted by either an external demand or an internal need, strives to reduce tension by maintaining the organismic balance between demands and needs.

Projection   The process by which the individual places in the outside world the parts of the personality that he or she refuses (or is unable) to identify.

Proximity   The Gestalt principle which states that objects or stimuli that are close together will be perceived as a unity. For example, a series of unconnected lines in a neon sign become a word or sentence.

Retroflection   The process by which some function that was originally directed from the individual toward the world changes direction and is bent back toward the originator. The result is a split between the self as doer and the self as receiver.

Self   The creative process that leads the person to actualizing behaviors by responding to emergent needs and environmental pressures. The fundamental characteristic of the self is the formation and distinction of gestures.

Self-image   The part of the personality that hinders creative growth by imposing external standards.

Similarity   When stimuli in the perceptual field causes us to group similar things together.

SUGGESTED READING

James, M., & Jongeward, D. (1971). *Born to win: Transactional analysis with Gestalt experiments*. Reading, MA: Addison-Wesley.

Korb, M.P., Gorrell, J., & Ban De Reit, V. (1989). *Gestalt therapy: Practice and theory* (2nd ed.). New York: Pergamon Press.

Latner, J. (1973). *The Gestalt therapy book*. New York: Bantam Books.

Passons, W. R. (1975). *Gestalt approaches in counseling*. New York: Holt, Rinehart & Winston.

Perls, F. (1969). *Gestalt therapy verbatim*. Moab, UT: Real People Press.

Perls, F. (1969). *In and out of the garbage pail*. Moab, UT: Real People Press.

Van Diert, V., & Korb, M. (1980). *Gestalt therapy: An introduction*. New York: Pergamon Press.

REFERENCES

Allen, H. A. (1985). The Gestalt perspective. *Journal of Applied Rehabilitation Counseling, 16,* 21–25.

Banks, W. P., & Krajicek, D. (1991). Perception. *Annual Review of Psychology, 42,* 305–331.

Bernard, J. M. (1986). Laura Perls: From ground to figure. *Journal of Counseling and Development, 64,* 367–373.

Burke, J. F. (1989). *Contemporary Approaches to Psychotherapy & Counseling: The Self-Regulation and Maturity Model.* Pacific Grove, CA: Brooks/Cole.

Bryant, D., Kessler, J., & Shirar, L. (1992). *The family inside: Working with the multiple.* New York: W. W. Norton.

Cadwallader, E. H. (1981). Values in Fritz Perls' Gestalt therapy: On the dangers of half-truths. *Counseling and Values, 28,* 192–201.

Covin, A. B. (1977). Using Gestalt psychodrama experiments in rehabilitation counseling. *Personnel and Guidance Journal, 56,* 143–147.

Dolliver, R. H. (1981). Some limitations in Perls' Gestalt therapy. *Psychotherapy, Research and Practice, 8,* 38–45.

Dolliver, R. H. (1991). Perls with Gloria re-reviewed: Gestalt techniques and Perls's practices. *Journal of Counseling and Development, 69,* 299–304.

Dolliver, R. H., Williams, E. L., & Gold, D. C. (1980). The art of Gestalt therapy or "What are you doing with your feet now?" *Psychotherapy: Theory, Research and Practice, 17,* 136–140, 142.

Epstein, W. (1988). Has the time come to rehabilitate Gestalt theory? *Psychological Research, 50,* 2–5.

Fagan, J. (1970). The task of the therapist. In J. Fagan & I. L. Shepherd (Eds.), *Gestalt therapy now.* Palo Alto, CA: Science and Behavior Books.

Graumann, C. F. (1989). Gestalt in social psychology. *Psychological Research, 51,* 75–79.

Greenberg, L. S. (1979). Resolving splits: Use of the two chair technique. *Psychotherapy: Theory, Research and Practice, 16,* 316–324.

Harman, R. L. (1975). A Gestalt point of view on facilitating growth in counseling. *Personnel and Guidance Journal, 53,* 363–366.

Hycner, R. (1987). An interview with Erving and Miriam Polster. *The Gestalt Journal, 10*(2), 27–66.

Jessee, R. E., & Guerney, B. G. (1981). A comparison of Gestalt and relationship enhancement treatments with married couples. *American Journal of Family Therapy, 9,* 31–41.

Jourard, S. (1964). *The transparent self.* Princeton, NJ: D. Van Nostrand.

Kastner, M., & Neumann, M. A. (1986). A model combining two psychotherapeutic approaches in group psychotherapy. *Psychotherapy, 23,* 593–597.

Kempler, W. (1973). Gestalt therapy. In R. Corsini (Ed.), *Current psychotherapies* (pp. 251–286). Itasca, IL: F. E. Peacock.

Köhler, W. (1973). *The mentality of apes* (2nd ed.) (E. Winter, Trans.). New York: Harcourt Brace & World. (Original work published 1927)

Korb, M. P., Gorrell, J., & Van De Riet, V. (1989). *Gestalt therapy: Practice and theory* (2nd ed.). New York: Pergamon Press.

Latner, J. (1973). *The Gestalt therapy book.* New York: Bantam Books.

Lawe, C. F., & Smith, E. W. L. (1986). Gestalt processes and family therapy. *Individual Psychology, 42,* 537–544.

Levitsky, A., & Perls, F. S., (1970). The rules and games of Gestalt therapy. In J. Fagan & I. L. Sheperd (Eds.), *Gestalt therapy now*. Palo Alto, CA: Science and Behavior Books.

Litt, S. (1978). Fritz Perls and Gestalt therapy. *American Psychologist, 33*, 958–959.

Little, L. F. (1986). Gestalt therapy with parents when a child is presented as the problem. *Family Relations, 35*, 489–496.

McClure, B. A., Merrill, E., & Russo, T. R. (1994). Seeing clients with an artist's eye: Perceptual simulation exercises. *Simulation and Gaming, 25*, 51–60.

McGoldrick, M., Pearce, J. K., & Giordano, J. (1982). *Ethnicity and family therapy*. New York: Guilford.

Naranjo, C. (1970). Present-centerdness: Technique, prescription, and ideal. In J. Fagan & I. Sheperd (Eds.), *Gestalt therapy now*. Palo Alto, CA: Science and Behavior Books.

Osborn, D. (1991). A return to Piaget: Guidelines for counselors. *Texas Association for Counselors and Development Journal, 19*, 13–19.

Passons, W. R. (1975). *Gestalt approaches in counseling*. New York: Holt, Rinehart & Winston.

Perls, F. S. (1969a). *In and out of the garbage pail*. Moab, UT: Real People Press.

Perls, F. S. (1969b). *Gestalt therapy verbatim*. Moab, UT: Real People Press.

Perls, F. S. (1970). Four lectures. In J. Fagan & I. L. Shepherd (Eds.), *Gestalt therapy now*. Palo Alto, CA: Science and Behavior Books.

Perls, F. S. (1976), *The Gestalt approach and eye witness to therapy*. New York: Bantam Books.

Perls, F. S., Hefferline, R. F., & Goodman, P. (1972). *Gestalt therapy: Excitement and growth in the human personality*. New York: Souvenir Press.

Phares, E. J. (1988). *Clinical psychology: Concepts, methods, and profession* (3rd ed.). Pacific Grove, CA: Brooks/Cole.

Prochaska, J. O. (1979). *Systems of psychotherapy: A transtheoretical analysis*. Homewood, IL: Dorsey Press.

Rock, I., & Palmer, S. (1990, December). The legacy of Gestalt psychology. *Scientific American, 84*–90.

Rice, L. N., & Greenberg, L. S. (1992). Humanistic approaches to psychotherapy. In D. K. Freedheim (Ed.), *History of psychotherapy: A century of change* (pp. 197–224). Washington, D.C.: American Psychological Association.

Saariluoma, P. (1992). Do visual images have Gestalt properties? *Quarterly Journal of Experimental Psychology, 45*, 399–420.

Sarris, V. (1989). Max Wertheimer on seen motion: Theory and evidence. *Psychological Research, 51*, 58–68.

Serok, S., & Levi, N. (1993). Application of Gestalt therapy with long-term prison inmates in Israel. *Gestalt Journal, 16*, 105–127.

Shepherd, I. L. (1970). Limitations and cautions in the Gestalt approach. In J. Fagan & I. L. Shepherd (Eds.), *Gestalt therapy now* (pp. 234–238). Palo Alto, CA: Science and Behavior Books.

Shostrom, E. L. (Producer). (1965). *Three approaches to psychotherapy: Part 2. Frederick Perls* [Film]. Orange, CA: Psychological Films.

Simkin, J. S. (1975). An introduction to Gestalt therapy. In F. D. Stephenson (Ed.), *Gestalt therapy primer*, Springfield, IL: Charles C Thomas.

Simkin, J. S. (1978). Gestalt therapy and the psychological abstracts. *American Psychologist, 33*, 705–706.

Thompson, C. D., & Rudolph, L. B. (1988). *Counseling children* (2nd ed.). Pacific Grove, CA: Brooks/Cole.

Tyson, G. M., & Range, L. M. (1987). Gestalt dialogues as a treatment for mild depression: Time works just as well. *Journal for Clinical Psychology, 43*(2), 227–231.

Wallen, R. (1970). Gestalt therapy and gestalt psychology. In J. Fagan & I. L. Shepherd (Eds.), *Gestalt therapy now.* Palo Alto, CA: Science and Behavior Books.

Watkins, C. E., Lopez, F. G., Campbell, V. L., & Himmell, C. D. (1986). Contemporary counseling psychology: The results of a national survey. *Journal of Counseling Psychology, 33,* 301–309.

Yontef, G. M. (1982). Gestalt therapy: Its inheritance from Gestalt psychology. *Gestalt Theory, 4,* 23–39.

Yontef, G. M. (1984). Modes of thinking in Gestalt therapy. *Gestalt Journal, 7*(1), 33-74.

Yontef, G. M., & Simkin, J. S. (1989). Gestalt therapy, In Corsini, R. J. & Wedding, D. *Current psychotherapies.* Itasca, IL: F. E. Peacock.

Zinker, J. (1978). *Creative process in Gestalt therapy.* New York: Random House.

CHAPTER 11

Transactional Analysis

Chapter Outline

Introduction
Brief Biography
Historical Development
View of Human Nature
Development of Maladaptive Behavior
Function of the Therapist
Goals of Therapy
Major Methods and Techniques
Application
Critical Analysis
Current Status
Chapter Summary
Key Terms
Suggested Reading

INTRODUCTION

During a single day, each of us negotiates our way through a myriad of inter-actions. Some negotiations are instantaneous, such as greeting the doorman, who returns the civility with a nod of recognition, and some negotiations, such as a first date or a request for a raise, have higher stakes and are more carefully sculpted. Daily life is a series of such negotiations.

These commonplace interactions are the concern of transactional analysis. Developing a language that is neither couched in theoretical concerns nor veiled in obtuse terminology, TA, as it is commonly called, seeks to take the mystery out of counseling. Indeed, the basic ideas of TA have long been acces-sible to the general public through two landmark books that remained on the national best-seller list for more than a year: Eric Berne's *Games People Play* and Thomas A. Harris' *I'm OK— You're OK.*

BRIEF BIOGRAPHY

Born in Montreal, Canada, in 1910, as a young lad Eric Lennard Bernstein often accompanied his father, a general practitioner of medicine, on his house calls. Berne admired his father's devotion to his patients and his lack of concern for money. Unfortunately, his father died at the age of 38, when Eric was barely 9 years old. Eric's desire to help others was born of his admiration for his father and nurtured by the memory of his happy relationship with him. Eric Berne

Eric Berne (1910–1970).
(AP/Wide World)

dedicated his first book to his father with these words: "He lived in dignified poverty as a country physician." As an adult, Eric inscribed an epigraph on his father's grave that read, "David Hillel Bernstein, M.D., a humane and conscientious physician. . . He loved his neighbor as himself and did no wrong." Fortunately, Eric's mother was a professional writer and editor, and she supported Eric and his younger and only sister after their father's death.

Inspired by the memory of his father, Eric followed his footsteps through medical school at McGill University, receiving his M.D. in 1935. Eric soon married his first of three wives, became an American citizen, and, in an accommodation to anti-Semitism, dropped the Lennard from his name and shortened Bernstein to Berne.

After his psychiatric residency at Yale University School of Medicine, Berne began psychoanalytic training at the New York Psychoanalytic Institute, a traditional Freudian stronghold that taught classical methods. His training, however, was cut short by World War II, which sent Berne to the U.S. Army Medical Corps in 1941, where he practiced medical psychiatry in several military hospitals.

After his discharge from the Army in 1946, Berne settled at the Veterans Administration Hospital in San Francisco and soon established a private practice in Carmel, California. It was there that he separated from his first wife and completed his first work, *The Mind in Action* (1947). He also resumed psychoanalytic training at the San Francisco Psychoanalytic Institute under Eric Erikson, who insisted that Berne not remarry until after the analysis was finished. Berne obliged, but did remarry in 1949 and fathered two children, as in his first marriage.

For more than 15 years, Berne pursued credentialing as a psychoanalyst without ever achieving official recognition. Indeed, he was humiliated and devastated when the San Francisco Institute said he was not yet ready and would need at least 3 or 4 years of further personal analysis and training. It was this rejection that propelled him into the development of his own orientation to psychotherapy. Turning his back on the obtuseness that seemed to be endemic in the classical method, Berne sought a more "rational" approach to therapy. He turned to the experiences he used in conducting group therapy during the war and gravitated toward a common-sense style, which characterizes his approach (Steiner, 1974).

> *I'm a head mechanic—that's all I am.*
>
> —Eric Berne

Eric Berne was single-minded and passionate in his vision for a new form of psychotherapy. Although he published many articles and monographs, he continued to insist that "there is only one paper to write which is called 'How to Cure Patients'—that's the only paper that's really worth writing if you're really going to do your job."

Berne built a study in his house away from the noise of his children. In 1950 he imposed a demanding schedule on himself, typically beginning on Monday and concluding on Sunday, which he followed until his death. Biographers describe him as indefatigable (Cheney, 1971). Most of his productive life he practiced in his two offices in Carmel and in San Francisco. His schedule was controlled and predictable: on Monday mornings he saw patients in Carmel; Tuesdays he counseled in San Francisco; Wednesdays he lectured at the University of California School of Medicine; Thursdays he was at Stanford or working with private clients or, later in the day, conducting a TA seminar in Monterey; and on Fridays he wrote, after which there was the inevitable game of poker in the evening. Weekends were devoted to more writing.

After a second divorce in 1964, Berne increased his writing time. Friends attributed the early wreck of his third marriage, and perhaps his untimely death at 60 years of age, to his frenetic work habits. At the time of his death, Berne was working on six different books. In fact, he called for page proofs and worked on them for 3 hours the day before suffering a fatal heart attack in 1970.

HISTORICAL DEVELOPMENT

Berne's long association with psychoanalysis helped form the ideas that eventually became transactional analysis. Although Berne denied any intentional borrowing from Freud, he admitted to thinking of psychoanalysis as "the core and transactional analysis as the apple" (Holland, 1973, p. 354).

But the roots of TA extend beyond its Freudian soil. Roots may also be found, for example, at McGill University in the neurological research on the brain conducted by Dr. Wilder Penfield. It was he who taught Berne that there was a neurological basis for the assumption that people existed in different ego states simultaneously and that these states were connected to memories (Penfield, 1952). Alfred Adler, whose lifestyle so closely parallels Berne's own script, also influenced Berne's theorizing (Simoneux, 1977). Berne's concern with feeling "not-OK" is strikingly similar to Adler's concept of feeling inferior. And when he turned to Carl Rogers, of course, Berne found a colleague who also rejected the Freudian diagnostic model and accepted the client as a problem-solving person. These assorted influences—Freud, Adler, and Rogers—were mixed, merged, and synthesized into transactional analysis.

Although Berne's first paper on TA was published in 1957, it took several years before the movement achieved public recognition. From the beginning, however, Berne strove to make his theory accessible. He wanted nothing to do with fancy language or "jazz," as he called it. After listening patiently to an elaborate report studded with jargon, Berne would often say, "That is all well and good. All I know is the patient is not getting cured" (Steiner, 1974, p. 14). At his seminars he banned theoretical jargon, which he labeled "bright ideas," polysyllabic vocabulary ("glossing over"), and hypothetical examples ("distractions"). He preferred short words, short sentences, short meetings, and short presentations. And, partly in reaction to his long years of psychoanalysis, short cures.

Dusay (1977) describes the formulation of TA as proceeding through four successive phases. In the first phase (1955–1962), influenced by his clients' descriptions of behaving as a child, as a parent, and as an adult, Berne developed the concept of ego states. In the second phase (1962–1966), he concentrated on ideas about transactions and games. It was during this time that the International Transactional Analysis Association was created (1964) and that Berne published the best-seller *Games People Play*. In the third phase (1966–1970), Berne explored the reasons some individuals choose to play certain games in life; and in the fourth phase (from 1970), just before his death, he studied action and energy distribution.

TA was the first therapy the lay public could understand. People soon began talking about "Child," "Parent," and "Adult" and about "games" and "scripts," as they described themselves in relationships. The diagrams, circles, and arrows that Berne used to explain interactions between people became increasingly commonplace in counseling offices, classrooms, management seminars, even Sunday School classes (Burke, 1989; Jongeward, 1973; Oden, 1974), and TA enjoyed wide appeal and great popularity. Unlike other casualties of the 1960s and 1970s, however, it has managed to survive its popularity and, in combination with other techniques, it is still considered a significant approach to counseling and psychotherapy.

VIEW OF HUMAN NATURE

Berne believed that basic psychological hungers motivate people to transcend patterns of behavior that begin early in life. "People are born princes and princesses and then their parents kiss them and turn them into frogs" (Steiner, 1974, p. 2), he once wrote. According to Berne, we transcend or overcome our "froggyness" by means of basic psychological hungers, especially by three fundamental needs: stimulus hunger, structure hunger, and position hunger.

Stimulus hunger is the need to be acknowledged or affirmed by others both psychologically and physically. Berne believed all persons have this basic need to be recognized, this need to receive *strokes*, whether positive (e.g., a smile) or negative (e.g., a frown). So powerful is the need for these strokes, which he described as basic units of social interaction, essential for life, that individuals deprived of positive reinforcement will actually seek negative strokes (Wollams and Brown, 1979). A child who misbehaves, for example, in order to receive the attention of parents may be punished, but he or she is still receiving strokes. Such strokes result in the collection of either good or bad feelings, which Berne called *stamps*, which can be cashed in when enough of them are collected. Individuals might collect enough bad feelings from failing grades, for instance, to justify their quitting school, or enough good feelings about studying hard to take time off to attend a party (Gladding, 1992).

Structure hunger refers to how we maximize the number of strokes we receive. The question "What do you say after you say hello?" distills Berne's thoughts about how we use time to maximize the number of strokes we receive. Berne (1972) identifies several options. Some individuals will *withdraw*, escaping into the safety of the self to avoid risk. The most restrictive and least re-

> *Of all those who preceded TA, Alfred Adler comes the closest to talking like a script analyst.*
>
> —Eric Berne

warding way to structure time, in this mode of withdrawal it is necessary to live on "stored" strokes or to fantasize "artificial" strokes. Others engage in so-called *rituals and pastimes:* interactions based on greetings, pleasantries, and other low-risk, noninvolving social conversations (e.g., "How are you?" "I'm fine, thanks"). Whereas these rituals provide some strokes, the yield is low. Still others will *take up activities:* time that is structured in terms of goals, work, and hobbies that typically bring strokes from others. And still others play *games,* which are interactions based on unwritten rules designed to create payoff. Usually covert and dishonest, these games typically generate negative payoffs, and Berne considered them to be the most common disturbance factor in interpersonal behavior. In contrast, *intimacy* is a method of structuring designed to bring people together. Based on honest, open, mutual relationships, such intimacy is as a result both the most risky and the most rewarding approach to increasing strokes.

Position hunger is the need to have our fundamental decisions about life validated and affirmed—to be told, as Berne put it, that we're either OK or not OK. It is a reflection of intrinsic self-worth. Early in life one makes basic decisions about the self: "I'm OK" or "I'm not OK." Once this decision about the self has been made, it provides a script for the ways in which a person structures time and seeks strokes.

Structure of Personality

According to Berne and his followers, personality is composed of three conscious or preconscious ego states: the *Parent,* the *Adult,* and the *Child.* Each ego state is an organized psychological system of feelings, thoughts, and behaviors (Drego, 1993), and each is distinct and mutually exclusive (Figure 11-1).

The Parent ego is the tape recorder–like composite of childhood memories, an audible record of how parents and significant others—parents and parent substitutes—acted, thought, and felt about us in childhood. This mindset is filled with values, injunctions, shoulds, oughts, and behaviors the individual

FIGURE 11-1 Parent, Adult, and Child.

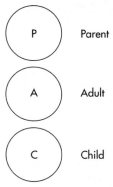

has internalized from significant others during childhood. Under the influence of such prohibitions as well as of permissions and nurturing messages, people behave as they believe their parents would want them to behave. Depending on the kinds of messages that the Parent has internalized, then, the Parent ego can be subdivided into the *Nurturing Parent,* the composite of messages that were loving, supportive, and accepting, and the *Critical Parent,* the composite of messages that were rejecting, controlling, and judgmental.

The second ego state, the Adult ego, is the computer-like processor of information from both the other two ego states as well as the external world. It acts to regulate the activities of the Child and Parent, mediating between them. Since its function is to test reality and since it is focused on data processing, probability estimating, and decision making, it does not deal with feelings but with facts. In fact, the Adult ego state is void of feelings. Its ultimate function is to present situations in an organized and intelligent way.

A further distinction between the Adult state and those of the Parent and Child, is that it is only in the Adult state that we possess a kind of "psychic energy" that Berne labeled *free energy.* This free energy is willed and deliberately enacted. Usually the Adult is thought of as a reservoir of free energy, whereas the Parent and the Child are composed of so-called *unbound energy,* which is active but is expressed without conscious choice and is therefore not under deliberate control. Another state of psychic energy, according to Berne, is *bound energy,* which holds the potential for activity (i.e., it is available), but is inactive (Shapiro, 1969).

The third ego state, that of the Child—the *child-within*—is the little boy or little girl portion of us that never grows up. This ego state is not about being childish, but about being childlike: about the fun-loving part of most individuals that is alternately inquisitive, affectionate, selfish, mean, playful, whiny, and manipulative. The Child ego state, which typically emerges in response to a communication from a Parent ego state (Clark, 1991), functions in two distinct forms. The *Natural Child* (or *Free Child*) strives for total freedom to do whatever it wants whenever it wants—to be loving, for example, affectionate, creative, aggressive, rebellious, and spontaneous. An uninhibited responder to the world, the Natural Child can also be intuitive and sensitive to nonverbal messages.

> *Maybe the reason people go into psychiatry is that they are not required to do very much except to have staff conferences to explain why they can't do very much.*
>
> —Eric Berne

On the other hand, the *Adapted Child* denies or ignores its own instincts and tries desperately to please parents by conforming to their demands. It uses compliance and procrastination to deal with feelings that will prevent reprimand from the Parent. As a result, the Adapted Child duplicates the original reactions individuals have toward parents during childhood, including such feelings as guilt, fear, anger, and frustration. Negotiating between the Natural Child and the Adapted Child is the emerging Adult in the Child, called the *Little Professor.* This childlike parallel to the Adult ego state is the source of intuition, creativity, and manipulation.

Gladding (1992) points out that these several ego states function simultaneously. He provides the example of a woman who observes an attractive man and goes through the following self-dialogue: "He is really good looking and well spoken [Adult], but he's probably stuck up [Critical Parent], although I've heard he's very sensitive [Nurturing Parent]. I wonder how I could attract him and get him to notice me [Natural Child]. I had better stop looking and get back to work or my boss will get mad at me [Adaptive Child]" (p. 126).

Although TA does not favor one ego state over another, the theory stresses the importance of being able to balance responses appropriately. TA also proposes that people are generally in one ego state or another. This functioning ego state can be identified by the content and expressions (especially nonverbal) of what we think, feel, say, and do.

Students often compare TA ego states with the three Freudian psychic structures: the id being the Child; the ego, the Adult; and the superego, the Parent. But Berne believed that all three structures were intrinsic to the ego and that, whereas Freud deemed only the ego to be conscious, Berne believed all three ego states were conscious or potentially so. So, although it is initially tempting to compare Freud's and Berne's three-part concepts, the overlap is not accurate (see Figure 11-2).

DEVELOPMENT OF MALADAPTIVE BEHAVIOR

Maladaptive behavior, according to Berne, is the result of confused ego states. This confusion occurs when a person vacillates between ego states without completing their transaction. When a young man is ineffective in maintaining a romantic relationship (an Adult function) because of lapses into inappropriate humor during potential times for romance (the Child), he is experiencing fuzzy ego boundaries and is blocking the free-flowing interaction among ego states. This person suffers from a "boundary problem."

Blocking, Contamination, and Exclusion

The two major boundary problems in TA are blocking and contamination. *Blocking* occurs when too much unbound or active energy is located in the

FIGURE 11-2 Comparison of Freud's and Berne's personality models.

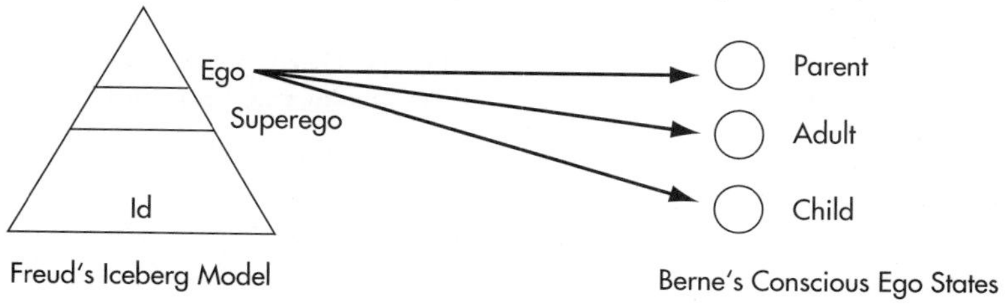

Freud's Iceberg Model   Berne's Conscious Ego States

Parent and/or Child, and the boundaries among ego states are too rigid and impermeable to deal with this excess energy (Figure 11-3). Blocking can lead to a dissociated condition in which individuals feel estranged from themselves, out of control. "I feel as though I'm in a dream," they may say, or "I feel that I'm doing this mechanically." When such a blocking of ego states occurs, people may seem peculiar and behave inappropriately. People who compulsively clean, for example, may be blocking the free energy of the Adult ego state. As a result they are tirelessly propelled by the unbound energy of their Parent. In its extreme form, blocking may lead to multiple personality disorder, in which the individual assumes alternate personalities, such as those of Dr. Jekyll and Mr. Hyde.

Contamination, on the other hand, occurs when one's boundaries break down, when they become too labile, too permeable to the unbound energy of the Parent and/or Child (Figure 11-4). The ego states invade and take command of each other and thereby create confusion—just the opposite of blocking. When the Parent takes over the Adult's rationality and judgment, for instance, the individual becomes highly legalistic and judgmental (Critical Parent). A Child contamination occurs when past experiences are incorrectly identified as current reality ("I'm a klutz"). A double contamination has occurred when the beliefs of the Parent ("everyone is bad") and the experiences of the Child ("I feel bad") invade the ego state of the Adult ("I am bad"). This may be the most common form of ego contamination (Shilling, 1984).

Exclusion takes place when one or two ego states dominate a personality. Whereas the constant Parent will be directive and authoritarian, for instance, the constant Adult may be devoid of feeling, and the constant Child will only want to play and to entertain others. It must be remembered, however, that no exclusion is total. The degree of intensity varies in time and place.

Games

In addition to boundary problems, maladaptive behavior can result from "the games people play." Berne used the term *game* because it suggests the idea of a contest that involves players, rules, moves, and predictable outcomes. Berne (1964, p. 125) defined a psychological game as a "recurring set of transactions, often repetitive, superficially rational, with a concealed motivation; or more

FIGURE 11-3 Blocking results from rigid and impermeable boundaries.

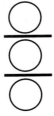

FIGURE 11-4 Contamination is the result of permeable ego boundaries.

colloquially, a series of transactions with a gimmick." On the surface, games appear to be *Complementary Transactions,* but they have a concealed motivation. The actual message of these games, however, is an *Ulterior Transaction,* and its real motivation is the predictable payoff or "gimmick" with which it concludes (Goldhaber & Goldhaber, 1976; Summerton, 1992).

This game playing is anything but enjoyable; it is serious and tragic. Games are not played for recreation; they are played compulsively over and over again. Every game, according to Berne (1964, p. 48), is "basically dishonest, and the outcome has a dramatic, as distinct from merely exciting, quality." Games occur when persons turn to others for confirmation of their negative "not-OK" position, and the result is the avoidance of intimacy.

Whereas intimacy is immensely rewarding, the difficulty is that it is spontaneous and thus involves considerable risks. It can be quite threatening. Since predictability outweighs the rewards of the risk, we settle for a lesser reward in order to be certain of achieving it. Instead of allowing unpredictable intimacy to occur, some people predetermine the outcome of their transactions by engaging in ulterior and crossed transactions, which ensure a predictable outcome. As the saying goes, a bird in the hand is worth two in the bush. For these people, it is better to be negatively discounted than to take the risk of not counting at all. This overwhelming fear of not being recognized or acknowledged by others leads people to the pain and isolation of playing games.

> *Information is of no value for its own sake, but only because of its personal significance.*
>
> —Eric Berne

Berne has analyzed numerous interaction games and, in his customary fashion, has labeled them with common-sense, straightforward names. One of the most common games people play is *Why Don't You—Yes But.* It is typically played like this:

A: "My husband always insists on doing our own repairs, and he never does anything right."
B: "Why doesn't he take a course in carpentry?"
A: "Yes, but he doesn't have the time."
B: "Why don't you buy him some good tools?"
A: "Yes, but he doesn't know how to use them."
B: "Why don't you have your building done by a carpenter?"
A: "Yes, but that would cost too much."
B: "Why don't you just accept what he does the way he does it?"
A: "Yes, but the whole thing might fall down"

Good players of *Why Don't You—Yes But* are able to wear people down. They give up because there is always one more problem, one more rejoinder.

Among the further, popular games that Berne describes is *Seduction,* which is played by a male and female who flirt with each other until one turns down the other, leaving both feeling slightly uncomfortable. *Uproar* is played by two persons who get increasingly angry until one or both cries "uproar." Although the game could have been stopped at any time by either player, the fracas continues with increasing decibels of sound until it finally ends in an uproar. Another game, called *Cops and Robbers,* is played by those who dare people in authority to catch them, although the players leave clues about where they can be found. In a game called *Blemish,* players do not feel comfortable with a new person until they have found his or her imperfection or foible, which can be as trivial as their style of dress. And individuals whose chief preoccupation is with the question "How will I look?" often play the game *Look How Hard I Tried.* If they are late, for example, they will take pains to arrive out of breath with a story that justifies their lateness.

People play these kinds of games with different degrees of vigor. Berne (1964) lists three levels of intensity: first-degree games are socially acceptable; second-degree games leave no permanent scars and the players would rather conceal the consequences; whereas third degree games, which are played for high stakes, usually lead to the emergency room, the courtroom, or the morgue.

Rackets

Each of us assumes a life position regarding our own OKness and the OKness of others. As another means of convincing themselves that they are "not OK" and to justify their never taking risks with real intimacy, people often develop habitual ways of feeling that Berne called *Rackets.* Originating in the experiences we had growing up as children, these Rackets are the unpleasant chronic feelings we hold onto after game playing. They are the feelings we get from the strokes we received when we acted in certain ways and observed how our parents responded. Eventually, these feelings become a basic part of our life script, a veritable collection of Rackets: the Guilt Racket, the Depression Racket, the Worry Racket, to name a few. Of course, these habitual feelings are inauthentic, that is, they are wholly unrelated to reality as currently experienced.

Was it a friend or foe that spread these lies?
Nay, who but infants question in such wise?
'Twas one of my most intimate enemies.
        —Dante Gabriel Rossetti

Injunctions

Injunctions can also contribute significantly to maladaptive behavior. Typically the signals that children pick up from their parents' internal child are "don't" messages that tell children what they need to do to be recognized. Since these messages stem from the parents' own anxiety, frustration, and unhappiness, they are often nonverbal, usually inferred from observation, but nonetheless powerful. According to Mary Goulding (1987), we decide as children to accept certain injunctions, or to challenge them. The basic list of common injunctions (Goulding, 1987; Goulding & Goulding, 1979) includes: Don't be, Don't succeed, Don't be you, Don't be sane, Don't be well, Don't belong. When children decide to accept them, these injunctions result in patterns of maladaptive behavior. But with help, these injunctions can be identified and rejected.

FUNCTION OF THE THERAPIST

The TA counselor works at being a catalyst for enabling clients to mobilize their resources (Dusay & Dusay, 1989). Acting very much like a "teacher, trainer, and resource person with heavy emphasis on involvement" (Harris, 1967, p. 239), the therapist explains key concepts such as structural analysis, transactional analysis, script analysis, and game analysis. In addition the counselor employs various techniques to help clients make full and effective use of all three ego states and to live game-free lives with intimate, rewarding relationships.

The TA therapist takes a significant amount of time to do both structural and transactional analysis. *Structural analysis* involves recognizing the influence of each ego state on thinking and behaving, so that people who are psychologically healthy can activate any one of the ego states whenever it is deemed appropriate. By identifying which ego state is in power at any given time, we are better able to understand our own behavior and the behavior of others (George & Cristiani, 1990; Knox & Lichtenberg, 1991).

But transactions are units of social action as well (Berne, 1964), and *transactional analysis* is concerned with diagnosing the ego states that emerge in a social interchange. TA therapists explore three kinds of transactions. The first of these, *complementary transactions,* occur when the lines of communication are parallel. When one person encounters another, for instance, and provides a *transactional stimulus*—an opening statement—from the Adult ego state, and the listener responds with an appropriate reply that is also from the Adult state, that is a complementary transaction. (In the terminology of TA, this reply is known as a *transactional response.*) The key to such transactions is that the *transactional response* be appropriate, whether Adult to Adult or Parent to Child and then Child to Parent. As long as transactions are complementary, communication can proceed smoothly and indefinitely:

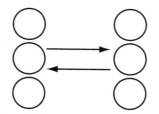

Complementary Transactions

When Linda asks, "What time is it?" for example, she is speaking as an Adult, and Roy's parallel response, "I think it's about 9:30," completes a complementary transaction. Or, similarly, Child to Child, as when Wayne urges his friend, "Party on, Garth!" and Garth appropriately responds, "Party on, Wayne!" At other times, of course, it may be utterly appropriate for the Child to complain to the Parent—the spouse coming home from a hard day at the office, for instance—and for the Parent to respond to the Child with a hug and words of comfort.

Crossed transactions, however, are a different story. When the lines of communication are crossed, communication is broken off, and the relation typically shuts down. The most common crossed transaction occurs when an Adult–Adult transactional stimulus is coupled with a Parent–Child or Child–Parent response. Unless the respondent is able to mobilize his or her Adult to complement the Adult in the other person, deadlock is inevitable, and the transaction concludes with one or both of the parties feeling hurt, angry, or misunderstood:

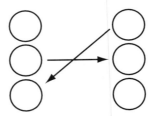

Crossed Transactions

When a student, for example, asks a professor, "How is this different from the concept we discussed yesterday?" he or she is speaking from the Adult ego state, and it is not appropriate for the professor to play the role of the Parent and angrily ask, "Where have you been for the past hour? Surely you heard what I just said!" Similarly, when Jerry says, "I am soo hungry! I'm like way starving!" he is speaking Child to Child, and a crossed transaction occurs when Alex's measured response is Adult to Adult: "You might consider a small nutritional snack to suppress your appetite." Such crossed transactions often occur out of negligence or preoccupation.

Ulterior transactions, which occur when more than two ego states operate simultaneously, are equally problematic. In ulterior transactions, one message is usually sent on a social level, usually Adult–Adult, while an implied subtext is sent on an unspoken level in another ego state:

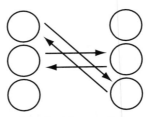

Ulterior Transactions

For example, when Julie the Adult solicitously asks her friend an overt question, "Are you sure you don't want to go out with him again?" the covert question may be coming from the Parent: "Don't you think it's about time you quit being so nit-picky and go out with a guy more than once?!"

Finally, the competent TA therapist is genuine. Berne was aware that his therapeutic approach could lead counselors into assuming a phony facade or even becoming disingenuous. To help his students understand just how important the quality of genuineness is for the therapist, Berne labeled several un-

Achievement is not the most
important thing. Authenticity is.
—M. James and D. Jongeward

healthy, nongenuine styles that professionals might develop (1966, p. 357). There is, for example, *Phallus in Wonderland*, who is fascinated by clients and what happens to them. The counselor who seemingly knows everything is *The Delegate*, with the "whole weight of psychoanalytic tradition behind him." Experimenting with clients, *The Smiling Rebel* tends to keep secret what's on his or her mind, whereas *The Jargon Junk Juggler* enjoys using large words that nobody understands. The therapist who gets along slowly, rescues somewhat, and never gets upset is *The Patient Clinician*, and *The Conservative*, who is so bland and passive that nothing much happens, is even less effective. And then there is *The Hypochondriac*, afraid to try anything new because of his or her own concern for comfort.

GOALS OF THERAPY

The fundamental goal of transactional analysis is to help clients achieve autonomy (Berne, 1964; James and Jongeward, 1971), which means assuming responsibility for one's own actions or feelings, taking control of one's life, planning and directing one's own destiny, and throwing off any perceptions that are inappropriate for living here and now. In other words, TA helps to free one's Adult from the influence of the Child and Parent, allowing the Adult the autonomy to be in control of decision making (James, 1977).

Autonomy is characterized by three qualities. *Awareness,* a realistic understanding of one's world, "requires living in the here and now," says Berne (1964, p. 179), "and not in the elsewhere, the past or the future." Second, *spontaneity,* the ability to express emotion in an uninhibited, game-free fashion, allows us to choose which ego state we want to express. *Intimacy,* the capacity to share love and closeness with others, can occur only when all games have been discarded and only when we truly relate to each other with unguarded acceptance and warmth.

Life Positions

Another goal of TA is to help clients analyze their relationships, that is, their transactions. This involves determining the predominant Life Position one has taken, since it causes a given transaction to go one way or another. Harris (1967) suggests that all of these Life Positions are intentional: that we decide what we are willing to compromise in order to satisfy our needs or our stimulus hunger.

These decisions lead to the position we take toward ourselves and others. According to Harris, individuals choose one of four basic life positions (Harris, 1967):

- *"I'm okay—you're okay"*: These people have formed self-concepts, are acknowledged as individuals, and have positive self-identities as well as a positive image of others.
- *"I'm okay—you're not okay"*: These people have positive self-images, but see everyone else as the enemy who threatens their existence. This position is paranoid because of the distrust it requires.
- *"I'm not okay—you're okay"*: These people blame themselves for everything that goes wrong and are drowning in guilt. They view themselves as polluted, and they feel unworthy of positive feedback from significant people in their lives. This depressive position is the most prevalent in contemporary society.
- *"I'm not okay—you're not okay"*: These people have a poor self-image and harbor hostility and anger toward the outside world. This position is futile. Prisons, psychiatric hospitals, and morgues are filled with people in this basic life position (Wollams & Brown, 1979).

It is the goal of TA to replace each of the three maladaptive life positions with the healthy "I'm OK—you're OK" position, which is "the *most* reality oriented" (Oden, 1974, p. 83). It is the original state of the baby at birth, and TA is optimistic about the human ability to recapture this birthright. "We do not drift into a new position," Harris writes (1967, p. 50). "It is a decision we make. In this respect it is like a conversion experience."

Scripts

These life positions are acted out in *scripts*, which are the dramas that tie together the games and transactions of our lives. A script is "a person's ongoing program for his life drama which dictates where he is going with his life and how he is to get there. It is a drama compulsively acted out, though his awareness of it may be vague" (James and Jongeward, 1971, p. 65). A life script is built uniquely on how one answers three questions: "Who am I?" "What am I doing here?" and "Who are all those others?"

This idea of a life script may be illuminated by the "Parable of the Eagle." James and Jongeward (1971) tell of an eagle who had grown up among chickens and did not know his true identity. A passing naturalist said, "It has the heart of an eagle and surely it can learn to fly." He took the eagle to the top of a mountain, saying, "You belong to the sky and not the earth. Stretch forth your wings and fly."

Preparation of the therapist must precede preparation of the patient.
—Eric Berne

The eagle hesitated, looked back toward the barnyard, began to tremble and slowly stretched his wings. At last, with a triumphant cry, he soared away into the heavens. James and Jongeward call those who discover their real potential, "winners."

Sidebar 11-1

THE OK CORRAL

Franklin Ernst (1973) uses this concept in a grid diagram, colloquially called "The OK Corral."

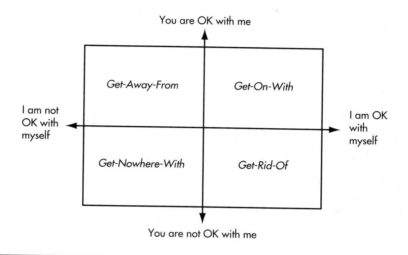

MAJOR METHODS AND TECHNIQUES

"The basic interest of transactional analysis," said Eric Berne (1972), "is the study of ego states" (p. 11) around which most TA methods revolve. These TA methods have been applied to numerous clinical problems and settings (Jensen, Baker, & Koepp, 1980): to treating personality disorders, for instance (Bonds-White, 1984), to trauma survival (Jacobs, 1991), asthma (Lammers, 1990), adult children of divorce (Silvestri, 1992), physical disability (Chapeau, 1992), eating disorders (Martin, 1990; Rumney & Steckel, 1985), childhood anxiety (LaFreniere & Dumas, 1992), family relationships (James, 1984), group processes (Nykodym, Longenecker, & Ruud, 1991), and so on.

Contracting

TA typically begins with the client and therapist initiating a contract, which includes a statement about what the client hopes to achieve in counseling, a statement about what the counselor will do to facilitate the process, and some specific criteria for knowing when the goal has been achieved. This strategy helps to prevent the client from shifting total responsibility to the counselor and establishes positive expectations. "A contract is an agreement between counselor and client which specifies the goals, stages, and conditions of treatment" (Wollams & Brown, 1979, p. 221).

The contract must meet several specific requirements (Dusay & Steiner, 1971; Hansen, Stevic, & Warner, 1982). At the outset both the counselor and the client, through Adult–Adult transactions, must mutually agree on the objectives. Second, the contract must call for mutual considerations: the counselor must give of his or her professional skill and time; and the client must give of his or her time and effort as well. Third, the contract defines the competencies of both parties. The counselor identifies the skills that will be applied in the situation, and the client commits his or her mind, time, and energy toward fulfilling the contract. Finally, the objective(s) of the contract must be within ethical limits.

Structural Analysis

In structural analysis clients are taught to identify their ego states and to become aware of how they function. During this initial, highly didactic stage of therapy, clients learn the terminology of TA. They are encouraged to read TA literature and to attend TA workshops (Friday, 1977). At this time, the counselor often makes use of audiovisual devices to demonstrate the ways in which the ego state functions. It is the purpose of structural analysis to help clients look at the developmental history of each of their ego states and at their innate capacity for expression. The counselor may even "give permission" to their clients to express all of their ego states.

One way of assessing how much energy exists in the five functional ego states of any person—Critical Parent, Nurturing Parent, Adult, Free Child, and Adapted Child—is through the use of an *egogram* (Dusay, 1972; Dusay & Dusay, 1989). Essentially a portrait of psychological energy, an egogram is constructed on a bar graph with five positions, each of which represents an ego state (Figure 11-5). Because each person has a distinct and unique personality, the five psychological forces differ within each individual. Ideally, a psychologically healthy individual will produce an egogram that is shaped like a bell curve. A

FIGURE 11-5 Egogram of a person who responds mostly from the Adult ego state.

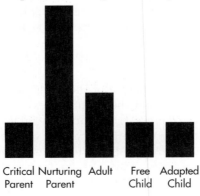

Critical Nurturing Adult   Free   Adapted
Parent   Parent   Child   Child

person with such an egogram is capable of Adult-to-Adult transactions, is more likely to become a Nurturing rather than a Critical Parent, and exhibits, not the passivity and resentment of the Adapted Child, but the acceptance and aliveness of the Free Child (Burke, 1989).

Functional Analysis

Less didactic than the first stage, the next stage of therapy is still insight oriented. Functional analysis describes transactions, whether complementary, crossed, or ulterior: that is, it describes the way people use their ego states to relate to themselves and others. Wollams and Brown (1979) outline three fundamental rules of communication that clients learn during this stage: first, as long as transactions remain complementary, communication may continue indefinitely; second, wherever the transaction is crossed, a breakdown in communication results and something different is likely to follow; and third, the outcome of the transactions will be determined not on the social, but on the psychological level.

The patient must undertake the task of living in a world in which there is no Santa Claus.

—Eric Berne

Game Analysis

Wollams and Brown (1979) have identified five different methods of analyzing the dynamics of game playing: (1) Formal game analysis involves exploring the "advantages" of playing specific games. (2) Drama triangle analysis involves focusing on the various game positions of Persecutor, Rescuer, or Victim (Karpman, 1968) as illustrated in the following diagram:

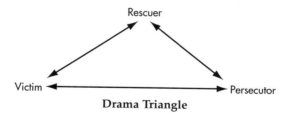

Drama Triangle

(3) Transactional game diagramming involves the diagnosis of ego states with an emphasis on the psychological level of communication. (4) Symbiosis diagramming identifies the preferred ego states of each player. (5) Formula G involves describing the flow of a game and the steps it will take once the initial moves are begun.

Script Analysis

TA therapists believe that poor transactions, rackets, and games are not random occurrences, but that they are patterned toward a desired end. Created in order to achieve this end, scripts are written at an early age, usually by parents, and they often consist of grand injunctions against certain healthy life developments (e.g., Don't Feel, Don't Get Close). Scripts may also be defined in terms of a life-theme cliché, such as Getting Even, Being Helpful, Carrying My Cross, or Looking for the Pot of Gold. In addition, scripts may be understood in terms of childhood mythologies or fairy tales. TA therapists believe that adults live out literary metaphors from childhood that symbolize their lives. Snow White, for instance, spends her life waiting for her prince to come along to remove her from difficulties, and Cinderella sighs and waits for the invitation to arrive. Meanwhile, the golden-haired Prince spends his life looking for Sleeping Beauty, whereas Peter Pan simply refuses to grow up (Karpman, 1968).

> *What was once decided can be undecided.*
>
> —Thomas A. Harris

Other kinds of scripts set out considerably more negative patterns of interaction (Gladding, 1992, p. 130): the *never script*, which forbids one to do what one wants because the parent forbids it; the *until script*, which requires waiting until a certain time to do something before one can have a reward; the *always script*, which compels its subject to repeat the same activity over and over again; the *after script*, which expects difficulty after a certain event; and the *open-ended script*, which involves not knowing what one is supposed to do after a given time.

The analysis of scripts like these requires a detailed exploration of the decisions clients have made about their life positions. In this process, clients are made to understand their life positions and to make decisions that allow them to adjust their scripts: to rid themselves of self-defeating behavior and to achieve more autonomy, spontaneity, and intimacy. Often such analysis leads to learning about early childhood scripts, which are updated for the contemporary situations (Goulding and Goulding, 1979).

In addition, Claude Steiner (1984) talks about our need for *emotional literacy* as a rationale for changing past life scripts. Emotional literacy is the ability to experience all of one's emotions with appropriate intensity and to understand what is causing these feelings. The systematic steps toward this emotional understanding include asking the client for permission to explore feelings; providing strokes; making a feeling/action statement ("I feel … about …"), in which emotion and action are closely tied; and ensuring that the feeling/action statement is heard by the other.

Redecision

A major branch of contemporary TA is Mary McClure Goulding's and Robert L. Goulding's "redecision school" (Barnes, 1977). Practitioners who follow the "classical" TA work of Berne do counseling with the Parent primarily on an intellectual level as they identify and change scripts. But the Gouldings believe that individuals can change their own scripts through *redecision:* an emotional, intellectual, and behavioral process that takes place in the Child with the support of the Adult and Parent. This approach emphasizes self-direction and incorporates concepts and techniques from Gestalt therapy and other techniques.

Goulding and Goulding (1979) use redecision "scenes" to change life scripts. As a means of freeing up the Child, the client and therapist select a real or imaginary scene and then act it out, allowing the client to make or remake decisions about which scripts to live out and which to abandon.

Group Therapy

The preferred form of treatment for TA-based programs, however, appears to be the group setting. The counselor observes individuals as they interact in a quasi-natural and spontaneous way with a group, which typically numbers about eight individuals who meet once a week for 2 hours. This provides rich and immediate data on which to illustrate and demonstrate the TA approach as it applies to interpersonal situations.

In a TA group the leader assumes the role of teacher to a greater extent than in most other forms of group therapy. The leader may begin a group session with a general introduction to TA concepts, or it may be a traditional group therapy situation in which members take turns discussing personal problems, while others offer help and suggestions. In any event the leader focuses on both verbal and nonverbal behavior as members interact about their individual problems. As "transactions" within the group emerge, the leader uses them as data to illustrate various types of interactions (Berne, 1968; Freedman, 1993), often using a blackboard to diagram transactions among the members.

APPLICATION

To a large extent, then, TA has focused its attention on nonclinical applications such as social and organizational situations, often at the expense of providing substantial case material. The following case study of "Mrs. Enatosky," however, from Eric Berne's *Transactional Analysis in Psychotherapy* (1961), is considered a classic TA counseling situation. Although it does not represent every aspect of the TA approach, it is distinctly TA and it illustrates many of Eric Berne's major counseling applications.

Mrs. Enatosky, a 34-year-old high school graduate whose husband was a mechanic, complained initially of "depressions" of sudden onset. She had previously been in Alcoholics Anonymous, hypnosis, and psychotherapy combined with Zen and yoga. Berne noted that she showed a special aptitude for transactional analysis and soon began to exert social control over the games that went on between herself and her husband, and herself and her son. Berne's formal diagnosis was "schizo-hysteria." The case will now be reviewed session by session with excerpts in Berne's own words.

April 1

The patient arrived on time for her initial interview. She stated that she had been an alcoholic for ten years and had been cured by Alcoholics Anonymous. She dated the onset of her drinking from her mother's psychosis when she was nineteen. She said that her depressions began at the same time. A preliminary search for traumatic events elicited that her father drank heavily and that her parents separated when she was seven years old. The medical history revealed headaches, and numbness of one arm and leg.

The history-taking was carefully planned so that at all times the patient seemed to have the initiative and the therapist at most was curious rather than formal or openly systematic in gathering information. This means that the patient was not required to play a game of psychiatric history-taking.

April 8
The neurologist suspected cervical arthritis, but did not recommend any specific treatment. The patient spontaneously mentioned wanting approval and rebelling "like a little girl," as some "grown-up part" of her judged it. She said the "little girl" seemed "childish." It was suggested that she let the "little girl" out, rather than try to clamp down on her. She replied that that seemed brazen. She sees the two most important "parents" in her life as her husband and her father. She is seductive toward her husband and recognizes that she was the same with her father.

The patient's special aptitude for structural analysis is already evident. She herself makes the separation between "the little girl" and "a grown-up part" and recognizes the compliance of "the little girl" toward certain people whom she relates to her parents. It was only necessary, therefore, to reinforce this trichotomy in a non directive way. With many other patients this might not have been undertaken until the third or fourth session, perhaps even later.

April 15
She resents people who tell her what to do, especially women. This is another reaction to "Parents." She mentions a feeling of "walking high." It is pointed out that this is the way a very small girl must feel, that this is again the child. It was emphasized that there was no mysterious or metaphysical aspect to these diagnostic judgments.

The patient has now experienced some of the phenomenological reality of the child and has added to the behavioral, social, and historical reality she established in the previous interviews. The indications, therefore, are favorable for treatment with transactional analysis.

April 22
"This week I've been happy for the first time in fifteen years. I don't have to look far to find the child, I can see it in my husband and in others too. I have trouble with my son." The game with her son was clarified in an inexact but timely and illustrative way in terms of parent (her disapproval and determination), child (her seductiveness and her sulkiness at his recalcitrance), and adult (her gratification when he finally did his work). It was hinted that an adult approach (good reason) rather than a parental approach (sweet reason) might be worth a try. The patent is now involved in transactional analysis proper and the idea of social control has been suggested.

April 28
She reports that things work better with her son. As the session ends she asks: "Is it all right to be aggressive?" Answer: "You want *me* to tell you?" She understands the implication that she should decide such things on adult grounds

rather than asking parental permission, and replies: "No, I don't." During this session some of the elements of her script are elicited. It gives the therapist an opportunity to decline to play and to reinforce her adult. The patient has made such good progress in understanding structural and transactional analysis that she is already considered adequately prepared for fairly advanced group therapy. The group she is to enter consists largely of women.

May 4
She liked the group but it made her uncomfortable during the rest of the week. She related some memories, including homosexual play during childhood. The experience in the group has activated sexual conflicts, and this is the first indication of their nature.

May 11
She felt highly excited on leaving the group meeting. Things are better at home. "I can kiss my son now and my daughter for the first time came and sat on my lap." The analysis of her family games had resulted in the establishment of some adult social control. It is evident that this improved control has been perceived by her children and for the first time in a long while they had the feeling that she can maintain her position and they react accordingly. An experience in the group later this week rather clearly showed her need for parental figures in some of her games. There was a new patient in the group, a male social worker, and she was very much impressed by his occupation. She asked him what they were supposed to do there. It was pointed out that she knew more than he did, since it was his first meeting and her third.

May 18
She has visited her mother only once in the past five or six years and it was suggested that it might be advisable for her to do that again. This suggestion was very carefully worded so as to be adult rather than parental. Any implication that she was a bad girl for not visiting her mother had to be avoided. She was able to understand the allure of such a visit as an exercise for her adult and as a means of preventing further difficulties between her parent and her child if her mother should die. The good reception of this suggestion was manifested by her bringing up new information. Her husband never washes his hair and always has a good excuse, which she accepts.

May 25
She said she has always been more afraid of sick animals than of sick people. This week her cat was sick, and for the first time she was not afraid of him. Once when she was little her father hit her, and her dog jumped on him, whereupon he gave the dog away. The import of this is not clear. Her maintenance of social control with the sick cat is evidence that a visit to her mother may be possible in the near future.

June 1
She wonders: "Why do I exist? Sometimes I doubted my existence." Her parents' marriage was a shotgun wedding and she has always felt that she was unwanted. The patient is now involved with existential problems. Her adult has evidently always been shaky because her child has implanted doubts about her existence, her right to exist, and the form in which she exists.

June 8
She describes her husband's alcoholic game. At AA she was told that she should bless him and comfort him, and that made her sick. She tried something different. "One day I said I would call the ambulance for the hospital, since he didn't appear to be able to take care of himself, so he got up and didn't drink again." He said he was only trying to help her stay sober by drinking himself. This comes up because he was drinking heavily last week and she had pain in her shoulders and wanted to hit him, but told him off instead. It appears from this that their secret marriage contract is based partly on the assumption that he will drink and she will function as a rescuer. This session helped to clarify for the patent the structure of her marriage and also emphasized the amount of time and effort that is required to keep marital games going, and equally, the amount of energy involved in their repression without conscious control.

July 6
There has been a interval of a month for summer vacation. She has some olfactory illusions. She thinks she smells gas in the office, but decides it is clean soap. During her recent yoga training, she developed imagery which was almost eidetic. She would see gardens and wingless angels with sparkling clarity of color and detail. Her existential doubts are less disturbing. These phenomena, and the auditory manifestations she had previously mentioned, are not necessarily alarming. They point to childhood restitutive tendencies related to a deeply disturbed relationship between her and her parents. The conventional approach would be to give her "supportive" treatment and help her repress this psychopathology and live on top of it. Structural analysis offers another possibility that requires some boldness: to allow this disturbed child to express herself and profit from the resulting constructive experiences.

July 13
She told her husband she was going to finger paint and he got angry and said: "Use pastels!" When she refused, he started to drink. She recognizes what happened here as a game of "Uproar" and feels some despair at having been drawn into this. She says, however, that if she does not play "Uproar" with him then *he* will feel despair, and it is a hard choice to make.

July 20
She is losing interest and feels tired. She reveals some family scandals she has never mentioned to anyone before and states now that her drinking did not begin after her mother became psychotic, but after these scandals. At this session a decisive move was made. The patient habitually sits with her legs in an ungainly exposed position. She complains that the men also made passes at her. She doesn't understand why, since she did nothing to bring this on. She was informed of her exposed position and expressed considerable surprise. At the subsequent group meeting she was silent most of the time. At the price of sacrificing the possibilities of normal family life, the patient has obtained a multitude of gains, primary and secondary, by playing games with her husband and other men and women.

August 10
The therapist returns after a two-week vacation. The confrontation has been successful. The patient now describes an assault by her father in her early pu-

berty while her stepmother pretended to be asleep. She relates this "assault" to her own seductiveness. This situation she discusses at some length, eliciting her feeling that sex is dirty or vulgar. She says she has always been very careful sexually with her husband because of this feeling and has tried to avoid sex with him for this reason. She understands that the games she plays with him are an attempt to avoid sex, as she feels she cannot let go enough to enjoy it and it is merely a burden to her.

August 17

The patient announces that this is her last session. She no longer fears that her husband will think she is dirty or vulgar if she acts lusty. During the week, she approached him differently and he responded with gratified surprise. For the last few days he has come home whistling for the first time in years. She also realizes something else. She has always felt sorry for herself and tried to elicit sympathy and admiration because she is a recovered alcoholic. She recognizes this now as a game of "wooden leg." She feels ready at this point to try it on her own. She reports that she is drawing instead of finger painting, doing what she wants; she feels this isn't wrong, it's like learning to live. "I don't feel sorry for people any more, I feel they ought to be able to do this too if they went about it right. I no longer feel I'm below everyone, although that feeling isn't completely gone. I don't want to come to the group any more; I'd rather spend the time with my husband. It's like we're starting to go with each other again when he comes home whistling. It's wonderful. I'll try it for three months and if I feel bad I'll call you." She was asked directly whether structural analysis helped and whether game analysis helped and in each case replied: "Oh, yes!" She added: "Also the script. For example, I said my husband had no sense of humor and you said 'Wait a minute, you don't know him and he doesn't know you because you've been playing games and acting out your scripts, you don't know what either of you is really like.' You were right because now I've discovered that he really has a sense of humor and that not having it was part of the game." (pp. 42-48)

In summing up the work he conducted with Mrs. Enatosky, Berne states: "Although in some current thinking the course of this case may not indicate

I'm not interested in progress ... I want to cure people.

—Eric Berne

that the improvement is stable, it requires only one assumption to take a more optimistic view, and that assumption is borne out by experience; namely, that playing games and playing through one's script are optional, and that a strong adult can renounce these in favor of gratifying reality experiences. This is the actionistic aspect of transactional analysis."

CRITICAL ANALYSIS

TA brings several advantages to the counseling field. It is conducive to short-term treatment, works well in a large variety of settings, can easily be adapted to group counseling, and provides opportunities even in brief-term treatment for developing effective problem-solving skills along with insight and personality change (Jensen et al., 1980). It is an approach that even counselors who do not view themselves primarily as TA practitioners can integrate into their therapeutic work (Massey, 1990). The combined use of TA and Gestalt therapy has been especially powerful (James & Jongeward, 1971; O'Hearne, 1992).

Since so much of our meaningful life experience is interpersonal, it is a major strength of TA that it is one of the only approaches that illuminates interpersonal, as opposed to intrapsychic, reality. This, coupled with TA's creative, catchy, and intuitively appealing terminology, is perhaps its greatest strength. Berne intended that his approach have practical value for the client and be accessible to the masses, that its concepts should be easily grasped and applied. Once people have learned the system and become more aware of their self-defeating patterns, they can almost immediately understand previously baffling interactions. (See Sidebar 11-2.)

More broadly, TA therapists have taken specific actions to make their approach sensitive to particular cultural needs, and as a result TA has experienced some success in applying itself to cross-cultural contexts. Berne's script types, for example, have been applied to Chinese myths (Chan, 1991) and to police work in Israel (Elaad, 1993). TA has also called for a continuous highlighting of ethical codes in different cultures (Chang, 1994; Pizer, 1994). When considering TA in a multicultural context, it must be pointed out that it also offers a structured approach that deals head-on with issues of power and control. And since in the dominant mainstream culture people of color often experience a sense of powerlessness, TA, with its emphasis on personal responsibility, can provide a means for a stronger sense of empowerment and increased personal power (Hlongwane & Basson, 1990). In addition, the contract used in the TA approach can serve as a means of preventing therapists from imposing their cultural values in a multicultural context.

There is, of course, a negative side to the accessibility of TA language: it can be used to excess, creating a barrier to the outsider, and there is a tendency to confuse labeling with counseling. The reader of TA literature is bombarded with phrases, concepts, lists, clichés, in-group language, or abbreviations that can baffle even the most ardent devotee. A hearty dose of second-degree games, second-order functional analyses of structural diagrams, Parent-in-Child ego states, drama triangles, and so forth can be particularly challenging. Perhaps more so than any other approach, TA is encumbered by an extraordinary number of "passwords" and awkward idiomatic expressions. The real danger is that we mistakenly believe that we have understood or explained something just because we have labeled it.

Do as I say and as I do, but don't be as I am!

—Eric Berne

As a result, the jargon of TA may often serve as a stumbling block, being foreign to many ethnic-minority groups and consequently cumbersome to implement. Berne obviously loved colorful language and frequently used myths and metaphors in his approach. Yet, whereas he claimed that TA vocabulary had basically only five words (Parent, Adult, Child, game, and script), *What Do You Say After You Say Hello?* (Berne 1972) lists nearly 100 terms in its glossary and *Principles of Group Treatment* (Berne, 1968) lists 127 terms. Although TA

Sidebar 11-2

PSYCHIC BORDERLINES

Erica E. Goode

Lavinia's dreams are vivid. In one, she is swimming, pursued by a man with a knife. She can feel the metal of the blade piercing her skin and see her blood filtering red in the bluegreen water. An artist in her late 20s, Lavinia is creative and vulnerable, passionate and flexible, freewheeling and unguarded. Her world is fluid: Thoughts and feelings run together, and at times she is uncertain where she leaves off and another person begins. Even as a child, she was extremely sensitive—not only to other people's feelings, but to violent images, even to loud noises. "I can't keep things out," she says.

In the language of a new personality theory proposed by Temple University psychiatrist Ernest Hartmann, Lavinia is a person with very *"thin boundaries"; the invisible membrane separating her from the outside world is highly permeable, more akin to gossamer than to iron* [italics added]. Charles, on the other hand, a 40-year-old businessman, has very "thick" boundaries. He is methodical and solid, his life a grid of precisely drawn lines. Charles dreams he is "in a room, squarish in shape, with concrete walls on three sides." He often speaks in engineering metaphors. In college, he had friends, he says, but he was never very close to them, and now "my only friend is my wife." Charles remembers his childhood only vaguely. Opening his eyes in the morning, he is instantly awake.

Psychic Poles

Lavinia and Charles, described in Hartmann's recently published book, *Boundaries in the Mind* (Basic Books, $23), are extremes. Lavinia is probably perceived by others as somewhat "flaky"; Charles, as unusually rigid. They scored at the poles of the Boundary Questionnaire, the test

Hartmann developed to measure what he calls a "basic and neglected dimension of personality." But most people, Hartmann says, fall somewhere in between, exhibiting "thickness" or "thinness" in more moderate forms.

Hartmann, of course, is not the first to divide the world into character types. Ever since the Greek philosopher and physician Empedocles sorted the personalities of his fellow citizens into the categories of air, earth, fire and water, there has been no shortage of ingenious ways to pigeonhole human variation. Swiss psychoanalyst *Carl Jung drew a basic distinction between introverts and extroverts* [italics added]. Psychologist *William James preferred the dichotomy of tough-minded and tender-minded.* [italics added]. And more recently, Americans have been able to divide themselves, often by merely filling in the blanks on a personality test, into *Type A's and Type B's, "sharpeners" and "levelers," right brains and left brains,* to name only a few [italics added].

Such systems for carving up the personality pie are not free from scientific controversy. Filling out a questionnaire, critics point out, is rarely a substitute for the complexities of life. And research based on personality tests, notes the *Oxford Companion to the Mind,* has "had little impact on the development of psychology, whether in the clinic or the lab." Yet bringing order to the chaos of individual differences is intuitively appealing. And Hartmann's studies have generated interest among clinicians, who recognize in his work their patients, their friends and even themselves. "It's an intriguing hypothesis," says Cornell University psychiatrist Robert Michels, "with confirmation awaited."

Hartmann, whose interest in "boundaries" grew out of his research on sleep and dreaming, argues that his theories

Continued.

Sidebar 11-2—cont'd

may prove more useful than previous attempts at personality taxonomy. For one thing, he says, the notion of boundaries cuts across many levels of human experience: There are boundaries between the states of sleep and waking, between thinking and feeling, between the conscious, rational processes of the ego and the chaotic unconscious world of the id.

Defensive Barricades

Repression and other psychological defense mechanisms can serve as boundaries to painful memories or unwanted feelings. (Freud himself, Hartmann points out, talked of "ego boundaries.") And in our daily interactions with partners, parents and co-workers, we constantly negotiate our boundaries, allowing people to come closer or preventing their approach.

But Hartmann goes further. The concept of boundaries, he believes, reflects something basic about the organization of the brain—a link missing from most personality theories. With its complicated interplay of nerve pathways and messenger chemicals, the brain both brings things together—integrating sensory information and mental processes—and keeps them apart, creating barriers that are protective and allowing the business of consciousness to proceed in an orderly fashion. Certain drugs—LSD, for example—can alter the efficiency of these processes. People's tendencies toward thickness or thinness, Hartmann speculates, may in some way relate to differences in functioning at the biological level.

In studying the responses of more than 2,000 people who have taken the Boundary Questionnaire, Hartmann finds that people differ greatly in the permeability of their boundaries. To a large degree, he says, "thickness" or "thinness" stretches across sensory, interpersonal and mental realms. A person who scores as "thin" on the test, for example, is likely to

agree that he is "unusually sensitive to loud noises and to bright lights," and also that he feels "unsure of who I am at times" and that "sometimes I don't know whether I am thinking or feeling." *Women, on the whole, have thinner boundaries than men* [italics added], Hartmann's studies indicate. People with thicker boundaries are more likely to be married but enjoy their sex lives less than "thinner" people. Those with porous boundaries report more symptoms of illness and are much more likely to dream vividly and recall their dreams upon waking. *Everyone's boundaries, says Hartmann, tend to thicken with age* [italics added].

The permeability of boundaries seems to have little to do with more traditional measures of mental illness. A thin personality may be creative, open to experience, a bit wacky and prone to unusual dreams, Hartmann finds, but not necessarily psychologically disturbed. Yet being either very thick or very thin has its risks: *"Having boundaries that are too thick and solid," he says, "makes you incapable of relationships and deprives you of dreams and fantasies. But having no boundaries at all is very dangerous"* [italics added]. Indeed, the subjects with very thin boundaries in Hartmann's studies often plunged deeply into destructive relationships; one woman said she *could not leave her physically abusive boyfriend because he was "part of her"* [italics added]. And *though thin boundary individuals appear no more prone to mental illness than others, extreme thinness of boundaries is characteristic of people who suffer the mental disintegration of schizophrenia or the volatile mood swings and identity confusion that clinicians label "borderline personality disorder."*

Childhood Origins

Many people with thin boundaries say they have been that way for as long as they can remember, Hartmann reports. And studies indicate that even children as

Sidebar 11-2—cont'd

young as 3 or 4 show differences in boundary thickness. But are thick or thin boundaries present at birth? There is scant evidence one way or the other, but the psychiatrist speculates that heredity plays some role, because the permeability of boundaries seems to run in families and shows a pattern characteristic of other genetically influenced traits. Thin boundary adults remember reacting unusually strongly, even as children, to quite normal traumatic events, such as the death of a pet or the birth of a sibling. Yet learning probably contributes, too. Some adults with thick boundaries, for example, recall great pressure to "catch up" to an older sibling.

Though boundary differences emerge early, they do not appear immutable. Hartmann and his colleagues have found that mental and emotional permeability can change over time. Individuals with

Source: *U.S. News & World Report,* January 20, 1992, p. 57–59

extremely thin boundaries, for example, sometimes develop thickness as protection against their vulnerability. And through long-term psychotherapy or psychoanalysis, the psychiatrist says, boundaries can shift, the thick person becoming more flexible, the thin person tougher and more thick-skinned.

Thick or thin, most people seem quite content to remain that way. Indeed, many have a sense of superiority about their approach to life. The thick research subjects Hartmann interviewed invariably assumed that the psychiatrist, like them, had thick boundaries. Thickness, they opined, was unquestionably the way to be, and they saw thinness as "weird and crazy." Similarly, thin subjects viewed thickness as "stolid, dull and dumb." Surely, as a creative scientist, Hartmann must have thin boundaries too, they said.

Has he taken the Boundary Questionnaire? Of course he has. "I come out in the middle," the psychiatrist says. "But a bit on the thin side of average."

therapists assert that their approach is simple and easy to understand, many clients have difficulty with the complexity of some of its concepts, such as crossed transactions. Consequently, before therapists challenge the life scripts of ethnic-minority clients, great care must be taken to build a trusting relationship that does not take the language of TA for granted.

A final critique of the TA approach must point out that it doesn't seem to appreciate the mysterious, conflicted dimensions of human life. In many respects, the TA therapists treat clients as objects: instead of beginning with trust, they begin with a contract; instead of attempting to understand the clients, they teach the language of TA so that their clients can understand them. The risk, then, is that TA counselors focus more on states, transactions, and scripts than on persons.

CURRENT STATUS

In the 1960s the best seller *Games People Play* propelled TA into such a groundswell of popularity that critics inevitably dismissed it as a fad. Instead,

TA matured and has shown no signs of fading. Thirty years later TA has developed an increasingly stable body of data; has its own respected professional journal, *Transactional Analysis;* and may be considered an important part of the background of a well-trained counselor. There are now over 14,000 members in the International Transactional Analysis Association (Ivey, Ivey, & Simek-Downing, 1987).

To be certified as a clinical member of the International Transactional Analysis Association (ITAA), the candidate must hold a regular current membership, pay dues and fees, and complete a training program of no less than 1 year, which includes 50 hours of advanced TA training, 50 hours of supervision of direct clinical service, 150 hours of clinical application, and participation in various TA seminars and other presentations.

Psychiatrists know many therapeutic procedures but less about what in a particular procedure is therapeutic.

—Eric Berne

To be certified as a clinical Teaching Member of ITAA, a candidate must hold a current clinical membership, pay fees and membership dues, complete a training program of no less than 2 years in association with three sponsoring Teaching Members, and hold a graduate degree in a "healing arts profession" or have 6 years full-time experience in the field of counseling.

The therapeutic approach developed by Eric Berne is both simple and profound. Although it is accessible to all counselors, it is understood fully only by those who are thoroughly trained. Regardless of its impact, however, TA is clearly past its heyday. In a survey of over 400 clinical and counseling psychologists, under 1% identified TA as their basic theoretical orientation (Smith, 1982). A survey of major American psychological and psychiatric journals between 1980 and 1986 indicates that research using TA is being published almost exclusively in a journal and newsletter dedicated entirely to transactional analysis. Still, TA interventions and the theories that underlie them continue to be included in all major counseling textbooks, and it is part of the eclectic repertoire of many practitioners.

CHAPTER SUMMARY

1. *Biography.* Born in Montreal, Canada, Berne (1910–1970) grew up admiring his father, who was a physician devoted to his patients. After his father's early death, Berne entered medical school, became an American citizen, and soon entered the Army Medical Corps as a psychiatrist. After World War II, Berne moved to San Francisco and resumed psychoanalytic training under Eric Erikson. Never achieving official recognition by the psychoanalytic association, however, Bern developed his own orientation to psychotherapy: transactional analysis, a more "rational" approach. He wrote many papers and books, including *Games People Play.*

2. *Historical Development.* The origins of TA can be found in a wide variety of sources. Berne merged, mixed, and synthesized the approaches of Freud, Adler,

and Rogers especially. From the beginning, Berne strove to make his theory accessible and he succeeded. The diagrams that Berne used to explain interactions between people have become increasingly commonplace in counseling offices, classrooms, and management seminars.

3. *View of Human Nature.* For Berne, people are motivated primarily by basic psychological hungers to transcend patterns of behavior that begin early in life: stimulus hunger (the need to be acknowledged or affirmed by others); structure hunger (how we use time to maximize the number of strokes we receive), and position hunger (the need to have our fundamental decisions about life validated and affirmed). Personality is composed of three conscious or preconscious ego states, each an organized psychological system of feelings, thoughts, and behaviors: the Parent, the Adult, and the Child.

4. *Development of Maladaptive Behavior.* Psychopathology, according to Berne, is the result of confused ego states. This confusion occurs when a person vacillates between ego states without completing his or her transaction (i.e., blocking the free-flowing interaction among ego states). In addition, maladaptive behavior can result from playing games, a recurring set of transactions with a concealed motivation. Games occur when persons turn to others for confirmation of their negative "not-OK" position, and the result is the avoidance of intimacy.

5. *Goals of Therapy.* The fundamental goal of TA is to help clients achieve autonomy, that is, to assume responsibility for their own actions or feelings, to take control of their lives, to plan and direct their own destinies, and to throw off any perceptions that are inappropriate for living here and now. In other words, TA helps to free one's Adult from the influence of the Child and Parent. Another goal of TA is to help clients analyze their relationships by discovering their predominant Life Positions (e.g., I'm Okay—You're Okay).

6. *Function of the Therapist.* The TA counselor works at being a catalyst for enabling clients to mobilize their resources. Acting very much like a teacher, the therapist explains key concepts such as structural analysis, script analysis, and game analysis. In addition the therapist helps clients make full and effective use of all three ego states, to live game-free.

7. *Major Methods and Techniques.* TA typically begins with a contract between client and therapist, which includes statements about what the client hopes to achieve and what the counselor will do, as well as specific criteria for knowing when the goal has been achieved. Structural analysis is then employed to identify the client's ego states and to become aware of how they function. Functional analysis is a didactic method used to describe transactions to the client. Game analysis looks at the methods of game playing in which a client may be involved. And script analysis examines the person's life direction, which is usually set at an early age.

8. *Application.* TA does not provide an abundance of case material. Nonetheless, the case of "Mrs. Enatosky," a 34 year old who had previously been in AA,

illustrates many of Berne's applications. Berne noted that she showed a special aptitude for TA and she soon began to exert social control over the games that occurred between herself and her husband and between herself and her son.

9. *Critical Analysis.* TA is conducive to short-term treatment and works well in a variety of settings. The use of TA and Gestalt therapy together has been especially helpful to many. It is one of the only approaches that illuminates interpersonal, as opposed to intrapsychic, reality. But although TA's language has made it accessible to a lay audience, it can be used to excess and the terminology threatens to create a barrier rather than a bridge. Cross-culturally, TA has shown some initiative in being sensitive to particular cultural needs and may lead to a greater sense of empowerment for minorities, but the TA jargon may also serve as a stumbling block for ethnic-minority groups.

10. *Current Status.* TA enjoyed a national groundswell of popularity in the 1960s and has been furthered by a body of data and a respected professional journal. Although it is often integrated into the work of a wide variety of therapists, few practitioners today would identify TA as their primary theoretical orientation. Nevertheless, its interventions continue to be used by many eclectic practitioners.

KEY TERMS

Activities   Any work or other goal-oriented behavior is an activity. In activity, the individual sets up a situation in which the accomplishment of the task brings the needed strokes.

Adapted Child   The Adapted Child becomes more controlled by interacting with parents.

Adult Ego State   Best characterized as being concerned with facts. It acts as an assimilator of information and is mature.

Child Ego State   The Child ego state is composed of all the feelings and ways of behaving that have been experienced during the early years of childhood.

Complementary Transaction   Sometimes called a parallel transaction, it is one in which stimulus and response vectors are parallel so that only two ego states are involved, one from each person.

Conditional Stroke   A stroke given for *doing* something.

Contamination   One of two ego-state boundary problems. It occurs when the logical, clear thinking of the Adult is interfered with by the prejudicial or irrational ideas and attitudes of the Parent or by the archaic feelings of the Child.

Contract   An agreement between counselor and client that specifies the goals, stages, and conditions of treatment. An agreement.

Controlling Parent   Opinionated, powerful, strongly protective, principled, punitive, and demanding.

Crossed Transaction   Occurs when the vectors are not parallel, or more than two ego states are involved.

Discounting   Involves ignoring or distorting some aspect of internal or external experience. One may discount the existence of a problem, the significance of a problem, the change possibilities of a problem, or one's own personal abilities.

Drama Triangle   A triadic interaction in which one person acts as persecutor, another as rescuer, and the third as victim.

Ego State   States of mind and their related patterns of behavior as they occur in nature.

Exclusion   This boundary problem exists when one or more ego states are effectively prevented from operating.

Filtered Stroke   A stroke that is distorted or containing irrelevant information.

Game   A series of "duplex transaction," which lead to a switch and a well-defined, predictable payoff that justifies a not-OK or discounted position.

Injunction   A type of negative parenting behavior: edicts that require children to behave in certain prescribed ways. They are usually "don't" messages.

Intimacy   A candid, game-free relationship with mutuality, free giving and receiving without exploitation.

Life Position   Early in life, people experience a need to take a position regarding their own intrinsic worth and that of others. There are four life positions: I'm OK—You're OK, I'm OK—You're Not OK, I'm Not OK—You're OK, I'm Not OK—You're Not OK.

Little Professor   The part of the Child ego state that is the forerunner of Adult reasoning.

Natural Child   This part of the Child ego state contains the young, impulsive, untrained, emotionally expressive child.

Negative Stroke   A painful stroke carrying a "You're not OK" message, and resulting in unpleasant feelings for the receiver.

Nurturing Parent   Caring, concerned, forgiving, reassuring, permissive, warmly protective, and worried.

Parent Ego State   Consists of a collection of tapes from significant others who had some kind of power relationship with the person.

Pastime   A pastime is a semiritualized conversation in which people share opinions, thoughts, or feelings about relatively safe topics that don't require them to act.

Position Hunger   The need to have one's basic decisions about life confirmed constantly—decision about the "OKness" of oneself and the world.

Positive Stroke   A pleasurable stroke carrying a "You're OK" message and resulting in good feelings for the receiver.

Racket   A habitual process (usually of complementary transactions) by which a person interprets or manipulates the environment to justify a life position of not-OKness.

Rituals   Highly stylized and predictable ways of exchanging low-involvement, low-risk strokes such as greetings.

Script   A personal life plan that each individual forms by a series of decisions early in life in reaction to his or her interpretation of the important things happening in his or her world.

Stamps   Feelings or strokes collected to justify some later behavior.

Stimulus Hunger   The universal need for stimulation or stroking.

Stroke   A unit of attention providing stimulation to a person.

Structure Hunger   People's need to use their time in ways that maximize the number of strokes they can receive.

Symbiosis   Two or more individuals behave as though they form a whole person.

Transaction   An exchange of strokes between two persons, consisting of a stimulus and a response between specified ego states.

Transactional Analysis   Psychotherapy that focuses on characteristic interactions that reveal internal ego states and the games people play in social situations.

Ulterior Transaction   A transaction that contains both an overt (social) and a covert (psychological) message. These may be either angular or duplex. An angular transaction involves three ego states and occurs when messages are sent simultaneously from one ego state of the initiator to two ego states of the respondent. A duplex transaction involves four ego states, two in each person. During the course of a duplex transaction, two sets of complementary transactions occur simultaneously, one on the social level and one on the psychological level.

Unconditional Stroke   Given for *being,* they pertain to conditions that occur naturally and do not require special effort.

Withdrawal   The most limiting and least rewarding way of structuring time. People who structure time by withdrawing live on strokes stored from the past or fantasized in the future.

SUGGESTED READING

Berne, E. (1961). *Transactional analysis in psychotherapy.* New York: Grove Press.

Berne, E. (1963). *The structure and dynamics of organizations and groups.* Philadelphia: J.B. Lippincott.

Berne, E. (1964). *Games people play.* New York: Grove Press.

Berne, E. (1972). *What do you do after you say hello?* New York: Grove Press.

Harris, T. (1967). *I'm OK—You're OK: A practical guide to transactional analysis.* New York: Harper & Row.

Harris, T. (1985). *Staying OK.* New York: Harper & Row.

REFERENCES

Barnes, G. (1977). *Transactional analysis after Eric Berne: Teachings of three TA schools.* New York: Harper & Row.

Berne, E. (1947). *The mind in action.* New York: Simon & Schuster.

Berne, E. (1961). *Transactional analysis in psychotherapy*. New York: Grove Press.

Berne, E. (1964). *Games people play*. New York: Grove Press.

Berne, E. (1966). *Principles of group treatment*. New York: Oxford University Press.

Berne, E. (1968). *Principles of group treatment*. New York: Grove Press.

Berne, E. (1972). *What do you say after you say hello?* New York: Grove Press.

Berne, E. (1977). *Intuition and ego states: the origins of transactional analysis*. San Francisco: TA Press.

Bonds-White, F. (1984). The special it: Treatment of the passive-aggressive personality. *Transactional Analysis Journal, 14*, 180–190.

Burke, J. F. (1989). *Contemporary approaches to psychotherapy and counseling: The self-regulation and maturity model*. Pacific Grove: Brooks/Cole.

Chan, D. W. (1991). Berne's script types and Chinese myths. *Transactional Analysis Journal, 21*, 220–226.

Chang, V. N. (1994). A transactional analysis decision-making model and ethical hierarchy. *Transactional Analysis Journal, 24*, 15–20.

Chapeau, T. (1992). Transactional analysis and rehabilitation: An integrative approach to disability. *Transactional Analysis Journal, 22*, 234–242.

Cheney, W. D. (1971). Eric Berne: biographical sketch. *Transactional Analysis Journal, 1*, 14–22.

Clark, B. D. (1991). Empathic transactions in the deconfusion of Child ego states. *Transactional Analysis Journal, 21*, 92–98.

Drego, P. A. (1993). Paradigms and models of ego states. *Transactional Analysis Journal, 23*, 5–29.

Dusay, J. M. (1972). Egograms and the constancy hypothesis. *Transactional Analysis Journal, 1*, 34–44.

Dusay, J. M. (1977). The evolution of transactional analysis. In G. Barnes (Ed.), *Transactional analysis after Eric Berne: Teachings and practices of three TA schools* (pp. 32–52). New York: Harper's College Press.

Dusay, J. M., & Dusay, K. M. (1989). Transactional analysis. In R. J. Corsini & D. Wedding (Eds.), *Current psychotherapies* (4th ed.) (pp. 405–453). Itasca, IL: F. E. Peacock.

Dusay, J. M., & Steiner, C. (1971). Transactional analysis in groups. In H. I. Kaplan & B. J. Sadock (Eds.), *Comprehensive group psychotherapy*. Baltimore: Williams & Wilkins.

Elaad, E. (1993). Detection of deception: A transactional analysis perspective. *Journal of Psychology, 127*, 5–15.

Ernst, F. H. (1973). Psychological rackets in the OK corral. *Transactional Analysis Journal, 3*, 19.

Freedman, L. D. (1993). TA tools for self-managing work teams. *Transactional Analysis Journal, 23*, 104–109.

Friday, P. J. (1977). A TA 101: Does it make a difference? *Transactional Analysis Journal, 7*, 176–177.

George, R. L., and Cristiani, T. S. (1990). *Counseling theory and practice* (3rd ed.). Englewood Cliffs, NJ: Prentice-Hall.

Gladding, S. T. (1992). *Counseling: a comprehensive profession* (2nd ed.). New York: Merrill.

Goldhaber, G. M., & Goldhaber, M. B. (1976). *Transactional analysis: Principles and applications*. Boston: Allyn & Bacon.

Goulding, M. M. (1987). Transaction analysis and redecision therapy. In J. K. Zeig (Ed.), *The evolution of psychotherapy* (pp. 258–299). New York: Brunner/Mazel.

Goulding, M. & Goulding, R. (1979). *Changing lives through redecision therapy*. New York: Brunner/Mazel.

Hansen, J. C., Stevic, R. R., & Warner, W. R., Jr. (1982). *Counseling: Theory and process* (3rd ed.). Boston: Allyn & Bacon.

Harris, T. A. (1967). *I'm OK—Your OK.* New York: Avon Books.

Hlongwane, M. M., & Basson, C. J. (1990). Self-concept enhancement of Black adolescents using transactional analysis in a group context. *School Psychology International, 11,* 99–108.

Holland, G. A. (1973). Transactional analysis. In R. Corsini (Ed.), *Current psychotherapies.* Itasca, IL: F. E. Peacock.

Ivey, A. E., Ivey, M. B., & Simek-Downing, L. (1987). *Counseling and psychotherapy: Integrating skills, theory, and practice.* Englewood Cliffs, NJ: Prentice-Hall.

James, J. (1984). Grandparents and family script parade. *Transactional Analysis Journal, 14,* 18–28.

James, M. (Ed.). (1977). *Techniques in transactional analysis for psychotherapists and counselors.* Reading, MA: Addison-Wesley.

James, M., & Jongeward, D. (1971). *Born to win: Transactional analysis with Gestalt experiments.* Reading, MA: Addison-Wesley.

Jensen, S. M., Baker, M. S., & Koepp, A. H. (1980). TA in brief psychotherapy with college students. *Adolescence, 15,* 683–689.

Jongeward, D. (1973). *Everybody wins: TA applied to organizations.* Reading, MA: Addison-Wesley.

Karpman, S. B. (1968). Fairy tales and script drama analysis. *Transactional Analysis Bulletin, 7,* 39–43.

Knox, P., & Lichtenberg, J. (1991). Order out of chaos: A structural analysis of group therapy. *Journal of Counseling Psychology, 38,* 279–288.

LaFreniere, P., & Dumas, J. E. (1992). A transactional analysis of early childhood anxiety and social withdrawal. *Development and Psychopathology, 4,* 385–402.

Lammers, W. (1990). From cure to care: Transactional analysis treatment of adult asthma. *Transactional Analysis Journal, 20,* 245–252.

Martin, F. E. (1990). The relevance of a systemic model for the study and treatment of anorexia nervosa in adolescents. *Canadian Journal of Psychiatry, 35,* 496–500.

Massey, R. F. (1990). Berne's transactional analysis as a neo-Freudian/neo-Adlerian perspective. *Transactional Analysis Journal, 20,* 173–186.

Nykodym, N., Longenecker, C. O., & Ruud, W. N. (1991). Improving quality of work life with transactional analysis as an intervention change strategy. *Applied Psychology: An International Review, 40,* 395–404.

Oden, T. A. (1974). *Game free: A guide to the meaning of intimacy.* New York: Harper & Row.

O'Hearne, J. (1992). How and why do transactional-gestalt therapists work as they do? *American Journal of Psychology, 4,* 163–172.

Penfield, W. (1952). Memory mechanisms. *Archives of Neurology and Psychiatry, 67,* 178–198.

Pizer, I. (1994). Ethics in Europe. *Transactional Analysis Journal, 24,* 60–63.

Rumney, A., & Steckel, T. (1985). Growing up and getting dependency needs met as an adult: Reparenting in anorexia nervosa. *Transactional Analysis Journal, 15,* 55–61.

Shapiro, S. B. (1969). Critique of Eric Berne's contributions to subself theory. *Psychological Reports, 25,* 283–296.

Silvestri, S. (1992). Treating adult children of divorce: A model based on redecision therapy. *Transactional Analysis Journal, 22,* 164–173.

Simoneux, J. (1977). Adlerian psychology and TA. In M. James (Ed.), *Techniques in transactional analysis for psychotherapists and counselors,* Reading, MA: Addison-Wesley.

Smith, D. (1982). Trends in counseling and psychotherapy. *American Psychologist, 37,* 802–809.

Steiner, C. (1974). *Scripts people live: Transactional analysis of life scripts.* New York: Grove Press.

Steiner, C. (1984). Emotional literacy. *Transactional Analysis Journal, 14,* 162–163.

Summerton, O. (1992). Game analysis in two planes. *Transactional Analysis Journal, 22,* 210–215.

Wollams, S., & Brown, M. (1979). *The total handbook of transactional analysis.* Englewood Cliffs, NJ: Prentice-Hall, 1979.

CHAPTER 12

Behavior Therapy

Chapter Outline

Introduction
Brief Biography
Historical Development
View of Human Nature
Development of Maladaptive Behavior
Function of the Therapist
Goals of Therapy
Major Methods and Techniques
Application
Critical Analysis
Current Status
Chapter Summary
Key Terms
Suggested Reading

INTRODUCTION

After years of living close to civilization, grizzly bears in Yellowstone National Park have lost their fear of humans. Before this region was so heavily populated by tourists and the garbage they leave behind, the bears, more or less, avoided all human contact. But recently the bears have become accustomed to people and an alarming number of human fatalities has been the result. This is not only a terrible human tragedy, but the bears involved in such attacks have to be destroyed. Because of this, there is concern that grizzly bears may become extinct.

Specialists have tried a number of strategies to protect the grizzlies, but all to no avail. Even when trapped and transported deep into the wild, these fear-

278

less bears will return to human habitats. More recently, however, officials have begun a promising, new program to reestablish fear of humans in these animals. Once trapped and caged, a human delivers a brief, electric shock to the bear in order to associate humans with pain and thus teach bears, once again, to fear people. It's working. These bears, who quickly learn to associate people with pain, are far more likely to stay away from humans.

But what does protecting grizzly bears have to do with behavior therapy, you may be asking. Actually, the principle used in protecting this endangered species, "learning by association," is basic to the process of learning in humans as well as animals. Perhaps you have received a ticket for speeding. If so, you can probably pinpoint the spot and even months later you still slow down as you near that location. You have "associated" it with an expensive penalty. Behavior therapy is built on the principle of association as well as a vast assortment of other laws of learning (e.g., shaping, punishment, reinforcement, etc.). In the theory and techniques of behavior therapy you will discover a treatment strategy distinct from all others—an approach that is precise in its application and thoroughly grounded in its reliance on research.

BRIEF BIOGRAPHY

Behavior therapy, unlike other theories in this book, is not closely identified with any single person. It has several important proponents: O. H. Mower (1947), A. Salter (1949), H. G. Jones (1956), V. Meyer (1957), H. J. Eysenck (1959), J. D. Krumboltz (1966), A. J. Yates (1958, 1980), and Arnold Lazarus (1958, 1971, 1989) are some of the most influential. But it is largely through the successive work of three psychologists that behavior therapy came to be. It was B. F. Skinner's creative ideas that allowed the behavioral approach to grow into a major force in psychology and gave behavioral therapy a solid platform to stand on. It was Joseph Wolpe who launched a vigorous program of research and training in behavior therapy, making it the most empirically validated approach to psychotherapy. And Albert Bandura stimulated the behavior therapy movement by drawing on social psychology as a source of innovative therapeutic strategies, opening the way for other theorists and researchers to expand the boundaries of behavior therapy.

B. F. Skinner

Burrhus Frederic Skinner was born on March 20, 1904, in Susquehanna, a small railroad town in northeastern Pennsylvania. His childhood was spent, as he described it, in a warm, stable family environment. His father was a lawyer; his mother, according to Skinner, was rigid, with high moral standards. While growing up, Skinner was an avid builder of things—sleds, rafts, seesaws, slingshots, blowguns, water pistols, scooters, wagons, model airplanes. He even built a gadget that confronted him with a sign in his bedroom closet whenever he failed to hang up his clothes (Skinner, 1976).

B. F. Skinner (1904–1990).
(AP/Wide World)

Skinner majored in English at a small liberal arts school in New York State, Hamilton College. After graduating in 1926, he attempted to make his mark as a writer of short stories. He even received encouragement from the noted poet, Robert Frost. Gradually, however, he gave up in literary attempts and came to realize that he was intensely interested in human behavior but "had been investigating it in the wrong way" (Skinner, 1976, p. 291). In the fall of 1928, Skinner entered Harvard University and began studying psychology. After earning a Ph.D. in 1931, he stayed on at Harvard for 5 years doing research. He then took a teaching position at the University of Minnesota and, later, as Chair of the Department of Psychology at Indiana University. In 1948 he returned to Harvard as a professor, where he remained the rest of his career (Nye, 1992).

Skinner's first important book was *The Behavior of Organisms*, published in 1938. Among his later works are *Walden Two* (1948), *Science and Human Behavior*

(1953), *Verbal Behavior* (1957), *The Technology of Teaching* (1968), *Beyond Freedom and Dignity* (1971), *About Behaviorism* (1974), and *Recent Issues in the Analysis of Behavior* (1989).

Skinner has been described as the most influential psychologist of this century and in one study (Goodell, 1975), 82% of college students could identify him. Skinner's last public appearance was on August 10, 1990, when he gave the keynote address at the opening ceremony of the American Psychological Association's annual convention. He died 8 days later in Cambridge, Massachusetts, at age 86, of complications from leukemia.

Joseph Wolpe

Born in Johannesburg, South Africa in 1915, Joseph Wolpe received his medical degree from the University of Witwatersrand in South Africa.

Although his initial work was psychoanalytically focused, by 1944, Wolpe was moving away from this approach in search of something more effective and began reading the work of Pavlov. By the late 1940s he had also been exposed to the writings of Clark Hull and Mary Cover Jones. The learning principles he discovered in his study became the basis for Wolpe's landmark work, *Psychotherapy by Reciprocal Inhibition* (1958). Wolpe not only developed specific therapy techniques but provided numerous case histories with outcome data in support of the efficacy of this *systematic desensitization* approach. At the University of Witwatersrand in South Africa, Wolpe met frequently with several colleagues and students who were excited about this new and effective way to treat anxiety and phobias. Arnold Lazarus and Stanley Rachman were among those in this group. They later helped to spread Wolpe's systematic desensitization technique to England and the United States, where Wolpe himself moved in 1963.

> *The world of the mind steals the show. Behavior is not recognized as a subject in its own right. In psychotherapy, for example, the disturbing things a person does or says are almost always regarded merely as symptoms, and compared with the fascinating dramas which are stated in the depths of the mind, behavior itself seems superficial indeed.*
>
> —B. F. Skinner

In 1966, Wolpe, by then at Temple University School of Medicine in Philadelphia, launched a program of research and training in behavior therapy. The same year, a nonprofit clinic and training center called the Behavior Therapy Institute headed by Arnold Lazarus opened in Sausalito, California; a new book, *Behavior Therapy Techniques* (1966), by Wolpe and Lazarus (his colleague at Temple), appeared; and the following year Wolpe and behavior therapy were introduced to the nation's intelligentsia by an article in the *New York Times Magazine.*

Albert Bandura

Born December 4, 1925, Albert Bandura grew up in the tiny hamlet of Mundare in northern Alberta, Canada. His parents were wheat farmers of Polish heritage,

Joseph Wolpe (1915–   ).
(Courtesy of the Milton H. Erickson Foundation, Inc., Phoenix, Arizona)

but little is known about his early life. We do not have an autobiographical statement from his own pen, nor has any other biographer contributed much information about Bandura's life. We do know, however, that Bandura was 1 of 20 students in a high school that had only two teachers and few resources. As a result, Bandura learned early to rely on his own academic initiative. After graduating from high school, Bandura got a summer job on a highway crew, patching holes in the Alaska highway, and then matriculated at the University of British Columbia in Vancouver. From there he chose the University of Iowa for graduate study because of its emphasis on learning and rigorous experimentation. Even then Bandura was interested in the application of learning theory to clinical phenomena. It was at Iowa that Bandura met his future wife, Virginia.

Albert Bandura (1925–   ).
(Courtesy of Albert Bandura)

Following completion of his Ph.D. in clinical psychology in 1952, Bandura joined the faculty at Stanford University. Under the influence of Robert Sears he began investigation of interactive processes in psychotherapy and on the family patterns that lead to aggressiveness in children. The work on familial causes of aggression, with Richard Walters, his first graduate student, gave rise to the emphasis on the central role of modeling influences in personality development and eventually culminated in their book, *Social Learning and Personality Development* (1963).

Bandura describes himself as conducting a multifaceted research program aimed at clarifying aspects of human capability that should be emphasized in a comprehensive theory of human behavior. His 1986 book, *Social Foundations of Thought and Action*, represents an effort to develop such a comprehensive theory. Professor Bandura is also known for *Principles of Behavior Modification* (1969) and his popular *Social Learning Theory* (1977). Today, Bandura continues to influence the field of behavior therapy in the post he has held at Stanford for more than 40 years.

HISTORICAL DEVELOPMENT

Behavior therapy has been described as having "a long past but a short history" (O'Leary & Wilson, 1987, p. 1), meaning that although many of its techniques have been in use for countless years, behavior therapy as a systemized approach dates back to only the 1950s. To understand this relatively new approach, however, one must begin with its "long past."

The beginnings of behavior therapy can be found in two converging historical events: the rise of behaviorism and the development of the experimental method in psychology (Wilson, 1989). Behaviorism, as a philosophy, is a metaphysical view based on *naturalism*, which assumes that the universe is composed exclusively of matter and energy, and hence there are no such things as supernatural entities. Human qualities such as mind, unconscious, soul, or will are in this view presumed either not to exist or to be understandable by the same physical laws that explain the rest of existence. Behaviorism's embrace of naturalism gave rise to the implication that all behaviors are caused by factors outside of themselves; all behavior is viewed as caused by events in the environment (Sechrest & Smith, 1994).

The leading figure in this movement was John B. Watson, professor at Johns Hopkins University, who directly challenged the prevalent introspectionist theories such as psychoanalysis and proposed that such mentalistic approaches were unscientific and irrelevant. For Watson, psychology would only make a significant contribution if it were to follow after the natural sciences in dealing exclusively with the study of overt behavior. He sought to discredit such ideas as unresolved Oedipal strivings and id–ego conflicts by proving that a phobia could be induced solely through external forces. Watson presented an 11-month-old infant named Albert with a tame white rat, and then crashed a hammer against a steel bar held just behind Albert's head. After only seven repetitions of this traumatic sequence, Albert was conditioned: he now showed a strong fear of the rat alone and also generalized his fear to other furry animals such as rabbits (Samelson, 1980; Watson, 1913, 1919, 1924). By the mid-1920s Watson carried his thinking into crusading perspectives. With examples like Albert, Watson postulated that behavior could be controlled scientifically and that traditional religious mores could be replaced by experimental

> *I am sometimes asked, "Do you think of yourself as you think of the organisms you study?" The answer is yea. So far as I know, my behavior at any given moment has been nothing more than the product of my genetic endowment, my personal history, and the current setting. That does not mean that I can explain everything I do or have done.*
>
> —B. F. Skinner

ethics. In his book *Behaviorism,* Watson stated: "Give me a dozen healthy infants, well formed ... and I'll guarantee you to take any one at random and train him to become any type of specialist I might select" (1924, p. 82).

In addition to the rise of behaviorism, experimental research on the psychology of learning also contributed to the development of behavior therapy. This is an approach based on a view known as *logical positivism,* under which everything that exists is empirically verifiable. From this perspective, if the material universe, understandable only as matter and energy operating according to universal laws, is all that is, then human beings are material beings only and hence explainable by natural laws. In a sense, the experimental method was putting behaviorism's philosophy into practice. This was first evident in 1879 when Wilhelm Wundt set up the first psychological laboratory in Leipzig, Germany. He decided to dispense with mental faculties and supernatural concepts such as the human soul and concentrate his attention on experience as the appropriate subject of psychology. But it was Russian physiologist Ivan Pavlov's turn-of-the-century experiment demonstrating classical conditioning principles, as revealed in the salivation responses of dogs, that was the most seminal event in the catalyst for this experimental movement in psychology. Around the same time in the United States, E. L. Throndike was developing his famous *law of effect,* in which he described how behavior was learned according to principles of reward and punishment, and Mary Cover Jones (1924) demonstrated how counterconditioning could be employed to help children overcome phobic reactions. In the late 1930s, B. F. Skinner elaborated the principles of instrumental learning with his work on operant conditioning. As did Pavlov and Watson, Skinner (1938) carried out innumerable experiments on animals to establish his behavioristic psychology. In 1932 he introduced what is now known as the Skinner box, with which he studied the learning habits of pigeons and rats, and in a dramatic display revealed that through proper reinforcement, pigeons could even learn to play Ping-Pong. Eventually Skinner's studies were also transposed to human learning, as described in his books, *Walden Two* (1948) and *Beyond Freedom and Dignity* (1971), where the so-called freedom and dignity of humankind are viewed simply as products of reinforcement.

The work of Ivan Pavlov with his salivating dogs, John Watson's discovery that phobias could be induced by scaring infants, and B. F. Skinner's fascination with teaching pigeons to play Ping-Pong are important milestones in the development of behavioristic thinking (Kanfer & Goldstein, 1980). But it was Joseph Wolpe (1958) who first translated those early research efforts into action techniques for promoting systematic client change. In 1958, he wrote one of the most important books in the development of behavior therapy, *Psychotherapy by Reciprocal Inhibition.* Until that time, no practitioner had systematically presented learning principles to the practice of counseling. Wolpe used a combination of classical conditioning theory and Clark Hull's then-popular learning theory as the basis for his work. Anxiety was learned through conditioned reactions, in Wolpe's view, and he devised several techniques to extinguish this anxiety. The most widely cited and used of these was Wolpe's systematic desensitization, which continues to be a powerful behavioral treatment today (discussed later).

It was not until the advent of systematic desensitization that behavior therapy as we know it today began to emerge. The term *behavior therapy* was introduced independently by three groups of researchers. Skinner and Lindsley (1954) referred to their use of operant conditioning principles with chronic schizophrenics as behavior therapy; Eysenck (1959) used the term in applying modern learning theory to treatment strategies; and Arnold Lazarus (1958) used it to refer to the addition of objective laboratory procedures to traditional psychotherapeutic methods. In this respect, Lazarus felt that behavior therapy was but one part of a total picture that could include certain elements of traditional psychotherapy with validated techniques from any source.

After its birth in the late 1950s, behavior therapy grew quickly in the 1960s as a significant alternative to psychodynamic approaches, causing John D. Krumboltz, a strong proponent and popularizer of this new therapy, to write *Revolution in Counseling* (1966). Behavioral strategies such as the token economy were applied to institutional settings (Ayllon & Azrin, 1968) and in 1969, Albert Bandura published the tremendously influential *Principles of Behavior Modification*, in which he describes the importance of behavioral modeling—learning by observing others and then being reinforced for performing as the model does. Concurrent with these developments were the formation of the Association for Advancement of Behavior Therapy and the emergence of several journals devoted exclusively to behavior therapy. In the 1970s behavior therapy gained widespread acceptance and by the 1980s, behavioral approaches were being refined and undergoing significant revisions, enough to make a common definition of behavior therapy next to impossible (Farkas, 1980; Follette & Houts, 1992; Masters, Burish, Hollon, & Rimm, 1987; Ross, 1985). By the end of the decade behavior therapy had basically split into three main theories: respondent learning (emphasizing Pavlov's and Watson's findings), operant conditioning (emphasizing Skinner's approach), and social modeling (emphasizing Bandura's vicarious learning). However, there are few purists in any of these schools; counselors who employ a behavioral approach usually integrate aspects of each of these theories.

All of life is nothing other than the realization of one purpose: the preservation of life itself, the tireless labor of which may be called the general life instinct.

—Ivan Pavlov

VIEW OF HUMAN NATURE

Despite the diversity of thought among behavior therapists, certain characteristics can be identified as basic to the overall approach. To begin with, the individual is seen as a product of his or her experience. Therefore, in the behavior therapy approach, people are neither good nor bad; they are essentially neutral. Because the laws of learning are emphasized, behavior therapists are less likely to emphasize commonalities of experience (e.g., stages of development, self-actualization, etc.) and instead focus on the way in which learning can lead to the development of practically any pattern of human behavior imaginable, depending on the person's learning history and biological potential. One implication of this is that behavior therapists tend not to employ a standard diagnostic nomenclature, which is judged to be rooted more in theory than reality.

The behavioral view of human nature is generally interactional; that is, it gives serious consideration to both personal and environmental determinants of human behavior. To the behavior therapist *inter*psychic views of personality underemphasize the pervasive effect that external events have upon persons. They believe instead that the behavior originates primarily from *intra*psychic causes.

Most behavior therapists would also argue that humans are basically hedonistic in nature. Therefore, behavior therapy is maximally responsive to requests to end or decrease personal suffering and to promote growth toward greater pleasure and enjoyment of life. Behavior therapists have no model of optimal human functioning toward which clients are led.

DEVELOPMENT OF MALADAPTIVE BEHAVIOR

From the behavior therapy perspective, psychopathology is defined as behavior that is disadvantageous or dangerous to the individual and/or to other people. Certain environmental circumstances shape the development of maladaptive behavior. Insufficient reinforcement, for example, occurs when a person acts but does not receive a reward. On the other hand, reinforcement for maladaptive actions is also a possibility. This occurs when an individual is reinforced for behavior that is actually negative. The child, who tells the truth about misbehaving and is immediately punished versus the child who lies about bad behavior and avoids punishment is an example.

Another cause of maladaptive behavior from the behavioral perspective is the reliance on a single, self-defeating reinforcer such as food, smoking, alcohol, or other addictive behaviors to cope with problems in life. Excessive punishment in place of positive reinforcement to control behavior can also lead to pathological behavior, for when punishment is used, anxiety and fear may develop (Krumboltz & Thoresen, 1976).

Insufficient cues to predict consequences occur when individuals do not know when certain behavior is appropriate. In other words, individuals may be unaware of the effect their behavior may have on others and on themselves, or they may incorrectly anticipate others' behaviors. This often results from poorly designed contingencies of reinforcement, punishment, or inappropriate generalizations, such as little Albert's fear of rabbits. A more clinical example might be the person who has one or two unpleasant experiences with their boss, for example, and becomes hostile and fearful toward all authority figures. The person then takes on a defensive stance with authorities and evokes true negative reactions from other authority figures the person meets, thereby perpetuating the faulty belief and self-defeating behavior (Marks, 1994).

From a Skinnerian perspective, maladaptive behavior is often shaped through reinforcement. For example, a child may engage in temper tantrums because the parents have reinforced such behavior with attention and concern. Or a busy parent may fail to respond to the child's polite request and answer only louder and louder calls, thereby shaping the child in the direction of becoming irritatingly noisy. According to Skinner (1953, p. 98), "[Such] differential reinforcement supplied by a preoccupied or negligent parent is very close to the procedure we should adopt if we were given the task of conditioning a child to be annoying." A shy child, on the other had, may be regarded by a well-meaning but misguided teacher who pays close attention to shy pupils only when they isolate themselves from their classmates and sulk.

Perhaps the most painful of all maladaptive behaviors stems from an overly severe set of self-standards, and the resulting attempt to avoid guilt or external punishments through excessive self-criticism. "There is no more devastating punishment than self-contempt," writes Bandura (1977, p. 141, 154).

Neurotic habits are distinguished by their resistance to extinction in the face of their unadaptiveness.

—Joseph Wolpe

"Linus, the security-blanketed member of the 'Peanuts' clan, also alluded to this phenomenon when he observed, 'There is no heavier burden than a great potential.'" Of course, Bandura differs from Skinner in his understanding of maladaptive behavior by attributing considerable importance to inner, cognitive causes of psychopathology. "Many human dysfunctions and ensuing torments stem from problems of thought. This is because, in their thoughts, people often dwell on painful pasts and on perturbing futures of their own invention. . . . They drive themselves to despondency by harsh self-evaluation. . . . And they often act on misconceptions that get them into trouble" (Bandura, 1986, p. 515).

FUNCTION OF THE THERAPIST

A behavior therapist may take on one of several roles, depending on the client's goals, but generally a counselor who takes a behavioral approach is very active in counseling. He or she serves as a consultant in behavior change, a supporter and motivator in the process of change, as a resource in clarifying the problem and designing change strategies, and as a model of more functional behavior (Gilliland, James, & Bowman, 1989). He or she may even work with people in the client's environment who are assisting in the behavioral change process.

To better understand the function of the behavior therapist, one can study the four major steps most behavior therapists take in the process of working with a client (Blackham & Siberman, 1971; Kazdin, 1978; Krumboltz, 1966). To begin with, the behavior therapist attempts to define the problem accurately and concretely. Thus, the therapist asks the client to specify when, where, how, and with whom the problem arises. The counselor may benefit from actually observing the problem behavior, but that is not absolutely necessary. It should be noted, by the way, that whereas counselors using a behavioral approach differ widely regarding the use of psychological tests and diagnoses, most rarely use paper-and-pencil personality profiles and, instead, attempt to measure the client's behavior and action. Next, the therapist conducts a developmental history of the client. In other words, the therapist tries to learn how the client has handled past circumstances and whether the presenting problem may be organically based.

After defining the problem and taking a developmental history, behavioral counselors help clients establish specific goals, breaking down large goals into small, achievable units. Counselors also set up learning experiences for clients to develop any needed skills (Krumboltz & Thoresen, 1976). For example, if a parent wants to avoid losing his or her temper with a son or daughter, the parent must first define what losing one's temper is and then make incremental steps toward reaching the major goal.

Finally, the behavioral therapist must determine the best methods for change. There are usually several behavioral methods that can help a client reach desired goals and some may work better than others in any client's particular case. Therefore the therapist must continually assess the effectiveness of selected methods and modify ones that are not working or try new ones.

GOALS OF THERAPY

Essentially, the goal of behavior therapy is to extinguish the client's identified maladaptive behavior and to introduce or strengthen adaptive behavior that can serve as a replacement and enable him or her to live a productive, happy life (Thoresen, 1969). The key to reaching this goal has nothing to do with uncovering psychological conflicts and everything to do with helping the client *learn* new behaviors. In behavior therapy, change comes simply through modifying one's behavior.

To understand the goals of behavior therapy more accurately, one must view the process of change through the three behavioral lenses of learning, three paradigms that can stand alone but are often integrated: respondent learning, operant conditioning, and social modeling.

Respondent learning was discovered by Pavlov. It occurs when a stimulus that is neutral is paired with a stimulus that has an effect until the neutral stimulus begins to elicit the same effects as the primary stimulus. In Pavlov's experiments with dogs, the bell became a *conditioned stimulus,* in that, just like the food, it elicited salivation in the dog. The dog's response to the food is called an *unconditioned response;* its response to the bell, once the bell became a conditioned stimulus, is called a *conditioned response.* Behavior then is a function of a stimulus. This reduces considerably the complex factors influencing human reactions to situations and allows the behaviorist to focus on a specific problem as a reaction to a given set of stimuli. So from this paradigm, the goal of behavior therapy is to pair stimuli that strengthen healthy behavior; it is to make adaptive generalizations. For example, the female client who has grown up with a destructive father has learned specifically to not trust her father. She may generalize her father's behavior to all men (making them a conditioned stimulus). Thus, learning to differentiate among stimuli becomes an important goal from the perspective of respondent learning (Wilson, 1995).

In *operant conditioning* a behavior occurs and some event follows the behavior that is reinforcing. This *positive reinforcement* increases the chance of the behavior's reoccurring in the future. If a counselor, for example, responds favorably when a client practices a relaxation exercise, and if such a favorable response is followed by the client performing the exercise more and more, the counselor's response is said to be a positive reinforcer. In similar fashion, *negative reinforcement* is anything that increases the probability of a response as a result of avoiding something negative that would have occurred had the behavior not been emitted (Rasnake, 1993). An example of this is a client whose avoidance of flying in airplanes is strengthened by the relief that comes from avoiding such activity. A similar concept, *punishment*, refers to the aversive consequences of a response and is often followed by a decrease in that response. For example, a child who is spanked by a parent after asking questions will likely decrease his or her questioning. It is important to note that, in operant conditioning, if no reinforcement is ever given, the probability of behavior change is unlikely. Thus, from this perspective the goal of therapy is to find reinforcers that strengthen adaptive behavior.

> *There is no scientific evidence for the Freudian conception of neurosis ... A neurosis is just a habit—a persistent habit of unadaptive behavior, acquired by learning.*
> —Joseph Wolpe

The third form of learning, *social modeling,* or *vicarious learning* as it is sometimes called, occurs independently of reinforcement when a person sees another's behavior that "teaches" him or her a new way of behaving. This approach was put forth by Albert Bandura (1977), who theorized that almost all important learning takes place through a social modeling approach that emphasizes the self-regulation of behavior and thus de-emphasizes the importance of external reinforcers. Bandura points out that millions of people, watching and imitating others at Toastmasters Clubs, have overcome their fear of public speaking. Commercials featuring admired athletes and celebrities are also vivid examples of the potency of imitative learning. From this perspective, the goal of therapy is to provide the client with models that strengthen adaptive behavior.

The specific goals of behavior therapy will vary with each client, but in all cases, the general goal is to create new conditions for learning to ameliorate problem behaviors (see Sidebar 12-1).

MAJOR METHODS AND TECHNIQUES

Because the quality of the counseling relationship is de-emphasized in behavior therapy, and because the main priority of this approach is the resolution of

Sidebar 12-1

B. F. SKINNER ON COUNSELING

In interviewing B. F. Skinner, Mary Harrington Hall asked about his view of clinical psychology and psychotherapy. Here is what he said.

Skinner: Well, they won't get anywhere if they don't get results. And you can't get results by sitting around and theorizing about the inner world of the disturbed. I want to say to those people: get down to the facts. But they seem to be threatened by facts. Operant conditioning—the proper arrangement and management of contingencies of reinforcement—has been fantastically successful with a number of problems of disordered behavior.

Take autistic children, for example. Our success in that area is a real threat, you see, to the people who think that the problem is something about the inner life, or the lack of identity, or alienation, or whatever all those things are that these kids are supposed to be suffering from.

What they are suffering from in fact is very bad schedules of reinforcement. That is something you can change for them, but this is not done. And you really can't expect mentalistic psychologists to do things

like that; their approach just simply destines them to inadequacy and failure.

Oh, but they are so sincere. They want to understand the boys, to sit and talk and gain their confidence, and all of this stuff. Meanwhile, there is a very simple way in which you can begin to get them to behave in a very respectable way and to learn the kinds of skills that will give them a chance to be effective citizens.

Take the problem in correctional institutions, for example. One of our people recently took over one of the buildings in a training school for boys and organized it on the basis of a point-reinforcement system. The boys were paid for their work, and they had to buy everything except basics. For free they could get the basic diet and a place to sleep in the dormitory, but anything else they had to buy. And the most points were given for learning something interesting with the help of teaching machines, or without. They got points for learning.

Don't you see, that's the point. It made them discover for the first time that they could learn something, and that learning something was valuable. This is a very important thing. Most of them had been convinced by our school systems that they were stupid. They discovered that they really weren't. It's remarkable, surprising, it really works! How very different it is from hand-holding and getting to know the boys.

Source: Hall, M. H. (1967). The behavioral view: A conversation with B. F. Skinner. In P. Chance & T. G. Harris (Eds.). *The best of Psychology Today* (p. 535). New York: McGraw-Hill.

---

the client's symptoms, the behavioral therapist relies heavily on a large repertoire of techniques to deal with client problems. Unlike those in other therapeutic schools, techniques in the behavioral approach must be effectively supported by empirical research as measured against specifiable ends. In fact, any technique that can be demonstrated to change behavior may be incorporated into a behavioral treatment plan, according to Arnold Lazarus (1989). He advocates the use of diverse techniques, regardless of their theoretical origin. Intervention methods associated with behavior therapy are so varied that there is a *Dictionary of Behavior Therapy Techniques* (Bellack & Hersen, 1987) that contains descriptions of more than 150 different techniques. The methods described in this section, therefore, are only a sample of the strategies available to the behavior therapist: behavioral assessment, positive reinforcement, token economies, assertiveness training, modeling, relaxation training, systematic desensitization, and flooding. These techniques are representative of some of the most common and effective techniques in the evolving field of behavior therapy.

Behavioral Assessment

Behavior therapists often begin work with clients by using a behavioral assessment developed to collect specific information about the client's presenting problem and accompanying behavior (Nelson & Barlow, 1981). After asking about the problem, the therapist will attempt to get as specific and concrete answers as possible by asking the client questions such as: "If I were watching you in this situation, what would I see you do?" The goal is to understand what the client does in particular situations. The purpose of behavioral interviewing is to identify the target behavior and the controlling variables, as well as to plan an appropriate intervention strategy. And whereas the therapist can work to define the presenting problem concretely, understanding its antecedents and consequences, the client may not be ready to reveal the true problem at the beginning of the behavioral assessment. For this reason a global assessment is sometimes used in which several structured interviews assess employment, sleep, stress, relationships, and so on (Lazarus, 1971). This allows the therapist to use information derived from the structured interview along with the initial description of the presenting problem to develop a more accurate picture of the problem.

> *At a recent cocktail party … [I] was cornered by an inquiring lady who expressed considerable puzzlement over adolescents' fascination for unusual and bizarre styles. The lady herself was draped with a sack, wearing a preposterous object on her head, and spiked high heel shoes that are more likely to land one in an orthopedic clinic, than to transport one across the room to the olives.*
>
> —Albert Bandura

Behavioral assessment may include the use of questionnaires and interviews with significant others (Nelson & Barlow, 1981). Self-monitoring is another often used assessment tool in which the client is asked to record his or her thoughts, feelings, and behaviors as they happen. This can provide valuable information in completing an accurate picture of the client's behavior. The bottom line of behavioral assessment is that specificity is necessary to develop individualized treatment plans (Galassi & Perot, 1992).

Positive Reinforcement

Positive reinforcement is probably the most widely used and most successful of all the behavior modification techniques. It involves providing a reward for positive behavior. The reward can be anything ranging from a token that can be used to purchase goods, to a star in one's book, to a verbal compliment, to a smile. The principle underlying positive reinforcement is that the tendency to repeat a response to a given stimulus will be strengthened as the response is rewarded. The key to successful positive reinforcement is selecting a reinforcer that will indeed strengthen the desired behavior. It is therefore necessary for the counselor to test out reinforcers and one of the best ways of doing this is simply by asking the client what will best serve as a reward.

Token Economies

Token economies can be applied to shape behavior when approval and other intangible reinforcers do not work. Under this system, appropriate behavior may be reinforced with "tokens" that can be later exchanged for desired objects or privileges. Tokens can be used to obtain candy and toys, or to participate in certain programs. The advantages of using a token economy are that tokens do not lose their incentive value and they are a concrete measure of the person's motivation to change certain behaviors. Tokens also give the person receiving them the opportunity to decide how to use them.

Assertiveness Training

The major tenet of assertiveness training is that a person should be free to express thoughts and feelings appropriately without feeling undue anxiety (Alberti & Emmons, 1982). The technique is especially helpful for timid clients and basically consists of counterconditioning their social anxiety and reinforcing their assertive behavior. The main method of assertiveness training is behavioral rehearsal, wherein the therapist helps the client practice behaving more assertively. The client is first taught that everyone has the right of self-expression and that there are differences among aggressive, passive, and assertive actions. The client and therapist then begin rehearsing assertive situations and the therapist offers feedback regarding the client's performance. Eventually the client is able to transfer the rehearsal to real situations where his or her behavior can become more adaptive with some assertiveness.

Modeling

Modeling is used to help a client acquire desired responses or to extinguish fears through observing the behavior of another person. This observation can be presented in a live modeling demonstration, in symbolic form through written and media-taped models, or via the client's own imagination. Through live modeling the counselor can demonstrate a behavior by role-playing, taking the part of the client and showing him or her a different way to respond or behave. A client who wishes to acquire self-expression skills, for instance, may benefit form seeing the counselor demonstrate such skills in role-played situations. Of course, live models other than the counselor can be equally effective. In fact it is best to select a model that is quite similar to the client in age, gender, ethnic background, social status, and so on. Researchers have found that arranging conditions so that clients hear or see themselves performing the desired response on tape can be a very powerful learning tool (Hosford & deVisser, 1974).

Although live models are often the best form for vicarious learning (Perry & Furukawa, 1980), they are often difficult to use because of the lack of control over ensuring their systematic demonstration of the desired behavior. To remedy this, many counselors make use of symbolic models, through audiotapes or videotapes in which a desired behavior is introduced and presented. For example, the client who wants to improve his or her ability to make public speeches can read about successful people and their ability to overcome struggles in learning to become effective speakers or the client can listen to an audiotape or watch a videotape of the same thing. Yet another way of using modeling as a technique in therapy is to have the client imagine a model performing a desired behavior or activity (Cautela, 1976). For example, if a client wants to be more vulnerable with his or her spouse, the client and therapist would develop a situation, a scene, to imagine. In this scene the client would be performing new behaviors (e.g., freely talking about his or her feelings) with favorable consequences. Of course, the favorable outcome must be something that is realistic and within the client's reach.

Relaxation Training

The most common form of relaxation training used by behavior therapists is called *progressive relaxation* or *muscle relaxation*. It is used to treat a wide variety of disorders, including headaches, psychosomatic pain, hypertension, and other anxiety-related problems. The basic premise of relaxation training is that muscle tension exacerbates anxiety and as a result individuals experience a reduction in felt anxiety by learning to discriminate between tense and relaxed muscle groups and thus relax them upon cue. The procedure involves training clients to tense and relax various muscle groups in their bodies successively while the counselor directs their attention to pleasant sensations. The training needs to occur in a quiet environment and the counselor uses a quiet soothing tone of voice when delivering the relaxation instructions. Each step in the process of alternating tension and relaxation of each muscle group takes about 10 to 15 s, with a 10- to 15-s pause between each of the steps. The entire procedure takes 20 to 30 min. After going through the procedure several times with the counselor's assistance, clients are encouraged to practice it on their own, daily if possible.

In using relaxation training, it is important for counselors to remember that many clients have developed a state of chronic muscular tension that may not disappear after only one or two attempts at muscle relaxation. Also, some clients may need more or less time to tense and relax muscles; others may prefer much less dialogue from the counselor. The point is that successful use of this technique requires that the counselor apply the procedure with each client in an individualized way.

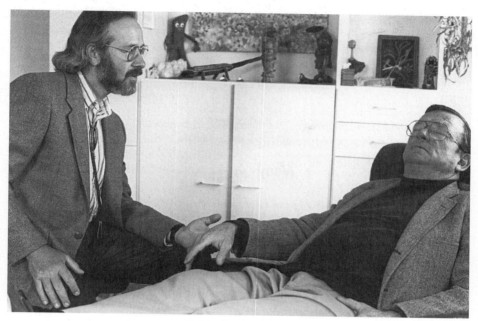

Relaxation training.
(Mimi Forsyth/Monkmeyer)

Systematic Desensitization

Systematic desensitization is an anxiety-reducing technique based on the learning principles of classical conditioning and developed by Joseph Wolpe (1958, 1982). It involves the pairing of a neutral event or stimulus with a stimulus that already elicits fear. Desensitization employs counterconditioning, substituting one type of response for another, to progressively lower the client's level of fear. In a relatively relaxed state, the client is exposed, step by step, to increasingly stronger stimuli until what used to bring about fear can now be experienced in a state of relaxation.

The procedure itself involves three basic steps and, on average, takes about 10 to 30 sessions to complete, depending on the client, the problem, and the intensity of the anxiety. There are three basic steps in desensitization: training in deep muscles relaxation (discussed above), constructing a hierarchy of emotionally provoking situations, and progressively pairing the items on the hierarchy with a state of relaxation in the client.

Hierarchy construction involves identifying various situations that evoke fear or anxiety. It involves situations the client has already experienced or anticipates experiencing in the future and usually consists of 10 to 20 different items arranged by the client in graduated order from the lowest or least anxiety-provoking to the highest. The following is an example of a hierarchy constructed to eliminate the fear of snakes:

See the word "snake" in a book

See a picture of a snake in a book

Hear someone talk about snakes

See a live snake in the zoo

See a dead snake as you walk down the road

See a live snake as you drive down the road

See a live snake as you walk down the road

Touch a dead snake on the road

Touch a live snake held by someone else

Hold a dead snake

Hold a live snake

Once the hierarchy has been constructed and the client has been trained in muscle relaxation, the counselor and client are ready to begin the pairing process. This starts with the counselor and client agreeing on a signal the client can use to let the counselor know if and when he or she is experiencing any anxiety during the pairing (usually the raising of an index finger). A state of relaxation is then induced for the client and the counselor then asks the client to imagine the first item on the hierarchy. The scene is presented for about 10 s, assuming the client does not signal anxiety before this time, and concludes when

Progressively reducing a fear of snakes through systematic desensitization.
(Susan Rosenberg/Photo Researchers)

the counselor says something such as, "Now stop imaging that scene." This is done several times until the client can imagine that scene without sensing any anxiety. Once this is achieved, the counselor moves up the hierarchy presenting the next scene until it can be imagined with no anxiety. Each desensitization session involving the pairing process typically begins with the last item successfully completed during the previous session and ends with a nonanxiety item. The pairing process is usually terminated in each session after successful completion of three to five hierarchy items. Because the pairing process may occur over several weeks, it is important for the counselor to keep accurate written notations about each item as it is presented to the client (Goldfried & Davison, 1976).

Flooding

Whereas systematic desensitization seeks to minimize anxiety by pairing small doses of it with a deep relaxation, flooding maximizes the anxious state of the client. The person who fears flying, for example, might be asked to imagine being on a plane high above the ocean, without first going through a hierarchy of scenes. Whereas the client's anxiety becomes extremely high while using the flooding technique, it usually dissipates and is eventually extinguished if the client stays with the scene long enough. The same strategy can be used, as can systematic desensitization, in real-life scenarios. For example, the counselor may actually make a plane trip with the client, encouraging him or her until the anxiety subsides. The principle is that anxiety disappears if it is not reinforced. Of course, this method is clearly anxiety-provoking and the client must also be in good physical condition to undergo such intense treatment. Inexperienced counselors should not try flooding without supervision.

> *The time seems to have come when psychology must discard all reference to consciousness; when it need no longer delude itself into thinking that it is making mental states the object of observation.*
>
> —John B. Watson

An example of one therapist's use of behavioral techniques on himself is recounted in Sidebar 12-2.

APPLICATION

Considerable research has shown different forms of behavior therapy to be effective in the treatment of numerous clinical problems in different populations (Kazdin & Wilson, 1978). For example, behavior therapy has been effectively applied to the treatment of anger (Moore & Shannon, 1993), obsessive–compulsive disorders (Fals & Lucente, 1994; Roth & Church, 1994), phobias (Emmelkamp, 1974; Emmelkamp, Brilman, Kuipers, & Mersch, 1986; Emmelkamp & Wessels, 1975; Stern & Marks, 1973; Turner, Beidel, Cooley, & Woody, 1994), depression (Gardner & Oei, 1981; Hersen, Bellack, Himmelhoch, & Thase, 1984; Jacobson, Fruzzetti, Dobson, & Whisman, 1993; Lewinsohn, 1975; Taylor & McLean, 1993; Rehm, 1977; Thase, Reynolds, Frank, &

A DIARY OF SELF-MODIFICATION

Israel Goldiamond

A distinguished teacher of behavior modification calmly explains how he turned a tragic automobile accident into a personal triumph.

One autumn afternoon in 1970, I found myself lying on my back, watching a white cloud moving slowly across a blue sky. My leg was bent back under my arm, totally devoid of feeling. I suspected, lying there on the grass near my wrecked car, that I might have suffered a spinal injury. Soon an ambulance arrived to take me to a nearby hospital, where I underwent surgery. A few weeks later I transferred to a rehabilitation hospital in the large city where my wife and I live. The hospital was to be my home for the next eight months.

During my hospitalization I observed my own behavior as a patient, as well as the behavior of my fellow patients. These observations did not occur in an intellectual vacuum, but in the context of my previous work as a psychologist. My approach to observation stemmed from the *experimental analysis of behavior,* or what might be called functional behaviorism. According to this viewpoint, if certain patterns of behavior occur on certain occasions, it may be because certain consequences can be observed to follow. On these occasions, the consequences are contingent on the behavior and maintain it. By understanding and changing these relations we can understand and change the behavior. This approach, when applied to clinical and classroom problems, is named *behavior modification;* when applied to courses of study, it is *programmed instruction;* and when applied to physiological problems, it is *biofeedback.*

In our laboratory and clinic at the University of Chicago, my colleagues and I have been applying behavior analysis to emotional and other problems of hospital outpatients. Our program requires self-analysis and self-control. We train the patient to discover and change the contingencies, the environmental conditions, that govern his behavior. By finding out what these contingencies are, the patient can analyze and understand his own responses.

When I awoke in the intensive-care unit after surgery, I realized that if I wanted to get back to the work I enjoy, work that I feel is important, I would have to exert the same type of self-control and analysis we had been applying in our clinic. I would have to specify the outcomes I wished to attain, discover the existing behaviors which were relevant to these outcomes, and develop a program to convert my current repertoire of behaviors to the desired repertoire. I would have to discover the contingencies governing my own behavior.

The patients enrolled in our self-control clinic must keep daily logs of their behaviors and other events, so I assigned myself this task as well. I kept a meticulous account of my physical abilities and progress. I made graphs. I described muscle movements. I recorded medications, surgery and X-rays. I noted some exercises I had imposed on myself ("9:15-9:20 a.m., shrugged shoulders 10 times"). Much later, I noted that when a person crawls forward the right arm and the left leg move together, but when he crawls backward the right arm and right leg move together.

I also recorded my own emotions— elation, annoyance, etc., and the contingencies responsible for producing them. Usually the contingencies were quite clear, but in one case they were not. Then the records I had kept proved to be valuable in clarifying them.

The problem was sleeplessness. The staff had to log-roll me every two hours during my sleep so that I would not develop skin ulcers, but I always fell asleep again. One evening in February I was unable to fall asleep for two hours after the final log-roll. The next night I was sleepless for four hours, the next for six, and on the fourth and fifth nights I was totally sleepless. My nurse attributed my mounting sleeplessness to mounting anxiety. What was I thinking about that kept me awake? Was I worried? What about?

Of course I was worried. If one can't sleep, one is liable to worry about it, and many of my thoughts were not pleasant; there is no reason why one's thoughts should be pleasant when one is lying sleepless in a hospital. But, as I have taught outpatients in our self-control program, emotions do not cause behavior. Contingencies determine both emotions and behavior. The solution had to be that something was keeping me awake at night. The nurse could find nothing in her record so I looked in mine. For the past four months I had been taking 40 milligrams of Valium (a tranquilizer and muscle relaxer) every day. This is a high dosage, and I had been told to kick it at my convenience, as I had previously kicked similar medications. I asked for 30 milligrams one day, and on the next day, the one preceding my first sleepless period, I switched to zero. My pattern of sleeplessness fit one of the many withdrawal symptoms that can occur upon termination of Valium treatment. When I discovered this, I promptly reinstated myself on a low dosage and began to sleep soundly all night. During the following month, I gradually faded the medication out completely.

Ongoing Professionalism
I kept up my professional activities while I was hospitalized. Even though I was immobilized, I conferred with a grant committee in my hospital room. By the start of the spring quarter, I was making weekend visits home, where I resumed my graduate seminar. When a small skin ulcer appeared on a buttock, I simply conducted class lying on my other side on the living room couch. I ran the laboratory and clinic from my hospital room, with research assistants, staff, students and colleagues constantly there during visiting hours. One weekend I addressed the annual banquet of the Association for Precision Teaching. I also took on a new client in a self-control weight program. My new roommate, John McWethy, editor of the Midwest edition of *The Wall Street Journal* and a severely impaired quadriplegic, caught my bad habits. He began to run his office from the same room and has since resumed his duties.

Resumption of my professional life was critical to me. Since doing so required that I participate in the rehabilitation program at the hospital, I participated above and beyond the call of duty. In other words, there was a contingency relation between my participation in the rehabilitation program and the resumption of my professional activities.

Problems as Goals
My laboratory office is on the second floor of a museum. To get there I go down a loading ramp to the basement, where there is a freight elevator. This requires that I telephone in advance to make sure the basement doors are open and the elevator is available. If calling every day became bothersome, I would arrange to arrive at definite hours so that my arrival could be anticipated, as is the arrival of visitors to the museum every morning when the guards unlock the main gates. The visitors too are dependent, in their case on the guard's completion of his duly appointed rounds.

Recently a nurse asked me to discuss the various difficulties of being disabled,

Continued.

because some patients were "not realistic about them." I declined indignantly. It is far more sensible, useful and fulfilling to define problems in terms of goals and ways to program getting them.

When the professional refers to a patient as being "unaware of," "not realistic about," or "repressing" his problem it is often the professional who is being unrealistic. If I choose not to discuss my pains, problems, and infections, it is not because I am unaware, unrealistic, or repressing. At times I am painfully aware of them, and I mean that literally. If a patient does not "face up" to these issues, it may be because he is facing, or trying to face, in a different direction, one that can help him achieve his goal.

The Crumbling Contingencies
Seated in my wheelchair, I very often feel a discomfort in my seat. I might call it pain. This occurs most frequently when I am not working. Now one way to talk about this is to say that the pain keeps me from working. Another way to talk about it is to say that because I am not working my attention has turned to my seat, and I feel discomfort. Either way I get sympathy and support, but neither approach is particularly helpful. A third way to talk about it is to say that the reason I am not working is because the contingencies which maintain productive work are absent or crumbling. The discomfort in my butt is a signal to me that something is lacking contingency-wise. My butt is apparently more sensitive to this state of affairs than is my intellect.

It follows that when I start to feel the discomfort, I should immediately attend to the contingencies before they break down completely. I should set up working conditions so that my writing can

progress. True, I will not get sympathy, but my behavior will get the same support of my colleagues which maintained it at a high rate before, and which I valued then and value now.

Reaction to one's own injury is supposed to cause depression. By considering apathy, depression or aggression as inevitable developmental stages in injury (or aging or illness), the professional staff can avoid asking how their actions might have been causal. The hospital told my wife to expect me to be profoundly depressed. When she protested that I was not depressed, the staff greeted the news with great skepticism.

Press the Right Levers
I submit that when depression does arise in the ill or disabled, it may be because consequences which used to be critical maintainers of behavior are no longer available, or the cost of obtaining these consequences may suddenly have become very high. A solution is to program actively either alternative consequences or alternative behavior patterns.

This viewpoint leads us to reinterpret the nature of a patient's symptoms. The question is, what contingencies are now governing the patient's behavior? Far from indicating pathology, the patient's behavior may actually be the most sensible one possible, given the particular reinforcement contingencies in effect. We know that a laboratory pigeon will peck at a disk, even though all previous pecks have produced electric shock, as long as he also occasionally gets food after a peck, and as long as he fails to get food after an unshocked response. We do not say that the pigeon is masochistic. His behavior is quite sensible. The pigeon is always right (Goldiamond, 1973).

Simmons, 1994; Wilson, 1982; Wilson, Goldin, & Charboneau-Powis, 1983; Zeiss, Lewinsohn, & Munoz, 1979); alcoholism (Baker & Cannon, 1979; Cannon & Baker, 1981; Elkins, 1980; Olson, Ganley, Devine, & Dorsey, 1981), sexual dysfunctions (Clement & Schmidt, 1983; Crowe, Gillan, & Golombock, 1981; Hartman & Dally, 1983; Obler, 1973), paraphilias (Brownell & Barlow, 1976; Brownell, Hayes, & Barlow, 1977; Evans, 1970; Levin, Barry, Camaro, Wolfinsohn, & Smith, 1977; Maletzky, 1980; Quinsey, Bergersen, & Steinman, 1976), marital distress (Babcock & Jacobson, 1993; Emmelkamp, Van der Helm, MacGillavry, & Van Zanten, 1984; Jacobson, 1984; Kelly & Halford, 1993; O'Leary & Turkewitz, 1978), and childhood disorders (Bijou, Birnbrauer, Kidder, & Tague, 1966; Bornstein & Kazdin, 1985; Craighead, 1982; Masters et al., 1987; Ross, 1981; Wolf, Risley, & Mees, 1964). Behavior therapy has been used successfully in hospital and prison settings, in rehabilitation counseling, and in special education environments. It also has broad applicability to problems in education, medicine, and community living (Liberman, Van Putten, Marshall, & Mintz, 1994).

The following case, written by Joseph Wolpe, illustrates two fundamental behavioral strategies: systematic desensitization and assertiveness training. It is the case of Mr. B, who is suffering from numerous somatic symptoms and has developed an obsession with his wife's sexual involvement with another man before their marriage. Dr. Wolpe will pick up the case from here:

> Mr. B. was a 31-year-old advertising salesman who four years previously had begun to notice himself [becoming] increasingly anxious in social and business situations from which it was difficult to get away. Within a few months, even five minutes in the office of a client would produce considerable anxiety accompanied by a strong desire to urinate. If he went out and relieved himself, the urge would return after a further five minutes, and so on. The only circumstances that could be associated with the onset of Mr. B's neurosis were the unsettlement of having moved to a new house in town, and his concern at the unexpected break-up of the marriage of close friends whom he had regarded as ideally mated. His only previous neurotic phase had been a brief one that had occurred upon moving to a new school at the age of 16. This could conceivably have conditioned anxiety to "new places." The Fear Survey Schedule revealed very high anxiety to the following stimulus classes: strange places, failure, strangers, bats, journeys—especially by train, being criticized, surgical operations, rejection, planes, being disapproved of, losing control, looking foolish, and fainting.
>
> Mr. B's early history was quite conventional. A feature of interest was a strong religious training with marked emphasis on "the good and the bad." Churchgoing had played a prominent part in his childhood and adolescence. In his middle teens he had come to resent it, but had never outwardly rebelled. He had done well in school and got on well with both classmates and teachers. He had been trained in journal advertising, but was now engaged in advertising salesmanship, which he greatly liked.
>
> At 18 he had met his wife who attracted him by her intelligence, good looks, and responsiveness to his jokes. The courtship was broken by Mr. B.

after she revealed that she had had an affair two years earlier. On reflection, he condoned the episode, and at the age of 20 married her. The relationship turned out to be a very congenial one, and sexually very satisfying to both; but Mr. B. was never really able to divest himself of the painful idea that he had been "dealt a dirty card."

At the second session, Mr. B. described how embarrassing and incapacitating he found his neurotic anxiety and the associated urge to urinate. Anxiety was greater in the presence of unfamiliar people and if there was no easy access to a toilet. Other factors that increased it were the importance of the occasion and the importance of the other person. On the whole, there was more anxiety in anticipation of a meeting than at the meeting itself. Since it was evident that a desensitization program would need to be undertaken, relaxation training was started at this interview.

At his next session, five days later, Mr. B. reported that he had practiced relaxing, and that by means of it had been able to desist from urinating while at home for a period of six and a half hours despite quite a strong urge. Relaxation training was now extended, and the general desensitization strategy worked out. It was apparent that the duration of interviews with his clients was an important factor determining the strength of Mr. B's anxiety. It was therefore decided to treat an "interview" hierarchy, using a time dimension for its easy quantifiability. I started the desensitization by having him image himself scheduled to a very brief meeting (of two minutes' duration) with the manager of an important firm. The first scene was presented to him as follows: "Imagine that you have just entered the office of a manager who has a rule that no representative is permitted to spend more than two minutes in his office." By the third presentation this scene produced no anxiety, and scenes of meetings of four minutes and six minutes were then presented in succession.

In subsequent interviews, the duration of these meetings was progressively extended, until by the ninth he could imagine being with an executive for 60 minutes without anxiety. He now found himself much better at real meetings and social situations. While visiting relatives, he urinated only three times in five hours. However, his anticipatory anxiety was almost as bad as ever. There was some measure of it several hours before a prospective meetings but it became much more noticeable 30 minutes to one hour beforehand, and then increased rather steeply. At the ninth interview, then, desensitization of anticipatory anxiety was started. Anxiety decreased to zero in two to three presentations of each of the following scenes:

1. In his office, 60 minutes before visiting a client.
2. In his office, 30 minutes before visiting a client and preparing to leave.
3. Twenty minutes before visiting a client, entering his car to allow ample time.
4. In his car on the way to a client ten minutes before the appointed time.
5. Emerging from his car at the premises of the client's office, with eight minutes in hand.
6. Entering the waiting room of the client's office six minutes before the appointed time.
7. Announcing himself to the client's secretary five minutes before the appointed time.

At his tenth interview, a week later, Mr. B. reported considerably less anxiety in relation to anticipated business meetings. He had for the first time in many months taken his wife to a downtown restaurant. During the 25-minute ride to that restaurant he had not, as in the past, had to stop to relieve himself in a rest room. At first slightly anxious in the restaurant, he had become almost entirely calm after the first ten minutes. Desensitization to the anticipation of interviews was continued to the point that he could calmly imagine himself in the client's waiting room two minutes before he was to be called in. This hierarchy was finally disposed of at the next session. Now Mr. B. spontaneously reported that he felt far greater confidence in all respects. He had been going out to get new business—at first feeling some strain, but later increasingly comfortably. He had spent one and a half hours with a new and imposing manager of an important new client firm, with hardly any anxiety before or during the interview. He was no longer bothered at going into strange places because it no longer mattered whether or not he knew where the toilet was. For the same reason, he had ceased to fear using trains, airlines, buses, and other public transportation.

Attention was now turned to Mr. B.'s difficulty in asserting himself with strangers. Assertive behavior was instigated. To facilitate it, he was desensitized to one relevant situation—telling a waiter "This food is bad." Anxiety disappeared at the second presentation. Two weeks later, at his 14th interview, B. stated that he was expressing himself where required with increasing ease. For example, he had immediately and effectively spoken up at a drugstore when another customer was taken ahead of him out of turn. He had become more and more comfortable making business calls, citing as an example a one-and three-quarter-hour interview with a particular executive. He commented that three months earlier he would in the course of so long a period have had to go out to urinate about 20 times. However, he still had to push himself to do some of the things he had become inured to avoiding.

From this point onward, the main focus of therapy was his distress about his wife's premarital affair. First, it was mutually agreed that Mr. B.'s reactions were irrational. Then, an attempt was made to employ imagery ... having Mr. B. project himself back to the time of his wife's affair and imagine that he was in the next room while she was amorously engaged with her lover in a hotel. He was to force the connecting door open and beat up the paramour. In doing this, it was supposed that angry emotions would be counterpoised to the anxiety that this image ordinarily evoked. Mr. B. was enjoined to practice this imaginary sequence 50 to 100 times a day. He felt himself making progressive improvement for about two weeks, when he stated that his obsession was about 20 percent less in incidence and 40 percent less in emotional intensity. But continuing the drill for a further four weeks yielded no further benefit. ...

I decided, therefore, to tackle the problem by systematic desensitization. In order to desensitize Mr. B. to this long-past situation, I employed images from a fictitious film supposed to have been taken of his wife's premarital amorous activities by a hidden camera in her family's living room. Relaxed and with his eyes closed, Mr. B. was asked to imagine that his wife was sitting on a couch with her lover who kissed her and then put his hand on one of her breasts over her dress for exactly five seconds. He felt no anxiety at this. A fair amount of anxiety was evoked by the next scene in which the duration of contact was made eight seconds, but at the third presentation of this scene anxiety disappeared. Two presentations were required to remove anxiety from him imagining the hand over the breast for 10 seconds, and five for 20 seconds.

At the following session, six weeks later, Mr. B. again felt anxiety to the 20-second hand contact, but it disappeared at the third presentation. Two weeks later, he reported that his feelings toward his wife were more detached and that he was thinking of her less. In general his thoughts were turning away from the past and toward the present and future. Mr. B. stated that "having got over the hump last time," he no longer cared what his wife had done in the past. Recovery from the obsession (as well as the other problems) had endured at last contact three years later. (Wolpe, 1982, pp. 309–312).

CRITICAL ANALYSIS

In critiquing behavior therapy, one must begin by understanding that its major appeal is to those who prefer a coherent conceptual framework rather than an approach based more on intuition, anecdotal evidence, and personal preference. In other words, a primary strength of behavior therapy has to be its commitment to systematization, objectivity, evaluation, and an exceptionally good research base. It demystifies the process of counseling and makes it possible for clients and outside evaluators to assess in a measurable way its level of accountability.

Behavior therapy deals directly with specific symptoms and thus is often able to assist clients more rapidly than some other approaches. It provides clients with an understanding of the treatment process by supplying them with concrete information about their role in that process and their level of progress through it. It also provides them with useful information about the reinforcements in their environment that maintain both adaptive and maladaptive behaviors.

Another strength of the behavioral approach is its abundance of available techniques and their applicability to a variety of settings. Its methods are constantly being evaluated and improved; new techniques evolve and are tested. In fact, between 1970 and 1980, the number of behavior therapy interventions available to counselors more than doubled (Groden & Cautela, 1981).

On the negative side, behavior therapy does not deal with the total person, only with his or her behavior. Critics contend that many behaviorists have taken the person out of personality and replaced it with an emphasis on laws that govern actions in specific environments. They ignore the clients' personal histories and unconscious, treating them more like pigeons than people. In other words, behavior therapy is too simple in its explanation of complex human interactions and is application is too mechanical (Erwin, 1992).

Although behavior therapists have been very productive in evaluting the efficacy of various techniques, relatively little attention has been devoted to the therapeutic process (Milne, Cowie, Gormly, & White, 1992). Therapists' qualities have been found, at least in one study (Ford, 1978), to account for more variance in treatment outcome than therapy type does. To be fair, many behavior therapists are careful to establish rapport with their clients and to make counseling a collaborative effort, but the fact that some behaviorists do not initially stress the relationship with the client has hurt the approach's image—with other therapists and with the public. Some even see behavior therapy as inhumane, particularly when practiced in institutions such as mental hospitals and prisons. The 1971 film, *A Clockwork Orange*, which depicted cruel, enforced behavioral control, was the image many had of behavior therapy. Some even equated it with brainwashing and torture (Turkat & Feuerstein, 1978). Of course, behavior therapists (Wolpe, 1981) have argued that it is inherently humane, in that the role of the therapist is to teach clients the means to reach their goals. The truth is that promoters of behavior therapy have always seen the need for a good therapist–client relationship (e.g., Goldfried & Davison, 1976; Wolpe, 1958); it is just that research articles and theoretical work, in contrasting this new approach with traditional ones, did not emphasize the therapeutic relationship. The image of behavior therapy, however, seems to have changed as it has matured—the *Clockwork Orange* image is not as prevalent as it was initially—but contemporary behavior therapy must continue to balance its demonstrated effectiveness with sensitivity to the human aspects of is work.

> *Twenty-five hundred years ago it might have been said that man understood himself as well as any other part of his world. Today he is the thing he understands least.*
>
> —B. F. Skinner

When it comes to multicultural counseling, behavior therapy has some clear advantages. To begin with, since it places emphasis not on lengthy introspection, emotions, and past history but on changing behaviors, behavior therapy can more quickly help the ethnic-minority client who has a specific behavioral problem. Behavior therapy, since it is a problem-solving approach, is not as likely to get bogged down in extraneous material that increases the likelihood of confusion and misunderstanding between client and therapist. Behavior therapy also allows for flexibility and adaptation of its techniques. This can be a tremendous plus in working with ethnic-minority clients. Because it does not force all clients into the same treatment program, it offers room to consider the unique background and needs of individual clients. On the downside, ethnic-minority clients who are functioning at relatively high levels but who are searching for meaning, purpose, or a better sense of identity within a particular culture will find little solace through behavior therapy. It simply does not take into account these issues unless they can be related directly to behavior.

CURRENT STATUS

Behavior therapy is no longer a radical alternative; it is part of the establishment. In only a few decades, an unknown and simplistic application of conditioning principles to the treatment of specific problems has become a highly sophisticated and generally accepted approach to a broad spectrum of individual disorders and societal concerns. Behavioral principles have been assimilated into the mainstream of therapeutic counseling to the extent that even insight-oriented counselors regularly use many of the techniques, for instance, goal setting, assertiveness training, relaxation training, and other methods of skill acquisition (Hundert, 1994; Kavanagh, 1994).

Behavior therapy today, however, is more complex than when it was practiced in the 1970s. It is now much broader than its original conception, more diverse with regard to theory, techniques used, and behaviorists' views on what the field should encompass (Adelsberg, 1994). It is becoming more comprehensive in its therapeutic scope, and considerably more sophisticated in its efforts to maintain therapeutic gains. Inspite of its broadening, or perhaps because of it, approaches to therapy that integrate a behavioral perspective continue to grow.

In the early 1960s there was not a single professional journal devoted exclusively to research on behavioral approaches in clinical psychology. Now there are more than a dozen, the most influential of which are *Behavior Research and Therapy, Journal of Applied Behavior Analysis, Behavior Therapy, Behavior Modification, Behavioral Assessment,* and *European Journal of Behavior Analysis and Modification.*

Similar growth has occurred in the publication of textbooks and handbooks dealing with behavior modification. The first book with "behavior therapy" in the title was Eysenck's *Behavior Therapy and the Neuroses,* published in 1960. Today there are hundreds of books about behavior therapy.

CHAPTER SUMMARY

1. *Biography.* Skinner (1904–1990) spent most of his professional life at Harvard. He has been described as the most influential psychologist of this century and he certainly set the stage for the development of behavior therapy. Wolpe (1915–) received his medical degree in South Africa and, after studying Pavlov, rebelled against his psychoanalytic training and devoted his career to an empirical approach to psychotherapy. He is best known for devising systematic desensitization. Bandura (1925–) has taught psychology his entire career at Stanford University, where he has developed a broader perspective on behavior therapy by bringing in a social learning component.

2. *Historical Development.* The beginnings of behavior therapy can be found at the crossroads of the rise of behaviorism as a philosophical view (due in great part to John B. Watson) and empiricism as a growing method in psychology (due in great part to Pavlov and Skinner). With the advent of systematic desensitization in the 1950s, however, behavior therapy came into its own and grew quickly during the 1960s as an alternative to psychodynamic approaches.

3. *View of Human Nature.* Behavior therapists view humans as products of their experience. People are neither good nor bad. But the behavior therapist does view humans as hedonistic in nature, responding to requests to end or decrease personal suffering or to promote greater pleasure and enjoyment in life. Behavior therapists have no model of optimal human functioning toward which clients are led.

4. *Development of Maladaptive Behavior.* Psychopathology, from the behavioral perspective, is defined as behavior that is disadvantageous or dangerous to the individual and/or to other people. It can result from insufficient cues to predict consequences or from inadequate reinforcement. One of the most painful of all maladaptive behaviors stems from an overly severe set of self-standards, and the resulting excess of self-criticism.

5. *Goals of Therapy.* The goal of behavior therapy is to extinguish the client's identified maladaptive behavior and to introduce or strengthen adaptive behavior that can serve as a replacement and enable him or her to live a productive life. The key to reaching this goal is learning new behaviors. This relies on three paradigms that can stand alone but are often integrated in this approach: respondent learning, operant conditioning, and social modeling.

6. *Function of the Therapist.* The behavior therapist is generally very active in counseling. He or she serves as a consultant, a supporter, a resource, and a model. Functionally, the behavior therapist facilitates a process involving four major steps: accurately defining the problem, gathering a developmental history of the client, establishing specific goals, and determining the best methods for change.

7. *Major Methods and Techniques.* Because its task is to resolve client symptoms, there are literally dozens and dozens of behavior therapy techniques. Some of the most common methods include behavioral assessment (specifying an individualized treatment plan), positive reinforcement (reward for positive behavior), token economies (using tokens to be exchanged for desired objects or privileges), assertiveness training (enabling clients to express thoughts and feelings more freely), modeling (learning through observing the behavior of another), relaxation training (discriminating between tense and relaxed muscle groups to relax on cue), systematic desensitization (pairing of a neutral stimulus with one that already elicits fear), and flooding (maximizing the anxious state of a client for eventual extinction).

8. *Application.* Research has shown different forms of behavior therapy to be effective in treating anger, obsessive–compulsive disorders, phobias, depression, alcoholism, sexual dysfunctions, paraphilias, marital distress, and childhood disorders. It has been used successfully in a wide variety of settings. The case of "Mr. B" summarized by Joseph Wolpe illustrates the effectiveness of systematic desensitization and assertiveness training.

9. *Critical Analysis.* Behavior therapy provides a relatively coherent conceptual framework of psychotherapy. It is committed to systematization, objectivity, evaluation, and a solid research base. It provides clients with an understanding of the treatment process and also supplies the practitioner with an abundance of effective techniques. Behavior therapy, however, is criticized for not dealing with the total person. Critics also point to the relatively little attention the behavioral approach has devoted to the therapeutic process. Whereas behavior therapy offers some advantages to multicultural counseling, it lacks

relevance for the ethnic-minority client who is searching for a better sense of identity within a particular culture.

10. *Current Status.* After only a few decades, behavior therapy is now part of the professional therapeutic establishment. It is also much more diversified than its founders might have imagined, encompassing a broad spectrum of individual disorders and societal concerns. It is also more sophisticated in its theory, techniques, and views. Because of this newer broadening and diversity, approaches to therapy that integrate a behavioral perspective continue to grow.

KEY TERMS

Assertiveness Training   A semistructured training approach that is characterized by its emphasis on acquiring assertiveness skills through practice. Assertiveness skills enable one to stand up for one's rights and beliefs more effectively.

Aversive Conditioning   A behavioral technique involving the association of the client's symptomatic behavior with a painful stimulus until the unwanted behavior is inhibited. The aversive stimulus is typically a mild electric shock or an emetic mixture, such as antabuse.

Aversive Control (Aversion Therapy)   Using an aversive stimulus, such as an electric shock, to reduce the probability of pathological behaviors (such as alcoholism). A relatively controversial form of behavior therapy.

Behavior Modification   A term referring specifically to Skinnerian methods for changing behavior, ones that need not necessarily involve psychopathology.

Behavior Rehearsal   A therapeutic technique that consists of acting out short exchanges between client and counselor in settings from the client's life. The aim of such rehearsing is an effective preparation for the client to deal with a real "adversary," so that the anxiety the latter evokes may be reciprocally inhibited.

Behavior Therapy   An approach to psychotherapy that seeks to change particular "target" behaviors and/or symptoms of the client, rather than trying to alter some unobservable or unconscious inner state.

Behaviorism   An approach to psychology that regards only actual behavior as suitable to scientific study.

Classical Conditioning (Respondent Conditioning)   A simple form of learning first demonstrated by Ivan Pavlov, wherein a conditioned stimulus (e.g., light) becomes capable of eliciting a particular conditioned response (salivation) by being repeatedly paired with an unconditioned stimulus (food).

Conditioned Reinforcement (Secondary Reinforcement)   Reinforcement that is provided by a conditioned stimulus.

Conditioned Stimulus   A previously neutral stimulus that acquires positive or aversive properties through conditioning.

Contingencies of Reinforcement   The interrelationships between stimuli in the external environment, a particular response, and the reinforcement that follows that response.

Continuous Reinforcement   Reinforcement given after every correct response. The converse of intermittent reinforcement.

Counterconditioning   A technique in which the experimenter (or therapist) presents an unconditioned stimulus that elicits an unconditioned response (UR) that is incompatible with the conditioned response (CR) and thus inhibits the conditioned response. For example, relaxation (UR) is incompatible with fear (CR).

Deprivation   Withholding a primary reinforcer (such as food or water) for some time, so that it may be used to reinforce and condition an operant.

Desensitization   A behavioral technique through which anxiety may be reduced by using relaxation as the counterconditioning agent. Graded anxiety-producing stimuli (in the anxiety hierarchy) are repetitively paired with a state of relaxation, until the connection between those stimuli and the response of anxiety is eliminated.

Extinction   The process of removing an unwanted response by failing to reinforce it.

Fixed-Interval Schedule (FI)   Reinforcing the first correct response that occurs after a specified interval of time, measured from the preceding reinforcement.

Fixed-Ratio Schedule (FR)   Reinforcing the last of a specified number of correct responses, counted from the preceding reinforcement. A schedule of intermittent reinforcement.

Flooding   A therapeutic technique in which repeated presentation of the conditioned stimulus without reinforcement brings about extinction of the conditioned response. It differs from desensitization in that no counterconditioning agent is used.

Generalization   Operates on the assumption that a reinforcement that accompanies a particular stimulus not only increases the probability of that stimulus eliciting a particular response, but also spreads the effect to other, similar stimuli. This process of generalization is extremely important, because no two stimuli or stimulus situations are exactly the same.

Hierarchy   A list of stimuli on a theme, ranked according to the amount of anxiety they produce. The hierarchy provides the therapist with a graded set of anxiety-producing stimuli to present to the client in conjunction with a counterconditioning agent in order to remove the anxiety attached to the stimuli.

Imitative (Social) Learning   A process whereby an observer learns a particular response by watching some other person (the model) in the environment perform the response.

Intermittent Reinforcement (Partial Reinforcement)   Reinforcement given after some correct responses, but not all. The converse of continuous reinforcement.

Negative Reinforcer   A stimulus that increases the probability of a response when removed following that response, such as an electric shock or disapproval.

Negative Reinforcement   A form of conditioning involving the removal of an aversive event as a result of the appearance (or disappearance) of the target behavior.

Neurotic Behavior   Any persistent habit of unadaptive behavior acquired by learning in a physiologically normal organism. Anxiety is usually the central constituent of this behavior, being invariably present in the causal situation.

Operant Conditioning   Operant conditioning is a theory of learning derived from the work of B. F. Skinner. The essential difference between operant and classical conditioning is that in operant conditioning, the unconditional stimulus follows some predetermined behavior when that behavior occurs spontaneously. In this procedure, the unconditioned stimulus is called a reinforcer.

Positive Reinforcer   A stimulus that increases the probability of a response when presented following that response, such as food or approval.

Positive Reinforcement   A form of conditioning in which the individual receives something pleasurable or desirable as a consequence of his behavior.

Programmed Instruction   A Skinnerian approach to education wherein specific correct responses are reinforced, often by a teaching machine, in a sequence designed to produce optimal learning.

Punishment   An interactional behavior involving the application of an aversive event as a result of the individual's engaging in a particular behavior. Punishment, the converse of reinforcement, is applied only to those behaviors that are to be eliminated.

Reciprocal Inhibition   The elimination or weakening of old responses by new ones. When a response is inhibited by an incompatible response and if a major drive reduction follows, a significant amount of conditioned inhibition of the response will be developed.

Reinforcement   A specified event that strengthens the tendency for a response to be repeated.

Response   A single instance of an operant, such as one peck on the disk in a Skinner box.

Response Induction   A change in the probability of a response that has not itself been conditioned, because it is similar to one that has.

Response Shaping   The process of moving from simple behaviors that are approximations of the final behavior to a final complex behavior. Through this process, certain behaviors that are close approximations of the desired behavior are reinforced, whereas other behaviors are not reinforced. At each stage of this process, a closer approximation of the desired behavior is required before reinforcement is given.

Satiation   Decreasing the probability of an operant by providing reinforcement without requiring the correct response to be made.

Schedules of Reinforcement   Programs of continuous or (more frequently) intermittent reinforcement, including interval schedules, ratio schedules, and various combinations thereof.

Spontaneous Recovery   A temporary increase in the probability of an operant that is undergoing extinction, which occurs at the beginning of a new experimental session without an additional reinforcement.

Systematic Desensitization   A form of behavior therapy, devised by Joseph Wolpe, wherein the client imagines a hierarchical sequence of feared stimuli and inhibits the resulting anxiety by practicing previously taught techniques of muscular relaxation. Alternatively, *in vivo* desensitization may be used with clients who are unable to imagine the feared situations vividly enough to feel anxious.

Token Economy   A detailed and complicated form of behavior therapy, based on Skinnerian operant conditioning, wherein desirable behaviors are followed with conditioned positive reinforcers (such as plastic tokens) that can later be exchanged for more primary reinforcers chosen by the client.

Unconditioned Response   An automatic, unlearned response elicited by an unconditioned stimulus.

Unconditioned Stimulus   A stimulus that automatically elicits a particular (unconditioned) response, without any learning or conditioning being necessary.

Variable-Interval Schedule (VI)   Reinforcing the first correct response that occurs after a varying interval of time, measured from the preceding reinforcement, with the series of intervals having a specified mean. A schedule of intermittent reinforcement.

Variable-Ratio Schedule (VR)   Reinforcing the last of a varying number of correct responses, counted from the preceding reinforcement, with the series of ratios having a specified mean. A schedule of intermittent reinforcement.

SUGGESTED READING

Bandura, A. (1969). *Principles of behavior modification.* New York: Holt, Rinehart & Winston.

Krumboltz, J. D. (Ed.) (1966). *Revolution in counseling: Implications of behavioral science.* Boston, MA: Houghton Mifflin.

Skinner, B. F. (1971). *Beyond freedom and dignity.* New York: Alfred A. Knopf.

Wolpe, J., & Lazarus, A. A. (1966). *Behavior therapy techniques.* New York: Pergamon Press.

REFERENCES

Adelsberg, M. (1994). The integration of behavioral principles and a psychodynamic viewpoint in the treatment of adolescents on an intermediate inpatient unit. *Psychiatric Quarterly, 65,* 135–147.

Alberti, R. E. & Emmons, M. C. (1982). *Your perfect right: A guide to assertive behavior* (4th ed.). San Luis Obispo, CA: Impact.

Ayllon, T., & Azrin, N. H. (1968). *The token economy: A motivational system for therapy and rehabilitation.* New York: Appleton-Century-Crofts.

Babcock, J. C., & Jacobson, N. S. (1993). A program of research on behavioral marital therapy: Hot spots and smoldering embers in marital therapy research. *Journal of Social and Personal Relationships, 10,* 119–135.

Baker, T. B., & Cannon, D. S. (1979). Taste aversion therapy with alcoholics: Techniques and evidence of a conditioned response. *Behavior Research and Therapy, 17,* 229–242.

Bandura, A. (1969). *Principles of behavior modification.* New York: Holt, Rinehart & Winston.

Bandura, A. (1977). *Social learning theory.* Englewood Cliffs, NJ: Prentice-Hall.

Bandura, A. (1986). *Social foundations of thought and action: A social cognitive theory.* Englewood Cliffs, NJ: Prentice-Hall.

Bandura, A., & Walters, R. (1963). *Social learning and personality development.* New York: Holt, Rinehart & Winston.

Bellack, A. S., & Hersen, M. S. (Eds.). (1987). *Dictionary of behavior therapy techniques.* New York: Pergamon Press.

Bijou, S. W., Birnbrauer, J. S., Kidder, J. D., & Tague, C. (1966). Programmed instruction as an approach to the teaching of reading, writing, and arithmetic to retarded children. *Psychological Record, 16,* 505–522.

Blackham, G. J., & Siberman, A. (1971). *Modification of child behavior.* Belmont, CA: Wadsworth.

Bornstein, P., & Kazdin, A. E. (Eds). (1985). *Handbook of clinical behavior therapy with children.* Monterey, CA: Brooks/Cole.

Brownell, K. D., & Barlow, D. H. (1976). Measurement and treatment of two sexual deviations in one person. *Journal of Behavior Therapy and Experimental Psychiatry, 7,* 349–354.

Brownell, K. D., Hayes, S. C., & Barlow, D. H. (1977). Patterns of appropriate and deviant sexual arousal: The behavioral treatment of multiple sexual deviations. *Journal of Consulting and Clinical Psychology, 45,* 1144–1155.

Cannon, D. S., & Baker, T. B. (1981). Emetic and electric shock alcohol aversion therapy: Assessment of conditioning. *Journal of Consulting and Clinical Psychology, 49,* 20–33.

Cautela, J. R. (1976). Behavior therapy and self-control: Techniques and implications. In C. Franks (Ed.), *Behavior therapy: Appraisal and status* (pp. 323–340). New York: McGraw-Hill.

Clement, U., & Schmidt, G. (1983). The outcome of couple therapy for sexual dysfunctions using three different formats. *Journal of Sex and Marital Therapy, 9,* 67–78.

Craighead, W. E. (1982). A brief clinical history of cognitive-behavior therapy with children. *School Psychology Review, 11,* 5–13.

Crowe, M. J., Gillan, P., & Golombock, S. (1981). Form and content in the conjoint treatment of sexual dysfunction: A controlled study. *Behavior Research and Therapy, 19,* 47–54.

Elkins, R. L. (1980). Covert sensitization treatment of alcoholism: contributions of successful conditioning to subsequent abstinence maintenance. *Addictive Behavior, 5,* 67–89.

Emmelkamp, P. M. G. (1974). Self-observation versus flooding in the treatment of agoraphobia. *Behavior Research and Therapy, 12,* 229–237.

Emmelkamp, P. M. G., Brilman, E., Kuipers, H., & Mersch, P. P. (1986). The treatment of agoraphobia: A comparison of self-instructional training, rational emotive therapy and exposure in vivo. *Behavior Modification, 10,* 37–53.

Emmelkamp, P. M. G., Van der Helm, M., MacGillavry, D., & Van Zanten, B. (1984). Marital therapy with clinically distressed couples: A comparative evaluation of system-theoretic, contingency contracting and communication skills approaches. In K. Hahlweg & N. Jacobson (Eds.), *Marital therapy and interaction.* New York: Guilford Press.

Emmelkamp, P. M. G., & Wessels, H. (1975). Flooding in imagination vs. flooding in vivo: A comparison with agoraphobics. *Behavior Research and Therapy, 13,* 7–16.

Erwin, E. (1992). Current philosophical issues in the scientific evaluation of behavior therapy theory and outcome. *Behavior Therapy, 23,* 151–171.

Evans, D. R. (1970). Subjective variables and treatment effects in aversion therapy. *Behavior Research and Therapy, 8,* 147–152.

Eysenck, H. J. (1959), Learning theory and behavior therapy. *British Journal of Medical Science, 105,* 61-75.

Eysenck, H. J. (1960). *Behavior therapy and the neuroses: Readings in modern methods of treatment derived from learning theory.* New York: Pergamon Press.

Fals, S., & Lucente, S. (1994). Treating obsessive-compulsive disorder among substance abusers. *Psychology of Addictive Behaviors, 8,* 14–26.

Farkas, G. M. (1980). An ontological analysis of behavior therapy. *American Psychologist, 35,* 364–374.

Follette, W. C., & Houts, A. C. (1992). Philosophical and theoretical problems for behavior therapy. *Behavior Therapy, 23,* 251–262.

Ford, J. D. (1978). Therapeutic relationship in behavior therapy: An empirical analysis. *Journal of Consulting and Clinical Psychology, 46,* 1302–1314.

Galassi, J. P., & Perot, A. R. (1992). What you should know about behavioral assessment. *Journal of Counseling and Development, 70,* 624–631.

Gardner, P., & Oei, T. S. (1981). Depression and self-esteem: An investigation that used behavioral and cognitive approaches to the treatment of clinically depressed clients. *Journal of Clinical Psychology, 37,* 128–135.

Gilliland, B. E., James, R. K., & Bowman, J. T. (1989). *Theories and strategies in counseling and psychotherapy* (2nd ed.). Boston: Allyn & Bacon.

Goldiamond, I. (1973). A diary of self-modification. *Psychology Today.* November, 188.

Goldfried, M. R., & Davison, G. C. (1976). *Clinical behavior therapy.* New York: Holt, Rinehart & Winston.

Goodell, R. (1975, August). The visible scientist. *APA Monitor, 1,* 8.

Groden, G., & Cautela, J. R. (1981). Behavior therapy: A survey of procedures for counselors. *Personnel and Guidance Journal, 60,* 175–179.

Hartman, L. M., & Dally, E. M. (1983). Relationship factors in the treatment of sexual dysfunction. *Behavior Research and Therapy, 21,* 153–160.

Hersen, M., Bellack, A. S., Himmelhoch, J. M., & Thase, M. E. (1984). Effects of social skill training, amitriptyline, and psychotherapy in unipolar depressed women. *Behavior Therapy, 15,* 21–40.

Hosford, R., & deVisser, L. (1974). *Behavioral approaches to counseling: An introduction.* Washington, DC: American Personnel and Guidance Press.

Hundert, J. (1994). The ecobehavioral relationship between teachers' and disabled preschoolers' behaviors before and after supervisor training. *Journal of Behavioral Education, 4,* 75–91.

Jacobson, N. S. (1984). A component analysis of behavioral marital therapy: The relative effectiveness of behavior exchange and communication/problem-solving training. *Journal of Consulting and Clinical Psychology, 52,* 295–305.

Jacobson, N. S., Fruzzetti, A. E., Dobson, K. S., & Whisman, M. (1993). Couple therapy as a treatment for depression. *Journal of Consulting and Clinical Psychology, 61,* 516–519.

Jones, H. G. (1956). The application of conditioning and learning techniques to the treatment of a psychiatric patient. *Journal of Abnormal and Social Psychology, 52,* 414–419.

Jones, M. C. (1924). The elimination of children's fears. *Journal of Experimental Psychology, 7,* 383–390.

Kanfer, F. H., & Goldstein, A. P. (1980). *Helping people change* (2nd ed.). New York: Pergamon Press.

Kavanagh, D. J. (1994). Issues in multidisciplinary training of cognitive-behavioral interventions. *Behavior Change, 11,* 38–44.

Kazdin, A. E. (1978). Behavior therapy: Evolution and expansion. *The Counseling Psychologist, 7,* 34–37.

Kazdin, A. E., & Wilson, G. T. (1978). *Evaluation of behavior therapy: Issues, evidence and research strategies.* Cambridge, MA: Ballinger.

Kelly, A., & Halford, W. K. (1993). Adapting behavioral therapy to the needs of a secondary marriage: A case evaluation. *Behavioral Psychotherapy, 21,* 115–125.

Krumboltz, J. D. (Ed.). (1966). *Revolution in counseling: Implications of behavioral science.* Boston, MA: Houghton Mifflin.

Krumboltz, J. D. & Thoresen, C. E. (Eds.). (1976). *Counseling Methods.* New York: Holt, Rinehart and Winston.

Lazarus, A. A. (1958). New methods of psychotherapy: A case study. *South African Medical Journal, 32,* 660–663.

Lazarus, A. A. (1971). *Behavior therapy and beyond.* New York: McGraw-Hill.

Lazarus, A. A. (1989). *The practice of multimodal therapy.* Baltimore: John Hopkins University Press.

Levin, S. M., Barry, S. M., Camaro, S., Wolfinsohn, L., & Smith, A. (1977). Variations of covert sensitization in the treatment of pedophilic behavior. A case study. *Journal of Consulting and Clinical Psychology, 45,* 896–907.

Lewinsohn, P. M. (1975). The behavioral study and treatment of depression. In M. Hersen, R. M. Eisler, & P. M. Miller (Eds.), *Progress in behavior modification* (Vol. 1, pp. 19–59). New York: Academic Press.

Liberman, R. P., Van Putten, T., Marshall, B. D., & Mintz, J. (1994). Optimal drug and behavior therapy for treatment-refactory schizophrenic patients. *American Journal of Psychiatry, 151,* 756–759.

Lindsley, O. R., Skinner, B. F., & Solomon, H. C. (1953). *Studies in behavior therapy, Status Report 1.* Waltham, MA: Metropolitan State Hospital.

Maletzky, B. M. (1980). Assisted covert sensitization. In D. J. Cox & R. J. Daitzman (Eds.), *Exhibitionism: Description, assessment and treatment.* New York: Garland.

Marks, I. M. (1994). Behavior therapy as an aid to self-care. *Current Directions in Psychological Science, 3,* 19–22.

Masters, J. C., Burish, T. G., Hollon, S. D., & Rimm, D. C. (1987). *Behavior therapy: Techniques and empirical findings* (3rd ed.) San Diego, CA: Harcourt Brace Jovanovich.

Meyer, V. (1957). The treatment of two phobic patients on the basis of learning principles. *Journal of Abnormal and Social Psychology, 55,* 261–266.

Milne, D., Cowie, I., Gormly, A., & White, C. (1992). Social supporters and behavior therapists: Three studies on the form and function of their help. *Behavioral Psychotherapy, 20,* 343–354.

Moore, K. J., & Shannon, K. K. (1993). The development of superstitious beliefs in the effectiveness of treatment of anger: Evidence for the importance of experimental program evaluation in applied settings. *Behavioral Residential Treatment, 8,* 147–161.

Mower, O. H. (1947). On the dual nature of learning—A reinterpretation of "conditioning" and "problem solving." *Harvard Educational Review, 17,* 102–148.

Nelson, R. O., & Barlow, D. H. (1981). Behavioral assessment: Basic strategies and initial procedures. In D. H. Barlow (Ed.), *Behavioral assessment of adult disorders* (pp. 13–43). New York: Guilford Press.

Nye, R. D. (1992). *The legacy of B. F. Skinner.* Pacific Grove, CA: Brooks/Cole.

O'Leary, K., & Wilson, G. (1987). *Behavior therapy: Application and outcome* (2nd ed.). Englewood Cliffs, NJ: Prentice-Hall.

O'Leary, K. D., & Turkewitz, H. (1978). The treatment of marital disorder from a behavioral perspective. In T. J. Paolino & B. S. McCrady (Eds.), *Marriage and marital therapy* (pp. 164–179). New York: Brunner/Mazel.

Obler, M. (1973). Systematic desensitization in sexual disorders. *Journal of behavior Therapy and Experimental Psychiatry, 4,* 93–101.

Olson, P. P., Ganley, R., Devine, V. T., & Dorsey, G. C. (1981). Long-term effects of behavioral versus insight-oriented therapy with inpatient alcoholics. *Journal of Consulting and Clinical Psychology, 49,* 866–877.

Perry, M. A., & Furukawa, M. J. (1980). Modeling methods. In F. H. Kanfer & A. P. Goldstein (Eds.), *Helping people change* (pp. 131–171). New York: Pergamon Press.

Quinsey, V. L., Bergersen, S. G., & Steinman, C. M. (1976). Changes in physiological and verbal responses of child molesters during aversion therapy. *Canadian Journal of Behavioral Science, 8,* 202–212.

Rasnake, L. K. (1993). Treatment acceptability research: Relevance to treatment selection decisions. *Child and Adolescent Mental Health Care, 3,* 31–47.

Rehm, L. P. (1977). A self-control model of depression. *Behavior Therapy, 8,* 787–804.

Ross, A. O. (1981). *Child behavior therapy.* New York: John Wiley.

Roth, A. D., & Church, J. A. (1994). The use of revised habituation in the treatment of obsessive-compulsive disorders. *British Journal of Clinical Psychology, 33,* 201–204.

Salter, A. (1949). *Conditioned reflex therapy.* New York: Farrar, Straus.

Samelson, F. J. B. (1980). Watson's Little Albert, Cyril Burt's twins, and the need for a critical science. *American Psychologist, 35,* 619–625.

Sechrest, L., & Smith, B. (1994). Psychotherapy is the practice of psychology. *Journal of Psychotherapy Integration, 4,* 1–29.

Skinner, B. F. (1938). *The behavior of organisms: An experimental analysis.* New York: Appleton-Century-Crofts.

Skinner, B. F. (1948). *Walden two.* New York: Macmillan.

Skinner, B. F. (1953). *Science and human behavior.* New York: Macmillan.

Skinner, B. F. (1957). *Verbal behavior.* New York: MacMillan.

Skinner, B. F. (1968). *The technology of teaching.* New York: Appleton-Century-Crofts.

Skinner, B. F. (1971). *Beyond freedom and dignity.* New York: Alfred A. Knopf.

Skinner, B. F. (1974). *About behaviorism.* New York: Alfred A. Knopf.

Skinner, B. F. (1976). *Particulars of my life.* New York: Alfred A. Knopf.

Skinner, B. F. (1989). *Recent issues in the analysis of behavior.* Columbus, OH: Charles E. Merrill.

Skinner, B. F., & Lindsley, O. R. (1954). *Studies in Behavior Therapy, Status Reports II and III.* Office of Naval Research Contracts, Norfolk, VA.

Stern, R., & Marks, I. M. (1973). Brief and prolonged flooding: A comparison in agoraphobic patients. *Archives of General Psychiatry, 28,* 270–276.

Taylor, S., & McLean, P. (1993). Outcome profiles in the treatment of unipolar depression. *Behavior Research and Therapy, 31,* 325–330.

Thase, M. E., Reynolds, C. F., Frank, E., & Simons, A. D. (1994). Response to cognitive-behavioral therapy in chronic depression. *Journal of Psychotherpay Practice and Research, 3,* 204–214.

Thoresen, C. E. (1969). The counselor as an applied behavioral scientist. *Personnel and Guidance Journal, 47,* 841–848.

Turkat, I. D., & Feuerstein, M. (1978). Behavior modification and the public misconception. *American Psychologist, 33,* 194.

Turner, S. M., Beidel, D. C., Cooley, M. R., & Woody, S. R. (1994). A multicomponent behavioral treatment for social phobia. *Behavior Research and Therapy, 32,* 381–390.

Watson, J. B. (1913). Psychology as the behaviorist views it. *Psychological Review, 20,* 158–177.

Watson, J. B. (1919). *Behavior from the standpoint of a behaviorist.* Philadelphia: J. B. Lippincott.

Watson, J. B. (1924). *Behaviorism.* New York: W. W. Norton.

Wilson, G. T. (1989). Behavior therapy. In R. Corsini & D. Wedding (Eds.), *Current psychotherapies* (4th ed., pp. 241–284). Itasca, IL: F. E. Peacock.

Wilson, G. T. (1995). Behavior therapy. In R. J. Corsini & D. Wedding (Eds.), *Current psychotherapies* (5th Ed.) (pp. 197–228). Itasca, IL: F.E. Peacock.

Wilson, P. H. (1982). Combined pharmacological and behavioral treatment of depression. *Behavior Research and Therapy, 20,* 173–184.

Wilson, P. H., Goldin, J. C., & Charboneau-Powis, M. (1983). Comparative efficacy of behavioral and cognitive treatments of depression. *Cognitive Therapy and Research, 7,* 11–124.

Wolf, M. M., Risley, T. R., & Mees, H. L. (1964). Application of operant conditioning procedures to the behavior problems of an autistic child. *Behavior Research and Therapy, 1,* 305–312.

Wolpe, J. (1958). *Psychotherapy by reciprocal inhibition.* Stanford, CA: Stanford University Press.

Wolpe, J. (1981). Behavior therapy versus psychoanalysis: Therapeutic and social implications. *American Psychologist, 36,* 159–164.

Wolpe, J. (1982). *The practice of behavior therapy* (3rd ed.). New York: Pergamon Press.

Wolpe, J., & Lazarus, A. A. (1966). *Behavior therapy techniques.* New York: Pergamon Press.

Yates, A. J. (1958). The application of learning theory to the treatment of tics. *Journal of Abnormal and Social Psychology, 56,* 175–182.

Yates, A. J. (1980). *Biofeedback and the modification of behavior.* New York: Plenum Press.

Zeiss, A. M., Lewinsohn, P. M., & Munoz, R. F. (1979). Nonspecific improvement effects in depression using interpersonal skills training, pleasant activity schedules, or cognitive training. *Journal of Consulting and Clinical Psychology, 47,* 427–439.

CHAPTER 13

Rational-Emotive and Other Cognitive Theories

Chapter Outline

Introduction
Brief Biography
Historical Development
View of Human Nature
Development of Maladaptive Behavior
Function of the Therapist
Goals of Therapy
Major Methods and Techniques
Application
Other Cognitively Based Theories
Critical Analysis
Current Status
Chapter Summary
Key Terms
Suggested Reading

INTRODUCTION

The comedian Mel Brooks tells the story of a crotchety grandfather who had troubled his family for years with an annoying, compulsive habit. He tore paper into bits and scattered the little pieces wherever he went. For years the family dragged him to world-renowned psychoanalysts, Adlerian therapists, Existential therapists, and so on—all to no avail. The man would not stop tearing paper. Finally, the family turned to an obscure, off-beat therapist. With the anxious family looking on, this modern therapist put his arm around the patient's should and said, "Let's take a little walk." The doctor walked with the old man from one end of the tiny office to the other, all the while whispering in his client's ear. Finally they stopped, and the doctor told the family: "You can take him home now. He's cured."

The man didn't tear paper for days. A year went by, and the habit still had not returned. The family was amazed and grateful, but remained curious about this new therapeutic technique. Finally they telephoned the therapist and begged him to repeat what he had said to the grandfather. The miracle worker said, "I told him, 'Don't tear paper.'"

More and more clients are seeking out commonsense therapeutic approaches that provide rapid and verifiable results. As a result, cognitive therapeutic strategies that emphasize logic and reason have become increasingly attractive. After all, who wouldn't want the benefits of simple problem-solving techniques that involve a short-term commitment and a minimal amount of angst?

The pioneer of these methods has been alternately described as "abrasive, impatient, and lacking in...social graces," and as "brilliant, sensitive, perceptive, humorous, and stimulating" (Weinrach, 1980, p. 152). His rugged language is more often found in a bar than a classroom. Despite his rough edges, or perhaps because of them, Albert Ellis blazed the trail for a new kind of counseling strategy known today as rational-emotive therapy, which remains one of the most popular contemporary approaches to counseling.

This chapter explores the history, theory, and application of Ellis's therapeutic technique, which is the most widely recognized cognitive approach, but it also presents other cognitively based therapeutic approaches that have made significant contributions to the counseling field.

BRIEF BIOGRAPHY

Albert Ellis, the founder and moving force behind rational-emotive therapy, was born into a devout Jewish family in Pittsburgh, Pennsylvania, in 1913. When he was 4 years old, his family moved to New York, where he grew up on the mean streets of the Bronx. Although his father was often absent, Ellis describes him in mostly positive terms, remarking that he acquired his intelligence, drive, and persistence from his father and his independent and often idiosyncratic behavior from his mother (Wiener, 1988). Describing her method of parenting as "benign neglect," Ellis credits his early independence of thought to his parents' hands-off approach to child rearing (Dryden, 1989). At age 5 years Ellis almost died from tonsillitis and later suffered from diabetes (Dryden, 1989; Morris & Kanitz, 1975). By age 7 years Ellis was largely on his own (Weinrach, 1980).

There's nothing either good or bad but thinking makes it so.

—Shakespeare

Ellis was 12 when his parents divorced. It was then that he questioned much of his early religious training and gave up plans to be a teacher of Hebrew. Instead he became a self-described "probabilistic atheist, " one who does not believe that God exists but would accept empirical evidence to the contrary.

Albert Ellis (1913–   ).
(Courtesy of The Milton H. Erickson Foundation, Inc., Phoenix, Arizona)

Even as a young adolescent in junior high school, Ellis dreamed of becoming a novelist. He planned to work as an accountant and save enough money to retire at age 30 to devote his time entirely to writing. And, in fact, he did complete a baccalaureate degree in business administration in 1934 at City College of New York. Despite the ravages of the depression, Ellis was gainfully employed in business until the mid-1940s. When he was not working, he wrote fiction, but his literary efforts were disappointing. After eight of his novels were rejected by publishers, Ellis decided to study psychology and write nonfiction. Ellis received a master's degree in 1943 and a Ph.D. in clinical psychology in 1947 from Columbia University. After earning his doctorate, Ellis became senior clinical psychologist at the New Jersey State Hospital and taught part-time at Rutgers University.

Inevitably, Ellis became interested in psychoanalysis. Since institutions that specialized in psychoanalytic training admitted only medical professionals, Ellis was hard pressed to find the training he desired. He finally succeeded in obtaining personal analysis for 3 years from the Karen Horney group. By the middle 1950s, however, Ellis' faith in psychoanalysis had deteriorated. Although his patients were gaining psychoanalytic insight and understanding, they seemed to continue in their dysfunctional behavior. Becoming increasingly more active and more directive with his patients, Ellis soon began practicing his own unique approach to therapy.

Ellis' original passion for writing would appear to have been rekindled by his study of psychology. He has served as editor for 10 journals, written over 600 articles, produced numerous films and tapes, and published nearly 50 books, some of which have been written for the general public, for example, *How to Live with a "Neurotic"* (1957) and *The Intelligent Woman's Guide to Dating and Mating* (1979a). His writings for professional therapists include *A Guide to New Rational Living* with Robert A. Harper (1975), *Humanistic Psychotherapy* (1973), *Overcoming Resistance* (1985), and *Rational-Emotive Couples Therapy* with Sichel, Yeager, DiMattio, & DiGuiseppe (1969).

Today Ellis lives in New York City, where he sees as many as 80 clients each week and supervises up to eight group sessions. He also gives about 200 workshops annually. Requests for his lectures, consultations, seminars, professional conferences, and personal appearances on radio and television continue unabated (Weinrach, 1980).

HISTORICAL DEVELOPMENT

The origins of rational-emotive therapy can be traced to the philosophy of Stoicism in ancient Greece, which distinguished an act from its interpretation. According to the Stoics, we are not so much disturbed by what happens to us, as by how we *interpret* what happens to us.

Whereas Stoics such as the Greek Epictetus and the Roman Marcus Aurelius planted the seeds of cognitive therapy, it wasn't until recently that these seeds were cultivated. Through personal and clinical experiences, Albert Ellis came to agree with the ancients that we are truly less influenced by the event itself than by what we choose to think about the event. Given this fundamental premise, Ellis developed a humanistic theory of psychotherapy that "squarely places man in the center of the universe and of his own emotional fate and gives him full responsibility for choosing to make or not to make himself seriously disturbed" (Ellis, 1973, p. 10).

Ellis' contemporary theory has flourished within the context of what is sometimes called the *cognitive revolution,* a scientific revolution that has assembled research in physiology, philosophy, linguistics, computer science, medicine, and various other areas of psychology (Dobson, 1988a, 1988b). There has been more research in human cognition over the past 20 years, writes Hunt (1982), than throughout all the previous history of scientific study.

Despite Ellis' original training and diligent practice of psychoanalysis, he remained dissatisfied when his patients' perfectionist and self-condemning behaviors remained unchanged. It was about this time that Ellis began studying learning theory, which he applied in his clinical practice. Although all the pieces of Ellis' therapeutic montage were not yet in place, his therapeutic effectiveness improved.

Ellis quietly observed that his patients' behaviors were not so much the singular result of their social learning and conditioning as of their attitudes and perceptions. A hunch led Ellis to a new hypothesis. He discovered that his patients' dysfunctional behaviors resulted from a predisposition to retain tenacious and irrational ideas and thoughts. Although to some, this assumption may have seemed little more than a classical commonplace, it motivated Ellis to work diligently toward a rational approach to psychotherapy (Ellis, 1993).

In recounting the beginnings of his theory, Ellis talks about his own decision to cope with profound shyness and fear of approaching women during his undergraduate days. As Ellis tells it, it was only by making himself extremely

Men are disturbed not by things, but by the views which they take of them.

—Epictetus

uncomfortable that he finally became comfortable in approaching women. Indeed, for 1 month he forced himself to approach and talk with more than 100 unfamiliar women in the Bronx Botanical Gardens, until he could do so comfortably. As he wryly explained, recalling the episode, his successful conquest of his social phobia was scarcely a matter of reinforcement: He managed to arrange for only a single date, and she never showed up. Nevertheless, he had taken action in the face of irrational doubts and fears.

Based as much on a philosophical as a psychological model, then, Ellis explained his new and radical approach to psychotherapy in a series of articles that culminated with the publication of *Reason and Emotion in Psychotherapy* in 1962. The therapeutic technique that emerged would come to be known as rational-emotive therapy, usually designated by its now-familiar acronym, RET. During his methodological pilgrimage, Ellis claims to have progressed from an improvement rate of 60% in 100 sessions with psychoanalytic techniques to 90% in only 10 or so sessions, because of this new approach (Ellis, 1979b).

VIEW OF HUMAN NATURE

Although Ellis believes that we are persistently buffeted by the unpredictable currents of living, he does not maintain that we are victims of the storms about us. Instead, he claims that we have final dominion over much of the pleasure and pain that comes from circumstances beyond our control. Since RET emphasizes that it is one's thoughts that affect, and often create, our feelings, the attention of the therapist is on the thought processes (Ellis, 1990). Although this theory does not ignore the emotional aspects of the human condition—the human psyche is considered to be intricately composed of both thoughts and feelings—it is nevertheless our thoughts that are central to RET's view of human nature. As a result, the efficacy of RET stems from our capacity to think rationally.

Ellis often summarized his view of human nature by means of a so-called A-B-C- theory of our behavior (Grieger, 1986a, 1986b). People frequently come to therapy because of a *consequence* (C), an emotional or behavioral condition that is disturbing them. It is common for them to attribute their emotional or behavioral consequence to *activating events* (A)—an external event, such as a financial setback or a fight with a friend, for instance, or a person's own thoughts or behavior—as if there were some necessary and invariable causal relationship between A and C. But according to Ellis, people are not disturbed by the events themselves, but by the *beliefs* (B) they hold about those events.

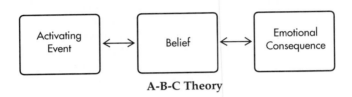

A-B-C Theory

From the point of view of RET, whenever the client is disturbed or dysfunctional at point C (the emotional consequence), it is not because of what is happening at point A (the activating event). Rather, "it is because of his own irrational and unvalidating suppositions at point B (his belief system)" (Ellis, 1971, p. 6). For example, if clients feel depressed at point C, it is not because they have been rejected by someone or have failed an exam at point A, but because they are convincing themselves of irrational beliefs at point B (e.g., "I'll never have a girlfriend" or "I'm stupid"). Ellis stresses that the ABC theory "is central to the whole field of RET and cognitive-behavior therapy and has an enormous amount of research that solidly supports it" (Ellis, 1977a, p. 3).

While the A-B-Cs of RET are central to its approach to personality, Ellis (1979b, 1979c, 1979d) makes several further assumptions about human nature as well. RET embraces a *soft determinism*, which allows human beings to resist only with great difficulty the strong pressures that surround them. Although human nature is, to some extent, determined by these extraordinary biological and social pressures, the fact remains that we do have free will and can create our own worlds. Ellis does not believe that human beings are good or evil, angels or devils; they are simply human beings, nothing more. Nevertheless, they are born with inner conflicting tendencies. They have a strong tendency to be reasonable and to find fulfillment while also being drawn to act irrationally and to thwart their own growth. One of the strongest human, innate tendencies is to be influenced by family and by culture.

Patterson (1980) notes several additional assumptions about the nature of humanity that are foundational to the cognitive approach to therapy. Most importantly, the RET therapist believes that individuals are uniquely rational and irrational. When they behave and think rationally, they are effective, happy, and competent. When they are irrational, however, they think illogically, resulting in psychological disturbance. And since thought and emotion accompany one another—since emotion is, in effect, biased, prejudiced, highly personalized, irrational thought—this is an emotional disturbance as well.

Such irrational thinking originates in the early illogical learning toward which children are biologically disposed and which they acquire from their parents and culture. In the process of growing up, children are taught to think and feel certain things about themselves and others. When emotions such as love and joy are associated with the idea of "This is good," they become positive human emotions; when emotions such as anger or depression become associated with "This is bad," they become negative emotions. As a result, it is not the situation, but that which we have been taught to associate with it, our perceptions of it, that make it negative or unpleasant.

We talk ourselves into this negative frame of mind, Ellis emphasizes. After all, human beings are verbal animals; we think in symbols and in language. Continuing states of emotional disturbance, then, are the result of self-verbalization, and they are determined, not by external circumstances or events, but by our perceptions and attitudes toward these events, which are incorporated in our internalized discussion of them. Disturbed individuals perpetuate this disturbance, maintaining illogical behavior by internally verbalizing irrational ideas and thoughts. And since, as noted above, thinking accompanies emotion, if the emotional disturbance persists, irrational thinking necessarily persists as well.

> *Reason is a light that God has kindled in the soul.*
>
> —Aristotle

But we are not victims of our circumstances, of past conditioning. In the same way in which people have been talked into—and have talked themselves into—their maladjustment, so they can talk and think their way out again. They can think and work until they actually make themselves different. The RET counselor believes, then, that people have the capacity to confront their value systems and reindoctrinate themselves with different beliefs, ideas, and values. Moreover, people have vast untapped resources for actualizing their potentials and for changing their personal and social destinies. According to Ellis, people have the power to understand their limitations, to change views and values that were uncritically accepted as a child, and to challenge self-defeating tendencies (see Sidebar 13-1).

Therefore, the goal of counseling is to enable clients to reorganize their perceptions and thought processes, so that their thinking becomes logical and rational. Only then can they truly understand how illogical (senseless) and irrational (without mental clarity) their self-verbalizations are. And only then can they begin to attack their negative and self-defeating thoughts. Ultimately, the goal is to clarify clients' thinking so self-verbalizations become more logical and efficient and are no longer producing negative emotions and self-defeating behavior.

TALKING TO YOURSELF

They say there's nothing wrong with talking to yourself, but when you start answering back, it's time to worry. They're wrong. Talking aloud to yourself in public isn't a sign of mental health, but holding an internal dialogue is quite normal and very useful. In fact, inner conversations have a powerful impact on emotional well-being and motivation. Becoming aware of exactly what you are saying to yourself about your self can help you understand why you react the way you do to events and people in your life. It can also give you a handle on controlling your moods, repeating your successes, and short-circuiting your shortcomings.

Positive self-talk can do a lot to give you the confidence that frees you to serve, and to use your talents to the fullest. If public speaking makes you nervous, use your inner voice to reassure yourself: "You can do it. You've done it well before. Why else would they have asked you to do it again?" Behind your nervousness may well be negative thoughts such as: "There are 300 people out there! I'll never hold their attention." Since self-talk has a way of becoming self-fulfilling prophecy, negative thinking can spell trouble. That's why it's important to monitor your inner voice.

Take the case of a 39-year-old mother who has persistent feelings of depression. Her inner voice tells her: "I'm lost. I feel like such a failure. I know I should be more patient with my kids, but they're such losers. I've given up even talking to them. It's just not fair. My friends' kids are perfect but mine are a mess and so is my life." These ruminations are a garbage bag of negatively loaded words and labels ("failure," "losers"); errors in the way she processes information ("My friends' kids are perfect"); faulty assumptions ("It's not

fair"—neither, of course, is life), and guilt-inducing expectations ("I should…").

This mother needs to identify these errors and distortions and develop a more accurate internal dialogue ("I know I'm not a perfect mother, but nobody is perfect. I do the best I can with my kids, and they're not perfect either. But, if I work on being more patient and communicating better, maybe the problems we've been having can be worked out"). The revised self-talk improves her mood and motivation, diffuses her anger, and directs her toward actions that can address some of her difficulties. This can eventually lead to positive changes in her behavior that improve her relationship with her family.

The real power of self-talk lies in how it changes behavior. Simply correcting your internal programming will improve your mood, but it won't do the most important job. The ultimate purpose of examining what is going on inside your head is to change actions that are self-defeating. Thinking correctly does alter your negative moods, but enduring change comes only with modifying your behavior.

If, for example. Your self-talk tells you, "I can't break up this relationship because I can't stand being alone, even though the relationship is harmful to me," You're likely to stay locked in the same unhappy situation. To make your self-talk more accurate, you might say, "I feel anxious about breaking up and facing the idea that I might be alone for awhile. But if I really want to give myself a chance for the kind of relationship that will make me happy, I must let go of the one I'm in."

Now comes the clincher: To activate the full power of your self-talk, you must follow the path that your new, accurate inner messages point. To find the behavior that goes with your new self-talk, ask yourself these questions: What behavior has my erroneous self-talk generated? How has it hindered me from reaching my goals? What actions does my corrected

Adapted from "The Power of Self-Talk," by Harriet B. Braiker, *Psychology Today* 23(12), 23–27. (December 1989).

self-talk suggest? How will my life be better when I change? When and how will I start to change?

Accurate self-talk should enable you to know how your behavior needs to change. And behavior is what counts. As an old proverb advises: "To know but not to act is not to know at all."

DEVELOPMENT OF MALADAPTIVE BEHAVIOR

The cognitive approach to psychopathology is based on the straightforward assumption that people are both "inherently rational and irrational, sensible and crazy" (Weinrach, 1980, p. 154). Because humans are self-conscious creatures, they observe their disturbance and then make themselves disturbed all over again about being disturbed (Burns & Nolen, 1992).

This theory is based on the premise that maladaptive behavior results from a number of major illogical ideas that are held and perpetuated until a new way of thinking is learned. These illogical ideas and thoughts are designated "inappropriate" or "self-defeating" and result in feelings of worthlessness, depression, rage, anxiety, mania, or self-pity (Ellis & Grieger, 1977; Garamoni, Reynolds, Thase, Frank, 1992; Russell, 1992).

According to Bard (1980, p. 23), the RET counselor will look for a number of symptoms, as evidence of maladaptive behavior. Some clients may report an abusive lifestyle, such as taking drugs, that threatens to shorten the span of enjoyable living. More broadly, they may become preoccupied with short-range enjoyment at the expense of long-range satisfaction. Or they may turn their back on the future altogether, refusing to acquire knowledge, for instance, which might increase their ability to maximize future enjoyment. Others tend to repeat actions, such as making themselves anxious when there is no real danger, which tend to generate immediate and unnecessary discomfort and pain. Still others may fail to cultivate innate capacities for different satisfactions, thus subjecting themselves to frequent periods of boredom, inertia, or dissatisfaction.

Whatever the symptoms, Albert Ellis found that specific, commonly occurring irrational beliefs typically lead to "various kinds of emotional disturbance" (Ellis, 1984a, p. 266):

Being loved and approved by virtually every significant person in our world is necessary for happiness and fulfillment. The need to be loved by everybody is an unattainable goal that renders people less self-directing and more insecure and self-defeating.

To be worthwhile, one should be thoroughly adequate, fully competent, and high achieving in all possible respects. This is another impossibility. People who base their worth on achievements, who turn every situation into a test, can never enjoy what they are doing. They are predestined to a sense of inferiority and constant fear of failure.

Certain people are bad, wicked, or villainous and should be severely blamed and punished. Everyone makes mistakes as a result of stupidity, ignorance, or emotional disturbance. Drawing the worst out of everyone, this blame-and-punishment approach often leads to unacceptable behavior and increased emotional disturbance.

It is awful and catastrophic when conditions are not the way one would very much like them to be. No situation is ever entirely perfect. Even in the best of circumstances, there is always something more that could be done. Treating an event as catastrophic will not change the event; in fact, it makes things worse. If people don't like the situation, they can try to change it, but if it cannot be changed, mature people will learn to adjust, to accept those things beyond their control. Under such circumstances, frustration is normal, of course, but prolonged stress over matters that cannot be altered is illogical.

Unhappiness is caused externally; therefore people have little or no ability to control their sorrows and disturbances. The reality is that most outside events, perceived as harmful, are only psychologically harmful. The events cannot hurt unless they are allowed to. Psychological hurt is a bilateral experience, demanding the cooperation of people's attitudes and reactions. When someone is unkind, rejecting, or annoying, for example, we disturb ourselves by perceiving their words and behavior as negative. Only when we realize that disturbances consist of our own perceptions and judgments does the locus of control shift from the other to ourselves.

If something is or may be dangerous or frightening, one should be terribly concerned about it and should keep dwelling on the possibility of its occurring. Thinking about something doesn't change it; in fact, obsessive concentration on the problem may evolve into a self-fulfilling prophecy, turning clients into victims of their own obsessions.

It is easier to avoid difficulties and responsibilities than to face them. On the other hand, turning our backs on troubles does not solve them either. Usually the difficulty remains, until it eventually looms larger, so that it must be dealt with anyway.

People need to be dependent on someone stronger than themselves. Everyone depends on others to some extent, but overdependency leads to a loss of independence, individualism, and self-expression, resulting in insecurity and an inability to learn.

One's personal history is an all-important determiner of one's present behavior; because something once strongly affected one's life, it will always have a similar effect.

Whereas the past may influence the present, it does not necessarily determine it; often it is used as an excuse to avoid changing our present behavior.

One should be personally upset over other people's problems and conditions. Beyond a general humanitarian concern, there is little to gain from dwelling on other people's problems. Usually they have nothing to do with us, and therefore should not seriously concern us. Even if there is a concern because of family connections or filial relationship, we are not upset by the behavior, but by our perception of the other's behavior, and mature people are able to control their own perceptions. In point of fact, getting upset usually prevents us from accurately understanding the circumstances into which others have fallen and keeps us from effectively helping them to resolve their problems.

There is always a right, precise, and perfect solution to human problems, and it is catastrophic if this perfect solution is not found. The perfect solution does not exist. The search for the final answer, the definitive solution, produces only anxiety and leaves us feeling dissatisfied and empty.

In summary, Goldfried (1988) holds that the two most common irrational beliefs involve approval from others (e.g., "If I am not liked and approved by others, that is terrible and I am no good") and perfection (e.g., "If I don't consistently do a perfect job, then I am no good").

Despite the fact that we are born with the potential to be rational and logical, Ellis (1973) believes that each of us, but especially the child, is gullible and highly suggestible to these various kinds of irrational thoughts. According to Ellis, these examples of "crooked thinking" are the result of distortions during childhood that have been reinforced by contemporary events and associations. "No matter what a person's past history may be, or how his parents, teachers, and other early associates may have helped him to become emotionally disturbed, he only remains disturbed because he still believes some of the unrealistic and illogical thoughts which he originally imbibed" (Ellis & Harper, 1975, p. 50).

As he thinketh in his heart, so is he.
—Proverbs 23:7

FUNCTION OF THE THERAPIST

Intentionally attempting to *lead* patients to a healthier perspective, the rational-emotive therapist is unequivocally directive. In keeping with his view that all psychotherapies are to some degree authoritarian, Ellis (1962, 1967) openly favors therapists' providing a high degree of direction to their clients. He does not mince words on this issue. An irrational belief, he writes, "can be elicited and demolished by any scientist worth his or her salt, and the rational-emotive therapist is exactly that: an exposing and nonsense-annihilating scientist" (1988, p. 199).

Therefore the RET therapist is quite verbal, often challenging or confronting clients, even in the first few sessions. To help them face their illogical thinking as quickly as possible, the therapist will use persuasion and debate in attacking clients' self-defeating patterns even at the outset of counseling (Harrell, Beiman, & Lapointe, 1986). However, he or she will not spend much time exploring the morbid details of the past, of who did what to whom, which are little more than a smoke screen, hiding the real issue of irrational thinking.

The task of the RET counselor is to help clients to straighten out crooked, irrational thinking, to rid themselves of illogical ideas, and to replace them with logical thoughts. Ellis (1973) calls this process, which begins by showing clients how and when they are irrational, Insight Number 1. The next insight, Number 2, occurs when clients understand and are convinced that they feed their own emotional disturbance by reindoctrinating themselves with the same repetitious, irrational ideas. Insight Number 3 allows clients to acknowledge fully that ridding themselves of their disturbances depends on their willingness to challenge their beliefs and develop new ways of thinking.

To accomplish this, the rational-emotive therapist must thoroughly understand belief systems and clearly distinguish rational and irrational beliefs if he or she is to lead clients to this new perspective. Rational beliefs, which are consistent with reality, can be supported with hard evidence and can be corroborated by a group of objective observers. Since irrational beliefs, such as those listed previously, are inconsistent with reality, they are not based on evidence. Both rational and irrational beliefs represent the client's evaluation of "reality," but they lead to different consequences. Irrational beliefs lead to dysfunctional emotional consequences, which interfere with the clients' goals.

In the world of minor lunacy the behavior of both the utterly rational and the totally insane seems equally odd.

—J. K. Galbraith

Although Ellis (1962) urges the therapist to attempt to understand the clients' world views, to see from their frame of reference, he believes it is harmful for the therapist actually to feel clients' disturbances or believe their irrationalities. "Indeed, it is precisely the therapist's ability to comprehend the patient's immature behavior without getting involved in or believing in it that enables him to induce the patient to stop believing in or feeling that this behavior is necessary" (1962, p. 115).

GOALS OF THERAPY

Thus the goal of RET is to "teach" clients to analyze and to correct their distortions of reality, to distinguish their irrational from their rational beliefs, so that they can challenge their irrational beliefs. The result is the reduction or elimination of undesirable emotions (Cohen, 1987). At this juncture, Ellis extends his A-B-C paradigm to include D, E, and F: after (A) teaching clients to recognize activating events, (B) corresponding beliefs, and (C) the emotional and behavioral consequences of these beliefs; the goal of RET is to teach a variety of ways to *dispute* (D) the emotional beliefs and to discriminate or attend to new emotional and behavioral *effects* (E), resulting in new *feelings* (F).

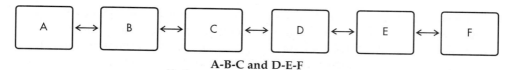

A-B-C and D-E-F

Disputation, which requires clients to challenge their irrational beliefs, aims to eliminate those beliefs and substitute them with a new, more rational philosophy. If disputation is effective, it will be apparent in the diminished emotional distress. The ultimate goal is to increase clients' awareness of these new effects and thus motivate them to continue using the disputational process in a self-directed manner, even after therapy is terminated.

In addition to disputing irrational thoughts, the cognitive approach has several other goals, according to Ellis (1979e, 1984b). First of all, RET urges clients to assume responsibility for their lives and work out their own problems. The goal is a self-directed life in which they can be true to themselves and, at the same time, aware of others. If therapy is successful, clients will accept themselves, not as they wish they were, but as they are. Only then can they become comfortable with themselves and find the courage to take risks. RET seeks to teach that worth does not depend on what one does or on the opinions of others.

Through RET therapy clients will become more accepting, more tolerant as well, allowing others to make mistakes without judging them and freeing themselves as well from both internal and external condemnation. They will find that it is possible to like people, without liking what it is that they do. Accepting themselves and accepting others, they will be able to accept random chance as a reality of life. Clients will learn to deal with uncertainty and chance with calmness. They will realize they can enjoy life in an imperfect world and still be mentally healthy. Healthy clients are also logical and objective and thus generally open-minded: open to change, open to engaging in meaningful commitments to both people and activities. RET therapists work to help clients turn their perspective outward and to absorb themselves in non-egocentric pursuits.

MAJOR METHODS AND TECHNIQUES

RET consists of three general modes or phases, the cognitive, emotive, and the behavioristic, each accompanied by its own set of techniques. During the *cognitive phase,* the counselor presents the cognitive rationale for the therapy to the client. (As Ellis has pointed out, an RET therapist can begin each therapeutic session by asking clients, "What problems have you been bothering yourself about?" During this initial stage clients are told they can learn to control their emotions by learning to become aware of their underlying thoughts and by learning to substitute alternative thoughts. The *emotive phase* of cognitive therapy is devoted to helping the client become aware of his or her thoughts. This is often done by asking clients to write down their troublesome thoughts. During the final *behavioristic phase* clients are trained to verbalize alternative cognitions and to change their behavior.

The following are some of the techniques used by RET and other cognitive therapists during these three phases.

Identifying Beliefs

The RET therapist is aware that clients often report their irrational beliefs as *feelings* and therefore have trouble responding to the counselor's questions about what thoughts have influenced their emotional consequence. When clients do not know what they are thinking, counselors facilitate the identification of irrational beliefs by asking questions such as; "If you bugged yourself, what would you hear?" "Suppose you were tape-recording. What is going on in your mind?" "Can you replay the tape? Tell me what it says."

Once clients begin to identify their irrational beliefs, the counselor can help group them into themes. The student who receives a C on an examination, for example, thinks he or she is an academic failure—a classic illustration of the theme of *all-or-nothing thinking*. Clients tend to categorize matters in terms of black or white, yes or no, for or against: a conversation that is less than perfect is a total failure. Others will engage in *mind reading:* making inferences about how people feel and think, imagining, for instance, that the president doesn't like people, that no one can get in to see him because he tells the Secret Service to keep them away. *Over-generalization,* seeing a single event as a never-ending pattern of defeat, is another theme that commonly emerges in RET sessions. Typically, clients overgeneralize by using the words *always* or *never*, e.g., "I am always in the wrong place at the wrong time." Still others will engage in *discounting,* rejecting positive experiences by insisting they "don't count." The perfectionist who earns high marks in a class will discount his or her experience by saying, "Anyone could have done it."

Further themes that RET therapists look for include *magnification,* exaggerating the importance of problems and shortcomings ("With my IQ I can never get a really good job"); *emotional reasoning,* assuming that negative emotions reflect the way things really are ("I feel guilty so I must be guilty"); and *self-blame,* taking personal responsibility for events that are beyond one's control ("If I had not made him get up he never would have been in the wreck").

Disputing

Disputation of irrational beliefs occurs in two stages. The *initial,* more specific stage requires a meticulous sentence-by-sentence examination and challenge of any irrational belief reported by the client. The *second,* general stage seeks to develop an alternate, more rational way of thinking. This disputation can take one of three forms: cognitive, imaginal, and behavioral. Regardless of the form(s) used, all disputations challenge the irrational beliefs of the clients and ask them to produce evidence to support the beliefs (Dryden, 1986; Dryden & Ellis, 1988; Ellis, 1982).

Cognitive disputation uses persuasion and direct questioning: "Can you prove it?" "How do you know?" "If that is true, what's the worst that can happen?" "How would that be so terrible?" "Where's the evidence?" "As long as you believe that, how will you feel?" (Walen, DiGuiseppe, & Wessler, 1980, pp. 97–99). Of course disputation can make some clients defensive, but the RET counselor is taught to be professionally sensitive to their responses.

Imaginal disputation, which is sometimes called *rational-emotive imagery*, is based on the assumption that the emotional consequences of clients' imaginings are similar to those produced by real stimuli. This technique is used to provide safe opportunities for trying new ways of thinking (Ellis 1984a, 1985, 1986a, 1989; Maultsby, 1975, 1984; Maultsby & Ellis, 1974). Using this technique, the therapist asks clients to imagine themselves in a problematic situation they dread. Once they have been guided into the feelings of that moment, they are asked to change their fear to mild apprehension, their anger to mild irritation, their depression to sadness, and so on. In other words, they are asked to imagine themselves feeling or behaving differently in this situation. As soon as clients receive the image of different feelings and behavior, they are instructed to signal to the counselor, who then asks them to notice what they are saying or thinking to themselves to produce those different emotions. These are the kinds of sentences or beliefs, the counselor will point out, that they need to use in real-life situations to produce different effects. For maximum results, Maultsby (1984) recommends that clients use this intervention on their own several times daily for at least a week or two to create positive habits leading to greater internal control of emotions (see Sidebar 13-2).

> *The whole world is a comedy to those who think, a tragedy to those who feel.*
>
> —Horace Walpole

Finally, *behavioral disputation* challenges clients to alter their irrational beliefs by behaving in different ways, a crucial step toward adopting a more rational philosophy. Behavioral disputation usually takes the form of reading books—bibliotherapy—and systematic homework assignments that include both written and *in vivo* practice (McMullin, 1986).

Countering

Countering asks clients to identify "counters" for each of their significant irrational beliefs and then to argue against these beliefs. Thus it provides for "thinking or behaving in an opposite direction, arguing in a very assertive fashion, and convincing oneself of the falsity of a belief" (McMullin & Giles, 1981, p. 6). McMullin and Giles (1981, pp. 67–68) have outlined several "rules" that must be followed in making use of this strategy. First of all, counters must be directly *opposite* to the false belief. For example, if the irrational belief is "I'm a failure if my wife leaves me," a directly opposite counter would be, "My wife's behavior is independent of my own success and accomplishments." Second, counters must be *believable* statements of reality. Although it may be reasonable to conclude, "I don't need to get straight A's in high school to get a reasonably good job after graduation," it is neither reasonable nor believable to conclude, "I don't have to go to high school to get a reasonably good job."

EMOTIONAL CONTROL CARD

To practice rational-emotive imagery an *emotional control card* is sometimes used (Sklare, Taylor, & Hyland, 1985). This wallet-sized card contains four emotionally debilitating categories (anger, self-criticism, anxiety, and depression) and a list of inappropriate feelings and a parallel list of appropriate feelings:

Inappropriate or Self-Destructive Feelings	Appropriate or Non-Defeating Feelings
Anger—Feelings of resentment, anger, madness, fury, rage	*Irritation*—Feelings of (mild or intense) irritation, displeasure, annoyance, frustration; anger at people's acts but not at their persons
Self-criticism—Feelings of humiliation, shame, embarrassment, inadequacy; discounting self as a person	*Criticism of one's behavior*—Feelings of (mild or intense) regret, sorrow, displeasure, doubt; criticism of one's behavior but not of one's total self
Anxiety—Feelings of anxiety, nervousness, hypertension, panic, helplessness, horror	*Concern*—Feelings of (mild or intense) concern, caution, vigilance; tension about one's performance but not about one's self
Depression—Feelings of depression, worthlessness, undeservingness, guilt, self-doubting	*Sadness*—Feelings of (mild or intense) sadness, sorrow, regret, discontentment, displeasure; feeling that one is a person who has performed badly but is not a bad person

Source: From "An Emotional Control Card for Inappropriate and Appropriate Emotions in Using Rational-Emotive Imagery" by Albert Ellis, 1986, *Journal of Counseling and Development, 65,* p. 206. Reprinted with permission.

In a potentially troubling situation, a client may refer to the card and change the quality of feelings about that situation. At the next session with the counselor, the client discusses the use of the card in cognitively restructuring thoughts to make them rational.

Furthermore, the RET therapist will urge clients to develop as many counters as possible to counteract the effects that the irrational beliefs have produced over time. Since lengthy, long-winded statements are easily forgotten, it is equally important that these counters be *concise,* capable of being summarized in a few words, and that they be stated with *assertive and emotional intensity.* They should not be said in a mechanical or unconvincing way. Finally, of course, it is essential that the clients create and *own* these counters. Because clients are likely to be more invested in counters that they themselves generate, the counselor's role in developing counters needs to be limited to coaching. As a result, effective countering is often highly idiosyncratic among different people.

Rational Self-Analysis

The cognitive practitioner will often ask clients to engage in *rational self-analysis,* which allows them to apply the A-B-C theory to their situations and helps them to actively dispute their own irrational beliefs. After all, realizing that A does not cause C is not enough. Not even accepting responsibility for disturbing emotions and self-defeating behavior is enough. Only the repeated investigation and disputation of irrational beliefs and the earnest practice of new and actualizing behaviors are likely to bring about positive change in thoughts, feelings, and behaviors (Ellis, 1990). Typically, this procedure involves asking clients to complete daily homework assignments. The following format is often used to facilitate this exercise:

	A Activating Event	C Consequence	B Belief	D Disputation	E Effects
Date and Time	Situation	Emotions	Automatic Thought	Rational Response	Outcome
2/19 8:00	Studying counseling theories	Confusion Frustration Anxiety	"I feel so stupid. I'll never be a good coun- selor since I already feel lost.	"Just because I don't under- stand every- thing about these theories doesn't make me stupid. Almost every introductory student feels overwhelmed."	Relief Mild tension

To help clients debate irrational thinking, they can be encouraged to ask a variety of questions: "Is my thinking here based on fact?" "Will my thinking here best help me protect my life and health?" "Will my thinking best help me achieve my short- and long-term goals?" "Will my thinking here best help me avoid my most unwanted conflict with others?" "Will my thinking best help me habitually feel the emotions I want to feel?"

Action Homework

In addition to rational self-analysis, specific action homework may also encourage clients to dispute their irrational ideas behaviorally. Since clients are often asked to do the very thing they fear most, these assignments nearly always involve some degree of risk. Clients who demand self-perfection, for example, may be instructed to select three tasks during the following week that they will intentionally do poorly. Those who anticipate the rejection of others are told to collect at least three rejections a day for three consecutive days and to note their self-talk immediately after each attempt. Others who have difficulty asking for help are assigned to request a helping hand once a day for 5 days in a row.

There are several important characteristics of these kinds of homework assignments: "consistency, specificity, systematic follow-through, and large steps" (Walen et al., 1980). That is to say, the homework must be consistent with the work of the session in which it is assigned. It needs to be both clear and concise. It expects clients to follow through with their assignments in structured, systematic ways that are to be reported at the beginning of the next session. And it calls for large steps, which are considered more effective in cognitive restructuring than gradual shaping.

Heightening Awareness

The RET therapist can also help clients become more aware of the *effects* of the A-B-C-D-E model through the use of numerical ratings and self-recording.

The soul of God is poured into the world through the thoughts of men.
—Ralph Waldo Emerson

For example, on a scale from 1 to 100—1 being "not intense distress" and 100 being "very intense distress"—clients are asked to record levels of emotional distress during actual situations they experience outside of counseling. The counselor may also rely on both self-reports and on the reports of significant others to observe the clients' new and different behaviors or responses.

Humor

Because the rational-emotive practitioner believes clients' problems stem from an exaggerated sense of the significance of unfortunate events, he or she will sometimes use humor to show clients how to "lighten up" and view their difficulties in the light of day (Ellis, 1977b, 1987a; Fry & Salameh, 1987; Mahoney, 1988).

In fact, the Institute for Rational-Emotive Therapy has produced an RET songbook and cassette recording entitled "A Garland of Rational Songs," featuring lyrics actually sung by a spirited Albert Ellis. Sometimes Ellis prescribes these "rational-humorous songs" to his clients, in order to highlight the absurdity of their irrational beliefs. Often clients are encouraged to sing the tunes to themselves or to each other in a group setting (Ellis, 1977b, 1987b). Sung to the tune of "I'm Just Wild About Harry," one of the most memorable lyrics of the RET collection is "I'm Just Wild About Worry":

> Oh, I'm just wild about worry
> And worry's wild about me!
> We're quite a twosome to make life gruesome
> And filled with anxiety!
> Oh, worry's anguish I curry
> And look for its guarantee!
> Oh, I'm just wild about worry
> And worry's wild about
> Never mild about,
> Most beguiled about me!

Lyrics by Albert Ellis, Copyright 1977, 1988 by Institute for Rational-Emotive Therapy.

APPLICATION

Part of what makes RET so stimulating is the effect of the therapist, especially when the therapist is Albert Ellis himself. Although a transcript cannot completely capture the essence of rational-emotive therapy, the following case portrays much of the dramatic momentum associated with its application. The client is a 26-year-old male, a commercial artist, who is homophobic. He has graduated from college, is doing well at his work, and has a steady girlfriend. Nevertheless, he is terribly afraid of becoming homosexual and is often obsessed with the idea. Whereas the pace of some approaches to this kind of issue would be quite slow, Ellis zeros in on the irrational, illogical thinking that has led to the obsession and quickly attempts to dismantle it. What follows are excerpts and adaptations from the sessions Ellis had with this client, interjected with Ellis's own commentary on the case.

THERAPIST: What's the main thing that's bothering you?

CLIENT: I have a fear of turning homosexual—a *real* fear of it!

THERAPIST: A fear of *becoming* homosexual?

CLIENT: Yeah.

THERAPIST: Because "*if* I become a homosexual—," what?

CLIENT: I don't know. It really gets me down. It gets me to a point where I'm doubting every day. I do doubt everything, anyway.

THERAPIST: Yes. But let's get back to—answer the question: "If I were a homosexual, what would that make me?"

CLIENT: [Pause] Less than a person?

THERAPIST: Yes. Quite obviously, you're saying: "I'm bad *enough*."

CLIENT: That's right.

THERAPIST: Now, why did you just say you don't know?

CLIENT: Just taking a guess at it, that's all. It's—it's just that the fear really gets me down! I don't know why.

THERAPIST: [Laughing] Well, you just *gave* the reason why. Suppose you were saying the same thing about—we'll just say—stealing: You hadn't stolen anything, but you *thought* of stealing something.

CLIENT: [Silence]

THERAPIST: If you believed that: "If I stole it, I would be a thorough jerk"— would you think of it often? Occasionally?

CLIENT: I'd think of it often.

THERAPIST: That's right! As soon as you say, "If so-and-so happens, I would be a thorough jerk!" you'll get *obsessed* with so-and-so. And the reason you're getting obsessed with homosexuality is this nutty belief, "If I *were* a homosexual, I would be a total jerk!" Now, look at that belief for a moment. And let's admit that if you were a homosexual, it would have real disadvantages. Let's assume *that*. But why would you be a thorough jerk if you were a homosexual? Let's suppose you gave up girls completely, and you were with guys. Now, why would you be a thorough jerk?

CLIENT: [Mumbles incoherently; is obviously having trouble finding an answer.]

THERAPIST: Think about it for a moment. The reason you're obsessed is the same reason you'd be obsessed with anything. I see people who are obsessed with five thousand different things. But in every single case, just about, I can track it down; and they're saying, "*If* I were so-and-so—" For example, "If I got up and made a public speech and fell on my face, I'd be a jerk!" "If I went to school and failed, I'd be a jerk!" "If I tried for a better job and failed, I'd be a jerk!" Now, you're doing the same thing about homosexuality: "If I ever *did* fail heterosexually and become a homosexual, I'd be an utter worm!" Now that will obsess you with homosexuality.

CLIENT: And that obsession brings me to doubt myself.

THERAPIST: Well—no. It's part of your general obsession. Your real obsession is: "If (1) I failed at something big, like heterosexuality, and (2) other people didn't like me—they really didn't like me—then I'd be no good!" Now, as a *subheading* under that, you've got the homosexuality. Your general fear is of being worthless—isn't it?

CLIENT: Yeah.

THERAPIST: And you don't only have it in the homosexual area—that's only dramatic and outstanding.

Although I, as the therapist, know very little about the client, I size him up quickly and decide to take a chance, on the basis of RET theory, and to try to get at one of the main cores of his problem quickly: his terrible feelings of inadequacy. I know fully that I may be barking up the wrong tree, and am prepared to back down later if I turn out to be mistaken. But I know, on the basis of considerable prior evidence, that there is an excellent chance that I may be right; and I want, by taking that chance, to try to save the client a great deal of time and pain. So I not only immediately try to educate him about his own magical beliefs in wormhood and its connection with his fear of homosexuality, but I also try to show him how human beings, in general, easily think the way he does and how so many of them, no matter what their abilities and talents, wind up by hating themselves because of this type of crooked thinking. I am thus exceptionally educational in the first minutes of this first session—just as, presumably, any good teacher would be.

CLIENT: [Pause] I mean, I—sit there and I try to prove what a homosexual is. Then I try to prove what a heterosexual is. And then I try to prove what *I* am. And to try to prove what *you* are, as a person—

THERAPIST: Yeah?

CLIENT: —is very hard to do.

THERAPIST: Because there is no way of doing it—except by some *definition:* "that if I were completely heterosexual, or if I were a *great* supervising artist, or if I were an Adonis, *then* I'd be a good guy!" That's the only way you can *prove* yourself: by some arbitrary definition of accomplishment.

CLIENT: Yeah, I kept, like—in the other therapy, I kept using the words *abnormal* and *homosexual.*

THERAPIST: Meaning—but what you mean is, "*If* I were abnormal—if everybody is normal but me—I'm no good!" Is that what you mean?

CLIENT: Yeah, I do mean that.

THERAPIST: But let's suppose that, now. Let's just suppose that. Let's suppose that ninety-nine out of one hundred guys are normal—which is not true, but we'll deliberately suppose it—and they all are with girls and having a ball and marrying and having children; and you're the one out of a hundred who can't do that, who really is homosexual. All you can do is go after boys, and you can't make it with girls. You're impotent; you just can't make it with girls. We'll deliberately assume that. Therefore, statistically you're abnormal. Right? Cause you're one out of a hundred, and they can do things that you can't do. Now, why would you be a no-goodnik? Not why would you be abnormal—we're just assuming that you would be; now why would you be a no-goodnik if that were so: you were the one out of a hundred who couldn't make it heterosexually?

CLIENT: Well—maybe fear of loneliness.

THERAPIST: That's why it would be *inconvenient*: because they'd get along with girls, and you wouldn't. So therefore you might be lonely. Though that's not true either: you might have a lot of homosexual guys. But let's suppose you're lonely. Now, why would you be a *louse* because you're lonely? Now why would you be failing? Because we're assuming you'd be failing. They're succeeding heterosexually; you're not. Now why would you be a louse?

CLIENT: For not falling in with what they're doing.

THERAPIST: But that's a definition! Now let's suppose the opposite, incidentally—that ninety-nine out of one hundred guys just about made it with girls—they got a girl here and they got a girl there, and they sort of succeeded—but you were outstanding, and you really were very good looking and bright and sexy, and girls just fell all over you. Now that would be *abnormal*, statistically. Right?

CLIENT: [Pause] It would be.

THERAPIST: Why would you be a jerk *then?* You'd be one out of a hundred!

CLIENT: So I'm going by the use of a definition?

THERAPIST: That's right! "That I have to be super good. Then I'm okay. But if I'm super bad—one out of a hundred on the bad side—then I'm a louse!" That's your definition. See? Now, is a definition—does a definition prove anything about a fact? Because it is a definition, and if you want to feel you're a jerk, you can feel you're a jerk. But does it really prove you are a jerk—if you can only get there by definition?

CLIENT: I dunno.

THERAPIST: Because it can really get absurd. I, for example, could say: "I'm a tuba." And you say, "You're a tuba? Well, how did you become a tuba? Prove it!" And I say, "Well, I'm going around oomp-oomp-oomp-bah. Therefore I'm a tuba!" Now does that prove I'm a tuba?

CLIENT: No.

THERAPIST: What does it prove? It does prove something. What?

CLIENT: That you're not one. You may want to be one—

THERAPIST: Yes, that I *think* I am a tuba. That's what it proves. Because if I'm going to go around acting like a tuba, whether I am or not, I think I am a tuba.

But it never proves I *am*, you see. Therefore, if you go around acting as if you are a jerk, it doesn't prove you *are* one; but it does prove that you *think* you are. And that's the story of your life! "If I'm not at *least* as good as others, and preferably much better, I *define* myself as an utter lowlifer! A Skunk!" Right?

CLIENT: Yes, that's true.

I, as the therapist, keep belaboring a single point here, until I am fairly sure that the client is getting it. For this is one of the main cores of RET: to show the client that his anxieties are *not* caused by his failing to achieve some goal that he wishes to achieve, but by his *demanding* that he achieve it. I feel, with practically all my clients, that if I can get over to them this single point, especially in one of the early sessions, that I have something of almost inestimable value: namely, the idea that *they* create their anxieties and other upsets, and they almost invariably do so by a single major irrational idea: the idea that they *must have* or *need* what they want. If they see this, then no matter what they are anxious, guilty, depressed, or angry about, they have a simple way of quickly discovering the *real* cause of their disordered emotion—their own demandingness—and of starting to challenge and attack it right away.

CLIENT: So as long as I keep thinking of a human being not being a jerk and yet one who makes mistakes, as long as I keep proving it to myself that that's all there is, and if I work at that, within time the problem will just leave. And I don't even think I'll have to work at it.

THERAPIST: Right.

CLIENT: I think it will just come now. So I see it more and more, yet I still have these lags of going back to a jerk. It's so much—so much more secure. But it makes for misery! And a lot of it. Something I don't need! But now that I've gotten over the problem, I really get along with my girl friend a lot better, and everything else. I've noticed that.

THERAPIST: Right.

CLIENT: And—I enjoy it more!

THERAPIST: Yes, because you're not spending the time doubting.

CLIENT: Yeah.

At the end of this eighth session, the client feels that he is doing so well that he decides on a two-week instead of a one-week gap between sessions. He continued therapy for five subsequent sessions, then felt that he wanted to try it on his own. A follow-up report, six months after therapy ended, showed that he was no longer obsessed with sexual ideas, and was continuing to get along better than ever with his girl friend. (Ellis, 1975, pp. 266–271.)

OTHER COGNITIVELY BASED THEORIES

Although rational-emotive therapy is the most widely known approach to cognitive therapy, it is not the only approach. About the same time that Albert Ellis was perfecting his therapeutic techniques, Aaron Beck, a Philadelphia psychiatrist, developed a cognitive theory based on the rationale that the way people

Aaron Beck.
(Leif Skoogfors/Woodfin Camp & Associates)

feel and behave is determined by how they structure their experience. In cases of depression and anxiety, for example, Beck tries to persuade his clients to generalize and project less often, so that they might become more realistic in their interpretation of events. Unlike Ellis, Beck does not try to dispute beliefs; instead, he employs specific profiles and treatment plans. In addition, Beck is more exploratory and more collaborative than Ellis (Beck, 1991), and he has a more positive attitude toward religion as well (Weinrach, 1988). As director of the Center for Cognitive Therapy at the University of Pennsylvania Department of Psychiatry, Beck has found his emphasis on *dysfunctional* thinking to be a highly effective means of achieving structured, active, short-term treatment (Beck, 1975, 1976, 1987, 1993; Beck & Emery, 1985; Beck, Rush, Hollon, & Shaw, 1979; Beck, Rush, Shaw, & Emery, 1979; Beck &

Weishaar, 1989; DeRubeis & Beck, 1988; Haaga & Davison, 1986; Rush, Beck, Kovacs, & Hollon, 1977; Weinrach, 1988).

Beck's cognitive approach is only one of several alternatives to RET. Another method, commonly referred to as *cognitive-behavioral therapy,* has emerged from out of the work of Albert Bandura's (1977, 1986) social learning and self-efficacy theory and Donald Meichenbaum's (1977, 1985) cognitive behavior modification or stress-inoculation training. The work of Bandura and Meichenbaum evolved from traditional behaviorism. However, whereas true behaviorists look to external factors as the ultimate cause of behavior, the cognitive-behavior practitioner believes that some human behavior is caused by internal or mental events. And whereas behaviorists focus greatly on *conditioning* as the explanation for all behavior, cognitive-behavioral practitioners assume that behavior transcends operant and classical conditioning, that it is more complex than pure reinforcement. As one might expect, the cognitive-behavior therapist believes that thoughts are equally important contributors to behavior (Beutler, Engle, Mohr, Daldrup, et al., 1991a; Meichenbaum, 1986; Meichenbaum & Cameron, 1982).

Men are apt to mistake the strength of their feeling for the strength of their argument. The heated mind resents the chill touch and relentless scrutiny of logic.

—William Gladstone

According to Meichenbaum (1977), the cognitive-behavioral therapist will encourage clients to become aware of how they think, feel, and behave in order to interrupt the scripted nature of their behavior, so that they can evaluate their behavior in various situations. Like RET, this approach assumes that distressing emotions are typically the result of irrational thoughts. Unlike RET, however, cognitive-behavior therapy is more integrated into the discipline of psychology, less dogmatic, and more scientific in its formulations (Emery, 1981; Jones & Butman, 1991; Wiser & Goldfried, 1993). Perhaps it is this that accounts for the therapist–client relationship being less personal than in many other approaches. The task of the therapist is to "act as a diagnostician, educator and technical consultant" to remedy dysfunctional cognitions (Kendall & Bemis, 1983, p. 566).

The practice of cognitive-behavior therapy features short-term interventions directed toward specifically defined targets. There are three major types of such interventions: *coping skill training,* in which clients are assisted in developing behavioral and cognitive skills for dealing with challenging situations; *cognitive restructuring,* which attempts to modify maladaptive thought patterns directly; and *problem-solving training,* in which people expand their general capacity for understanding and facing challenging problems (Dobson & Block, 1988; Neimeyer & Feixas, 1990).

Considerable research using strategies from cognitive approaches has supported its theoretical foundation (Beck, 1993). The very broad application of the theory and strategies bolsters the claim of cognitive therapy as a robust system of treatment. Consider the myriad of clinical situations to which it has been effectively applied in recent years: panic disorder (Barlow, 1990; Telch, Lucas, Schmidt, Hanna, 1993), insomnia (Morin, Kowatch, Barry, & Walson, 1993), bulimia nervosa (Hom & Giles, 1991; Jones, Peveler, Hope, & Fairburn, 1993; Wilson, Eldredge, Smith, & Niles, 1991), marital conflict (Denton, 1991;

Donald Meichenbaum.
(Courtesy of The Milton H. Erickson Foundation, Inc., Phoenix, Arizona)

Epstein, Baucom, & Rankin, 1993; Montag & Wilson, 1992), rape victims (Foa, Rothbaum, Riggs, & Murdock, 1991), kleptomania (Schwarz & Hoellen, 1991), social phobia (Bruch, Heimberg, & Hope, 1991), schizophrenia (Liberman & Green, 1992), sexual abuse (Deblinger, McLeer, & Henry, 1990), job-related distress (Barkham & Shapiro, 1990), and depression (Addis & Jacobson, 1991; Beardslee, Hoke, Wheelock, & Rothberg, 1992; Burns & Nolen, 1992; Propst, Ostrom, Watkins, & Dean, 1992; Thase & Simons, 1992).

CRITICAL ANALYSIS

The cognitive approach to therapy is one of the most effective and easily learned methods of counseling. Few would disagree that it is a largely successful means of preventing clients from seriously passing judgment on themselves based on some inconsequential or superficial aspect of their behavior, and this within a relatively short time period. The economy and efficiency of this approach are just as impressive. Because the cognitive approach fits instinctively with the rational aspect of human beings, it has generated a significant amount of bibliotherapeutic material and positive research findings.

Despite its many contributions to the field of counseling, however, RET and similar cognitive approaches present a number of critical concerns. To begin with, the almost exclusive focus of RET on cognition has been criticized for simplifying the complexity of the human experience. The A-B-C model may be attractive, but it may also be misleading: its linear and simple components may not always fit neatly into the complex emotional and cognitive environment that characterizes most people. The point is that in evaluating RET for its breadth of methods, one quickly sees that it is one of the narrower approaches. In combination with other behavioral approaches, however, this critique of RET begins to diminish.

Another criticism of RET is that it attempts to implement a truly value-free approach to therapy. Ellis (1978, p. 40) clearly states that "RET posits no absolutistic or invariant criteria of rationality." Paradoxically, the very article (Ellis, 1978, p. 55) that proclaims value openness concludes with a list of particular values and goals that clients "need to seek" if they want to obtain happiness and minimize emotional disturbance. Again refusing to identify arbitrarily the criteria by which therapists might distinguish rational from irrational thoughts, Ellis has argued elsewhere that "rational thoughts ... are defined in RET as those thoughts that help people to live longer and happier, particu-

Humans are highly suggestible, impressionable, vulnerable, and gullible.

—Albert Ellis

larly by ... choosing for themselves certain ... happiness-producing values, purposes, goals" (Ellis & Bernard, 1986, pp. 5–6). But to judge the efficacy of a belief, based on the criterion of whether it produces "happiness-producing values," on the one hand, or an irrational or inappropriate effect, on the other, is clearly an invitation to circular reasoning. After all, how does one recognize an inappropriate effect except by the irrationality of the belief that has produced it? And on what basis does the therapist determine a belief to be irrational, unless it is by the effect that it produces? If one has a depressive reaction to a belief that "My physician says I am seriously ill, and that is awful," an RET therapist cannot conclude that this reaction is excessive except by having a predetermined notion of exactly how upset one can legitimately be in such circumstances. Ellis has attempted to overcome this problem by defining an inappropriate emotional response as one that impedes rather than helps people overcome the obstacle that is causing their distress. The question remains, however: Who determines what emotions help and what emotions hurt our growth?

When it comes to therapy from a multicultural perspective, RET and other cognitive-behavioral therapies have fundamental advantages and disadvantages. Their most obvious contribution to multicultural counseling is the challenge to examine how one's thinking determines, to a large extent, how one feels and what one does. This is a nearly-universal human experience that transcends many cultural barriers (Beutler, Mohr, Grawe, & Engle, 1991; Rihani, 1987). Indeed, some have suggested that particular ethnic-minority cultures may even be more receptive to the directive style of RET than North Americans, who view counseling as a more exploratory and democratic process (Waxer, 1989). It has also become clear that the cognitive approach is frequently used in training practices around the world (Deane, 1992; Lloyd & Bhugra, 1993; Page, 1993). The difficulty is that the cognitive approach can easily misconstrue as "irrational" the values of ethnic-minority clients that are related to their particular world view. In addition, this approach may neglect the fact that many irrational environments in which clients reside and that exist beyond the counseling office continue to foster and reinforce irrational thoughts and maladaptive behaviors. When working with minority clients, the cognitive therapist needs to exercise considerable care to avoid this danger.

A critique of the cognitive approach to counseling must also take into account its frequently effective work with physically disabled clients. There is often a need for the counselor working with disability-related interventions, for example, to confront and interrupt the client's unrealistic and negative beliefs and expectations concerning the disability and its implications. The cognitive approach can further help clients to disassemble seemingly insurmountable problems into smaller and more manageable units (Halligan, 1983).

A final comment must be made concerning Ellis' bombastic style, which can become unnecessarily intertwined with one's understanding of how RET is practiced. There are many styles of doing rational therapy, however, and there are gentle, respectful ways to aid the process of cognitive change. It is vital in studying RET to separate the habits and manner of Ellis as a therapist from his ideas.

CURRENT STATUS

In recent years RET has come to enjoy wide acceptance. Although the approach certainly has its critics, Ellis has consistently countered attacks with a hearty spirit and with "innumerable studies" providing empirical evidence (Ellis, 1977b, p. 3; 1989). In general, research exploring the A-B-C theory is supportive (Burns & Nolen-Hoeksema, 1992; DiGuiseppe, Leaf, & Linscott, 1993; DiGuiseppe, Miller, & Trexler, 1979; Ellis, 1979e, 1986b; Ellis & Dryden, 1987; Ellis & Whiteley, 1979; Engels, Garnefski, & Diekstra, 1993; Folkins, 1970; Geer, Davison, & Gatchel, 1970; Hajzler & Bernard, 1991; Jordan & Kempler, 1970; McGovern & Silverman, 1986; Oei, Hansen, & Miller, 1993; Silverman, McCarthy, & McGovern, 1992; Steffy, Meichenbaum, & Best, 1970; Valins, 1970). The evidence shows that emotional difficulties do tend to be associated with specific irrational ideas (Dua, 1970; Haaga & Davison, 1989; Lipsky, Kassinove, & Miller, 1980; Moleski & Tosi, 1976; Reardon & Tosi, 1977; Rimm & Litvak, 1969; Tosi & Carlson, 1970; Tosi & Eshbaugh, 1976; Tosi & Reardon, 1976;

Velten, 1968). Today, a great deal of research on RET routinely appears in the *Journal of Rational-Emotive and Cognitive-Behavior Therapy.*

Two nonprofit institutes have been established by Ellis to promote RET: the Institute for Rational Living, a scientific and educational foundation established in 1959, and the Institute for Rational-Emotive Therapy, an institution for professional training and clinical services established in 1968. With headquarters in New York City, these institutes have branches in several cities in the United States and other countries. The Institute for Rational-Emotive Therapy offers several levels of training, including Primary and Intermediate Certificates, an Associate Fellowship, and a Fellowship. All levels involve instruction, individual supervision, and written and oral examinations. A register at the Institute for Rational-Emotive Therapy lists hundreds of psychotherapists who have received training in RET. In addition to therapists who have received formal training in RET, hundreds of others follow cognitive approaches. To obtain further information or a catalog of RET workshops and publications, contact:

> Institute for Rational-Emotive Therapy
> 45 East 65th Street
> New York, NY 10021-6593
> Telephone: (212) 535-0822

Some years ago, Aaron Beck asked, "Can a fledgling psychotherapy challenge the giants in the field—psychoanalysis and behavior therapy?" (Beck, 1976, p. 333). Since that question was asked, substantial empirical support has accumulated and thousands of practitioners subscribe to a form of cognitive therapy, making the cognitive approach one of the most popular modes of psychotherapy.

CHAPTER SUMMARY

1. *Biography.* Ellis (1913–) grew up in New York City, where as a young adolescent he dreamed of becoming a novelist. In 1934, he graduated from City College of New York with a BA in business administration. In his spare time, Ellis wrote fiction, but his literary efforts did not pay off. After eight of his novels were rejected by publishers, Ellis decided to study psychology and eventually earned his Ph.D. in clinical psychology from Columbia University. Ellis began practicing psychoanalysis but eventually became more active and directive with his patients, gradually developing his own approach to therapy.

2. *Historical Development.* Although the origins of RET can be traced as far back as ancient Greece, the approach more recently stems from cognitive learning theory. Despite Ellis's original training and practice of psychoanalysis, he remained dissatisfied with this approach and hypothesized that his patients' behaviors were influenced by their attitudes and perceptions. This hypothesis motivated Ellis to work diligently toward a rational approach to psychotherapy.

3. *View of Human Nature.* Ellis holds that human nature has the potential to control much of the pleasure and pain that seemingly results from life's circumstances. According to Ellis, the human psyche is intricately entwined with thoughts and feelings. Ellis' view of human nature can be summarized in his formulation of the A-B-C theory, which suggests that people come to therapy because of a disturbing consequence (C), which is attributed to an activating event (A), as if there were a causal relationship. According to Ellis, however, people are not disturbed by events themselves, but by the beliefs (B) they hold about those events.

4. *Development of Maladaptive Behavior.* Because humans are self-conscious creatures, they observe their disturbance and then make themselves disturbed all over again about being disturbed. Maladaptive behavior, therefore, results from a number of illogical ideas (e.g., that being loved and approved by everyone is necessary for happiness) that are held and perpetuated until a new way of thinking is learned. These illogical ideas result in feelings of worthlessness, depression, rage, anxiety, mania, or self-pity. Although we are born with the potential to be rational, we become illogical because of distortions during childhood and the contemporary reinforcement of those distortions.

5. *Goals of Therapy.* The ultimate goal of RET is to "teach" clients to analyze and correct their distortions of reality. It aims to help clients separate their rational from their irrational beliefs. Then the identified irrational beliefs are challenged; that is, the client is brought to a point of disputing irrational emotional beliefs. RET aims to eliminate the irrational beliefs and substitute them with a new, more rational philosophy. If this disputation is effective, it will be apparent in the diminished emotional distress, and it will result in clients assuming more responsibility for their own lives.

6. *Function of the Therapist.* In RET the therapist is unequivocally verbal and directive, intentionally attempting to lead the patient to a healthier perspective. By using persuasion and debate to attack self-defeating patterns, the therapist works as quickly as possible to help clients face their illogical thinking. Exploring the details of the past is only a smoke screen, hiding the real issue of irrational thinking. The process for the RET therapist, then, centers on showing clients how and when they are irrational.

7. *Major Methods and Techniques.* RET consists of three general phases. In the cognitive phase the therapist presents the rationale for therapy to the clients. The emotive phase is devoted to helping clients become aware of their thoughts. During the behavioristic phase clients are trained to verbalize alternative cognitions and to change their behavior. During each of these phases, techniques such as disputation, countering, and action homework may be used.

8. *Application.* A transcript cannot completely capture the role that Ellis' personality plays in how he applies RET, but the case of a 26-year-old male commercial artist who is homophobic portrays much of its dramatic momentum. In this case, Ellis quickly taps into the client's irrational, illogical thinking and

through disputation quickly attempts to dismantle it. After eight sessions, the client's obsession is relieved.

9. *Other Cognitively Based Theories.* Although RET is the most widely known cognitive approach, it is not the only one. Aaron Beck also developed a highly effective cognitive theory based on the rationale that the way people feel and behave is determined by how they structure their experience. Emphasizing dysfunctional thinking, he tries to help clients become more realistic in their interpretation of events by projecting less often. Donald Meichenbaum has inaugurated a cognitive-behavioral approach, which emphasizes that clients need to become aware of how they think, feel, and behave in order to interrupt the scripted nature of their behavior so that they can evaluate their behavior in various situations.

10. *Critical Analysis.* The cognitive approach to therapy is a proven short-term strategy for preventing clients from seriously passing judgment on themselves based on some inconsequential aspect of their behavior. But it has been criticized for simplifying the complexity of human experience and for trying to implement a truly value-free approach to therapy. Concerning multicultural counseling, the cognitive approach is capable of transcending many cultural barriers but runs the risk of misconstruing as irrational the values of ethnic minority clients that are related to their particular world views.

11. *Current Status.* In recent years RET and other cognitive approaches have come to enjoy wide acceptance. Much of their following and support can be attributed to the empirical evidence that undergirds their efforts. Also, Ellis' two nonprofit institutes, with headquarters in New York City, promote RET in many areas. Thousands of practitioners subscribe to a form of cognitive therapy today, making it one of the most popular modes of psychotherapy.

KEY TERMS

Action Homework   Assignments designed to encourage clients to dispute their irrational ideas behaviorally. These assignments nearly always involve some degree of risk since clients are often asked to do the very thing they fear most.

All-or-Nothing Thinking   Seeing things in black or white, yes or no, for me or against me categories. If a conversation is anything less than perfect, is it seen as a total failure? Example: A student who receives a C on a single exam thinks that he or she is a total academic failure.

Cognitive   Characteristic of putting importance on purpose, knowing, understanding, thinking, and reasoning in behavior.

Countering   A technique whereby clients are asked to identify "counters" for each of their significant irrational beliefs and then to argue against these beliefs. In other words, countering involves arguing in a very assertive fashion and convincing oneself of the falsity of a belief.

Discounting   Rejecting positive experiences by insisting they "don't count." Example: Earning high marks in a class are discounted by saying, "Anyone could have done it."

Emotion-Control Card   A wallet-sized card containing four emotionally debilitating categories (anger, self-criticism, anxiety, and depression) and a list of inappropriate feelings and a parallel list of appropriate feelings. It is used in practicing rational-emotive imaging.

Emotional Reasoning   Assuming that negative emotions reflect the way things really are. Example: "I feel guilty so I must be guilty."

Emotive   Having to do with emotion-provoking stimuli.

Insight Number 1   What Ellis calls showing clients how and when they are irrational.

Insight Number 2   What Ellis calls convincing clients that they maintain their own emotional disturbance by reindoctrinating themselves with the same repetitious, irrational ideas.

Insight Number 3   What Ellis calls leading clients to a full acknowledgment that ridding themselves of their disturbances depends on their willingness to join in challenging their beliefs and in developing new ways of thinking.

Irrational   Characterized by being influenced or guided by "crooked" thinking.

Magnification   Exaggerating the importance of problems and shortcomings. Example: "With my IQ I can never get a really good job."

Mind Reading   Making inferences about how people feel and think. Example: "The president doesn't like people; no one can get in to see him because he tells the Secret Service to keep them away."

Overgeneralization   Seeing a single event as a never-ending pattern of defeat by using the words *always* or *never* when thinking about it. Example: "I am always in the wrong place at the wrong time."

Rational   Characterized by being influenced or guided by reason.

Self-Blame   Taking personal responsibility for events that are beyond one's control. Example: "If I had not asked to go shopping he never would have been in the wreck."

Self-Efficacy   A comprehensive sense of one's own capability, effectiveness, strength, or power to attain desired results.

Social Learning   A modified form of behaviorism that stresses the importance of cognitive processes as causal agents in behavior. Albert Bandura is the leading contemporary exponent of this point of view.

SUGGESTED READING

Ellis, A. (1962). *Reason and emotion in psychotherapy.* New York: Lyle Stuart.

Ellis, A., & Dryden, W. (1987). *The practice of rational-emotive therapy.* New York: Lyle Stuart.

Ellis, A., & Grieger, R. (1977). *Handbook of rational-emotive therapy* (Vol. 1). New York: Springer.

Ellis, A., & Grieger, R. (1986). *Handbook of rational-emotive therapy* (Vol. 2). New York: Springer.

REFERENCES

Addis, M. E., & Jacobson, N. S. (1991). Integration of cognitive therapy and behavioral marital therapy for depression. *Journal of Psychotherapy Integration, 1,* 249–264.

Bandura, A. (1977). Self-efficacy: Toward a unifying theory of behavioral change. *Psychological Review, 84,* 191–215.

Bandura, A. (1986). *Social foundations of thought and action.* Englewood Cliffs, NJ: Prentice-Hall.

Bard, I. (1980). *RET in practice.* Edison, NJ: Resolute Press.

Barkam, M., & Shapiro, D. A. (1990). Brief psychotherapeutic interventions for job-related distress: A pilot study of prescriptive and exploratory therapy. *Counseling Psychology Quarterly, 3,* 133–147.

Barlow, D. H. (1990). Long-term outcome for patients with panic disorder treated with cognitive-behavioral therapy. *Journal of Clinical Psychiatry, 51,* 17–23.

Beardslee, W. R., Hoke, L., Wheelock, I., & Rothberg, P. C. (1992). Initial findings on preventive intervention for families with parental affective disorders. *American Journal of Psychiatry, 149,* 1335–1340.

Beck, A. T. (1975). *Depression: Causes and treatment.* Philadelphia: University of Pennsylvania Press.

Beck, A. T. (1976). *Cognitive therapy and emotional disorders.* New York: International Universities Press.

Beck, A. T. (1987). Cognitive therapy. In J. K. Zeig (Ed.), *The evolution of psychotherapy* (pp. 149–178). New York: Brunner/Mazel.

Beck, A. T. (1991). Cognitive therapy: A 30-year retrospective. *American Psychologist, 46,* 368–375.

Beck, A. T. (1993). Cognitive therapy: Past, present, and future. *Journal of Consulting and Clinical Psychology, 61,* 194–198.

Beck, A. T., & Emery, G. (1985). *Anxiety disorders and phobias: A cognitive perspective.* New York: Basic Books.

Beck, A., Rush, A., Hollon, S., & Shaw, B. (1979). *Cognitive therapy of depression.* New York: Guilford Press.

Beck, A., Rush, A., Shaw, B., & Emery, G. (1979). *Cognitive therapy of depression.* New York: Guilford Press.

Beck, A. T., & Weishaar, M. E. (1989). In R.J. Corsini & D. Wedding (Eds.), *Current psychotherapies* (4th ed., pp. 285–320). Itasca, IL: F. E. Peacock.

Beutler, L. E., Engle, D., Mohr, D., & Daldrup, R. J., (1991a). Predictors of differential response to cognitive, experiential, and self-directed psychotherapeutic procedures. *Journal of Consulting and Clinical Psychology, 59,* 333–340.

Beutler, L. E., Mohr, D. C. Grawe, K., & Engle, D., (1991b). Looking for differential treatment effects: Cross-cultural predictors of differential psychotherapy efficacy. *Journal of Psychotherapy Integration, 1,* 121–141.

Bruch, M. A., Heimberg, R. G., & Hope, D. A. (1991). States of mind model and cognitive change in treated social phobics. *Cognitive Therapy and Research, 15,* 429–441.

Burns, D. D., & Nolen-Hoeksema, S. (1992). Therapeutic empathy and recovery from depression in cognitive-behavioral therapy: A structural equation model. *Journal of Consulting and Clinical Psychology, 60,* 441–449.

Burns, D. D., & Nolen-Hoeksema, S. (1992). Therapeutic empathy and recovery from depression in cognitive-behavioral therapy: A structural equation model. *Journal of Consulting and Clinical Psychology, 60,* 441–449.

Cohen, E. D. (1987). The use of syllogism in rational-emotive therapy. *Journal of Counseling and Development, 66,* 37–39.

Deane, F. P. (1992). Pretreatment expectations of New Zealand clients receiving cognitive-behavioral psychotherapy: Comparison with a North American sample. *International Journal of Social Psychiatry, 38,* 138–149.

Deblinger, E., McLeer, S. V., & Henry, D. (1990). Cognitive behavioral treatment for sexually abused children suffering post-traumatic stress: Preliminary findings. *Journal of the American Academy of Child and Adolescent Psychiatry, 29,* 747–752.

Denton, W. H. (1991). The role of affect in marital therapy. *Journal of Marital and Family Therapy, 17,* 257–261.

DeRubeis, R. J., & Beck, A. T. (1988). Cognitive therapy. In K. S. Dobson (Ed.), *Handbook of cognitive-behavioral therapies* (pp. 273–306). New York: Guilford Press.

DiGuiseppe, R. A., Leaf, R., & Linscott, J. (1993). The therapeutic relationship in rational-emotive therapy: Some preliminary data. *Journal of Rational Emotive and Cognitive Behavior Therapy, 11,* 223–233.

DiGiuseppe, R. A., Miller, N. J., & Trexler, L. D. (1979). A review of rational-emotive psychotherapy outcome studies. In A. Ellis & J . M . Whiteley (Eds.), *Theoretical and empirical foundations of rational-emotive therapy* (pp. 218–235). Pacific Grove, CA: Brooks/Cole.

Dobson, K. S. (Ed.). (1988a). *Handbook of cognitive-behavioral therapies.* New York: Guilford Press.

Dobson, K. S. (1988b). The present and future of the cognitive-behavioral therapies. In K. S. Dobson (Ed.), *Handbook of cognitive-behavioral therapies* (pp. 387-414). New York: Guilford Press.

Dobson, K. S., & Block, L. (1988). Historical and philosophical bases of the cognitive-behavioral therapies. In K. S. Dobson (Ed.), *Handbook of cognitive-behavioral therapies* (pp. 3–38). New York: Guilford Press.

Dryden, W. (1986). Vivid methods in rational-emotive therapy. In A. Ellis & R. Grieger (Eds.), *Handbook of rational-emotive therapy* (Vol. 2, pp. 221–245). New York: Springer.

Dryden, W. (1989). Albert Ellis: An efficient and passionate life. *Journal of Counseling and Development, 67,* 539–546.

Dryden, W., & Ellis, A. (1988). Rational-emotive therapy. In K. S. Dobson (Ed.), *Handbook of cognitive-behavioral therapies* (pp. 214–272). New York: Guilford Press.

Dua, P. S. (1970). Comparison of the effects of behaviorally oriented action and psychotherapy reeducation on introversion-extroversion, emotionality, and inter-external control. *Journal of Counseling Psychology, 17,* 567–572.

Ellis, A. (1957). *How to live with a neurotic at work or home.* New York: Crown.

Ellis, A. (1962). *Reason and emotion in psychotherapy.* New York: Lyle Stuart.

Ellis, A. (1971). *Growth through reason.* Hollywood, CA: Wilshire Books.

Ellis, A. (1973). *Humanistic psychotherapy: The rational-emotive approach.* New York: Julian Press.

Ellis, A. (1975). *Growth through reason.* Hollywood, CA: Wilshire Books.

Ellis, A. (1977a). The basic clinical theory of rational-emotive therapy. In A. Ellis & R. Grieger (Eds.), *Handbook of rational-emotive therapy* (Vol. 1, pp. 3–34). New York: Springer.

Ellis, A. (1977b). *A garland of rational songs.* New York: Institute for Rational-Emotive Therapy.

Ellis, A. (1979b). The practice of rational-emotive therapy. In A. Ellis & J. Whiteley (Eds.), *Theoretical and empirical foundations of rational-emotive therapy* (pp. 61–100). Pacific Grove, CA: Brooks/Cole.

Ellis, A. (1979c). Rational-emotive therapy. In A. Ellis & J. M. Whiteley (Eds.), *Theoretical and empirical foundations of rational-emotive therapy* (pp. 1–6). Pacific Grove, CA: Brooks/Cole.

Ellis, A. (1979d). The theory of rational-emotive therapy. In A. Ellis & J. Whiteley (Eds.), *Theoretical and empirical foundations of rational-emotive therapy* (pp. 33–60). Pacific Grove, CA: Brooks/Cole.

Ellis, A. (1979e). Rational-emotive therapy: Research data that support the clinical and personality hypotheses of RET and other modes of cognitive-behavior therapy. In A. Ellis & J. M. Whiteley (Eds.), *Theoretical and empirical foundations of rational-emotive therapy* (pp. 101–173). Pacific Grove, CA: Brooks/Cole.

Ellis, A. (1982). Rational-emotive family therapy. In A. M. Horne & M. M. Ohlsen (Eds.), *Family counseling and therapy*. Itasca, IL: F. E. Peacock.

Ellis, A. (1984a). Is the unified-interaction approach to a cognitive-behavior modification a reinvention of the wheel? *Clinical Psychology Review, 4*, 215–217.

Ellis, A. (1984b). Maintenance and generalization in rational-emotive therapy. *The Cognitive Behaviorist, 6*, 2–4.

Ellis, A. (1985). *Overcoming resistance: Rational-emotive therapy with difficult clients*. New York: Springer.

Ellis, A. (1986a). Rational-emotive therapy and cognitive behavior therapy: Similarities and differences. In A. Ellis & R. Grieger (Eds.), *Handbook of rational-emotive therapy* (Vol. 2, pp. 31–45). New York: Springer.

Ellis, A. (1986b). Rational-emotive therapy. In I. L. Kutash & A. Wolf (Eds.), *Psychotherapist's casebook* (pp. 277–287). San Francisco: Jossey-Bass.

Ellis, A. (1987a). The evolution of rational-emotive therapy (RET) and cognitive behavior therapy (CBT). In J. K. Zeig (Ed.), *The evolution of psychotherapy* (pp. 107–132). New York: Brunner/Mazel.

Ellis, A. (1987b). The impossibility of achieving consistently good mental health. *American Psychologist, 42*, 364–375.

Ellis, A. (1988). *How to stubbornly refuse to make yourself miserable about anything—yes, anything!* New York: Lyle Stuart.

Ellis, A. (1989). Rational-emotive therapy. In R. J. Corsini & D. Wedding (Eds.), *Current psychotherapies* (4th ed., pp. 197–238). Itasca, IL: F. E. Peacock.

Ellis, A. (1990). Rational and irrational beliefs in counselling psychology. *Journal of Rational-Emotive and Cognitive-Behavior Therapy, 8*, 221–223.

Ellis, A. (1993). Reflections on rational-emotive therapy. *Journal of Consulting and Clinical Psychology, 61*, 199–201.

Ellis, A., & Abrams, E. (1978). *Brief psychotherapy in medical and health practice*. New York: Springer.

Ellis, A., & Bernard, M. E. (1986) . What is rational-emotive therapy (RET)? In A. Ellis & R. Grieger (Eds.), *Handbook of rational-emotive therapy* (Vol. 2, pp. 3–30). New York: Springer.

Ellis, A., & Dryden, W. (1987). *The practice of rational-emotive therapy*. New York: Lyle Stuart.

Ellis, A., & Grieger, R. (1977). *Handbook of rational-emotive therapy* (Vol. 1). New York: Springer.

Ellis, A., & Grieger, R. (1986). *Handbook of rational-emotive therapy* (Vol. 2). New York: Springer.

Ellis, A., & Harper, R. A. (1975). *A new guide to rational living* (Rev. ed.). Hollywood, CA: Wilshire Books.

Ellis, A., & Whiteley, J. M. (Eds.). (1979). *Theoretical and empirical foundations of rational-emotive therapy.* Pacific Grove, CA: Brooks/Cole.

Ellis, A., Sichel, J., Yeager, R., DiMattio, D., & DiGiuseppe, R. (1969). *Rational emotive couples therapy.* New York: Pergamon Press.

Ellis, A., Yeager, R. J. (1989). *Why some therapies don't work.* Buffalo, NY: Prometheus Books.

Emery, G. (1981). *A new beginning: How you can change your life through cognitive therapy.* New York: Simon & Schuster (Touchstone Books).

Engels, G. I., Garnefski, N., & Diekstra, R. F. (1993). Efficacy of rational emotive therapy: A quantitative analysis. *Journal of Consulting and Clinical Psychology, 61,* 1083–1090.

Epstein, N., Baucom, D. H., & Rankin, L. A. (1993). Treatment of marital conflict: A cognitive-behavioral approach. Special Issue: Marital conflict. *Clinical Psychology Review, 13,* 45–57.

Foa, E. B., Rothbaum, B. O., Riggs, D. S., & Murdock, T. B. (1991). Treatment of post traumatic stress disorder in rape victims: A comparison between cognitive-behavioral procedures and counseling. *Journal of Consulting and Clinical Psychology, 59,* 715–723.

Folkins, C. H. (1970). Temporal factors and the cognitive mediators of stress reaction. *Journal of Personality and Social Psychology, 14,* 173–184.

Fry, W. R., Jr., & Salameh, W. A. (Eds.). (1987). *Handbook of humor and psychotherapy.* Sarasota, FL: Professional Resource Exchange.

Garamoni, G. L., Reynolds, C. F., Thase, M. E., Frank, E. (1992). Shifts in affective balance during cognitive therapy of major depression. *Journal of Consulting and Clinical Psychology, 60,* 260–266.

Geer, J. H., Davison, G. C., & Gatchel, R. L. (1970). Reduction of stress in humans through non-veridical perceived control of aversion stimulation. *Journal of Personality and Social Psychology, 14,* 731–736.

Goldfried, M. R. (1988). Application of rational restructuring to anxiety disorders. *The Counseling Psychologist, 16,* 50–68.

Grieger, R. M. (1986a). From a linear to a contextual model of the ABC's of RET. In A. Ellis & R. Grieger (Eds.), *Handbook of rational-emotive therapy* (Vol. 2, pp. 59–80). New York: Springer.

Grieger, R. M. (1986b). The process of rational-emotive therapy. In A. Ellis & R. Grieger (Eds.), *Handbook of rational-emotive therapy* (Vol. 2, pp. 203–212). New York: Springer.

Haaga, D. A., & Davison, G. C. (1986). Cognitive change methods. In F. H. Kanfer & A. P. Goldstein (Eds.), *Helping people change: A textbook of methods* (3rd ed., pp. 236–282). New York: Pergamon Press.

Haaga, D. A., & Davison, G. C. (1989). Outcome studies of rational-emotive therapy. In M. E. Bernard & R. DiGiuseppe (Eds.), *Inside rational-emotive therapy.* San Diego, CA: Academic Press.

Hajzler, D. J., & Bernard, M. E. (1991). A review of rational-emotive education outcome studies. *School Psychology Quarterly, 6,* 27–49.

Halligan, F. G. (1983). Reaction depression and chronic illness: Counseling patients and their families. *The Personnel and Guidance Journal, 61,* 401–406.

Harrell, T. H., Beiman, I., & Lapointe, K. (1986). Didactic persuasion techniques in cognitive restructuring. In A. Ellis & R. Grieger (Eds.), *Handbook of rational emotive therapy* (Vol. 2, pp. 213–220). New York: Springer.

Hom, P. H., & Giles, T. R. (1991). Performance-based intervention for non-purging bulimia: Some implications for the treatment of binge eating and obesity. *Psychology and Health, 5,* 183–191.

Hunt, M. (1982). *The universe within.* New York: Simon & Schuster.

Jones, R., Peveler, R. C., Hope, R. A., & Fairburn, C. G. (1993). Changes during treatment for bulimia nervosa: A comparison of three psychological treatments. *Behaviour Research and Therapy, 31,* 479–485.

Jordan, B. T., & Kempler, B. (1970). Hysterical personality: An experimental investigation of sex-role conflict. *Journal of Abnormal Psychology, 75,* 172–176.

Jones, S. C. & Butman, R. E. (1991). *Modern psychotherapies.* Downer's Grove, IL: Intervarsity Press.

Kendall, P., & Bemis, K. (1983). Thought and action in psychotherapy: The cognitive-behavioral approaches. In M. Hersen, A. Kazdin, & A. Bellack (Eds.), *The clinical psychology handbook* (pp. 565–592). New York: Pergamon.

Liberman, R. P., & Green, M. F. (1992). Whither cognitive-behavioral therapy for schizophrenia? *Schizophrenia Bulletin, 18,* 27–35.

Lipsky, M, J., Kassinove, H., & Miller, N. J. (1980). Effects of rational-emotive therapy, rational role reversal, and rational-emotive imagery on the emotional adjustment of community mental health center patients. *Journal of Consulting and Clinical Psychology, 48,* 366–374.

Lloyd, K., & Bhugra, D. (1993). Cross-cultural aspects of psychotherapy. *International Review of Psychiatry, 5,* 291–304.

Mahoney, M. J. (1988). The cognitive sciences and psychotherapy: Patterns in a developing relationship. In K. S. Dobson (Ed.), *Handbook of cognitive-behavioral therapies* (pp. 357–386). New York: Guilford Press.

Maultsby, M. C. (1975). *Help yourself to happiness.* New York: Institute for Rational-Emotive Therapy.

Maultsby, M. C. (1984). *Rational behavior therapy.* Englewood Cliffs, NJ: Prentice-Hall.

Maultsby, M. C., & Ellis, A. (1974). *Technique for using rational-emotive imagery.* New York: Institute for Rational-Emotive Therapy.

McGovern, T. E., & Silverman, M. S. (1986). A review of outcome studies of rational emotive therapy from 1977 to 1982. In A. Ellis & R. Grieger (Eds.), *Handbook of rational-emotive therapy* (Vol. 2, pp. 81–102). New York: Springer.

McMullin, R. E. (1986). *Handbook of cognitive therapy techniques.* New York: W. W. Norton.

McMullin, R. E. & Giles, T. R. (1981). *Cognitive-behavior therapy.* New York: Grune & Stratton.

Meichenbaum, D. (1977). *Cognitive behavior modification: An integrative approach.* New York: Plenum Press.

Meichenbaum, D. (1985). *Stress inoculation training.* New York: Pergamon Press.

Meichenbaum, D. (1986). Cognitive behavior modification. In F. H. Kanfer & A. P. Goldstein (Eds.), *Helping people change: A textbook of methods* (pp. 346–380). New York: Pergamon Press.

Meichenbaum, D., & Cameron, R. (1982). Cognitive-behavior therapy. In G. T. Wilson & C. M. Franks (Eds.), *Contemporary behavior therapy: Conceptual and empirical foundations* (pp. 310–338). New York: Guilford Press.

Moleski, R., & Tosi, D. J.(1976). Comparative psychotherapy: Rational-emotive therapy versus systematic desensitization in the treatment of stuttering. *Journal of Consulting and Clinical Psychology, 44,* 309–311.

Montag, K. R., & Wilson, G. L. (1992). An empirical evaluation of behavioral and cognitive-behavioral group marital treatments with discordant couples. *Journal of Sex and Marital Therapy, 18,* 255–272.

Morin, C. M., Kowatch, R. A., Barry, T., & Walton, E. (1993). Cognitive-behavior therapy for late-life insomnia. *Journal of Consulting and Clinical Psychology, 61,* 137–146.

Morris, J. B. & Kanitz, F. (1975). *Rational emotional therapy.* New York: Houghton Mifflin.

Neimeyer, R. A., & Feixas, G. (1990). The role of homework and skill acquisition in the outcome of group cognitive therapy for depression. *Behavior Therapy, 21,* 281–292.

Oei, T. P. S., Hansen, J., & Miller, S. (1993). The empirical status of irrational beliefs in rational emotive therapy. *Australian Psychologist, 28,* 195–200.

Page, A. C. (1993). To whom should cognitive-behavior therapies be taught? *Australian Psychologist, 28,* 51–54.

Patterson, C. H. (1980). *Theory of counseling and psychotherapy* (3rd ed.). New York: Harper & Row.

Propst, L. R., Ostrom, R., Watkins, P., & Dean, T. (1992). Comparative efficacy of religious and nonreligious cognitive-behavioral therapy for the treatment of clinical depression in religious individuals. *Journal of Consulting and Clinical Psychology, 60,* 94–103.

Reardon, J. P., & Tosi, D. J. (1977). The effects of rational stage directed therapy on self concept and reduction of psychological stress in adolescent delinquent females. *Journal of Clinical Psychology, 33,* 1084–1092.

Rihani, S. (1987). Irrational ideas among Jordanians and Americans: A cross-cultural study of Ellis' theory of rational-emotive therapy. *Dirasat, 14,* 73–102.

Rimm, D. C., & Litvak, S. B. (1969). Self-verbalization and emotional arousal. *Journal of Abnormal Psychology, 74,* 181–187.

Rush, A.J., Beck, A. T., Kovacs, M., & Hollon, S. (1977). Comparative efficacy of cognitive therapy and pharmacotherapy in the treatment of depressed outpatients. *Cognitive Therapy and Research, 1,* 17–37.

Russell, L. A. (1992). Comparisons of cognitive, music, and imagery techniques on anxiety reduction with university students. *Journal of College Student Development, 33,* 516–523.

Schwartz, D., & Hoellen, B. (1991). "Forbidden fruit tastes especially sweet": Cognitive-behavior therapy with a kleptomaniac woman: A case report. *Psychotherapy in Private Practice, 8,* 19–25.

Silverman, M. S., McCarthy, M., & McGovern, T. E. (1992). A review of outcome studies of rational-emotive therapy from 1982–1989. *Journal of Rational-Emotive and Cognitive-Behavioral Therapy, 10,* 111–186.

Sklare, G., Taylor, J., & Hyland, S. (1985). An emotional control card for rational-emotive imagery. *Journal of Counseling and Development, 64,* 145–146.

Steffy, R. A., Meichenbaum, D., & Best, J. A. (1970). Aversive and cognitive factors in the modification of smoking behavior. *Behavior Therapy and Research, 8,* 115–125.

Telch, M. J., Lucas, J. A., Schmidt, N. B., & Hanna, H. H. (1993). Group cognitive-behavioral treatment of panic disorder. *Behavior Research and Therapy, 31,* 279–287.

Thase, M. E., & Simons, A. D. (1992). Cognitive behavior therapy and relapse of non-bipolar depression: Parallels with pharmacotherapy. *Psychopharmacology Bulletin, 28,* 117–122.

Tosi, D. J., & Carlson, W. A. (1970). Dogmatism and perceived counselor attitudes. *Personnel and Guidance Journal, 48,* 657–660.

Tosi, D. J., & Eshbaugh, D. M. (1976). The personal beliefs inventory: A factor-analytic study, *Journal of Clinical Psychology, 32,* 322–327.

Tosi, D. J., & Reardon, J. P. (1976). The treatment of guilt through rational stage directed therapy. *Rational Living, 11,* 8–11.

Valins, S. (1970). The perception and labeling of bodily changes as determinants of emotional behavior. In P. Black (Ed.), *Physiological correlates of emotion* (pp. 134–142). New York: Academic Press.

Velten, E. A. (1968). A laboratory task for induction of mood states. *Behavior Research and Therapy, 6,* 473–482.

Walen, S., DiGuiseppe, R., & Wessler, R. (1980). *A practitioner's guide to RET.* New York: Oxford University Press.

Waxer, P. H. (1989). Cantonese versus Canadian evaluation of directive and non-directive therapy. *Canadian Journal of Counselling, 23,* 263–272.

Weinrach, S. G. (1980). Unconventional therapist: Albert Ellis. *Personnel and Guidance Journal, 59,* 152–160.

Weinrach, S. G. (1988). Cognitive therapist: A dialogue with Aaron Beck. *Journal of Counseling and Development, 67,* 159–164.

Wiener, D. N. (1988). *Albert Ellis: Passionate skeptic.* New York: Praeger.

Wilson, G. T., Eldredge, K. L., Smith, D., & Niles, B. (1991). Cognitive-behavioral treatment with and without response prevention for bulimia. *Behavior Research and Therapy, 29,* 575–583.

Wiser, S. L., & Goldfried, M. R. (1993). Comparative study of emotional experiencing in psychodynamic-interpersonal and cognitive-behavioral therapies. *Journal of Consulting and Clinical Psychology, 61,* 892–895.

CHAPTER 14

Reality Therapy

Chapter Outline

Introduction
Brief Biography
Historical Development
View of Human Nature
Development of Maladaptive Behavior
Function of the Therapist
Goals of Therapy
Major Methods and Techniques
Application
Critical Analysis
Current Status
Chapter Summary
Suggested Reading

INTRODUCTION

Many counselors, disillusioned with a perceived ineffectiveness of unconditional positive regard, wary of approaches involving the unconscious, and put off by the presumed inhumaness of behavioral techniques, have looked for a viable alternative to these methods. They have sought a straightforward theoretical approach that could make a practical difference in people's lives and many have found that alternative in reality therapy.

Reality therapy holds that people can do something about their fate if they will consider themselves and their environment realistically. In a sense it is a straightforward, action-oriented, pragmatic approach to counseling that is relatively uncomplicated and easy to understand (Osipow, Walsh, & Tosi, 1984). Although it seems simple, proponents of reality therapy remind us that "simple" should not be mistaken for "simplistic."

Reality therapy is based on an explanation of brain functioning known as *control theory*. This theory accounts for human behavior, not on the basis of past conflicts, external stimuli, or rational thinking, but on the principle that we act in an attempt to fulfill our current needs: belonging, power, pleasure, freedom, and survival. Actions, thoughts, emotions, and even human physiology are continuously generated to fulfill these generic needs and specific wants. Some behavior is helpful; some is ineffective or harmful. Through the process of reality therapy, clients learn to travel on a more effective path, to make more realistic choices, to satisfy their needs—a journey often unseen by clients in the beginning of therapy. In a trusting environment in which they can define and express their needs and wants, clients are able to self-evaluate and choose alternatives leading to a more effective life.

Like many of the other approaches we have examined in this text, reality therapy is largely the product of a single man, Dr. William Glasser.

BRIEF BIOGRAPHY

William Glasser was born in Cleveland, Ohio, on May 11, 1925, the third and youngest child of Ben and Betty Glasser. Little has been written about Glasser's childhood, which he speaks of as being relatively uneventful and happy. After graduating from Cleveland Heights High School, where he played cornet in the band and developed a lasting interest in sports, he majored in chemical engineering at Case Institute of Technology. While still a student, he married Naomi Judith Silver. After graduation he pursued a Ph.D. in clinical psychology, but his advisers rejected his dissertation and he gained admission to medical school at Western Reserve University instead. In 1953, he received

> *A therapy that leads all patients toward reality, toward grappling successfully with the tangible and intangible aspects of the real world, might accurately be called …*
> Reality Therapy.
>   —William Glasser

his M.D. degree at the age of 28. He completed a psychiatric residency at UCLA in 1957, spending the last year of his residency at the West Los Angeles Veterans Administration Hospital. In 1961 he became board-certified.

While in residency, Glasser became increasingly pained over the disjunction between the Freudian methods he had studied and the approaches that truly seemed to help the patient. Increasingly disillusioned with the efficacy of traditional psychoanalytic procedures, Glasser began experimenting with alternative treatments. In 1962, Glasser joined the staff of an institute for adolescent girls in Ventura, California. Three years later he published *Reality Therapy: A New Approach to Psychiatry*, which made ample use of his experiences at the Ventura school to illuminate the details of his therapeutic approach. In 1969 he published, with considerable success, *Schools Without Failure*, which applied the principles of reality therapy to the school setting (Parish, 1988).

Glasser was married to his wife, Naomi, for 46 years before she died of cancer in 1992. Their three children have followed in their father's footsteps: one in counseling, another in teaching, a third in medicine. Naomi Glasser has also contributed to her husband's work by editing two important texts that explain

William Glasser (1925–   ).
(Courtesy of The Milton H. Erickson Foundation, Inc., Phoenix, Arizona)

how reality therapy is done: *What Are You Doing? How People Are Helped by Reality Therapy* (1980) and *Control Theory in the Practice of Reality Therapy: Case Studies* (1989). Dr. Glasser continues to lecture around the globe on his ideas. He recently wrote a book for couples, *Staying Together* (1995), which is a control theory guide to a lasting marriage.

HISTORICAL DEVELOPMENT

Although the presupposition that justifies reality therapy is an earlier account of brain functioning called control theory, the two phrases—"control theory" and "reality therapy"—are now sometimes used interchangeably. Norbert Wiener, a Harvard University mathematician, who formulated many of the principles that have been subsumed under control theory, has described the importance of feedback to both engineering and biological systems (1948) as well as the sociological implications for human beings (1950).

Central to Glasser's approach is his belief in the potential for and the necessity of individuals to choose their own direction (see Sidebar 14-1). One writer argues that the roots of this notion can be found in Ralph Waldo Emerson's concept of self-reliance (Croll, 1992); others have suggested that Alfred Adler's model of psychotherapy is a direct ancestor of reality therapy (Rozsnafsky, 1974; Whitehouse, 1984). But when asked about the historical development of reality therapy, Glasser is more likely to point to his basic dislike of and objections to psychoanalytic therapy, which focuses primarily on neurosis and mental illness. Rejecting the medical model of mental illness developed by his Freudian colleagues, Glasser began to argue that patients are not ill, but weak. Only if patients' abilities were strengthened, he thought, could they function as healthy members of society.

Sidebar 14-1

UNDERSTANDING CONTROL THEORY

Wubbolding (1988) has provided a standard summary of Glasser's control theory as it applies to counseling and psychotherapy:

1. *Human beings are born with five needs:* belonging, power (competence, achievement, recognition, self-esteem, and so on), fun or enjoyment, freedom or independence (autonomy), and survival. These needs are general and universal. Along with wants, which are specific and unique for each person, they serve as the motivators or sources of all behavior.
2. *The difference between what individuals want and what they perceive they are getting (input) is the immediate source of specific behaviors at any given moment.* Thus reality therapy rests on the principle that human behavior springs from internal motivation, which drives the behavior moment to moment (Wubbolding, 1988). Another consequence of this principle is that human behavior is not an attempt to resolve unconscious, early childhood conflicts.

The sources of effective behaviors ("I'll do it," positive symptoms, and negative symptoms and negative addictions) are current, internal, and conscious.

3. *All human behaviors are composed of doing (acting), thinking, feeling, and physiology.* Behaviors are identified by the most obvious aspect of this total behavior. Thus, someone counseled for poor grades in school is seen with a presenting action problem. People are labeled psychotic because the primary and most obvious aspect of their total behavior is dysfunctional thinking. Depression, anger, resentment, and fear are most obvious in other persons, so their behavior is called a feeling behavior. The most obvious component of others' behavior is the physiological element, including heart disease, high blood pressure, and other ailments. Because behavior is total—that is, made up of four components—and because it is generated from within, it is useful to see behavior not as static but as ongoing. Therefore, total behavior is often expressed in "ing" words. Feelings, for example, are described as "depress-

ing," "guilting," "anxietying," and so on. Another implication of this principle is that all behavior has a purpose. Human choices are not aimless or random. They are all teleological; in other words, they serve a purpose: to close the gap between the perception of what a person is getting and what he or she wants at a given moment.

4. *Human behavior, originating from within, means that human beings are responsible for their behaviors.* In other words, we are all capable of change. This change is brought about by choosing more effective behaviors. The aspect of human behavior over which we have the most direct control is that of acting, and secondarily that of thinking. Therefore,

Adapted from Wubbolding, R. E. (1988). *Using reality therapy.* New York: Harper & Low.

in counseling and psychotherapy, the focus is on changing total behavior by discussing current actions—along with the evaluation of their effectiveness in fulfilling needs, current wants, and the evaluation of their realistic attainability—and current perceptions or viewpoints along with their helpfulness to the individual.

5. *Human beings see the world through a perceptual system that functions as a set of lenses.* At a low level of perception, the person simply recognizes the world, i.e., gives a name to objects and events, but does not make a judgment about them. At a high level of perception, the person puts a positive or negative value on the perception. Exploring the various levels of perception and their helpfulness is part of the counseling process.

While Glasser was in the valley of doubt, Dr. G. L. Harrington, his teacher at UCLA, was having his own troubled thoughts about the merits of psychoanalysis as a curative science. Since Harrington believed that there was no significant proof that psychoanalysis had any curative powers, he, too, was seeking a more effective psychotherapy. Harrington's doubts inspired Glasser to develop what finally emerged as reality therapy. Glasser gives full credit for many of reality therapy's ideas to his supportive and sympathetic teacher.

Actually, the ever-practical Glasser arrived at his treatment theory at least in part because he was not optimistic about starting a private practice. Glasser knew that his open resistance to the psychoanalytic approach during his residency at UCLA would not make him a top choice for referral among his former professors. Yet these were the very referrals on which he would need to rely, if he were to succeed as a beginning psychiatrist. Believing referrals would not be forthcoming, Glasser gave up the idea of starting a private practice in favor of a position as head psychiatrist at a youth facility run by the state of California for female delinquents: the Ventura School for Girls. It was here that Glasser had the freedom to practice his treatment strategies without hindrance. He began using techniques he had developed earlier—techniques that met with such amazing success, that Glasser (1965) managed to cut recidivism in the institution to an unheard of 20%.

Shortly after publishing *Reality Therapy* in 1965, Glasser founded the Institute of Reality Therapy in Canoga Park, California, to train human service professionals in his new therapeutic approach. Glasser also joined with California educators to apply the principles of reality therapy to both the ghetto schools of Watts and the upscale schools of Palo Alto.

So successful were Dr. Glasser's efforts in education, that he soon began lecturing extensively on reality therapy throughout the United States and Canada. He has worked with communities and school districts to establish teacher-training centers, and has served as a consultant for courts, police bureaus, and welfare departments. His frequent appearances on television and his writings, which have been translated into numerous languages, have carried the practical message of reality therapy around the world.

VIEW OF HUMAN NATURE

Reality therapy assumes that every person wants to be different—to feel somehow separate and distinct from every other living being—and it underscores this desire by identifying the unique needs of the individual. "No matter where the search may go, no other person exists who thinks, looks, acts, and talks exactly as we do" (Glasser & Zunin, 1979, p. 292). This intrinsic and inherited need to be unique transcends cultures and is the driving force for all behavior (Peterson & Woodward, 1992).

According to Glasser, during the first 6 years of our lives, we develop either a negative or a positive identity. People with a positive self-image believe that they are worthwhile, that there is at least one other person in the world who cares about them (Glasser & Wubbolding, 1995). "When a man acts in such a way that he gives and receives love, and feels worthwhile to himself and others, his behavior is right and moral," writes Glasser (1965, p. 57). People with positive identities tend to associate with other people who also have positive identities.

Negative identities are formed by individuals who do not think well of themselves and who, as a result, also have problems caring about other people.

Conventional psychiatry wastes too much time arguing over how many diagnoses can dance at the end of a case history.

—William Glasser

Characterized by irresponsible and self-defeating behavior that hurts themselves and others, these people engage in behavior that often denies reality (Protheroe, 1992). "In their unsuccessful effort to fulfill their needs," Glasser (1965, p. 219) argues, "no matter what behavior they choose, all patients have a common characteristic: they all deny the reality of the world around them." According to Glasser (1981), it is this denial and the formation of a negative identity that leads to maladaptive behavior.

As a result reality therapy views identity through one's behavior. Unlike behavioristic theory, which focuses on a stimulus–response paradigm, reality therapy measures behavior against the objective standard of reality, with which individuals are either in consonance or dissonance.

DEVELOPMENT OF MALADAPTIVE BEHAVIOR

Reality therapists reject the medical model, arguing against the existence of nearly all forms of mental illness. According to Glasser (1961, 1984), mental illness is not like a case of the measles: It is not so much something that happens to individuals, as it is an attempt to deal with external events. That is to say, people choose mental illness. Despite heavy criticism, Glasser ignores biology as a factor in mental illness and instead views maladaptive functioning as the consequence of irresponsibility. Problems arise when people are not taught, or do not accept, responsibility for their behavior. When some people refuse to accept or ignore that responsibility, the price they pay is high: No longer feeling worthwhile, they establish a *failure identity*.

In contrast, to have a *success identity* and feel worthwhile, healthy individuals will conscientiously maintain a satisfactory standard of behavior. "To do so," Glasser says, "we must learn to correct ourselves when we do wrong and to credit ourselves when we do right. If we do not evaluate our behavior . . . we do not act to improve our conduct where it is below our standards, we will not fulfill our need to be worthwhile and we will suffer" (1965, p. 10).

There was a time when human behavior, according to Glasser, was controlled by the *old brain* needs of survival. In contemporary times, however, our behavior is associated with *new brain* needs for belonging, power, freedom, and pleasure. People have images of these needs, and these images in their minds behave according to whether or not their needs are being satisfied. Thus, personal actions are based on perceptions. "Our behavior is our constant attempt to control perceptions," Glasser writes (1981, p. 53). In his model of maladaptive behavior, Glasser posits that individuals *create* behaviors, including mentally disturbing ones such as delusions and hallucinations, in order to create identities for themselves that meet their expectations.

FUNCTION OF THE THERAPIST

Thus the reality therapist attaches direct values to behavior, measuring clients' success or failure in treatment against their ability to meet these values (Thatcher, 1987). For the reality therapist, responsibility serves as a foundational value. "Responsibility is considered the basic concept of reality therapy and is defined as the ability to meet one's needs without depriving others of the ability to meet theirs" (Rachin, 1974, p. 47).

Because the reality therapist believes that a change in behavior must precede a change in identity, the focus is on changing irresponsible, self-defeating behavior. If, according to Glasser, "we are what we do," to change "who we are" (identity), we must change "what we do" (behavior): that is, change in identity follows change in behavior (Glasser & Wubbolding, 1995). The reality therapist's task is therefore to help clients identify and change self-defeating behavior.

As might be expected, Glasser (1965) describes the role of the reality therapist in concrete terms. The work of the therapist is difficult because a "firm
emotional relationship" must be built with clients who have failed to establish
such relationships in the past. However, the therapist is "aided by recognizing
the patient is desperate for involvement and suffering because he is not able
to fulfill his needs" (p. 21). In fact, the therapist's participation is the "major
skill of doing reality therapy" (p. 21). The counselor needs to be tough, interested, warm, understanding, sensitive, and genuine. To provide clients with examples of responsible behavior, the therapist must fulfill his or her own needs
and be willing to talk about personal struggles. In short, he or she must provide
clients with a genuine person who cares. "Unless the requisite involvement exists between the responsible therapist and the irresponsible patient, there can
be no therapy" (Glasser, 1965, p. 21). In the counseling relationship, then, the
counselor's role is to communicate warmth, understanding, and concern.

Nevertheless, the reality therapist must withstand clients' requests for
sympathy or a "justification of his actions no matter how the patient pleads or
threatens" (p. 22). Irresponsible action must never be condoned. The therapist
must also be "willing to watch the patient suffer, if that helps him toward responsibility" (p. 22). Glasser also writes that therapists must "never be frightened or rebuffed by the patient's behavior" (p. 23).

Assuming the warm, caring mindset of this therapist, Glasser characterizes
the function of the reality therapist in several ways (Glasser, 1965; Glasser &
Wubbolding, 1995). First of all, the focus is on behavior, and since the past cannot be changed, the focus is on behavior in the present tense. Although the
counselor will not punish clients for failure, they must finally learn to identify
their irresponsible patterns of behavior before being open to change. Once this
self-defeating behavior is identified, the counselor will assist clients in developing a plan to change behavior. It is important for this plan to be in writing.
Finally, making it clear that excuses are unacceptable, the counselor will help
clients to make a commitment to carry out their plan.

Because interviews with clients are likely to take place in settings other
than the typical counseling office, with its carpet, desk, and bookshelves, the
personhood of the reality therapist is vitally important. In fact, reality therapy
is often practiced in such atypical places as schools, street clinics, and prisons:
on the playground, for example, with young people in a delinquent detention
center, or in a prison yard with inmates. The circumstances often determine the
therapy in these settings. These varied environments require a reality therapist
to be a consistent model of personal responsibility, in or out of the counseling
office (Clagett, 1992).

GOALS OF THERAPY

Because clients are unable to achieve a healthy identity without becoming
aware of their behavior, the overarching goal of reality therapy is to help them
identify and change their self-defeating behavior. In fact, Glasser believes that

clients have more control over their behavior than over their thinking or feeling responses. To this end, reality therapy seeks to help clients to interact constructively by accepting the reality of their existence, by developing a keen sense of responsibility, and by making appropriate choices. Unlike clients in existential therapy, however, individuals in reality therapy are not viewed as creating their own existence and destiny through such choices. Instead, they are directed to conform to standards of reality in order to behave and thus to live more productively and harmoniously.

Glasser (1976) lists several criteria for behavior that is suitable and healthy. First of all, the behavior has such real, specific value for the clients that they believe their lifestyles will improve if they practice the behavior. Clients should be able to engage in this behavior without being self-critical and without being competitive. And they should be able to accomplish this behavior on their own, without an extraordinary amount of mental effort.

The final, broad goal of enabling clients to live productive, harmonious lives is realized through three separate but interwoven procedures, according to Glasser. First, the counselor helps clients face reality head-on, and then he or she helps them test their behavior against that reality. Second, without rejecting them as people, the counselor rejects their unrealistic behavior. And finally, the counselor teaches them better ways to fulfill their needs within the parameters of reality. In these several ways the reality therapist strives to help clients clarify their life goals, to identify what they want in life. After examining the obstacles that lie in the path of those goals, the therapist will then help clients to discover the personal assets and environmental supports that will facilitate the successful completion of their goals.

We constantly gripe, complain, and struggle with reality.

—William Glasser

Only when clients assume responsibility for their personal behavior, only when they manage to meet their personal needs without hurting themselves or others, can it be said that they have made progress toward reaching their goals (Wubbolding, 1975).

MAJOR METHODS AND TECHNIQUES

Glasser (1965) conceives of the process of reality therapy in eight general steps that therapists can apply very flexibly in helping clients face reality and become more responsible. At the outset of therapy it is crucial that the therapist *be involved,* that he or she establish a caring rapport within the context of a professional helping relationship, and that the therapist remain positive and emphasize the clients' strengths. Not until then can the therapist find out what it is that clients really want and whether the "want" is possible to fulfill. Second, the therapist will *focus, not on feelings, but on behavior.* Because the clients' behavior is presumed to be an attempt at some form of control, a means of satisfying a want or need, the therapist then needs to persuade them to own up to what they are doing now and to deal with evasions and abstractions. Third, it is essential that the therapist *focus on the present* in order to help clients realize that what they are doing is ineffectual. This is not to be viewed as a callous judgment by the therapist; it is simply a means of subordinating clients' histories to the present, so that they can examine what they are doing now. Next, the therapist needs to *make a plan.* Functioning as a resource for solutions and as a concrete planner, the therapist helps clients to devise a plan to control their lives more effectively. Nevertheless, the effective therapist knows that he or she can never solve anything for clients; that is the clients' work. And it is the clients, not the therapist, who must learn to evaluate their behavior to know whether what they are doing is helping their situation.

But such a plan is not worthwhile, Glasser believes, unless the therapist manages to *get a commitment* from clients to carry it out. Clients with failure identities are particularly reluctant to commit to change. At this point, the therapist will brook *no excuses,* which are always part of the ineffectual patterns of the past. Reality therapists are interested in the future and maintain an attitude of "no excuses." Even if the plan is failing, the emphasis needs to lie not on dissecting the old plan, but on developing a new strategy for success. This the therapist can, and should, accomplish without being punitive. The therapist needs to *eliminate punishment,* which usually involves another person controlling the client's life. Besides, natural consequences are punishment enough. We are better motivated, then, if we are able to do things without the fear of being punished if we do not do them. Last, the effective therapist will *never give up.* To give up is to be controlled by the client's ineffectual behavior, Glasser writes, so the therapist must always look toward the possibility of change.

> *I went to the woods because I wished to live deliberately, to confront only the essential facts of life, and see if I could not learn what it had to teach, and not, when I came to die, discover that I had not lived.*
>
> —Henry David Thoreau

Glasser does not rely on these procedures as a "cookbook" for therapeutic intervention. If ideas from other theoretical orientations can help clients confront reality, practitioners of reality therapy will use those techniques as well. Wallace (1986) and Wubbolding (1988, 1991) note a number of strategies, often shaped by a therapist's personality, that are used as part of the approach in reality therapy.

Structuring

Reality therapists help clients to *structure* their expectations, to understand the nature, limits, and goals of therapy. This structuring helps clients adjust their expectations and gives them a realistic hope for change. Providing clients with confidence in their therapist, structuring lets them know their well-being is valued by their therapist. Simple descriptions of the counseling process or brief explanations—discussing fees, for example, or talking about the expected number of sessions—may help alleviate the anxiety that clients feel. In fact, Glasser (1965) suggests that setting a predetermined time limit or stipulating the number of sessions may motivate clients to focus better and work more intensely.

By helping clients accept the responsibility for their behavior and by allowing them to face the reality of their situation, structuring, encourages them to remain in therapy and to face the reality of their situation.

Confrontation

Confrontation is inevitable in reality therapy. At the outset of therapy clients will be immediately confronted with present reality, and eventually they will need to face the question: Is what I am currently doing right or wrong for me? Most confrontations in reality therapy are reflected by a variety of questions that call clients to action and that place responsibility for the action squarely on their shoulders. These questions will confront clients with the issue of how they plan to meet their goals or with whether they are truly committed to meeting their goals at all. Clients are also confronted with the consequences of their actions, whether internal (e.g., feeling depressed) or external. This critical aspect of reality therapy teaches individuals what they can expect when they act in certain ways. Sometimes clients are even confronted with a contract requiring their signature as evidence of their commitment.

Contracts

Although verbal agreements, confirmed with a handshake, may suffice for some clients, a written contract signed by both the client and his or her therapist further reinforces a commitment to follow through. An ongoing reminder of the specific sequence and schedule in the clients' plans, a signed contract provides concrete evidence of their intention to change their behavior. And once the conditions of a written contract are fulfilled, it serves as a record of the person's capacity to work responsibly and successfully meet his or her goals.

Instruction

In reality therapy, clients will inevitably need specific skill development to implement their courses of action. If the therapist is competent to teach the desired skill, he or she will use time in the therapy sessions to instruct the client; if not, clients may be referred elsewhere for skill instruction. Whatever the alternative, as long as both the therapist and the clients assume mutual responsibility in the learning process, reality therapy will not avoid providing whatever instruction is needed for clients to meet their goals.

Skillful Questioning

A major intervention in reality therapy centers on the question: "Does your present behavior enable you to get what you want now, and will it take you in the direction you want to go?" (Glasser, 1989). The practitioner of reality therapy helps clients to evaluate their behavior by asking a number of direct questions, for example, "Is what you are doing helping or hurting you?" "Is what you are doing now what you want to be doing?" "Is your behavior working for you?" "Is what you are doing against the rules?" "Is what you want realistic or attainable?" "How committed are you to the therapeutic process, and to changing your life?" (Wubbolding, 1988). Direct questions like these begin to highlight the importance of choice. Wubbolding (1988) notes that such skillful questioning not only allows the therapist to enter the client's world, where he or she can gather important information, but also helps the client take more effective control of his or her life.

Emphasizing Choice

By emphasizing the freedom of clients to live by their own personal standards, reality therapy keeps the responsibility for clients' behavior on themselves. To sharpen this emphasis on personal responsibility, the counselor often turns adjectives into verbs. Instead of saying clients are angry, for instance, as if anger were an inescapable situation, he or she will use verbs, such as *angering* or *bullying*, that highlight the clients' responsibility for this frame of mind. Likewise, instead of having a headache, clients are said to be *headaching*. The emphasis here is on personal choice. Through changing adjectives and nouns,

The therapist must teach the patient that therapy is not primarily directed toward making him happy.
—William Glasser

which describe attributes or states of being, to active verbs, individuals can finally begin to understand that they are "choosing to depress." Therefore fewer choices will be made that result in depression. The emphasis is on positive, constructive actions that stem from choosing to live by standards of reality (Glasser, 1989).

Role-Playing

When clients are struggling to put recently acquired skills into practice, the reality therapist may turn to role-playing techniques that help *presentize* clients' behavior and that allow them to rehearse the events that cause their anxiety. During a role-playing activity, clients learn to prepare for the consequences of their behavior, including their feelings, while performing the activity. Difficulties in interpersonal relationships are often relieved through role-playing specific situations with the reality therapist (Cockrum, 1993).

Support

Clients with a failure identity, who have learned to expect failure, often need encouragement in anticipating successful outcomes of their efforts. As they put their new plans into action, support can assist them in achieving an optimistic outlook. Once they see that their therapist encourages and supports them, that he or she believes in them, their motivation and self-efficacy increases. Inevitably the therapist's trust and support communicates a sense of self-worth, and it is this growing feeling of being worthwhile that gives clients more energy to live responsibly.

Constructive Debate

A client's self-concept can be enhanced through constructive debate. When therapists and clients challenge one another's ideas and values, it demonstrates that they have values worth defending, that what they have to say is worthwhile and is taken seriously. Through constructive debate, clients learn they can contribute meaningfully to the therapeutic process. Their voices are significant.

Humor

Knowing that clients can be brought closer to reality through the therapeutic use of humor, the reality therapist occasionally uses humor in a sensitive manner. Used appropriately, humor can help clients gain a healthy ability to laugh at themselves—to become less introspective and more objective. When humor is used improperly, however, when it is sarcastic, punitive, or demeaning, it will dismantle whatever trust, confidence, and credibility has been established (Saper, 1987). Such inappropriate humor certainly undermines the process of reality therapy.

Self-Disclosure

Requiring equal and active participation of both client and therapist, reality therapy is a collaborative effort. As a result reality therapists share personal experiences and struggles and open themselves up to reveal their humanity, even to the point of questioning their own values or uncovering their own weaknesses. When therapists make themselves vulnerable, clients feel less vulnerable. Such appropriate self-disclosure brings clients closer to reality.

Positive Addictions

Glasser encourages his clients to choose positive "addictions" that lead to more satisfactory ways of living—jogging, for instance, movies, meditation, or visiting with friends, anything that may help them reach a "healthy high." Of course, our world offers opportunities for negative or positive addictions, but, according to Glasser, our addictions and our fates are up to us. We are in control of our addictions: we can choose pain or we can choose joy (Glasser, 1976).

Assessment

Although the counselor in reality therapy makes little attempt to test, diagnose, interpret, or otherwise assess clients, he or she does evaluate their progress toward desired goals. Although the basic requirement on the part of the client is responsibility, almost any constructive, responsible change in clients' behavior is defined as a step in that direction. Termination of therapy is warranted "if the patient can act in increasingly responsible ways, resolve crises and adjustment problems through accepting that he is responsible for himself and his behavior

and that he can fulfill his needs without hurting himself or other people"
(Glasser & Zunin, 1979, p. 327).

APPLICATION

Reality therapy has been effectively applied to a wide variety of clinical issues,
including suicidal ideation (Lester, 1994), school discipline and motivation
(Benshoff, Poidevant, & Cashwell, 1994; Glasser, 1990; Parish, 1992), self-esteem
(Williamson, 1992), alcohol abuse (Barrett, 1992; Honeyman, 1990; Hulbert,
1992; Peacock, 1992), drug abuse (Mickel, 1993; Reuss, 1985), anxiety (Udry,
1992), mental illness (Garner, 1983), burnout (Edelwich, 1980; Wubbolding,
1979), grief recovery (Stanwood, 1992), rape recovery (McArthur, 1990), exercise initiation (Hart, 1992), sexual offenders (Stanton, 1992), neurolinguistic
hypnosis (Ignoffo, 1994), and autonomy training (Newton, Brack, & Brack,
1992).

Whereas reality therapy is able to treat effectively a variety of clients,
William Glasser illustrates the essentials of his approach—involvement, rejection of irresponsibility, relearning, and so on—in the following case. Glasser is
quick to point out, however, that the application of his theory does not follow
a static formula; it is uniquely determined by the personality of each client. The
following are Glasser's own words in describing how he applied his approach
to "Pat."

> A wealthy, young, overindulged, satisfactorily married mother of two whose
> only obvious problem was overweight, Pat is typical of the fairly responsible
> patients whom the psychiatrist sees. Extremely pleasant, with an agile, intelli-
> gent mind, she was skeptical of psychiatry yet hopeful that perhaps through
> therapy she might gain more from her life. Notwithstanding her material well-
> being, she felt that there was much she was missing.
>
> The first part of reality therapy with Pat was difficult for both of us as I tried
> to create involvement between us and she tried to understand what I was dri-
> ving at. Expecting to discuss her childhood, she found it difficult to understand
> that I was not particularly interested in historical material. Attempting at times
> to talk about her dreams and unconscious mind, she found me equally uninter-
> ested. Restricting the discussion to the present seemed sterile to her because her
> life was the rather humdrum existence of the rich suburban housewife who had
> difficulty in filling her days. Nevertheless we did find much to discuss about the
> current status of her large, complex family and also about books, plays, movies,
> and current events. Stimulated to think about what was going on in the world
> outside of her limited existence, she enjoyed our discussions, but she continu-
> ally questioned the therapy and the lack of progress toward a better life.
>
> Her favorite diversion was to take me to task for not helping her to reduce.
> In addition to her own direct comments, she quoted her husband as saying he
> could not see one apparent benefit from therapy. According to him she was as
> fat and difficult to live with as ever. To these attacks on my therapeutic skill I
> would answer that psychotherapy does not reduce people, that it does not
> make them happier, and it does not solve their problems. If she wanted to re-

duce, she was free to do so and I would encourage her, but weight reduction was not my responsibility. I emphasized that if she wanted to change she had to come regularly because I knew that we had to become involved before anything could happen. I did not care what she talked about as long as it had to do with the present. I had to stress both that she must come and that I could do little directly for her because I did not want her to become involved with me as a dependent. Without magic to help her, I would stay with her until the problems she came for were solved. As with every patient, I let her know that I was there as a person who would not desert her or give her false hope.

Discussing her rather irresponsible existence in which she did everything to please herself only, Pat seemed to revel in the long descriptions of her childish behavior toward her husband, her family, and even some other friends. It was very important to her to tell me how much better she would be if she could act in a more mature way, but how she absolutely would not do so. She was anxious for me to tell her to do something different, which I was tempted to do, but I refrained because I knew she was trying to cast me in the role of reformer so that she could reject me as she had rejected everyone else who had tried to correct her.

Therapy continued slowly, little seemed to be happening, yet the relationship was growing. Unable to make me assume a role she could reject, she began to develop some respect and trust for me and what I was doing. Although she started to come late in an effort to show how little she cared, she did come. I paid no attention to her lateness, or to her insincere apologies or excuses. Finally, one day during a rather innocuous conversation she burst out and said, "There's nothing you can do to make me responsible." Here was a remarkable statement because I had never mentioned the word responsibility to her. Nevertheless, the months of subtle pressure had had their effect. She was now very slightly on the defensive, because she was beginning to understand what I was trying to do. I was able to increase the pressure on her to change by discussing my work with the delinquent girls. When I pointed out how similar she was to these girls, she readily agreed, saying, "If you help them so much why can't you help me?" To this little pleasantry I replied, "because I can't lock you up. If I could, you know as well as I do that you would change." Not denying my claim, she countered by stating that all I had was these two hours a week in the office and that's all I ever would have. Since I had no control it was up to her. I added, "I'll wait, I have all the time in the world."

Next, Pat attacked my fees by saying that they were too low, another depreciation of my worth. She said she could afford more, other psychiatrists were getting larger fees, why didn't I ask for more. I answered her charge by asking if therapy had helped her. When she replied that it hadn't, I said that considering my ineffectiveness I could hardly change more, I wasn't worth it. Having thus passed the test of avarice, I was not again challenged on my fees. Through this gambit and countless others we became more deeply involved. She tried everything to prove me irresponsible. I responded by admitting any apparent shortcomings but never giving up. All her efforts were really directed toward having me commit one of two fatal errors—giving up or giving in. Either one would have finished therapy.

After almost a year, we began to be more involved; I could point out her irresponsibilities. My regular presence and my stand for greater responsibility encouraged her to take a chance and change. During the whole of the second year she slowly became more responsible. Although the change was not dramatic, she was less self-centered and more able to give to others, especially to her husband and children, who needed her far more than she was originally able to admit to herself. She felt a keener sense of achievement and she lost fifty pounds. She tried to credit me with the weight loss, but as I refused to take the blame for her inability to lose earlier, I refused to take the credit then.

It was a difficult, though rewarding, case. With her intelligence and energy, Pat certainly had great capacity for more worthwhile behavior within her immediate surroundings, and perhaps she will have a chance to do more in the larger world. In the final part of therapy we were both groping toward the goal of even greater responsibility (Glasser, 1965, pp. 143–148).

CRITICAL ANALYSIS

The strengths of reality therapy are quite apparent. To begin with, it has great versatility. It can be applied to many different populations—children, adolescents, adults, and the aged—and in almost any setting that emphasizes mental health and adjustment, such as hospitals, schools, prisons, and crisis centers (Glasser, 1989). In addition, Glasser's approach is concrete. Both counselor and clients are able to assess how much progress is being made and in what areas, especially if a goal-specific contract has been drawn up. If clients are doing well in modifying one behavior and not another, increased attention can be given to the underdeveloped area. Another strength of reality therapy is that it has successfully challenged the medical model of psychotherapy, providing a refreshing alternative to pathology-centered approaches to counseling.

> *The therapist freely gives praise when the patient acts responsibly and shows disapproval when he does not.*
>
> —William Glasser

Reality therapy, however, is not without its pitfalls. For example, it has been criticized for exaggerating observable behavior traits, while ignoring other valuable therapeutic concepts such as the unconscious. Linked to this shortcoming is Glasser's view that all forms of mental illness are attempts to deal with external events; in short, that people choose mental illness. The result is, of course, a reluctance to consider the biological factors that contribute to mental illness, a stance that critics find naive or even irresponsible. In addition, reality makes little allowance for the need of some clients to resolve past events. A traumatic experience, for example, may need to be dealt with in the context of treatment.

And more than some approaches, reality therapy has the potential to be misused by practitioners who are insufficiently involved with their clients or who settle for general goals, force a plan on the client, or proceed too quickly to commitment (Wubbolding, 1975). In other words, reality therapy runs the risk of being abused in the hands of an authoritarian counselor, the "expert" who is frantically straightening out everyone else. Whereas Glasser believes that in reality therapy the counselor should not judge clients' behavior—that the counselor is to support them in their personal exploration of values—an overzealous practitioner could easily impose values on clients. Although this is always a potential danger, it is perhaps most hazardous when applying reality therapy within a cross-cultural context.

In fact, when practiced appropriately, Glasser's approach readily lends itself to cross-cultural counseling in a number of ways. Because its focus is on acting and thinking rather than on identifying and exploring feelings, and since it is not burdened with a great deal of technical jargon, many ethnic-minority clients can find reality therapy relatively inviting. Not surprisingly, then, reality therapy is taught in many countries. The Institute for Reality Therapy has ties to Japan, Korea, Ireland, Norway, the United Kingdom, Australia, New Zealand, Hong Kong, Singapore, and the former Yugoslavia (Glasser & Wubbolding, 1995).

Because it is up to clients to determine what they want, reality therapy has the potential to help ethnic-minority clients integrate into their lives desirable "foreign" values and practices, while allowing them to retain their ethnic values and identity. However, because the approach depends considerably on effective two-way communication, it does have limitations in helping clients who, for any reason, cannot adequately express their needs. Some ethnic-minority clients are reluctant to say what they need; their culture has not reinforced an assertive stance and they may have been socialized to think more socially than personally.

Glasser's emphasis on personal freedom gives rise to yet a further caution in applying reality therapy to ethnic minorities: His radical view on one's ability to choose may cause the therapist not to comprehend fully the ways in which social forces have systematically repressed members of minority groups. A brutal fact of life for many minorities, discrimination is a real barrier that prevents minority clients from getting what they want.

In regards to counseling diverse populations, reality therapy can work effectively with people adjusting to a disability and with their ensuing rehabilitation as well. During the early phases of counseling, for example, clients are required to learn and face the reality of their disabilities, which are never to be used as excuses for personal failures and dependency. Then they are provided with the means of living within its framework (Ososkie & Turpin, 1985; Walker, 1987). In later phases of adaptation, the reality therapist may further assist clients in setting time-limited personal, social, and vocational goals and in teaching and practicing community-based problem-solving and decision-making skills.

CURRENT STATUS

Although Glasser's thinking has expanded through the years, he has remained true to the basic constructs of his early methods and theory. Already in 1981, for instance, in *Stations of the Mind,* Glasser built a comprehensive picture of the workings of the "internal world" of the mind, which can be understood only by how we relate to external reality. And in 1984, in *Take Effective Control of Your Life,* Glasser revealed the importance of thinking in terms of control theory, which enables people to avoid problems that require professional help and to take more effective charge of their lives.

Since 1965 reality therapy has achieved a substantial following, especially among teachers and youth guidance counselors, substance-abuse treatment counselors, and rehabilitation counselors. Today reality therapy is recognized as an effective therapeutic approach and has been successfully applied in school settings, correctional institutions, psychiatric hospitals, convalescent homes, vocational rehabilitation centers, psychiatric clinics, and social service settings (see Sidebar 14-2) (Bassin, Bratter, & Rachin, 1976; Bratter, Bratter, Radda, & Steiner, 1993; Cohen & Sordo, 1984; Edens & Smryl, 1994; Evans, 1984; Heuchert, 1989; Vogt, 1985). Between the years of 1970 and 1990, 82 doctoral dissertations were written on this therapeutic approach (Franklin, 1993).

Sidebar 14-2

REALITY THERAPY WITH RAPE VICTIMS

Margaret J. McArthur

In a rape victim group, members have an opportunity to learn how others with similar experiences have been able to recover and work through similar problems. The peer support from members all along the continuum of recovery gives an individual a sense of hope (Roth, Dye, & Lebowitz, 1988). This instillation and maintenance of hope is crucial in all forms of psychotherapy (Yalom, 1985). Group therapy is extremely effective when the members have similar problems, but are at different stages of resolution (Kaltenbach & Gazda, 1975). Collective problem-solving in a peer support group is presumed to be very effective (Coates & Winston, 1983).

Reality therapy groups provide individuals greater opportunities for involvement, both in having others care for them and in providing opportunities for them to care for many others. The group assists the individual in making value judgments about whether or not previous behavior is working. The group is a tremendous resource when individuals make plans, offering ideas without advising. Commitment to a group is a powerful motivator,

and peer support aids the individual in successfully completing her or his plan. The never-ending support of a nonpunishing group of peers is vital in achieving a success identity.

Rape has an impact on the sense of self, effecting a loss of self-esteem, creation of guilt and shame, mistrust in interpersonal relationships and distorted perceptions of self-worth. Because of this massive injury to the self, rape victims may very quickly become isolated and lonely. They may experience their pain in any of the modes previously listed: disturbances of emotions, behavior problems, disturbances of thoughts, or somatic complaints. While other therapeutic approaches for rape victims focus on alleviating symptoms of psychiatric illness, reality therapy treats the sense of self. The intrusive thoughts, feelings, and actions a rape victim experiences may lead her to believe she is going crazy (Rose, 1986). Other frameworks reinforce this belief by placing a value judgment on her symptoms of illness. In contrast, reality therapy changes the point at which this value judgment is made, moving the assessment up to step three in the process of asking the victim to determine for herself if what she is doing is moral, legal, and is working to fulfil her needs. Reality therapy teaches the victim she is not crazy, but that she may be having difficulty in meeting her basic needs. Emphasis in reality therapy is on effective and ineffective behavior, not on the signs and symptoms of mental illness. Reality therapy offers the victim opportunities to regain self-esteem, resolve guilt and shame, rebuild trusting relationships, and renew her sense of self-worth by changing the point at which value judgments are made.

Loss of the sense of competence results in loss of self-esteem for rape victims. Reality therapy helps rebuild lost self-esteem. The rape victim is given opportunities to make plans to meet her needs, plans in which she can succeed and feel powerful over her environment again. When she succeeds, her success identity is reinforced. She regains mastery over her environment.

Loss of self-determination creates guilt and shame. Control was taken away from the victim at the time of the rape, but control over her behavior is now back in her hands. The feelings of helplessness and loss of control reported by rape victims may lead to depression as Seligman's learned helplessness model suggests (1985). Many victims appear to use what happened as an excuse for acting out, isolating themselves from others and withdrawing into depression. Victims often develop a passive life-style because of chronic feelings of helplessness and powerlessness (Goodman & Nowak-Scibelli, 1985). They feel their lives are out of their control. The reality therapy group actively confronts this passive style in a warm, supportive atmosphere. The group doesn't allow excuses for acting out or isolative behavior. The responsibility for the victim's behavior is not with the family who doesn't understand or the assailant who has ruined her life forever. The opportu-

nity for making a success of her life, for becoming a survivor instead of a victim, is hers. Reality therapy by no means attempts to minimize the real pain and loss of the victim, but does help the victim to see that her behavior is no longer under someone else's control. Now, it is up to her to continue to choose how this event will affect her behavior and life-style. Reality therapy reinforces her responsibility for fulfilling her needs and, in doing so, returns her sense of self-determination.

Following rape, the victim may have difficulty trusting others. She is sensitive to the reactions of others. Sensing their discomfort, she may want to withdraw and isolate herself. Women who have shared similar traumas quickly develop empathic rapport (Sadock, 1983). Members in rape groups form a common bond around their experience. However so-called crazy may seem their thoughts, feelings, and behaviors, they soon learn they are common to others. Reality therapy groups require involvement with other victims, as involvement with others is proposed to be the key to developing a success identity. Along with this involvement comes recognition and respect for themselves and others. They begin to trust others as they realize they are not alone. Members realize they are able to help others, because they understand each other's problems. In helping others they find a sense of purpose and belonging that restores their own self-esteem. They are able to rediscover the dignity they lost. They begin to meet their needs to love and be loved while giving and receiving support from others.

Evans (1978) says a supportive, nonpunishing atmosphere is necessary for maintaining a healthy ego after rape. Those to whom the rape victim discloses herself may be critical and nonsupportive. Reality therapy groups pride themselves

Continued.

Sidebar 14-2—cont'd

on being supportive and nonpunishing. The affirmation a victim receives in a reality therapy group allows for a return of feelings of self-worth and begins the repair of her distorted self-perception.

The role of the leader in a reality therapy group for rape victims is the same as in any reality therapy group. The leader serves as a model of a responsible person (Kaltenbach & Gazda, 1975). The leader becomes highly involved with each group member, and focuses on here-and-now behavior and relationships. The leader assists members clearly to define what they want, to make value judgments at the right time, and to make plans for which success is guaranteed. In addition, the leader rewards successes, makes sure no excuses are accepted, and helps the group guard against criticism. In teaching the group the principles of reality therapy, the members are able to learn new behavior, accept responsibility, and ensure long-lasting, successful life-styles. The fact that reality therapy is a simple, straightforward technique for meeting one's needs makes it possible for individuals to continue to use reality therapy as a self-help coping strategy once the group has ended.

The Institute for Reality Therapy offers seminars that lead to certification for practitioners of reality therapy: an 18-month training program consisting of workshops, supervised practice, video and audio taping, small-group practice, feedback, and other experiences. More than 4500 people have completed the reality therapy certification process worldwide (Glasser & Wubbolding, 1995). Further information on these training programs can be obtained through:

The Institute for Reality Therapy
7301 Medical Center Drive, Suite 407
Canoga Park, CA 91307
Telephone: (818) 888-0688

or

The Center for Reality Therapy
777 Montgomery Road
Cincinnati, OH 45236
Telephone: (513) 561-1911

Launched in 1981, the *Journal of Reality Therapy* is devoted to publishing articles concerning research, theory, and practical applications of reality therapy in field settings. During the past decade and a half, more than 200 essays, articles, and research studies have been published on the applications of reality therapy. For further information on this journal, contact:

The *Journal of Reality Therapy*
203 Lake Hall
Boston-Bouve College
Northeastern University
360 Huntington Avenue
Boston, MA 02115

Never content to allow his approach to remain without constant scrutiny, additions, and changes, Dr. Glasser continues to be a quite active student, especially of educational systems. In fact, many of today's school districts are looking to his work in formulating curricula and school policies.

CHAPTER SUMMARY

1. *Biography.* Glasser (1925–) was born in Cleveland, Ohio, and his early years were characterized by a happy childhood in a loving family. He majored in chemical engineering and after graduation pursued a Ph.D. in clinical psychology. However, when Glasser's advisers rejected his dissertation, he gained admission to medical school and received his M.D. degree from Western Reserve University in 1953. He completed a psychiatric residency at UCLA in 1957. During this time, Glasser became disillusioned with the efficacy of traditional psychoanalytic procedures and began experimenting with alternative methods of treatment.

2. *Historical Development.* The origins of reality therapy are found in Glasser's basic dislike of the psychoanalytic approach, which focuses primarily on neurosis and mental illness. Glasser rejected the medical model of mental illness and argued that the patient is weak, not ill. It was Glasser's teacher, however, G. L. Harrington, who spurred him on in his unorthodox beliefs and his rejection of the medical model. Eventually taking a position as head psychiatrist at a youth facility for female delinquents run by the state of California, Glasser was finally free to practice his treatment strategies without hindrance. After he cut recidivism dramatically in the institution, he began writing about his unique approach.

3. *View of Human Nature.* Reality therapy assumes everyone wants to be different and has an intrinsic and inherited need to feel somehow separate and distinct from every other living being. Glasser defines two kinds of identity—positive and negative—which he views through behavior, testing it against reality. Individuals function either in consonance or dissonance with reality.

4. *Development of Maladaptive Behavior.* According to Glasser, a person chooses mental illness. He ignores biology as a factor in mental illness and instead views maladaptive functioning as the consequence of irresponsibility. According to Glasser, individuals must maintain a satisfactory standard of behavior if they are to have a success identity, feel worthwhile, and avoid forms of maladaptive behavior.

5. *Goals of Therapy.* The primary goal of reality therapy is to help clients identify and change self-defeating behavior, to help them make appropriate choices, and to develop a sense of responsibility. Reality therapy strives to help clients clarify what they want in life and then examine obstacles that stand in the way of their reaching what they want.

6. *Function of the Therapist.* Viewing responsibility as a foundational value, the therapist attempts to help clients change irresponsible behavior. To do so the therapist works to build a solid emotional relationship with the client by being tough, interested, warm, understanding, sensitive, and genuine. The bottom line is that the reality therapist must be an excellent example of responsible behavior.

7. *Major Methods and Techniques.* Glasser outlines eight general procedures that therapists can apply in helping their clients face reality and become more responsible: establishing a caring rapport, focusing on behavior (not feelings), focusing on the present (not the past), making a specific plan, getting a commitment, accepting no excuses, eliminating punishment, and never giving up. In addition, the reality therapist may employ a variety of techniques such as writing a contract with the client, role-playing, finding positive addictions, and so on.

8. *Application.* Reality therapy has been applied to a wide variety of clinical issues, but the essentials of Glasser's approach can be illustrated in the case of "Pat," a wealthy, young, overindulged, satisfactorily married mother of two. It is a typical case in that it begins with Glasser investing in Pat and then helping her become responsible for what she wants, weight reduction. The therapy continued slowly because Pat was unable to make Glasser assume a role she could reject. This helped her develop some respect and trust in the process and eventually come to accept that only she could make herself responsible. After almost a year, Glasser could point out Pat's irresponsibilities and truly encourage her to take a chance and change. Pat felt a keener sense of achievement and she lost 50 pounds.

9. *Critical Analysis.* Reality therapy has great versatility with applications to different populations and in a variety of settings. It is also goal-specific, allowing for accessible monitoring of progress. Another strength is that it provides a refreshing alternative to pathology-centered approaches. On the other hand, reality therapy does not validate other valuable concepts such as personal history and the unconscious as well as biological factors contributing to mental illness. However, when reality therapy turns to ethnic-minority clients, it offers an approach that is free from jargon and relatively inviting. Because the approach leaves it to the client to determine what he or she wants, it allows ethnic-minority clients to retain their ethnic identity and values while integrating other desired values and practices.

10. *Current Status.* Glasser's thinking on reality therapy continues to expand and is being undergirded more firmly by control theory. The research base continues to grow, with a steady stream of doctoral dissertations being written on reality therapy. The Institute for Reality Therapy offers seminars that lead to certification for its practitioners, and there is a journal devoted to publishing articles on reality therapy. Today Glasser's approach is being successfully applied in schools, correctional institutions, hospitals, clinics, and social service settings, while Dr. Glasser continues to be active in writing about his unique approach to counseling.

SUGGESTED READING

Glasser, W. (1965). *Reality therapy: A new approach to psychiatry.* New York: Harper & Row.
Glasser, W. (1969). *Schools without failure.* New York: Harper & Row.
Glasser, W. (Ed.). (1989). *Control theory in the practice of reality therapy: Case studies.* New York: Harper & Row.
Wubbolding, R. E. (1988). *Using reality therapy.* New York: Harper & Row.

REFERENCES

Barrett, C. (1992). Substance abuse: A window of opportunity. *Journal of Reality Therapy, 11,* 20–21.
Bassin, A., Bratter, T. E., & Rachin, R. L. (Eds.). (1976). *The reality therapy reader: A survey of the work of William Glasser.* New York: Harper & Row.
Benshoff, J. M., Poidevant, J. M, & Cashwell, C. S. (1994). School discipline programs: Issues and implications for school counselors. *Elementary School Guidance and Counseling, 28,* 163–169.
Bratter, B. I., Bratter, T. E., Radda, H. T., & Steiner, K. M. (1993). The residential therapeutic caring community. *Psychotherapy, 30,* 299–304.
Clagett, A. F. (1992). Group-integrated reality therapy in a wilderness camp. *Journal of Offender Rehabilitation, 17,* 1–18.
Coates, D., & Winston, T. (1983). Counteracting the deviance of depression: Peer support groups for victims. *Journal of Social Issues, 39,* 160–194.
Cockrum, J.R. (1993). Teaching role playing and critiquing. *Journal of Reality Therapy, 12,* 70–75.
Cohen, B., & Sordo, I. (1984). Using reality therapy with adult offenders. *Journal of Offender Counseling, Services & Rehabilitation, 8,* 25–39.
Croll, M. (1992). The individualist roots of reality therapy: A textual analysis of Emerson's "Self-Reliance" and Glasser's reality therapy. *Journal of Reality Therapy, 11,* 22–26.
Edelwich, J. (1980). *Burn-out.* New York: Human Sciences Press.
Edens, R. M., & Smryl, T. (1994). Reducing disruptive classroom behaviors in physical education: A pilot study. *Journal of Reality Therapy, 13,* 40–44.
Evans, D. B. (1984). Reality therapy: A model for physicians managing alcoholic patients. *Journal of Reality Therapy, 3,* 20–26.
Evans, H. I. (1978). Psychotherapy for the rape victim: Some treatment models, *Hospital and Community Psychiatry, 29,* 309–312.
Franklin, M. (1993). Eighty-two Reality Therapy doctoral dissertations written between 1970-1990. *Journal of Reality Therapy, 12,* 76–83.
Garner, A. (1983). Living with mental patients. *Journal of Reality Therapy, 2,* 27–31.
Glasser, N. (Ed.). (1980). *What are you doing? How people are helped through reality therapy.* New York: Harper & Row.
Glasser, N. (Ed.). (1989). *Control theory in the practice of reality therapy: Case studies.* New York: Harper & Row.
Glasser, W. (1961). *Mental health or mental illness?* New York: Harper & Row.
Glasser, W. (1965). *Reality therapy: A new approach to psychiatry.* New York: Harper & Row.
Glasser, W. (1969). *Schools without failure.* New York: Harper & Row.
Glasser, W. (1972). *The identity society* (Rev. ed.). New York: Harper & Row.
Glasser, W. (1976). *Positive addiction.* New York: Harper & Row.

Glasser, W. (1981). *Stations of the mind.* New York: Harper & Row.

Glasser, W. (1984). *Take effective control of your life.* New York: Harper & Row.

Glasser, W. (1990). *The quality school.* New York: Harper & Row.

Glasser, W. (1995). *Staying together: The control theory guide to a lasting marriage.* New York: Harper Collins Publishers.

Glasser, W., & Wubbolding, R. E. (1995). Reality therapy. *Current psychotherapies* (5th ed.). Itasca, IL: F. E. Peacock.

Glasser, W., & Zunin, L. (1979). Reality therapy. *Current psychotherapies.* Itasca, IL: F. E. Peacock.

Goodman, B., & Nowak-Scibelli, D. (1985). Group treatment for women incestuously abused as children. *International Journal of Group Psychotherapy, 35,* 531–544.

Hart, E. A. (1992). Using reality therapy for exercise initiation. *Journal of Reality Therapy, 12,* 24–31.

Heuchert, C. M. (1989). Enhancing self-directed behavior in the classroom. *Academic Therapy, 24,* 295–303.

Honeyman, A. (1990). Perceptual changes in addicts as a consequence of reality therapy based group treatment. *Journal of Reality Therapy, 9,* 53–59.

Hulbert, R. J. (1992). The Iowa therapeutic community model of chemical dependency treatment. *Journal of Substance Abuse Treatment, 9,* 389–393.

Ignoffo, M. (1994). Two compatible methods of empowerment: Neurolinguistic hypnosis and reality therapy. *Journal of Reality therapy, 13,* 20–25.

Kaltenbach, R.F., & Gazda, G.M. (1975). Reality therapy in groups. In G.M. Gazda (Ed.), *Basic approaches to group psychotherapy and group counseling* (2nd ed., pp. 196–233). Springfield, IL: Charles C. Thomas.

Lester, D. (1994). Psychotherapy for suicidal clients. *Death Studies, 18,* 361–374.

McArthur, M. J. (1990). Reality therapy with rape victims. *Archives of Psychiatric Nursing, 4,* 360–365.

Mickel, E. (1993). Parent assistance workshops (P.A.W.S.) reality based intervention for the crack exposed child. *Journal of Reality Therapy, 12,* 20–28.

Newton, F. B., Brack, C.J., & Brack, G. (1992). Autonomy training: A structure group experience. *Journal of College Student Development, 33,* 371–373.

Osipow, S. H., Walsh, W. B., & Tosi, D. J. (1984). *A survey of counseling methods.* Homewood, IL: Dorsey Press.

Ososkie, J. N., & Turpin, J. O. (1985). Reality therapy in rehabilitation counseling. *Journal of Applied Rehabilitation Counseling, 16,* 34–38.

Parish, T. S. (1988). Why reality therapy works. *Journal of Reality Therapy, 7,* 31–32.

Parish, T. S. (1992). Ways of assessing and enhancing student motivation. *Journal of Reality Therapy, 11,* 27–36.

Peacock, J. A. (1992). Using RT/CT to enhance alcohol use/abuse awareness. *Journal of Reality Therapy, 12,* 19–23.

Peterson, A. V., & Woodward, G. D. (1992). Basic needs—competitive or complementary: A statistical study of psychological needs. *Journal of Reality Therapy, 11,* 41–45.

Protheroe, D. (1992). Reality therapy and the concept of cognitive developmental stages. *Journal of Reality Therapy, 12,* 37–44.

Rachin, R. L. (1974). Reality therapy: Helping people help themselves. *Crime and Delinquency, 20,* 45–53.

Reuss, N. (1985). Alternatives to cocaining. *Journal of Reality Therapy, 4,* 8–11.

Rose, D. (1986). Worse than death: Psychodynamics of rape victims and the need for psychotherapy. *American Journal of Psychiatry, 143,* 817–824.

Roth, S., Dye, E., & Lebowitz, L. (1988). Group therapy for sexual-assault victims. *Psychotherapy, 25*, 82–93.

Rozsnafsky, J. (1974). The impact of Alfred Adler on three "free-will" therapies of the 1960's. *Journal of Individual Psychology, 30*, 65–80.

Sadock, V.A. (1983). Group psychotherapy with rape victims and battered women. In H. I. Kaplan & B. J. Sadock (Eds.), *Comprehensive group psychotherapy* (2nd ed., pp. 282–285). Baltimore, MD: Williams & Wilkins.

Saper, B. (1987). Humor in psychotherapy: Is it good or bad for the client? *Professional Psychology: Research and Practice, 18*, 360–367.

Seligman, M.E.P. (1975). *Helplessness: On depression, development, and death.* San Francisco, CA: W. H. Freeman.

Stanton, D. T. (1992). Treating sexual offenders: Reality therapy as a better alternative. *Journal of Reality Therapy, 12*, 3–10.

Stanwood, D. L. (1992). Grief and the process of recovery. *Journal of Reality Therapy, 12*, 11–18.

Thatcher, J. A. (1987). Value judgments: A significant aspect of reality therapy. *Journal of Reality Therapy, 7*, 23–25.

Udry, E. M. (1992). Interventions for the anxious and depressed: Suggested links between control theory and exercise therapy. *Journal of Reality Therapy, 12*, 32–36.

Vogt, S. (1985). Reality therapy in a convalescent home. *Activities, Adaptation & Aging, 6*, 55–59.

Walker, G. (1987). Rehabilitation counseling with dual diagnosis clients. *Journal of Applied Rehabilitation Counseling, 18*, 35–37.

Wallace, W. A. (1986). *Theories of counseling and psychotherapy: A basic issues approach.* Boston: Allyn & Bacon.

Whitehouse, D. (1984). Adlerian antecedents to reality therapy and control theory. *Journal of Reality Therapy, 3*, 10–14.

Wiener, N. (1948). *Cybernetics.* New York: John Wiley.

Wiener, N. (1950). *The human use of human beings: Cybernetics and society.* Boston: Houghton Mifflin.

Williamson, R. S. (1992). Using group reality therapy to raise self-esteem in adolescent girls. *Journal of Reality Therapy, 12*, 37–44.

Wubbolding, R. E. (1975). Practicing reality therapy. *Personnel and Guidance Journal, 53*, 164–165.

Wubbolding, R. E. (1979). Reality therapy as an antidote to burn-out. *American Mental Health Counselors Association, 1*, 39–43.

Wubbolding, R. E. (1988). *Using reality therapy.* New York: Harper & Row.

Wubbolding, R. E. (1991). *Understanding reality therapy.* New York: Harper Collins.

Yalom, I. (1985). *The theory and practice of group psychotherapy* (3rd ed.). New York: Basic Books.

CHAPTER 15

Conclusion:

Comparing the Major Therapeutic Theories

Chapter Outline

Comparing Therapeutic Approaches
Does Psychotherapy Work?
Is One Therapy Better Than Another?
Integrating Therapeutic Approaches
The Challenge of Contemporary Psychotherapy

Once considered the exclusive province of the very rich and the very disturbed, psychotherapy now reaches not only people who are afflicted with severe mental illness but throngs of everyday people who suffer from the problems associated with "normal" living. The demand for therapy has increased 400% in the last three decades and more than 80 million people, at a cost of over $4 billion annually, seek psychotherapy.

The wide variety of therapeutic options has become such an establishment in contemporary society, it is easy to forget that this was not always so. In 1920 there was one basic theory of psychotherapy, Sigmund Freud's psychoanalysis. Over the next two decades, several versions of neopsychoanalytic theory emerged and began competing for dominance. Today, there are literally dozens, if not hundreds (Corsini, 1981; Gabbard, 1995; Herink, 1980) of therapies striving for recognition—some say there are almost as many approaches to counseling as there are counselors (Ivey, 1980). It is even possible to buy consumer's guides to today's myriad of therapies. (For a brochure on choosing a psychologist, contact the APA Public Affairs Office at 750 First St., N.E., Washington, DC 20002.) In this book, however, we have examined the most well-known, most documented, and most reputable approaches: psychoanalytic, Adlerian, existential, behavioral, person-centered, gestalt, transactional analysis, rational-emotive, and reality therapy. And we have seen that each theory provides a structure or framework from which counselors can work in a systematic fashion. But we are still left with a question: How does a student, or for that matter, a client, choose one theoretical orientation over another?

COMPARING THERAPEUTIC APPROACHES

A well-known study conducted in 1950 found that experienced helpers of different theoretical persuasions tended to have more in common than inexperienced helpers of the same persuasion. These common elements included the relationship dimensions of genuineness, empathic understanding, respect, and acceptance of the client (Fiedler, 1950). More recently, other studies have described the same phenomenon after comparing counselors using different approaches (Lieberman, Yalom, & Miles, 1973; Truax & Carkhuff, 1967).

To help you gain a clearer picture of the various counseling approaches you have studied in this book and to stimulate your thinking about how they compare and contrast, consider Table 15-1 (Gladding, 1992; Pietrofesa, Hoffman, & Splete, 1984).

After you have reviewed the comparison table, you may notice several emphases and strategies that cut across therapeutic boundaries. If so, you are not alone. Practitioners have sought commonalties and have found much overlap among the various theories. For example, many of the terms used in transactional analysis stem from psychoanalytic thinking. Gestalt therapy and person-centered therapy both focus on the present and emphasize positive directions and goals of living. One can find many, many similarities among theories. Some have even argued that the various approaches may be emphasizing different aspects of the same process (Patterson, 1980).

We shall not cease from exploration and the end of all our exploring will be to arrive where we started and know the place for the first time.

—T. S. Eliot

Strategies may take different forms when implemented under a different orientation, but some of them are similar enough to be seen as common factors for therapeutic effectiveness. Notwithstanding theoretical differences, here are some of the overarching factors most frequently noted by practitioners.

1. *Developing an expectancy for change.* Perhaps the most common factor of effective therapy involves raising the client's level of expectance for change. In fact, many therapists attribute the success of psychotherapy more to a heightened expectancy level than to any specific technique. Simply translated, hope seems to cut across therapeutic borderlines. It brings about a belief within clients that fosters a curative power. In other words, therapy achieves its success, in part, because of its capacity to generate a client's expectancy of improvement. Part art and part science, psychotherapy profits from the mystique that surrounds both fields. Also, clients often approach therapy with a large emotional investment in making it work, and effective therapy, no matter what its modality, capitalizes on this hopeful investment. The perception

TABLE 15-1

	Psychoanalysis	Adlerian	Existential	Person Centered
View of human nature	Emphasizes early childhood and psychosexual development, the unconscious, and ego defense mechanisms. Its focus is on biological, deterministic aspects of behavior.	Emphasizes social interests as a primary motivator while focusing on birth order, family constellation, and style of life as major influences on personal growth and development.	Emphasizes a belief in human freedom and choice of lifestyle. The primary focus is on meaning as it relates to anxiety, life, death, and the relevance of individual experience.	Emphasizes the positive, forward moving, and good aspects of human nature and a phenomenological view of the self, which demonstrates a growth orientation if provided with the right conditions.
Role of the counselor	The counselor encourages transference and exploration of the unconscious. The counselor, who uses interpretation, is viewed as the expert.	The counselor works with the client, modeling, teaching, and assessing the client's situation. Homework is often assigned and encouragement is given freely.	The counselor focuses on being authentic and understanding with the client while stressing a personal relationship of shared experience.	The counselor works to cultivate an environment that emphasizes personal warmth, empathy, acceptance, and genuineness.
Goals of therapy	Goals include making the unconscious conscious, working through unresolved developmental stages, and reconstructing the personality.	Goals include cultivating social interest, correcting faulty assumptions and mistaken goals, and bringing about behavioral change through acting "as if."	Goals include helping clients realize their responsibility, awareness, freedom, and an outward frame of reference.	Goals include self-exploration and acceptance, openness to self and others, self-direction, and a focus on the here and now.
Methods and techniques	Free association; dream analysis; analysis of transference; analysis of resistance; interpretation.	Empathy, support, collaboration; stressing client responsibility; examination of memories, family constellation.	Inquiringness; acceptance of client uniqueness; confrontation; awareness exercises; imagery.	Acceptance; clarification; reflection of feeling; positive regard, self-disclosure; open-ended questions.

Behaviorism	Gestalt	Rational-Emotive	Transactional Analysis	Reality
Emphasizes that human behaviors are learned and that old behaviors can be extinguished while new ones are established.	Emphasizes the importance of wholeness and completeness in human life while stressing the importance of affect, phenomenology, and anti-determinism.	Emphasizes that humans are both inherently rational and irrational; that they can disturb themselves by what they think.	Emphasizes the ego states of Parent, Adult, and Child while stressing the importance of interpersonal integration and analysis of transactions.	Emphasizes that problems occur when people do not take responsibility for behavior and that people need to love and be loved and act in control of their environment.
The counselor serves as a teacher, director, and expert who actively participates in session and assists clients in clarifying goals and modifying behaviors.	The counselor uses an energetic demeanor to emphasize the here and now while helping clients resolve unfinished business.	The counselor is active and directive in teaching, confronting, and correcting the client while also concentrating on the A-B-Cs of self-talk.	The counselor contracts with the client for specific change and instructs in the language of interpersonal transactions.	The counselor, being active, practical, and didactic, serves as a model and teacher who focuses on establishing a relationship.
Goals include helping clients modify maladaptive behavior, learn productive responses, and establish and achieve specific concrete goals.	Goals include immediacy of experience, making choices in the now, resolving the past, becoming congruent, and growing up mentally.	Goals include putting an end to irrational thinking; eliminating oughts, shoulds, and musts; and eliminating self-defeating habits.	Goals include relative attainment of autonomy, increased personal health, becoming more aware, game free, and intimate.	Goals include becoming psychologically strong and rational, taking responsibility, clarifying goals, formulating a realistic plan, and eliminating excuses.
Reinforcement; shaping, extinction; self-monitoring; punishment; systematic desensitization; flooding; stress inoculation.	Exercises and experiments; fantasy and role playing; dream work; taking responsibility; confrontation, exaggeration.	Disputing; instruction of emotion construction; imagery; persuasion; logical reasoning; homework assignments.	Treatment contracts; interrogation; illustration and specification; confrontation; often combined with Gestalt techniques.	Focusing; evaluating; making a plan and a commitment to follow it; not blaming; role-playing; confronting; role modeling.

by a client that "I have been heard and understood and can be helped" can be as important as any other therapeutic intervention. Whatever the means, the objective of therapy is almost always to bring about the kind of change the client expects.

2. *Reducing emotional discomfort.* Most who find their way into a therapist's office are truly unhappy, beleaguered by depression, anxiety, phobias, or some other distress from the long list besetting the human race. Whatever the discomfort, therapists of all stripes are dedicated to alleviating it. Of course, therapists, to greater and lesser degrees, do not strive to eliminate all discomfort; in so doing, they might also eliminate motivation for working toward more lasting change. The challenge is to diminish extreme distress without sapping the client's desire to deal with enduring problems. The therapeutic relationship can be used as a means to this end by serving as a buffer against outside hostility. The form this takes will certainly differ among therapists (from direct reassurances to more subtle alliances), but each is using the relationship to reduce the client's emotional discomfort.

3. *Fostering insight.* Whereas Freud focused almost exclusively on bringing about insights from an analysis of unconscious influences, most current therapists aim for insight in a general sense of greater self-understanding. By learning why they behave as they do, clients can became empowered to choose a different way of behaving. Therapists of all theoretical persuasions seek to promote self-examination and self-knowledge in their clients. Some deal with a specific type of content, whereas other therapists try to promote insight by asking their clients to examine the implications of specific behaviors.

4. *Encouraging catharsis.* Most therapists encourage their clients to express emotions freely in their presence. Releasing pent-up emotions that the client has not acknowledged brings about a desired cathartic effect whereby the client's pain is eased and the client becomes more comfortable with his or her emotions. Most therapeutic modalities, in their own ways, value the understanding that comes from expressing emotions in constructive ways and modifying those emotions that have become so maladaptive that the client's functioning is impaired. However catharsis is brought about, the goal is for the evoked emotions to be reexamined and be made to work for, rather than against, the client.

5. *Providing new information.* Many theoretical approaches involve an educational component, sometimes subtly, sometimes not. So in general terms, the therapist provides new information to correct gaps of distortion in a client's understanding or self-knowledge. Misinformation about countless issues can be cleared up relatively quickly in many cases where a therapist adapts a teacher-like role. In some approaches this is accomplished through providing reading material about a topic, a process known as bibliotherapy (Marx, Gyorky, Royalty, & Stern, 1992). New information, regardless of the theoretical orientation from which it is received, gives clients an added perspective on their issues and allows them to be seen as more solvable.

Although there is no one fully acceptable theoretical model of therapy, these therapeutic factors form the backbone of most practitioners' counseling and psychotherapy. As you compose your own integrationist model of therapy, or even if you devote yourself to one primary mode, these fundamentals remain fairly consistent. They may be revealed, emphasized, and altered in different ways, depending on their theoretical undergirdings, but they are the factors common to most therapeutic work. Which, by the way, begs the question: Does therapy really work?

DOES PSYCHOTHERAPY WORK?

In 1995 the American Psychological Association commissioned a study to determine how many people seek help from a professional psychotherapist or counselor. A random telephone survey revealed that 46% of those questioned had seen a mental health professional at some point in their lives. In 1977, a

A little experience often upsets a lot of theory.

—Samuel P. Cadman

similar survey revealed that 33% of those queried had sought psychological help. And going back to 1957, only 13% (Cavaliere, 1995). It appears that the stigma associated with seeing a professional is lessening and more people are seeking help. Likewise, perhaps, it may be that the general population is discovering that help from a counselor can make a difference. Whatever the reason, the increasing numbers cannot necessarily be correlated with therapeutic success. To determine this, other studies are needed and, fortunately, have been conducted for a number of decades.

One of the first studies to consider the effectiveness of counseling was done by Hans Eysenck (1952), who surveyed 19 published reports covering more than 7000 cases. Eysenck concluded that individual psychotherapy was no more effective against neurotic disorders than no therapy at all: "Roughly two-thirds of a group of neurotic patients will recover or improve to a marked extent within about two years of the onset of their illness whether they are treated by means of psychotherapy or not" (p. 322).

Although Eysenck's conclusions caused a storm of controversy in the psychological community, his study immediately stimulated more research. A later review of the literature done by Meltzoff and Kornreich (1971) found more "good" or acceptable results than did Eysenck and therefore concluded that psychotherapy was effective and superior to no treatment. Bergin and Lambert (1978) also found evidence of treatment-related improvement. They questioned the "spontaneous recovery" of the control subjects in the studies that Eysenck surveyed, noting that even though they received no formal therapy, many of them did get help from friends, clergy, physicians, and teachers. They concluded that the improvement rate among people in psychotherapy was greater than that of untreated control subjects. Sloane and his colleagues (1975), who compared people who had received psychoanalytic psychotherapy, those who had had behavior therapy, and a control group of people who were on a

Hans Eysenck.
(London Times/Archive Photos)

waiting list for therapy, found that both therapies were superior to the control condition in reducing major symptoms.

In 1977, a dramatically new approach was taken to the effectiveness question. Smith and Glass (1977) reported an averaging of the results of a large number of studies, from which they concluded that the typical therapy client is better off than 75% of untreated controls. But is this simply because the clients believed they would be helped, or is it because of the actual treatment itself? Landman and Dawes (1982) concluded that although initiating any treatment creates a small improvement, actually receiving therapy leads to a much greater improvement. In other words, the effects of receiving therapy appear to be a result of more than just believing that one is going to get better.

Today, researchers have enough data to refute Eysenck's 1952 charge with conviction. Investigators have repeatedly shown that clients with diverse problems who receive a broad range of therapies improve more than they would with no treatment, with placebo treatment, or through spontaneous recovery, and the gains are lasting. A recent University of Pennsylvania study of the major modes of psychotherapy, including a dynamic psychotherapy, behavior therapy, and cognitive therapy, concluded that they all had similar outcomes and that 80% of the treated patients showed improvement (Gabbard, 1995). An even more comprehensive and recent study published in *Consumer Reports* (1995) provides strong evidence in favor of psychotherapy's effectiveness. The study concluded that most patients who receive psychotherapy benefit from it and that those who receive more, benefit more. In examining *Consumer Reports* methodology, Martin Seligman (1995) has concluded that the results of the study are quite robust and may provide the most effective answer yet to the question "Does psychotherapy work?" The answer appears to be yes.

| *The only therapy is life.*
—Otto Rank

IS ONE THERAPY BETTER THAN ANOTHER?

The global issue of effectiveness raises the question of how the effectiveness of particular theories stack up against one another. Is psychoanalytic therapy, for example, more effective than person-centered therapy? Logically, you might expect the different approaches to therapy to vary in effectiveness. Several reviews, however, have concluded that there are few differences in the results obtained by various forms of therapy (Casey & Berman, 1985; Cross, Sheehan, & Khan, 1982; DiLoreto, 1971; Garfield, 1983; Michelson, 1985; Smith, Glass, & Miller, 1980). One group of researchers (Luborsky, Singer, & Luborsky, 1975), after reviewing the evidence, quoted the dodo bird who had just judged a race in *Alice and Wonderland:* "Everyone has won and all must have prizes." However, other psychologists question these conclusions; they point out that there is no agreement on appropriate methods for determining the relative effectiveness of different types of therapy (Eysenck, 1985; Piroleau, Murdoc, & Brody, 1983; Shapiro, 1985). It is dismaying that the debate over such an important issue has not yet been resolved, but the debate itself continues to spur careful well-managed studies conducted in the hope of making a breakthrough.

What is clear, however, is that some kinds of psychotherapy appear to be more appropriate for certain kinds of people and problems. Psychoanalytic therapy, for example, seems to be best suited to people seeking extensive scrutiny of themselves or profound self-understanding, relief of inner conflict, or better relationships with others. On the other hand, behavior therapy is probably more appropriate for clients who have a specific behavioral problem. Desensitization, for example, is most effective with conditioned avoidance responses such as phobias and anxiety disorders. Studies show that cognitive therapy brings moderate relief from unipolar depression as well as panic disorder.

Perhaps more crucial than therapeutic modality in predicting whether psychotherapy is a success for certain clients is the client's motivation itself. The old joke is true: It takes only one therapist to change a light bulb, but the light bulb has to *want* to change. Another consideration beyond matching a specific therapeutic issue with a specific modality is whether the length of treatment may be more important than the type of therapy that is implemented (see Sidebar 15-1). The *Consumer Reports* survey (1995) found that long-term therapy produced significantly more improvement than short-term therapy. This finding is not without its critics, however. They attribute this to "therapy junkies" who are so committed to therapy as a way of life that they bias the results in this direction.

When comparing different therapeutic approaches, one must not lose sight of the fact that not all therapists are created equal. Some counselors are unquestionably more effective than others and the variation in effectiveness depends more on therapists' personal skills than on differences in theoretical orientation. Effective therapy, generally speaking, has as much or even more to do with the chemistry between therapist and client and with the strength of the working alliance than it does with the theoretical constructs subscribed to. Good, bad, and mediocre therapists are found within each therapeutic approach.

Sidebar 15-1

IS A SINGLE SESSION ENOUGH?

In keeping with the mood of the times to economize in all things, some therapists are saying that a single session of psychotherapy is enough for most people.

The approach capitalizes on the fact that on average about a third of the people who consult a therapist never return for a second session, making one session the most frequent length of therapy. The advocates of single-session therapy argue that what is so often a person's only therapeutic encounter should be used to maximize its effect. But they also contend that for many, if not most, people, one therapy session can leave them with the tools and the encouragement to handle their problems on their own. For example a single session may be all that is required to give a person the resolve to end a destructive relationship.

"It's not hard to be helpful to somebody in a single session," said Dr. Bernard Bloom, a psychologist at the University of Colorado, who is an originator of the approach.

For most psychoanalysts and other psychotherapists who routinely do therapy lasting months or years, the idea seems absurd. And even some therapists who have milder reactions are skeptical.

Typical was the reaction of Dr. Robert Michels, dean at the Cornell Medical School, and a former chairman of the psychiatry department. "In my clinical experience," he said, "a single session of therapy is unlikely to be enough for most patients."

Even so, Dr. Simon Budman, a psychologist at the Harvard Community Health Plan in Boston, said: "There is more single-session therapy going on than many therapists realize. I find that 10–15% of my clients only need a single session."

Recently, Dr. Budman treated a college senior who had been suffering from panic attacks. The first occurred in the initial meeting of a second-semester course, when the instructor asked students to introduce themselves and tell their plans for their future. "He got so panicked, he had to walk out," Dr. Budman said, after which the student became increasingly anxious because of the fear that he would have more attacks.

In talking to the student, Dr. Budman discovered that he was worried about his future. "Here it was, the end of his senior year and he was unsure about what he would do next," Dr. Budman said. "I pointed out that it was entirely appropriate for him to be anxious in his situation."

Sometimes, Dr. Budman said, all a person needs to hear is that his or her reaction is normal given the circumstances. Four months after their single meeting, Dr. Budman called the student and found that he had not had any more panic attacks.

Normally, therapists use the first session, or several sessions, to gather information about a client, delaying therapeutic intervention until later. But single-session advocates argue that, in addition, therapists should use the initial session to make interventions and suggestions that can have therapeutic effect. "You can say from the outset, let's see what I can do to be helpful to you in an hour or so," Dr. Bloom said. "When the hour is over, the person can have gotten enough to make a change in his life."

To be sure, even the most enthusiastic supporters of single-session therapy admit limitations. Perhaps the most impor-

tant is how long a person expects the therapy to last.

"If a client comes in the door expecting long-term therapy, single-session therapy can't work," said Dr. Moshe Talmon, a psychologist at the Kaiser Permanente Medical Center in Hayward, California, a leading advocate of the approach. But he said that most first-time patients in community clinics and prepaid medical plans do not expect therapy to last long. Dr. Talmon said most people who go to therapists are appropriate candidates for a single session, especially those who have a specific problem, such as family conflicts.

"At the beginning I thought single-session therapy would be most helpful for less severe and acute problems," Dr. Talmon said, "but when a problem is very urgent and painful, people are motivated to change quickly."

Data supporting the single-session treatment have come from a variety of studies, often unexpectedly. For example, one of the earliest was a follow-up of 141 people who had consulted therapists on only one occasion in community clinics in New York City. Done in the 1950s, the study found that two thirds said they had been helped, although their therapists thought of them as "dropouts."

Indirect evidence of benefit came from a 1979 study of 304 patients in a prepaid medical plan in California. The study found that people who consulted a psychotherapist for a single session had a 60% decline in their use of all other medical services over the next 5 years.

And in recent research, 200 patients who had consulted a therapist just once at a California prepaid medical plan were called several months later; 78% said they got what they wanted out of that single session and felt better about the problem. The research is reported in Dr. Talmon's book *Single Session Therapy*.

Adapted from Goleman, D. (1991, May 2), Therapists Say a Single Session May Be Enough. *The New York Times*, p. 38.

ι these findings and others, it is no wonder that the followers of partic-
ιories are beginning to ease their boundaries.

INTEGRATING THERAPEUTIC APPROACHES

There is a significant trend in counseling to move away from strong loyalty to
individual schools of thought and a corresponding move toward integrating
different approaches to therapy (Beitman, Goldfried, & Norcross, 1989). Most
clinicians used to depend exclusively on one system of therapy while rejecting
the utility of all others. This era of fragmentation may be drawing to a close. For
more than a decade, researchers have found that the greatest proportion of psychologists responding to a survey described themselves as *eclectic* in approach
(Jensen, Bergin, & Greaves, 1990; Norcross & Prochaska, 1982; Smith, 1982) (see
Figure 15-1). The relatively new *International Journal of Eclectic Psychotherapy*
and the Society for the Exploration of Psychotherapy Integration are two indi-
cators that eclecticism is thriving among today's clinicians.

Eclectic means, quite literally, "drawn from many sources." Counselors
who embrace this approach are well acquainted with all the theories involved
and they use various theories to match the needs of various clients. An eclectic
approach, however, does not mean the absence of an orientation. Nor does an
eclectic orientation permit an ill-defined, inconsistent, or random collection of
philosophies, purposes, and techniques. When this is the method, it is sometimes sarcastically referred to as "electric," implying that the practitioners are
trying any and every method that "turns them on." Understandably, this kind
of counselor can do more harm than good if he or she does not thoroughly understand the theories being drawn from. A "healthy" eclectic approach requires

FIGURE 15-1 The pooled data from a survey of 415 clinical and counseling psychologists (Smith, 1982) and another survey of 479 clinical psychologists
(Norcross & Prochaska, 1982) indicate that the most widely employed approaches to therapy are (in order) the eclectic, the psychodynamic, the behavioral, the cognitive, and the client-centered approaches.

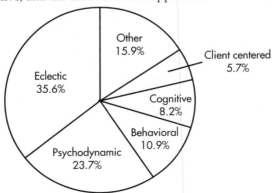

counselors to have a sound knowledge of the counseling theories used, a basic integrative philosophy of human behavior, and a flexible means of fitting the approach to the client, not vice versa (Cavanaugh, 1990). After mastering the various theories, the key is to know what approach to use when, where, and how (Harman, 1977).

Some scholars advocate a hierarchy of eclectic practices (McBride & Martin, 1990). The first level of eclecticism is termed *syncretism,* which is an unsystematic, sloppy process of fitting unrelated clinical concepts together. The second level is *traditional* and incorporates an orderly combination of compatible features into a harmonious whole. The third level is described as *professional* and requires the counselor to master at least two theories before ever trying to make any combinations. And the final level of eclecticism is called *theoretical,* where it is conceptualized as a type of metatheory that underlies and explains the overall practice of counseling in a unifying manner. Arnold Lazarus (1967, 1971, 1976, 1981, 1985) has done more than any other theorist to provide this kind of an encompassing approach to eclecticism.

> *The important thing is not to stop questioning. Curiosity has its own reason for existing. One cannot help but be in awe when he contemplates the mysteries of eternity, of life, of the marvelous structure of reality. It is enough if one tries merely to comprehend a little of this mystery every day. Never lose a holy curiosity.*
>
> —Albert Einstein

Lazarus initially defined his approach as *technical eclecticism* but it is now commonly known as multimodal therapy. With his approach, therapists use whatever techniques are most appropriate for given problems regardless of the theoretical system from which the techniques are derived. Although he carries a strong behavioral emphasis, Lazarus may view behavioral techniques as appropriate for one type of difficulty, and Gestalt or psychoanalytic procedures as preferred for another.

According to Lazarus, a client's personality is organized by seven modes of functioning. These can be summarized by the acronym BASIC ID, which stands for behavior, affect, sensation, imagery, cognition, interpersonal relations, and drugs. Each of these areas of functioning (with the exception of drugs, which is a form of treatment) may call for different techniques, ranging across several schools of therapy. Treatment focuses on influencing each of these areas of functioning, but the choice of what systematic approach to use with a client depends on where the client is experiencing the most difficulty. Human areas of functioning are interactional, Lazarus believes, and there is a "firing order" by which one mode influences another. The goal of treatment, then, is multifaceted and involves influencing the behavior of the entire person by selectively working in one or two primary areas.

Although widely respected, Lazarus' method of trying to achieve a healthy eclecticism should not be viewed as the only way this can be done. In a national survey of psychotherapists (Jensen et al., 1990), it was found that 72% of "eclectics" reported using psychodynamic principles within their version of eclectic therapy, 54% reported cognitive approaches as their foundation, and 45% reported using behavioral methods as their underlying structure for eclecticism (as does Lazarus). The point is that eclectic therapy does not come in only one

Arnold Lazarus (1932–   ).
(Courtesy of The Milton H. Erickson Foundation, Inc., Phoenix, Arizona)

form; there are analytic eclectics and behavioral eclectics and humanistic eclectics. Eclectic psychotherapy is a diverse orientation that embraces many different combinations fitting the style of individual therapists.

As you examine the various approaches to counseling, it is hoped that you have begun thinking of ways to integrate some of the theories and techniques into your own orientation as a counselor. It is vital for each counselor to discover what systematic approaches work best for him or her as a personal style develops. In your continued studies of professional counseling and psychotherapy, and perhaps as you develop a careful eclectic approach, let me remind you that your choice of techniques should be principled. Your integration of strategies should be based on each individual case rather than on the dictates of a general theoretical system to be imposed on every client. In other words, your integration of strategies should model Lazarus' method of drawing on the combined and complementary wisdom of different theoretical approaches because you understand how each one can be used in given situations and for differing human needs and functions.

THE CHALLENGE OF CONTEMPORARY PSYCHOTHERAPY

When one of the Disney theme parks was opened a few months after Walt Disney's death, an impressed visitor reportedly expressed his appreciation to one of the park's designers. "It is sad that Mr. Disney did not live to see this," the visitor said.

"Oh, but he did see it," the designer replied. "That's why the park is here."

Visionaries like Walt Disney are able to anticipate the future, imagine the possibilities, and then work to make them a reality. The field of professional counseling and psychotherapy needs visionaries—realistic people who understand change, who see possibilities that others miss, and who refuse to dispense yesterday's answers to today's questions.

Contemporary society, often rootless, cynical, and sometimes hopeless, breeds apprehensive apathy. But contemporary counselors cannot allow this toxin to contaminate the field of psychotherapy. Nor can we, as counselors, retreat into a therapeutic cocoon that is dedicated solely to looking inward. For too long, some say, psychotherapy has traced unhappiness and dysfunction to the subjective world of the "interior self." We have been warned of the hazards of gazing perpetually within—that the flip side of self-awareness is self-absorption, narcissism, and the tendency to interpret everything in individual terms.

Psychotherapy is the systematic use of a human relationship for therapeutic purposes.

—Hans Strupp

In their 1985 volume *Habits of the Heart,* for example, University of Berkeley sociologist Robert Bellah and his colleagues correlated the spread of the inward psychotherapeutic ethic with the erosion of values, arguing that it "posits an individual who is able to be the source of his own standards" and "denies all forms of obligation and commitment in relationships." Similarly, James Hillman and Michael Ventura, authors of *We've Had a Hundred Years of Psychotherapy—and the World's Getting Worse,* see therapy's emphasis on self-analysis as a holdover from 19th-century individualism, an approach inappropriate to a late–20th century society in which active social involvement is imperative.

As we stand on the edge of the 21st century, it is an appropriate time for the next generation of counselors to reassess the field and envision its future. The process of human change and transformation will remain much the same; it will always be arduous, always a matter of steps taken forward, steps back. But we cannot give in to the temptation to look only back in order to avoid the future. Our profession cannot afford to withdraw and watch from the sidelines.

The next generation of counselors and psychotherapists must move forward with confidence, squarely facing the challenges our changing society presents. The truth is that the future does not depend so much on the dreams we dream or the plans that we conceive. The future depends more on the choices that we make. And so I leave you, the next generation of counselors, with a challenge.

As we have seen throughout the chapters of this book, theories cannot be developed apart from the contexts of the theorists and their original backgrounds. The most widely respected and significant counseling theories, therefore, reflect the spirit of the era and region in which the theorists who developed them have lived. It is no wonder, then, that these theories have been developed by white men in Western cultures primarily for middle- and upper-middle-class clients. Thus, it has been up to individual practitioners in contemporary society to bear the onus for developing cultural awareness and applicability in the context of these theories (see Sidebar 15-2).

Sidebar 15-2

MAKING ROOM ON THE COUCH FOR CULTURE

The patient seemed psychotic, complaining in a listless ramble, "My soul is not with me anymore—I can't do anything." Seriously disturbed, she had been taken to a psychiatric hospital by her relatives. The psychiatrist who interviewed the woman discovered the problem had begun when she got bad news from her native Ecuador: an uncle she was close to had died unexpectedly.

"I realized that her clinical picture fit a syndrome known in Latin American cultures as 'susto,' or loss of the soul," said Dr. Juan Mezzich, a psychiatrist at the Mount Sinai School of Medicine in Manhattan, who treated the woman. "In facing the tragic news, the soul of the patient departs with the dead person, leaving the person soulless. In our psychiatric terms, we would say she was depressed."

Dr. Mezzich is at the forefront of a new movement in psychiatry to recognize the cultural trappings that patients bring with them, and to shape diagnosis and treatment accordingly. In the last 5 years the movement, which comes at a time when an increasing proportion of psychiatric patients in America come from an array of cultures, has led to a growing stream of books and scholarly articles on cultural influences in mental health. Virtually every professional convention for psychotherapists now offers a workshop on how culture affects psychiatric problems.

The American Journal of Psychiatry has recently published guidelines for psychiatric evaluation that for the first time explicitly recommend that a patient's cultural or ethnic background be considered, including how the patient understands the symptoms he or she is having.

For example, the woman from Ecuador was at first misdiagnosed as psychotic by another psychiatrist. But Dr. Mezzich, who is from Peru, not only knew about the susto syndrome but also devised a treatment for her that drew upon his understanding of her background. "Instead of just giving her antidepressants, I tried an approach based on Hispanic culture," he said. "There, for susto, you would expect to have a mourning ritual to help the person assimilate the loss. So, with her family, we organized a sort of wake where everyone talked about the loss of her uncle and what it meant to them."

The wake "was quite powerful for her," Dr. Mezzich said. "She didn't need any antidepressants, and within a few meetings, including two with her family, her symptoms lifted and she was back participating fully in life once again."

The anthropological study of psychiatric disorders like susto has yielded a fascinating list of syndromes known only in one or another culture, like the sudden, violent outburst known as "amok" in Malaysia; or "koro," the East Asian term for intense anxiety that one's sexual organs will recede into one's body with fatal consequence. Anthropologists say these are not mere ethnographic curiosities. Rather, they say, the syndromes illustrate a broader point, that notions of mental disorder, if not the disorders themselves, are shaped by culture.

Indeed, some disorders of the mind that are well recognized in some cultures simply have no equivalent in Western psychiatry. One such is "taijin kyofusho," a Japanese malady that loosely translates as "fear of people." The name describes a morbid dread that one will do something that will embarrass other people.

"The syndrome revolves around social shame," said Dr. Arthur Kleinman, a medical anthropologist and psychiatrist at Harvard Medical School. "The closest equivalent Western psychiatric diagnosis is social phobia, but that is an anxiety disorder, a fear that people will criticize you. It's not at all the same thing. Japanese clinicians say this psychological problem simply has no parallel in our own culture or diagnostic system—we don't think of the fear of embarrassing other people as a psychological syndrome."

The stamp of culture on mental disorders extends to America itself, Dr. Kleinman asserts. Although it is difficult to see for those immersed in American culture, he contends that there are psychiatric syndromes unique to Western industrialized societies. "Anorexia nervosa seems as culture-bound to America and similar industrialized cultures as amok is to Malaysia," Dr. Kleinman said.

Dr. Spero Manson, a medical anthropologist in the psychiatry department at the University of Colorado Health Science Center and himself a Chippewa, said: "There is simply no such thing as anorexia among native peoples in North America. The overconcern with body stereotypes isn't relevant in Indian cultures—the grave concern with slenderness is itself seen as absurd. Native people would be very concerned about a person who was willfully wasting away, but you just don't find it, except perhaps among highly acculturated Indians."

Dr. Kleinman says that although exotic disorders exist, most mental health workers will not confront them directly, but will have to deal instead with differences in how patients describe or experience universal problems like depression. "You need to understand the idiom of distress—how a person talks about his problem," Dr. Kleinman said. For Hopi Indians, for example, there are five terms that refer to types of depression. Dr. Manson said the nearest English equivalents were "deep worry," "pouting," "Drunken like craziness," "unhappiness," and "heartbroken."

Most of these categories bear only a surface resemblance to psychiatry's concepts of depression, Dr. Manson says. "The term 'heartbroken' translates also as 'heart is dying' or 'spiritual death'— there's really no match for this in the diagnostic manual," Dr. Manson said.

The most common cause of "heartbreak" is a rupture in a close relationship, such as a child being ignored by its mother or the breakup of a teenage romance. The typical reactions range from being shocked and perplexed to feeling despair and exhaustion.

"Depending on which of these sicknesses a Hopi patient thinks he is

Continued.

suffering from, some treatments would make better sense than others," Dr. Manson said. "Heartbreak, for example, has mainly physiological manifestations, like disturbed sleep and loss of appetite. Typically it's treated with herbs, so a medication would make sense. But for unhappiness the appropriate treatment for a Hopi would be a combination of psychotherapy and group support.

"Take a psychiatrist aware only of the standard psychiatric approaches," Dr. Manson continued. "In comes a Hopi patient, and the questions asked and treatment approach taken may mesh poorly at best with that patient's understanding of what should happen. The psychiatrist's lens might lead him to call it major depression, but that imposes another way of thinking about it."

Adapted from Goleman, D. (1995, December 5) Making room on the couch for culture. *The New York Times*, p. B5.

Many of the syndromes specific to one culture refer to some kind of brief psychosis, Dr. Mezzich said. "In countries like India and Egypt, for example, about half of psychiatric patients have a temporary psychotic state, typically a well-recognized syndrome in those cultures, that had no matching diagnosis in American psychiatry until the diagnosis of acute, transient psychosis was added last year," he said.

Not only has the diagnostic manual changed to take account of disorders specific to one culture, the training of mental health workers is also changing.

"At San Francisco General Hospital, we offer residents training on units that are focused on different cultural groups," said Dr. Francis Lu, codirector of the Cultural Competence and Diversity Program at the hospital and a psychiatrist at the University of California. And, for the first time, the national guidelines for training psychiatry residents this year specify that they be trained in assessing any cultural impact on their patients' problems.

(Shirley Zeiberg/Photo Researchers)

Classic counseling theories, as we have seen, do not specifically address the racial, ethnic, and cultural considerations of today's American minority groups. However, before we disown or discard these traditional therapeutic theories because of their original context, we can work to integrate these theories with cultural considerations. Pedersen (1991) put it succinctly when he stated, "Until and unless the multicultural perspective can be understood as not only generic to all counseling but also increasing the accuracy of counseling, culture will remain an exotic concept" (p. 250). He calls multiculturalism "the fourth force"—a force that will carry the next generation of counselors.

A theory is no more like a fact than a photograph is like a person.

—Ed Howe

This fourth force will undoubtedly require a redefinition of current theories and a major integration of multicultural considerations into our current theories. A theoretical framework that incorporates multicultural aspects is no longer just a goal, but a necessity. As counselors and therapists, we cannot wait for the evolution of a new theory to do the work for us. The reality of the changing demographics of our clientele presents this generation of practitioners with the challenge of integrating multicultural components into theoretical understanding (Ridley, 1995; Wehrly, 1995).

Where will the future of psychotherapy take us? In an attempt to extract and amplify salient counseling trends, 40 experts in the field were asked just that. They predicted that present-centered, structured, and directive techniques would increase in the years to come (Norcross & Freeheim, 1993). Whether they are correct or not only time will tell, but one thing is certain: All therapies have the ultimate common goal of helping clients reduce their suffering, improve their relationships, and take action to live a more fulfilling life. By facing the future and developing your own approach to counseling—whether it be psychoanalytic, behavioral, person-centered, eclectic, or something else—you will be joining ranks with a diverse group of professionals who are basically headed in the same direction.

REFERENCES

Beitman, B. D., Goldfried, M. R., & Norcross, J. C. (1989). The movement toward integrating the psychotherapies: An overview. *American Journal of Psychiatry, 146,* 138–147.

Bellah, R. N., Madsen, R., Sullivan, W. M., Swidler, A., & Tipton, M. (1985). *Habits of the heart: Individualism and commitment in American life.* New York: Harper & Row.

Bergin, A. E., & Lambert, M. J. (1978). The evaluation of therapeutic outcomes. In S. L. Garfield & A. E. Gergin (Eds.), *Handbook of psychotherapy and behavior change: An empirical analysis.* New York: John Wiley.

Casey, R. J., & Berman, J. S. (1985). The outcome of psychotherapy with children. *Psychological Bulletin, 98,* 388–400.

Cavaliere, F. (1995, June). APA brochure offers tips on choosing a psychologist. *APA Monitor,* 9.

Cavanaugh, M. E. (1990). *The counseling experience.* Monterey, CA: Brooks/Cole.

Corsini, R. J. (Ed.). (1981). *Handbook of innovative psychotherapies.* New York: John Wiley.

Cross, D. G., Sheehan, P. W., & Khan, J. A. (1982). Short- and long-term follow-up of clients receiving insight-oriented therapy and behavior therapy. *Journal of Consulting and Clinical Psychology, 50,* 103–112.

DiLoreto, A. O. (1971). *Comparative psychotherapy: An experimental analysis.* Chicago: Aldine-Atherton.

Eysenck, H. J. (1952). The effects of psychotherapy: An evaluation. *Journal of Consulting and Clinical Psychology, 16,* 319–324.

Eysenck, H. J. (1985). *The decline and fall of the Freudian empire.* London: Pelican Books.

Fiedler, F. (1950). A comparison of therapeutic relationships in psychoanalytic, nondirective and Adlerian therapeutic relationships. *Journal of Counseling and Psychology, 14,* 436–445.

Gabbard, G. (1995). Are all psychotherapies equally effective? *The Menninger Letter, 3,* 1–2.

Garfield, S. L. (Ed.). (1983). Special section: Meta-analysis and psychotherapy. *Journal of Consulting and Clinical Psychology, 51,* 3–75.

Gladding, S. T. (1992). *Counseling: A comprehensive profession.* (2nd ed.). New York: Merrill.

Harman, R. L. (1977). Beyond techniques. *Counselor Education and Supervision, 17,* 157–158.

Herink, R. (Ed.). (1980). *The psychotherapy handbook.* New York: New American Library.

Hillman, J. & Ventura, M. (1993). *We've had a hundred years of psychotherapy—and the world's getting worse.* San Francisco: Harpers.

Ivey, A. E., with Simeck Downing, L. (1980). *Counseling and psychotherapy: Skills, theories, and practice.* Englewood Cliffs, NJ: Prentice-Hall.

Jensen, J. P., Bergin, A. E., & Greaves, D. W. (1990). The meaning of eclecticism: New survey and analysis of components. *Professional Psychology: Research and Practice, 21,* 124–130.

Landman, J. C., & Dawes, R. M. (1982). Psychotherapy outcome: Smith and Glass' conclusions stand up under scrutiny. *American Psychologist, 37,* 504–516.

Lazarus, A. A. (1967). In support of technical eclecticism. *Psychological Reports, 21,* 415–416.

Lazarus, A. A. (1971). *Behavior therapy and beyond.* New York: McGraw-Hill.

Lazarus, A. A. (1976). *Multimodel behavior therapy.* New York: Springer.

Lazarus, A. A. (1981). *The practice of multimodel therapy: Systematic, comprehensive, and effective psychotherapy.* New York: McGraw-Hill.

Lazarus, A. A. (1985). *Casebook of multimodel therapy.* New York: Guilford Press.

Lieberman, M., Yalom, I., & Miles, M. (1973). *Encounter groups: First facts.* New York: Basic Books.

Luborsky, L., Singer, B., & Luborsky, L. (1975). Comparative studies of psychotherapies: Is it true that everyone has won and all must have prizes? *Archives of General Psychiatry, 32,* 995–1008.

Marx, J. A., Gyorky, Z. K., Royalty, G. M., & Stern, T. E. (1992). Use of self-help books in psychotherapy. *Professional Psychology: Research and Practice, 23,* 300–305, 652.

McBride, M. C., & Martin, G. E. (1990). A framework for eclecticism: The importance of theory to mental health counseling. *Journal of Mental Health Counseling, 12,* 495–505.

Meltzoff, J., & Kornreich, M. (1971, July). It works. *Psychology Today,* 57–61.

Mental health: Does therapy help? (1995, November). *Consumer Reports,* 734–739.

Michelson, L. (Ed.). (1985). Meta-analysis and clinical psychology. *Clinical Psychology Review, 5,* 1.

Norcross, J. C., & Freeheim, D. K. (1993). Into the future: Retrospect and prospect in psychotherapy. In D. K. Freedman, *History of Psychotherapy*. Washington, DC: American Psychological Association.

Norcross, J. C., & Prochaska, J. O. (1982). National survey of clinical psychologists: Affiliations and orientations. *Clinical Psychologist, 35*, 4–6.

Patterson, C. H. (1980). *The therapeutic relationship: Foundations for an eclectic psychotherapy*. Monterey, CA: Brooks/Cole.

Pedersen, P. B. (1991). Concluding comments to the special issue. *Journal of Counseling and Development, 70*, 250.

Pietrofesa, J. J., Hoffman, A., & Splete, H. H. (1984). *Counseling: An introduction*. (2nd ed.). Boston: Houghton Mifflin.

Piroleau, L., Murdoc, M., & Brody, N. (1983). An analysis of psychotherapy versus placebo studies. *Behavioral and Brain Sciences, 6*, 275–310.

Ridley, C. R. (1995). *Overcoming unintentional racism in counseling and therapy: A practitioner's guide to intentional intervention*. Thousand Oaks, CA: Sage Publications.

Seligman, M. E. P. (1995). The effectiveness of psychotherapy: The *Consumer Reports* study. *American Psychologist, 50*, 965–974.

Shapiro, B. A. (1985). Recent applications of meta-analysis in clinical research. *Clinical Psychology Review, 5*, 13–34.

Sloane, R. B., Staples, F. R., Cristol, A. H., Yorkston, J. J., & Whipple, K. (1975). Short-term analytically oriented psychotherapy versus behavior therapy. *American Journal of Psychiatry, 132*, 373–377.

Smith, D. (1982). Trends in counseling and psychotherapy. *American Psychologist, 37*, 802–809.

Smith, M. L., & Glass, G. V. (1977). Meta-analysis of psychotherapy outcome studies. *American Psychologist, 32*, 752–760.

Smith, M. L., Glass, G. V., & Miller, T. I. (1980). *The benefits of psychotherapy*. Baltimore: Johns Hopkins University Press.

Talmon, M. (1990). *Single session therapy*. San Francisco: Jossey-Bass.

Truax, C., & Carkhuff, R. (1967). *Toward effective counseling and psychotherapy*. Chicago: Aldine.

Wehrly, B. (1995). *Pathways to multicultural counseling competence: A developmental journey*. Pacific Grove, CA: Brooks/Cole.

Acknowledgments

CHAPTER 1

Sidebar 1-1, *pages 9–10:* Berger, J. (1995). Therapy on wheels. *The New York Times,* May 23. Copyright © 1995 by The New York Times Company. Excerpted by permission. / Sidebar 1-2, *pages 12–13:* Fischer, E., & Turner, J. (1970). Attitudes toward seeking professional help: Development and research utility of an attitude scale. *Journal of Consulting and Clinical Psychology, 35,* 82–83. Copyright © 1970 by the American Psychological Association. Reprinted by permission. / Sidebar 1-3, *page 19:* Weiten, W., Lloyd, M. A., & Lashley, R. (1991). *Psychology applied to modern life: Adjustment in the 90s,* 3rd ed. Reprinted by permission of Brooks/Cole Publishing Co., Pacific Grove, California.

CHAPTER 2

Sidebar 2-1, *page 27:* Patterson, C. H. (1985). *The therapeutic relationship: Foundations for an eclectic psychotherapy.* Reprinted by permission of Brooks/Cole Publishing Co., Pacific Grove, California. / Sidebar 2-3, *page 32:* Johnson, D. W. (1981). *Reaching out: Interpersonal effectiveness and self-actualization,* 6th ed. Copyright © 1997 by Allyn and Bacon. Adapted by permission.

CHAPTER 3

Sidebar 3-1, *page 48:* Beck, M., Springer, K., Foote, D., et al. (1992). Sex and psychotherapy. *Newsweek,* April 13, 53–55. Copyright © 1992, Newsweek, Inc. All rights reserved. Excerpted by permission.

CHAPTER 4

Sidebar 4-1, *pages 57–58:* Gleick, E. (1996). Rehab centers run dry. *Time Magazine,* February 5. © 1996 TIME Inc. Reprinted by permission. All rights reserved. / Text, *page 60:* Sue, D. W., & Sue, D. (1990). *Counseling the culturally different: Theory and practice,* 167–168. Copyright © 1990, 1981 by John Wiley & Sons, Inc. All rights reserved. /

Sidebar 4-2, *pages 63–65:* Leerhsen, C. (1990). Unite and conquer. *Newsweek,* February 5, 50–55. © 1990, Newsweek, Inc. All rights reserved. Reprinted by permission.

CHAPTER 6

Sidebar 6-3, *page 108:* Gelman, D. (1990). A fresh take on Freud. *Newsweek,* October 29, 84. © 1990, Newsweek, Inc. All rights reserved. Reprinted by permission. / Text, *page 111:* Auden, W. H. (1939). © 1939 by W. H. Auden. Reprinted by permission of Curtis Brown Ltd., New York.

CHAPTER 7

Sidebar 7-2, *page 132:* Mosak, H. (1971). Lifestyle. In A. G. Nikelly (Ed.), *Techniques for behavior change,* 77–81. Reprinted courtesy of Charles C Thomas, Publisher, Ltd., Springfield, Illinois. / Sidebar 7-3, *pages 135–139:* Huyghe, P. (1985). Voices, glances, flashbacks: Our first memories. *Psychology Today,* September, 48–52. Copyright © 1985 (Sussex Publishers, Inc.) Reprinted by permission.

CHAPTER 8

Sidebar 8-2, *page 163,* and Margin Quote: Frankl, V. E. (1959). *Man's search for meaning,* 58–60. Copyright © 1959, 1962, 1984, 1992 by Viktor E. Frankl. Reprinted by permission of Beacon Press, Boston. / Sidebar 8-3, *pages 169–170:* Gendlin, E. T. (1981). *Focusing.* Copyright © 1978, 1981 by Eugene T. Gendlin, Ph.D. Used by permission of Bantam Books, a division of Bantam Doubleday Dell Publishing Group, Inc.

CHAPTER 9

Sidebar 9-1, *pages 191–192:* Jones, A., & Crandall, R. (1986). Validation of a short index of self-actualization. *Personality and Social Psychology Bulletin,* **12,** 63–73. Copyright © 1986. Abridged by permission of Sage Publications. / Text, *page 198:* Rogers, C. R. (1942). *Counseling and psychotherapy,* 116–117 and 135–136. Copyright © 1942. Reprinted by permission of Houghton Mifflin Company.

CHAPTER 10

Text, *pages 228–230:* Perls, F. (1969). *Gestalt therapy verbatim.* Reprinted by permission of The Gestalt Journal. / Sidebar 10-3, *page 233:* Yontef, G. M, & Simkin, J. S. (1989). Gestalt therapy. In Corsini, R. J., & Wedding, D. (Eds.), *Current psychotherapies,* 4/e, 323–361. 1989 copyright. Reproduced by permission of the publisher, F. E. Peacock Publishers Inc., Itasca, Illinois.

CHAPTER 11

Sidebar 11-1, *page 257:* Ernst, F. H. Psychological rackets in the OK corral. *Transactional Analysis Journal,* **23,** 104–109. Published by International Transactional Analysis Association, San Francisco. Reprinted by permission of F. H. Ernst, Jr. / Text, *pages 261–265:* Berne, E. (1961). *Transactional analysis in psychotherapy.* Copyright © 1961. Reprinted by permission of Random House, New York. / Sidebar 11-2, *pages 267–269:* Goode, E. E. (1992). Psychic borderlines. *U.S. News & World Report,* January 20, 57–59. Copyright, Jan. 20, 1992, U.S. News & World Report. Used by permission.

CHAPTER 12

Sidebar 12-1, *page 291:* Hall, M. H. (1967). The behavioral view: A conversation with B. F. Skinner. In Chance, P., & Harris, T. G. (Eds.), *The best of Psychology Today,* 535. Copyright © 1967 (Sussex Publishers, Inc.). Reprinted by permission. / Sidebar 12-2, *pages 298–300:* Goldiamond, I. (1973). A diary of self-modification. *Psychology Today,* November, 188. Copyright © 1973 (Sussex Publishers, Inc.). Reprinted by permission. / Text, *pages 301–304:* Wolpe, J. (1982). *The practice of behavior therapy,* 3rd ed., 309–312. London: Pergamon Press of Elsevier Science Ltd. Copyright © 1969 Joseph Wolpe. All rights reserved.

CHAPTER 13

Braiker, H. B. (1989). The power of self-talk. *Psychology Today,* December. Copyright © 1985 (Sussex Publishers, Inc.) Adapted by permission. / Text, *pages 325–327, 334, 335–338:* All materials © Albert Ellis, Ph.D. Used by permission of Albert Ellis and Institute for Rational-Emotive Therapy, New York. / Sidebar 13-2, *page 332:* Ellis, A. (1986). An emotional control card for inappropriate and appropriate emotions in using rational-emotive therapy. *Journal of Counseling and Development,* **65,** 206. © American Counseling Association. Reprinted with permission. No further reproduction authorized without written permission of the American Counseling Association.

CHAPTER 14

Sidebar 14-1, *pages 358–359:* Wubbolding, R. E. (1988). *Using reality therapy.* Copyright © 1991 by Robert E. Wubbolding. Reprinted by permission of HarperCollins Publishers, Inc. / Text, *pages 368–370:* Glasser, W. (1965). *Reality therapy: A new approach to psychiatry,* 143–148. Copyright © 1965 by William Glasser, M. D. Reprinted by permission of HarperCollins Publishers, Inc., and the author. / Sidebar 14-2, *pages 372–374:* McArthur, M. J. (1990). Reality therapy with rape victims. *Archives of Psychiatric Nursing,* **IV:6.** Reprinted by permission of W. B. Saunders Co. and the author.

CHAPTER 15

Sidebar 15-1, *pages 388–389:* Goleman, D. (1991). Is a single session enough? *New York Times,* May 2, B8. Copyright © 1991 by The New York Times Company. Excerpted by permission. / Sidebar 15-2, *pages 394–396:* Goleman, D. (1995). Making room on the couch for culture. *New York Times,* December 5, B5. Copyright © 1995 by The New York Times Company. Excerpted by permission.

Name Index

Abeles, N., 49
Abramowitz, S. I., 200
Abrams, D., 102
Abrego, P. J., 14
Addis, M. E., 341
Adelsberg, M., 306
Adler, A., 4, 119–146, 245
Afresti, A. A., 71
Albee, G. W., 5
Albers, G. R., 68
Alberti, R., 293
Alexander, C. M., 59–60
Alexander, F., 101
Allen, D., 59
Allen, H. A., 233
Allen, T., 28
Allman, L. S., 173
Anderson, C. A., 39
Anderson, W. P., 27
Angel, E., 165
Ansbacher, H. L., 123, 126, 127, 145
Ansbacher, R., 126
Antill, J. K., 61
Aponte, H. J., 59
Aristotle, 6, 50, 79, 323
Arlow, J. A., 88
Arnold, K., 57
Arredondo, P., 60
Ascher, L. M., 171
Asher, J., 61
Ashmead, D., 137
Aspey, D. N., 29
Atkinson, D. R., 56
Auden, W. H., 111

Ayllon, T., 286
Azrin, N. H., 286

Babcock, J. C., 301
Bacon, F., 61
Baker, M. S., 257, 268
Baker, T. B., 301
Baldwin, M., 32
Balente, S. M., 45
Ball-Rokeach, S. J., 34
Bandura, A., 27, 279, 281–284, 288, 290, 292, 340
Banks, W. P., 213
Baradell, J. G., 202
Bard, I., 325
Barkam, M., 341
Barlow, D. H., 292, 301, 340
Barnes, G., 260
Barrett, C., 368
Barrett-Lennard, G. T., 29, 196
Barry, H., 134
Barry, S. M., 301
Barry, T., 340
Bassin, A., 372
Basson, C. J., 266
Batchelor, W., 70
Bates, C. M., 47, 50
Baucom, D.H., 341
Beardslee, W. R., 341
Beauchamp, T. L., 45
Beck, A. T., 338–340, 344
Becker, E., 155
Beckerman, N. L., 69
Beidel, D. C., 297
Beiman, I., 328

Beitman, B. D., 390
Belkin, G. S., 11, 16, 33
Bellack, A. S., 292, 297
Bellah, R. N., 393
Bemis, K., 340
Benshoff, J. M., 368
Berdyaev, N., 159
Berenson, B. G., 25, 27
Berger, J., 10
Berger, M., 50
Bergersen, S. G., 301
Bergin, A. E., 25, 30, 45, 66, 168, 385, 390, 391
Berman, A. L., 46
Berman, J. S., 387
Bernard, J. M.,16, 224, 227
Bernard, M. E., 342, 343
Bernays, M., 88
Berne, E., 5, 243–252, 255–257, 259, 261–265, 266
Bernstein, B. L., 59
Best, J. A., 343
Beutler, L. E., 11, 340, 343
Bhugra, D., 343
Bibring, G., 107
Biggs, D., 15
Bijou, S. W., 301
Binder, J. L., 100
Binswanger, L., 155, 161
Birnbrauer, J. S., 301
Bishop, D. R., 134, 144
Blackham, G. J., 288
Blanck, G., 101, 109
Blanck, R., 101, 109
Blane, H. T., 134
Blau, B., 50
Blocher, D. H., 15, 16, 46, 49, 50
Block, J., 194
Block, L., 340
Bloom, B., 388
Bohmer, P., 133
Bonaparte, M., 7
Bonds-White, F., 257
Bordin, E. S., 30
Bornstein, P., 301
Borys, D. S., 47
Boss, M., 155, 161
Bowman, J. T., 288
Boy, A., 30
Bozarth, J. D., 191
Brack, C. J., 368
Brack, G., 368
Bradford, A. E., 66
Bradley, J. R., 16
Braiker, H. B., 324–325

Brammer, L., 80
Brammer, L. M., 14, 29, 38
Bratter, B. I., 372
Bratter, T. E., 372
Brecher, E. M., 89
Bremner, R., 39
Brennan, T. P., 322
Brenner, C., 88
Breuer, J., 7, 90–91
Brilman, E., 297
Brodesky, A. M., 47, 50
Brodley, B. T., 191
Brody, N., 387
Broveman, I. K., 61
Broverman, D. M., 61
Brown, M., 246, 256, 258, 259
Brownell, K. D., 301
Browning, D. S., 67
Bruch, H., 11
Bruch, M. A., 341
Brunswick, R. M., 7
Bryant, D., 231
Buber, M., 159, 160, 165
Budman, S., 388–389
Bugental, J. F. T., 155, 169
Buie, J., 98
Burish, T. G., 286, 301
Burk, J. F., 145
Burke, H. F., 10
Burke, J. F., 122, 202, 220, 234, 246, 259
Burns, D. D., 325, 341, 343
Burton, M. V., 202
Butler, K., 66
Butler, R. N., 71
Butman, R. E., 186, 340
Bylski, N. C., 168
Byrd, B., 133
Byrne, G., 68

Cadman, 385
Cadwallader, E. H., 234
Cain, D. J., 187, 201, 203
Callanan, P., 35, 45
Camaro, S., 301
Cameron, R., 340
Campbell, J., 66
Campbell, V. L., 202, 234
Camus, A., 157, 159, 168, 174
Cannon, D. S., 301
Caplan, P. J., 107
Carkhuff, R. R., 15, 25, 27, 29, 30, 381
Carlson, W. A., 343
Carroll, L., 11
Carter, J. A., 25
Carter, R. T., 59

Casas, J. M., 59–60
Casey, R. J., 387
Cashwell, C. S., 368
Cautela, J. R., 294, 304
Cavaliere, F., 11, 385
Cavanaugh, M. E., 25, 26, 28, 31, 32, 51, 391
Chan, D. W., 266
Chance, P., 291
Chang, V. N., 266
Charboneau-Powis, M., 301
Charcot, J., 91
Cheney, W. D., 244
Childress, J. S., 45
Christensen, A., 17
Christopher, S. B., 94
Church, J. A., 297
Cicero, M. T., 16, 83
Clagett, A. F., 362
Clark, B. D., 248
Clark, C., 49
Clark, R. W., 89, 90
Clarkson, F. E., 61
Claxton, R. P., 133
Clement, U., 301
Cloud, H., 37
Coates, D., 372
Cockrum, J. R., 366
Cogswell, J. F., 160
Cohen, B., 372
Cohen, E. D., 49, 328
Cohen, J., 62
Cohen, K., 44
Collins, G. R., 66
Comas-Diaz, L., 108
Combs, A., 35
Cook, R. E., 36
Cooley, M. R., 297
Coonerty, S. M., 35
Cooper, A. M., 111
Cooper, G. F., 45
Corey, G., 25, 35, 45
Corey, M. S., 25, 35, 45
Corlis, R. B., 166
Cormier, L. S., 10, 17, 28, 32, 35, 46, 51
Cormier, W. H., 17, 32, 35, 46, 51
Cornell, W. F., 47
Corrigan, J. D., 25
Corsini, R. J., 7, 120, 134, 140, 380
Cotton, S., 61
Coven, A., 62
Covin, A. B., 224
Cowell, D. R., 133
Cowie, I., 304
Cozad, L., 155

Craig, S. S., 133
Craighead, W. E., 301
Cramer, D., 196
Crane, B. B., 25
Crane, F., 49
Cristiani, T. S., 14, 35, 62, 253
Crockett, J., 133
Croll, M., 358
Cross, D. G., 387
Crow, M. J., 301
Cunningham, C., 39
Cunningham, L. M., 167
Curlette, W. L., 131
Curtis, J. M., 133
Cushman, P., 7

Daldrup, R. J., 343
Dally, E. M., 301
Davenport, L., 63–65
Davis, J. R., 39
Davison, G. C., 20, 297, 305, 340, 343
Dawes, R. M., 386
Dean, T., 341
Deane, F. P., 343
Deblinger, E., 341
DeCarvalho, R. J., 167
DeCasper, A., 138
DeCsipkes, R.A., 25
DeForest, C., 61
DeKraai, M. B., 49
de La Fontaine, J., 84
de la Rocha, O., 173
de La Rochefoucauld, F., 45
Dell, D. M., 25
Denkowski, G. C., 49
Denkowski, K. M., 49
Denton, W. H., 340
DeRosa, A. P., 133
DeRubeis, R. J., 340
Deutsch, D., 150
Deutsch, H., 7, 8, 107
Devine, V. T., 301
deVisser, L., 294
Devore, W., 56
Dewey, E. A., 134
Diekstra, R. F., 343
DiGuiseppe, R. A., 320, 331, 334, 343
DiLoreto, A. O., 387
DiMattio, D., 320
Dinkmeyer, D., 124, 131, 132, 134, 140
Dinkmeyer, D. Jr., 131
Dobson, K. S., 297, 320, 340
Dolliver, R. H., 221, 231
Dopson, L., 158
Dorsey, G. C., 301

Drego, P. A., 247
Dreikurs, R., 130, 140
Dreyfus, E. A., 28, 140
Drumheller, P., 49
Dryden, W., 318, 330, 343
Dua, P. S., 343
Dubois, P., 7
Dulchin, J., 49
Dumas, J. E., 257
Duncan, L., 145
Dunn, K. W., 39
Durant, W., 4
Durrance, P., 68
Dusay, J. M., 245, 253, 258
Dusay, K. M., 253, 258
Dye, E., 372
Dymond, R. F., 194

Eash, U., 62
Edelwich, J., 368
Edens, R. M., 372
Edison, T., 40
Edkins, W., 110
Egan, G., 28–30, 196
Einstein, A., 136, 391
Eisenberg, S., 25
Elaad, E., 266
Eldredge, K. L., 340
Eliot, T. S., 28, 381
Elkins, D., 173
Elkins, R. L., 301
Ellenberger, H., 120, 130, 165
Elliott, H., 184
Elliott, J. E., 145
Ellis, A., 66, 119, 120, 145, 318–322, 325–338,
    342–344
Emerson, R. W., 334
Emery, G., 339, 340
Emmelkamp, P. M. G., 297, 301
Emmons, A. L., 293
Engels, G. I., 343
Engle, D., 340, 343
Epictetus, 321
Epstein, N., 341
Epstein, R., 122
Epstein, W., 234
Erikson, E., 71, 109
Ernst, F. H., 257
Erwin, E., 304
Eshbaugh, D. M., 343
Evans, D. B., 372
Evans, D. R., 301
Evans, H. I., 373
Evans, T. D., 144

Evison, I. S., 67
Eysenck, H. J., 107, 279, 286, 306,
    385–387

Fagan, J., 221
Fairbairn, W. R. D., 109
Fairburn, C. G., 340
Fals, S., 297
Farkas, G. M., 286
Farson, R., 186
Feixas, G., 340
Fell, M., 68
Fenichel, O., 214
Feuerstein, M., 305
Fielder, F., 196, 381
Filer, P., 62
Fine, R., 111
Fink, J., 201
Fischer, E., 13
Fizel, D., 10
Foa, E. B., 341
Folkins, C. H., 343
Follette, W. C., 286
Fong, K., 59
Ford, J. D., 304
Foreyt, J. P., 107
Foxworth, C. L., 202
France, A., 20
Frank, A., 214
Frank, E., 325
Frank, J. D., 7, 30, 81
Frankl, V. E., 4, 145, 155, 160–165, 167, 168,
    170–172
Franklin, M., 372
Franks, C. M., 107
Freedman, L. D., 261
Freeheim, D. K., 397
Freeman, L., 91
Freeman, S. C., 201
Freimuth, V. G., 61
French, T., 101
Fretz, B. R., 14, 45, 49, 202
Freud, A., 4, 107, 109
Freud, S., 3, 4, 48, 66, 88–113, 119, 123, 124
Frey, D. H., 167
Friday, P. J., 258
Frizzell, K., 49
Fromm, E., 5, 35, 99, 119, 145
Fromm-Reichmann, F., 47, 107
Fruzzetti, A. E., 297
Fry, W. R. Jr., 334
Fujino, D. C., 59
Furrow, B. R., 45
Furtmuller, C., 122

Furukawa, M. J., 294
Futterman, D., 70

Gabbard, G., 386, 387
Gade, E., 158
Galassi, J. P., 292
Galbraith, J. K., 328
Gambrill, E., 36
Ganley, R., 301
Garamoni, G. L., 325
Gardner, L. E., 144
Gardner, P., 297
Garfield, S. L., 30, 387
Garfinkle, M. I., 142
Garnefski, N., 343
Garner, A., 368
Gartrell, N., 48
Garza-Perez, J., 171
Gatchel, R. L., 343
Gates, L., 133
Gay, P., 89–91, 111
Gazda, G. M., 15, 31, 51, 372, 374
Geer, J. H., 343
Gehring, D. D., 50
Gelman, D., 108
Gelso, C. J., 14, 25, 45, 49, 202
Gendlin, E. T., 25, 169, 196
George, R. L., 14, 35, 253
Gibb, J. R., 29
Gibson, D. R., 68
Gibson, R. L., 5, 7
Gilbert, L. A., 61
Giles, T. R., 331, 340
Gillan, P., 301
Gilliland, B. E., 288
Gilmore, S. K., 62
Giordano, J., 59, 232
Gladding, S. T., 66, 246, 249, 260, 381
Gladstein, G. A., 196
Gladstone, W., 340
Glass, G. V., 387
Glass, J., 71
Glasser, N., 356–357, 359–371, 374
Gleick, E., 57–58
Glenn, J., 97
Goethe, 37
Gold, D. C., 221
Gold, L., 141
Goldfried, M. R., 297, 305, 327, 340,
    390
Goldhaber, G. M., 251
Goldhaber, M. B., 251
Goldiamond, I., 298–300
Goldin, J. C., 301

Goldman, W., 57
Goldrick, M., 59
Goldstein, A. P., 31, 285
Goldstein, K., 184, 191, 214
Goleman, D., 388–389, 394–396
Golombock, S., 301
Good, G., 155
Good, G. E., 61
Goode, E. E., 266–268
Goodell, R., 281
Goodman, B., 373
Goodman, P., 214, 224
Goodyear, R. K., 16, 201
Gormly, A., 304
Gorrell, J., 217, 219
Gottman, J., 11
Goulding, M., 252, 260, 261
Goulding, R., 252, 260, 261
Gove, W. R., 60
Grant, K., 71
Grater, H., 133
Graumann, C. F., 213
Graves, S., 50
Grawe, K., 340
Gray, L. A., 49
Greaves, D. W., 390, 391
Green, M. F., 341
Green, S. W., 46
Greenberg, J., 111
Greenberg, L. S., 214, 227
Greenblatt, L., 61
Greenlee, R. W., 165
Greenson, R. R., 101
Grieger, R. M., 322, 325
Groden, G., 304
Grube, J. W., 34
Guerney, B. G., 231
Guntrip, H., 109
Gurman, A. S., 28
Gyorky, Z. K., 384

Haaga, D. A., 340, 343
Hackney, H., 10, 28, 46, 56, 196
Hajzler, D. J., 343
Halford, W. K., 301
Hall, J., 59
Hall, M. H., 291
Halligan, F. G., 343
Hanna, H. H., 340
Hansen, J., 343
Hansen, J. C., 258
Harackiewicz, J., 135
Harding, A. K., 49
Hare-Mustin, R. T., 61

Harman, R. L., 221, 391
Harper, R., 99
Harper, R. A., 320, 327
Harrell, T. H., 328
Harrington, G. L., 359
Harris, S., 38
Harris, T. A., 243, 253, 255, 256, 260
Harris, T. G., 291
Hart, E. A., 368
Hartley, D., 200
Hartman, H., 109
Hartman, L. M., 301
Hartmann, E., 267–269
Hasenauer, J. E., 61
Hatton, C. L., 45
Hayashi, S., 201
Hayden, D., 201
Hayes, S. C., 301
Hearst, N., 68
Hefferline, R. F., 224
Heidegger, M., 159, 161, 164
Heimberg, R. G., 341
Hein, K., 70
Heitzmann, C., 68
Hemingway, E., 18
Hendrick, S. S., 61
Henry, D., 341
Heppner, P. P., 27
Heraclitus, 68
Herink, R., 380
Herlihy, B., 49
Hersen, M. S., 62, 292, 297
Heslett, F. E., 167
Hess, B. B., 71
Heuchert, C. M., 372
Higginbitham, H. N., 31
Hill-Hain, A., 201
Hillman, J., 393
Himmelhoch, J. M., 297
Himmell, C. D., 202, 234
Hippocrates, 6, 84
Hlongwane, M. M., 266
Hoellen, B., 341
Hoffer, E., 59
Hoffman, A., 28, 381
Hoke, L., 341
Holland, G. A., 245
Hollender, M. H., 91
Hollon, S. D., 286, 301, 339, 340
Holmes, O. W., 14
Hom, P. H., 340
Honeyman, A., 368
Hope, D. A., 341
Hope, R. A., 340

Horney, K., 7, 98, 107, 119, 214
Hornstein, G., 103
Hosford, R., 294
Hosie, T., 62
Houts, A. C., 286
Howe, E., 397
Hu, L., 59
Hubbard, J., 133
Hubbard, M. G., 61
Hulbert, R. J., 368
Hull, C., 281, 285
Hulley, S., 68
Hundert, J., 306
Hunt, M., 320
Hurding, R., 108
Huyghe, P., 135–139
Hycner, R., 219
Hyland, S., 332

Ibrahim, F. A., 35, 173
Ignoffo, M., 368
Ivey, A. E., 171, 270, 380
Ivey, M. B., 171, 270

Jacobs, A., 257
Jacobs, M. D., 65
Jacobson, N. S., 17, 297, 301, 341
James, J., 257
James, M., 255, 256, 266
James, R. K., 288
James, W., 35
Jameson, B., 65
Janet, P. M. F., 7, 123
Jaspers, K., 159
Jensen, J. P., 390, 391
Jensen, S. M., 257, 266
Jessee, R. E., 231
Jevne, R., 25
Jewell, L. N., 16
Jobe, T., 67
Jobes, D. A., 46
Johnson, D. W., 32
Jones, E., 88, 90
Jones, H. G., 279
Jones, J., 88
Jones, M. C., 281, 285
Jones, R., 340
Jones, S. C., 340
Jones, S. L., 186
Jongeward, D., 246, 255, 256, 266
Jordan, A. E., 45
Jordan, B. T., 343
Jourard, S., 219
Jung, C. G., 4, 48, 71, 94, 97

Kaam, A. L. Van, 155, 160
Kahn, E., 199
Kaltenbach, R. F., 372, 374
Kanfer, F. H., 31, 285
Kanitz, B., 29
Kanitz, F., 318
Kant, I., 85
Kaplan, H. B., 126
Karpman, S. B., 259 260
Kassinove, H., 343
Kastner, M., 231
Kaufman, W., 145
Kavanagh, D. J., 306
Kazdin, A. E., 288, 297, 301
Kelly, A., 301
Kelly, T. A., 35
Kemp, C. G., 168
Kempler, B., 343
Kempler, W., 217, 221
Kendall, P. C., 11, 107
Kendall, R., 340
Kern, R. M., 131
Kernberg, O., 109
Kessler, J., 231
Khan, J. A., 387
Kidder, J. D., 301
Kierkegaard, S., 157–159, 174, 190
Kiesler, D. V., 25
Kihlstrom, J., 135, 136
King, M. L. Jr., 174
Kirchner, R., 33
Kirk, F. S., 62
Kirschenbaum, H., 183–185
Klein, G. S., 109
Kleinman, A., 395
Knapp, S., 49
Knox, P., 253
Kobasa, S. C., 160
Koepp, A. H., 257, 268
Koffka, K., 215
Köhler, W., 215, 222
Kohut, H., 109, 110
Kompf, M., 49
Kopala, M., 51
Korb, M. P., 217, 219
Korchin, S., 88
Kornreich, M., 385
Kottler, J. A., 25
Kottman, T., 130, 143
Kovacs, M., 340
Kowatch, R. A., 340
Krajicek, D., 213
Krumboltz, J. D., 10, 80, 279, 286–289
Kuipers, H., 297

Kunins, H., 70
Kuno, T., 201

LaCrosse, M. B., 31
LaFreniere, P., 257
Laing, R. D., 164
Lamb, D. H., 49
Lambert, M. J., 25, 385
Lambert, W. W., 34
Lammers, W., 257
Landman, J.C., 386
Lantz, J., 165
Laplanche, J., 92, 101
Lapointe, K., 328
Larson, D., 15
Latner, J., 222
Lawe, C. F., 231
Lazarus, A. A., 20, 279, 281, 286, 291, 292, 391, 392
Leaf, R., 343
Leak, G. K., 94, 144
Lebowitz, L., 372
Ledwidge, B. L., 171
Lee, C. C., 59
Leerhsen, C., 63–65
Lennox, S., 9
Lepper, M. R., 39
Leslie, R., 50
Lester, D., 368
Levant, R., 189
Levi, N., 232
Levin, S. M., 301
LeVine, P., 167
Levitsky, A., 224
Lewin, K., 79, 212
Lewinsohn, P. M., 297, 301
Lewis, K. N., 25
Lewis, M. I., 71
Lewis, S. D., 63–65
Liberman, R. P., 301, 341
Lichtenberg, J., 253
Lieberman, M., 381
Liff, Z. A., 109
Lincoln, A., 46
Lindsley, O. R., 286
Lineberger, M. R., 133
Linscott, J., 343
Lipschitz, F., 102
Lipsey, M., 14
Lipsky, M. J., 343
Litt, S., 214
Little, L. F., 221
Litvak, S. B., 343
Lloyd, K., 343

Loesch, L. C., 25
Loftus, P. E., 168
Lombana, J. H., 71, 72
London, J., 68
London, P., 8
Longenecker, C. O., 257
Lonner, W. J., 5
Lopez, A., 59
Lopez, F. G., 202, 234
Lopez, R., 59
Losoncy, L. E., 131
Lovell, M., 200
Lowe, C. M., 80
Lu, F., 396
Luborsky, L., 387
Lucas, J. A., 340
Lucente, S., 297
Ludden, J., 58
Lukas, E., 170, 171

MacDevitt, J. W., 28
MacDonald, D., 51
MacDonald, G., 38
MacGillavry, D., 301
MacNair, R. R., 49
Maddi, S. R., 160
Mahler, M., 107, 109
Mahoney, M. J., 334
Maletzky, B. M., 301
Malony, H. N., 66
Malpass, R., 5
Manaster, G J., 134, 140
Manson, S., 395
Marcel, G., 159
Markman, H., 11
Marks, I. M., 288, 297
Marrow, A., 79
Marshall, B. D., 301
Martin, F. E., 257
Martin, G. E., 391
Martin, L. J., 71
Maruyama, G., 134
Marx, J. A., 384
Marx, K., 124
Maslow, A., 26, 28, 145, 186, 192, 193
Massey, R. F., 142, 266
Masters, J. C., 286, 301
Maultsby, M. C., 331
May, R., 5, 111, 155–157, 159, 160, 162,
    164–166, 172
Mays, V. M., 5
McArthur, M. J., 368, 372–374
McBride, M. C., 391
McCarthy, M., 343
McClure, B. A., 221

McDavis, R. J., 60
McDowell, W., 62
McGoldrick, M., 232
McGovern, T. E., 343
McGuire, J. M., 50
McGuire, W., 123
McKinney, H., 59
McLean, P., 297
McLeer, S. V., 341
McLeod, J., 173, 189
McMullin, R. E., 331
Mead, M., 98
Meador, B., 185, 186
Meara, N. M., 45
Meares, R., 101
Meehl, P. R., 8
Mees, H. L., 301
Meichenbaum, D., 340, 341, 343
Meir, G., 136
Meissner, W., 100
Meltzoff, J., 385
Mendel, E., 142
Mendoza, D., 29
Merrill, E., 221
Mersch, P. P., 297
Meyer, V., 279
Mezzich, J., 394–395
Michels, R., 266, 388
Michelson, L., 387
Mickel, E., 368
Miles, M., 381
Miller, F. E., 65
Miller, M. J., 202
Miller, N., 134
Miller, N. J., 343
Miller, S., 343
Miller, T. I., 387
Milliken, R. L., 33
Milne, D., 304
Minrath, M., 108
Mintz, J., 301
Miranda, A. O., 144
Mitchell, K. M., 25, 196
Mitchell, M. H., 5, 7
Mitchell, S., 111
Modell, A., 109
Mohr, D. C., 340, 343
Moldawsky, S., 14
Moleski, R., 343
Montag, K. R., 341
Moore, K. J., 297
Moreira, V., 188
Morin, C. M., 340
Morris, J. B., 318
Morten, G., 56

Mosak, H. M., 126, 130–133, 140, 142
Moschetta, P. V., 126
Moscovitch, M., 137
Moyers, B., 66
Mullis, F. J., 131
Munoz, R. F., 301
Munroe, R., 99
Murdoc, M., 387
Murdock, T. B., 341
Murphy, H. B., 25
Myers, J. E., 71

Naranjo, C., 219
Narayan, C., 133
Nathanson, R., 62
Neal, N., 49
Neimeyer, R. A., 340
Neisser, U., 136, 137
Nelson, K., 138–139
Nelson, M., 63–65
Nelson, R. O., 292
Nemiah, J. C., 101
Neumann, M. A., 231
Newman, J., 200
Newman, J. L., 47
Newman, S., 68
Newton, F. B., 368
Nicoll, W. G., 144
Nietzsche, F., 123–124, 157–159, 171, 172, 174
Nikelly, A. G., 127, 131, 133, 134, 139, 140
Niles, B., 340
Nolen, S., 325, 341
Nolen-Hoeksema, S., 343
Norcross, J. C., 155, 174, 175, 390, 397
Nowak-Scibelli, D., 373
Nye, R. D., 99, 111, 188, 280
Nykodym, N., 257

O'Brien, M., 61
O'Connell, W. E., 126
O'Hearne, J., 266
O'Leary, K., 284
O'Leary, K. D., 301
O'Meara, D. P., 47
Obler, M., 301
Oden, T. A., 246, 256
Oei, T. P. S., 343
Oei, T. S., 297
Okun, B. F., 35
Olson, P. P., 301
Orgler, H., 122, 123, 128
Osawa, M., 201
Osborn, D., 213

Osipow, S. H., 16, 29, 30, 167, 168, 355
Ososkie, J. N., 371
Oss, M., 57
Ostrom, R., 341
Otero, Z. T. M., 47
Owen, I. R., 160

Page, A. C., 343
Palmer, S., 215
Papert, S., 136
Pappenheim, B., 90
Parish, T. S., 356, 368
Parker, R. W., 202
Parrott, L., 29, 120
Partenheimer, D., 157
Patterson, C., 35
Patterson, C. H., 14, 27, 81, 201, 322, 381
Patterson, L. E., 25
Pavlov, I., 285, 286, 306
Payne, I., 168
Peacock, J. A., 368
Pearce, J. K., 59, 232
Peck, M. S., 66
Pedersen, P. B., 60, 397
Pegram, M., 165
Penfield, W., 276
Perez, J. F., 25
Perlin, M., 133
Perlman, L. G., 62
Perlmutter, M., 137
Perls, F. S., 5, 213–215, 217–230, 232, 235
Perls, L., 231
Perot, A. R., 292
Perry, M. A., 294
Perry, W., 83
Pervin, L. A., 160
Peters, H. J., 167
Peterson, A. V., 360
Peveler, R. C., 340
Pew, W., 124, 132, 134, 140
Pfost, K. S., 162
Phares, E. J., 223
Phares, L. A., 160
Phillips, L., 15
Piaget, J., 135
Piechowski, M. M., 32
Pietrofesa, J. J., 28, 61, 381
Pine, F., 91, 109
Pine, G., 30
Piroleau, L., 387
Pitt, W., 52
Pizer, I., 266
Plato, 6
Poddar, P., 50
Poidevant, J. M., 368

Pomper, S., 63–65
Pontailis, J., 92, 101
Ponterotto, J. G., 59–60
Pope, K. S., 45, 47, 48
Potts, M. K., 162
Pounds, B., 144
Prochaska, J. O., 109, 144, 174, 222, 390
Propst, L. R., 341
Protheroe, D., 360
Purkey, W. W., 143

Quinsey, V. L., 301

Rabe, P., 166
Rabinowitz, F. E., 155
Rachin, R. L., 361, 372
Rachman, S., 107, 281
Radda, H. T., 372
Ranft, V. A., 44
Range, L. M., 222, 231
Rank, O., 48, 84, 387
Rankin, L. A., 341
Rapaport, D., 109
Raskin, N. J., 186, 199
Rasnake, L. K., 290
Rausch, H. L., 30
Raymond, C., 196
Reardon, J. P., 343
Regan, J. F., 35
Rehm, L. P., 297
Reich, T., 96
Remer, P., 60
Reuss, N., 368
Reynolds, C. F., 297, 325
Rice, L. N., 214
Richards, P. S., 67
Richardson, B. L., 59
Ridley, C. R., 29, 59, 397
Riessman, F., 65
Riggs, D. S., 341
Rihani, S., 343
Rimm, D. C., 286, 301, 343
Rink, A., 45
Risley, T. R., 301
Roazen, P., 123
Roback, H. B., 200
Roberts, R. C., 184
Rock, I., 215
Rogers, C. R., 5, 25, 28–30, 35, 39, 120, 145,
    183–201, 245
Rokeach, M., 34, 35
Rose, D., 372
Rosenkrantz, R., 61
Rosenthal, H. R., 140
Rosenthal, R., 35

Ross, A. O., 286, 301
Ross, L., 39
Rossetti, D. G., 252
Roth, A. D., 297
Roth, S., 372
Rothbaum, B. O., 341
Rothberg, P. C., 341
Rowe, W., 25
Royalty, G. M., 384
Rozsnafsky, J., 358
Rubin, D., 136
Rucker, B. B., 25
Rudolph, L. B., 217
Rule, W. R., 144
Rumney, A., 257
Runyan, W. McK., 88
Rusalem, H., 62
Rush, A. J., 339, 340
Russell, L. A., 325
Russo, T. R., 221
Ruud, W. N., 257
Ryan, A., 173
Rychalk, J., 186
Rzasa, T., 39

Sadock, V. A., 373
Salameh, W. A., 334
Sales, B. D., 49
Salter, A., 279
Samelson, F.J. B., 284
Samler, J., 35
Sampson, H., 88, 109
Saper, B., 367
Sarris, V., 215
Sartre, J. P., 155, 159, 160, 162, 165, 174
Satir, V., 32
Schacter, D., 137
Scheler, M., 164
Scher, M., 61
Schiffer, F., 58
Schlesinger, E. G., 56
Schlossberg, N. K., 61
Schmidt, G., 301
Schmidt, J. J., 143
Schmidt, L. D., 25
Schmidt, N. B., 340
Schutz, B., 46, 47
Schwartz, D., 341
Schwartzberg, S., 165
Schwarzlose, J., 58
Sechrest, L., 284
Sederer, L., 58
See, J. D., 202
Segal, A. J., 49
Seligman, L., 51, 143, 201

Seligman, M. E. P., 25, 27, 373, 387
Serok, S., 232
Sexton, T. L., 25
Shafranske, E., 66
Shah, S., 49
Shakespeare, 134, 318
Shannon, K. K., 297
Shapiro, B. A., 387
Shapiro, D. A., 341
Shapiro, S. B., 248
Shaw, B., 339
Sheehan, P. W., 387
Sheehy, M., 57
Sheeley, B. L., 49
Shepherd, I. L., 231
Shilling, L. E., 250
Shimizu, M., 208
Shirar, L., 231
Shlien, J. M., 189
Shostrom, E. L., 14, 29, 221
Shulman, B. H., 133
Siberman, A., 288
Sichel, J., 320
Siegel, M., 49
Siegel, S., 48
Sileo, F. J., 51
Silverman, M. S., 343
Silverstein, S., 106
Silvestri, S., 257
Simek-Downing, L., 171, 270, 380
Simkin, J. S., 223, 228, 233, 234
Simoneux, J., 245
Simons, A. D., 297, 341
Simonton, D. K., 71
Singer, B., 387
Sitton, S., 133
Skinner, B. F., 279–281, 284–286, 288, 291, 305, 306
Sklare, G., 332
Sloane, R. B., 385
Small, J., 25
Smith, A., 301
Smith, B., 284
Smith, D., 145, 202, 270, 340, 390
Smith, D. C., 68
Smith, E. W. L., 212, 231
Smith, M. L., 386
Smryl, T., 372
Solomon, R. L., 34
Solyom, C., 171
Solyom, L., 171
Sommers, P., 62
Sordo, I., 372
Sorenson, J. L., 68
Spero, M. H., 66

Sperry, L., 131
Spicer, J., 58
Spitz, R., 109
Splete, H. H., 28, 381
St. Clair, M., 109
Stanton, D. T., 368
Stanwood, D. L., 368
Staples, F. R., 385
Steckel, T., 257
Steffy, R. A., 343
Steiner, C., 244–246, 258, 260
Steiner, K. M., 372
Steinman, C. M., 301
Stepansky, P. E., 123
Stern, E. M., 66
Stern, R., 297
Stern, T. E., 384
Stevens, M. J., 162
Stevic, R. R., 258
Stone, G. L., 61
Stone, M., 127
Storr, A., 106
Strain, P. S., 62
Strauss, U., 9
Strupp, H. H., 100, 393
Stunkard, A. J., 107
Sue, D., 56, 59, 60, 201
Sue, D. W., 36, 56, 59, 60
Sue, S., 59
Surrey, L., 49
Suzuki, L. A., 59–60

Tague, C., 301
Takeuchi, D. T., 59
Talmon, M., 389
Tan, S. Y., 66, 67
Tarasoff, T., 50
Taylor, J., 332
Taylor, R. E., 51
Taylor, S., 297
Telch, M. J., 340
Tharp, R. G., 15, 32
Thase, M. E., 297, 325, 341
Thatcher, J. A., 361
Thompson, C., 7, 98, 107
Thompson, C. D., 217
Thoreau, H. D., 364
Thoresen, C. E., 287, 289
Throndike, E. L., 285
Tillich, P., 156, 160
Tobin, S. A., 111, 173
Todd, C., 137
Tosi, D. J., 16, 29, 30, 167, 343, 355
Tournier, P., 201
Townsend, J., 37

Tramel, D., 33
Trexler, L. D., 343
Trezza, G. R., 70
Trotzer, J. P., 25
Truax, C. B., 25, 30, 196, 381
Tudor, J. F., 60
Turkat, I. D., 305
Turkewitz, H., 301
Turner, J., 13
Turner, R. M., 171
Turner, S. M., 297
Turpin, J. O., 371
Twain, M., 84
Tyler, L. E., 29
Tyson, G. M., 222, 231

Udry, E. M., 368
Usher, C. H., 201

Vaihinger, H., 123
Valins, S., 343
VandeCreek, L., 49
Vandergriff, A., 62
Van der Helm, M., 301
Van De Riet, V., 217, 219
Van Hasselt, V. B., 62
Van Putten, T., 301
Van Zanten, B., 301
Vasquez, M. J. T., 45
Velten, E. A., 343
Ventura, M., 393
Verger, G., 134, 139
Vetter, V. A., 47
Vogel, S. R., 61
Vogt, S., 372
von Bismarck, O., 83
von Ehrenfels, C., 215
Vontress, C. E., 59

Wachtel, P., 199
Wachtel, P. L., 92
Wade, P., 59
Walen, S., 331, 334
Walker, G., 371
Wallace, W. A., 145, 167, 174, 364
Wallen, R., 216
Wallerstein, R. S., 107
Walpole, H., 331
Walsh, W. B., 16, 29, 30, 167, 168, 355
Walters, R., 283
Walton, E., 340
Warlick, J., 130, 143
Warner, D. L., 16
Warner, R. E., 202
Warner, W. R., Jr., 258

Watkins, C. E., 202, 234
Watkins, C. E. Jr., 139, 145
Watkins, P., 341
Watson, D. L., 32
Watson, J. B., 284, 297, 306
Watson, J. F., 285
Watson, P. D., 34
Watson, T., 36
Waxer, P. H., 343
Weathers, R. S., 173
Wedding, D., 7, 120
Wehrly, B., 397
Weinrach, S. G., 318, 320, 325, 339, 340
Weishaar, M. E., 339–340
Wessels, H., 297
Wessler, R., 331, 334
Westman, A. S., 162, 168
Wetzel, R. J., 15
Wheelock, I., 341
Whisman, M., 297
Whiston, S. C., 25
White, C., 304
White, P. E., 144
Whitehouse, D., 358
Whiteley, J. M., 343
Wiener, D. N., 318
Wiener, N., 357
Wilder, J., 120, 145
Williams, E. L., 221
Williams, J. H., 60, 61
Williams, M. H., 47
Williamson, E., 35
Williamson, R. E., 358–359, 363, 364, 366, 368, 370
Wilson, D., 14
Wilson, G., 284
Wilson, G. L., 341
Wilson, G. T., 107, 284, 290, 297, 340
Wilson, L. S., 44
Wilson, P. H., 301
Wilson, W., 88
Winnicott, D. W., 102
Winston, T., 372
Wiser, S. L., 340
Wittmer, J. M., 145
Wolf, M. M., 301
Wolfinsohn, L., 301
Wollams, S., 246, 256, 258, 259
Wollner, J. M., 202
Wolpe, J., 279, 281, 282, 285, 288, 290, 295, 301–305
Woodward, G. D., 360
Woody, S. R., 297
Wordsworth, W., 85
Worell, J., 60

Worthington, E. L., 66
Wrenn, C. G., 45, 56
Wubbolding, R. E., 360–362, 371, 374
Wundt, W., 7, 285

Yalom, E. D., 155, 165, 169
Yalom, I., 372, 381
Yalom, I. D., 155
Yates, A. J., 279
Yau, T., 201

Yeager, R., 320
Yontef, G. M., 215, 223, 233
Young-Bruehl, E., 108

Zane, N. W. S., 59
Zeiss, A. M., 301
Zimring, F. M., 186
Zinker, J., 221
Zucker, H., 109
Zunin, L., 360, 368

Subject Index

A-B-C theory of behavior, 322
About Behaviorism (Skinner), 281
Acceptance, person-centered therapy and, 195
Acknowledgment, defined, 237
Acting "as if", 141
Action homework, 333–334
  defined, 346
Activities, defined, 272
Actualizing tendency, 187
  defined, 205
Adaptation, defined, 237
Adapted child, 248
  defined, 272
Adlerian therapy, 119–146
  acting "as if", 141
  application, 142–143
  asking "The Question", 141
  birth order, 133–134
  biography of Adler, 121–123
  catching oneself, 141–142
  compared to other therapies, 382
  contribution to modern psychology, 120
  creative self, 144
  critical analysis of, 143–145
  current status, 145–146
  developing self-understanding, 140
  development of maladaptive behavior, 127–129
  differences with Freud, 122–124
  dreams, 139–140
  early recollections, 134–139
  finalism, 125–126
  function of therapist in, 129–131
  goals of therapy, 130
  guiding fiction, 124

  historical development of, 123–124
  inferiority, 124–125
  inferiority complex, 120, 127–128
  initiating therapeutic relationship, 130–131
  introduction to, 119–120
  lifestyle investigation, 123, 129, 131–140
  major methods and techniques, 130–142
  paradoxical intention, 141
  push button, 142
  reorientation, 140–142
  social interest, 124, 126
  societies of, 146
  spitting in client's soup, 141
  superiority complex, 128
  teleology, 123
  view of human nature, 124–126
Adler School of Professional Psychology, 146
Adult ego state, 248, 272
Affirmation in Gestalt therapy, 224
Aggression, defined, 237
AIDS, 49, 67–70
  confidentiality and, 69
  facts on, 70
Alcoholics Anonymous, 64–66
All-or-nothing thinking, 330, 346
Ambiguity, tolerance of and effective counselors, 33
American Association for Marriage and Family Therapist, 52
American Association of Retired Persons, 71
American Counseling Association, 52
  address for, 21
  establishment and membership of, 20–21
American Mental Academy for Certified Clinical Mental Health, 52

419

American Psychological Association, 52
 establishment and membership of, 20–21
 guidelines for treatment of women, 61
American Psychologist, 20
Americas Institute of Adlerian Studies, 146
Anal-expulsive personality, 97
Anal-retentive personality, 97
Anal stage, defined, 113
Analysis of the Self, The (Kohut), 111
Antichrist, The (Nietzsche), 158
Anxiety:
 defined, 113, 177
 ego and, 93–94
 existential therapy and, 162
 Gestalt therapy and, 223
 psychoanalytic theory and, 99
APA Monitor, The, 20
Approbation, defined, 237
Assertiveness training, 293, 301–304
 defined, 308
Assessment, reality therapy and, 367–368
Association for Religious and Value Issues in
     Counseling, 66
Attitudinal values, existential therapy, 167
Aversion therapy, defined, 308
Aversive conditioning, defined, 308
Aversive control, defined, 308
Awareness:
 defined, 237
 gestalt therapy, and, 218–219
 lack of, 220
 transactional analysis and, 255

*Becoming Partners: Marriage and Its
     Alternatives* (Rogers), 185
Behavioral disputation, 331
Behavioral rehearsal, defined, 308
Behaviorism (Watson), 285
Behaviorism, defined, 308
Behavior modification, 298
 defined, 308
Behavior of Organisms, The (Skinner), 280
Behavior therapy, 278–306
 application of, 297–304
 assertiveness training, 293, 301–304
 behavioral assessment, 292
 behavior modification, 298
 biofeedback, 298
 biography of Bandura, 281
 biography of Skinner, 279–281
 biography of Wolpe, 281
 cognitive behavioral therapy, 340
 compared to other therapies, 383
 conditioned response, 289
 conditioned stimulus, 289

critical analysis of, 304–305
current status of, 305–306
defined, 308
development of maladaptive behavior,
     287–288
effectiveness of, 387
flooding, 297
function of therapist, 288–289
goals of therapy, 289–290
historical development of, 284–286
introduction to, 278–279
major methods and techniques, 290–297
modeling, 293–294
negative reinforcement, 290
operant conditioning, 290
positive reinforcement, 290, 292–293
programmed instruction, 298
punishment, 290
relaxation training, 294
respondent learning, 289
social modeling, 290
systematic desensitization, 295–297,
     301–304
token economies, 293
unconditioned response, 289
vicarious learning, 290
view of human nature, 286–287
Behavior Therapy and the Neuroses (Eysenck),
     306
Behavior Therapy Techniques (Wolpe), 281
Being-in-the-world, 161
Betty Ford Center, 57
Beyond Freedom and Dignity (Skinner), 281,
     285
Beyond the Pleasure Principle (Freud), 89
Biofeedback, 298
Birth order:
 Adlerian therapy and, 133–134
 defined, 148
 dethroned, 133
 first-born, 133
 last-born, 134
 second-born, 133–134
Boundaries, 267–269
Boundaries in the Mind (Hartmann), 267
Bound energy, 248

Carl Rogers on Encounter Groups (Rogers), 185
Carl Rogers on Personal Power (Rogers), 185
Castration anxiety, 97
 defined, 113
Catching oneself, 141–142
Catharsis, 7, 102
 defined, 113
Center for Reality Therapy, 374

Child ego state, defined, 272
Childhood amnesia, 136
Children, early memory and, 135–139
Child-within, transactional analysis and, 248
Choice and integration in Gestalt therapy, 224
Civilization and Its Discontents (Freud), 90
Classical conditioning, defined, 308
Client-counselor relationship, informed
    consent, 46–47
Clinical psychologists, training and
    therapeutic setting for, 17
Clinical Treatment of the Problem Child
    (Rogers), 184, 185
Clockwork Orange, A, 305
Closure:
    defined, 237
    principle of, 215
Code of Ethics for Mental Health Counselors, 52
Cognitive, defined, 346
Cognitive-behavioral therapy, 340
Cognitive disputation, 331
Cognitive restructuring, 340
Cognitive revolution, 320
Cognitive theories, 338–341. *See also* Rational-
    emotive therapy
    dysfunctional thinking, 339
    effectiveness of, 387
Community mental health centers, as sources
    of therapeutic services, 19
Compensation, defined, 148
Complementary transactions, 253, 272
Conditional positive regard, 205
Conditional stroke, 272
Conditioned reinforcement, 308
Conditioned response, 289
Conditioned stimulus, 289, 308
Confidentiality, 47, 49–50
    AIDS and, 69
    defined, 47
Confrontation, reality therapy and, 365
Confrontation, Gestalt therapy and, 228
Congruence, 28, 193–194, 205
Conscious, defined, 113
Consciousness, defined, 92
Consultation, 15
Contamination, 250, 272
Contemporary issues in counseling, 56–72
    AIDS, 67–70
    differently abled, 62–63
    gender differences, 60–61
    multicultural counseling, 56, 59–60
    older adults, 71–72
    religious clients, 66–67
Contingencies of reinforcement, 309
Continuous reinforcement, 309

Contract, 257–258
    defined, 272
    reality therapy and, 365
Controlling parent, defined, 272
*Control Theory in the Practice of Reality
    Therapy: Case Studies* (Glasser), 357
Control therapy, 356 *See also* Reality therapy
    understanding, 358–359
Coping skills training, 340
Counseling:
    common features in, 11
    defined, 8, 10–11
    multicultural, 56, 59–60
    non-western tradition of, 5–7
    vs. psychotherapy, 14
    "willingness to seek" quiz, 12–13
Counseling and Psychotherapy (Rogers), 184,
    185
Counseling Psychologist, 20
Counseling psychologists, training and
    therapeutic setting for, 17
Counselors:
    consultation, 15
    functions of, 15–16
    group therapy, 15
    organizational development, 15–16
    professional growth and development,
        19–21
    supervision, 16
    training of, and therapeutic setting of,
        15–19
    triadic consultation, 15
    types of, and training for, 16–19
Counselors, common pitfalls faced by
    beginning, 36–40
    fear of silence, 38
    impatience, 39
    interrogating, 38–39
    moralizing, 39–40
    not setting limits, 37
    premature problem solving, 37
    reluctance to refer, 40
Counselors, effective, 24–40
    awareness of values, 34–36
    empathic abilities, 29–30
    genuine interest in others, 28–29
    personal qualities of, 24–36
    personal warmth, 30–32
    psychological health of, 26–28
    role-free, 28–29
    self-actualizing, 27
    self-awareness, 32–33
    tolerance of ambiguity, 33
Countering, 331–332
    defined, 346

Countertransference, 103
defined, 114
Gestalt therapy, 232
Courage to Create, The (May), 157
Creative power of self, 144
Adlerian therapy and, 144
defined, 148
Cross-cultural counseling, 50–60. *See also*
Multicultural counseling
defined, 59
Crossed transaction, 254, 273

Dasein, 161, 162, 177
Daseinsanalysis, 177
Death, existential therapy and, 161
Defense mechanisms, 93
defined, 114
denial, 95
displacement, 95
intellectualization, 95
projection, 95
rationalization, 95
reaction formation, 95
regression, 95
repression, 95
sublimation, 95
Denial, 95
Denial of needs, 110
Deprivation, defined, 309
Dereflection, 170–171, 177
Desensitization:
defined, 309
effectiveness of, 387
Dethroned, 133
Dictionary of Behavior Therapy Techniques
(Bellack & Hersen), 292
Differentiation in Gestalt therapy, 224
Differently abled. *See also* Physically
disabled
cognitive approach, 343
counseling issues of, 62–63
Discounting, 330
defined, 273, 347
Displacement, 95
Disputing, 330–331
Divided Self, The (Laing), 164
Doctor and the Soul, The (Frankl), 170
Drama triangle, defined, 273
Dream analysis, 102
defined, 114
latent content, 102
manifest content, 102
Dreams:
Adlerian therapy and, 139–140
Gestalt therapy and, 224–225

Duty to warn, 50
Dysfunctional thinking, 339

Early memory, 135–139
ability to retain, 136–137
Adlerian therapy, 134–139
defined, 148
Freud and, 135, 136
Eclectic therapy, 390–393
professional, 391
syncretism, 391
technical, 391
theoretical, 391
Ego, 93–94
anxiety and, 93–94
contamination, 250
defense mechanisms, 93
defined, 114
exclusion, 250
reality principle, 93
secondary process thinking, 93
strength of, 99
Ego and the Id, The (Freud), 89–90
Egogram, 258
Ego ideal, 99
defined, 114
Ego psychology, 109
Ego state, defined, 273
Eigenwelt, 161, 162, 164, 177
Elderly, counseling issues and, 71–72
Electa complex, 97, 114
Emotional control card, 432
Emotional literacy, 260
Emotional reasoning, 330
defined, 347
Emotional reeducation, 103
Emotion-control card, defined, 347
Emotive, defined, 347
Empathic abilities, 195–196
defined, 29
of effective counselor, 29–30
importance of, in counseling, 29
levels of, 29–30
vs. sympathy, 29
Empathy, defined, 205
Empty chair, 227
Encounter group, 200, 205
Erogenous zones, 94
Eros, 93
Essays in Individual Psychology (Wilder), 120
Ethical Guidelines for Group Counselors, 52
Ethical issues, 44–52
client-counselor relationship, 46–47
confidentiality and privileged
communication, 47, 49–50

Ethical issues *(Cont.)*
    duty to warn, 50
    foundations of, 45–46
    informed consent, 46
    principles and guidelines, 52
    sexual intimacies with clients, 47
    virtue and, 45
    when in doubt, 51–52
Ethical Principles of Psychologists and Code of
    Conduct Standards, 52
Ethical Standards for School Counselors, 52
Ethics, 11
Exaggeration, Gestalt therapy and,
    227–228
Exclusion:
    defined, 273
    in transactional analysis, 250
Existential Psychology (May), 157
Existential therapy, 154–175
    "I and Thou", 159
    "I-Thou" encounter, 165
    anxiety and, 162
    application of, 172–173
    attitudinal values, 167
    being-in-the-world, 161
    biography of May, 155–157
    compared to other therapies, 382
    confrontation of life issues, 168–169
    course of therapy, 168
    critical analysis of, 173–174
    current status of, 174–175
    dasein, 161, 162
    death, 161
    development of maladaptive behavior, 162,
        164–165
    eigenwelt, 161, 162, 164
    felt sense, 169–170
    focusing, 169
    function of therapist, 165–166
    goals of therapy, 166–167
    historical development of, 157–159
    introduction, 154–155
    logotherapy, 170–172
    major methods and techniques and,
        167–172
    mitwelt, 161, 162, 164
    nature of authentic person, 162
    process of change and, 166
    responsibility, 160–161
    umwelt, 161, 162, 164
    view of human nature, 160–162
Experience, defined, 205
Experiential values, existential therapy and,
    167
Explosive layer, 220

Expression in Gestalt therapy, 224
Extinction, defined, 309

Failure identity, 361
Father, role in Adlerian theory, 127
Felt sense, 169–170
Fictional finalism, 126
    defined, 148
Figure, 217
    defined, 237
    in gestalt therapy, 216
Filtered stroke, defined, 273
Finalism, 125–126
First-born child, 133
Fixation, 96
    defined, 114
Fixed-interval schedule, defined, 309
Fixed-ration schedule, defined, 309
Flooding, 297, 309
Focusing, 169, 177
Free association, 101–102
    catharsis, 102
    defined, 114
Freedom To Learn (Rogers), 185
Freedom to Learn for the 80's (Rogers), 185
Free energy, 248
Freudian slip, 102, 114
Fuller Graduate School of Psychology, 67
Fully functioning persons, 190, 192–193
    defined, 205
Functional analysis, 259

Game, defined, 273
Game analysis, 259
Games, 250–252
    Blemish, 252
    Cops and Robbers, 252
    Look How Hard I Tried, 252
    Seduction, 251
    transactional analysis and, 247
    Ulterior Transaction, 251
    Uproar, 251
    Why Don't You-Yes But, 251
Games People Play (Berne), 243, 269
Gender difference, counseling and, 60–61
Generalization, defined, 309
Genital stage of psychosexual development,
    97–98, 114
Genuineness, defined, 206
Gestalt:
    defined, 212, 237
Gestalt therapy, 211–235
    affirmation, 224
    "Aha!" experience, 222
    application of, 228–231

Gestalt therapy *(Cont.)*
    assuming responsibility, 226
    awareness, 218–219
    biography of Perls, 213–215
    choice and integration, 224
    compared to other therapies, 383
    confrontation, 228
    converting questions to statements, 226
    countertransference, 232
    critical analysis of, 231–234
    current status, 234–235
    denial of needs, 220
    development of maladaptive behavior,
        219–220
    dichotomizing dimensions of self, 220
    differentiation, 224
    dream work, 224–225
    empty chair, 227
    exaggeration, 227–228
    explosive layer, 220
    expression, 224
    figure and, 216
    function of therapist, 221–222
    goals of therapy, 222–223
    ground, 216
    "Here and Now" principle, 223
    historical development of, 215–217
    "I and Thou" principle, 223
    impasse layer, 220
    implosive layer, 220
    inability to complete unfinished business,
        220
    introduction to, 211–213
    lack of awareness, 220
    lack of self-responsibility, 220
    lose contact with the environment, 220
    major methods and techniques, 224–228
    making the rounds, 117
    "may I feed you a sentence", 228
    meaningful whole, 215
    moral precepts of, 219
    organism-environment field, 217
    organismic self-regulation, 217–218
    phobic layer, 220
    phony layer, 219–220
    playing the projection, 226–227
    psychological homeostasis, 218
    safe emergency, 221
    top dog, 219
    underdog, 219
    unfinished business and, 223
    use of personal pronouns, 226
    view of human nature, 217–219
    "What and How" principle, 223
    workshop, 233

Gestalt Therapy Verbatim (Perls), 228
Great American Values Test, The, 34
Ground, 216, 217, 238
Group therapy, 15, 261
Guidepost, 21
Guiding fiction, 124
Guilt, defined, 177

Habits of the Heart (Bellah), 393
Hartford Institute of Living, 57
Hazelden Foundation, 57
Hear and now, defined, 238
Helplessness, Adlerian therapy and, 128
"Here and Now" principle and, 223
Hierarchy, defined, 309
Hierarchy construction, 295–296
Historical development of therapies:
    Adlerian therapy, 123–124
    existential therapy, 157–159
    Gestalt therapy, 215–217
    person-centered therapy and, 185–187
    psychoanalytic therapy, 90–91
    transactional analysis, 245–246
Homeostasis, defined, 238
Hospitals, as sources of therapeutic services,
    19
Humanistic approach. *See* Person-centered
    therapy
Human nature, view of:
    Adlerian therapy, 124–126
    behavior therapy, 286–287
    existential therapy, 160–162
    gestalt therapy and, 217–219
    person-centered therapy, 187–188
    psychoanalytic theory, 91–98
    rational-emotive therapy, 321–325
    reality therapy and, 360
    transactional analysis and, 246–249
Human service agencies, as sources of
    therapeutic services, 19
Humor, reality therapy and, 367
Hypnosis, birth of psychoanalysis, 91

I'm OK—You're OK (Harris), 243
I and Thou (Buber), 159
"I and Thou" principle, 223
Id, 92–93
    defined, 114
    eros, 93
    libido, 93
    pleasure principle, 93
    primary process thinking, 92
    thanatos, 93
Ideal self, defined, 206
Identifying beliefs, 330

Imaginal disputation, 331
Imitative learning, defined, 309
Impasse, defined, 238
Impasse layer, 220
Implosive layer, 220
Inability to complete unfinished business, 220
In and Out of the Garbage Pail (Perls), 215
Incongruence, defined, 206
Indirect helping, 15
Individual psychology, 119, 124. *See also* Adlerian therapy
   defined, 148
Industrial/organizational psychologists, training and therapeutic setting for, 18
Inferiority, 124–125
   striving for superiority, 125
Inferiority complex, 120
   neglect and, 127
   pampering and, 127
Informed consent, 46–47
Injunction, 252, 273
Insight number 1, 347
Insight number 2, 347
Insight number 3, 347
Insight therapy, 101
Institute for Rational-Emotive Therapy, 344
Institute for Rational Living, 344
Institute for Reality Therapy, 374
Instruction, reality therapy and, 365
Intellectualization, 95
Intentionality, defined, 177
Interiority complex, 148
Interiority feelings, 148
Intermittent reinforcement, 309
Internal frame of reference, 206
International Transactional Analysis Association, 270
Interpretation of Dreams, The (Freud), 89
Interrogation, beginning counselors and, 38–39
Intimacy:
   defined, 273
   transactional analysis and, 247, 251, 255
Introjection, 94
   defined, 206, 238
Irrational, defined, 347
Irrational beliefs, 325–327
   most common, 325–327
"I-Thou" encounter, 165

Journal of Counseling and Development, 21
Journal of Counseling Psychology, 20

Journal of Professional Psychology, 20
Journal of Vocational Behavior, 20

Last-born child, 134
Latency stage of psychosexual development, 97, 114
Latent content, defined, 102, 114
Legal issues, 44–52
   client-counselor relationship, 46–47
   confidentiality and privileged communication, 47, 49–50
   duty to warn, 50
   foundations of, 45–46
   informed consent, 46
   virtue and, 45
   when in doubt, 51–52
Libido, 93, 114
Life positions, 255–256, 273
Life style:
   Adlerian therapy and, 129
   behaviors associated with, 132
   birth order, 133–134
   defined, 131, 148
   ethical convictions, 133
   investigation of 131–140
   picture of the world, 133
   self-concept, 131
   self-ideal, 131
Limits:
   beginning counselors and, 37
Little professor, 248, 273
Logotherapy, 164, 170–172, 175
   defined, 177
   dereflection, 170–171
   modify clients' attitudes, 170–171
   paradoxical intention, 170–171
Lose contact with environment, 220
Love, defined, 177
Love and Will (May), 157

Magnification, 330, 347
Maladaptive behavior, development of:
   Adlerian therapy, 127–129
   behavior therapy and, 287–288
   existential therapy, 162, 164–165
   Gestalt therapy and, 219–220
   person-centered therapy, 188–189
   psychoanalytic therapy, 98–99
   rational-emotive therapy and, 325–327
   reality therapy and, 361
   transactional analysis, 249–255
Malpractice, defined, 46
Man's Search for Himself (May), 157
Man's Search for Meaning (Frankl), 163

Managed-care companies, substance-abuse treatment and, 57–58
Manifest content of dreams, 102, 114
Marriage and family therapists, training and therapeutic setting for, 18
Masculine protest, defined, 149
Meaning and purpose, psychological method, 26
Meaningful whole, 215
Memory, early, 135–139
Mind in Action, The (Berne), 244
Mind reading, 330, 347
Mitwelt, 161, 162, 164, 177
Mobile Psychological Services, 9–10
Modeling, 293–294
Morality principle, 94
Moralizing, beginning counselors and, 39–40
Mother, role in Adlerian theory, 127
Multicultural counseling, 56, 59–60. See also Cross-cultural counseling
  behavior therapy and, 305
  existential therapy and, 173
  Gestalt therapy and, 232
  psychoanalysis therapy and, 107–108
  therapy and, 394–397
  transactional analysis and, 268–269
Muscle relaxation, 294

National Academy for Certified Clinical Mental Health Counselors, 52
National Board of Certified Counselors, 52
Natural child, 248, 273
Negative reinforcement, 290, 310
Negative stroke, 273
Neglect, defined, 149
Neurotic behavior, defined, 310
Neurotic Constitution, The (Adler), 124
Nondirective therapy, defined, 206
Nonverbal cues of personal warmth and coldness, 32
North American Society of Adlerian Psychology, 145–146
Nurturing parent, 273

Object relations theory, 109–110
Occupational counselors, training and therapeutic setting for, 18
Oedipus complex, 97, 114
OK corral, 257
On Becoming a person (Rogers), 185
Ontological characteristics, 177
Ontology, 177
Operant conditioning, 290, 310
Oral-aggressive trait, 96
Oral-receptive trait, 96

Oral stage of psychosexual development, 96, 114
  oral-aggressive trait, 96
  oral-receptive trait, 96
Organ inferiority, 124–125, 149
Organismic self-regulation, 238
Organismic valuing process, 187–188
  defined, 206
Organizational development, counselors and, 15–16
Overgeneralization, 330, 347

Pampering, 149
Paradoxical intention, 141, 170–171, 178
Paraprofessional counselors, training and therapeutic setting for, 19
Parent ego, 247–248
Parent ego state, defined, 273
Partial reinforcement, defined, 309
Pastime, defined, 273
Pastoral counselors, training and therapeutic setting for, 18
Penis envy, 97, 114
Perceived self-efficacy, 27
Perfection, Adlerian theory and 125
Personality:
  comparison of Freud's and Berne's personality models, 249
  development of, and psychoanalysis, 94–98
  structure of, and transactional analysis, 247–249
  structure of psychoanalytic theory and, 92–94
Personal responsibility, psychological health and, 26–27
Personal warmth:
  effective counselors and, 30–32
  nonpossessive warmth, 30
  nonverbal cues of, 32
Person-centered therapy, 182–203
  actualizing tendency, 187
  application of, 196–199
  biography of Roger, 183–185
  compared to other therapies, 382
  congruence, 193–194
  critical analysis of, 199–202
  current status of, 202
  defined, 206
  development of maladaptive behavior, 188–189
  empathic understanding, 195–196
  encounter groups, 200
  fully functioning person, 190, 192–193
  function of therapist, 189
  goals of therapy, 190–193

Person-centered therapy *(Cont.)*
historical development of, 185–187
introduction, 182–185
major methods and techniques, 193–196
moving away from self one is not, 190–191
moving toward one's true self, 191–193
organismic valuing process, 187
Q-sort technique, 194
self-actualization, 191–192
unconditional positive regard, 195
view of human nature, 187–188
Persuasion and Healing (Frank), 11
Phallic stage of psychosexual development, 97, 114
Phenomenological, 178
Phenomenology, 206
Phobic layer, 220
Phony layer, 219–220
Physical disabilities. *See also* Differently abled
counseling issues of, 62–63
Gestalt therapy, 232–233
person-centered therapy and, 201–202
Pleasure principle, 93, 114
Position hunger, 247, 273
Positive addictions, reality therapy and, 367
Positive regard, defined, 206
Positive reinforcement, 290, 292–293
defined, 310
Positive stroke, 273
Power and Innocence (May), 157
Practice, vs. theory, 79
Preconscious, 92, 114
Primary process thinking, 92, 115
Principles of Behavior Modification (Bandura), 284, 286
Principles of Group Treatment (Berne), 266
Private practitioners, as sources of therapeutic services, 19
Privileged communication, 49
Problem-solving training, 340
Programmed instruction, 298, 310
Progressive relaxation, 294
Projection, 95
defined, 238
Gestalt therapy and, 226–227
Proximity, principle of, 215, 238
Psychiatric nurse, training and therapeutic setting for, 18
Psychiatrists, training and therapeutic setting for, 17
Psychoanalytic therapy, 87–111
anal stage, 96–97
anxiety and, 99
application of, 103–105
biography of Freud, 88–90

birth of, 91
compared to other therapies, 382
comparison of Freud's and Berne's personality models, 249
critical analysis of, 105–108
current status of, 109–111
defense mechanisms, 93–95
development of maladaptive behavior, 98–99
development of personality, 94–98
dream analysis, 102
effectiveness of, 107–108, 387
ego, 93–94
ego psychology, 109
Electra complex, 97
emotional reeducation, 103
free association, 101–102
function of therapist, 100–101
genital stage, 97
goals of therapy, 99
historical development of, 90–91
id, 92–93
impact of, 3–5
insight therapy, 101
interpretation of resistance, 103
interpretation of transference, 102–103
introduction, 87–88
latency stage, 97
major methods and techniques of, 101–103
modern-day session of, 106
multicultural counseling and, 107–108
object relations theory, 109–110
Oedipus complex, 97
oral stage, 96
penis envy, 97
phallic stage, 97
psycho sexual development, 96–98
self-psychology, 110–111
structure of personality, 92–94
superego, 94
supportive therapy, 101
training and therapeutic setting for, 17
unconscious, 92
uncovering therapy, 101
view of human nature, 91–98
womb envy, 98
women's role in development in, 7, 107, 108
Psychological health:
meaning and purpose, 26
of effective counselors, 26–28
perceived self-efficacy, 27
personal responsibility, 26–27
Psychologists, training and therapeutic setting for, 17

Psychologists Interested in Religious Study, 66
Psychology:
    ego, 109
    individual, 119
Psychology and the Human Dilemma (May), 157
Psychology of "As If", The (Vaihinger), 123
Psychopathology of Everyday Life, The (Freud), 89
Psychophysical stage in Gestalt theory, 217
Psychosexual development, 96–98
    anal stage, 96–97
    genital stage, 97–98
    latency stage, 97
    oral stage, 96
    phallic stage, 97
Psychotherapist:
    professional growth and development, 19–21
    training of, and therapeutic setting of, 16–19
Psychotherapy:
    challenges of contemporary, 393–397
    vs counseling, 14
    effectiveness of, 385–387
    historical view of, 4–8
    non-western tradition of, 5–7
Psychotherapy by Reciprocal Inhibition (Wolpe), 281, 285
Punishment, 290
    defined, 310
Push-button technique, 142

Q-sort technique, 194
Questioning:
    Gestalt therapy and, 226
    reality therapy and, 365–366

Rackets, 252, 273
Rape victims, reality therapy and, 372–374
Rational, defined, 347
Rational-emotive imagery, 331
Rational-emotive therapy. *See also* Cognitive therapies
    A-B-C's of, 322
    action homework, 333–334
    application of, 335–338
    biography of Ellis, 318–320
    compared to other therapies, 383
    countering, 331–332
    critical analysis of, 341–343
    current status of, 343–344
    D-E-F and, 328–329
    development of maladaptive behavior, 325–327

disputing, 330–331
emotional control card, 332
function of therapist, 327–328
goals of therapy, 328–329
heightening awareness, 334
historical development of, 320–321
humor, 334
identifying beliefs, 330
introduction to, 317–318
irrational beliefs, 325–327
major methods and techniques, 329–334
rational self-analysis, 332–333
self-talk, 324–325
soft determinism, 322
view of human nature, 321–325
Rationalization, 95
Rational self-analysis, 332–333
Reaction formation, 95
Reality principle, 93, 115
Reality Therapy: A New Approach to Psychiatry (Glasser), 356, 359
Reality therapy, 355–375
    application of, 368–370
    assessment and, 367–368
    biography of Glasser, 356–357
    compared to other therapies, 383
    confrontation, 365
    constructive debate and, 367
    contracts and, 365
    control theory, 356
    critical analysis of, 370–371
    current status of, 371–375
    development of maladaptive behavior, 361
    emphasizing choice, 366
    failure identity, 361
    function of therapist in, 361–362
    goals of therapy, 362–363
    historical development of, 357–360
    humor and, 367
    instruction and, 365
    introduction to, 355–356
    major methods and techniques, 363–368
    positive addictions and, 367
    rape victims and, 372–374
    role-playing and, 366
    self-disclosure and, 367
    skillful questioning and, 365–366
    steps in, 363–364
    structuring, 364–365
    success identity, 361
    support and, 366
    view of human nature, 360
Reason and Emotion in Psychotherapy (Ellis), 321

Recent Issues in the Analysis of Behavior
  (Skinner), 281
Reciprocal inhibition, 310
Redecision, 260–261
Referrals:
  beginning counselors and, 40
  ethics and, 46
  situation likely to call for, 51
Regression, 95
Rehabilitation centers, 57–58
Reinforcement, defined, 310
Relaxation training, 294
  muscle, 294
  progressive, 294
Religion, counseling and, 66–67
Reorientation, Adlerian therapy and,
  140–142
Repression, 95
Resistance:
  defined, 115
  interpretation of, 103
Respondent conditioning, 308
Respondent learning, 289
Response, defined, 310
Response induction, 310
Response shaping, 310
Responsibility:
  existential therapy and, 160–161
  Gestalt therapy and, 226
Restoration of the Self, The (Kohut), 111
Retroflection, defined, 238
Revolution in Counseling (Krumboltz), 286
Rituals:
  defined, 273
  transactional analysis and, 247
Road Less Traveled, The (Peck), 66
Role-playing, reality therapy and, 366
Rosemead Graduate School of Psychology, 67

Safe emergency, 221
Satiation, defined, 310
Schedules of reinforcement, 311
School counselors, training and therapeutic
  setting for, 18
School psychologists, training and
  therapeutic setting for, 18
Schools, as sources of therapeutic services, 19
Schools Without Failure (Glasser), 356
Science and Human Behavior (Skinner), 280
Scripts:
  after, 260
  always, 260
  defined, 274
  never, 260
  open-ended, 260

transactional analysis and, 256
  until, 260
Script analysis, 259–260
Secondary process thinking, 93, 115
Secondary reinforcement, 308
Second-born child, 133–134
Self:
  defined, 238
  moving away from self one is not, 190–191
  moving toward one's true self, 191–193
  person-centered therapy and, 190–193
Self-actualization:
  characteristics of therapists and, 27
  defined, 206
  scale for, 192
Self-awareness, effective counselors and,
  32–33
Self-blame, 330, 347
Self-concept, defined, 206
Self-disclosure, reality therapy and, 367
Self-efficacy, 347
Self-image, 238
Self-psychology, 110–111
Self-responsibility, lack of, 220
Self-talk, 324–325
Self-understanding, Adlerian therapy, 140
Sexual intimacies, with clients, 47–48
Sierra Tucson, 57
Significant other, 206
Similarity, principle of, 215, 238
Single-session therapy, 388–389
Skinner box, 285
Social Foundations of Thoughts and Action
  (Bandura), 283
Social interest, 124, 126, 149
Social learning, 309, 347
Social Learning and Personality Development
  (Bandura), 283
Social Learning Theory (Bandura), 284
Social modeling, 290
Social stage in Gestalt theory, 217
Social workers, training and therapeutic
  setting for, 18
Soft determinism, 322
Spiritual stage in Gestalt theory, 217
Spitting in the client's soup, 141
Spontaneity, transactional analysis and, 255
Spontaneous recover, defined, 311
Stamps, defined, 274
Stations of the Mind (Glasser), 371
Stimulus hunger, 246
  defined, 274
Stop Abuse By Counselors in Seattle, 48
Striving for superiority, 125
  defined, 149

Stroke, defined, 274
Structural analysis, 253, 258–259
Structure hunger, 246–247
Structuring, reality therapy, 364–365
Studies of Hysteria (Freud & Breuer), 91
Sublimation, 95
Substance abuse counselors, training and
    therapeutic setting for, 19
Substance-abuse treatment, rehabilitation
    centers for, 57–58
Success identity, 361
Superego, 94
    defined, 115
    introjection, 94
    morality principle, 94
Superiority complex, 128, 149
Supervision, counselors and, 16
Support, reality therapy and, 366
Support groups, 63–65
    categories of, 65
Supportive therapy, 101
Susto, 394–395
Symbiosis, 274
Sympathy, vs. empathy, 29
Systematic desensitization, 295–297, 301–304
    defined, 311
    hierarchy construction, 295–296

Take Effective Control of Your Life (Glasser), 371
Tarasoff decision, 50
Technical eclecticism, 391
Technology of Teaching, The (Skinner), 281
Teleological, 149
Teleology, 123, 178
Thanatos, 93, 115
Theories, 79–83
    discovering within you, 81–83
    importance of studying, 80–81
    vs. practice, 79
Therapeutic theories, comparing, 380–397
    challenge of contemporary psychotherapy,
        393–397
    eclectic approach, 390–393
    effectiveness of psychotherapy, 385–387
    effectiveness of specific therapies, 387–390
    factors in, 381, 384–385
    integrating therapeutic approaches,
        390–393
    single-session therapy, 388–389
    table of, 382–383
Therapist, function of:
    Adlerian therapy and, 129–131
    behavior therapy and, 288–289
    existential therapy and, 165–166
    Gestalt therapy and, 221–222

person-centered therapy, 189
in psychoanalytic therapy, 100–101
rational-emotive therapy and, 327–328
reality therapy and, 361–362
transactional analysis and, 253–255
Therapy:
    insight, 101
    supportive, 101
    uncovering, 101
Therapy goals:
    Adlerian therapy, 130
    behavior therapy, 289–290
    existential therapy and, 166–167
    Gestalt therapy, 222–223
    person-centered therapy and, 190–193
    psychoanalytic therapy, 99
    rational-emotive therapy and, 328–329
    reality therapy and, 362–363
    transactional analysis, 255–256
Therapy methods and techniques:
    Adlerian therapy, 130–142
    behavior therapy, 290–297
    existential therapy and, 167–172
    Gestalt therapy, 224–228
    person-centered therapy and, 193–196
    psychoanalytic therapy, 101–103
    rational-emotive therapy and, 329–334
    reality therapy and, 363–368
    transactional analysis and, 257–261
Three Approaches to Psychotherapy (Rogers,
    Ellis & Perls), 221
Token economies, 293, 311
Top dog, 219
Transaction, defined, 274
Transactional analysis, 242–270
    adapted child, 248
    adult ego, 248
    application of, 261–265
    awareness and, 255
    biography of Berne, 243–245
    child-within, 248
    compared to other therapies, 383
    comparison of Freud's and Berne's
        personality models, 249
    complementary transactions, 253
    contamination, 250
    contracting, 257–258
    critical analysis of, 265, 168–169
    crossed transactions, 254
    defined, 274
    development of maladaptive behavior,
        249–255
    egogram, 258
    emotional literacy, 260
    exclusion, 250

Transactional analysis *(Cont.)*
   free energy, 248
   functional analysis, 259
   function of therapist, 253–255
   game analysis, 259
   games, 250–252
   goals of therapy, 255–256
   group therapy, 261
   historical development of, 245–246
   injunctions, 252
   intimacy and, 251, 255
   introduction to, 242–243
   life positions, 255–256
   little professor, 248
   major methods and techniques, 257–261
   natural child, 248
   OK corral, 257
   parent ego, 247–248
   position hunger, 247
   rackets, 252
   redecision, 260–261
   script analysis, 259–260
   scripts, 256
   spontaneity and, 255
   stimulus hunger, 246
   structural analysis, 253, 258–259
   structure hunger, 246–247
   structure of personality, 247–249
   ulterior transactions, 254–255
   view of human nature, 246–249
Transactional Analysis in Psychotherapy
   (Berne), 261
Transactional response, 253
Transactional stimulus, 253
Transference:
   defined, 115
   interpretation of, 102–103
   therapist and, 100–101
Triadic consultation, 15
Trust, client-counselor relationship
   and, 46

Ulterior transactions, 254–255, 274
Umwelt, 161, 162, 164, 178
Unbound energy, 248

Unconditional positive regard, 30
   defined, 206
   person-centered therapy and, 195
Unconditional stroke, 274
Unconditioned response, 289, 311
Unconditioned stimulus, 311
Unconscious, 92, 115
Uncovering therapy, 101
Underdog, 219
Unfinished business, 223

Values:
   awareness of, and effective counselors,
      34–36
   defined, 34
   test of, 34
Variable-interval schedule, 311
Variable-ratio schedule, defined, 311
Verbal Behavior (Skinner), 281
Vicarious learning, 290
Virtue, defined, 45
Virtue ethics, 45
Vocational counselors, training and
   therapeutic setting for, 18

Walden Two (Skinner), 280, 285
Warmth, defined, 206
Way of Being, A (Rogers), 185
*We've Had a Hundred Years of Psychotherapy—
   and the World's Getting Worse* (Hillman &
   Ventura), 393
"What and How" Principle, 223
*What Are You Doing? How People Are Helped
   by Reality Therapy* (Glasser), 357
What Do You Say After You Say Hello? (Berne),
   266
Will, defined, 178
Withdrawal, defined, 274
Womb envy, 98, 115
Women:
   APA guidelines for treatment of, 61
   historical role in psychotherapy
      development, 7, 107, 108
Workplaces, as sources of therapeutic
   services, 19